ATLANTIC OCEAN

Loch
Olabhat

Kunda

Star Carr

Tollund
Aamosen
Svaerdborg
York
Rothwell
Gallehus
Flag Fen
Brandon
Thorpe
Nonsuch
Clacton
Somerset
Danebury
Swancombe
Levels
Stonehenge
Kent's Cavern
Winchester
Meer II
Neanderthal
Cranborne Chase
Abbeville
Koln Lindenthal
Maiden Castle
Buster Hill
St. Acheul
Mezhirich
Carnac
Somme R.
Speyer
Dolní Věstoníce
Grand Pressigny
Wasserburg
Hallstatt
Combe Grenal
Solutré
La Téne
La Quina
Similaun
Lascaux
Abri Pataud
Cassegros
Dordogne R.
Opovo
Altamira
BLACK
SEA
Douro R.
Hvar
Terra Amata
Torralba/Ambrona
Grotte De
Herculaneum
Samothrace
MITANNI
Chauvet
Pompeii
Troy
THESSALY
Sounion
MEDITERRANEAN SEA
Laurion
Aphrodisias
Hacilar
Olympia
Siphnos
Athens
Mycenae
Helos
Epidauros
Knossos

——— Ice limit at height of Würm Glaciation

Archaeological Sites in Europe

IN THE BEGINNING

IN THE BEGINNING

AN INTRODUCTION TO ARCHAEOLOGY

NINTH EDITION

BRIAN M. FAGAN

UNIVERSITY OF CALIFORNIA, SANTA BARBARA

 LONGMAN

An imprint of Addison Wesley Longman, Inc.

New York • Reading, Massachusetts • Menlo Park, California • Harlow, England
Don Mills, Ontario • Sydney • Mexico City • Madrid • Amsterdam

To

Milton Johnson
Who started it all

Acquisitions Editor: Alan McClare
Text Design and Project Management: Interactive Composition Corporation
Cover Design: Kay Petronio
Art Studio: Interactive Composition Corporation
Photo Researcher: Mira Schachne
Electronic Production Manager: Eric Jorgensen
Manufacturing Manager: Hilda Koparanian
Electronic Page Makeup: Interactive Composition Corporation
Printer and Binder: RR Donnelley & Sons Company
Cover Printer: Phoenix Color Corp.

For permission to use copyrighted material, grateful acknowledgment is made to the
copyright holders on pp. 516-519, which are hereby made part of this copyright page.

Library of Congress Cataloging-in-Publication Data

Fagan, Brian M.
    In the beginning : an introduction to archaeology / Brian M. Fagan. —9th ed.
        p. cm.
    Includes bibliographical references and index.
    ISBN 0-673-52524-4 (hardcover)
        1. Archaeology—Methodology. 2. Archaeology—History. I. Title.
CC75.F34   1996
930.1—dc20   95-53828
                                                                        CIP

ISBN 0-673-52524-4

2345678910—DOC—9998

CONTENTS

BASIC PROCESSES AND PRINCIPLES 57

RECOVERING ARCHAEOLOGICAL DATA   149

9 FINDING AND ASSESSING ARCHAEOLOGICAL SITES   150

ANALYZING THE PAST: ARTIFACTS AND TECHNOLOGY 209

RECONSTRUCTING PAST LIFEWAYS 263

CULTURAL RESOURCE MANAGEMENT 435

TO THE READER

Many people think of archaeology as a romantic subject, a glamorous pastime spent with pyramids, mysterious inscriptions, and buried treasure. This stereotype originated in the nineteenth century, when both archaeologists and the ancient civilizations they uncovered became legendary. Today, more than 150 years of archaeological investigations have turned archaeology into a meticulous discipline. But the excitement is still there, in the many diverse and highly detailed reconstructions of life in the past that come from scientific inquiry. Archaeologists have reconstructed the lifeways of the earliest humans, documented some of the earliest art in the world, outlined the processes of plant domestication, and even examined the garbage produced in modern urban America. In this book I describe how archaeologists make and study such finds to illuminate the human past.

In the Beginning introduces the history and methods of archaeology and its significance today. I discuss archaeological concepts and procedures and show how archaeologists describe cultures as part of time and space to interpret the prehistoric past. One objective in this book is to provide a comprehensive summary of the field for people who have little or no experience with it. A second objective is to alert you to a major crisis facing archaeology in our time. All archaeological sites are finite records of the past; once destroyed, they can never be replaced. But treasure hunting by individuals and an explosive increase in the construction of buildings, roads, dams, and the like have destroyed thousands of archaeological sites all over the world. Without access to intact sites, we cannot possibly complete a picture of the human past. The crisis of site destruction is, in its way, as important as the ecological crisis we face. *In the Beginning* is meant to alert you to the need for living responsibly with your cultural heritage.

Archaeology has become a highly sophisticated, "high-tech" discipline in recent years, and there are many more professional archaeologists working in the field than even a decade ago. The result has been not only a knowledge explosion but also the development of ever more sophisticated and fine-grained methods for studying the past. We cannot examine even a small fraction of these elaborate, often expensive, and invariably fascinating methods within the compass of this relatively short book. Nor do we delve deeply into the powerful statistical methods and computerized approaches that are commonplace in archaeology today. This book focuses on the basic principles of our discipline, on the fundamental tenets that are as important whether one uses a trowel, a laser recording system, or a complicated computer graphics program in pursuit of the past. I hope that you will pursue the topics that interest you in more advanced and specialized archaeology courses or in the many excellent books and articles listed in the bibliography at the back of the book and in the guide to further reading at the end of each chapter.

The chapters close with summaries highlighting the major themes and concepts. Whenever practicable, drawings and photographs illustrate the subjects the text describes in words. I use specialized terminology as little as possible and define every new term when it first appears. In addition, a glossary at the back of the book provides definitions of the words used in the book as well as some words you may encounter in other reading.

I have written this book from predominantly English-language sources for two main reasons. First, my reading in the vast archaeological literature has been necessarily selective and mostly in English. Second, for most of you, English is your native tongue. Although linguistic abilities and time have thus biased this volume toward the achievements and writings of English-speaking archaeologists, archaeology is indeed a global activity, conducted with great energy and intelligence by every nation and in every corner of the world.

May you enjoy the world of the past as much as I have! Good luck with your adventures in archaeology!

Brian M. Fagan

TO THE INSTRUCTOR

When I started writing the first edition of *In the Beginning* in 1968, I had no idea that it would still be in print after a quarter century and that I would one day be revising it for the ninth time. Any book like this is the work of far more than one person, for many instructors and students have written to me, or button-holed me at a meeting, to make suggestions or to offer criticism or even reprints of their own work. I am deeply grateful for their constant input, and for both their critical and kind words. *In the Beginning* is truly a product of both author and readers.

TRENDS IN ARCHAEOLOGY

The ninth edition of *In the Beginning* reflects a number of important trends in archaeology in recent years, including a growing emphasis on nondestructive methods of studying the past, as remote sensing acquires increasing sophistication and becomes more affordable. There is also a growing awareness that we must devote more attention and energy to the conservation of a rapidly vanishing archaeological record. At the same time, new antiquities legislation and a rising tide of protest from Native Americans and others have set off a long, drawn-out, and passionate debate not only about the morality of archaeology and about the ways in which we practice North American archaeology, but also about the relationships between archaeologists everywhere and indigenous peoples. It is no coincidence that archaeological theory is moving in new directions, toward a new emphasis on the archaeology of people rather than more general issues of processes of culture change. This is reflected in new research into gender, ethnicity, and inequality, and also in the slow acceptance of "cognitive archaeology," sometimes called the "archaeology of mind," as a major theoretical trend.

We are at a fascinating point in archaeological method and theory, with archaeologists divided into a minority engaged in intensive theoretical debate and the remainder continuing to carry out empirical research, albeit in more sophisticated ways, that have been commonplace for generations. Archaeologists are engaged in intense debates about the future of the discipline and about its role in the contemporary world, debates stimulated in part by the divisive and fractious times in which we live. What is happening in archaeology has already happened in many other sciences and is still taking hold in much of biology: the development of distinctive and scientific archaeological methods and theories that not only enrich our understanding of the past but add to our understanding of ourselves. Inevitably, this has led to ever more intense specialization in ever more high-tech methods and increasingly esoteric research. Please encourage your students to think of archaeology as one enterprise, not as dozens of unrelated activities! Above all, encourage them to look at the broad picture as well as the local one, for the greatest advances in archaeology, as in other sciences, have come not from slavish specialization, but from inspirations born of broad vision.

CHANGES IN THE NINTH EDITION

I have made hundreds of small changes in this edition, many of them updated discussions of methods, theories, and case studies. At the suggestion of reviewers, I have retained the format and coverage of earlier editions. Despite attempts to telescope some chapters into others, the existing organization, honed as it has been over eight editions, seems to work well for most users. However, at the suggestion of reviewers, I have moved coverage of the archaeological record and other basic principles further forward in the book, so they are covered before the two chapters on space and time. The illustrations have been updated and revised throughout, although one suffers from the continual frustration of writing about a visual subject and being restricted by space and budget as to the number of pictures one can include. This ninth edition sees a number of major changes. I have expanded coverage of remote sensing, added more material on social organization, trade, and religion, and added a new chapter on the archaeology of gender and groups, an expanding interest in the field. The emergence of cognitive archaeology as a major theoretical approach is an encouraging signpost for the future. I have updated Chapter 20 on cultural resource management to reflect the latest legislative changes, as well as the intense debate over the repatriation of burials and funerary artifacts. As in earlier editions, I suggest a brief list of further readings and cross-reference the text to a bibliography for those who wish to delve more closely into topics treated briefly in the book. Space restrictions prevent me from adopting any other approach.

This is a long book and a complex one. It would be easy to make it a dreary catalog of method and theory, and to stretch it to a thousand pages. But, as the great archaeologist Sir Mortimer Wheeler once said, "dry archaeology is the driest dust that blows," so I have done everything I can to make this book an interesting read, keeping jargon to a minimum. In the interest of brevity, I have had to cover some topics, such as population carrying capacity and sampling, in almost indecent haste. I have also omitted discussion of the more exotic experimental methodologies that now crowd the pages of archaeological literature. While valuable, many of them are not strictly relevant to the basic goals of archaeology outlined in these pages. I leave it to you to fill in details on topics that you think are inadequately covered here. I urge you, however, to give full coverage to the growing crisis of the archaeological record. This subject demands full factual and moral coverage in all introductory courses, where many students arrive with the notion of finding buried treasure or collecting beautiful artifacts. Every course in archaeology must place responsibility for preserving the past emphatically in public, as well as professional, hands. It is for this reason that this book ends with a stark statement of basic archaeological ethics for everyone.

In the Beginning surveys the broad spectrum of archaeological method and theory. With the very first edition, I decided not to espouse any one theory of archaeology, but to give each instructor a basis for amplifying the text with his or her own viewpoint and theoretical persuasion. This decision has been endorsed by many users. A reviewer said some editions ago: "This is the fun with this book." Long may it continue to be so.

ANCILLARIES

An Instructor's Manual and Test Bank by Professor Kathryn Cruz-Uribe of Northern Arizona State University is available to faculty members. It includes chapter summaries, teaching suggestions, lists of key terms with definitions, and a test bank consisting of multiple-choice, short answer, and essay questions.

ACKNOWLEDGMENTS

As always, this edition is the result of input and advice from many people, both professional archaeologists and students. I have even received correspondence from Australia, Slovakia, and Japan, and am gratified to learn that *In the Beginning* has been translated into Indonesian. The comments of my correspondents are always challenging and provocative, and I only hope that my efforts to navigate between conflicting viewpoints and priorities meet with their approval. I am deeply grateful to my good friend George Michaels for constant encouragement and stimulating debate, and to the reviewers who read the text: Elliot Abrams, Ohio University; D. Bruce Dickson, Texas A&M University; Allan S. Gilbert, Fordham University; Julia A. King, St. Mary's College of Maryland; Carolyn G. Koehler, University of Maryland-Baltimore County; Jon Muller, Southern Illinois University and Richard W. Yerkes, Ohio State University.

Finally, many thanks to Alan McClare, my editor at Longman, who puts up with so much and endures my wife's titillating faxes, and to his colleagues in production and design, especially Bill Mahaffey, who turned my computer disks into reality. Special thanks to Joel Hatch and Deril Johnson for their splendid design. I am deeply grateful for their skills, and for their friendship, too.

Brian M. Fagan

PART 1

BACKGROUND TO ARCHAEOLOGY

Of all ruins, possibly the most moving are those of long-deserted cities, fallen century by century into deeper decay, their forsaken streets grown over by forest and shrubs, their decadent buildings quarried and plundered down the years, gaping ruinous, the haunt of lizards and owls ... the marble and gold of palaces, the laurel and jasmine of gardens, are now brambles and lagoons; the house built for Caesar is now dwelt in by lizards ...

Rose Macaulay
The Pleasure of Ruins

Why study archaeology? What is the importance of this popular and apparently romantic subject? We begin to answer these questions by looking at the place of archaeology in the twentieth-century world, at its important role in our cultural enrichment and in the writing of world history. Unfortunately, the discipline faces a crisis brought about by rapid destruction of important sites by industrial development and treasure hunting. Furthermore, the credibility of archaeologists is undermined by all sorts of pseudo-archaeologies purporting to tell the truth about lost worlds, ancient astronauts, and sunken continents.

The reality of archaeology is much less romantic but just as fascinating. We define archaeology by placing it within its broad context as part of anthropology and history.

1

INTRODUCING ARCHAEOLOGY

Archaeology is the stuff dreams are made of—buried treasure, gold-laden pharaohs, the romance of long-lost civilizations. Many people believe archaeologists are romantic heroes, like the film world's Indiana Jones. Cartoonists depict them as elderly, eccentric scholars in sun helmets digging up inscribed tablets in the shadow of Egyptian temples. They are thought to be typical absentminded professors, so deeply absorbed in the details of ancient life that they care little for the pressures and frustrations of modern life. Archaeology is believed to open doors to a world of romance and excitement, to discoveries like the spectacular tomb of the Egyptian pharaoh Tutankhamun, opened by English archaeologists Howard Carter and Lord Carnarvon in 1922.

The first archaeologists were, indeed, adventurers (Figure 1.1a). The Mayan civilization of Mexico and Guatemala was first described by American travel writer John Lloyd Stephens, who traveled in the forests of the Yucatán with artist Frederick Catherwood in 1839 (Figure 1.1b). Stephens tried to buy the Maya city of Copán for fifty dollars, so he could mount an exhibit to sell his book. The deal fell through because there was no way of shipping his finds to New York. Some dug for profit, others out of intellectual curiosity. None was more single-minded than Heinrich Schliemann, a German businessman (Ceram, 1953). In his early forties he gave up business, married a young Greek woman, and set out to find Homer's legendary city of Troy in 1871. His hectic search ended at the mound of Hissarlik in northwestern Turkey. Schliemann recruited 150 men and moved 325,000 cubic yards of soil in his early seasons, but he proved the Homeric legends had some basis in reality. His archaeological methods were brutal—he destroyed almost as much as he discovered.

Archaeology has come a long way since the days when one could find a lost civilization in a month. In this chapter we explore archaeology's role in the twentieth-century world and the crisis of destruction that archaeology faces. We define archaeology in relation to anthropology and history, and look at different types of archaeologists.

WHY STUDY ARCHAEOLOGY?

Few archaeologists are fortunate enough to discover a royal burial or a forgotten civilization. Most excavate for a lifetime, finding nothing more spectacular

FIGURE 1.1A   The nineteenth-century archaeologist as adventurer. Englishman Austen Henry Layard floated his Assyrian finds from ancient Nineveh down the Tigris River on wooden rafts supported by inflated goatskins. When the raft reached the Persian Gulf, the skins were deflated and packed upstream on donkeys, while the wood was sold. The Assyrians themselves had used similar river vessels.

than some fine pottery or delicately made stone tools. British archaeologist Stuart Piggott called archaeology "the science of rubbish," and there is much truth in that statement. Archaeologists spend their lives investigating the surviving and abandoned remains of ancient societies. It is not gold or fine objects that interest them, though, but the information that comes from digging up finds and properly recording them. The archaeologist today is as interested in why people lived the way they did as in the objects they made and the buildings they erected.

On the face of it, the study of archaeology, however fascinating, seems a luxury we can ill afford in a world beset by economic uncertainties and widespread poverty and famine. But to regard archaeology in such a way would be to treat the entire cultural heritage of humanity as irrelevant and unnecessary to the quality of our lives; in reality, it is integral, as we shall see below. (Trigger, 1984a).

ARCHAEOLOGY IS FASCINATING

The great public fascination with archaeology began with the classic archaeological discoveries of the nineteenth century (Figure 1.1), with the finding of the Biblical Assyrians of Mesopotamia and ancient Troy. Today, archaeology is as much a part of popular culture as football or the automobile. Thousands of people

FIGURE 1.1B   The nineteenth-century archaeologist as adventurer. A lithograph by artist Frederick Catherwood, who accompanied John Lloyd Stephens, of the Castillo at Chichén Itzá, Mexico.

read archaeology books for entertainment, join archaeological societies, and flock to popular lectures on the past. Recent discoveries like the spectacular Sipán burials in Peru (Figure 1.2) (Alva and Donnan, 1993) and the Stone Age rock paintings of Grotte de Chauvet in France made front page headlines around the world.

Armchair archaeology is one thing; to experience the sites and objects of the past firsthand is another. The monuments of antiquity cast an irresistible spell. The jetliner and the package tour have made archaeological tourism big business. Fifty years ago only the wealthy and privileged could take a tour up the Nile, visit Classical Greek temples, and explore Mayan civilization. Now package tours can take you to Egypt, to the Parthenon (Figure 1.7), and to Teotihuacán, Mexico (Figure 15.7). The immense Pyramids of Giza in Egypt (Figure 16.8), and the prodigious labor that built them; the white columns of the Temple of Poseidon at Sounion, Greece, touched with pink by the setting sun; the ruins at Tikal bathed in the full moon's light—as sights alone, these overwhelm the senses. To sit in the great amphitheater at Epidauros, Greece, and to hear Euripides' stanzas recited in the perfect acoustics of the highest seats is a deeply moving experience. Tutankhamun's golden mask (Figure 1.3) or a giant Olmec head with snarling face head (Figure 16.12) lifts us to a realm where achievement endures and perceptions seem of a higher order. There are moments when the remote past reaches out to us, comforting, encouraging, offering precedent for human existence. We marvel at the achievements of the ancients, at their awesome legacy to all humankind.

FIGURE 1.2   A mannequin wears replicas of the ceremonial regalia of a
Moche warrior priest, similar to those found in a royal tomb of A.D. 400 at
Sipán, Peru. The Lords of Sipán are one of the greatest archaeological
discoveries of the twentieth century.

FIGURE 1.3   The golden coffin of Egyptian king Tutankhamun.

ARCHAEOLOGY STUDIES OUR COMMON CULTURAL HERITAGE

Every society on earth has some form of origin myth: folklore that is the official, sanctioned account of how it came into being. Our own society is no exception. "And God said, 'Let us make man in our image, after our likeness: and let them have dominion over the fish of the sea, and over the fowl of the air, and over the cattle, and over all the earth, and over every creeping thing that creepeth on the earth.'" Thus reads the first chapter of Genesis in the biblical Old Testament, a majestic account of the Creation that was accepted as the authorized version of human origins for centuries.

Origin myths, such as that of Genesis, developed in response to humanity's deep-seated curiosity about its origins. They also reflect each society's perspective on human existence. For many, existence is defined by their close relationship to the natural world, and by the endless cycles of passing seasons. Such definitions assume human existence is unchanging, that both past and future generations will share the same existence as those alive today. In contrast, Western civilization has a linear view of human existence, which unfolds in all parts of the world over an enormously long period of time. As a result, for more than two thousand years, Westerners have speculated about their ancestry and tried to develop theoretical models to explain their origins, humankind's collective cultural heritage. Some of these models are purely philosophical; others are based on archaeological data. Archaeology is fascinating because it enables us to test theoretical models of evolving societies: why some people have flourished, others have vanished without a trace, and still others have sunk into obscurity.

Western curiosity about the past stems not only from preoccupation with our ultimate origins but from strong feelings of nostalgia as well. We live in a world of rapid change and diminishing natural resources, in a crowded, overpopulated urban environment. As population increases and ecological problems deepen, we find ourselves nostalgic for simpler, earlier times. Archaeology gives insight into those seemingly less complicated societies of the past (Trigger, 1984a).

The earliest written records of the human past date back about 5,000 years in Egypt and Mesopotamia. Yet the vast landscape of the remote past extends back more than 2.5 million years, with documentary history little more than a century old in much of the African interior, New Guinea, and the Americas. Archaeology is the only way to study the earlier chapters of human history, for it is unique among the sciences in its ability to study changes in human societies over long periods of time. It provides an objective way of studying the collective cultural heritage of humankind, which is independent of the dictates of any religious faith. Why are we biologically and culturally diverse? In what ways are we similar or different? When did the great diversity of humanity come into being, and why? These are fundamental questions about humankind that archaeologists can attempt to answer.

Archaeology is a product of Western science, and, as such, is sometimes considered irrelevant by some non-Western societies, which believe profoundly in the cyclical nature of human existence. Many Native Americans consider archaeology unnecessary, even insulting to their ancestors. But the fact remains that it offers the only scientific way of understanding the ancient world, and the linear histories of many Native American and other societies, which came into contact with literate Western civilization only in the past five centuries, during the European Age of Discovery. Before European contact, North American Indian history was not written; it consisted mostly of oral traditions handed down from generation to generation. Archaeology and archaeological sites are the only other possible sources for very early American Indian history.

One of the most remarkable examples of archaeology's ability to reveal the history of Native Americans comes from Ozette, Washington, where Richard Daugherty has excavated the remains of a Makah Indian village that was buried by mud slides about 500 years ago (Figure 4.3) (Kirk, 1974). Conditions for preservation at the site were so exceptional that archaeologists were able to recover complete details of the village's plank houses and their contents, down to stored food and whalebone harpoons. By working closely with the tribal council, Daugherty was able not only to interpret the objects found on the site, but also to help the council raise a large sum of money for a local museum in which to display the finds. In this way he brought the hitherto forgotten history of the Makah into the consciousness of the Indians themselves and of the public as well.

The Ozette example is by no means unique, for more and more archaeologists are working closely with American Indian communities, and Southwestern groups, among others, have retained archaeologists and anthropologists to work on land claim cases currently in the courts. The Hopi and Zuni nations, for example, have formed their own archaeology units to investigate sites on their land (Chapter 20).

Archaeological excavations reveal much about the diversity of early historic American society. In Florida, Kathleen Deagan has excavated the site of Fort Mose, the first free black community in North America. This tiny hamlet of some 37 families, 2 miles (3.2 km) from Spanish St. Augustine on the Atlantic coast, was founded in 1738, overrun by the British in 1740, and rebuilt in 1753. A walled fort enclosed a large church, the priest's house, a well, and guardhouses, while the villagers lived in 22 thatched houses (Figure 1.4). Many of the inhabitants were of West African origin, and excavations have recovered military artifacts and domestic items, offering the prospect that one day archaeologists will be able to identify what African, English, Indian, and Spanish cultural elements the black inhabitants retained. Fort Mose was occupied until the Spanish abandoned Florida in 1763. Other excavations in the South and the Southeast have investigated plantation life and slave communities, a rich archaeological record of very culturally diverse African-American populations (L. Ferguson, 1992).

Many newly independent nations, eager to foster nationalism, are encouraging archaeological research as the only way to uncover the early roots of the peoples who lived there before colonial times. For years the Tanzanian and Zambian governments in Africa have sponsored excavations, whose results soon will appear in university textbooks and schoolbooks. The primary goal of archaeology there, as in many parts of the world, is to write unwritten history, not from archives and dusty documents, but from long-abandoned villages and rubbish heaps (Trigger, 1984a).

ARCHAEOLOGY HAS POLITICAL VALUE

They called Tlacalel the "Woman Snake." He was the right-hand man of a series of fifteenth-century Aztec rulers in highland Mexico, a brilliant diplomat who prevailed on his masters to burn all earlier tribal records. In their place, he concocted a convincing rags-to-riches story which recounted the Aztecs' mercurial rise from obscurity to become masters of Mexico, chosen by Huitzilopochtli, the Sun God himself. Tlacalel was not the first official in history to rewrite the past to serve the present. Archaeology has long been used to foster nationalism, to aid political propaganda. The Nazis used archaeology to produce "evidence" for the existence of a white master race in Europe in the 1930s (B. Arnold, 1992). The Roman siege of Masada with its tragic ending has long been a focus for Israeli nationalism (Yadin, 1966). During the late 1960s, the white settler govern-

FIGURE 1.4   Artist's impression of the Fort Mose settlement in the mid-eighteenth century.

ment of Rhodesia in southern Africa claimed that the Zimbabwe ruins, a famous complex of stone buildings, were the work of Phoenician colonists who had settled south of the Zambezi River more than 2,000 years ago. They chose to ignore half a century and more of archaeological research that showed Zimbabwe had been built by indigenous African peoples between A.D. 1000 and 1500. The reason for the claim was easily discerned: a Phoenician date for Zimbabwe would be evidence for white settlement in southern Africa long before the local people arrived (Garlake, 1973).

Interpretations of the past are rarely value-neutral (Fowler, 1987). Inevitably, archaeologists themselves bring to their work values and perspectives from their own culture, even if they are much more conscious of this than they were a generation ago (Shanks and Tilley, 1987a). Such subliminal biases are very different from the deliberate use of archaeology to establish historical fact and to support claims against governments or nationalist goals.

ARCHAEOLOGY IS VALUABLE IN THE CONTEMPORARY WORLD

Archaeologists have played an important role in economic development in South America. As early as 1000 B.C., farmers living on the altiplano along Lake Titicaca in southern Peru were using raised fields, elevated planting surfaces that were used to grow crops in areas that were subject to seasonal flooding (Erickson, 1992). The soils were rich, and by elevating them and building a canal network, prehistoric cultivators were able to grow potatoes, quinoa, and other indigenous crops with impressive yields. The raised fields were abandoned before the Spanish Conquest, and the modern economy of the same environment is based on pastoralism. Archaeologists' experiments with reconstructions of ancient raised gardens showed that excellent crop yields could be obtained from the prehistoric plots, in areas considered marginal by modern agricultural authorities. The traditional system has many advantages—high yields, no need for fertilizer, and much-reduced risks of frost or flood damage. Furthermore, high yields can be obtained with local labor, local crops, and no outside capital. At last count, nearly 2,125 acres (860 ha) had been rehabilitated and many more fields are planned. Archaeologists are actively involved in several other such projects in the Americas.

Archaeology has also worked directly for contemporary American society, especially in the management of resources and waste. University of Arizona archaeologist William Rathje has studied the garbage dumps in Tucson and other cities for a long time (Rathje and Murphy, 1992). His team examines patterns in garbage disposed of by city households, analyzes evidence from the dump with the latest archaeological research designs and techniques, and joins to it data gleaned from interviews with householders and other sources. His study has revealed startlingly wasteful habits in Arizona households of many economic and social backgrounds, information that could be used to suggest better strategies for consumer buying and resource management. Because the objects we use shape our lives in many ways, we need to understand how they affect us to learn about the past and anticipate the future.

THE CRISIS IN ARCHAEOLOGY

Archaeologists bring a unique tool to the social sciences of which they are a part: a perspective that enables us to understand how people have dealt with the world around them, and with each other, from the earliest times. This contributes to a much better understanding of our own history, as well as that of the environment, the world climate, and the landscape. The long-abandoned settlements that archaeologists study are repositories of precisely dated geological, biological, and environmental data that can add a vital time depth to studies of the contemporary world. Unfortunately, archaeological sites are an endangered species. Ancient settlements are being destroyed so rapidly that a sizable portion of the world's archaeological heritage has already vanished forever.

Unlike trees or animals, archaeological sites are a finite resource. Once a bulldozer or a treasure hunter moves in, archaeological evidence is wiped out. The archaeologist's archives are buried in the soil, and the only way to preserve them is to leave them alone, intact, until they can be investigated with rigorous scientific care. Both human nature and the insatiable needs of the world's growing population have wrought terrible destruction on the archaeological record everywhere. Pothunters and treasure hunters have left thousands of archaeological sites looking like rabbit burrows and have so damaged them that archaeological inquiry is impossible. The ravages of industrial activity, strip mining, and agriculture have also taken their catastrophic toll on many sites. In some parts of the United States, damage of sites is an uncontrolled epidemic. Those of us alive today may be the last to see undisturbed archaeological sites in North America and many other parts of the world (McGimsey, 1972).

COLLECTORS AND THE MORALITY OF COLLECTING

Our materialistic society greatly emphasizes wealth and the possession of valuable things. Many people feel an urge to possess the past, to keep a piece of antiquity on the mantel. Projectile points, prehistoric hand axes, Benin bronzes, or Maya pots add an exotic touch to the prosaic American living room. Many archaeological artifacts, such as those Benin bronzes, have high antique and commercial value. They are "buried treasure," valued as museum pieces and by the world's major collectors, commanding enormous prices at auction and in salerooms. High commercial prices and the human urge to own have incited unscrupulous treasure hunting and a flourishing illegal trade in antiquities, resulting in the rape of sites for gold and other precious ornaments, as well as pottery, sculpture, and all other artifacts that today's covetous collectors seek to own and sell. In some countries, such as Egypt, Italy, Costa Rica, and Peru, tomb robbing is a full-time, if technically illegal, profession. The Italian *tombaroli* concentrate on Etruscan tombs (Meyer, 1992). Entire Inka cemeteries have been dug up for gold ornaments. Thousands of Egyptian tombs have been rifled for papyri and statues.

North America bristles with pothunters who think nothing of ravaging sacred Indian sites for their projectile points and potsherds. Despite increasingly comprehensive legislation, illegal looting continues unabated. In a recent scandalous episode, an undisturbed Mississippian site at Slack Farm, close to the Ohio River in Kentucky, was looted by a group of pothunters who paid the landowner a large sum for the right to dig up Indian burials and the valuable grave goods associated with them. It was two months before their nefarious activities were halted, by which time the site looked like a battlefield (Fagan, 1995a) (Figure 1.5). The offenders were never convicted. (See also Chapter 19 and Munson, Jones, and Fry, 1995.)

FIGURE 1.5   Slack Farm, Kentucky, showing the damage wrought by looters before archaeologists moved in.

Why do people collect antiquities? In 1921, Henri Codet, a French medical doctor, wrote a pioneering dissertation on collecting. He concluded that it has four underlying motives: "the need to possess, the need for spontaneous activity, the impulse to self-advancement, and the tendency to classify things" (Meyer, 1992). Another Frenchman said of collecting: "It is not a pastime, but a passion and often so violent that it is inferior to love or ambition only in the pettiness of its aims." People collect everything from beer-bottle caps to oil paintings, and anything collectible is considered by collectors to be portable and private—and it is their duty to preserve it. It follows that everything has a market value and can be purchased, the market value depending on the demand for the category of artifact or its rarity or aesthetic appeal (Muensterberger, 1994). The archaeological context of the artifact is often quite unimportant, and information about the people who made it is usually irrelevant: all that matters is the object itself (Figure 1.6 top).

Protecting antiquities is complex and incredibly difficult, for in the final analysis, it involves appealing to people's moral values and requires almost unenforceable legislation that ultimately would take away a potential source of livelihood, however illegal, from thousands of poverty-stricken peasants and more prosperous intermediaries who have some political influence. Most countries have museums, and many have antiquities services and stringent laws controlling the export of archaeological finds—at least in theory. The trouble is that the laws cost a fortune to administer and enforce, and even relatively developed countries such as Mexico are unable to police even the most famous sites.

FIGURE 1.6   The wrong and the right ways to dig. Archaeology is a hobby for both of these groups, but the top group is destroying evidence of the past through its digging "techniques," whereas the bottom group is preserving it. The latter, alas, happens all too rarely.

But public opinion in Egypt and other countries shows some pride in the national heritage. It is galling to see the prized sculptures and antiquities of one's past adorning museums in distant capitals. Yet the tide of public opinion cannot stem the collectors' mania or the ruthless policies of some museums. Fortunately, some universities and museums have adapted more stringent acquisitions policies, although it is too early to say whether they have had any effect. Changing public attitudes, more cautious policies, and a shortage of fine antiquities may slow the traffic, but significant damage has already been done.

PSEUDO-ARCHAEOLOGIES

Modern archaeology is highly technical and—let us be honest—sometimes rather dull. In contrast, the flood of "pseudo-archaeologies" that has appeared in recent years positively drips with romance and excitement, with "unexplained" secrets, lost civilizations, and great temples buried in dense rain forests. The Lost Continent of Atlantis, the Ten Lost Tribes of Israel, expeditions in search of Noah's Ark—all provide superb raw material for the armchair adventurer (Feder, 1996).

Popular writer Erich von Däniken (1970; 1971) created a famous pseudo-archaeology during the 1970s. He took advantage of the public's general fascination with space to argue that people from other worlds lived on earth long before our civilization arose. With his books and films he earned millions of dollars by arguing that foreign astronauts visited the earth thousands of years ago. They found primitive humans on earth and fertilized some of the females. Millennia later the spacemen returned and found *Homo sapiens* scattered over the earth. They repeated their breeding experiment and eventually produced a "creature intelligent enough to have the rules of society imparted to it" (von Däniken, 1970). These new beings started art and agriculture and eventually their own civilizations, regarding their progenitors as "benevolent gods who were interested in their welfare." But soon warfare began, and people began to destroy many of the sacred places.

The world at large adored von Däniken's incredible hypotheses, but archaeologists were puzzled. His extravagant theories—they are nothing less—are a superb example of misused archaeological data. Most scholars find it impossible to follow von Däniken's reasoning, for his archaeological "evidence" is laced with biblical allusions, in one of which he claims that Sodom and Gomorrah were destroyed by an atomic bomb! The Ark of the Covenant, he contends, was an electrified transmitter that enabled Moses to communicate with the astronauts. He identified a space-suited astronaut at the controls of a rocket on a Maya sarcophagus lid at Palenque in Mesoamerica. Von Däniken was totally unfamiliar with ancient Maya culture and examined Maya art with the expectation that he would find spacemen. In fact, Maya experts know from their knowledge of ancient cosmography that the carving represents a Maya king poised between life and death on his journey to the spiritual world (Feder, 1996).

Von Däniken's brand of pseudo-archaeology is unusual only because he has moved into space for his heroes. Like his predecessors, and like many people fascinated by escapism and space fiction, he is intoxicated with the mystery and lure of vanished tribes and lost cities engulfed in swirling mists (Wauchope,

1972). Of course, the pseudo-archaeologists do not all turn to space for their explanations. British journalist Graham Hancock (1995) has claimed that a great civilization flourished under Antarctic ice 12,000 years ago. (Of course, its magnificent cities are buried under deep ice sheets, so we cannot excavate them!) Colonists spread to all parts of the world from their Antarctic home, colonizing such well-known sites as Tiwanaku in the Bolivian highlands and building the Sphinx by the banks of the Nile. Hancock weaves an ingenious story by piecing together all manner of controversial geological observations and isolated archaeological finds. He waves aside the obvious archaeologist's reaction, which asks where traces of these ancient colonies and civilizations are to be found in Egypt and other places. Hancock fervently believes in his farfetched theory, and being a good popular writer, he has managed to piece together a best-selling book which reads like a "whodunit" written by an amateur sleuth.

Flamboyant pseudo-archaeology of the type espoused by von Däniken and Hancock will always appeal to people who are impatient with the deliberate pace of science and to those who believe in faint possibilities. Some of these "cult archaeologies" show all the symptoms of becoming personality cults, even religious movements. The theories espoused by the leaders become articles of faith, the object of personal conversion. They are attempts to give meaning to being human and are often steeped in symbolism and religious activity. Almost invariably the cultists dismiss archaeologists as "elitists" or "scientific fuddy-duddies" because they reject wild theories that are unsupported by scientifically gathered evidence.

This kind of pseudo-archaeology forms a distinctive literary genre, in which the author is the reader's guide behind the pathetic facade put up by science along the path to the Real Historical Truth. Far more insidious are pseudo-archaeologies that masquerade as serious "alternative" histories. Some years ago, linguist Martin Bernal (1987) published a detailed scholarly analysis of Egyptian civilization, in which he claimed that this earliest of states, and Western civilization for that matter, owed much to black African inspiration. Bernal's "Black Athena" hypothesis caused a sensation in African-American circles and has become an important rallying point for Afrocentrists, historians who believe that Africa was at the center of world history, the fountain not only of humanity, but of civilization itself. According to Egyptologists and others with detailed knowledge of Bernal's linguistic arguments, the entire Black Athena hypothesis is seriously flawed on methodological and historical grounds. Egyptian civilization was an entirely indigenous development within the narrow confines of the Nile Valley below the first cataract, with only sporadic, usually commercial, contacts with black African kingdoms upstream until very late in Egyptian history.

Along even more extreme lines Native American activist Vine DeLoria Jr. (1995) has denounced archaeologists for their hypotheses that the first Americans crossed the Bering Strait from Siberia some 15,000 years ago. He has used discredited geological theories and carefully selected and edited oral traditions to claim that Native Americans settled their homeland very much earlier, and that both giants and white people lived in North America and slaughtered Ice Age big-game animals 9,000 years ago. Unlike Bernal, who attempted scholarly analysis of archaeological and linguistic evidence, DeLoria merely creates a mythic fantasy from what he chooses to consider reliable data, which bears no resemblance to any form of historical reality whatsoever.

While von Däniken and Hancock work within a distinctive and escapist literary genre, Bernal and Deloria's works appeal to very different audiences, to people whose perspectives on history are tied to establishing cultural identities in the modern world. To many Native Americans, for example, the use of archaeology to investigate their history is totally repugnant. They argue that their own religious beliefs and creation legends provide them with an adequate perspective on their history. Archaeology, they argue correctly, is a phenomenon of Western science, a dispassionate way of looking at the past without spiritual faith, something alien to many Native Americans. DeLoria tries to fill this vacuum with an alternative history based on oral traditions and what he calls "Indian memories." He made no critical evaluation of his sources and produced what is basically historical fiction which is just as disrespectful of Native American history as he claims archaeologists have been.

Unfortunately, popular attitudes toward archaeology tend toward the romantic and the exotic. A public nurtured on television, sound bites, and instant gratification prefers mystical adventure stories of lost civilizations to scientific reality. Archaeologists often fight an uphill battle to convince a wider audience of the value of their work, even if the magazine *Skeptical Inquirer* regularly debunks the more outrageous pseudo-archaeologies. Today's archaeology may be far from exotic, but although it is highly technical, it is still extremely fascinating. This book will give you an understanding of how scientific archaeologists go about their work, of the ways in which they strive to reconstruct the past as it actually happened, not as an author believes it happened.

ARCHAEOLOGY, ANTHROPOLOGY, AND HISTORY

ANTHROPOLOGY AND ARCHAEOLOGY

Anthropology is the scientific study of humanity in the widest possible sense. Anthropologists study human beings as biological organisms and as people with a distinctive and unique characteristic—culture. They carry out research on contemporary human societies and on human development from the very earliest times. This enormous field is divided into subdisciplines:

Physical anthropology involves the study of human biological evolution and the variations among different living human populations. Physical anthropologists also study the behavior of other living primates, such as the chimpanzee and the gorilla, research that can suggest explanations for behavior among the earliest human beings.

Cultural anthropology deals with the analysis of human social life, both past and present. It is primarily a study of human culture and how culture adapts to the environment. A number of specialists work within cultural anthropology:

Ethnographers spend most of their time describing the culture, technology, and economic life of living and extinct societies.

Ethnologists engage in comparative studies of societies, a process that involves attempts to reconstruct general principles of human behavior.

Social anthropologists analyze social organization, the ways in which people organize themselves.

Linguistics, the study of human language, sometimes has an important role to play in the study of the past. Many early archaeologists were deeply concerned with such major problems as the origins of the Indo-Europeans, speakers of primeval European languages (A.C. Renfrew, 1987).

Many of the archaeologist's objectives are the same as those of the cultural anthropologist, one difference being that archaeologists study ancient societies. For example, archaeologist Payson Sheets has excavated an ancient Maya village at Cerén in San Salvador that was buried in ash by a volcanic eruption in about A.D. 580. His excavations have revealed a perfectly preserved Maya settlement, in such detail that he has even recovered maize in the gardens around houses and tools that were stored in the rafters of the houses (Figure 4.7) (Sheets, 1992). The site offered a unique opportunity to study prehistoric Maya family and village life, but Sheets and his colleagues are studying this long-forgotten community and its people using the material remains of their lives, for, unlike ethnologists, they cannot talk to their subjects. One could describe an archaeologist as a special type of anthropologist, one who studies the past. This definition is some-what inadequate, however, for archaeologists use many theoretical frameworks to link their excavated evidence to actual human behavior and do far more than merely use data different from that used by cultural anthropologists.

ARCHAEOLOGY

Archaeologists build theories and apply scientific techniques and theoretical concepts in studying the material remains of culture (Renfrew and Bahn, 1996; Sharer and Ashmore, 1995). They cover all of human history, from the time of the earliest human beings right up to the present.

To understand what archaeology involves requires some knowledge of the material evidence we examine. As we shall see in Chapter 4, some raw materials survive much longer than others. Stone and clay vessels are nearly indestructible; wood, skin, metals, and bone are much more friable. In most archaeological sites, only the most durable remains of human material culture are preserved for the archaeologist to study. Any picture of life in the prehistoric past derived from archaeological investigations is likely to be very one-sided. As a result, the unfor-tunate archaeologist is like a detective fitting together a complicated collection of clues to give a general impression and explanation of prehistoric culture and society. Often, it can be like taking a handful of miscellaneous objects—say, two spark plugs, a fragment of a china cup, a needle, a grindstone, and a candle-holder—and trying to reconstruct the culture of the people who made these diverse objects on the basis of these objects alone.

Some people think that archaeology is an assortment of techniques, such as accurate recording, precise excavation, and detailed laboratory analysis. This narrow definition, however, deals only with "doing archaeology," the actual work of recovering data from the soil. Modern archaeology is far more than a gathering of techniques, for it involves not only recovering, ordering, and describing things from the past, but also interpreting the evidence from the earth. In fact, it is an interactive discipline that strikes a balance between practical excavation and description and theoretical interpretation.

THEORY IN ARCHAEOLOGY

The word *theory* has many uses among social scientists. In archaeology it is the overall framework within which a scholar operates. Theory is still little developed in archaeology, as in the other social sciences, partly because working with variable human behavior is difficult and also because of inadequate research methods. Truly interactive archaeology is a constant dialogue between theory and observation, a more or less self-critical procedure that is very much based on inferences about the past, in turn built on phenomena found in the contemporary world. Theoretical approaches to archaeology are numerous; these are some of them:

Cultural materialism seeks the causes behind sociocultural diversity in the modern world. Thus technoeconomic and technoenvironmental conditions exert selective pressures on society and its ideologies (M. Harris, 1968). Cultural materialism is closely associated with the teachings of Engels and Marx. It is especially attractive to archaeologists because it stresses technology, economy, and environment, for these kinds of data survive in the archaeological record. Most archaeologists would probably consider themselves cultural materialists (Chapter 19).

Structural approaches treat human cultures as shared symbolic structures that are cumulative creations of the human mind. Structural analyses are designed to discover the universal principles of the human mind, an approach associated in particular with famed French anthropologist Claude Lévi-Strauss. The difficulty with this approach is that the intangibles of the human mind are difficult to verify from the archaeological record (Chapter 19).

Ecological approaches stress the study of ancient societies within their natural environments (Chapter 15). They are fundamental to contemporary archaeology.

Evolutionary approaches have been popular in archaeology since the nineteenth century. The concepts that form multilinear cultural evolution are inextricable from modern archaeological research (Chapters 3 and 19).

Much archaeological research and theory is strongly influenced by contributions made by people in other academic disciplines, such as specialists in other fields of anthropology and in biology, chemistry, geography, history, physics, and computer technology.

ARCHAEOLOGY AND PREHISTORY

The term *archaeology* originally embraced the study of ancient history as a whole, but the word was gradually narrowed to its present definition—the study of material remains and human cultures using archaeological theory and techniques. *Prehistory* refers to the period of human history extending back before the time of written documents and encompasses the enormous span of human cultural evolution that extends back at least 4 million years. This is the time frame studied by prehistoric archaeologists.

ARCHAEOLOGY AND HISTORY

Archaeology is our primary source of information for 99 percent of human history. Written history describes less than one-tenth of 1 percent of that enormous time span. Although written records extend back 5,000 years in the Near East, the earlier portions of that period are but dimly illuminated by available documents. In other parts of the world, prehistory ended much later. Continuous written history in Britain began with the Roman conquest some 2,000 years ago; the ancient Maya of Mesoamerica developed a complex written script centuries before Christopher Columbus brought Western civilization in contact with Native American society. Some parts of the world did not come into contact with Western society until much more recently. The tribes of the Central African interior had their first outside contact in 1855, with David Livingstone. Continuous government records in this area did not begin until late in the nineteenth century, and parts of New Guinea and the Amazon basin are still in the process of leaving their prehistoric past.

Documentary history contrasts sharply with archaeology. First, historians work with accurate chronologies. They can date an event with certainty to within a year, possibly even as closely as to the minute or the second. Second, their history is that of individuals, groups, governments, and even several nations interacting with each other, reacting to events, and struggling for power. They are able to glimpse the subtle interplay of human intellects, for their principal players have often recorded their impressions or deeds on paper. But the historian's record often has gaps. Details of political events are likely to be far more complete than those of day-to-day existence or the trivia of village life, which often mattered little to contemporary observers. Artifacts and material culture are central to understanding historic cultures, and archaeologists are experts in studying broad patterns of human change and early cultures (Orser and Fagan, 1995).

THE DIVERSITY OF ARCHAEOLOGISTS

Because no one could possibly be expert in the entire time span of archaeology, most archaeologists specialize, pursuing one of the following specialties:

Prehistoric archaeologists (prehistorians) study prehistoric times, from the time of the earliest human beings right up to the frontiers of documentary history. Their dozens of specialties include **paleoanthropologists,** who are experts in the culture and artifacts of the earliest human beings. Others are authorities in stone technology, studying the early peopling of the world and the lifeways of prehistoric hunter-gatherers. Those who specialize in the origins of agriculture and literate civilization work with pottery, domesticated grains, and animal bones, and a wide range of site types and economic lifeways.

Because modern prehistoric archaeology covers the globe, it is divided between New and Old World archaeologists, each focusing on specific regions such as the North American Southwest, Mesoamerica, or Peru. These large areas are too big for specialist researchers to work alone, so they tackle a specific region, site, or detailed problem within a larger site, region, or area. Our knowledge of world prehistory today was gathered by hundreds of archaeologists working in all parts of the world, on small problems or larger ones, on a regional survey or a ten-year excavation at one settlement. And, of course, some prehistorians are experts on soil analysis, ancient animal bones, computer applications and statistical methods in archaeology, or simply excavation itself.

Classical archaeologists study the remains of the great Classical civilizations of Greece and Rome (Figure 1.7). Traditionally, Classical archaeologists have given much attention to art objects and buildings, but many are now beginning to study the types of economic, settlement, and social problems, of interest to prehistoric archaeologists, that are discussed in this book (Snodgrass, 1987; Soren and James, 1988).

Egyptologists and Assyriologists are among the many specialist archaeologists who work on specific civilizations or time periods. These specialties require

FIGURE 1.7   The Parthenon in Athens. Recent Classical research pays close attention to the social, political, and economic contexts of ancient architecture.

unusual skills. Egyptologists must acquire a fluent knowledge of hieroglyphs to help them study the ancient Egyptians, and Assyriologists, experts on the Assyrians of ancient Iraq, must be conversant with cuneiform script.

Historical archaeologists study archaeological sites from periods from which written records exist. They examine Medieval cities, such as Winchester and York in England; they excavate Colonial American settlements (Figure 1.8), Spanish missions, and nineteenth-century forts in the American West; and they study a range of interesting historical artifacts, from bottles to uniform buttons (Orser and Fagan, 1995).

Historical archaeology is concerned with the study of ancient material culture, for artifacts and technology can tell us much about the diversity of historic societies. Much text-aided archaeology is a multidisciplinary enterprise, like the long-term research projects conducted in the historic district of Annapolis, Maryland. The excavations in the city have investigated a tavern, eighteenth-century residences, and many other sites, including a lot now occupied by a modern hotel. This property was first occupied about 1690; bottles, cups, and plates dating to that decade have come from the site

FIGURE 1.8   Foundations for the Public Hospital for the Insane at Colonial Williamsburg, Virginia, which were revealed by meticulous excavation in 1972.

(Yentsch, 1994). The archaeologists revealed intricate layers of occupation, including a timber house of the early 1700s. Governor Calvert's brick house, the first floor of which now forms part of the modern hotel, was subsequently built on the same site in the 1720s. Most of this structure was drastically rebuilt in the nineteenth century, but the walls were preserved within the Victorian building. The excavations also revealed a brick heating system for channeling hot air to a greenhouse. This was partly torn up in the 1760s and filled with domestic refuse before being covered over by an addition to the 1720 house. The refuse proved a rich treasure trove for the archaeologist; it included bones, pins, buttons, hair, pieces of paper, cloth, and fish scales. Ann Yentsch's Calvert House investigations are important because she attempted to move past the study of mere artifacts to the study of the complex culture in the house, where rich and poor, free and enslaved, men and women, lived in close juxtaposition. European cities like Winchester and York offer magnificent opportunities to combine historical records such as title deeds with excavations, making it possible to identify the owners of individual Medieval houses (Keene, 1985).

Historical records can also be important in telling us about societies that had limited written records. The Classic Maya civilization, which flourished in Mesoamerica between about A.D. 200 and 900, had developed a complex writing system. With it the Mayans could record religious, political, and astronomical events with elaborate glyphs sculpted on stone and wood and set down in large books. Although still only partly deciphered, these records are revealing the hitherto unknown political history of the Mayans (Schele and Friedel, 1990; Schele and Miller, 1992).

Underwater archaeologists study sites and ancient shipwrecks on the sea floor and lake bottoms, even under rapids in Minnesota streams (Bass, 1970, 1988; Gould, 1983). Scuba-diving archaeologists now have an array of specialist techniques for recording and excavating these underwater sites. There is a tendency to think of underwater archaeology as something different, but in fact it is not. The objectives of such archaeology remain the same—to reconstruct and interpret past cultures, also the scientific study, through material remains, of all aspects of ancient seafaring. Some modern underwater excavations, such as the investigation of the Bronze Age Uluburun ship off southern Turkey (Figure 1.9) and the reconstruction of the Kyrenia ship from northern Cyprus, are superb examples of scientific archaeology (Steffy, 1994).

Biblical archaeologists study the archaeology of a variety of ethnic groups living in Syro-Palestine, linking accounts in the Bible and Canaanite literature with archaeological sites in the Near East. This complex specialization requires a detailed knowledge not only of history and several languages, but of archaeology as well (R.L. Harris, 1995).

Industrial archaeologists study buildings and other structures dating to the Industrial Revolution or later, such as Victorian railway stations, old cotton plantations, windmills, and even slum housing in England (Hudson, 1982; C. M. Clark, 1987). Anyone entering this field needs at least some training as an architectural historian.

FIGURE 1.9 Recovering copper ingots from the Bronze Age shipwreck at Uluburun, off southern Turkey. The ship, dating from the fourteenth century B.C., contained objects from all over the Near East, testifying to the international nature of eastern Mediterranean trade at the time.

These are but a few of the specialties in archaeology. The modern science is so complex as to have experts in dozens of aspects of the subject, from mouse bones to soil profiles to techniques in ancient metallurgy. All are unified by their common interest in studying humanity in the past.

GOALS OF ARCHAEOLOGY

Whether they concentrate on the most ancient human societies or those of more recent centuries, all archaeologists agree that their fundamental responsibility is to conserve the past for future generations. Their research has four broad goals:

1. Studying sites and their contents in a context of time and space to reconstruct descriptions of long sequences of human culture. This descriptive activity reconstructs cultural history.
2. Reconstructing past lifeways.
3. Explaining why culture change takes place, or why cultures remain the same over long periods of time.
4. Understanding sites, artifacts, food remains, and other aspects of the archaeological record as it relates to our contemporary world.

By no means would every scholar agree that all four of these objectives are equally valid or indeed that they should coexist. In practice, however, each objective usually complements the others, especially when archaeologists design their research to answer specific questions, rather than merely dig as a precursor to describing rows of excavated objects.

CULTURE HISTORY

The expression **culture history** means, quite simply, the description of human cultures as they extend backward thousands of years into the past. An archaeologist working on the culture history of an area describes the prehistoric cultures of that region. Culture history is derived from the study of sites and the artifacts and structures in them in a temporal and spatial context. By investigating groups of prehistoric sites and the many artifacts in them, it is possible to erect local and regional *sequences* of human cultures that extend over centuries, even millennia (see Chapters 11 and 18). Most of the activity is descriptive, accumulating minute chronological and spatial frameworks of archaeological data as a basis for observing how particular cultures evolved and changed through prehistoric times. Descriptive culture history is an essential preliminary to any work on lifeways or cultural process (see Chapter 19).

Many archaeologists who work on culture history feel inhibited by poor preservation of artifacts and sites about making inferences on the more intangible aspects of human prehistory, such as religion and social organization. They argue that archaeologists can legitimately deal only with the material remains of ancient human behavior. Unfortunately, this rather narrow view of culture history has sent many people off in unprofitable directions, into a long and painstaking preoccupation with artifact types and local chronologies that has turned much of archaeology into a glorified type of classification.

PAST LIFEWAYS

The study of past lifeways—the ways in which people have made their livings in the changing environments of the past—has developed into a major goal in recent years. The study of artifacts and structures without environmental context gives a one-sided view of humanity and its adaptations to the environment. Studying past lifeways is a multidisciplinary enterprise, reconstructing ancient subsistence patterns from animal bones, carbonized seeds, and other food residues recovered in meticulous excavation. Pollen analysts, soil scientists, and botanists cooperate in looking at archaeological sites in a much wider, multidisciplinary context. The context of such studies is still descriptive archaeology, preoccupied with space and time, but the emphasis is different: the contexts supplied by space and time related to changing patterns of human settlement, subsistence strategies, and ancient environments. As long ago as 1948, Gordon Willey surveyed in detail the coastal Virú Valley in Peru, where he plotted the distributions of hundreds of prehistoric sites from different chronological periods against the valley's changing environment (Willey, 1953). This was a pioneer attempt at reconstructing prehistoric patterns of settlement, obviously a key part in any attempts to reconstruct prehistoric lifeways.

The intent in this goal of archaeology is still, however, descriptive, within a theoretical framework that sees human cultures as complicated, ever-changing systems. These systems interact with one another and with the natural environment as well.

CULTURAL PROCESS

A third archaeological goal not only describes the past but also explains culture change in prehistory. Archaeologists working toward this goal attempt to explain cultural change, process, and evolution in the past, topics that we explore more fully in Chapter 19 (definitions are in the Glossary). The ultimate goal is to explain why human cultures in all parts of the world reached their various stages of cultural evolution. Human tools are seen as part of a system of related phenomena that include both culture and the natural environment. Thus, prehistoric archaeology is a science in which research methods must be much more rigorous than hitherto. Archaeologists design their research work within a framework of testable propositions that may be supported, modified, or rejected when they review all of the excavated and analyzed archaeological data.

This "processual" approach to archaeology ("processual archaeology") is based on an assumption that the past is inherently knowable, provided that rigorous research methods and designs are used and that field methods are impeccable. Thus, archaeology is more than a descriptive science and archaeologists can explain cultural change in the past (Binford, 1983a).

In recent years, a reaction against "processual archaeology" has emerged, which is sometimes called "post-processual" or "cognitive archaeology" (see Chapter 19).

UNDERSTANDING THE ARCHAEOLOGICAL RECORD

"The archaeological record is here with us in the present," writes Lewis Binford (1983a). He emphasizes how much a part of the contemporary world the artifacts and sites that make up the remains of our past are. Our observations about the past are made today, in the 1990s, for we are describing sites and artifacts as they come from the soil today, centuries, often millennia, after they were abandoned. In this way the archaeologist differs from the historian who reads a document written in, say, 1492, which conveys information written by a contemporary observer that has not changed since that year. The archaeological record is made up of material things and arrangements of material objects in the soil. The only way we can understand this record is by knowing something about how the individual finds came into being. Binford likens archaeological data to a kind of untranslated language that has to be decoded if we are to make statements about human behavior in the past. "The challenge that archaeology offers, then, is to take contemporary observations of static material things and, quite literally, translate them into statements about the dynamics of past ways of life and about the conditions in the past," writes Binford (1983a). Archaeologists cannot study the past directly but must consider it with reference to the present. For this reason, controlled experiments, observations of contemporary hunter-gatherers and horticulturists, and the formulation that Binford and others call "middle-range theory" are vital to archaeologists (Chapter 14).

DIFFERING GOALS: NEW AND OLD WORLD ARCHAEOLOGISTS

Not only do disagreements about goals divide archaeologists as a whole, but American scholars have a viewpoint different from that of many Old World prehistorians as well. In the United States, archaeologists have long considered their discipline as part of anthropology. European archaeologists, by contrast, lean toward defining archaeology as part of history. In Europe, the arts of excavation have been highly developed by a historical tradition that began with A. H. L. Fox Pitt-Rivers and continued with Sir Mortimer Wheeler and many post-World War II archaeologists. Both British and Continental prehistorians have greatly emphasized recovery of data from the ground, tracing settlement patterns and structures, reconstructing economies, and analyzing in detail artifact types and complicated typologies. The archaeologist is seen as an artisan with diverse skills, not the least of which is effective reconstruction of the past, both to amplify the written record and to create a historical story, albeit incomplete, for periods when no archives record the deeds of chiefs or the attitudes of individuals.

One reason for the difference in approach may be that European archaeologists think of prehistory as their own history, whereas prehistorians in the Americas are conscious that they are studying prehistoric peoples from a background completely different from their own, a non-Western tradition. But for all the differences in approaches and goals, every archaeologist, of whatever viewpoint, would agree that we cannot hope to carry out archaeological research without a body of sound theory, good descriptive archaeology, and detailed information from both the contemporary world and prehistoric lifeways. Above all, the present and the phenomena of the world we live in are there to help us achieve better understanding of the major issues in archaeology:

- What were our earliest ancestors like, and when did they come into being? How old is "human" behavior, and when did such phenomena as language evolve? What distinguishes our behavior from that of other animals?
- How and when did humanity people the globe? How can we account for human biological and cultural diversity?
- What were the conditions and when and how did human beings domesticate animals and plants, becoming sedentary farmers?
- What caused complex societies to evolve—the urban societies from which, ultimately, our own industrial civilization grew?

- Last, a long-neglected question: How did the expansion of Western civilization affect the hunter-gatherer, agricultural, and even urban states of the world that it encountered after Classical times?

In the Beginning is not meant to describe these major developments in human prehistory. Rather, I summarize the multitude of methods and theoretical approaches that archaeologists have used to gain a better understanding of our long past.

SUMMARY

- Modern archaeology is the scientific study of past cultures and technologies—whether ancient or recent—by scientific methods and theoretical concepts devised for that purpose.
- Archaeology covers the human past, from the earliest peoples up to modern times.
- Archaeology had its origins in treasure hunting, Renaissance classicism, and grave robbing, but it has evolved into a highly precise discipline. It has become an integral part of twentieth-century life as a component of popular culture and modern intellectual curiosity.
- Archaeology provides the only viable means of discovering the history of many of the world's societies whose documented past began in recent times. As such, it is a vital support for nationalist feeling and for fostering cultural identity.
- Archaeologists have major contributions to make to the resolution of modern land disputes and to modern management of resources.
- The destruction of sites, fostered by greedy collectors and industrial development, is the crisis that archaeology is faced with today. Archaeological sites are a finite resource that can never be replaced. If the present rate of destruction continues, the danger is real that few undisturbed archaeological sites will remain by the end of this century.
- Archaeologists also face a challenge from people who promote "pseudo-archaeologies" purporting to explain the past, such as extravagant theories that ancient Egyptians or Phoenicians landed in the New World thousands of years before Columbus.
- Archaeology is part of the science of anthropology, which is the study of humanity in the widest possible sense. Archaeologists use a battery of special methods and techniques to examine human societies of the past.
- There are many types of archaeologists. Prehistoric archaeologists study prehistory, that is, human history before written records; historical archaeologists study the material archive of historic cultures; and Classical archaeologists study ancient Greece and Rome.
- Modern archaeology has four basic goals: studying culture history, reconstructing past lifeways, explaining cultural process, and understanding the archaeological record as it relates to the contemporary world.
- In contrast to American archaeologists, many Old World scholars think of archaeology as extending documentary history into the remote past.

GUIDE TO FURTHER READING

These books may be helpful as general reading about archaeology today, but I advise you to consult a specialist before starting in on them:

Binford, Lewis R. *In Pursuit of the Past*. New York: Thames and Hudson, 1983. A closely argued essay on archaeology that integrates ethnoarchaeology with the archaeological record. Recommended for more advanced readers.

Ceram, C. W. *Gods, Graves, and Scholars*. New York: Knopf, 1953. A classic account of early archaeologists; a wonderful introduction to the heroic days of archaeology.

Fagan, Brian M. *Time Detectives*. New York: Simon and Schuster, 1995. A popular book on archaeology which shows how science and archaeology interact.

Feder, Kenneth L. *Frauds, Myths, and Mysteries*. 2nd ed. Mountain View, Calif.: Mayfield, 1996. A useful survey of the phenomenon of pseudo-archaeology.

Meltzer, David J., Don D. Fowler, and Jeremy A. Sabloff, eds. *American Archaeology Past and Future*. Washington, DC: Smithsonian Institution Press, 1986. A series of essays on American archaeology that range over many of the topics in this chapter.

Orser, C.E., and Brian M. Fagan, *Historical Archaeology*. New York: HarperCollins, 1995. An introduction to the basic principles of historical archaeology. Many case examples.

Renfrew, A. C., and Paul Bahn. *Archaeology: Theories, Methods, and Practice*. 2nd ed. New York: Thames and Hudson, 1996. A superb handbook of archaeological method and theory, comprehensively illustrated.

PART 2

A SHORT HISTORY OF ARCHAEOLOGY

SIXTH CENTURY B.C. THROUGH 1990

The Four Stages of Public Opinion

I (Just after publication)
The Novelty is absurd and subversive of Religion & Morality. The propounder both fool & knave.

II (Twenty years later)
The Novelty is absolute Truth and will yield a full & satisfactory explanation of things in general—The propounder man of sublime genius & perfect virtue.

III (Forty years later)
The Novelty won't explain things in general after all and therefore is a wretched failure. The propounder a very ordinary person advertised by a clique.

IV (A century later)
The Novelty a mixture of truth & error. Explains as much as could reasonably be expected. The propounder worthy of all honour in spite of his share of human frailties, as one who has added to the permanent possessions of science.

Thomas Huxley, *Notes,* 1873

No one can fully understand modern scientific archaeology without having some notion of its roots. The first archaeologists were little more than philosophers and antiquarians who were searching for curiosities, buried treasure, and intellectual enlightenment. These treasure hunters were the predecessors of the early professionals, scholars who concentrated on site description and believed that human society evolved through simple stages, the final stage being modern civilizations. Since World War II, archaeology has undergone a major transformation, from a basically descriptive discipline into a many-sided activity that is greatly absorbed in trying to understand how human cultures changed and evolved in the past. If there is one major lesson to be learned from the history of archaeology, it is that no development in the field took place in isolation. All innovations in archaeology are the result of steady advances in the quality of scientific research.

2

THE BEGINNINGS OF SCIENTIFIC ARCHAEOLOGY: SIXTH CENTURY B.C. TO THE 1950s

This chapter examines the early development of archaeology from its beginnings in the philosophical speculations of the Greeks to the development of radiocarbon dating and theories of cultural ecology in the 1950s. We see how archaeology began as little more than treasure hunting, and how successive innovations led archaeologists in new directions, away from simple descriptions toward multilinear evolutionary frameworks for prehistoric times.

BEGINNINGS

People have speculated about human origins and the remote past for thousands of years. As early as the eighth century B.C., the Greek philosopher Hesiod wrote about a glorious, heroic past of kings and warriors. He described five great ages of history, the earliest one of Gold, when people "dwelt in ease." The last was an Age of War, when everyone worked hard and suffered great sorrow (Daniel, 1981). Speculations of this type were widespread in Classical and early Chinese writings. New Kingdom officials in Ancient Egypt restored and conserved Old Kingdom monuments from 1,000 years earlier, while King Nabonidus of Babylon dug into the temples of his predecessors in search of antiquities, which he displayed in his palace.

During the Renaissance, people of wealth and leisure began to travel in Greece and Italy, studying antiquities and collecting examples of Classical art. A new era in Classical archaeology began with the first archaeological excavations into the depths of the famed Roman city of Herculaneum in 1783 (Ceram, 1953). The Herculaneum excavations revealed incredibly full details of one of several Roman towns buried by ash from an eruption of Vesuvius in A.D. 79. At Pompeii, the choking ash preserved the bodies of people fleeing the eruption in panic (Figure 2.1).

Wealthy collectors made a beeline for Mediterranean lands, while their less wealthy colleagues stayed at home and speculated about ancient European history,

FIGURE 2.1   Body of a beggar smothered by volcanic ash outside the Nucerian Gate at Pompeii, Italy.

and about the builders of burial mounds, fortifications, and occasionally more spectacular monuments such as Stonehenge in southern England (Figure 2.2). How old were the builders of such structures? Had they resembled the American Indians, South Sea islanders, and other living nonliterate peoples? There was only one way to find out—excavate ancient sites. These chaotic excavations yielded a mass of stone and bronze axes, strange clay pots, gold ornaments, and skeletons buried with elaborate objects (Figure 2.3). This jumble was confusing. Some graves contained gold and bronze, others held only stone implements, and still others housed cremated remains in large urns. Many questions were unanswered. Which burials were earliest? Who had deposited the bodies, and how long ago? No one yet had a way of putting in order the thousands of years of prehistoric times that preceded the Greeks, Romans, and ancient Egyptians of biblical fame.

SCRIPTURES AND FOSSILS

One reason early archaeologists were confused was that they had no idea how long people had been living on earth. Most people believed that Genesis, chapter 1, told the true story of the Creation. God had created the world and its inhabitants in six days. The story of Adam and Eve provided an entirely consistent

FIGURE 2.2   Stonehenge, the Bronze Age ceremonial center in southern England that was an early focus of antiquarian interest.

explanation for the creation of humankind and the peopling of the globe. In the seventeenth century, Archbishop James Ussher used the genealogies in the Old Testament to calculate that the world was created on the night preceding October 23, 4004 B.C. (Grayson, 1983). Ussher's chronology became theological dogma. It allowed approximately six thousand years for all of human history.

At the time when antiquarians were digging into European burial mounds, Captain James Cook and other Western navigators were exploring the Americas and the Pacific, bringing back new information about all manner of societies flourishing at various levels of cultural development, none of them as advanced as eighteenth-century Europe. A few scholars began to put prehistory in a new perspective, in terms of human progress over time, from the simple to the more complex. But could all of this progress have occurred within a mere 6,000 years?

At the same time, new archaeological discoveries were casting doubt on biblical chronologies. The bones of tropical animals such as the elephant and the hippopotamus came from the gravels of European rivers. Soon the same types of bone turned up in the same strata as carefully chipped stone axes of obvious human manufacture (Figure 2.4). But until the 1860s, the shackles of theological dogma confined human existence within a few millennia.

THE ANTIQUITY OF HUMANKIND

The eighteenth century saw an awakening of interest in archaeology, geology, and the natural sciences. A knowledge explosion in science coincided with the Industrial Revolution. Geologists were in the forefront, their field studies stimulated by deep cuts into the earth resulting from vast engineering projects such

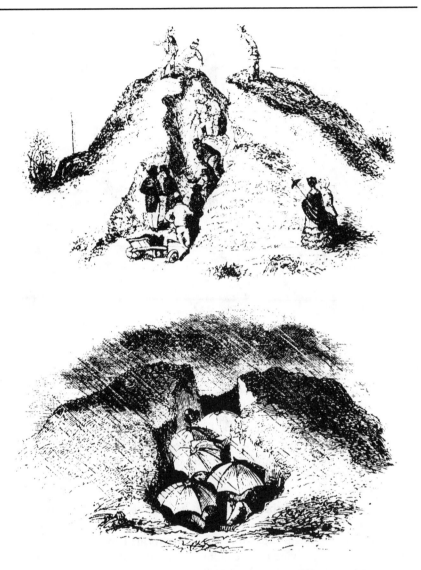

FIGURE 2.3   A nineteenth-century British burial mound excavation as depicted in *Gentleman's Magazine,* 1840. "Eight barrows were examined . . . Most of them contained skeletons, more or less entire, with the remains of weapons in iron, bosses of shields, urns, beads, brooches, armlets, bones, amulets, and occasionally more vessels."

as railroad and canal building. William "Strata" Smith (1769–1839) was one of many field observers who studied these exposures, identifying geological strata and fossil animal types that appeared and disappeared at the same time everywhere on earth. Smith emphasized that the rocks of the earth had been formed by continuous natural geological processes. Every gale that battered the coast, every flash flood or sandstorm, and every earthquake movement were among

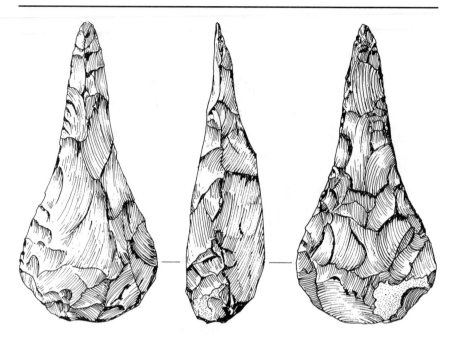

FIGURE 2.4   A stone hand ax of the type found in the same geological layers as the bones of extinct animals. This example was discovered by John Frere at Hoxne, England, in 1797.

the natural phenomena that had gradually shaped the earth into its modern form. Thus, as James Hutton argued in his *Theory of the Earth* (1784), the earth was formed entirely by natural processes, not by divine intervention or catastrophic floods that earlier scientists had considered the nemesis of long-extinct animals.

Hutton's and Smith's theories of what became known as "uniformitarianism" caused a furor, for they attacked the very essence of the Ussherian chronology with their arguments that the earth was formed by long-term natural processes and not by divine intervention. If one accepted the new theories, one accepted the notion that humankind had lived on Earth for many thousands of years. The debate over the antiquity of humankind culminated in 1859 with two major scientific developments—the publication of Darwin's theory of evolution and natural selection and the verification of the contemporaneity of humans and extinct animals.

Charles Darwin began to formulate his theories as a result of a five-year scientific voyage around the world aboard the HMS *Beagle* in 1831–1836 where he witnessed firsthand the incredible biological diversity of the world. Back in England, Darwin delved more deeply into what he called the "species question." He realized his theory would imply that accumulated favorable variations in living organisms over long periods must result in the emergence of new species and the extinction of old ones. Darwin was a timid man, and he procrastinated

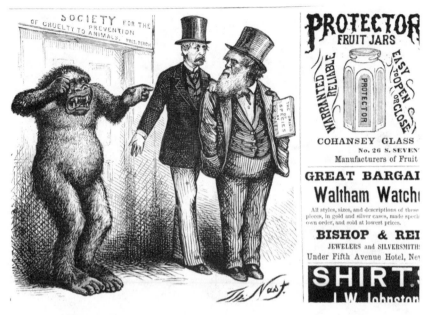

FIGURE 2.5   A period cartoon by Thomas Nast lampooning Darwin's linking apes with human beings.

publishing his results. Evolution, even more than uniformitarianism, flew right in the face of the sacrosanct interpretation of the account of the Creation in Genesis. He sat on his ideas for 20 years until another biologist, Alfred Wallace, sent him an essay that reached much the same conclusions. Reluctantly, Darwin penned a "preliminary sketch," as he called it, in 1859—*On the Origin of Species*.

This scientific classic described evolution and natural selection, giving a theoretical explanation for the diversity of both living and fossil forms. Evolution by natural selection does not, of course, entirely explain biological phenomena, but natural selection does provide a direct way of accounting for biological change as time passes. Predictably, Darwin's theories caused a furor, horrifying many people by assuming that human beings were descended from apelike ancestors (Figure 2.5). But they were soon widely accepted by the scientific community and formed a theoretical background for some important contemporary archaeological discoveries (Van Riper, 1993).

Discoveries of human artifacts in association with extinct animals were nothing new by 1859, for many such finds had been reported over the years, mostly at the hands of enthusiastic amateur diggers. One of the most persistent was French customs officer Jacques Boucher de Perthes, who collected stone tools and animal bones from sealed gravels of the Somme River near Abbeville, in northern France, between 1837 and the 1860s. De Perthes was ridiculed by the scientific establishment when he claimed that the makers of his axes had lived before the biblical flood.

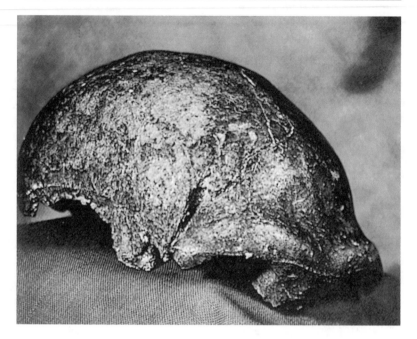

FIGURE 2.6   The Neanderthal cranium from Germany, found in 1856.

Rumors of his finds reached the ears of British antiquarian John Evans and geologist Joseph Prestwich. They visited de Perthes and examined his collections and sites. In one place John Evans actually removed a hand ax from the same sealed level as a hippopotamus bone. The two visitors were convinced that de Perthes's many finds were proof of long antiquity for humankind, something that the new theories of uniformitarianism and evolution made intellectually possible. As John Evans said: "This much appears established beyond doubt, that in a period of antiquity remote beyond any of which we have hitherto found traces, this portion of the globe was peopled by man." Rapid scientific acceptance of the long antiquity of humankind followed, an established antiquity that is one of the intellectual and practical foundations of all scientific archaeology (Grayson, 1983).

If the Somme hand axes and other such finds were of great antiquity, who were the people who had manufactured and used them? Were they modern-looking humans or apelike beings that were closer to apes than people? Part of what was soon to become an intricate fossil jigsaw came to light in a cave near Düsseldorf in Germany's Neanderthal ("Neander Valley") region in 1856, when quarry workers unearthed a primitive-looking human skull (Figure 2.6). It had a huge, beetling brow ridge and a squat skull cap that were quite unlike the smooth, rounded cranium of modern *Homo sapiens*. Many scientists dismissed the Neanderthal skull as that of a modern pathological idiot. But a minority, among them the celebrated English biologist Thomas Huxley, believed that the skull was from a primitive human being, perhaps one of those who had made early stone tools. Huxley himself not only championed the theories of evolution but also expressed what has become one of the fundamental questions archaeologists confront to this day: "the ascertainment of the place which man occupies in nature and of his relations to the universe of things" (Huxley, 1863). At the time Huxley wrote these words, scientists were finally realizing that humanity had evolved both biologically and culturally over a very long period of time indeed. The achievements of early nineteenth-century archaeology were summarized by French archaeologist Gabriel de Mortillet in a guidebook to the archaeology exhibits at the Paris Exposition of 1867: "A Law of Human Progress, a Law of Similar Human Development, and A High Antiquity for Humanity" (Daniel, 1981).

THE THREE-AGE SYSTEM

The spectacular social and economic changes generated by the Industrial Revolution in the nineteenth century generated much interest in human progress. As early as the late sixteenth century, some antiquarians were writing about prehistoric ages of stone, bronze, and iron. Two centuries later, Scandinavian scholars like Sven Nilsson proposed stages of savagery, barbarism, and civilization in ancient societies. These general concepts were refined by Danish archaeologist Christian Jurgensen Thomsen (1788–1865), curator of the National Museum in Copenhagen. He put the confusing collection of artifacts from bogs, burial chambers, and shell middens in order by classifying them into three groups, representing ages of stone, bronze, and iron, using finds in previously undisturbed graves as a basis for his classification.

Thomsen's bold classification was taken up by another Dane, J. J. A. Worsaae, who proved the system's basic stratigraphic validity. By studying archaeological finds from all over Europe, Worsaae demonstrated the widespread validity of the method that became known as the three-age system (Worsaae, 1843). This system was a technological subdividing of the prehistoric past. It gave archaeologists a broad context within which their own finds could be placed. The three-age framework for Old World prehistory, in modified form, survives today (Figure 7.1).

The three-age system of the Scandinavians was not adopted in North America, where almost no metals and no very early Stone Age sites were found. The foundations of accurate stratigraphic and chronological studies in American archaeology were soundly laid by Thomas Jefferson, Harvard archaeologist F. W. Putnam in Ohio, and in the classic archaeological laboratory of the Southwest (Willey and Sabloff, 1993).

HUMAN PROGRESS

By the time Charles Darwin wrote *On the Origin of Species,* the three-age system was well established throughout Europe. It was but a short step from the three ages to doctrines of human progress. In 1850 the sociologist Herbert Spencer (1820–1903) was already declaring that "progress is not an accident, but a necessity. It is a fact of nature" (Spencer, 1855). Darwin's theories of evolution seemed to many people a logical extension of the doctrines of social progress. The new theories opened up enormous tracts of prehistoric time for Victorian archaeologists to fill. The oldest finds were de Perthes's crude axes from the Somme Valley. Later in prehistory, apparently, other people started to live in the great caves of southwestern France, at a time when reindeer, not hippopotamuses, were living in western Europe. And the famous "lake dwellings," abandoned prehistoric villages found below the water's edge in the Swiss lakes during the dry years 1853 and 1854, were obviously even more recent than the cave sites of France (Daniel, 1981). What was the best theoretical framework for all these finds? Could notions of human progress agree with the actual archaeological discoveries? Did prehistoric peoples' technology, material culture, and society develop and progress uniformly from the crude tools of the Somme Valley to the sophisticated iron technology of the much more recent La Tène culture in Europe? Had cultures evolved naturally along with the biological evolution that lifted humanity through all the stages from savagery to civilization? French archaeologist Gabriel de Mortillet even went so far as to proclaim that the progress of humanity was governed by laws akin to those that deposited geological strata (Daniel, 1981).

As archaeological research extended beyond Europe and into the New World, the incredible diversity in early human experience became visible in the archaeological record. The great civilizations of the Near East were recovered by Henry Layard and others, and the great Mesoamerican religious complexes were described anew (Figure 1.1). Stone Age art was accepted as authentic some years after the Altamira paintings were discovered in northern Spain in 1879 (Figure 2.7). Yet many parts of North America and Africa showed no signs of higher civilizations. Furthermore, the New World civilizations and European cave art seemed to imply to nineteenth-century scientists that humanity sometimes "regressed." The

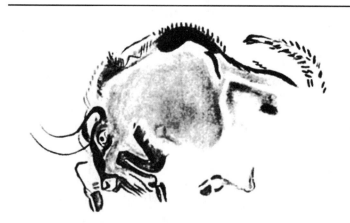

FIGURE 2.7   Bison in a polychrome cave painting in Altamira, Spain. The Altamira style is the ultimate artistic achievement of the late Ice Age peoples of western Europe, about 12000 B.C.

great religious centers of Mesoamerica had been abandoned, for instance, and art equal to that from the French caves did not reappear there for many thousands of years. Scientists became less and less certain that people had a common, consistently progressing universal prehistory.

But, obviously, humankind had progressed considerably overall since the remote millennia of its simple origins, and life had improved for humanity—for the Victorians, at any rate. The pioneer anthropologist Sir Edward B. Tylor (1832–1917) surveyed human development in all of its forms, from crude stone axes of the Somme Valley in France to Maya temples and Victorian civilization. The origins of civilized institutions, he argued (1871), might be found in the simpler institutions of "ruder peoples." If the stone axes made by Australian Aborigines were like those found in ancient European river terraces, then perhaps marriage customs of the native Australians were similar to those among the Stone Age inhabitants of Europe. Tylor used accounts of contemporary primitive peoples and archaeological findings to reemphasize a three-level sequence of human development popular with eighteenth and early nineteenth-century scholars, including Herbert Spencer: from simple hunting "savagery," through a stage of simple farming, "barbarism," to "civilization," the most complex of human conditions. "Although the three divisions of savage, barbaric, and civilised man do not correspond at all perfectly with the stone, bronze, and iron ages, the classification of civilization thus introduced by [Sven] Nilsson and Thomsen has proved a guide of extraordinary value in arranging their proper order of culture in the nations of the Old World," he wrote in his famous article on Anthropology in *Encyclopedia Britannica* (1878).

American anthropologist Lewis Henry Morgan (1818–1881) went even further than Tylor. He outlined no fewer than seven ethnic periods of human progress in his famed book *Ancient Society* (1877). Like Tylor, however, Morgan's stages began with simple savagery and had human society reaching its highest achievements in a "state of civilization." His seven stages, he said, had developed quite rationally and independently in different parts of the world. Morgan's work was to influence modern North American archaeology, with its strong evolutionary bias.

Such notions of human progress were easy to defend in a world whose frontiers were still being explored. There was no such thing as a "world prehistory" in the 1870s, merely thousands of scattered archaeological finds, most of them from Europe, the Mediterranean, or North America. Even expert scientists turned to the comfortable framework of biological and social evolution to explain the astonishing diversity of humankind.

UNILINEAR EVOLUTION AND DIFFUSIONISM

UNILINEAR EVOLUTION

Anthropology formed from several diverse intellectual philosophies. These included biological evolution, the notion of social progress, and the idea of cultural evolution. A most important influence was the constant contact between Western civilization and other human societies with completely different social institutions. It was easy for anthropologists, corresponding as they did with missionaries and pioneer settlers from all over the world, to argue that Victorian civilization was the pinnacle of human achievement. The huge volume of anthropological and archaeological data they collected was used to build a universal scheme of unilinear cultural evolution. In other words, all human societies had the potential to evolve from a simple hunter-gatherer way of life to a state of literate civilization, but many of them had never made it.

Today unilinear evolution seems far too simple an explanation for evolving society. But one must remember that every generation of archaeologists looks at the world through its own perceptions of the social and political environment around it. The early archaeologists were no exception, assuming that their own civilization was the contemporary high point of human achievement. As more and more data accumulated from anthropological research and archaeological excavations all over the world, however, it became clear that a universal scheme of unilinear evolution was a totally unrealistic and ethnocentric way of interpreting world history.

DIFFUSION AND DIFFUSIONISTS

As archaeological knowledge blossomed late in the nineteenth century—and in America, particularly, early in the twentieth—scholars realized prehistoric humanity was also very diverse. But they still faced many hard questions. What were the origins of human culture? When and where was metallurgy introduced? Who were the first farmers? If people did not develop according to universal evolutionary rules, how, then, did culture change and cultural diversity come about? Archaeologists began to expect that population movements, migrations, and invasions would explain prehistory.

The diffusion of ideas and objects from one people to another was recognized early as a valid explanation for cultural change in prehistory. It was especially popular with late-nineteenth-century archaeologists, who reacted against the idea that cultures changed uniformly and also realized that culture change could be explained by outside influences. Many archaeologists began to go along with diffusionist theories when they tried to explain why Near Eastern civilizations were so much richer than the apparently poor European cultures of the same period. Furthermore, they argued, how could the brilliant New World civilizations in Mexico and Peru have arisen if not by long-distance migration from the civilized centers in the Near East?

In its more extreme forms, diffusionism is the assumption that many major human inventions originated in one place and then diffused to other parts of the world by trade, migrating populations, cultural contact, or bold explorers. Early in the twentieth century, British anatomist Grafton Elliot Smith became obsessed with the techniques of Egyptian mummification, sun worship, and monumental stone architecture. The achievements of ancient Egyptian civilization were so unique, he argued in *The Ancient Egyptians,* published in 1911, that all of world civilization and much of modern Western culture diffused from the Nile Valley. It was the "People of the Sun" who had achieved all of this, people who were not afraid of voyaging widely in search of gold, shells, and precious stones. Thus sun worship and early civilization spread over the world.

Smith's diffusionist views of human history were much oversimplified and at least as inadequate as unilinear cultural evolution. Slowly, the first professional archaeologists of the twentieth century realized that they were dealing with very complex problems. Fortunately, they set aside attempts to write universal histories and concentrated on collecting basic data from archaeological sites.

Diffusionist theories have remained popular, albeit in a modified form. In their most extreme manifestations, they still reach incredible heights of absurdity, as in seeking to prove that black Africans colonized America before Columbus or that the Vikings settled Minnesota thousands of years ago (Chapter 1).

DESCRIPTIVE ARCHAEOLOGY

The first professional archaeologists and anthropologists lived when the traditional cultures of non-Western societies were being erased by modern technological civilization. They felt their overwhelming priority to be collecting basic information about vanishing cultures. These data were an essential preliminary to the elaborate theoretical approaches used in archaeology today. American anthropologist Franz Boas (1858–1942) and his students helped establish anthropology—and, by implication, archaeology along with it—as a form of science, by applying more precise methods to collecting and classifying data. They collected an incredible quantity of data on Native American pot designs, basketry, and thousands of other cultural details. Artifacts and customs were meticulously studied and used as the basis for explanations of the past.

These collections led to some quite false interpretations of American Indian culture, later disproved by archaeological research. For instance, ethnologists of this period saw the European arrival, especially with domestic horses, as of unparalleled importance, causing the Great Plains to become filled with nomadic buffalo hunters and raiders of the type made familiar to us by Hollywood films. They described the Plains as sparsely populated up to that time. They were partly right, for the Plains population did indeed swell rapidly as horses came into use. But subsequent work by such archaeologists as W. D. Strong, who dug at Signal Butte, Nebraska, revealed that the Great Plains had been inhabited by hunter-gatherers and horticulturalists for many hundreds of years before the Europeans and horses turned the Plains into a carnival of nomads (Strong, 1935). Archaeology, then, became a source of information against which one checked the historical reconstructions produced by ethnologists.

VERE GORDON CHILDE (1892–1957)

Perhaps the most brilliant of these archaeologists was an Oxford-trained Australian, Vere Gordon Childe. A gifted linguist, he acquired an encyclopedic knowledge of the thousands of prehistoric finds in museums from Edinburgh to Cairo. Once he had mastered the data, Childe set out to describe European prehistory, using "cultures, instead of statesmen, as actors and migrations instead of battles" (Childe, 1958).

Gordon Childe classified cultures by the surviving culture traits—pots, implements, house forms, ornaments—known to be characteristic because they were constantly found together. Cultural successions were reconstructed within limited geographic areas and compared with those from neighboring regions; the culture traits—presumed to have spread from one area to another—were carefully checked. This type of methodology spread in the 1930s and 1940s, when archaeology was still mainly a descriptive discipline. But Childe went further, for he was one of the few archaeologists who realized that cataloging artifacts was useless unless conducted within some frame of reference. He therefore used data from hundreds of sites and dozens of cultures to formulate a comprehensive viewpoint of Old World prehistory that became a classic. The origins of agriculture and domestication and of urban life were, he felt, two great revolutionary turning points in world history. He described two major stages, the Neolithic and Urban revolutions. Each so-called revolution saw new and vital inventions that could be identified in the archaeological record by characteristic artifacts. The Neolithic and Urban revolutions were really a technological and evolutionary model, combined with an economic one, in which the way people got their living was the criterion for comparing stages of world history.

Childe dominated archaeological thinking in Europe until the late 1950s. But his ideas were less influential in the New World because Childe himself never studied or wrote about American archaeology (Trigger, 1980).

CULTURE HISTORY

Boas, Childe, and their disciples made collecting data a primary objective in both New and Old World archaeology. But archaeology itself evolved somewhat differently on each side of the Atlantic.

OLD WORLD ARCHAEOLOGY

The Europeans were studying their prehistoric origins, concentrating on constructing descriptive, historical schemes tracing European society from its hunter-gatherer origins up to the threshold of recorded history. The earliest sites were the hand ax sites in the Thames and Somme river valleys, followed by Ice Age cave dwellings in southwestern France that showed that the Neanderthalers were followed by modern humans with a much more sophisticated hunter-gatherer culture. A similar culture history sequence was postulated for all of Europe and the Near East as well. As Childe showed, the later prehistoric peoples of the Near East and temperate Europe were the logical ancestors of the Greeks, Romans, and other civilizations. It was no coincidence that Arnold Toynbee and other world historians adopted the archaeologists' universal schemes when they made prehistoric times the first chapter in their great historical syntheses.

THE NEW WORLD: THE DIRECT HISTORICAL APPROACH

New World archaeologists were in a very different position. Their most logical way to work was from the known, historical Indian cultures backward into prehistoric times (Summary of literature, see Willey and Sabloff, 1993). The early Southwestern archaeologists adopted this approach in their 1890s research tracing modern Indian pottery styles centuries into the past. This work culminated in the excavations at Pecos Pueblo carried out by Harvard archaeologist A. V. Kidder between 1915 and 1929 (Kidder, 1924). These excavations established a cultural sequence still used in modified form today. Later researchers, such as W. D. Strong, applied similar methods to Plains archaeology with great success (Strong, 1935).

This **direct historical approach**—working from known, historic sites to unknown, prehistoric settlements, preferably those of known peoples—has strict limitations, however. It works satisfactorily as long as one is dealing with the same cluster of finds, such as pottery forms. Once one excavates sites occupied by people with totally different cultures, however, continuity is lost, and the direct historical approach can no longer be used.

NEW WORLD: THE MIDWESTERN TAXONOMIC SYSTEM

Franz Boas's influence was strong from the 1920s to the 1950s among archaeologists who concentrated on collecting and classifying enormous numbers of prehistoric finds from hundreds of sites all over the Americas. They began to arrange these in increasingly elaborate regional sequences of prehistoric cultures, but ran into trouble because no two archaeologists could agree on how to handle enormous quantities of new data emerging from large-scale dam surveys and other Depression-era "make-work" projects in the East and Midwest. Thus no one could compare one area to another using common terminology. Scholars in the Southwest, and a group in the Midwest headed by W. C. McKern, wrestled with the problem, trying to find explicit and formal descriptive terms for groups of archaeological finds. McKern's group prepared definitions that soon became known as the "Midwestern Taxonomic System" (McKern, 1939). By correlating sequences of artifacts and hundreds of sites through long prehistoric periods, using seriation methods (Chapter 7), users of the system were able to compare cultural sequences throughout the Midwest and the eastern United States. The system was highly effective in linking cultural sequences but was limited as a means of interpreting the past, simply because it relied on artifacts, subsistence patterns, and stratigraphic evidence, paying little attention to other lines of evidence about the past.

By the 1940s, James Ford, James Griffin, and Gordon Willey had begun to look farther afield than local regions. At their disposal was a mass of unpublished archaeological data from hundreds of sites excavated during the Depression (Willey and Sabloff, 1993). Their studies in the eastern United States revealed steady development in prehistoric material culture over many thousands of years. They distinguished periods within which broad similarities in prehistoric culture could be found and designated those as developmental stages.

Just as the Midwestern Taxonomic System was reaching the potential limits of its effectiveness, Gordon Willey and Philip Phillips extended earlier survey work in a landmark monograph (1958) that applied essentially the same techniques to the entire New World. Most importantly, they devised developmental stages for the whole continent. These proposed stages were defined by technology, economic data, settlement patterns, art traditions, and social factors rather than by chronology, which, to their way of thinking, was a less important consideration (Chapter 18).

NEW WORLD ARCHAEOLOGY: CHRONOLOGY AND TIME SCALES

No question worried the archaeologists of the 1920s to the 1950s more than establishing an age for their sites and finds (Dating methods: Chapter 8). Once they reached the limits of direct historical ties, they had no means of dating early American cultures. The first breakthrough came in the early years of this century, when University of Arizona astronomer A. E. Douglass started his now-famous studies of annual growth rings in southwestern trees. By 1929, Douglass had developed an accurate chronology for Southwestern sites that was eventually extended back from modern times into the first century B.C. Unfortunately, however, tree-ring dating could be used only in the dry areas of the Southwest, where trees had a well-defined annual growth season. (It has now been applied with success to northern areas.)

Elsewhere, archaeological chronology was mostly done by intelligent guess-work until 1949, when University of Chicago scientists J. R. Arnold and W. F. Libby (1949) described the radiocarbon method for dating organic materials from archaeological sites. Within a few years, radiocarbon dates were processed from hundreds of sites all over the world. For the first time, a widely accepted chronological framework for New World archaeology superseded the guesswork of earlier years. Archaeologists could finally compare widely separated sites and cultures with an unbiased time scale. They could now deemphasize chronology and classification and concentrate instead on why American and Indian cultures had changed in the past.

CULTURAL ECOLOGY

Before and after radiocarbon dating arrived, new emphases in archaeology slowly developed, on the study of human settlement against the changing landscape, pioneered by Cyril Fox and other field workers in Britain (Fox, 1932) and on interpretation, based on carefully studied regional sequences. One conclusion was obvious: human material culture and social organization had developed from the simple to the infinitely complex. From then on, many accounts of world prehistory or broad syntheses of large culture areas allowed for the general notion of progress in prehistory (Braidwood and Braidwood, 1983; Childe, 1942; Willey, 1966, 1971).

JULIAN STEWARD: MULTILINEAR EVOLUTION

At about this time, anthropologist Julian Steward started asking himself: Are there ways of identifying common cultural features in dozens of societies distributed over many cultural areas? Disagreeing with the ardent evolutionists, who insisted that all societies passed through similar stages of cultural development, Steward assumed that certain basic culture types would develop in similar ways under similar conditions. Very few actual concrete features of culture, though, would appear among many human societies in a similar, regular order repeated again and again. In other words, cultural evolution was multilinear; that is, it had proceeded on many courses and at different rates, not just on one universal track, as Tylor and others had believed.

Before Steward, such people as Alfred Kroeber, Lewis Morgan, and Leslie White had long thought of culture as like a layered cake, with technology as the bottom layer, social organization the middle, and ideology the top (L. White, 1949). Steward added the environment to the cake and also looked to it for causes of cultural change. To do so, he developed a method for recognizing the ways in which such change is caused by adaptation to the environment.

Calling his study of environment and culture change **cultural ecology,** Steward laid down three principles (1955):

1. Similar adaptations may be found in different cultures in similar environments.
2. No culture has ever achieved an adaptation to its environment that has remained unchanged over any length of time.
3. Differences and changes during periods of cultural development in any area can either add to societal complexity or result in completely new cultural patterns.

Steward used these principles as a basis for studying cultures and culture change in widely separated areas. To study different cultures, he would isolate and define distinguishing characteristics in each culture, a nucleus of traits he called the *cultural core*. He observed that African San, Australian Aborigines, and Fuegian Indians were all organized in patrilineal (descent through the father) bands, forming a cultural type. Why? Because their ecological adaptation and social organization were similar. Although their environments differed greatly, from desert to cold and rainy plains, the practical requirements of the hunting and gathering lifeway grouped all these people in small bands, each with its own territory. In each area, the social structure and general organization of the bands were very similar, and their adaptation to their environment was fundamentally the same, despite many differences in detail. Steward used his cultural-core device to isolate and define distinguishing characteristics of the hunter-gatherer and of other specific culture types from all of the miscellaneous data he had.

Steward spent much time studying the relationships between environment and culture that form the context and reasons for critical features of culture. Though a culture trait, be it a new type of house or a form of social organization, might be found at one location because it diffused there, that did not explain why the people accepted the trait in the first place. Steward applied cultural ecology to such questions, and also to problems such as why the adjustment of human societies to different environments results in certain types of behavior. To diffusion and evolution he added a new concept: changing adaptations to the natural environment. In other words, the study of culture change involved studying human cultures and their changing environmental conditions as well.

A STUDY OF ARCHAEOLOGY

When Steward's work appeared, American archaeology was completely preoccupied with chronology and artifacts. It was as if archaeologists were classifying insects or collecting postage stamps. Then, in 1948, archaeologist W. W. Taylor published his famed work *A Study of Archaeology,* a devastating critique of American archaeologists' preoccupation with chronology. This landmark essay was the culmination of a debate about functionalism (Chapter 19), which had been unfolding quietly in anthropological and archaeological circles for more than a decade.

Taylor called for shifting emphasis from chronological sequences and distributions to detailed, multilevel studies of individual sites and their features, such as cultural layers, floors, or hearths. The conjunctive approach brought together all possible sources of evidence on a site—technology, style, ecological evidence, architecture, and information on social life—to focus on the people who lived at the site and on the changes in their culture.

Studying the people meant seeing their artifacts in context, as products of entire cultural systems, and reconstructing these systems as completely as possible, including even the less tangible parts, such as their social organization and religious institutions. This view contrasted with that of Childe and his contemporaries on the other side of the Atlantic, who preferred to limit their study to artifacts. Taylor tried to introduce into archaeology a view of culture envisaging the discipline as integral to anthropology. He felt that the disciplines should work together to arrive at general truths about human culture (Kluckhohn, 1940).

Julian Steward's and W. W. Taylor's research brought twentieth-century archaeology to the threshold of great theoretical change. They established, once and for all, the close relationship between archaeology and anthropology. *A Study of Archaeology* showed, with incisive clarity, that one of archaeology's primary goals must be to develop adequate explanations for human prehistory, an aim far more sophisticated than mere excavation, collection, and description.

SUMMARY

- Archaeology originated in the intellectual curiosity about the past felt by a number of Classical writers, such as Hesiod, who engaged in much speculation about the stages in early human history.
- After the Renaissance this curiosity manifested itself in excavations at Herculaneum and elsewhere. But speculations about early prehistory were shackled by the dogma of the Christian church.
- With greater knowledge of human biological and cultural diversity late in the eighteenth century, people began to speculate about the relationships among different groups and about the notion of human progress from simple to complex societies.
- From the discoveries in the Somme Valley, France, and elsewhere, we have proof from the bones of extinct animals directly associated with tools made by human beings, that humanity had existed for more than 6,000 years. These discoveries could not be placed in a scientific context, however, until both uniformitarian geology—the new science of paleontology—and the theory of evolution by natural selection were created.
- The notion of human social evolution followed that of biological evolution. Many archaeologists thought of prehistoric cultures as arranged in stratum-like layers of progress from the simple to the complex. A simple form of unilinear evolution was espoused by such pioneer anthropologists as Sir Edward B. Tylor and Lewis Morgan, who portrayed humanity as having progressed from simple savagery to complex, literate civilization.

- Unilinear evolution was far too simple a scheme to satisfactorily explain prehistory. Some scholars turned to diffusionist schemes, assuming that many cultural innovations had emanated from Egypt and similar centers of higher civilization.
- These diffusionist explanations proved just as unsatisfactory. Influenced by Franz Boas and Vere Gordon Childe, archaeologists began to describe artifacts and sites much more precisely and preoccupied themselves with culture history and chronologies.
- American archaeologists used extensively the direct historical approach to prehistory, working back in time from known historical cultures to prehistoric societies. Standard taxonomic systems were also developed in the 1930s and were widely used. Radiocarbon dating arrived in the late 1940s, coinciding with greater interest in the natural environment and the study of human ecology.
- Anthropologist Leslie White devised a theory of multilinear evolution to explain the past, and his colleague Julian Steward formulated the principles of cultural ecology, studying the relationships between human cultures and their natural environments.
- W. W. Taylor's *Study of Archaeology,* published in 1948, was a landmark critique of American archaeology, chiding archaeologists for preoccupation with description and chronology rather than with cultural change. This pioneer work and the research of Julian Steward and of Leslie White established once and for all the close relationship between archaeology and anthropology.

GUIDE TO FURTHER READING

Fagan, Brian M. *The Adventure of Archaeology.* Washington, D.C.: National Geographic Society, 1985. A lavishly illustrated account of the history of archaeology that is ideal for beginners.

Grayson, Donald. *The Establishment of Human Antiquity.* Orlando, Fla.: Academic Press, 1983. A definitive and scholarly study of human antiquity based on contemporary sources. Strongly recommended for the advanced reader.

Lewin, Roger. *Human Evolution,* 3d ed. Oxford, England: Blackwell, 1995. An authoritative summary of biological and cultural evolution.

Meltzer, David J., Don D. Fowler, and Jeremy A. Sabloff, eds. *American Archaeology Past and Future: A Celebration of the Society for American Archaeology, 1935–1985.* Washington, D.C.: Smithsonian Institution Press, 1986. A set of essays that review the development of American archaeology since the 1930s.

Trigger, Bruce G. *A History of Archaeological Interpretation.* Cambridge: Cambridge University Press, 1989. A brilliant and definitive intellectual history of archaeology.

Willey, Gordon, and Jeremy Sabloff. *A History of American Archaeology,* 3d ed. New York: Freeman, 1993. A detailed account of New World archaeology from the Spanish occupation until recent times.

3

SCIENCE, ECOLOGY, AND DECODING THE PAST: THE 1950s TO THE 1990s

Archaeology, like the other social sciences, has changed almost beyond recognition in four decades. The computer, statistical methods, and the philosophy of science have transformed archaeology from a primarily descriptive discipline into a much more comprehensive system. Chapter 3 starts with these developments and shows how more sophisticated ecological and evolutionary approaches and the greater application of deductive scientific methods and theory building took archaeology in new directions.

SCIENCE AND ARCHAEOLOGY

COMPUTERS AND STATISTICAL METHODS

The advent of the FORTRAN programming language and much readier access to computers and more sophisticated statistical methods began to change archaeology and anthropology in the 1950s (Spaulding, 1953). Both changing interests among researchers and application of the computer to order and handle enormous numbers of tools brought about this new approach to archaeological evidence. Statistical methods rapidly came into fashion as archaeologists realized that with these they could prepare far more meticulous and detailed descriptions of finds than had ever been carried out without them (for quantitative methods, see Chapter 11).

LEWIS BINFORD AND THE SCIENTIFIC METHOD

Doing graduate work at the University of Michigan, Lewis Binford and his then-wife Sally came into contact with eminent scholars who had done much to develop archaeology in the 1940s and 1950s. Among them were James Griffin, who taught them descriptive archaeology; Albert Spaulding, who introduced them to statistical techniques for handling specific problems; and Leslie White, who exposed them to logic and urged them to steep themselves in the philosophy of science. Lewis Binford learned the importance of theory and recognized the close links between archaeology and ethnography. The ultimate objective of archaeology, he believed, was to search for universal laws that govern cultural change.

In the 1960s, Binford wrote theoretical papers that caused ferment in archaeological circles. He advocated more rigorous scientific testing, using formal scientific methods. (The scientific method establishes facts about the natural world by observing objects, events, and phenomena using inductive and deductive reasoning). Binford agreed that statements about the significance of the archaeological record used to be evaluated according to how far back our knowledge of contemporary peoples could be projected onto prehistoric contexts, and according to our judgment of how professionally competent and honest the archaeologists interpreting the past were (Binford, 1962, 1972, 1983a). Inferences about the archaeological record had been made by simple induction, along with guidance from ethnographic data and experimental archaeology. Binford argued that although induction and inference are perfectly sound methods for understanding the past, the real need was for independent methods for testing propositions about the past, commonly used in science, and that these must be far more rigorous than the time-honored value judgments arrived at by assessing professional competence. His approach was soon called the "new archaeology." (For more on archaeology as a science and the scientific method, see Chapter 5.)

With a scientific approach providing interaction among old data, fresh ideas, and new data, we can approach a research problem with a collection of observed data that enables us to pose research hypotheses. Some general problems may have to do with change: How and why did the hunter-gatherers of the Near East turn to agriculture and domestic animals for their livelihood? Or the problems may touch on cultural relationships: Did a new pottery type suddenly appearing in a Midwest cultural sequence get there by trade, population movement, or independent invention?

Working hypotheses were nothing new in archaeology. Binford's approach was different because he advocated that these hypotheses be tested explicitly against archaeological data collected in the field and against other alternatives that have been rejected. Once a hypothesis is tested against raw data, it can join the body of reliable knowledge upon which further hypotheses can be erected. These in turn may require additional data or even entirely new approaches to the excavation and collection of archaeological information. Binford suggested that the explicit scientific method should now be applied to archaeological research.

Binford's papers, lectures, and seminars provoked interest among many American archaeologists, many of whom joined him in reevaluating the methods of archaeology. He and his disciples challenged the assumption that because the archaeological record is incomplete, reliable interpretation of the nonmaterial and perishable components of prehistoric society and culture were impossible. All artifacts found in an archaeological site functioned at one time in a particular culture and society. They occur in meaningful patterns that are systematically related to the economies, kinship systems, and other contexts within which they were used. Moreover, all these artifacts were at the mercy of transient factors such as fashion or decorative style, each of which itself has a history of acceptance, use, or rejection within the society. Thus artifacts are far more than mere material items;

rather, they reflect many of the often intangible variables that go into determining the actual form of the objects preserved. Binford (1968) argued that "data relevant to most, if not all, of the components of past sociocultural systems are preserved in the archaeological record." The archaeologist's task is to devise methods for extracting this information that deal with all determinants in the society or culture being studied (for a British perspective, see D. L. Clarke, 1968).

Binford's "new archaeology" was really a synthesis of many diverse trends, among them cultural ecology, multilinear evolution, and the new emphasis on scientific methods and computers.

LIVING ARCHAEOLOGY (ETHNOARCHAEOLOGY)

A spin-off from this drive for greater scientific rigor was renewed interest among archaeologists in living peoples. The direct historical approach evolved from American archaeologists' recognition that modern Native American cultures had long roots in prehistory. Binford (1978, 1983a) urged, however, that once researchers compare past behavior with that of modern peoples, they should explicitly state the implications and then test each against archaeological data. The conditions for making such tests were best in the field, observing cultural adaptations among living hunter-gatherers and subsistence agriculturalists. Before long, he argued, archaeology would be the only source of explanations for cultural variations among nonindustrial societies. Binford really cared most about how the archaeological record came into existence and how it, as a static phenomenon, was linked to ever-changing human systems.

Richard Lee was among the anthropologists who studied the !Kung San of the Kalahari. He realized archaeologists' difficulties, and arranged to take a prehistorian, John Yellen, to study the remains of long-abandoned campsites and compare them to modern settlements (Lee, 1979; Yellen, 1977). Lewis Binford himself has worked among the Nunamiut Eskimo and the Navajo, comparing living cultures and archaeological materials and trying to develop workable models of culture as rigorous yardsticks for studying variability (Binford, 1978). More recent research has focused on hunter-gatherer groups like the Hadza of northern Tanzania (Figure 3.1); on farming societies, like the Kalinga of the Philippines (Longacre, 1991); and on several Near Eastern groups.

SYSTEMS THEORY AND ECOLOGY

SYSTEMS THEORY

Another element creating a more scientific archaeology was the influence of both philosophers of science and advocates of general systems theory (D. L. Clarke, 1968; Flannery, 1968; Watson and others, 1984). As archaeologists moved away from simple explanations and models of unilinear evolution toward much more elaborate theories, they began to examine the delicate and complex relationships between human societies and their ever-changing environments. Systems approaches involved thinking of human cultures as complicated systems of inter-acting elements, such as technology and social organization, which interacted, in turn, with the ecological systems of which they were part (see Chapter 19). The

FIGURE 3.1 A team of archaeologists and anthropologists records details of a successful hunt by Hadza hunter-gatherers in northern Tanzania, East Africa. Data from surveys like these are of great value for interpreting the archaeological record of prehistoric hunter-gatherers.

systems approach has strongly influenced archaeology because of intense interest in relationships between prehistoric peoples and their environments. (More on systems theory in Chapter 6.)

ECOLOGY AND ARCHAEOLOGY

Ecological thinking about archaeology has a long history. Much of it is based on the assumption that human cultures can affect their environments, and vice versa. One school of thought, environmental determinism, held that forms in nature, which are active, determined human culture, which is passive. However, Franz Boas and other anthropologists rejected this and went so far as to argue that the environment was passive and that human culture developed because some environmental possibilities were selected and others ignored.

Modern ecology, with its focus on ecosystems, caused these simple notions to be rejected in favor of more holistic views of culture and environment. These assume that cultural ecology studies the whole picture of the way in which human populations adapt to and transform their environments. Human cultures are thought of as open systems because their institutions may be connected with those of other cultures and with the environment. Open-system ecology is very realistic, assuming a great deal of variation between individual modern and archaeological cultures. Any explanation of culture has to be able to handle the real patterns of variation found in living cultures, not just the artificial ones erected by classifiers of archaeological cultures. So many factors influence cultural systems that order can be sought only by understanding the system—those processes by which cultural similarities and differences are generated. Many complex factors are external to the culture and cannot be controlled by the archaeologist; one cannot reconstruct the whole cultural system from only one part of it (in archaeological cultures, the surviving artifacts and food residues). Every facet of the cultural system has to be reconstructed separately, using the evidence specifically relevant to that facet, making available, in time, a picture of the whole cultural system, as comprehensive as possible. The issue is a society's total adaptation to both its natural and cultural environments. Developments affecting any one aspect of the culture can ultimately produce further adjustments throughout the system and affect the system's relationship with the natural environment.

Studying prehistoric societies in context—in their natural environments—involves examining the relationships between prehistoric settlements and their surrounding landscape. For working purposes, archaeologists divide human societies into state-organized and pre-state societies, two broad categories distinguished by their social complexity (Chapter 16). In both cases, the relationship between the society, however complex, and its environment is of vital importance.

Important studies in Mexico have assumed that the patterns of human settlement throughout time provide a reliable way of studying the changing adaptations of human cultures to an environment over a long period (Flannery, 1976; Sanders and others, 1979) (see Chapter 15). Such studies can be conducted only with detailed background knowledge of the specific environment in which the culture flourished, changed, and eventually died. Some of the most sophisticated research in archaeology is being done in the open-system ecology format as archaeologists wrestle to develop a meeting ground between a broad view of cultural change and the need to look at each changing culture and its microadaptation to a dynamic environment; both are clearly needed (Flannery, 1976).

WHAT'S TO BE DONE: LIVING ARCHAEOLOGY

The emphasis on systems theory, scientific method, and new approaches to ecology sparked intense debate about the tactics of archaeological research in the 1960s and 1970s. Some people argued that archaeology was a science, which aimed to study basic laws of human behavior. But other archaeologists viewed archaeology as examining the activities of past human beings, as a discipline that was less a science than a historical discipline with its own limitations, resources, and explanatory methods (Flannery, 1973). Everyone agrees, however, that mathematical models, statistical approaches, and rigorous scientific methods will be more and more vital in archaeology.

The fervor of debate and controversy quieted somewhat in the 1980s, partly because some of the basic tenets put forward by Lewis Binford and other scholars had by then been accepted. Most younger archaeologists practicing today were trained by scholars brought up in the new thinking. The scientific method is

widely used; research designs are far more sophisticated than those of a generation ago; and highly technical scientific techniques like remote sensing are
common. But frustration remains, for most of the rich theoretical expectations of
the 1960s remain unfulfilled (Dunnell, 1982). Archaeologists today seem divided
into two camps: a smaller group who write about "theoretical" issues and
concentrate on concepts, methods, and techniques, which are occasionally
applied to a body of data; and a much larger group who carry out empirical studies of the same type that have been done for generations. More "scientific" methods may be used, true, but the effect is mostly superficial. Little integration seems
to link the two groups. In this sense, the "new" archaeology of the 1960s has
failed. Many archaeologists wonder whether archaeology is, in fact, a theoretical
discipline. They must be wrong, for it seems to be undergoing the change that
occurred in biology a generation ago and is now taking place throughout the
social sciences—a serious attempt to assemble a body of theory for archaeology
as distinctive as those of physics and the other experimental sciences.

The innovators who started the revolution in archaeology in the 1960s had no
idea the task they were undertaking was so enormous (Meltzer and others, 1986).
What exactly has been achieved, and where do we go from here? Some of the
achievements of archaeology since the 1960s are indeed impressive: much raw
data, a new emphasis on regional surveys, and widespread use of quantitative
methods. Ecological theory and human ecology itself are fundamental parts of
archaeology in the 1990s. The "new" archaeology, not coincidentally, is no longer
called that. Its most important and rigorous elements have survived. Other
elements, such as the search for general laws of human behavior and the more
extreme manifestations of general systems theory, have less significance. No one
would now question that human cultures should be thought of as ever-changing
systems interacting with their natural environment and one another. The difference
today is that archaeologists are thinking much more profoundly about the archaeological record itself and how it came into being. We can study the remote past only
by means of material evidence that has been changed by centuries, even millennia,
underground. How do we explain the archaeological record? How was it formed?
Archaeologists have turned to "living archaeology" for some answers.

Living archaeology (Chapter 14) includes experimental archaeology and
study of living peoples (ethnoarchaeology). Much of experimental research
focuses on obvious problems like the tree-felling power of stone axes or the
cultural ecology of modern hunter-gatherers in the Kalahari, often referred to in
these pages. But these projects have led a number of investigators to ask the question of questions: How can the present, with its rich data on modern subsistence,
climate, soil qualities, and a myriad of other phenomena, be used to interpret the
past? Not only that, under our world with its varied landscape lies the archaeological record—thousands of sites and artifacts buried since they were abandoned by
their makers. Theoretically, at any rate, we have a wealth of data that could be
used to interpret the past, to bridge the gap between sites and peoples as they were
in prehistoric times and the surviving archaeological record of today. Some people
are puzzled as to why archaeologists are busy studying modern Australian
Aborigines or the city dump in Tucson, Arizona. The reason is that archaeologists
are investigating the relationship between the static archaeological record and the

dynamic, ever-changing world in which we live—and they are doing it while simultaneously developing a new body of archaeological theory, which Binford (1983a), borrowing from sociology, named middle-range theory.

Middle-range theory is best defined as a body of theoretical constructs designed to bridge the gap between the archaeological record in the past and the modern world (see Chapter 14). In the final analysis, archaeological research is an interaction between observed facts (the archaeological record) and research to give meaning to these observations (by means of experimental archaeology, ethnoarchaeology, and historical documents). This interaction involves the archaeologist in all manner of seemingly exotic inquiries: Inuit (Eskimo) subsistence in the 1990s, patterns of wear on the edges of prehistoric tools and modern replicas, and the effects of various geological deposits on the survival of animal bone parts. Much of this research, dealing with basic global problems in the origins of humanity or of more complex societies, must be worldwide in scale. Certainly the sort of research carried out by the archaeologist in 2020 will differ from that of a colleague in the 1990s, but middle-range theory and studies of the contemporary world will continue to be important themes in archaeological research at least for the remainder of the twentieth century (Meltzer and others, 1986).

CURRENT THEORETICAL TRENDS

Some archaeologists have reacted strongly against the ardent materialism of the new archaeology and have embarked on a search for "meaning" or "structure" in the archaeological record (Leone, 1986). They believe that people are like actors, assuming an active role in the shaping of their culture, their society. Thus one must search for the structure behind the artifacts, the overarching patterns that guided people in their interactions with their own culture. Sometimes called "cognitive archaeology" or the "archaeology of mind," this kind of approach is still in its infancy (see Chapter 19), with some of the most notable research coming from studies of the cosmology of the ancient Maya civilization of Central America (Schele and Friedel, 1990, 1993).

Ecological approaches to archaeology are concerned with processes of culture change, with general phenomena. In recent years, some archaeologists, often called "post-processualists," have reacted against this concern with general processes, and they are focusing their attention on the role of the individual in ancient cultures and on the study of ethnic diversity in the archaeological record. Some interesting research involves delving into gender roles in prehistoric societies and into early African-American history in the Americas (Gero and Conkey, 1991, 1996; Ferguson, 1991) (Chapter 16).

At the same time, more archaeologists are thinking hard about the role that archaeology plays in contemporary society, about the ideologies that they, as active members of contemporary society, seek to impose on their interpretations of the past (Chapter 19). They realize that the past can be interpreted in many different ways, including some that actually manipulate archaeology for political and other ends.

Contemporary archaeology is in considerable theoretical turmoil, as those on the cutting edge of current thinking about the past search for a body of original theory that is effective as a way of studying and interpreting prehistory. So far the search has been largely unsuccessful. It is possible that many inspirations will come from recent advances in evolutionary biology, for, as Kent Flannery has pointed out, archaeology is second to none as a discipline for studying cultural change over long periods of time (Flannery and Marcus, 1983). In the meantime, archaeology has come a long way since the antiquarian digs of eighteenth-century Britain. The chapters which follow describe the basic principles of what is now a highly demanding and scientific discipline.

SUMMARY

- In the 1950s, statistical methods long used in the natural and physical sciences came to archaeology. With the new approaches these techniques engendered, archaeologists could perform more detailed analyses and manipulate larger quantities of data.
- Lewis Binford formulated new approaches to archaeology using explicitly scientific methods. He emphasized that archaeological data be tested against formal hypotheses and that careful research designs be used for planning all inquiries.
- This more scientific archaeology included a new interest in living archaeology—ethnoarchaeology. Studying surviving hunter-gatherers gives some insights into prehistoric societies. Before long, it was clear archaeology would be the only means for explaining cultural variations in nonindustrial societies over long periods of time.
- Moving away from simple explanations of the past, archaeologists chose systems approaches to help them depict a human culture as a complicated system of interacting elements that in turn interacted with the ecological system of which it was a part.
- Systems approaches developed hand in hand with cultural ecology, that is, with studies of the changing relationships between prehistoric societies and the environments in which they flourished.
- Current theoretical debates are more concerned with the archaeology of individuals and groups than with processes of cultural change.

GUIDE TO FURTHER READING

Binford, Lewis R. *In Pursuit of the Past.* New York: Thames and Hudson, 1983. An account of archaeology in the 1980s, with a personal record of intellectual developments in recent years.

——. *Working at Archaeology.* Orlando, Fla.: Academic Press, 1983. Binford's major papers arranged in historical order. Read in conjunction with *In Pursuit of the Past.*

Flannery, Kent V., ed. *The Early Mesoamerican Village.* Orlando, Fla.: Academic Press, 1976. A volume of essays with fascinating dialogues about the various approaches to archaeology.

Gero, Joan, and Margaret Conkey, eds. *Engendering Archaeology*. Oxford: Blackwell, 1991. Thought-provoking essays on the study of gender in the archaeological record.

Renfrew, Colin, Peebles, Christopher, S. Hodder, Ian, Bender, Barbara, Flannery, Kent V., and Marcus, Joyce. "What is Cognitive Archaeology?" *Cambridge Archaeological Journal* 3 (2) (1993): 247–270. A series of essays on the emerging approach called "cognitive archaeology." Invaluable as a thoughtful analysis of current theory.

Trigger, Bruce G. *A History of Archaeological Interpretation*. Cambridge: Cambridge University Press, 1989. An authoritative account of the development of explanation in archaeology.

PART 3

BASIC PROCESSES AND PRINCIPLES

Excavators, as a rule, record only those things which appear to them important at the time, but fresh problems in archaeology and anthropology are constantly arising . . . Every detail should, therefore, be recorded in the manner most conducive to facility of reference, and it ought at all times to be the chief object of an excavator to reduce his own personal equation to a minimum.

General Augustus Lane Fox Pitt Rivers,
Excavations in Cranborne Chase (1887)

Part Three describes the basic processes and principles of archaeological research. What is the archaeological record? How do archaeologists carry out their research? What are the basic principles upon which archaeology is based? In this section of the text, we define the archaeological record, look at factors that affect it, and examine the concept of culture in archaeology, the nature of archaeological data, and the ways in which people have established archaeological contexts. Fundamental to context are methods of defining human activities in space and, especially, of measuring prehistoric time. We describe the various methods that have been devised for dating prehistoric cultures from the very earliest times.

4

THE ARCHAEOLOGICAL RECORD

W e begin our discussion of the basic principles of archaeology with the archaeological record of sites, artifacts, and other phenomena. This record is incomplete and biased, for complex and still little-understood processes have transformed the abandoned artifacts, structures, and sites of our forebears. In this chapter, we examine the makeup of the archaeological record, site-formation processes, and the nature of archaeological data.

ARCHAEOLOGICAL DATA

Archaeological data consist of any material remains of human activity—a scatter of broken bones, a ruined house, a gold mask, a vast temple plaza. Archaeological data result from two processes. The first is human behavior, the result of human activity. The other is what are often called transformational processes. As we have seen, the archaeologist identifies and reconstructs ancient human behavior, such as the occupation of a hunter-gatherer camp. The band decides on a location, gathers building materials—sticks, brush or sod, mammoth bones—erects a dwelling, occupies it, then destroys or just abandons the settlement. Archaeologists reconstruct sequences of ancient human behavior not only from archaeological data itself but also from the circumstances under which they are found.

Human behavior is the first stage in the formation of the archaeological record. But what happens when the site is deserted? The collapsed brush shelters, a scatter of stone tools, the remains of a ceremony are abandoned, being of no further use to their owners. All manner of natural processes take hold. The bodies of the buried dead decay; toppled shelters rot away in the sun. Subsequently, a nearby lake may rise and cover the remains, or windblown sand may accumulate over the stone artifacts. Another group may come and build a farming village on the same spot or may simply pick up and reuse some of the artifacts left by the earlier occupants. All these cultural and noncultural developments are *transformational processes*— continuous, dynamic, and unique processes that vary with each archaeological site. Of course, there are wide differences in the preservation of various artifacts, raw materials, and other finds. Thus the archaeologist's data are always biased and incomplete, altered by a variety of transformational, or site-transformation, processes. It follows that anyone investigating an archaeological site has to look closely at both natural and human agents of transformation. For example, World Wars I and II destroyed thousands of archaeological sites, whereas wet conditions in Scandinavian bogs have preserved prehistoric corpses in excellent condition.

SITE-FORMATION PROCESSES

The objects from the past that survive come down to us in two forms, either as historically documented artifacts, such as Orville and Wilbur Wright's first airplane, or in the archaeological record as culturally deposited artifacts that are no longer part of a living society. This past, in the form of artifacts, does not come down to us unchanged, for complex processes have acted on these objects, be they tools, dwellings, burials, food remains, or other humanly manufactured or modified items. Archaeologists must not only study these artifacts but also untangle the many events and processes that contribute to the great variability in the archaeological record as we know it today (Butzer, 1982; Schiffer, 1987). The factors that create the historical and archaeological records are known as site-formation processes.

Site-formation processes are those agencies, natural or cultural, that have transformed the archaeological (or historical) record since a site was abandoned. There are two basic forms of site-formation processes: cultural and noncultural.

Cultural transformations are those in which human behavior has transformed the archaeological record. They can vary widely in their impact and intensity. For example, later occupants of a surface that was a hunter-gatherer camp in the Near East may have been farmers and goatherds rather than hunters. The foundations of their houses cut deeply into underlying strata, while the hooves of their penned goats trampled on and scattered small stone artifacts lying on the surface. And, of course, the archaeologist's excavations are cultural processes, too.

On a more specific level, people reuse artifacts—to conserve precious tools and valuable raw materials, changing the use of an artifact from a knife to a scraper, recycling a projectile point to another use. Sometimes prestigious or valuable objects become prized heirlooms passed down from generation to generation or buried with the dead, as soapstone pipes and other precious artifacts were with Hopewell kin leaders in the Midwest more than 2,000 years ago. Reuse, especially of such commodities as building materials, can become a potent factor in settlements that are occupied for longer periods of time, where people recycle old bricks and other materials for new dwellings. Then there is the dumping of trash, some of it underfoot, much of it elsewhere, in secondary locations where trash heaps may form. These heaps often tend to cluster in specific locations that can be used for many generations, perhaps using a convenient, abandoned storage pit or an old dwelling. Disposal of the dead can be viewed as another form of discard behavior. The archaeologist must decipher the complicated behavioral processes—perhaps the logic, if you will—behind the accumulation of trash heaps, the disposal of the dead, and many other activities.

In short, the archaeological record is not a safe place for artifacts, for a myriad of human activities can disturb them after deposition—plowing, mining, digging of foundations, land clearance, even artillery bombardment, to say nothing of pothunting and site looting.

Noncultural processes are the events and processes of the natural environment that affect the archaeological record. The chemical properties of the soil or bacteria may accelerate the decay of organic remains such as wooden spears or dwellings or may even increase the chances of superb preservation. Rivers may overflow and inundate a settlement, mantling the abandoned remains with fine silt. A great earthquake can topple a settlement in a few minutes, as happened to the Roman town at Kourion in Cyprus on July 21, A.D. 365 (Soren and James, 1988). Windblown sands, ice disturbances, and even the actions of earthworms can disturb the archaeological record.

Whether site-formation processes are cultural or noncultural, the important point is that one can never take the archaeological record at face value. In other words, what you see in the ground is not necessarily a direct reflection of human behavior. The archaeologist must not only record, analyze, and interpret the archaeological record at face value but also investigate the formation processes that altered the record from the moment of its deposition.

Site-formation processes are always important in archaeology, but they assume special importance under circumstances in which it is necessary to document precise associations between, say, human activity and extinct animals. Of no controversy is this more true than the ongoing debates about the date of the first human settlement of the Americas (Dillehay and Meltzer, 1991). The earliest well-attested occupation of the Americas dates to about 12,000 years ago, perhaps a couple of millennia earlier, documented by an archaeological record that is beyond question. It is a different matter with earlier claims, claims as early as 40,000 years ago or more, notably from sites in South America. The Boqueirão da Pedra Furada site in northeastern Brazil is claimed to contain evidence of human occupation, including hearths, dating to before 40,000 years ago. However, the excavators have failed to scrutinize the site-formation processes that have acted on the artifacts from the lower levels of the site (Guidon and Delibrias, 1986). The claimed 40,000-year-old occupation and associated artifacts result from natural geological phenomena such as water action, which filled the lower levels of the cave (Meltzer and others, 1994).

The environment is a hostile place for human artifacts, for the process of interacting with it causes deterioration and drastic modification of the many properties of artifacts, affecting everything from color and texture to weight, shape, chemical composition, and appearance. The environmental agents of deterioration can be grouped into chemical, physical, and biological categories (Schiffer, 1987). Chemical agents are universal, for the atmosphere contains water and oxygen, which create many chemical reactions—corrosion of some metals is an example. Different water temperatures, irradiation of materials by sunlight, and atmospheric pollutants all cause chemical reactions. Buried objects are often subject to rapid chemical change, especially as a result of dampness. Soils also contain reactive compounds such as acids and bases that contribute to many deterioration processes. Acidic soils dissolve bones, for example. Many archaeological deposits are somewhat salty, a condition caused by salts derived from wood ash, urine, and the neutralization of acids and bases. Such saline conditions can retard some decay, but copper, iron, and silver can decay severely.

Physical agents of deterioration are also universal, agents such as water, wind, sunlight, and earth movement. Water is especially potent, for it can tumble artifacts on the shores of oceans or lakes or from riverbank encampments, sometimes even fracturing them in ways that suggest human manufacture. Rainwater can cascade off roofs and tunnel deep prooves into walls. The cycle of wetness followed by drying cracks many woods and causes rot; melting and freezing ice cracks rocks, even concrete. Physical agents operate on scales small and large. For example, the effects of the Kourion earthquake flattened the small port and also affected the landscape for miles around. The site-formation processes at shipwreck sites like the Late Bronze Age Uluburun wreck off southern Turkey are of vital importance in understanding the cultural significance of the ship.

Living organisms are the main agents of biological decay. Bacteria occur almost everywhere and are usually the first to colonize dead organic matter and begin the processes of decay. Fungi also occur widely and are especially destructive to wood and other plant matter, particularly in damp, warmer climates. Beetles, ants, flies, and termites infest archaeological sites, especially middens and abandoned foods. Animals such as dogs and hyenas chew, gnaw, and scavenge bones and other organic materials from the surfaces of abandoned sites and game kills.

Archaeological sites are also affected by the processes within the natural environment of which they are a part. The first human activity at any site took place on a natural surface, on natural sediments themselves sitting on underlying bedrock. Sometimes this underlying sediment was weathered over a long time and may contain pollen grains, plant remains, or other sources of environmental information. For instance, some Bronze Age burial mounds in Europe were erected on undisturbed soils that contained forest pollen grains, giving a picture of the local environment at the time of construction. After the site is abandoned, additional sediments usually accumulate on top of the archaeological remains through the action of wind or water, such as the windblown sands that accumulate in the rooms of Southwestern pueblos. Human feet or animal paws, burrowing animals, earthworms, wall flakings from overhanging cliffs, and the deteriorating elements of artifacts and structures contribute to the alteration of archaeological deposits. Rock shelters in southwestern France, for example, were occupied intermittently by hunter-gatherer groups between 30,000 and 15,000 years ago. Some of the larger ones contain densely packed layers of hearths, ash accumulations, boulders, and decaying structures (Laville and others, 1980). Untangling how these levels were formed is a complex process.

The site-formation processes at each individual site must be considered separately, usually in the context of the different deposits within the site. The first stage is to identify the specific cultural and noncultural formation processes that created each deposit or set of deposits. This involves thinking of the artifacts as an integral part of the deposits in which they are found. The investigator records and analyzes such phenomena as reductions in size, patterns of damage, and distribution within the deposit as ways of trying to understand the complex "package" of evidence about cultural and environmental materials that makes up that deposit. In other words, the archaeologist has to establish what cultural and noncultural processes led to the formation of each deposit in the site. The fundamental point about studying site-formation processes is that they have to be identified before behavioral or environmental inferences can be made about any archaeological site. The identification of specific site-formation processes is difficult, even under ideal circumstances, and involves not only geoarchaeological research but also data acquired from ethnoarchaeology, controlled experiments, and other sources. It is not enough, then, to observe conditions of unusually good preservation or to describe the complex layers of a prehistoric rock shelter. One must also analyze and interpret the ways in which the archaeological record was created through site-formation processes.

THE MATRIX: PRESERVATION AND HUMAN ACTIVITY

All archaeological finds, from a humble stone chopper to an Egyptian pharaoh's tomb, occur within a **matrix** (the physical substance which surrounds the find) from natural phenomena such as a river flood or from human behavior such as the building of a new community on top of an older one. The chemistry and physical characteristics of the matrix can have a profound effect not only on the **provenance** (the precise three-dimensional position of the find in the matrix as recorded by the archaeologist) of an archaeological find, but also on its context and association with other subjects. For example, the physical characteristics of the deposits in which they were found tell us that fast-running waters of the River Thames in England rolled dozens of Stone Age hand axes downstream from where they were originally dropped by their makers and deposited them in river gravels, to be recovered by archaeologists more than 250,000 years later. Human behavior also determines the context and provenance of archaeological finds in the matrix. Many Hopewellian culture burials of 1,800 years ago were deposited in mound platforms in the Ohio Valley. Careful excavation of the surrounding deposits shows that many people were laid to rest before a large earthwork was erected over the sepulchral platform where the dead lay (Fagan, 1995e).

Evaluating the natural formation processes that have contributed to the archaeological record involves geoarchaeological research (Chapter 15). Deciphering human activities from artifact patterns in the matrix requires careful evaluation of many subtle behaviors from the remote past. The following are some common instances where human activity has affected the archaeological record.

DISCARDS

The patterns of artifact discard can be very subtle; understanding them often requires knowledge that is still beyond our grasp. For example, at the Maya trading center on Cozumel, off the coast of the Yucatán peninsula, the people invested very little material wealth in temples, tombs, or other permanent monuments (Friedel and Sabloff, 1984). Their capital in obsidian (volcanic glass) was kept fluid and on hand, an investment in resources different from that found at other Maya ceremonial centers, which invested heavily in religious monuments and tangible displays of wealth. The different investment in resources reflects the activities and their significance in each type of locality. Interpreting such patterns of discard, the remains that are left for interpretation after the long centuries and millennia of natural destruction have taken place, presents huge difficulties for archaeologists. Any archaeologist working anywhere has to face the kind of peculiar problems that Friedel and Sabloff identified at Cozumel. What are the distorting effects of human discard patterns on the archaeological record, on surface site survey, and on the limits to which we can take the interpretation of sites and finds?

RECYCLING

People discard artifacts, and they recycle them as well. A stone ax can be sharpened again and again until the original, large artifact is just a small stub that has been recycled into extinction. It takes a great deal of effort to build a mud-brick house from scratch. Very often, an old house is renovated repeatedly, its precious wooden beams used again in the same structure or in another building. Such recycling can distort the archaeological record, for what appears to be a one-time structure might in fact have been used again and again. Tree-ring dating of pueblos in the Southwest is complicated by the constant reuse of wooden beams. Sometimes, too, the Pueblo Indians would cut beams and stockpile them for later use.

Not only individual artifacts but also entire archaeological sites can be recycled. A settlement flourishes on a low ridge in the Near East. After a generation or two the site is abandoned, and the inhabitants move elsewhere. Later, people return to the site, level the abandoned houses, and build their own dwellings right on top of the site. This type of recycling can seal and preserve earlier levels, but it can also result in the reuse of building materials from earlier houses.

HEIRLOOMS

Successive generations may also find a structure or an artifact so valuable that they consciously preserve it for the benefit of their descendants. The great temple, or *ziggurat,* of the city of Eridu in Mesopotamia was first erected around 5000 B.C. This important shrine was visible for miles around and was rebuilt on the same site time and time again for more than 2,000 years. Tracing the complex history of this mud-brick structure has consumed many hours of excavation time (Lloyd, 1963).

CEREMONIAL ARTIFACTS

Many prehistoric societies valued ritual objects, such as masks, ceremonial axes, and other symbolic artifacts that were associated with ancestor worship. These ceremonial artifacts were sometimes buried with a dead priest or leader, as with Tutankhamun and with the Lords of Sipán in Peru. It is easy enough to tell their age and association with a grave dug at a particular period. In other instances, ceremonial artifacts can be treasured for generations, displayed only on special occasions or kept in a special relic hut. By treasuring such objects, however, the owners can unwittingly distort the archaeological record. Fortunately, in most cases it is possible to identify instances of **curation,** or preservation, by the style of the artifacts. In Tutankhamun's tomb, Howard Carter found among the grave furniture objects that had belonged to earlier pharaohs. Presumably, they had been placed in the tomb to fill in gaps in the royal inventory caused by the king's unexpected death.

DELIBERATE AND ACCIDENTAL DESTRUCTION

The many other potential causes of human distortion of the archaeological record can include deliberate destruction of cemeteries, erasure of inscriptions from temples at royal command, or the ravages of warfare, both ancient and modern. Even more destructive are depredations by treasure hunters and antiquities dealers satisfying the greed of museums and private collectors (Meyer, 1977).

PRESERVATION CONDITIONS: INORGANIC AND ORGANIC MATERIALS

We must now examine preservation conditions, some of the circumstances under which the archaeological record comes down to us in exceptional condition. Under highly favorable circumstances, many kinds of artifactual materials are preserved, including such perishable items as leather containers, baskets, wooden arrowheads, and furniture. But under normal circumstances, only the most durable artifacts survive. Generally, the objects found in archaeological sites are of two broad categories: inorganic and organic materials.

Inorganic objects are of such materials as stone, metals, and clay. Prehistoric stone implements, such as the choppers of the earliest humans, made more than 2 million years ago, have survived in perfect condition for archaeologists to find. Their cutting edges are just as sharp as they were when abandoned by their makers. Clay pots are among the most durable human artifacts, especially if they are well fired. It is no coincidence that much of prehistory is reconstructed from chronological sequences of changing pottery styles. Fragments (potsherds) of well-fired clay vessels are practically indestructible; they have lasted as long as 10,000 years in some Japanese sites.

Organic objects are made of living substances, such as wood, leather, bone, or cotton. They rarely survive in the archaeological record. When they do, the picture of prehistoric life they give us is much more complete than that from inorganic finds.

ORGANIC MATERIALS AND THE ARCHAEOLOGICAL RECORD

Most of the world's archaeological sites preserve little more than the inorganic remains of the past, the most durable artifacts to survive the centuries and millennia. Sometimes, however, especially favorable preservation conditions result in the survival of highly informative organic materials—artifacts, food remains, and environmental data.

WATERLOGGED ENVIRONS AND WETLANDS

Waterlogged or peat-bog conditions are particularly favorable for preserving wood or vegetal remains, whether the climate is subtropical or temperate. Tropical rain forests, such as those of the Amazon Basin in South America and Zaire in Africa, are far from kind to wooden artifacts. In contrast, a significant number of archaeological sites occur near springs or in marshes where the water table is high and perennial waterlogging of occupation layers has occurred since they were abandoned (Coles and Coles, 1986; Purdy, 1988). Numerous shipwrecks have yielded valuable archives of information, for conditions underwater have preserved even insignificant artifacts. King Henry VIII's warship *Mary Rose* yielded priceless information on Tudor ship construction and gunnery, and the skeletons of archers, their weaponry, and a myriad of day-to-day artifacts, large and small. The Uluburun Bronze Age ship from southern Turkish waters has provided a unique portrait of eastern Mediterranean trade more than 3,300 years ago, while the ship's timbers will add much to our knowledge of early marine architecture (Figure 1.9) (Chapter 16).

Wetlands look like dreary, waterlogged countryside, far from appealing. In prehistoric times, wetlands were often just used for hunting or were traversed by pathways. Others were exploited for crops, for grazing, or even for settlement and such industries as gathering thatching grass. Wetlands come in an infinite variety, each type formed by different depositional processes, with a highly varied archaeological content. Many wetland sites have been well protected from the ravages of animal and human scavengers and from the severe noncultural processes that have acted on more exposed locations. In some cases, as in the Somerset Levels of southwestern England, archaeologists have been able to reconstruct entire landscapes traversed by wooden walkways, using not only walking but also aerial photographs, remote sensing, and subsurface boring (Coles and Coles, 1986).

SOMERSET LEVELS   The Somerset Levels in England were once a bay of the nearby Severn River, a bay filled with thick peat deposits between 6,000 and 1,500 years ago (Coles and Coles, 1986). Conditions on the Levels fluctuated constantly, so the inhabitants built wooden trackways that traversed their traditional routes across the Levels (Figure 4.1). Some 6,000 years ago, the Neolithic builders of the Sweet Track needed a raised walkway to join two islands in a marsh. They felled trees on dry ground, prepared them as required, and carried the wood to the marsh edge. Then they placed long poles end to end on the marsh surface along the preferred route, usually alder, ash, or hazel trunks pegged into the underlying wet ground with stout stems about every 3 feet (1 m). The pegs were driven in obliquely in pairs, crossing over the poles in a V shape. The builders then lodged planks into these crossed pegs on top of the poles, forming a mile-long walkway about 16 inches (41 cm) wide and about the same height above the poles. The Sweet Track excavations have provided a unique opportunity for paleoenvironmental reconstruction and also for tree-ring analyses. A chronology from the ash trees has established that all the timber for the track was expertly felled at one time, with the track being used for about ten years. So detailed were the investigations that the excavators were able to show that part of the track, over a particularly wet portion, was repaired several times. Wooden

FIGURE 4.1   Neolithic track in the Somerset Levels, southwestern England.

wedges, wooden mallets, and stone axes were used for splitting the planks; other artifacts came from the crevices of the track, among them stone arrowheads, complete with traces of shaft, glue, and binding; hazelwood bows; and imported stone axes.

TOLLUND MAN   Danish bogs have yielded a rich harvest of wood-hafted weapons, clothing, ornaments, traps, and even complete corpses, such as that of Tollund Man (Glob, 1969). This unfortunate individual's body was found by two peat cutters in 1950, lying on its side in a brown peat bed in a crouched position, a serene expression on his face and eyes tightly closed (Figure 4.2). Tollund Man wore a pointed skin cap and a hide belt—nothing else. We know

FIGURE 4.2   Tollund Man, preserved for 2,000 years in a Danish bog.

that he had been hanged, because a cord was found knotted tightly around his neck. The Tollund corpse has been shown to be about 2,000 years old and to belong to the Danish Iron Age. A formidable team of medical experts examined his cadaver, among them a paleobotanist who established that Tollund Man's last meal consisted of a gruel made from barley, linseed, and several wild grasses and weeds, eaten 12 to 24 hours before his death. The reason for his execution or sacrifice is unknown.

OZETTE   Richard Daugherty of Washington State University worked at the Ozette site on the Olympia Peninsula in the Pacific Northwest for more than a decade (Kirk, 1974). The site first came to his attention in 1947 as part of a survey of coastal settlements. Ozette had been occupied by Makah Indians until 20 or 30 years before, and traces of their collapsed houses could be seen on top of a large midden. It was not until 1966 that Daugherty was able to start excavations

FIGURE 4.3   Ozette, Washington. Excavation of the walls, sleeping benches, and planks of a prehistoric house uncovered by a mud slide. The waterlogged conditions preserve wood and fiber perfectly.

at the site, which was being threatened with obliteration by wave action and mud slides. A trial trench revealed large deposits of whale bones and yielded radiocarbon samples dating back 2,500 years. Most importantly, the muddy deposits had preserved traces of wooden houses and the organic remains in them. Then, in 1970, a call from the Makah Tribal Council alerted Daugherty to a new discovery. High waves had cut into the midden and caused the wet soil to slump, revealing collapsed wooden houses buried under an ancient landslide.

Daugherty and his colleagues worked for more than ten years to uncover the remains of four cedarwood longhouses and their contents (Figure 4.3). The excavations were fraught with difficulty, and high-pressure hoses and sprays were needed to clear the mud away from the delicate woodwork. All the finds were then preserved with chemicals before final analysis. The wet muck that mantled the houses had engulfed them suddenly in a dense, damp blanket that preserved everything except flesh, feathers, and skins. The houses were perfectly preserved, one uncovered in 1972 measuring 69 feet long and 46 feet wide (21 m by 14 m). There were separate hearths and cooking platforms, and hanging mats and low walls served as partitions. More than 40,000 artifacts came from the excavations, including conical rain hats made of spruce roots, baskets, wooden bowls still impregnated with seal oil, mats, fishhooks, harpoons, combs, bows and arrows,

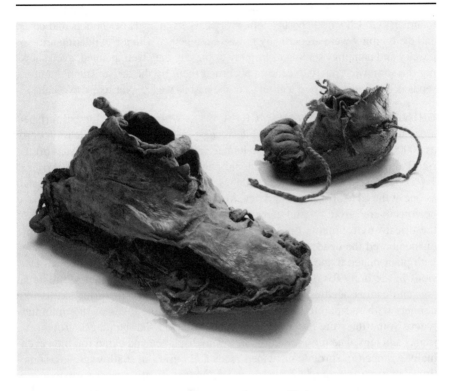

FIGURE 4.4   A fiber sandal from Hogup cave, Utah.

even fragments of looms, and ferns and cedar leaves. A fine artistic tradition in wood excited the excavators: the trove included a whale fin carved of red cedar and inlaid with 700 sea otter teeth (Figure 12.19).

The Ozette site is a classic example of how much can be recovered from an archaeological site in waterlogged conditions. But Ozette is important in other ways, too, for the Makah Indians who lived there had a tangible history, extending back at least 2,000 years before the whites came. Oral traditions and written records for the Makah go back no further than A.D. 1800. The Makah abandoned Ozette only in modern times, to move nearer a school in the 1920s. The archaeological excavations have traced the continuity of this village of whale catchers and fisherfolk far back into prehistory, giving a new sense of identity to the Makah of today.

DRY CONDITIONS

Very arid environments, such as those of the American Southwest or the Nile Valley, are even better for preservation than waterlogged localities (Figure 4.4).

THE TOMB OF TUTANKHAMUN   Undoubtedly one of the most famed of all archaeological discoveries is the amazing tomb of Tutankhamun (c. 1323 B.C.), unearthed by Lord Carnarvon and Howard Carter in 1922 (Carter and others, 1923–1933; Reeves, 1990). The undisturbed burial chamber was opened, revealing the grave furniture in exactly the same state as it had been laid out by the king's mourners. Gilded wood chests, cloth, ivory caskets, models of chariots and boats, and the mummy were all perfectly preserved, together with a bewildering array of jewelry and paintings shining as brightly as the day they were painted, even showing the somewhat hasty execution accorded them by the artist. Tutankhamun's sepulcher provides as vivid a glimpse of the past as we are ever likely to obtain.

CHINCHORRO MUMMIES, CHILE   The Chinchorro culture flourished along the southern Peruvian and Chilean coast of South America at least as early as 7000 B.C. The Chinchorro were a hunter-gatherer society that subsisted off the rich Pacific inshore fisheries and local patches of wild plant foods (Arriaza, 1995). They settled in permanent villages, burying their dead in cemeteries such as one at the El Morro site near Arica. More than 280 Chinchorro mummies have been recovered from coastal cemeteries, astonishingly well preserved in one of the driest environments on earth. Beginning in about 5000 B.C., the people dismembered the dead, skinned, and eviscerated them, then packed the bodies with plant material and reinforced them with sticks. Later, they made neat incisions in the body for removing organs, then sewed them together with human hair and cactus needles. They attached wigs of human hair to the skulls like helmets with red-painted ash paste, often painting the faces of the mummies black. Sometimes the mourners reattached the skin like bandages around the trunks and legs. The mummified bodies were displayed and cared for, then eventually wrapped in shrouds of twined reeds and buried in shallow graves, sometimes in family groups of six or more. Mummification ceased among the Chinchorro in about 1500 B.C., centuries before Tutankhamun ruled Egypt. The bone chemistry and bowels of the Chinchorro mummies reveal a diet heavy in seafood, and evidence of tapeworm infestations and auditory exostosis, caused by diving in deep water.

ARCTIC CONDITIONS

Arctic sites, too, are excellent for preserving the human past. The circumpolar regions of Siberia and the New World have acted like a giant freezer in which the processes of decay have been held in check for thousands of years. Close to the Arctic Ocean, dozens of deep-frozen mammoth carcasses have survived thousands of years in a state of perennial refrigeration. Perhaps the most famous is the Beresovka mammoth, which became mired on the swampy banks of a Siberian river one spring some 10,000 years ago. The Russian expedition that recovered the carcass in 1901 found the meat so fresh that the scientists fed it to their dogs. The mammoth's hair was perfectly preserved, and the remains of its last meal were found on its tongue and in its stomach (Digby, 1926).

"THE ICE MAN"   A combination of dry winds and extreme cold dried out and preserved a 5,300-year-old Bronze Age corpse found high on the Similaun glacier in the European Alps in 1991 (Barfield, 1994; Spindler, 1994) (Figure 4.5). The 20-year-old man's body was first dried out by cold winds, then buried by snow and ice before being exposed in modern times as the glacier melted in warm weather. He was in a crouched position, as if he had taken shelter in bad

FIGURE 4.5 "Otzi the Ice Man" from the Similaun glacier in the European Alps. A reconstruction of his appearance at the time of his death.

weather when lost. Experts believe the man was either hunting or looking for minerals like copper, which is plentiful in the Alps. The man carried a copper ax with a wooden shaft, a leather quiver with 14 bone- and wood-pointed arrows, and replacement heads and a puttylike substance for mounting them. He wore leather boots lined with hay for warmth, a stone necklace, and leather and fur garments. His knee and back bore small tattoos. An international team of experts will examine the body, decipher its DNA, and examine its connective tissues. The Similaun corpse has been radiocarbon-dated to between 3350 and 3300 B.C.

FRANKLIN EXPEDITION, CANADIAN ARCTIC   On May 19, 1845, veteran arctic explorer Sir John Franklin left London in command of the most completely equipped arctic expedition ever to search for the famed Northwest Passage across far northern Canada. HMS Erebus and HMS Terror sailed into the remote north from western Greenland in July of the same year and were never seen again. A couple of years passed before concern was felt, as the ships were equipped for a prolonged absence. By 1850, however, several expeditions were combing the Hudson Bay region for traces of the missing explorers. Three graves were found on remote Beechey Island, close to where the searchers discovered traces of the expedition's first winter camp, but these were of men who had died before the expedition ran into trouble. It was not until 1859 that other searchers on King William Island at the foot of the Boothia Peninsula, the western arm of Hudson Bay, came across a cairn and an abandoned ship's boat filled with dead sailors who had perished while on a last desperate journey to safety. Sporadic searches until the 1880s yielded occasional European artifacts and nonnative human bones. No records of the expedition were ever recovered, and it was assumed that Franklin and his men had perished from malnutrition, for they refused to live off food resources such as sea mammals, which the indigenous Inuit had subsisted on for thousands of years even in the depth of winter.

Anthropologist Owen Beattie is an expert in forensic anthropology who has worked on many criminal cases in his native Canada. In 1981 he mounted the first of a series of field trips in search of new evidence about the demise of the Franklin expedition. At first he concentrated his search in the King William Island area but recovered little more than some startling evidence for cannibalism among the last survivors of the expedition. He also recovered a skeleton from the boat site that displayed unusually high lead levels, to the point that he suspected its owner had suffered from chronic lead poisoning. Beattie needed more complete anatomical information. So he applied for permission to exhume the graves of the three men who had been interred on Beechey Island—Petty Officer John Torrington, Able Seaman John Hartnell, and Marine Private William Brain. It was a spectacular exercise in cold-climate archaeology and forensic medicine which furnished new clues to the fate of the Franklin expedition.

The wooden coffins of the three men were well preserved, Torrington's covered with blue wool fabric decorated with white tape. A hand-painted, wrought-iron plaque, perhaps fashioned from a tin can, bore the inscription "John Torrington, died January 1st, 1846, aged 20 years." The excavators had to thaw ice around the coffin lid and shear the nails. The body was encased in a block of ice that was melted with buckets of heated water. Soon Torrington's perfectly

FIGURE 4.6   John Torrington.

preserved toes and the front of his shirt came into view. The head was covered with a fold of blue wool. When the cloth was drawn back with tweezers, John Torrington's perfectly preserved countenance stared at them (Figure 4.6). For the first time, scientists gazed not at a crude drawing or a primitive photograph of their forebears but at the face of an actual nineteenth-century human being. It was a startling and emotional experience.

Torrington had been buried in simple, gray linen trousers. He wore a white shirt with blue stripes, a high collar, and a pleated waist. A white, polka-dotted kerchief covered his medium-brown hair. An on-site autopsy revealed that he had stood 5 feet 4 inches tall and had been very emaciated at the time of his death. Laboratory tests on his organs told a tale of serious medical problems for such a young man. His lungs were blackened by inhalation of coal dust, smoke, and other atmospheric pollutants. Since Torrington was a stoker, this is hardly surprising. He had suffered from emphysema and tuberculosis and had probably died of pneumonia. However, the real cause of death was probably the severe mental and physical problems caused by lead poisoning, for trace-element analyses of his hair gave readings of more than 600 parts per million, evidence of acute lead poisoning.

The bodies of John Hartnell and William Brain, exhumed in 1986, also bore signs of serious lead poisoning. Beattie's detailed autopsies painted a picture of an expedition plagued by catastrophic health problems, almost certainly resulting from lead poisoning. Loss of energy and poor appetites, neurotic and illogical behavior, acute depression—these symptoms, especially the mental ones, were deadly in the stressful conditions of the Arctic. The lead concentrations probably came from the solder used to seal the tinned foods consumed by the expedition, and many of the foods may have been spoiled, owing to poor can sealings.

There were, of course, many causes for the failure of the Franklin expedition, but the near-perfect preservation conditions of the Arctic have provided modern science with a possible underlying cause for one of the great tragedies of nineteenth-century exploration (Beattie and Geiger, 1986).

TRAGEDY AT UTQIAGVIK   Another spectacular discovery, this time on a bluff overlooking the Arctic Ocean near Barrow, Alaska, also records a tragedy, this from recent prehistory. Two Inupiat women, one in her forties, the other in her twenties, were asleep in a small driftwood-and-sod house on a bluff overlooking the ocean on a stormy night in the 1540s (Dekin, 1987). A teenage boy and two young girls slept nearby. The sea ice was crashing against the shore, the ice pack driven against the coast by high waves. Suddenly, a giant mass of ice chunks broke free in a violent surge and was carried over the bluff, crashing tons of ice down on the tiny house. The roof collapsed, killing the inhabitants immediately. At dawn, the neighbors found the house silent and left it buried under the ice. Later, other members of the family removed some utensils and food from the ruins, and the timber uprights projecting through the ice were salvaged. The rest was undisturbed for five centuries, a deep-frozen prehistoric tragedy.

Five centuries ago, Utqiagvik was a sizable settlement, but it is now buried under much of an expanding Barrow, Alaska. There are at least 60 house mounds. In 1982 the remains of an Inupiat winter house came to light, intact and still mostly frozen. The house was formed of hand-hewn driftwood used for both floorboards and wall panels. Everything was held together with a matrix of frozen earth and insulated with a sod roof. The well-preserved bodies of the women were autopsied. Both had been in reasonably good health, although their lungs were blackened with anthracosis, a condition caused by inhaling smoke and oil-lamp fumes in closed-in winter houses. They ate a heavy diet of whale and sea blubber, which had narrowed their arteries and caused atherosclerosis. The older woman had given birth about two months before the disaster and was still lactating. Both of them had suffered periods of poor nutrition and illness. The older had recovered from pneumonia and a painful muscle infection called trichinosis, perhaps contracted from eating raw polar bear meat.

The women had slept naked under their bed robes, probably to avoid moisture buildup in their daily garments that would freeze when they went outside.

Outside, they had worn caribou parkas, snow goggles, and mittens, and waterproof sealskin inner boots, all found in the entrance tunnel to the house. Much of their time was spent making and repairing clothing and maintaining the hunting gear that was well preserved in the ruins. There were bone harpoon heads for hunting seals and other sea mammals, with the remains of a bola, a sinew throwing device weighted with bone weights used to snare birds in flight. A wooden bucket stitched together with baleen and a wood and bone pick for clearing ice were recovered near the house entry.

VOLCANIC ASH

Everyone has heard of Roman Herculaneum and Pompeii, entire towns overwhelmed in A.D. 79 by an eruption of nearby Vesuvius. The volcanic ash and lava buried both communities, even preserving the body casts of fleeing victims (Figure 2.1). Such sites are rare, but when they are discovered they yield remarkable finds. In the sixth century A.D., a volcanic eruption in a nearby river suddenly buried a small Maya village at Cerén in San Salvador (Sheets, 1992). The people had eaten their evening meal, but had not yet gone to bed. They abandoned their houses and possessions and fled for their lives. Not only did the ash bury the village, it also smothered the nearby crops, burying corn and agave plants as they stood in the fields. Payson Sheets and a research team from many disciplines have recovered entire dwellings and outhouses and the artifacts within them just as they were abandoned, for the ash was too thick for the people to rescue their possessions. Each Cerén household had a building for eating, sleeping, and other activities, and also a storehouse, kitchen, and sometimes other structures (Figure 4.7). Substantial thatched roofs projected far beyond the walls, providing not only covered walkways, but places for processing grain and for storage. Each household planted maize, cacao, agave, and other crops in gardens close to their homes, setting most crops in neat rows. They stored grain in clay vessels with tight lids, some corn and chilis were suspended from the roof, and many implements were also kept in the rafters. So far, the excavations have uncovered three public buildings, one, perhaps, a community center, as well

FIGURE 4.7   Artist's reconstruction of the dwelling, workshop (right), and storehouse (left), Household 1, Cerén, San Salvador.

as outlying maize fields where the plants were doubled over, with the ears still attached to the stalk, a "storage" technique still used in parts of Central America today. Judging from the mature maize plants, the eruption occurred at the end of the growing season, in August.

Cerén provides an unusually complete look at life in a humble Maya settlement far removed from the great ceremonial centers where the elite lived. It is remarkable for its complete artifact inventories and food supplies, finds so well-preserved that even minute details of village architecture are preserved. We even know where the Cerén people kept their sharp knives—in the rafters of their houses!

SUMMARY

- Site-formation processes are factors that create the historical and archaeological records, natural or cultural agencies that have transformed the archaeological record during and since a site was abandoned.
- There are two basic types of site-formation processes. Cultural transformations are those in which human behavior has transformed the archaeological record through such acts as rebuilding houses or reusing artifacts. Noncultural processes are events and processes of the natural environment that affect the archaeological record, such as the chemical properties of the soil and natural phenomena such as earthquakes and wind action.
- Later human activity can radically affect archaeological preservation. People may selectively discard some types of artifacts, and many variables can affect the layout of settlements and other considerations.
- Some people, such as the Southwestern Indians, recycled wooden beams and other materials, distorting the archaeological record. Sites are reused, lower strata are often disturbed, and succeeding generations may preserve an important building, such as a temple, for centuries. Modern warfare, industrial activity, even deep agriculture and cattle grazing can affect the preservation of archaeological remains.
- Preservation conditions depend mostly on the soil and general climatic regime in the area of a site. Inorganic objects, such as stone and baked clay, often survive almost indefinitely. But organic materials, such as bone, wood, and leather, survive only under exceptional conditions, such as in dry climates, in permafrost areas, and when waterlogged. The surviving picture of the past obtained from excavations is often confined to inorganic materials.
- Waterlogged and peat-bog conditions are especially favorable for preserving wood and vegetal remains. In this chapter we discussed the Somerset Levels, Danish bog corpses, and the Ozette site in Washington State as sites of these types.
- Dry conditions can preserve almost the full range of human artifacts, the best examples being the remarkably complete preservation of ancient Egyptian culture and the comprehensive finds made in desert caves in the American West.
- Arctic conditions can literally refrigerate organic materials in the soil. We described the recent discovery of the "Ice Man" in the European Alps as well

as a buried Eskimo family from Alaska, and modern findings on the fate of the Franklin expedition.

- Volcanic ash has preserved the Maya village at Cerén in San Salvador. A sudden eruption mantled the settlement in thick ash, so that entire houses and their contents, as well as gardens, survived intact.

GUIDE TO FURTHER READING

Beattie, Owen, and John Geiger. *Frozen in Time: The Fate of the Franklin Expedition.* London: Bloomsbury Publications, 1986. A popular account of the excavation of the graves of three members of the Franklin expedition. Gives an excellent description of the difficulties of excavating in arctic environments.

Coles, Bryony, and John Coles. *Sweet Track to Glastonbury.* New York: Thames and Hudson, 1986. An exemplary account of the Coles' excavations in England's Somerset Levels. Excellent illustrations.

Reeves, Nicholas. *The Complete Tutankhamun.* London: Thames and Hudson, 1990. All you need to know about this most famous of archaeological discoveries, superbly illustrated.

Schiffer, Michael. *Site Formation Processes of the Archaeological Record.* Tucson: University of Arizona Press, 1987. A synthesis of site-formation processes in archaeology and some of the research problems associated with them. Comprehensive bibliography.

Sheets, Payson. *The Cerén Site.* New York: Harcourt, Brace, Jovanovich, 1992. A short case study of this Maya village buried by volcanic ash. Ideal for readers unfamiliar with archaeological methods.

5
DOING ARCHAEOLOGICAL RESEARCH

This chapter describes how archaeologists do archaeological research. Modern archaeology makes use of scientific methods developed by archaeologists themselves and also by scientists in many other disciplines. It is a complex process involving research design, field surveys, and actual excavation, as well as lengthy laboratory analysis of many types of finds.

After discussing the qualifications of a good archaeologist, we look at the relationship between science and archaeology, at inductive and deductive reasoning, and then examine the process of archaeological research itself. This short chapter is an important preliminary to the discussions of archaeological data acquisition that follow.

THE ARCHAEOLOGIST'S SKILLS

Early archaeologists needed few qualifications beyond a liking for the past, some experience in excavation, and an ability to classify artifacts. Sir Leonard Woolley, famed excavator of Ur-of-the-Chaldees in Mesopotamia in the 1920s, was completely self-trained and learned excavation in a few seasons in the Sudan. In an interview with an Oxford college president, he was told: "I have decided that you shall become an archaeologist!" Fortunately for science, Woolley obeyed him.

The archaeologists of the 1990s, however, need specialist training in administrative, technical, and academic skills of many types. Modern archaeology has become so complex that few individuals can possibly master all the skills needed to excavate a large city or even a medium-sized settlement where preservation conditions are exceptionally complete. In the 1920s, Woolley excavated Ur with a handful of Europeans, three expert Syrian foremen, and several hundred workers. An expedition to an equivalent site today would consist of a carefully organized team of experts whose skills reflect the precise hypotheses about the site that are to be tested in the field.

Let us examine, then, some of the basic skills an archaeologist needs.

THEORETICAL SKILLS

The archaeologist must be able to define research problems in their context: everything that is known about them. This knowledge includes the current status of research on a specific problem, such as the origins of humanity or the earliest human settlement of Ohio, and also the latest theoretical and methodological advances in archaeology that could affect the definition and solution of the problem. The research problem will be defined by the specific objectives to be achieved. The archaeologist must have the expertise to formulate the precise hypotheses to be tested in the research. As the research proceeds, he or she will have to be able to evaluate and put together the results of the work in the context set by the original objectives.

METHODOLOGICAL EXPERTISE

Every archaeologist must have the ability to plan the methods to be used in the research to achieve the theoretical goals initially laid out. Methodological skills include being able to select among methods of data collection and to decide which analytical methods are most effective for the data being handled. Excavating sites requires a large range of methodological skills, from deciding which sampling and trenching systems to use to devising recording methods to dealing with special preservation conditions where fragile objects have to be removed intact from their matrix.

One important aspect of methodological expertise requires selecting and working with specialists from other disciplines. This task involves understanding multidisciplinary research and knowing the uses and limitations of the work done by, say, geologists or zoologists for the specific problems one is investigating.

TECHNICAL SKILLS

Methodological and technical skills overlap, especially in the field. The scientific excavation of any site or a large-scale field survey requires more than the ability to select a method or a recording system; one needs also to execute it under working conditions. Archaeological excavations require great precision in measurement and excavation, deployment of skilled and unskilled labor, and implementation of find-recovery systems that keep artifacts in order from the moment they are found until they are shipped to the laboratory for analysis. At issue here is provenance of the artifacts and features and of the associated ecofacts. (An **ecofact** consists of nonartifactual materials such as food residues and other finds that throw light on human activities.) The field archaeologist has to assume the roles of supervisor, photographer, surveyor, digger, recorder, writer, and soil scientist, as well as be able to deal with any unexpected jobs, such as uncovering the delicate bones of a skeleton or setting up details of a computer program. On large sites, expertly trained students or fellow archaeologists may assume such specialist tasks as photography; on small sites, the archaeologist must often perform this and all other tasks single-handedly.

ADMINISTRATIVE AND MANAGERIAL SKILLS

Modern archaeology requires—or actually demands—that its practitioners exercise high-grade administrative and managerial skills. Today's archaeologist has to be able to coordinate the activities of specialists from other disciplines, organize and deploy teams of volunteer students and paid laborers, and raise and administer research funds obtained from outside sources. He or she must always be aware of all aspects of a research project as it progresses, from arranging for permits and supplies of stationery and digging tools to doing the accounts.

Above all, anyone working on an archaeological project has to be an expert in human relations, in keeping people happy at demanding work, which is often carried out under difficult and uncomfortable conditions. The diplomatic side of archaeological excavations is often neglected. But the folklore of archaeology abounds with stories of disastrous excavations run by archaeologists with no sensitivity to their fellow workers. A truly happy excavation is a joy to work on, a dig on which people smile, argue ferociously over interpretations of stratigraphic profiles through an endless day, and enjoy the companionship of a campfire in the evenings.

WRITING AND ANALYTICAL SKILLS

If there is one basic lesson to be learned at the beginning of any archaeological endeavor, it is that all excavation is destruction of finite archives in the ground that can never be restored to their original configuration. Every archaeologist is responsible not only for analyzing his or her finds in the laboratory but also for preparing a detailed report on the fieldwork that has been done—an important part of the permanent record of archaeological research. Regrettably, the shelves in museums all over the world are filled with finds from sites that have been excavated but never written up. An unpublished site is effectively destroyed. At first glance, the list of qualifications a professional archaeologist needs can be formidable. In practice, though, sound classroom training combined with a great deal of fieldwork experience can provide the necessary background.

ARCHAEOLOGY, SCIENCE, AND THE SCIENTIFIC METHOD

At various places we have referred to scientific archaeology, the scientific method, and the testing of hypotheses against data collected in the field (Kelley and Hanan, 1988). It is now time to ask a fundamental question: Is archaeology a science? The answer is a qualified yes. In the sense that archaeologists study human societies of the past by scientifically recovering and analyzing data that consist of the material remains of these societies, it is a science. But in the sense that archaeology, as part of anthropology, studies the intangible philosophic and religious beliefs of a society, it is not a science.

What do we mean by *scientific*? Science is a way of acquiring knowledge and understanding about the parts of the natural world that can be measured. It is a disciplined and carefully ordered search for knowledge, carried out in a systematic manner. This is a far cry from the ways in which we acquire our personal experience of religious philosophies, social customs, or political trends. Science involves using methods of acquiring knowledge that are not only cumulative but also subject to continuous testing and retesting. Over the years, scientists have developed the general procedures for acquiring data, known as the scientific method, which have come into wide use. Even though the scientific method may be applied in somewhat different ways in botany, zoology, and anthropology, the basic principles are the same: the notion that knowledge of the real world is both cumulative and subject to constant rechecking. The scientific method, when used, has many applications to archaeological data, and its use classifies much of archaeology as a science.

THE SCIENTIFIC METHOD

Science establishes facts about the natural world by observing objects, events, and phenomena. In making these observations, the scientist proceeds by using both inductive and deductive reasoning.

Inductive reasoning takes specific observations and makes a generalization from them. I once found nearly 10,000 wild vegetable remains in a 4,000-year-old hunter-gatherer camp in central Zambia. More than 42 percent of them were from the *bauhinia,* a shrub currently prized for its fruit and roots, which flowers from October to February. The *bauhinia* is still eaten by San hunter-gatherers in the Kalahari today. From these observations, I used the process of induction to hypothesize that *bauhinia* has been a preferred seasonal food for hunter-gatherers in this general area for thousands of years (Fagan and Van Noten, 1971).

Deductive reasoning follows from hypotheses formulated through induction. That is, the researcher forms specific implications from the hypotheses. In the Kalahari, I would have formulated a hypothesis (or series of hypotheses) about *bauhinia* eating by San and prehistoric hunter-gatherers and then tested it with ethnographic fieldwork and archaeological investigations. My hypothesis would then be confirmed, rejected, or refined.

A classic example of applying the scientific method comes from field studies done in the Great Basin in the Western United States by anthropologist Julian Steward, who spent much of the 1920s and 1930s working on Shoshonean ethnography. The mass of field data he collected led him to formulate hypotheses about the ways in which the Shoshoneans moved their settlements throughout the year (Steward, 1938).

In the late 1960s this pioneer work was greatly refined by David Hurst Thomas, who deduced densities and distributions of artifacts in the various ecological zones of the Great Basin from Steward's hypotheses about Shoshonean settlement patterns. "If the late prehistoric Shoshoneans behaved in the fashion suggested by Steward, how would the artifacts have fallen on the ground?" he asked (Thomas, 1983b). He constructed more than 100 predictions relating to Steward's original hypotheses. Next, he devised tests to verify or invalidate his predictions. He expected to find specific forms of artifacts associated with particular types of activity, such as hunting, in seasonal archaeological sites where hunting was said to be important. Aware of local preservation conditions, he strongly emphasized the distribution and frequency of artifact forms. Then he collected in the field the archaeological data needed for his tests. Finally, Thomas tested each of his predictions against the field data and rejected about 25 percent of his original ones. The remainder were supported by the data and provided a major refinement of Steward's original hypotheses. Later fieldwork gave him abundant opportunities to refine these hypotheses and to collect more data to test them further.

Thomas's Great Basin research is a good example of the benefits of the scientific method in archaeological research.

The importance of the scientific method, however, should not be overestimated. A balanced view is this: "Science advances by disproof, proposing the most adequate explanations for the moment, knowing that new and better explanations will later be found. This continuous self-correcting feature is the key to the scientific method" (Doran, 1987).

THE PROCESS OF ARCHAEOLOGICAL RESEARCH

We must now describe the process of archaeological research from formulation of the research design to publication of the final report (See Figure 5.1).

RESEARCH DESIGNS

A **research design**, whether simple or complex, is a formal procedure whose purpose is to direct the execution of an archaeological investigation. It has two objectives: to ensure that the results will be scientifically valid and to carry out the research as efficiently and economically as possible (Binford, 1964). The process of archaeological research, then, is controlled by the research design, which takes the project through stages. These stages, to be described shortly, are by no means common to all research projects; for although "research design" sounds rigid and inflexible, in practice the design for any project has to be flexible enough to allow changes in the overall project as field research proceeds.

FORMULATION

Any archaeological research begins with fundamental decisions about the problem or area to be studied. A research problem can be as grandiose as determining the origins of agriculture in the Southwest—a truly enormous project—or as specific as determining the date of the second phase in Stonehenge's construction. The initial decisions will identify both the problem and the geographic region in which it will be investigated. The latter can be one site or an entire region. These decisions immediately limit the scope of the research design.

Once the problem and the area are identified, the researcher must do a great deal of background research, involving both library work and field investigations. He or she must read up on previous archaeological research on the problem and study the geology, climate, ecology, anthropology, and general background of the area. Several field visits are essential, both to examine fieldwork conditions and to get a feel for the region. Water supplies, campsites, and sources of labor have to be identified. Landowners' permissions to dig and survey are essential, and government permits may be needed. At least some preliminary fieldwork is needed to aid in formulating the research design, especially in areas where no archaeology has been carried out before.

The objective directing all this preliminary work is to refine the problems being investigated until the archaeologist can begin to define the specific research goals. These goals will almost inevitably include testing specific hypotheses, which can be related to research carried out by previous investigators, or entirely new hypotheses that come out during the preliminary formulation of the research problem. Yet others will be added as the research work proceeds. Generating hypotheses at this stage is vital, for they determine the types of data that will be sought in the field. These types must be defined, at least in general, before one goes into the field.

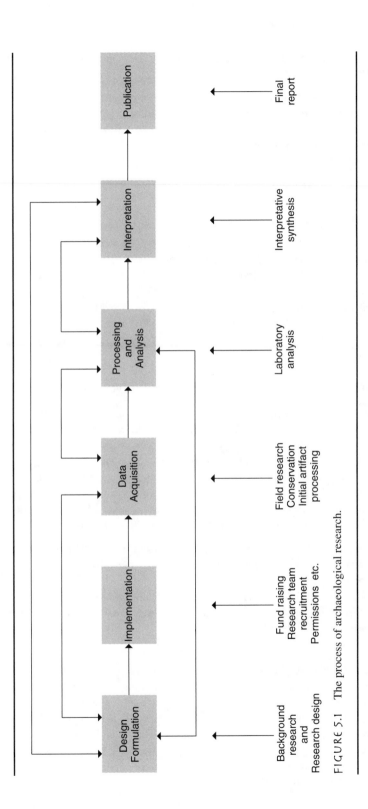

FIGURE 5.1   The process of archaeological research.

Let us take two hypotheses designed as part of a research project involving early food production in Egypt:

1. The earliest cereal agriculture near Kom Ombo developed among hunter-gatherers who had been exploiting wild vegetable foods very intensively.
2. The emergence of agriculture came about as a result of the intensification of gathering and rapid population growth, causing shortages of wild cereals. So people began to grow wild cereals for themselves.

What sorts of data would be needed to test these hypotheses at Kom Ombo? The archaeologist formulating the project of which this hypothesis is a part would be looking for:

- Sites in areas where wild cereals could have grown, where preservation conditions would allow for survival of vegetal remains.
- Food residues in the form of carbonized and discarded vegetable foods and the bones of domesticated animals.
- Implements used for harvesting and processing both wild and domesticated grains—grindstones, sickles, and so on.
- Evidence for such features as storage pits or baskets, indicating deliberate conservation of food supplies.
- Sites that were occupied longer than the relatively short periods favored by most hunter-gatherers, since farmers have to watch over their crops.

Armed with both hypotheses and lists of the types of evidence likely to be encountered in the field, the archaeologist can plan for the equipment, facilities, and people needed to carry out the job. Even more important, the project can be formulated with advice from experts, whose specialist knowledge will be needed either in the field or in the laboratory. The necessary contacts with experts are best made before the fieldwork begins and funds are obtained. A surprising number of specialists are needed for even quite simple investigations. The Kom Ombo hypothesis could ideally require the long- or short-term services of these specialists:

- A geologist to assist in geological dating of sites in the Nile Valley.
- A soil scientist to study occupation levels and organic soils.
- A radiocarbon dating laboratory to date carbon samples.
- A botanist to supervise recovery of vegetal remains and to identify them.
- An expert on pollen analysis to work on any such samples recovered in the excavations.
- A zoologist to study the animal bones.

The larger-scale project may take an integrated team of experts from several disciplines into the field—an expensive enterprise that often yields important results. The study of early agriculture in the Near East was revolutionized by Robert Braidwood of the University of Chicago in the 1950s when he took such a team of experts with him to the Zagros Mountains. The research team was able to trace agriculture and animal domestication from their beginnings among nomadic hunter-gatherers on the highlands more than 9,000 years ago (Braidwood and Braidwood, 1983).

Research design has a critical part in cultural resource management (Chapter 20). Regional research designs for large areas such as the San Juan Basin in Colorado provide a long-term framework for hundreds of minor environmental impact studies and research projects. These designs are not cast in concrete; they are ever-changing documents that are brought up to date regularly to accommodate changing methodologies and new circumstances in the field (Fowler, 1982).

The final stage in formulating the research project is acquiring the necessary funding. This can be frustrating and time-consuming work, for sources of money for archaeological fieldwork are always in short supply. Most excavations organized in the Americas are funded either by the National Science Foundation or, if within the United States, by some other government agency, such as the National Park Service. Some private organizations, such as the National Geographic Society or the Wenner Gren Foundation for Anthropological Research, support excavations. Many excavations, such as the regular seasons at Aphrodisias in Turkey or Crow Canyon in the American Southwest, rely heavily on private donations. The organizers spend considerable time seeking private gifts to support each field season and the laboratory work that follows it.

DATA COLLECTION

Once the field team is assembled and the funds are in hand, actual implementation of the project begins. The first stage is to acquire equipment, set up camp, and organize the research team in the field. Once that procedure is complete, collection of archaeological data can begin.

Collection of data involves two basic processes: locating and surveying sites and scientifically excavating carefully selected sites.

Locating archaeological sites is obviously the first stage in collecting data. As we will see in Chapter 9, reconnaissance can be carried out on foot, in vehicles, even on the back of a mule. A variety of techniques are used to ensure that a representative sample of sites is located and investigated before excavation. Then the surfaces of the sites are carefully examined and samples of artifacts lying at ground level are collected to record as much as possible about the location without the expense of excavation. This recording can include photographs, some surveying and measurement, and even some probing of the site with borers or remote-sensing devices. Obviously, much less information is collected from surface surveys than from excavations.

Archaeological excavations are ultimately a recording of subsurface features and the provenance, or precise spatial relationships, of the artifacts within the site. Varied techniques are used to collect and record archaeological data from beneath the ground, as described in Chapter 10. Obviously, the scope of archaeological excavation can range from a small test pit to a large-scale investigation at an ancient city.

DATA PROCESSING, ANALYSIS, AND INTERPRETATION

The end products of even a month's excavation on a moderately productive site are a daunting accumulation. Box upon box of potsherds, stone tools, bones, and other finds are stacked in the field laboratory and must be cleaned, labeled, and sorted. Hundreds of slides and photographs must be processed and cataloged. Computer disks and rolls of drawings with important information on the provenance of finds from the trenches must also be cataloged. Then there are radiocarbon and pollen samples, burials, and other special finds that need examination by specialists. The first stage in processing the data, then, occurs at the site, where the finds are washed, sorted, and given preservation treatment sufficient to transport them to the archaeological laboratory for more thorough examination.

The detailed analysis of the data is carried out, often for many months, in a laboratory with the facilities for such research work. These analyses include not only classifying artifacts and identifying the materials from which they were made, but also studying food remains, pollen samples, and other key sources of information. All these analyses are designed to provide information for interpreting the archaeological record. Some tests, such as radiocarbon dating or pollen analysis, are carried out in laboratories with the necessary technical equipment. We describe various approaches to archaeological analysis in Chapters 11 through 17.

Interpreting the resulting classified and thoroughly analyzed data involves not only synthesizing all the information from the investigation but also final testing of the basic hypotheses formulated at the beginning of the project. These tests produce models for reconstructing and explaining the prehistory of the site or region. We look at some of these models and interpretations in Part 7.

PUBLICATION

The archaeologist's final responsibility is publishing the results of the research project. Archaeological excavation destroys all or part of a site; unless the investigator publishes the results, vital scientific information will be lost forever. The ideal scientific report publishes not only the research design and hypotheses that have been formulated but also the data used to test them and to interpret the site or region so that the same tests can be replicated by others.

All archaeological research is cumulative, in the sense that everyone's investigations are eventually superseded by later work, which uses more refined methods of recovery and new analytical approaches. But unless every archaeologist publishes the results of his or her completed work, the chain of research is incomplete, and a fragment of human history will vanish into oblivion. It is sad that the pace of publication has been far behind that of excavation. The reason is not hard to discern: excavation is far more fun than writing reports!

SUMMARY

- Modern archaeology makes use of scientific methods devised by archaeologists and also by scientists in many other disciplines.
- A well-qualified archaeologist commands many skills, both in archaeological method and theory and in practical methodology. This expertise includes the ability to select and work with specialists in other academic disciplines.

Practical fieldwork experience and considerable administrative and managerial skill are also required on even the smallest research project. All archaeologists have to acquire precise analytical and writing skills to enable them to communicate their results and record them for posterity.

• Archaeologists use science as a means of acquiring knowledge and understanding about the parts of the natural world that can be observed. They do so by working with two forms of reasoning: inductive reasoning, which takes specific observations and makes a generalization from them; and deductive reasoning, which starts with a generalization and proceeds to specific implications.

• The process of archaeological research begins with formulating highly specific research designs that are flexible enough to allow changes in the overall project as field research proceeds.

• The research project is formulated to fit the problem to be investigated and the geographic area involved. Formulation means carrying out background research and then developing hypotheses to be tested against data acquired in the field.

• Once the field team is assembled, members acquire data by reconnaissance, site survey, and excavation. This acquisition requires them to record provenance, archaeological context, and a great deal of basic information about the site, its natural environment, and its archaeological finds.

• The processing of archaeological data requires analyzing and interpreting the archaeological finds, which involves sorting, classifying, and ordering the finds, then testing the hypotheses developed as part of the research design.

• The final stage in archaeological research is publishing the results for posterity.

GUIDE TO FURTHER READING

Dancey, W. S. *Archaeological Field Methods: An Introduction.* Minneapolis: Burgess, 1981. Probably the best and most up-to-date manual on American field methods around. Especially good on research design.

Hester, Thomas R., Harry J. Shafer, and Robert F. Heizer. *Field Methods in Archaeology.* Palo Alto, Calif.: Mayfield, 1987. A basic field manual on survey and excavation for the beginner.

Renfrew, Colin, and Paul Bahn. *Archaeology: Theories, Methods, and Practice.* 2nd ed. New York: Thames and Hudson, 1996. A comprehensive exploration of archaeological methods that explores the issues in this chapter in more detail.

6

CULTURE, DATA, AND CONTEXT

In this chapter we introduce you to some basic concepts of archaeological research, to culture, to data in the form of artifacts, and their matrix, provenance, and context. The provenance and context of all archaeological data are based on the two fundamental laws, superposition and association. From basic concepts, we move on to discuss spatial context—not the limitless frontiers of the heavens, but a precisely defined location for every find made during an archaeological survey or excavation.

THE CONCEPT OF CULTURE

In Chapter 1, I stated that "anthropologists study human beings as biological organisms and as people with a distinctive and unique characteristic—culture. . . . Archaeologists are, in fact, a special type of anthropologist, specializing in past human culture." Few concepts in anthropology have generated as much controversy and academic debate as those expressed in that statement (Kroeber and Kluckhohn, 1952). All definitions of this most elusive of theoretical formulations are a means of explaining cultures and human behavior in terms of the shared ideas a group of people may hold. One of the best definitions was written by the great Victorian anthropologist Sir Edward Tylor more than a century ago. He stated that culture is "that complex whole which includes knowledge, belief, art, morals, law, custom, and any other capabilities and habits acquired by man as a member of society" (Tylor, 1871). To that definition, modern archaeologists would add the statement that culture is our primary means of adapting to our environment.

Culture is a distinctively human attribute, for we are the only animals to use our culture as our primary means of adapting to our environment. It is our adaptive system. Although biological evolution has protected the polar bear from arctic cold with dense fur and has given the duck webbed feet for swimming, only human beings make thick clothes and igloos in the Arctic and live with minimal clothing under light, thatched shelters in the tropics. We use our culture as a buffer between ourselves and the environment, a buffer that became more and more elaborate through the long millennia of prehistory. We are now so detached from our environment that removal of our cultural buffer would render us almost helpless and probably lead to extinction of the human race in a very short time. Thus human cultures are made up of human behavior and its results; they obviously consist of complex and constantly interacting variables. Human culture, never static, is always adjusting to both internal and external change, whether environmental, technological, or societal (Deetz, 1967). Increasingly, humans have modified the natural environment to such an extent that they have created their own.

THE NATURE OF CULTURE

Culture can be subdivided in all sorts of ways—into language, economics, technology, religion, political or social organizations, and art. But human culture as a whole is a complex, structured organization in which all our categories shape one another. All cultures are made up of myriad tangible and intangible traits, the contents of which result from complex adaptation to a wide range of ecological, societal, and cultural factors. Much of human culture is transmitted from generation to generation by sophisticated communication systems that permit complex and ceaseless adaptations to aid survival and help rapid cultural change take place—as when less-advanced societies come into contact with higher civilizations.

Everyone lives within a culture of some kind, and every culture is qualified by a label, such as "middle-class American," "Eskimo," or "Masai." The qualification conjures up characteristic attributes or behavior patterns typical of those associated with the cultural label. One attribute of a middle-class American might be the hamburger; of the Eskimo, the kayak; of the Masai, a long-handled, fine-bladed spear. Our mental images of cultures are associated with popular stereotypes, too. To many Americans, Chinese culture conjures up images of paper lanterns and willow-pattern plates; French culture, good eating and fine wines. We are all familiar with the distinctive "flavor" of a culture that we encounter when dining in a foreign restaurant or arriving in a strange country. Every culture has its individuality and recognizable style, which shape its political and judicial institutions and morals.

Archaeologists think of culture as possessing three components:

1. The individual's own version of his or her culture, the diversified individual behavior that makes up the myriad strains of a culture.
2. Shared culture: elements of a culture shared by everyone. These can include cultural activities like human sacrifice or ritualized warfare or any shared human activity, as well as the body of rules and prescriptions that make up the sum of the culture (Figure 6.1). Language is critical to this sharing; so is the cultural system.
3. The **cultural system,** the system of behavior in which every individual participates. The individual not only shares the cultural system with other members of society but also takes an active part in it.

Culture, then, can be viewed as either a blend of shared traits or a system that permits a society to interact with its environment. To do anything more than merely work out chronological sequences, the archaeologist has to view culture as a group of complex, interacting components. These components remain static unless the processes that operate the system are carefully defined. Archaeologists are deeply involved with **"cultural process,"** the processes by which human societies changed in the past.

FIGURE 6.1   The Aztec Indians of Mexico sacrificed hundreds of human victims to the sun god Huitzilopochtli each year in the belief that the blood of human hearts nourished the sun on its journey across the heavens. This belief was part of the shared culture of this society, even if such sacrifices are totally alien to other societies.

A cultural system was well defined by archaeologist Stuart Struever (1971): "Culture and its environments represent a number of articulated [interlinked] systems in which change occurs through a series of minor, linked variations in one or more of these systems." For example, an Eskimo cultural system is part of a much larger arctic ecosystem. The cultural system itself is made up of dozens of subsystems: an economic subsystem, a political subsystem, and many others. Let us say that the climate changes suddenly. The Eskimo now switch from reindeer hunting to fishing and sealing. The change triggers all sorts of linked shifts, not only in the economic subsystem but in the technological and social subsystems as well. A cultural system is in a constant state of adjustment within itself and with the ecosystem of which it is a part. The concept of cultural systems is derived from general systems theory, a body of theoretical concepts formulated as a means of searching for general relationships in the empirical world (Watson and others, 1984). The notion of cultural systems has come into use in archaeology purely as a general concept to help us understand the ever-changing relationship between human cultures and their environment.

Many of the interacting components of culture are highly perishable. So far, no one has been able to dig up an unwritten language. Archaeologists have to work with the tangible remains of human activity that still survive in the ground. But these surviving remains of human activity are radically affected by intangible aspects of human culture. For example, the Hopewell people of the American Midwest traded finely made ornaments fashioned out of hammered copper sheet over enormous distances 1,800 years ago. These ornaments turn up in Hopewell burial mounds. The copper technology that made them was simple, but the symbolism behind the artifacts was not. They were probably exchanged between important individuals as symbolic gifts, denoting kin ties, economic obligations, and other social meanings that are beyond the archaeologist's ability to recover (Fagan, 1995). The archaeologist thus faces much greater limitations in research than the ethnographer, who works with living societies and can talk to individuals in society.

NORMATIVE, FUNCTIONAL, AND PROCESSUAL MODELS OF CULTURE

NORMATIVE MODELS

Anthropologist Franz Boas had a profound influence on early American archaeology, for he developed what is often called a "normative" view of culture. This was the first concept of culture to be applied to archaeology, the notion that all human behavior is patterned, the forms of the patterns being determined very largely by culture. This rubric envisages a set of rules, or norms for behavior, within any society that pass from one generation to the next. There are, of course, individual variations, for all the norms do is define the range of acceptable behavior.

Boas applied the normative view of culture to contemporary societies, but archaeologists often use it to examine societies evolving over long periods of time. Anthropologists try to abstract the norms of human behavior by observing societies over many months, even years. They are searching, as it were, for the "grammar" of a society. Archaeologists use the material remains of the archaeological record, such as pottery or stone tools, to infer human behavior, arguing that such durable artifacts represent norms of technological behavior, if nothing else. They assume implicit rules governed the manufacture of all kinds of artifacts over many generations.

This descriptive approach allowed archaeologists to reconstruct and observe variations and changes in what they called behavioral norms. It has been very successful in working out detailed, descriptive outlines of human prehistory at the local and regional levels. However, it does not address two critical goals of archaeology—reconstructing past lifeways and explaining cultural change.

FUNCTIONAL MODELS

Bronislaw Malinowski was one of the great anthropologists of the early twentieth century, famous for his observations of the Trobriand Islanders in the western Pacific and for his functional model of culture. Culture to Malinowski and other functionalist anthropologists like E. E. Randcliffe-Brown, who worked among the Nurer of the Sudan, was "inherited artifacts, goods, technical processes, ideas, habits, and values." He went much further than Boas, arguing that each human culture was a set of closely interrelated mechanisms designed to satisfy both social and survival needs, not just for individuals but for society as a whole. Thus, the nature of that society could be understood only by looking at the network of complex relationships that formed the underlying structure of that society. Each component of a cultural system, living or prehistoric, has a specific function, be it stone technology, ways of growing crops, or residence rules after marriage. Each function is connected to a myriad of others by a network of relationships, forming an ever-adjusting cultural system.

Functionalism can be a somewhat ahistorical way of looking at human societies, but archaeologists have found it of considerable use in examining individual artifacts and cultural traits as part of a much larger network of functional relationships. However, in one aspect functionalism diverges greatly from more recent ecological models of culture, which view cultural systems not as self-regulating but as undergoing constant change as they adapt to their natural environments.

PROCESSUAL MODELS

The changing models of culture in archaeology reflect a gradual shift in emphasis from mere description of the past to processual models based on hypothesis-testing strategies, cultural ecology, and multilinear evolution (Chapters 3 and 18). Some archaeologists are even toying with the idea of not using the concept of culture at all.

CULTURAL PROCESS

Systems theory deals with relationships and variations in relationships; in other words, it deals with precisely the phenomena involved in explaining the processes by which cultures change. Modern scientific archaeology analyzes the causes of cultural change, that is, cultural process.

The word *process* implies a patterned sequence of events that leads from one state of affairs to another. This patterned sequence is determined by a decision-making process that sets the order of events. A 40-foot sailing yacht starts as a pile of materials—wood, aluminum, copper, bronze—and then a patterned sequence of manufacturing events turns the material into a gleaming new ship. Archaeology is a process, too. It involves designing the research project, formulating the hypothesis from prior research, collecting and interpreting new data to test the hypothesis, and finally, publishing the results.

Conditions are events that force people to make decisions about how to deal with new situations. As such, they are distinct from the actual process of decision making—the mechanisms that lead to any kind of change. A change in the natural environment from year-round rainfall to a seasonal pattern is a condition.

In archaeology, cultural process refers to the "identification of the factors responsible for the direction and nature of change within cultural systems" (Sharer and Ashmore, 1995). Processual archaeology is analysis of the conditions of culture change, which involves looking at relationships between variables that could lead to cultural change. These possible conditions are then tested against actual archaeological data, sometimes in a systems theory context.

Clearly, no one element in any cultural system is the primary cause of change; instead, a complex range of factors—rainfall, vegetation, technology, social restrictions, population density—interact and react to changes in any element in

FIGURE 6.2   A San hunter-gatherer in the Kalahari Desert searches in the bole of a tree for water. Human culture is, from the ecologist's viewpoint, merely one element in the ecosystem.

the system. It follows, then, that human culture, from the ecologist's viewpoint, is merely one element in the ecosystem, a mechanism of behavior whereby people adapt to an environment (Figure 6.2) (Dunnell, 1980).

THE ARCHAEOLOGICAL RECORD

The **archaeological record** is the general name denoting the more or less continuous distribution of artifacts over the earth's surface, in highly variable densities. Variations in artifact densities reflect the character and frequency of land use, making them an important variable that the archaeologist can measure (Dunnell and Dancey, 1983). Some high-density clusters of artifacts may be subsumed under the term *site*. Although "archaeological record" refers specifically to distributions of artifacts, it can include:

- *Artifacts:* in the strict sense, objects manufactured or modified by humans (Figure 6.3).
- *Features:* artifacts and artifact associations that cannot be removed intact from the ground, such as postholes and ditches.
- *Structures:* houses, granaries, temples, and other buildings that can be identified from standing remains patterns of postholes and other features in the ground.

FIGURE 6.3   A Moche ceramic portrait head from coastal Peru, dating to c. A.D. 600. Such portraits are realistic depictions of Moche leaders and nobles, some of whom are known to have been warrior priests. Most Moche portraits have come from looted graves, so their contexts in time and space are unfortunately unknown.

- *Ecofacts:* sometimes refers to food remains, such as bones, seeds, and other finds, which throw light on human activities.

Data are the natural materials recognized by the archaeologist as significant evidence, all of which are collected and recorded as part of the research. Data are different from "facts," which are simply bits of observable information about objects, conditions, and so on.

Archaeological data are sometimes referred to as *evidence.*

Archaeological data do not consist of artifacts, features, structures, and ecofacts alone, however; they consist also of their context in space and time.

MATRIX AND PROVENANCE

All scientifically collected or excavated archaeological finds, be they a complete site or a lone object, occur within a matrix and have a specific provenance.

The **matrix** is the physical substance that surrounds the find. It can be gravel, sand, mud, or even water. Most archaeological matrices are of natural origin— passing time and external phenomena, such as wind and rainfall, create them. The early bone caches at Olduvai Gorge in Tanzania were at the edge of a shallow and ever-fluctuating lake 1.75 million years ago. The scatters of tools and bones left by the departing hominids were soon covered by a layer of thin lake sand carried by advancing shallow water. This matrix preserved the tools in their original positions for thousands of millennia (Leakey, 1971). An archaeological matrix can also be human-made, such as the huge earthen platforms of Hopewell burial mounds in the Midwest.

Provenance (or provenience) is the precise three-dimensional position of the find within the matrix as recorded by the archaeologist. It is derived from accurate records kept during excavations and site surveys, from evidence that is inevitably destroyed once a site is dug or artifacts are collected from a surface site. Every human artifact has a provenance in time and space. The provenance in time can range from a radiocarbon date of $1,400 \pm 60$ years before the present for a Maya temple to a precise reading of A.D. 1996 for a dime released by the United States Mint.[1] Frequently, it can simply be an exact position in an archaeological site whose general age is known. Provenance in space is based, finally, on associations between tools and other items that were results of human behavior in a culture. Provenance is determined by applying two fundamental archaeological principles: the principle of association and the principle of superposition.

THE PRINCIPLE OF ASSOCIATION

The archaeological principle of **association** (Figure 6.4) was first stated by Danish archaeologist J. J. A. Worsaae when excavating prehistoric burials in 1843:

> The objects accompanying a human burial are in most cases things that were in use at the same time. When certain artifact types are found together

---

[1] Conventional archaeological usage is B.P. (years before present) "present" being A.D. 1950 by international agreement, and also A.D./B.C., dates calculated relative to the date of Christ's death. Some archaeologists use CE/BCE ("Common Era," "Before Common Era") instead of A.D./B.C.

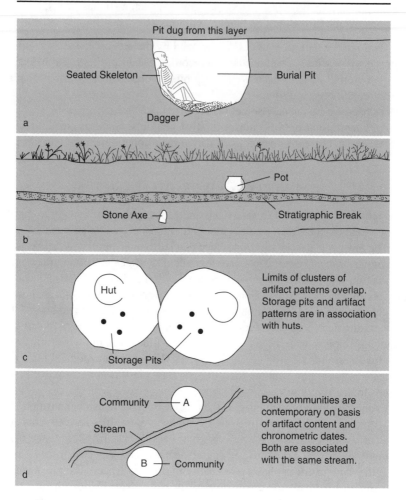

FIGURE 6.4 Some instances of archaeological associations. (a) The burial pit, dug from the uppermost layer, contains not only a skeleton but also a dagger that lies close to its foot. The dagger is associated with the skeleton, and both finds are associated with the burial pit and the layer from which the grave pit was cut into the subsoil. (b) In contrast, a pot and a stone ax are found in two different layers, separated by a sterile zone, a zone with no finds. The two objects are not in association. (c) Two different household clusters with associated pits and scatters of artifacts. These are in association with one another. (d) An association of two contemporary communities.

in grave association after grave association, and when more evolved forms of the same tools are found in association with other burials, then the associations provide some basis for dividing the burials into different chronological groups on the basis of association and artifact styles.

Instances of archaeological associations are legion. The first evidence of high antiquity for humankind came from associations of stone axes and the bones of extinct animals discovered in the same geological layers. Many early Mesoamerican farmers' houses are associated with storage pits for maize and other crops. In this and many other cases, the horizontal association between artifacts and houses, dwellings and storage pits, or artifacts and food residues provides the archaeological association. Much of the most valuable archaeological data are derived from precise studies of associations between different finds in the ground.

THE PRINCIPLE OF SUPERPOSITION

The time dimension of archaeology is erected on basic principles of stratigraphic geology and the principle of **superposition** set down by the uniformitarians early in the nineteenth century (Chapter 2).

The principle of superposition states that the geological layers of the earth are stratified one upon another, like the layers of a cake. Cliffs by the seashore and quarries are easily accessible examples. Obviously, any object found in the lower-most levels, whether a stone or something humanly made, was deposited there before the upper levels were accumulated. In other words, the lower strata are earlier than the upper strata. The same principle applies to archaeological sites: The tools, houses, and other finds in the layers of a site can be dated relative to the layers by their association with the stratum in which they are found (Figure 6.4).

The basis of all scientific archaeological excavation is the accurately observed and carefully recorded stratigraphic profile (Chapter 7).

ARCHAEOLOGICAL CONTEXT

Archaeological **context** is derived from careful recording of the matrix, provenance, and association of the finds. Context is far more than just a find spot, a position in time and space. It involves assessing how the find got to its position and what has happened since its original owners abandoned it. Anyone wanting to reconstruct human behavior or ancient cultural systems must pay careful attention to the context of every find.

Context is affected by three factors:

1. The manufacture and use of the object, house, or other find by its original owners. The orientation of a house may be determined by the position of the sun on summer afternoons. Because the archaeologist's objective is to reconstruct ancient behavior, this aspect of context is vital.
2. The way in which the find was deposited in the ground. Some discoveries, like royal burials or caches of artifacts, were deliberately buried under the ground by ancient people; others vanished as a result of natural phenomena. Dilapidated houses that have been abandoned are slowly covered by blowing sand or rotting vegetation. The Roman city of Herculaneum in Italy, however, was buried quickly by a catastrophic eruption of Vesuvius in August of the year A.D. 79.
3. The subsequent history of the find in the ground. Was the burial disturbed by later graves, or was the site eroded away by water?

PRIMARY AND SECONDARY CONTEXT

The context of any archaeological find can be affected by two processes: the original behavior of the people who used or made it and events that came later.

Primary context is the original context of the find, undisturbed by any factor, human or natural, since it was deposited by the people involved with it. The Iron Age warrior depicted in Figure 6.5, who was buried at Maiden Castle in A.D. 43, died from his wounds in a battle against a Roman legion. The survivors buried him swiftly in a shallow grave. The skeleton survived intact in its primary context until Sir Mortimer Wheeler excavated the undisturbed burial late in the 1930s (Wheeler, 1943).

Secondary context refers to the context of a find whose primary context has been disturbed by later activity. Very frequently, excavators of a burial ground will find incomplete skeletons whose intrusive graves have been disturbed by deposition of later burials. As in the tomb of pharaoh Tutankhamun, tomb robbers may disturb the original grave furnishings, frantically searching for gold or precious oils. In still other instances, finds can be shifted by the natural forces of wind and weather. Many of the Stone Age tools found in European river gravels have been transported by floodwaters to a location far from their original place of deposition. All these disturbed finds are in a secondary context.

FIGURE 6.5   An iron arrowhead embedded in the backbone of a skeleton from the battle cemetery at Maiden Castle, Dorset, England. The artifact comes from a Roman cultural context; the skeleton, native British. Nevertheless, they are associated in the archaeological record.

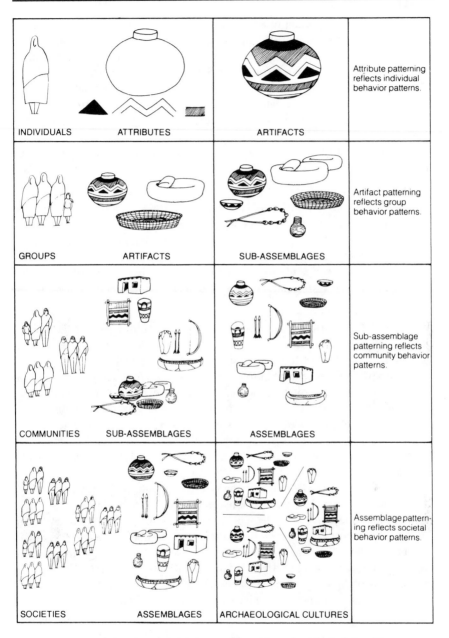

FIGURE 6.6   Human behavior as reflected in archaeological classifications. The hierarchy begins with attributes and artifacts and ends with entire archaeological cultures.

SPATIAL CONTEXT

Spatial context is important to archaeologists because it enables them to determine the distance between different objects or features, between entire settlements, or between settlements and key vegetational zones and landmarks. Important distances can be a few inches of level ground between a dagger and the associated skeleton of its dead owner, a mile separating two seasonal camps, or a complicated series of interrelated distance measurements separating dozens of villages that are part of an elaborate trading system carrying luxury goods through several geographic regions hundreds of miles apart.

One can identify four dimensions of variability in human behavior reflected in spatial context:

1. *Artifact*: individual human activity.
2. *Structure:* household or group activities (structures can, of course, include public buildings, such as temples, which are used by more than one household).
3. *Site:* community activity, groups of contemporary houses, stores, temples, and other structures.
4. *Region:* the activities of groups of people reflected by sites distributed on the landscape. These are sometimes referred to as a settlement pattern.

These four levels of spatial context are closely tied to actual cultural behavior (Figure 6.6). An artifact itself can provide valuable information on technology and actual use. But to infer cultural behavior we must know the artifact's association, both with other artifacts and with the matrix in which it was found. The patterning of artifacts in space around an abandoned iron-smelting furnace or near the bones of a slaughtered bison kill is tangible evidence for specific human behavior. An unassociated projectile point will never give you anything more specific than the inference that it was used as a weapon. But a patterning of projectile points, scraping tools, and large boulders associated with a bison skeleton has a context in time and space that allows much more detailed inferences.

The basic assumption behind all studies of artifacts in space is that they were used for different purposes and that characteristic groups of them were used for specific activities, such as ironworking, butchery, and hunting. It follows that similarly patterned groups of artifact types found on other sites resulted from similar activities, even if they show differences in detail. During the earlier millennia of the Stone Age, people enjoyed much the same level of hunting and gathering culture throughout Africa, Europe, and India. This parallel is reflected in thousands of similar-looking stone axes found in sites as widely separated as the Thames Valley in England and the Cape of Good Hope in South Africa.

ARTIFACTS, SUBASSEMBLAGES, AND ASSEMBLAGES

As we saw in Chapter 4, archaeological data comprise the material remains of ancient human behavior. This data comes in many forms, and a fundamental part of archaeological research involves classifying and interpreting the data, creating order out of a jumble of artifacts and other finds.

The process of classification involves making judgements about different categories of finds (Chapter 11). Archaeologists have terms that define these remains for research purposes, arbitrary groupings used for archaeological analysis, which may, or more often may not, represent "real" things in the past. In other words, data groups are instruments used in research, not actual cultural phenomena, even if sometimes they coincide with them.

ARTIFACTS

Artifacts are commonly defined as items that exhibit any physical attributes that can be assumed to be the result of human activity. This definition implies that the term artifact covers every form of archaeological find, from stone axes, bronze daggers, and clay pots to butchered animal bones, carbonized seeds, huts, and all other manifestations of human behavior that can be found in archaeological sites. Some archaeologists define artifacts by breaking them down into four categories: portable artifacts, features, structures, and ecofacts.

Whichever definition is preferred, all assume that any object or any event of manufacture or consumption is a product of human activity if its location or any other of its features cannot be accounted for by natural processes (Deetz, 1967). In other words, artifacts are compared to natural objects and distinguished from them, not by individual features but by a patterning of different, human-caused features. It is this patterning that is important. A simple flake removed from an elaborate ceremonial obsidian knife blade may not necessarily show evidence of human modification. But the patterned, consistently repeated removal of several dozen or hundreds of small flakes—the pattern forming a knife—is highly diagnostic of human activity. Normally there is no difficulty at all in telling artifacts made or caused by humans from those caused by water action, fire, animal kills, or other natural phenomena (but see Lyman, 1994).

SUBASSEMBLAGES

An artifact, such as an arrowhead or a basket, is made up of a combination of attributes (see Chapter 12), which make up a constant pattern of behavior reflected in the finished artifact. When such artifacts are found in patterned associations reflecting the shared cultural behavior of minimal groups, they are commonly classified in **subassemblages.** A hunter uses a bow, arrows, and a quiver; a blacksmith uses hammers, tongs, and bellows to make hoes or spears; and so on. Subassemblages represent the behavior of individuals, and are often tool kits.

ASSEMBLAGES

When a number of subassemblages of artifacts—say, a collection of hunting weapons, baskets, pounders, and digging sticks, traces of windbreaks, and stone vessels—are found in a contemporary association, they reflect in their patterning the shared activities of a total community and are known as **assemblages.** With assemblages, one is looking at the shared behavior of a community as a whole, which frequently is reflected in the remains of houses, the features associated with them, and community settlement patterns.

ARCHAEOLOGICAL SITES

Archaeological **sites** are places at which traces of past human activity are to be found. They represent accumulations of the remains of human behavior over periods of time. Sites are normally identified by the presence of artifacts. They can range in size from a large city, such as Teotihuacán, in the Valley of Mexico, to a tiny scatter of hunter-gatherer artifacts in Death Valley, California. There are millions of archaeological sites in the world, many of them still undiscovered. Some were occupied for a few hours, days, or weeks; some were occupied for a generation or two and then abandoned forever. Other localities, such as Mesopotamian occupation mounds, or tells, were reoccupied again and again for hundreds, even thousands, of years and contain many stratified layers (Figure 6.7). In contrast, the occupation site may contain little more than a surface scatter of potsherds or stone tools or an occupation layer buried under a few inches of topsoil. Archaeological sites can consist of a simple association (an isolated burial and one pot), many associations making up an assemblage of artifacts representing one community, or a series of assemblages stratified one above another. In a sense, archaeological sites are a paradox. They may represent long-term communal behavior over, say, 300 or 1,000 years, but what the archaeologist actually finds may be the remains of a very brief episode of such behavior, perhaps the filling of a storage pit, which took ten minutes on July 4, A.D. 1250.

FIGURE 6.7   The central area of the great Mesopotamian city of Uruk, one of the earliest cities in the world. The temples atop ziggurats were at the center of the city, which was surrounded by a massive defensive wall.

CLASSIFYING SITES

Archaeological sites can be classified in these ways:

By archaeological context. The context of artifacts in the site can be used to distinguish between sites such as surface locations, single-level occupations, and stratified settlements.

By artifact content. The site is labeled according to its specific artifact content: pottery, stone tools, milling stones, and so on. The associations, assemblages, and subassemblages of artifacts in the site are used to label it as Stone Age, Maya, and so on.

By geographic location. Most human settlements have been concentrated in well-defined types of geographic locations, and these sites can be referred to as cave sites, valley bottom sites, foothill sites, and the like.

By artifact content related to site function. Because subassemblages reflect individual human behavior, sites can be classified by the characteristic patterning of the artifacts found in them, such as kill sites and habitations.

Using these criteria, researchers identify several broad site functions, which are commonly used by archaeologists everywhere.

COMMON SITE FUNCTIONS

These are some common site functions:

Living or habitation sites are the most important sites, for they are the places where people have lived and carried out a multitude of activities. The artifacts in living sites reflect domestic activities, such as food preparation and tool-making. Dwellings are normally present. The temporary camps of California fisherfolk are living sites, as are Stone Age rockshelters, Southwestern pueblos, and Mesopotamian tells. Habitation sites of any complexity are associated with other sites that reflect specialized needs, such as agricultural systems, cemeteries, and temporary camps.

Kill sites are places where prehistoric people killed game and camped around the carcasses while butchering the meat. They are relatively common on the Great Plains; the Olsen-Chubbock site is a good example. Projectile points and butchery tools are associated with kill sites.

Ceremonial sites may or may not be integral to a living site. The Mesopotamian *ziggurat* dominated its mother city, and Maya cities such as Tikal boasted of imposing ceremonial precincts surrounded by habitation areas. Other famous ceremonial sites, such as Stonehenge in England or the Great Serpent Mound in Ohio, are isolated monuments. Ceremonial artifacts, such as stingray spines used in mutilation rituals, and statuary may be associated with sacred sites.

Burial sites include both cemeteries and isolated tombs. People have been burying their dead since at least 50,000 years ago and have often taken enormous pains to prepare them for the afterlife. Perhaps the most famous burial sites of all are the Pyramids of Giza in Egypt. Royal burials, such as that of the Egyptian pharaoh Tutankhamun, absorbed the energies of hundreds of people in their preparation. Many burials are associated with special grave furniture, jewelry, and ornaments of rank.

Trading, quarry, and art sites form a special category in that some kind of specialist activity was carried out. The special tools needed for mining copper, obsidian, and other metals identify quarry sites. Trading sites are identified by large quantities of exotic trade objects and by their strategic position near major cities. The Assyrian market that flourished outside the Hittite city of Kanesh in 1900 B.C. is one of these. *Art sites,* which abound in southwestern France, southern Africa, Australia, California, and other areas, are identified by paintings on the walls of caves and rockshelters.

CULTURES, REGIONS, AND SETTLEMENT PATTERNS

The spatial units we have referred to thus far are all confined to the boundaries of one community. They reflect the activities of the maximum number of people who occupied a settlement at some time during a cycle of settlement. Although a great deal of archaeological research is carried out on single sites, archaeologists often seek to understand the prehistory of a much wider area. Several communities or a scattered population living in a well-defined region may be linked in the same subsistence or settlement system. Such commonly held systems, and the human activities that derive from them, make up an entire culture. Cultural behavior is identified by the patterning that appears in an entire assemblage. Studying an entire culture involves working with much larger bodies of archaeological information, as well as with background geographic and environmental data. Cultures, regions, and settlement patterns are both spatial and integrative units, which involve chronological, social, and cultural dimensions also.

ARCHAEOLOGICAL CULTURES AND OTHER UNITS

A number of units commonly subsume such larger scale information:

Archaeological cultures are consistent patternings of assemblages, the archaeological equivalents of human societies. Archaeological cultures consist of the material remains of human culture preserved at a specific space and time at several sites.

Culture areas are large geographic areas in which artifacts characteristic of an archaeological culture exist in a precise context of time and space. One can refer to both a Maya cultural system and a Maya culture area.

Archaeological regions are generally described as well-defined geographic areas bounded by conspicuous geographic features, such as an ocean, lakes, or mountains. Once having defined a region geographically, the researcher will try to identify its ecological and cultural boundaries throughout prehistoric times.

Most regional approaches involve far more than comparing the artifacts from a few scattered settlements. They are based on a research strategy aimed at sampling the entire region and on objectives intended to reconstruct many more aspects of prehistoric life than those uncovered at a single site. These include both social organization and economic strategies (see Chapter 16).

SETTLEMENT PATTERNS

A **settlement pattern** is the distribution of sites and human settlement across the natural landscape (Chapter 15). Settlement patterns are determined by many factors: the environment, economic practices, and technological skills. Settlement archaeology is part of the analysis of interactions between people and their environment (Figure 15.10).

In determining spatial relations, archaeologists base their studies of the behavior of a human society as a whole on models and hypotheses tested by data from many disciplines. These data bear on the ways in which communities and their associated contemporary assemblages are grouped into larger units on the landscape (Figure 15.13). They bear, too, on the ways in which prehistoric societies interacted with the ever-changing natural environment.

Spatial context is vital to scientific archaeology, for it provides one of the critical dimensions of archaeological data. The other critical dimension is time, which we will consider in Chapter 7.

SUMMARY

- Culture is humanity's primary means of adapting to the natural and cultural environment. Human culture is made up of our behavior and its results and is also the way in which we assign meaning to our lives. Our culture is always adjusting to both internal and external change.
- Archaeologists work with the tangible remains of human activity that survive in the ground. Archaeological finds are not culture in themselves but products of it, and they are linked to culture in a systematic way.
- Archaeologists think of human cultures as complex systems of interacting variables. This viewpoint is based loosely on principles of general systems theory, a way of searching for general relationships in the empirical world.
- A major objective of archaeology is to understand the complex linkages between human cultures and the environments in which they are found.
- Cultural process involves identifying the factors responsible for the direction and nature of change within cultural systems. Processual archaeology is the analysis of the causes behind cultural change.
- In this chapter we defined the archaeological record, data, and provenance, discussed the fundamental principles of association and superposition, and examined context in archaeology.

GUIDE TO FURTHER READING

The literature on basic archaeological concepts is sketchy at best, but these are some key works.

Deetz, James. *Invitation to Archaeology.* Garden City, N.Y.: Natural History Press, 1967. A classic exposition of basic archaeological concepts.

Renfrew, Colin, and Paul Bahn. *Archaeology: Theories, Methods, Practice.* 2nd ed. New York: Thames and Hudson, 1996. A comprehensive handbook to archaeological method and theory. Hundreds of illustrations.

Sharer, R. J., and Wendy Ashmore. *Archaeology: Discovering the Past,* 3rd ed. Mountain View, Calif.: Mayfield, 1995. A comprehensive text with good coverage of the subject matter of this chapter.

Watson, Patti Jo, Steven Le Blanc, and Charles L. Redman. *Archaeological Explanation,* 2d ed. New York: Columbia University Press, 1984. A fundamental source that describes processual archaeology in rather technical language.

Willey, Gordon R., and Philip Phillips. *Method and Theory in American Archaeology.* Chicago: University of Chicago Press, 1958. A classic essay on basic culture history in North American archaeology.

7

TIME: RELATIVE CHRONOLOGY

The measurement of time and the ordering of prehistoric cultures in chronological sequence have been one of the archaeologist's major preoccupations since the very beginnings of scientific research. In this chapter we examine the ways in which archaeologists establish chronological relationships among artifacts, sites, and other features.

How does one classify the past and measure the age of the great events of prehistory?

Consider for a moment how you view time. What is the earliest date you can remember? Mine is my third birthday—I have a vague memory of balloons and lots of people. My continuous memory of people as individuals and of day-to-day events begins at age eight. Most adults have a somewhat similar span of recollection and a chronological perspective on their lives extending back into early childhood. Our sense of personal involvement in human history, too, extends only over our lifetimes. We have only indirect involvement with the lives of our parents, relatives, or other friends, some of whom may have been alive 50 to 70 years before we were born. Perhaps our most profound involvement with time occurs toward the end of our lives, with a period covering the lives of our immediate family. But we also have a marginal sense of longer chronologies and a perspective on events within them—our family ancestry, the history of our community, of our nation, and in these days of ardent internationalism, of the world as well—though few people have a sense of perspective for the whole span of human experience.

CHRONOMETRIC (ABSOLUTE) AND RELATIVE DATING

Prehistoric chronologies cover enormous periods of time—millennia and centuries. Some idea of the scale of prehistoric time can be gained by piling up a hundred quarters. If the whole pile represents the time humankind has been on earth, the length of time covered by historical records would be considerably less than the thickness of one coin.

Archaeologists commonly refer to dates expressed in years as **chronometric** or **absolute** dates. Julius Caesar landed in Britain in 55 B.C.; Washington, D.C., was founded in A.D. 1800. The current chronometric dates for the earliest tool-making humans begin about 2.5 million years ago. Though not nearly as precise as the date for Caesar, they are nevertheless expressed in years. Dating experts draw widely on techniques invented by chemists and physicists and used by geologists for chronometric dating (see Chapter 8).

Relative dates correlate prehistoric sites of cultures with one another by their relative age. They are based on the law of superposition.

Relative dates are simpler to establish than chronometric dates. If I place a book on the table and then pile another on top of it, clearly the upper of the two was placed on the table at a later moment in time than the original volume. The second book became part of the pile after the first—though how long afterward we have no way of telling. At the foundation of relative chronology lie stratigraphy and the principle of superposition.

STRATIGRAPHY AND SUPERPOSITION

Most relative chronology in archaeology has its basis in large- or small-scale stratigraphic observations in archaeological sites of all ages. These were the observations which led to the wide acceptance of the Three Age System in the Old World, and Willey and Phillips' system (1958) of Paleo-Indian, Formative, Classic, and Postclassic in the Americas (Chapter 2) (Figure 7.1).

Superposition is fundamental in studying archaeological sites, for many settlements, such as Near Eastern mounds, Native American villages in the Ohio Valley, or cave sites, contain multilevel occupations whose decipherment is the

Approximate Age	Geological epoch	Three-age terminology	Important Events
3000 B.C. – 7800 B.C. –	HOLOCENE	Iron Age Bronze Age Neolithic Mesolithic	Writings in the Near East Origins of food production
12,000 B.C. – 35,000 B.P. –	END OF PLEISTOCENE	Upper Paleolithic	Settlement of the Americas Origins of blade technology
70,000 B.P. – 400,000 B.P. –	PLEISTOCENE	Middle Paleolithic	Emergence of *Homo sapiens sapiens* (150,000 B.P.) Hand axes in widespread use
1.75 million B.P. – 5 million B.P. –		Lower Paleolithic	Origins of toolmaking (2.5 million B.P.)
13 million B.P. –	PLIOCENE		
25 million B.P. –	MIOCENE		No humans
34 million B.P. –	OLIGOCENE		

FIGURE 7.1   Some nomenclature of Old World archaeology and geology.

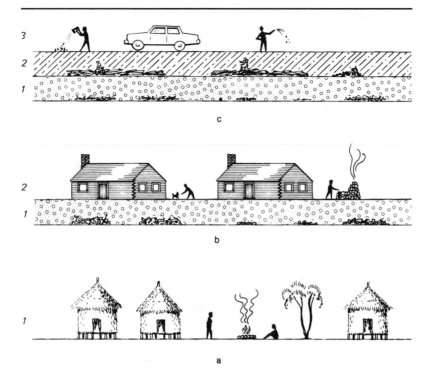

FIGURE 7.2 Superposition and stratigraphy: (a) A farming village flourishes five thousand years ago. After a time, the village is abandoned, and the huts fall into disrepair. Their ruins are covered by accumulating earth and vegetation. (b) After an interval, a second village is built on the same site, with different architectural styles. This village in turn is abandoned; the houses collapse into piles of rubble and are covered by accumulating earth. (c) Twentieth-century people park their cars on top of both village sites and drop litter and coins that when uncovered reveal to the archaeologist that the top layer is modern. An archaeologist digging this site would find that the modern layer is underlaid by two prehistoric occupation levels; that square houses were in use in the upper of the two, which is the later (principle of superposition); and that round huts are stratigraphically earlier than the square ones here. Therefore, village 1 is earlier than village 2, but when either was occupied or how many years separate village 1 from village 2 cannot be established without additional data.

key to their relative chronology (Figure 7.2). Wheeler (1954) describes the process of human occupation as applied to stratigraphy:

The human occupation of a site normally results in the accumulation of material of one kind or another on and about the area occupied. Objects are lost or discarded and become imbedded in the earth. Floors are renewed and old ones buried. Buildings crumble and new ones are built on the ruins. A flood may destroy a building or a town and deposit a layer of alluvium on its debris and later, when the flood has subsided, the level site may be reoccupied. Sometimes, the process is in the reverse direction. Evidences of occupation may be removed as in the deepening of an unsurfaced street by traffic, or the digging of a pit for the disposal of rubbish or for burial. . . . In one way or another the surface of an ancient town or village is constantly altering in response to human effort or neglect; and it is by interpreting rightly these evidences of alteration that we may hope to reconstruct something of the vicissitudes of the site and its occupants.

Stratigraphy, as applied to archaeological sites, is on a much smaller scale than that of geology, but it is often correspondingly more complicated (E. C. Harris, 1989). Most archaeological relative chronology employs careful observation of sequences of occupation levels as well as correlation of these with cultural sequences at other sites in the same area. Successive occupation levels may be found at the same spot, as in a cave, fort, or mound site, where many generations of settlers lived within a circumscribed or restricted area. In other sites, however, the chronological sequence can be horizontal, as when economic or political conditions dictate regular movement of villages when fields are exhausted or residence rules are modified. In this case, a cultural sequence may be scattered throughout a series of single-level occupation sites over a large area and can be put together only by judicious survey work and careful analysis of the artifacts found in the different sites.

The artifacts, food bones, or other finds recovered from the layers of a site are as critical as the stratigraphy itself. Each level in a settlement, however massive or small, has its associated artifacts, the objects that the archaeologist uses as indicators of cultural and economic change. Indeed, the finds in each layer—and their associations—often provide the basic material for relative chronology. Furthermore, the relative dating of many sites is complicated by other questions. Has the site been occupied continuously? Do stratigraphic profiles reflect continuous occupation over a long time or a sequence that has been interrupted several times by warfare or simple abandonment of the site? Such problems can be resolved by careful examination of excavated profiles (Figures 7.3 and 7.4).

Another factor that may affect interpretation of stratigraphy is the breaks or disruptions in the layering caused by human activity and by natural phenomena. These disruptions in a site form a vital part of the context of archaeological data.

Cultural transformations are those resulting from human behavior. For example, later occupants of a village may dig rubbish pits or graves into earlier strata. Cattle may be kept on the site, their hooves removing the soil and disturbing the upper levels of the underlying horizons; this disturbance may also be caused by later people cultivating the rich soils of an abandoned village site. Building activities may cause foundation trenches and even stone walls to be sunk into earlier levels. The local inhabitants' technological level has a direct bearing on their ability to destroy evidence of earlier occupation. The inhabitants of a Near Eastern city are obviously more likely to have destroyed evidence of earlier occupation with constant rebuilding than a group of farmers without metal tools who merely reoccupy earlier village sites, minimally disturbing the underlying

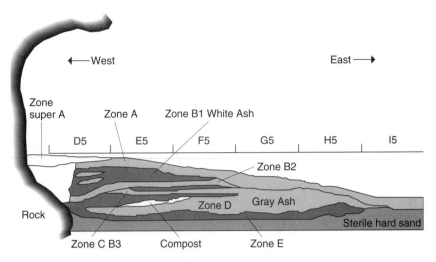

FIGURE 7.3 An idealized section through Guilá Naquitz Cave, Valley of Oaxaca, Mexico, showing the different occupation zones. Most cave and rock shelter sections are more complex than this one.

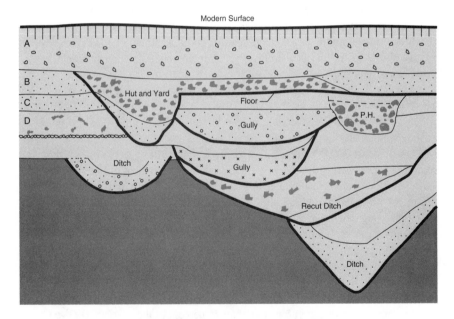

FIGURE 7.4 A stratigraphic section through the original town center in Cambridge, England, showing profiles of prehistoric and Roman enclosures and huts with a posthole (P.H.), gullies, and ditches. The complex stratigraphy is interpreted by correlating the various features with their horizontal layers, a difficult task in this case because of the jumbled layers. The lowest ditch was cut into bedrock (E) and was truncated by a later ditch. (1/32 actual size)

levels. Modern construction activity, road building, or deep plowing can also disturb a site and its contents, as can depredations by pot and treasure hunters, who care not at all about scientifically collected data.

Natural transformations are those caused by natural phenomena. A sudden flood can cover an abandoned village with a thick layer of mud. Volcanic ash buried Roman Pompeii in A.D. 79. Burrowing animals, too, enjoy archaeological sites, working their way through the soft, organic soils of caves and village sites and disrupting stratigraphy over large areas of the settlement. Natural transformations are vital, for they determine the preservation of data. Preservation conditions differ widely from site to site and must be assessed carefully for each location. We must understand conditions of both cultural and natural transformation to interpret archaeological data precisely (Chapter 7).

PLEISTOCENE GEOCHRONOLOGY: THE ICE AGE

Most people have heard of the Great Ice Age, known to geologists as the Pleistocene, a period of recent geological time when much of Europe and North America experienced a bitter, arctic climate (Butzer, 1974, 1982; Goudie, 1992; Waters, 1993). It was during this period that most of human prehistory was played out—against a background of complex and often dramatic climatic change that radically affected the pattern of human settlement. The science of Pleistocene geochronology (from the Greek geos, "earth"; chronos, "time") allows us to develop relative chronologies for early prehistory, and to attempt paleoenvironmental reconstructions (Loew and Walker, 1985).

The Ice Age began about 1.6 million years ago, during a long-term cooling trend in the world's oceans (Nilsson, 1983). These years were ones of constant climatic change. The Pleistocene is conventionally split into three subdivisions: the Lower, Middle, and Upper Pleistocene (Figure 7.5).

Until about 700,000 years ago, climatic fluctuations between warmer and colder regimens were still relatively minor. These were critical millennia, for it was during this long period that archaic humans emerged in Africa and spread from tropical regions into temperate latitudes in Europe and Asia. About 730,000 years ago the earth's magnetic polarity reversed abruptly. This important event, the so-called Matuyama-Brunhes boundary, has been recognized in deep-sea cores and in land deposits in many parts of the world. Since then, there have been at least eight cold (glacial) and warm (interglacial) cycles, the last cold cycle ending about 12,000 years ago. (Strictly speaking, we are still in an interglacial today.) These cycles were so constant that it can be said that the world's climate has been in transition from cold to warm and back again for more than 75 percent of the past 700,000 years.

Vegetational changes have mirrored climatic fluctuations. During glacial episodes, treeless arctic steppe and tundra covered much of Europe and parts of

FIGURE 7.5   Diagram showing the major climatic events of the Ice Age.

Temperature (Lower ← → Higher)	Dates (B.P.)	Periods	Epochs	Subdivisions	European Glacials/Interglacials	North American Glacials/Interglacials	Human Evolution	Prehistory	Three-Age System
		Holocene	Holocene	Holocene	Holocene	Holocene		Cities, agriculture Settlement of New World	Iron Age Bronze Age Neolithic Mesolithic
	10,000	Quaternary	Brunhes (Pleistocene)	Upper Pleistocene	Weichsel (Würm)	Wisconsin	*Homo sapiens sapiens*		Upper Paleolithic
	118,000				Eemian	Sangamon			
	128,000			Middle Pleistocene	Saale (Riss)	Illinoian			
					Holstein	Yarmouth	*Homo sapiens*	Hunter-gatherers	Lower and Middle Paleolithic
			Matuyama	Lower Pleistocene	Elster (Mindel)	Kansan	*Homo erectus*		
	730,000								
		Tertiary	Pliocene / Olduvai Event				Early hominids and *Australopithecus*		
	1,600,000								

Uncertain climatic detail before 130,000 years ago →

Note for the advanced reader and the instructor: Throughout this book I have used the glacial terminology applied to northern Europe in discussing the successive glaciations and interglacial periods in the Old World. This system follows Karl Butzer's definitive synthesis, *Environment and Archeology*, 3d ed. (Hawthorne, N.Y.: Aldine, 1974). Many still use the Alpine names preferred in earlier literature, but I have chosen to reduce confusion and recognize that not everyone will agree. For the newcomers, here are the equivalent names. Alpine terms: Würm, Riss, and Mindel; northern European terms: Weichsel, Saale, and Elster.

North America but gave way to temperate forest during interglacials. In the tropics, Africa's Sahara Desert may have supported grassland during interglacials, expanding dramatically during dry, cold spells.

The last interglacial lasted from 128,000 to 118,000 years ago, when a slow cooling trend brought full glacial conditions to Europe and North America, which persisted until about 10,000 years ago, when there was a rapid return to more temperate conditions. The final Ice Age (Würm) glaciation was the backdrop for some of the most important developments in human prehistory, notably the spread of anatomically modern *Homo sapiens sapiens* from the tropics to all parts of the Old World and into the Americas (Fagan, 1990). Between about 25,000 and 15,000 years ago, northern Eurasia's climate was intensely cold. A series of brilliant Stone Age hunter-gatherer cultures evolved both on the open tundra and in the sheltered river valleys of southwestern France and northern Spain, cultures famous for their fine antler and bone artifacts and exceptional artwork. The world's geography was dramatically different 20,000 years ago, and the differences had a major impact on human prehistory. For example, one could walk from Siberia to Alaska across a flat, low-lying plain, the Bering Land Bridge (Figure 7.6). This was the route by which humans first reached the Americas more than 12,000 years ago (Dillehay and Meltzer, 1991).

From the archaeological perspective, the major climatic events of the past 1.5 million years provide a broad framework for a relative chronology of human culture. Although almost no human beings lived on, or very close to, the great ice

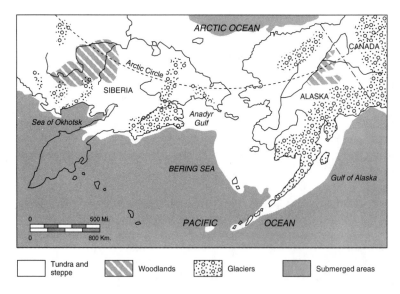

FIGURE 7.6   The Bering Land Bridge, as reconstructed by the latest research.

sheets that covered so much of the Northern Hemisphere, they did live in regions affected by geological phenomena associated with the ice sheets: coastal areas, lakes, and river floodplains. When human artifacts are found in direct association with Pleistocene geological features of this type, it is sometimes possible to tie in archaeological sites with the relative chronology of Pleistocene events derived from geological strata. And thanks to sophisticated geochronological methods like pollen analysis, it is often possible to reconstruct local environments during the Ice Age with remarkable precision.

RECONSTRUCTING THE ICE AGE

DEEP-SEA CORES

The world's ocean floors are a priceless archive of ancient climatic change. Deep-sea cores produce long columns of ocean-floor sediments that include skeletons of small marine organisms that once lived close to the ocean's surface. These plank-tonic foraminifera consist largely of calcium carbonate. When alive, their minute skeletons absorb organic isotopes. The ratio of two of these isotopes—oxygen 16 and oxygen 18—varies as a result of evaporation. When evaporation is high, more of the lighter oxygen 16 is extracted from the ocean, leaving the plankton to be enriched by more of the heavier oxygen 18. When great ice sheets formed on land during glacial episodes, sea levels fell as moisture was drawn off for continental ice caps. During such periods, the world's oceans contained more oxygen 18 in proportion to oxygen 16, a ratio reflected in millions of foraminifera. A mass spectrometer is used to measure this ratio, which does not reflect ancient temperature changes but is merely a statement about the size of the oceans and about contemporary events on land. It is possible to confirm climatic fluctuations by using other lines of evidence as well. You can analyze the changing frequencies of foraminifera and other groups of marine microfossils in the cores. By using statistical techniques, and assuming that relationships between different species and sea conditions have not changed, climatologists have been able to turn these frequencies into numerical estimates of sea surface temperatures and ocean salinity over the past few hundred thousand years and produce a climatic profile of much of the Ice Age (Figure 7.7). These events have been fixed at key points by radiocarbon dates (see Chapter 8) and by studies of paleomagnetism (ancient magnetism). The Matuyama-Brunhes magnetic reversal of 730,000 years ago is a key stratigraphic marker, which can be identified both in sea cores and in volcanic strata ashore, where it can be dated precisely with potassium-argon samples (Chapter 8).

GLACIATIONS, INTERGLACIALS, AND SEA LEVELS

The glaciers and ice sheets that make up the framework for geochronological stud-ies were formed in mountainous, high-latitude areas and on continental plains during the Pleistocene. Prolonged periods of arctic climate and abundant snowfall caused glaciers to form over enormous expanses of northern Europe, North America, and the alpine areas of France, Italy, and Switzerland. These alternated with shorter interglacial phases, when world climate was considerably warmer than

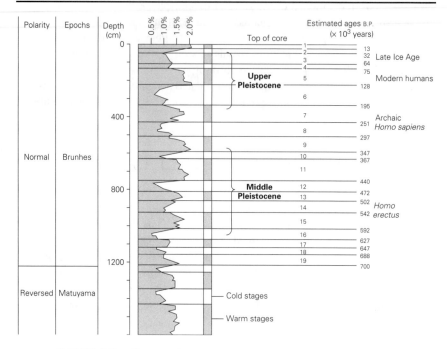

FIGURE 7.7   The core that serves as the standard reference for events during the past 700,000 years comes from the Solomon Plateau in the Pacific Ocean, core V28–238 (Shackleton and Opdyke, 1973). The Matuyama-Brunhes boundary occurs at a depth of 39.3 feet (1,200 cm) in the core. Above it a sawtoothlike curve identifies eight complete glacial and interglacial cycles, a far more complicated picture of the Middle and Upper Pleistocene than comes from land sediments. Scientists believe that these changes are triggered by long-term astronomical changes, especially in the earth's orbit around the sun. These affect the seasonal and north-south variations of solar radiation the earth receives.

it is today. Every ice sheet had a **periglacial** zone, an area affected by glacial climatic influences. Some 25,000 years ago, the persistent glacial high-pressure zone centered over the northern ice sheet caused dry, frosty winds to blow over the periglacial regions. The dry winds blew fine particles of dust, known as **loess,** onto the huge, rolling plains of central and eastern Europe and Northern America.

The loess plains of central and eastern Europe were inhabited by hunter-gatherers who preyed on mammoths and other big game (Soffer, 1985). The relative dates of these settlements have been established by correlating the occupation levels with the different periods of loess accumulation that took place during the Pleistocene. Much later, in about 6000 B.C., Danubian peoples, the first farmers of temperate Europe, settled almost exclusively on these same light loess soils, for they were eminently suitable for the simple slash-and-burn agriculture practiced by these pioneer farmers (Figure 7.8) (Champion and others, 1984).

The ice sheet growing on land had effects beyond the formation of loess plains. The water that falls as snow to form the ice sheets and glaciers ultimately

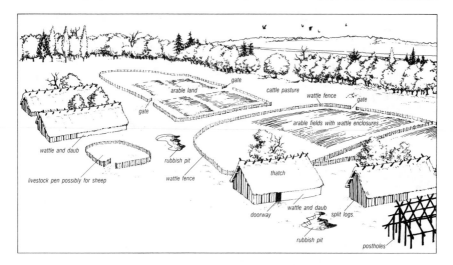

FIGURE 7.8 Reconstruction of a central European farming village of about 6000 B.C., of a type built on the soft loess soils of the late Ice Age.

comes from the oceans. When large areas in the northern latitudes were covered with ice, enormous quantities of water—enough to reduce the general level of the oceans by many meters more than 90 meters at the height of the last glaciation 18,000 years ago—were immobilized on land. This eustatic effect was accompanied by an isostatic effect as well. The sheer dead weight of the massive ice sheets sank the loaded continental blocks of the land masses into the viscous underlying layers of the earth that lie some 6 miles (10 km) below the surface. The world looked very different 10,000 years ago. Until as late as 7000 B.C., Britain was joined to the continent by a strip of marsh, covering the area that is now the North Sea and part of the English Channel (Figure 7.9).

Many prehistoric settlements occupied during periods of low sea level are, of course, buried deep beneath the modern oceans. Numerous sites on ancient beaches have been found dating to times of higher sea level. American archaeologist Richard Klein excavated a coastal cave at Nelson Bay in the Cape Province of South Africa that now overlooks the Indian Ocean (Klein, 1983). Large quantities of shellfish and other marine animals are found in the uppermost levels of the cave. But in the lower levels, occupied roughly 11,000 to 12,000 years ago, fish bones and other marine resources are very rare. Klein suspects that the seashore was many miles away at that time, for world sea levels were much lower during a long period of arctic climate in northern latitudes. Today the cave is only 50 yards (45 m) from the sea.

ICE AGE ANIMALS

Throughout the millennia of the Ice Age, humans subsisted on game animals and plant foods. Archaeologists have found hunters' weapons and butchery tools in association with the fragmented bones of animals large and small. During the Ice Age, these prey were often extinct species, such as the giant pigs and buffalo

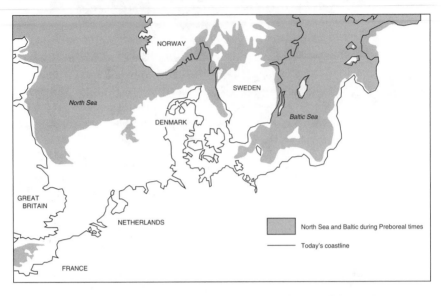

FIGURE 7.9   Great Britain and Scandinavia at the end of the Ice Age, showing sea levels around 7000 B.C.

found at Olduvai Gorge in Tanzania, East Africa. Paleontologists have tried to build up relative chronologies of the Ice Age from evolutionary changes in such animals as the elephant and the pig. Species vary greatly in their tolerance of environmental conditions, and faunal change can sometimes relate to time or climatic change. For example, a study of the changing fossil-pig forms at the early hominid site at Omo in southern Ethiopia showed that potassium-argon dates for *Homo habilis,* a very early human form in northern Kenya, were too early. Birds and rodents can also be useful chronological markers.

At several points during the Ice Age, large-scale extinctions of mammals large and small occurred. The most dramatic of these extinctions occurred at the end of the Ice Age, some 11,000 years ago, when many large arctic mammals like the woolly rhinoceros and more than 50 other species of American animals vanished within a short time. Herein lies one of the great controversies of American archaeology, for some experts believe that it was human big-game hunters who were responsible for the disappearance of many large mammals in the New World. Some 12,000 years ago, goes the argument, human predators spread throughout the Americas, hunting big game. Populations rose quickly and slow-breeding animals like mammoth and mastodon were rapidly hunted into extinction. This is probably a simplistic view, for while humans may have accelerated the process of extinction, complex environmental factors also came into play. Current thinking tends to underplay the human role in the extinction process (Martin and Klein, 1984).

More information on the study of animal bones can be found in Chapter 13.

PLANTS AND POLLEN ANALYSIS

Vegetation is one of the best indicators of ecological change and relative chronology, for it depends on climate and soil for survival and is a sensitive barometer of climatic alteration. Pollen analysis, or **palynology,** is a comprehensive way of studying ancient vegetation; it was developed in 1916 by a Swede, Lennart van Post, who used forest trees. Subsequently, this analysis was extended to all pollen-liberating vegetation. The principle of pollen analysis is simple (Dimbleby, 1985). Large numbers of pollen grains are dispersed in the atmosphere and have remarkable preservative properties if deposited in an unaerated geological horizon. The pollen grains can be identified microscopically (Figure 7.10) with great accuracy and can be used to reconstruct a picture of the vegetation that grew near the spot where they are found.

Pollen analysis begins in the field. The botanist visits the excavation and collects a series of closely spaced pollen samples from the stratigraphic sections at the site. Back in the laboratory, the samples are examined under a very powerful microscope. The grains of each genus or species present are counted, and the resulting figures subjected to statistical analysis. These counts are then correlated with the stratigraphic layers of the excavation to provide a sequence of vegetational change for the site. Typically, this vegetational sequence lasts a few centuries or even millennia. It forms part of a much longer pollen sequence for the area that has been assembled from hundreds of samples from many different sites. In northern Europe, for example, botanists have worked out a complicated series of vegetational time zones that cover the past 10,000 years. By comparing the pollen sequences from individual sites with the overall zone chronology, they can give a relative date for the site. For example, the famous Star Carr hunter-gatherer site in northeast England yielded pollen samples that placed it in the pre-Boreal vegetational zone of some 10,000 years ago. This was a time when birch trees dominated the local landscape (J. G. D. Clark, 1954).

Palynology has obvious applications to prehistory, for sites are often found in swampy deposits where pollen is preserved, especially fishing or fowling camps and settlements near water. Isolated artifacts, or even human corpses (such

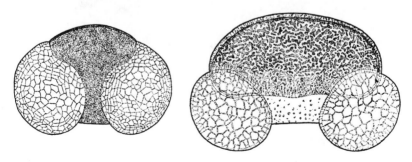

FIGURE 7.10   Pollen grains: left, spruce; right, silver fir. Both 340 times actual size.

as that of Tollund Man found in a Danish bog), have also been discovered in these deposits; pollen is sometimes obtained from small peat lumps adhering to crevices in such finds (Bryant and Holloway, 1983). Thus botanists can assign relative dates even to isolated finds that would otherwise remain undated. An archaeological site having a pollen graph coinciding with that of a particular vegetational zone clearly belongs within that period. Unfortunately, pollen from archaeological sites is sometimes heavily contaminated by cultural activities, especially if there has been later occupation at the same location, so such samples must be used with care.

As Figure 7.11 shows, palynology is a powerful tool for modeling Ice Age and later climatic change, especially when combined with deep-sea cores. Pollen analysis has important applications for later prehistory as well. Improved recovery and excavation methods have opened up all sorts of new possibilities. Southwestern archaeologists now have a regional pollen sequence that provides not only climatic information but also valuable facts about the functions of different pueblo rooms and different foods that were eaten by the inhabitants.

Identifying cultural activities from pollen archaeological sites can be extremely tricky, for the tiny grains can be transported to a site in many ways—by wind, water, rodents, even people bringing ripe fruit home. Sometimes, too, people

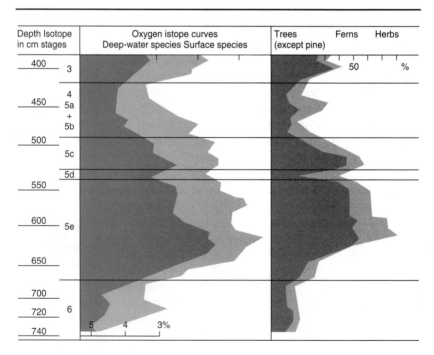

FIGURE 7.11   A long-term pollen sequence for the Ice Age from Spain (left) compared to oxygen-isotope curves taken from a deep-sea core in the nearby Bay of Biscay, showing close correlation between the two.

will use surface soil from neighboring areas, complete with its pollen content, to make a house floor. Some species like the sunflower have heavy pollen that can cling to ripe fruit. Such factors are likely to contaminate the pollen samples from many sites, unless one has other plant evidence, such as, say, squash rind or seeds, to confirm the palynological data.

Pollen analysis is providing new perceptions of Stone Age life at the height of the last glaciation in southwestern France, some 15,000 to 20,000 years ago. This was, we are told, a period of extreme arctic cold, when Europe was in a deep freeze, people subsisting off arctic animals and taking refuge in deep river valleys like the Dordogne and the Vézère, where some of the earliest cave art in the world has been discovered. In fact, pollen grains from the rock shelters and open camps used by Stone Age hunter-gatherers of this period paint a very different picture of the late Ice Age climate in this area. It is a portrait of a favored arctic environment in which the climate fluctuated constantly, with surprisingly temperate conditions, especially on the south-facing slopes of deep river valleys. Here, people used rock shelters that faced the winter sun, where snow melted earlier in the spring, within easy reach of key reindeer migration routes and of arctic game that wintered in the valleys. The vegetational cover was not treeless, as is commonly assumed, but included pine, birch, and sometimes deciduous trees, with lush summer meadows in the valley floors (Laville and others, 1980). (For more on pollen, see Chapter 13.)

ARTIFACTS AND RELATIVE CHRONOLOGY

Manufactured artifacts are the fundamental data with which archaeologists study human behavior in the past. These artifacts are reflections of ancient human behavior and how it has changed throughout time. You need only look at the simple stone chopper of the earliest human beings and compare it to the latest and most sophisticated computer to get the point. Most artifact changes in prehistory, however, are extremely gradual. They are cumulative, minor changes in such elements as, say, shape, decoration, or lip angle of clay pots that lead ultimately to a vessel quite different in form, hardly recognizable as related.

STYLISTIC SERIATION

Typology is a method used in natural science to work out relationships in the form and structure of organisms within an evolutionary sequence. Archaeologists use typology to analyze human-made objects. Archaeologists base their typologies on another important assumption, too: some technological trends are irreversible. An obvious example is an airplane enthusiast who, given a series of photographs of aircraft types dating from the beginnings of aviation to the present, could place them in approximately correct order, even if he had no idea of the dates of the photographs. It simply would be impossible to envision a typological sequence in which the earliest aircraft was a supersonic jet and the latest a 1912 Blériot monoplane: the modifications needed would be both illogical and incredible.

Egyptologist Sir Flinders Petrie was a pioneer student of artifact change. In the 1880s he wanted to arrange a large number of pre-Dynastic tombs from the Nile Valley in chronological order. He eventually placed them in sequence by studying groups of pots found with the skeletons, arranging the vessels so their *stylistic* differences reflected gradual change (Petrie, 1889). The handles on the jars were particularly informative, for they changed from functional appendages into more decorative handles and, finally, degenerated into painted lines. Petrie built up a series of pottery stages at Diospolis Parva to which he assigned "sequence dates," the 50 stages running from SD 30 to SD 80. The SD 30 was the oldest in the group. Petrie started his sequence with the number 30 because he assumed correctly that the earliest of his wares was not, in fact, the most ancient Egyptian pottery. His sequence dates were subsequently applied over wide areas of the Nile Valley, providing an admirable relative chronology for early Egyptian pottery that remained in use for many years. When a pot of a known type in the sequence date series was found, the pot itself and all objects associated with it could be dated to that stage in the sequence.

FREQUENCY SERIATION

In the past half-century **seriation,** a technique for ordering items by their morphology, has evolved swiftly, relying increasingly on changing frequencies of artifact traits. Archaeologists generally use seriation to study relative chronology (L. Johnson, 1968; Marquardt, 1978). Recent studies of seriation are based on the assumption that popularity of any artifact or culture trait is transient. The miniskirt becomes the midi or maxi, dancing styles change from month to month, recordings hit the Top 40 but are forgotten in a short time, and each year's "all new" automobile model is soon relegated to the secondhand lot. Other traits may have far longer lives. The crude knives of the earliest people were a major element in early toolkits for hundreds of thousands of years. Candles were used for centuries before kerosene and gas lamps came into fashion. But each had its period of maximum relative frequency, or popularity. Figure 7.12 shows how such popularity distributions are made up with bar graphs plotted against strata or other archaeological associations. Each distribution of artifacts or culture traits plotted has a profile that has been described as resembling a battleship's hull viewed from the air.

The technique of seriation is based on the assumption that popularity of pottery types, forms of stone artifacts, and other culture traits peaks in such a battleship curve, the widest part of the graph representing the period of maximum popularity. A second assumption holds that different types of artifacts maintain some continuity over a period of time. Thus sites within a restricted and uniform geographic area showing similar plots of pottery or other artifact types are of broadly the same relative date. A series of sites or surface collections can be linked in a relative chronology (even though, without chronometric dates, one cannot tell when they were occupied) provided that the samples of artifacts used are statistically reliable. Edwin Dethlefsen and James Deetz tested the battleship-curve assumption against some historical data, using a series of Colonial grave-stones from a New England cemetery (Dethlefsen and Deetz, 1966) (Figure 7.13). The gravestones, dated by the inscriptions on them, show three decorative styles—death's head, cherub, and urn and willow—that yield an almost perfect series of battleship curves following one upon the other. Seriation is also applied to stylistic change in a single series of artifacts that may in themselves form a

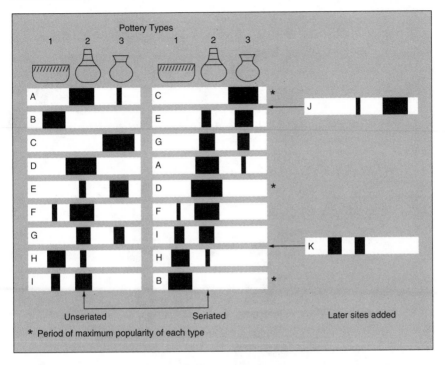

FIGURE 7.12   Seriation. At the left, nine excavated sites (A to I) contain different percentages of three distinct pottery types. At the right, the nine sites have been seriated by rearranging the bars of type percentages into battleship-curve order. At the far right, later excavations are eventually fitted into the sequence.

battleship curve. The same principle used by Petrie with his pre-Dynastic jars applies, and a battleship curve results. Once the sequence of artifact types has been established, it is possible to insert new sites or single components from multilevel settlements into the carefully correlated sequence of seriated artifact types. These are added simply by comparing the percentages of types found in the new site with those in the correlated sequence as a whole. The new site is inserted into the sequence with considerable precision, on the assumption that closely similar artifacts were made at approximately the same time and that the lifetime of these tools coincides, albeit approximately, at all sites in a restricted culture area. If the collections are radiocarbon-dated, the seriation can also be given an accurate date in years.

The so-called battleship-curve seriation method has been widely applied in American archaeology. Figure 7.14 illustrates a fine example of a seriated pottery sequence, from the Tehuacán Valley in Mexico, famed for its evidence of early maize cultivation (MacNeish, 1970). It shows how three distinctive phases of

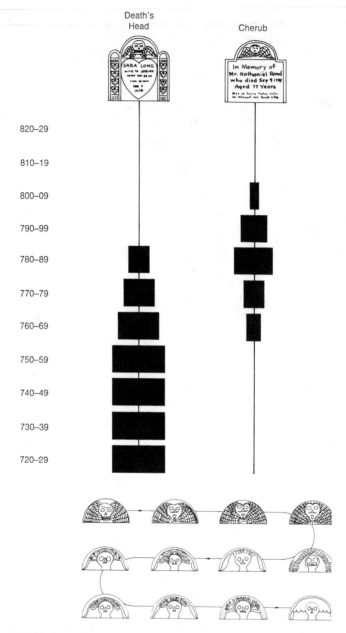

FIGURE 7.13 (top) Deetz's classic seriation of stylistic sequences of gravestones in Stoneham, Massachusetts. These dated battleship curves prove that all objects have a period of maximum popularity. (bottom) Seriation of a stylistic change within one New England gravestone motif. This type of seriation deals with the minute changes in a motif and shows how cultural traits change very gradually over time.

Approximate Age	Geological epoch	Three-age terminology	Important Events
3000 B.C. – 7800 B.C. –	HOLOCENE	Iron Age Bronze Age Neolithic Mesolithic	Writings in the Near East Origins of food production
12,000 B.C. – 35,000 B.P. –	END OF PLEISTOCENE	Upper Paleolithic	Settlement of the Americas Origins of blade technology
70,000 B.P. – 400,000 B.P. –	PLEISTOCENE	Middle Paleolithic	Emergence of *Homo sapiens sapiens* (150,000 B.P.) Hand axes in widespread use
1.75 million B.P. – 5 million B.P. –		Lower Paleolithic	Origins of toolmaking (2.5 million B.P.)
13 million B.P. –	PLIOCENE		
25 million B.P. –	MIOCENE		No humans
34 million B.P. –	OLIGOCENE		

FIGURE 7.14   The battleship-curve principle was used to develop this seriated ceramic sequence from the Tehuacán Valley in Mexico.

Tehuacán culture were ordered in a relative chronology with the seriated counts of many pottery types.

You will notice that Figure 7.14 contains no absolute dates; the illustrated seriation is based on changing pottery forms and nothing else. In fact, of course, the chronological validity of the Tehuacán sequence has been confirmed by radiocarbon dating. Today's seriators use sophisticated statistical techniques to produce the seriation and to test the viability of their conclusions (L. Johnson, 1968; Marquardt, 1978).

Although seriation can work well with undated artifact sequences, it works even better when radiocarbon dates or other accurate dating methods are available. When artifact types change rather predictably throughout a period and these changes are well-documented and dated in such a way that the direction of change is established, it is possible to assign undated sites with similar artifacts to an approximate relative position on the crude time scale. It works well, of course, only when the artifacts being studied are of a type that changed in a distinctive and readily identifiable way.

CROSS-DATING

One of the classic relative dating techniques of archaeological research, cross-dating has been applied to many sites in the New World and Old World. In its classic application, cross-dating is based on dated objects, such as coins or pottery types, whose precise ages are known in the localities of ultimate origin (Childe, 1956).

When a dated artifact, such as a coin, turns up in an otherwise undated prehistoric occupation level far from its place of origin, it is safe to conclude that the horizon was laid down no earlier than the date of the article of known age. A Native American village site in Virginia that yielded an Elizabethan coin bearing the date 1588 obviously dates to 1588 or later.

Such items as Chinese porcelain, Roman glass vessels, faience or glass beads, cotton and flax fabrics, bronze daggers, and Greek wine amphoras (and more importantly, their contents) were diffused widely throughout the Old World, often to the barbarian tribes on the fringe of the unknown. The dates of styles of Chinese porcelain or Greek vases, changing according to fashion's dictates, are firmly established in historical records. For example, imported Chinese porcelain found in the deposits of Great Zimbabwe in south central Africa date the heyday of that great trading center to before A.D. 1450 (Garlake, 1973).

Cross-dating has also been widely applied to sites where objects of known age are absent. In these instances, a well-studied sequence of different artifacts, whose development throughout time has been established by excavation, seriation, and stratigraphy, can be used to fit sites in neighboring areas into the master sequence simply by taking the artifacts in them and matching them with the dated collections from the central area. A well-known study of this type was conducted in the Tehuacán Valley in Mexico, where the excellent artifacts and seriations from Richard MacNeish's many excavations were combined with radiocarbon dates to fix the chronological time span of each cultural phase in the valley (MacNeish, 1970). Armed with the precise chronological sequence, MacNeish's team was able to fit new sites and their artifactual contents into the sequence by both radiocarbon dating and cross-dating of the seriated artifacts in the site. In some instances, the relative chronology established by cross-dated artifacts was more accurate than a radiocarbon date that was out of line with the master chronology established on the long Tehuacán sequence. This sequence was used as a cross-dating yardstick to correlate sites and cultural sequences all over Mexico. Obviously, individual trade artifacts with a short life at Tehuacán are best for such cross-datings, for their short life gives the cross-dating considerable precision. Artifacts such as ceramics or stone tools give less accurate results, for entire pottery styles may be copied only in part by others or may take time to spread from one area to another. But approximations are better than no relative chronology at all.

Relative chronology is a valuable tool for archaeological research. Unfortunately, however, it does not provide accurate dates in years, the ultimate objective of all chronological research. Chapter 8 outlines the major methods used to date archaeological sites in calendar years.

SUMMARY

• Chronological ordering of prehistoric times was a major problem for early archaeologists. In an attempt to deal with this difficulty, C. J. Thomsen refined the three-age system, a technological framework that was widely used in the Old World. New World archaeologists used the direct historical approach to determine the framework for the Americas.

- Chronometric (absolute) dates are expressed in years. In contrast, relative dates represent relationships in time that are used to correlate prehistoric sites or cultures with one another. These are based on the law of superposition.
- Cultural disturbances, which result from human behavior, can affect stratigraphy. Natural disturbances, such as erosion or flooding, can change stratigraphic contexts by natural means.
- The Pleistocene, or Great Ice Age, has been relatively dated by such geological events as the major glaciations and interglacials as well as by fluctuations in sea level and climatic evidence from deep-sea caves.
- Pollen analysis, or palynology, uses the fossil pollens of grasses and forest trees to study prehistoric vegetational cover with great accuracy. Pollen samples provide ecological information about glaciations and interglacials, and insights on the environments surrounding archaeological sites.
- Early archaeologists studied the evolution of artifact styles over time. This approach has developed into formal ordering, the technique of seriation. This technique is based on the assumption that artifacts come into fashion, have a period of maximum popularity, and then slowly go out of style. Tested against the evidence of New England tombstones and other modern artifacts, seriation has become an effective way of ordering sites in chronological sequence.
- Cross-dating, widely applied in Europe and Mesoamerica, uses artifacts of a known age, such as coins and other items that were widely traded, to provide relative dates for sites in areas that have no historical chronology.

GUIDE TO FURTHER READING

Butzer, Karl. *Environment and Archaeology*, 3d ed. Hawthorne, N.Y.: Aldine, 1974. The fundamental synthesis of Pleistocene geochronology; recommended for advanced readers.

————. *Archaeology as Human Ecology*. Cambridge: Cambridge University Press, 1982. Excellent treatise on the basics of geoarchaeology, especially environmental context.

Deetz, James. *Invitation to Archaeology*. Garden City, N.Y.: Natural History Press, 1967. The best account of seriation for the lay reader yet written, by someone closely involved with basic research in this field.

Michels, J. W. *Dating Methods in Archaeology*. Orlando, Fla.: Academic Press, 1973. A useful summary of major dating methods.

8

TIME: CHRONOMETRIC DATING

More effort has been devoted to inventing methods of chronometric dating in archaeology than to almost any other aspect of the subject (Bailey, 1983). The reason for this interest is that fundamental questions about the past are involved. How old is this tool? How long ago was that site occupied? Are these villages contemporary? These are probably the first questions asked by anyone curious about an artifact or a prehistoric village, as well as by the archaeologist. They remain among the most difficult to answer (Geyh and Schleicher, 1990).

Figure 8.1 summarizes the major dating methods for human cultural history and the spans of time they cover. Let us now look at the principal methods of chronometric dating used to develop absolute chronologies for prehistory. Our discussion starts with the chemical and physical methods used to date the earlier millennia of prehistory and ends in modern times with objects of known age.

POTASSIUM-ARGON DATING (EARLIEST TIMES TO c. 50,000 YEARS AGO)

PRINCIPLES

The only viable means of chronometrically dating the earliest archaeological sites is the potassium-argon method (Dalrymple and Lamphere, 1970). Geologists use this radioactive counting technique to date the age of the earth from rocks as much as 2 billion years old and as little as 50,000 years old. Potassium (K) is one of the most abundant elements in the earth's crust and is present in nearly every mineral. In its natural form, potassium contains a small proportion of radioactive potassium 40 atoms. For every hundred potassium 40 atoms that decay, 11 become argon 40, an inactive gas that can easily escape from its material by diffusion when lava and other igneous rocks are formed. As volcanic rock forms through crystallization, the concentration of argon 40 drops to almost nothing. But regular and reasonable decay of potassium 40 will continue, with a half-life of 1.3 billion years. It is possible, then, to measure with a spectrometer the concentration of argon 40 that has accumulated since the rock formed. Because many archaeological sites were occupied during a period when

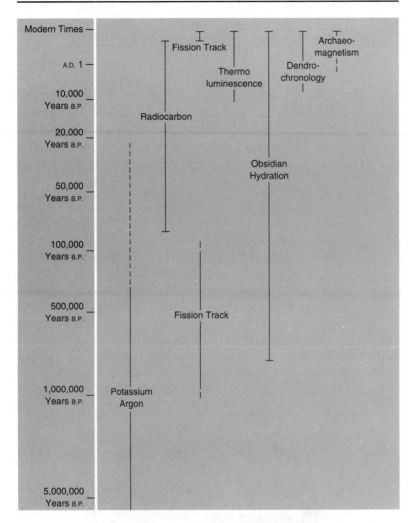

FIGURE 8.1 Chronological span of major chronometric methods used in archaeology. At the right, a column shows the immense span of prehistory when compared with historic times, illuminated by written documents.

extensive volcanic activity occurred, especially in East Africa, it is possible to date them by associations of lava with human settlements.

DATABLE MATERIALS AND PROCEDURES

Potassium-argon dates have been obtained from many igneous minerals, of which the most resistant to later argon diffusion are biotite, muscovite, and sanidine. Microscopic examination of the rock is essential to eliminate the possibility of contamination by recrystallization and other processes. The samples are processed by crushing the rock, concentrating it, and treating it with hydrofluoric acid to remove any atmospheric argon from the sample. The various gases are then removed from the sample and the argon gas is isolated and subjected to mass spectrographic analysis. The age of the sample is then calculated using the argon 40 and potassium 40 content and a standard formula. The resulting date is quoted with a large standard deviation—for early Pleistocene sites, on the order of a quarter of a million years.

In recent years, computerized argon laser fusion has become the technique of choice. By steering a laser beam over a single irradiated grain of volcanic ash, a potassium-argon specialist can date a lake bed layer, or even a small scatter of tools and animal bones left by an early hominid. The grain glows white hot and gives up a gas, which is purified, then charged by an electron beam. A powerful magnet accelerates the charged gas and hurls it against a device which counts its argon atoms. By measuring the relative amounts of two isotopes of the element, researchers can calculate the amount of time which has elapsed since the lava cooled and the crystals formed.

ARCHAEOLOGICAL APPLICATIONS

Fortunately, many early human settlements in the Old World are found in volcanic areas, where such deposits as lava flows and tuffs are found in profusion. The first archaeological date obtained from this method came from Olduvai Gorge, Tanzania, where Louis and Mary Leakey found a robust Australopithecine skull, *Australspitheans boisei*, stone tools, and animal bones in a Lower Pleistocene lake bed of unknown age. Lava samples from the site were dated to about 1.75 million years, doubling the then-assumed date for early humans

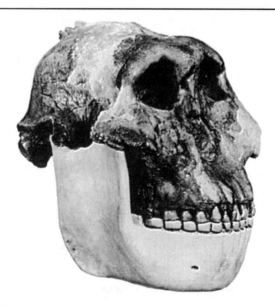

FIGURE 8.2   Skull of *Australopithecus boisei,* with reconstructed jaw, from Bed I at Olduvai Gorge, Tanzania, East Africa, potassium-argon dated to about 1.75 million years ago.

(Figure 8.2) (Tobias, 1971). Stone flakes and chopping tools of undoubted human manufacture have come from Koobi Fora in northern Kenya, dated to about 2.5 million years, the earliest date for human artifacts. Still earlier *Australopithecus* fossils have been dated at Aramis near the Hadar in Ethiopia to about 4.5 million years ago (White et al., 1994). Recently, a team of Berkeley scientists have dated *Homo erectus*-bearing levels at Modjokerto in southeast Asia to 1.8 million years using the laser fusion technique (Swisher and others, 1994).

LIMITATIONS

Potassium-argon dates can be taken only from volcanic rocks, preferably from actual volcanic flows. Archaeologically, it is obviously vital that the relationship between the lava being dated and the human settlement it purports to date be worked out carefully.

RADIOCARBON DATING (c. 45,000 YEARS AGO AND EARLIER TO A.D. 1500)

PRINCIPLES

Radiocarbon dating is the best known and most widely used of all chronometric dating methods, providing a chronology for human prehistory after 45,000 years ago and earlier (Libby, 1955).

The radiocarbon dating method is based on the fact that cosmic radiation produces neutrons that enter the earth's atmosphere and react with nitrogen. They produce carbon 14, a carbon isotope with eight rather than the usual six neutrons in the nucleus. With these additional neutrons, the nucleus is unstable and is subject to gradual radioactive decay. Willard Libby calculated that it took 5,568 years for half the carbon 14 in any sample to decay, its so-called half-life. (The half-life is now more accurately measured to be 5,730 years.) He found that the neutrons emitted radioactive particles when they left the nucleus, and he arrived at a method for counting the number of emissions in a gram of carbon.

Carbon 14 is believed to behave exactly like ordinary carbon from a chemical standpoint, and together with ordinary carbon it enters into the carbon dioxide of the atmosphere. The tempo of the process corresponds to the rates of supply and disintegration. Because living vegetation builds up its own organic matter through photosynthesis and by using atmospheric carbon dioxide, the proportion of radiocarbon present in it is equal to that in the atmosphere. As soon as an organism dies, no further radiocarbon is incorporated into it. The radiocarbon present in the dead organism will continue to disintegrate slowly, so that after 5,730 years only half the original amount will be left; after about 11,100 years, only a quarter; and so on. Thus, if you measure the rate of disintegration of carbon 14 to nitrogen, you can get an idea of the age of the specimen being measured. The initial amount of radiocarbon in a sample is so small that the limit of detectability is soon reached. Samples older than 50,000 years contain only minuscule quantities of carbon 14.

DATABLE MATERIALS AND PROCEDURES

Radiocarbon dates can be taken from samples of many organic materials. About a handful of charcoal, burnt bone, shell, hair, skin, wood, or other organic substance is needed. The samples themselves are collected with meticulous care during excavation from particular stratigraphic contexts so that an exact location, specific structure, or even a hearth is dated. Several dates must be taken from each level, because one or more may have been contaminated by a variety of factors. Modern rootlets, disturbances in the stratigraphy, and even packing with tissue paper or newspaper can introduce younger carbon into an ancient sample, although some of the more obvious contaminations are eliminated by careful laboratory treatment.

The first stage in the dating procedure is physical examination of the sample. The material is then converted into gas, purified to remove radioactive contaminants, and then piped into a proportional counter. The counter itself is sheltered from background radiation by massive iron shields. The sample is counted at least twice at intervals of about a week. The results of the count are then compared with a modern count sample, and the age of the sample is computed by a formula to produce the radiocarbon date and its statistical limit of error. A date received from a radiocarbon dating laboratory is in this form: 3,621 ± 180 radiocarbon years before the present (B.P.)

The figure 3,621 is the age of the sample (in radiocarbon years) before the present. Notice that the sample reads in radiocarbon years, not calendar years. Corrections must be applied to make this a chronometric date.

The radiocarbon age has the reading ± 180 attached to it. This is the *standard deviation*, an estimate of the amount of probable error. The figure 180 years is an estimate of the 360-year range within which the date falls. Statistical theory provides that there is a 2-out-of-3 chance that the correct date is between the span of one standard deviation (3,441 and 3,801). If we double the deviation, chances are 19 out of 20 that the span (3,261 and 3,981) is correct. Most dates in this book are derived from carbon 14-dated samples and should be recognized for what they are—statistical approximations.

The conventional radiocarbon method relies on measurements of a beta-ray decay rate to date the sample. Accelerator mass spectrometry (AMS) allows radiocarbon dating to be carried out by direct counting of carbon 14 atoms, rather than by counting radioactive disintegrations (Figure 8.3) (Gowlett, 1987). This has the advantage that samples up to 1/1,000 the size can be dated, especially for the time span between 10,000 and 30,000 years ago. Accelerator dating distinguishes between carbon 14 and carbon 12 and other ions through its mass and energy characteristics, requiring far smaller samples to do so. Even more important, the problem of background radiation is eliminated, and the sample sizes are the same for all time periods, the small quantity of organic material required allowing retesting of different parts of the same sample if this proves necessary. The samples needed are so small that it is possible, for example, to date an individual tree ring, a seed, or an actual artifact.

Accelerator dating is especially useful for dating the amino acids from bone collagen, but almost any material can be dated, even tiny wood fragments preserved in the haft sockets of metal spearheads, for example.

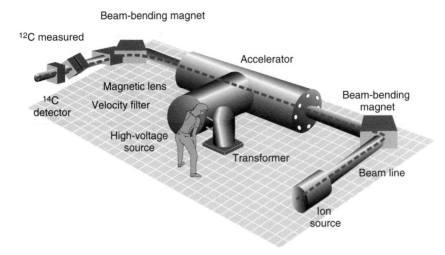

FIGURE 8.3 Accelerator mass spectrometry (AMS) radiocarbon dating. Ionized carbon atoms from the sample are first pulled in beam form toward the accelerator. As the beam passes through the first beam-bending magnet, lighter atoms turn more sharply than heavier ones. They move to the inside of the diverging beam, where a filter blocks the further progress of all charged particles except those of atomic mass 14. When the beam enters the accelerator, it is stripped of all molecules of mass 14 that might be indistinguishable from single carbon 14 atoms. The accelerator pushes the remaining ions through a second beam-bending magnet, filtering out more non-carbon 14 particles. Then the beam is focused before reaching an extremely sensitive detector that counts the number of remaining ions.

ARCHAEOLOGICAL APPLICATIONS

Radiocarbon dates provide the basic chronology for the past 45,000 years, but AMS dating provides an additional advantage in that it can date individual maize cobs and other seeds, providing very accurate dates for the origins of agriculture. For example, AMS dates of early maize cobs in Mexico's Tehuacán Valley have shown maize was first domesticated in southwestern Mexico about 3000 B.C. (B.D. Smith, 1994).

LIMITATIONS

Radiocarbon dates can be obtained only from organic materials, which means that relatively few artifacts can be dated. But associated hearths with abundant charcoal, broken animal bones, and burnt wooden structures can be dated. Artifacts contemporary with such phenomena are obviously of the same age as the dated samples. Having a block of samples from the same division is preferable because they can be treated statistically and tested for probable degree of accuracy. All radiocarbon dates are, of course, statistical computations, and, if uncalibrated, are merely the radiocarbon age that is statistically most likely.

CALIBRATION OF RADIOCARBON DATES

Libby made a false assumption when he originally formulated the radiocarbon method. He had argued that the concentration of radiocarbon in the atmosphere remained constant as time passed, so that prehistoric samples, when alive, would have contained the same amount of radiocarbon as living things today. In fact, changes in the strength of the earth's magnetic field and alterations in solar activity have considerably varied the concentration of radiocarbon in the atmosphere and in living things. Thus samples of 6,000 years ago were exposed to a much higher concentration than are living things today. It is possible, fortunately, to correct radiocarbon dates by using accurate dates from tree rings.

Since 1966, dendrochronology experts have been systematically applying radiocarbon analysis to tree-ring samples of known age and have plotted calibration curves, which are used for converting radiocarbon dates into actual dates in years (Stuiver and Reimer, 1993). This tool is likely to receive universal acceptance in coming years; it calibrates dates between A.D. 1950 and 6500 B.C. The discrepancies between radiocarbon and calibrated dates are wide. Here is an example: 10 B.C. ± 30 has a calibrated interval of 145 B.C. to A.D. 210. Calibration by tree ring goes back as far as about 6800 B.C. German oaks may take the calibration curves to about 8000 B.C. very shortly (Stuiver and Pearson, 1993). Earlier dates are still uncalibrated, but recently scientists have used a new, highly accurate technique based on the decay of uranium into thorium to date fossil coral near Barbados in the Caribbean. They compared these dates to radiocarbon results, and found that dates between 10,000 and 25,000 years ago may be as much as 3,500 years too recent. The new coral researches are beginning to provide calibrations back to 21,950 years ago, which is about 18,400 years ago in radiocarbon years.

Calibration tables are now in widespread use, so most people think of uncalibrated dates as radiocarbon ages, not dates in actual years.

BRIDGING THE GAP: TL, ESR, AND OTHER METHODS

A variety of experimental methods have been used in attempts to bridge the long gap between the limits of potassium-argon and radiocarbon chronologies. These include thermoluminescence, electronic spin resonance, and uranium series dating.

THERMOLUMINESCENCE (TL) (AFTER 40,000 YEARS AGO)

PRINCIPLES, DATABLE MATERIALS, AND PROCEDURES

Thermoluminescence, a method with a formidable-sounding name for dating pottery, is still in the developmental stage in archaeology (Aitken, 1984, 1990). The principle is simple. The materials from which pottery is made have the property of storing energy by trapping electrons as atomic defects or impurity sites. This stored energy can be released by heating the pottery, at which time visible light rays, known as thermoluminescence, are emitted. All pottery and ceramics contain some radioactive impurities at a concentration of several parts per million. These materials emit alpha particles at a known rate, depending on how densely concentrated they are in the sample. When an alpha particle is absorbed by the pottery minerals around the radioactive impurities, it causes mineral atoms to ionize. Electrons are then released from their binding to the nuclei and later settle at a metastable (relatively unstable) stage of higher energy. This energy is stored, unless the parent material is heated—as when the pot is being fired—when the trapped electrons are released and thermoluminescence occurs. After the pot is fired, alpha particles are again absorbed by the material, and the thermoluminescence potential increases until the pot is heated again. Thus a clay vessel is dated by measuring the thermoluminescence of the sample, as well as its alpha-radioactivity and its potential susceptibility to producing thermoluminescence. In the laboratory, the trapped electrons are released from a powdered pottery fragment by sudden and violent heating under controlled conditions.

ARCHAEOLOGICAL APPLICATIONS AND LIMITATIONS

Thermoluminescence has been used with reasonable success to date heat-altered stone tools, burned hearths, and pottery, and also to determine the date of last exposure of unheated sediments to sunlight. As with other dating methods, results have been obtained initially from vessels of known age; because of these results, several investigators claim accuracies of $\pm$ 10 percent for prehistoric dates; other proponents of the method are more cautious, however. Thermoluminescence dating has considerable potential for dating artifacts older than 50,000 years, far beyond the outer limits of radiocarbon dating. The oldest pottery in the world is about 10,000 years old, but TL can be applied to stone artifacts fabricated from rock with a crystalline structure, provided they were heated at their time of use or manufacture. By using TL on burnt flint tools you can date individual artifacts, for the burning has effectively set the TL clock to zero, thus allowing you to date actual artifacts. This approach has been used on 70,000- to 40,000-year-old stone tools made by Neanderthal people in Europe, but perhaps the most dramatic example comes from Qafzeh cave in the Near East, where French archaeologist Helene Valladas dated some burnt flints associated with the bones of fully modern humans to 92,000 years ago. Valladas's dates caused a sensation, for they showed that archaic Neanderthals and fully modern humans had lived alongside each other in the Near East for at least 30,000 years.

TL dating has serious limitations under these circumstances. For example, one has to know the sensitivity of individual flint types to radiation, something that can be established by assaulting them with artificial radiation in the laboratory. Then there is the problem of the annual dose of radiation that came from the radiation around the sample in the ground and from the atmosphere. In the case of the Qafzeh dates, however, most of the radiation dose came from within the flints, so the dates appear relatively secure. TL dates of 36,000 years ago have also been obtained from Neanderthal artifacts in France, and readings of 60,000 years are claimed for possible early human occupations in Australia.

ELECTRON SPIN RESONANCE (ESR) (2 MILLION YEARS AGO AND LATER)

ESR measures the electrons trapped within a bone or shell sample without the necessity of heating them. All electrons spin in one of two opposite directions. Each electron's spin creates a tiny magnetic force pointing in one direction—like a compass needle. The electrons are paired under normal circumstances, so their spins cancel each other out. By manipulating an external magnetic field placed around the sample, the researcher can reverse the spin of the electrons, a process that causes them to absorb a finite amount of energy from a microwave field that is also applied to the sample. This loss of microwave energy can be measured with a detector, giving a direct count of the number of electrons caught in the traps, and hence a date for the sample. The larger the number of electrons, the older the sample, the number being determined by the known decay rate of radioactive elements.

ESR is still in its experimental stages, and has been found to work well on tooth enamel dating from 1,000 to 2 million years old. Like TL, it suffers from serious uncertainties, for moisture and radiation absorption rates vary greatly from site to site. It is best in dry environments like the Near East, where it has been used to date modern-looking human remains at Skhul cave on Mount Carmel, Israel, to about 100,000 years ago—confirmation of the TL dates from nearby Qafzeh.

URANIUM SERIES DATING (1 MILLION TO 50,000 YEARS AGO)

Uranium dating is based on the radioactive decay of uranium isotopes. It measures the steady decay of uranium into various daughter elements inside any formation that is made up of calcium carbonates, such as limestone or cave stalactites. Since many early human groups made use of limestone caves and rockshelters, bones and tools embedded in calcium carbonate layers can sometimes be dated by this method, using techniques somewhat similar to those employed in radiocarbon dating. Uranium series dates are still experimental, and have large statistical errors, but they have potential, especially when combined with other techniques such as thermoluminescence.

The best approach to dating sites between about a million and 50,000 years ago is to use a combination of dating methods, which, between them, may provide an acceptable absolute chronology (Shreeve, 1992). One of the most remarkable, and tantalizing, examples of this approach involves the Katanda site in Zaire, central Africa. Here, Alison and John Yellen unearthed beautifully made barbed-bone fish points from the same layers as dense piles of catfish remains and simply made stone tools. The Yellens were astonished by their discovery, for everyone believed bone fishing harpoons were first made at least 40,000 years later. Only 4 miles (6.5 km) downstream from Katanda lies Ishango, a 25,000-year-old fishing camp. By correlating geological layers from Ishango to Katanda, the Yellens are convinced their site is much earlier. They are using a combination of TL and ESR dates, the latter taken from hippopotamus teeth, in an attempt to date a site that may throw light on the origins of modern humans. So far no dates have been announced, for the Yellens want to have a firm chronology in place before they publish the discovery.

FISSION-TRACK DATING (3 MILLION TO 100,000 YEARS AGO)

PRINCIPLES

Fission-track dating is a new chronometric method that promises to have important archaeological applications in the future. The principle of the method is that many minerals and natural glasses, such as obsidian, contain very small quantities of uranium that undergo slow, spontaneous decay. Most uranium atoms decay by emitting alpha particles, but spontaneous fission causes the decay of about one atom in every 2 million. The fission decay rate and its extent are constant, and the date of any mineral containing uranium can be obtained by measuring the amount of uranium in the sample, which is done by counting the fission tracks in the material. These tracks are narrow trails of damage in the material caused by fragmentation of massive, energy-charged particles. The older the sample, the more tracks it has. It is possible to examine fission tracks under high magnification and to calculate the sample's age by establishing the ratio between the density of the tracks and the uranium content of the sample.

DATABLE MATERIALS AND PROCEDURES

Two counts of fission tracks are needed for each sample. The materials used, which must have a high uranium content, can be either volcanic rock, as in lava flows that originated more recently than the beginnings of prehistory, or manufactured materials, such as certain types of artificial glass. In rocks, it is the time of origin of the rocks that is being dated, not the time of their utilization. An optical microscope is used to examine the tracks in the sample, which have first been etched with hydrofluoric acid. This procedure enlarges the tracks to make them more visible. The first count establishes the density of the tracks; the second, by inducing fission of uranium 235 through neutron irradiation, makes a count of the uranium content in the sample. The age of the sample is the ratio of the number of observed tracks resulting from natural fission to those resulting from induced fission.

ARCHAEOLOGICAL APPLICATIONS

Fission-track dating has been invaluable to paleoanthropologists. The volcanic tuff under Bed I at Olduvai Gorge, where the early hominid fossils were found, was dated to 2.03 ± 0.28 million years using the fission-track method, which agreed reasonably well with potassium-argon dates of about 1.8 million years. The same method also dated the volcanic level above a *Homo habilis* skull at Koobi Fora in northern Kenya to 1.88 million years ago, settling a vigorous controversy over the date of this earliest human. Modern manufactured glass with high uranium content, used to make a nineteenth-century candlestick, has been dated accurately to the last century (Fleischer, 1975).

LIMITATIONS

Only volcanic rocks contemporary with a human settlement and formed at the time the site was occupied can be used.

OBSIDIAN HYDRATION (7,800,000 YEARS AGO TO PRESENT)

PRINCIPLES

Obsidian is a natural glass substance formed by volcanic activity. It has long been prized for its sharp edges and other excellent qualities for toolmaking. Projectile heads, hand axes, blades, and even mirrors were made from this widely traded material in both the New World and the Old. A new dating method makes use of the fact that a freshly made surface of obsidian (no other known artifact material has this property) will absorb water from its surroundings, forming a measurable hydration layer that is invisible to the naked eye. Because the freshly exposed surface has a strong affinity for water, it keeps absorbing until it is saturated with a layer of water molecules. These molecules then slowly diffuse into the body of the obsidian. This hydration zone contains about 3.5 percent water, increasing the density of the layer and allowing it to be measured accurately under polarized light. Each time a freshly fractured surface is prepared, as when a tool is being made, the hydration begins again from scratch. Thus the depth of hydration achieved represents the time since the object was manufactured or used (Leute, 1987).

Hydration is observed with microscopically thin sections of obsidian sliced from artifacts and ground down to about 0.003 inch. The thickness of the layer is measured through the microscope at eight spots, the mean value being calibrated into units of microns (micrometers). These thickness readings can be used in both absolute and relative chronologies (Friedman and Trembour, 1983). Unfortunately, this promising dating method has some problems, mostly because we still do not fully understand hydration. Little is known about how temperature changes or chemical composition affect hydration, so it is impossible to use the method without calibrating it against tree-ring dates or some other established archaeological procedure. In recent years, basic research into the hydration process has led to much refinement of what was once an experimental dating method. Neutron activation analysis is now commonly used, which provided not only dates, but sourcing information that can be used to monitor changes in trade networks (Chapter 16).

ARCHAEOLOGICAL APPLICATIONS

Obsidian hydration dating has been used with great success in Mesoamerica, notably at Copán, where a major 10-year dating campaign using this method was based on a specific chronology research agenda (Freter, 1993). This approach differs from more traditional dating projects in the culture area, which rely on seriated potsherds and chronometric dates obtained from hearths and other in-situ features. Such a deductive research design was essential, for there were critical environmental variables such as temperature, rainfall, and soil acidity to be assessed. Data on these factors came from such sources as weather stations, wet and dry thermal cells buried at various depths in the sites to be dated, and soil composition measurements, collected for as many years as possible. At the same time, a comprehensive sampling strategy ensured that obsidian artifacts spanning the entire span of the deposits and a variety of tools were dated. The sampling strategy also allowed for obsidian sourcing studies, so that the chemical characterizations from the dated artifacts also provided information on changes in obsidian trade through time. AnnCorinne Freter calls this a "conjunctive approach," that brought all kinds of chronological data and a formal investigation of all the variables which could affect hydration into a single chronological project. Thus, the accuracy of obsidian hydration dates was checked at every turn.

The Copán Obsidian Dating Project began in 1984 and has yielded over 2,300 dates from 252 sites, over 17 percent of the sites in the Copán Valley (Freter, 1994). The method was ideal for Copán, where radiocarbon and archaeomagnetic dates are rare and expensive, while obsidian hydration is relatively cheap. At the same time, the abundance of obsidian in both the central core and in outlying rural settlements allowed the economical dating of large numbers of sites. Thus, Freter (1994) and her research team were able to plot changing settlement patterns from A.D. 500 to 1150 with such chronological accuracy that they were able to show that the collapse of the Copán state was rapid between 800 and 850, accompanied by a graded, 200-to-250-year outmigration from the central precincts where the elite resided as their power and prestige declined, probably as a result of environmental stress (more on the Copán survey in Chapter 15). Freter also points out that given constant environmental conditions within a site, obsidian hydration has great potential for providing relative chronologies and identifying sites with disturbed occupation layers.

DENDROCHRONOLOGY (10,000 YEARS AGO OR EARLIER TO PRESENT)

PRINCIPLES

Dendrochronology, or tree-ring dating, was originated in Arizona by A. E. Douglass in about 1913. Douglass developed a tree-ring chronology for Southwestern pueblos, linking ancient and modern trees and beams. Both the slow-growing sequoia and the California bristlecone pine provide long tree-ring sequences, the latter a continuous chronology of 8,200 years. One pine tree has been reported to be 4,900 years old.

Everyone is familiar with tree rings—concentric circles, each circle representing annual growth—visible on the cross-section of a felled trunk. These rings are formed on all trees, but especially where seasonal changes in weather are marked, with either a wet and dry season or a definite alternation of summer and winter temperatures. As a rule, trees produce growth rings each year, formed by the cambium, or growth layer, lying between the wood and the bark. When the growing season starts, large cells are added to the wood. These cells develop thicker walls and become smaller as the growing season progresses; by the end of the growth season, cell production has ceased altogether. This process occurs every growing year, and a distinct line is formed between the wood of the previous season, with its small cells, and the wood of the next, with its new, large cells. The thickness of each ring may vary according to the tree's age and annual climatic variations, thick rings being characteristic of good growth years.

Weather variations within a circumscribed area tend to run in cycles. A decade of wet years may be followed by five dry decades. One season may bring a 40-year rainfall record. These cycles of climate are reflected in patterns of thicker or thinner rings, which are repeated from tree to tree within a limited area. Dendrochronologists have invented sophisticated methods of correlating rings from different trees so they can build up long master sequences of rings from a number of trunks that may extend over many centuries (Figure 8.4). By using modern trees, whose date of felling is known, they are able to reconstruct accurate dating as far back as 8,200 years. Actual applications to archaeological wood are much harder, but archaeological chronology for the American Southwest now goes back to 322 B.C.

DATABLE MATERIALS AND PROCEDURES

The most commonly dated tree is the Douglas fir. It has consistent rings that are easy to read and was often used in prehistoric buildings. Piñon and sagebrush are usable, too. Because the latter was commonly used as firewood, its charred remains are of special archaeological interest. The location of the sample tree is important. Trees growing on well-drained, gently sloping soils are best, for their rings display sufficient annual variation to make them more easily datable. The rings of trees in places with permanently abundant water supplies are too regular to be usable.

Samples are normally collected by cutting a full cross-section from an old beam no longer in a structure, by using a special core borer to obtain samples from beams still in a building, or by V-cutting exceptionally large logs. Delicate or brittle samples are impregnated with paraffin or coated with shellac before examination.

Once in the laboratory, the surface of the sample is leveled to a precise plane. Analyzing tree rings consists of recording individual ring series and then comparing them against other series. Comparisons can be made by eye or by plotting the rings on a uniform scale so that one series can be compared with another. The series so plotted can then be computer-matched with the master tree-ring chronology for the region. Measuring the tree rings accurately can also add precision to the plottings.

ARCHAEOLOGICAL APPLICATIONS

Extremely accurate chronologies for Southwestern sites have been achieved by correlating a master tree-ring sequence from felled trees and dated structures

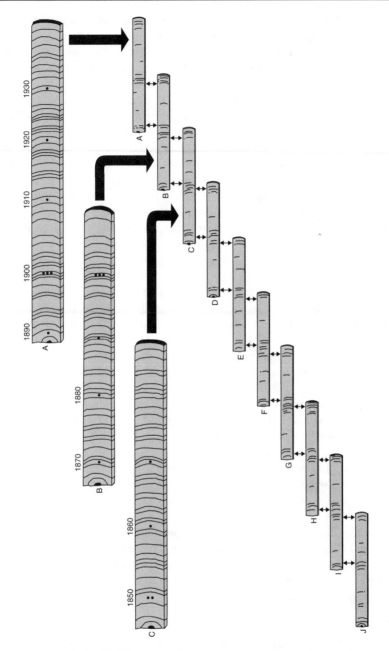

FIGURE 8.4 Building a tree-ring chronology: A shows a boring taken from a living tree after the 1939 growing season; B through J are specimens taken from old houses and progressively older ruins. The ring patterns match and overlap back into the past.

with beams from Indian pueblos. The beams in many such structures have been used again and again, and thus some are very much older than the houses in which they were most recently used for support. The earliest tree rings obtained from such settlements date to the first century B.C., but most timbers were in use between A.D. 1000 and historic times.

In one classic example, Jeffrey Dean (1970) collected numerous samples from wooden beams at Betatakin, a cliff dwelling in northeastern Arizona dating to A.D. 1270. He used 292 samples to reconstruct the history of the cliff dwelling, room by room. He found that three room clusters were built in 1267, and a fourth was added a year later. In 1269 the inhabitants trimmed and stockpiled beams for later use. These were not actually used until 1275, when ten more room clusters were added to Betatakin. Such intrasite datings are possible when a large number of samples can be found. Similar research at Walpi Pueblo, a Hopi site in Arizona founded in A.D. 1400 and still inhabited today, proved the essential validity of Dean's methods, but highlighted the difficulties of dating complex sites where beams are reused frequently, when salvaged beams have been trimmed (Ahlstrom and others, 1991).

Dendrochronology has been used widely in Alaska, the Chesapeake Bay area, northern Mexico, Canada, Scandinavia, Ireland, the British Isles, the Aegean Islands and Greece, and Germany (Baillie, 1982). Recent European research has been especially successful. What the bristlecone pine is to the Southwest, oaks are to Europe. European tree-ring experts have collected large numbers of tree-ring records from oaks that have lived for 150 years or so. Through visual and statistical comparison, they have linked living trees to ancient ones from bogs and prehistoric sites and also to farmhouse and church beams, providing a tree-ring sequence that goes back 10,021 years in Germany and 7,289 years in Ireland. Dutch tree-ring experts have even tried dating the oak panels used by old masters for their oil paintings as a way of authenticating works of art! The Aegean Dendrochronology Project has developed a tree-ring sequence covering 6,000 of the past 8,500 years, which will allow greater precision for the chronology of the Minoan and Mycenaean civilizations and earlier cultures.

Finally, dendrochronology has great potential to aid the study of drought cycles and climatic change since the Ice Age throughout western North America (Fritts, 1976). Along the California coast, tree-ring data is being combined with deep-sea core temperature information to provide a promising record of climatic fluctuations in later prehistory.

LIMITATIONS

Dendrochronology traditionally has been limited to areas with well-defined seasonal rainfall. Where the climate is generally humid or cold, or where trees enjoy a constant water supply, the difference in annual growth rings is either blurred or insignificant. Again, the context in which the archaeological tree-ring sample is found affects the usefulness of the sample. Many house beams have been reused several times, and the outside surface of the log has been trimmed repeatedly. The felling date cannot be established accurately without carefully observing the context and archaeological association of the beam. For this reason, several dates must be obtained from each site. Artifacts found in a structure whose beams are dated do not necessarily belong to the same period, for the house may have been used over several generations.

ARCHAEOMAGNETIC DATING (LAST 2,000 YEARS, PERHAPS EARLIER)

The study of paleomagnetism has revolutionized geology in recent years, confirming theories of continental drift and showing that the earth's geomagnetic field has reversed its polarity many times in the past. By dating unoriented samples of fired clay, it may one day be possible to date sites at least 10,000 years old, perhaps much earlier. This type of *paleointensity dating* has the potential for dating potsherds, among the most common of all archaeological finds (Wolfman, 1984), but has not yet been widely used.

In the past 25 years, information on polarity has been recorded from stratified rocks up to a billion years old. These igneous (volcanic) rocks are independently dated using potassium-argon methods, providing a relatively accurate polarity scale for the world over the past 5 million years. The current epoch of normal polarity is called the Brunhes and began about 700,000 years ago. As research into archaeological applications of paleointensity dating accelerates, we can expect some dramatic results, especially from more recent sites where pottery is to be found. Archaeomagnetic dating has a much shorter time frame and is based on measurements of secular variation in fired clays.

PRINCIPLES

We know that the direction and intensity of the earth's magnetic field has varied throughout prehistoric time. Many clays and clay soils contain magnetic minerals, which when heated to a dull red heat will assume the direction and intensity of the earth's magnetic field at the moment of heating. Thus if the changes in the earth's magnetic field have been recorded over centuries, or even millennia, it is possible to date any suitable sample of clay material known to have been heated by correlating the thermoremanent magnetism of the heated clay with records of the earth's magnetic field (Wolfman, 1984). Archaeologists frequently discover structures with well-baked clay floors—ovens, kilns, and iron-smelting furnaces, to name only a few—whose burned clay can be used for archaeomagnetic dating. Of course, reheated clays (clays used again after their original heating) will change their magnetic readings and are thus useless for archaeomagnetic dating.

Thermoremanent magnetism results from the ferromagnetism of magnetite and hematite, minerals found in significant quantities in most soils. When the soil containing these minerals is heated, the magnetic particles in magnetite and hematite change from a random alignment to one that conforms with that of the earth's magnetic field. In effect, the heated lump of clay becomes a very weak magnet that can be measured by a parastatic magnetometer. A record of the magnetic declination and dip similar to that of the earth's actual magnetic field at the time of heating is preserved in the clay lump. The alignment of the magnetic particles fixed by heating is called thermoremanent magnetism.

DATABLE MATERIALS AND PROCEDURES

Selecting a kiln or other baked structure for magnetic dating is far from straightforward. Substantial floors of well-baked clay are best for the purpose. Tiny pillars of burnt clay that will fit into a brass-framed extraction jig are extracted from the floor. The jig is oriented to present-day north-south and fitted over the pillars, which are then encapsulated in melted dental plaster. The jig and pillar are carefully removed from the floor, and then the other side of the jig is covered with dental plaster as well. The clay sample is placed under suspended magnets and rotated. The scale will record the declination and dip of the remanent magnetism in the clay. An absolute date for the sample can then be obtained if the long-term, or secular, variation of the earth's field for the region is known.

ARCHAEOLOGICAL APPLICATIONS AND LIMITATIONS

From an archaeological point of view, archaeomagnetism has but limited application because systematic records of the secular variation in the earth's magnetic field have been kept for only a few areas. Declination and dip have been recorded in London for 400 years, and a very accurate record of variations covers the period from A.D. 1600. France, Germany, Japan, and the Southwestern United States have received some attention. From the last, clay samples associated directly with dendrochronological or radiocarbon samples have been tested, with one set of readings from 16 pre-Columbian villages extending back almost 2,000 years.

CALENDARS AND OBJECTS OF KNOWN AGE
(AFTER 3,000 B.C.)

CALENDARS

A calendar developed by an ancient civilization provides an excellent way of dating archaeological sites, if the calendar can be linked to our own chronology. The Mesopotamians and the ancient Egyptians fashioned sophisticated calendars, and the Maya of the Yucatán had a calendric system that is justly admired (Schele and Friedel, 1990). Calendars were used to regulate the agricultural and religious year in Egypt and Mesopotamia and were vital in organizing secular and religious life in the Yucatán.

The Maya used both a 365-day secular calendar and a 260-day religious calendar for timing religious ceremonies (Figure 8.5). Their system of dating their own civilization in years started from a mythical date long before their own society existed. Known as the Long Count, the system is recorded on many stelae, along with inscriptions that signal important events or transfer of priestly power. Attempts made to link the Long Count and the Christian calendar place the span of the Mayan calendar from about 3113 B.C. to A.D. 889. Much of this time is, of course, long before the Maya themselves were a fully fledged state. But the Long Count stelae are a useful check on the dates of such well-known Maya sites as Tikal and Palenque.

The most reliable chronometric dates are, of course, those obtained from historical documentation of archaeological sites. We know that King Henry VIII

FIGURE 8.5   Many Maya stelae (carved stone monuments) record important dates in the lives of their rulers. This stela carries a date equivalent to A.D. 771.

began to build his palace at Nonsuch, England, in A.D. 1538. The chronology of Plimoth Plantation in Massachusetts is also well-established from contemporary records, and our primary interest lies in discovering details of settlement layout or day-to-day life. Many later sites yield easily dated artifacts, such as coins dropped by the inhabitants on the floors of buildings or elsewhere in the settlement's strata. Such objects can provide accurate dates for the earliest age of the archaeological sites being investigated.

OBJECTS OF KNOWN AGE

Objects of known age found in African, North American, and European prehistoric sites include a bewildering array of artifacts, from dated coins and glass

1730-1770

1780-1820

FIGURE 8.6   Representative evolutionary changes in the designs on the bowls of English tobacco pipes dating to between 1730 and 1830.

bottles to Chinese porcelain and all manner of imported ceramics. The latter include American domestic tableware, English imported china, and Spanish majolica vessels in historic sites in North America (Noël Hume, 1969). Some of these types of finds can act as artifacts for cross-dating prehistoric sites.

One of the most useful Colonial American artifacts is the imported English kaolin pipe (Figure 8.6). Not only were pipes manufactured, imported, smoked, and thrown away within a very short time, but the shape of the pipe body changed in an easily recognizable evolutionary chain. Clay pipes were so cheap that everyone, however poor, used and discarded them almost like cigarettes. Not only the bowl but the length of the stem and the diameter of the hole changed between A.D. 1620 and 1800, and these characteristics have been used to date these artifacts and the sites associated with them with considerable precision.

The potential range of historic objects that can be dated to within surprisingly narrow chronological limits is enormous (Orser and Fagan, 1995). Many people collect beer cans, bottle caps and openers, barbed wire, firearms, uniform buttons, and even horseshoes. All these artifacts, to say nothing of such prosaic objects as forks, electrical switch plates, and scissors, can be dated to within a few years with mail-order catalogs, U.S. patent records, and a great deal of patient detective work. Bottles, buckets, and horseshoes may be the unrespectable artifacts of archaeology, but unlike many of their prehistoric equivalents, they can be dated with great accuracy. What better way to learn about archaeology than to study and date our own material culture!

SUMMARY

- Although historical records provide a fairly accurate chronology for much of the past 5,000 years, archaeologists rely heavily on chemical and physical chronometric dating methods.
- Potassium-argon methods are used for dating the earliest human beings. These can be used to determine dates from the origins of the earth up to about 400,000 years ago. This radioactive counting method is based on measuring accumulations of argon 40 in volcanic rocks. It has been used to date early human fossils.

- Radiocarbon dating is the most widely used method. It can be applied at sites from between 75,000 and 400 years ago. Based on the rate at which carbon 14 decays to nitrogen in organic objects, it can be used to date such materials as charcoal and bone and even skin and leather. The accuracy of radiocarbon dating is subject to statistical errors. Dates up to 8,000 years ago are calibrated against tree-ring chronologies, owing to variations in the carbon 14 content of the atmosphere.
- Thermoluminescence may prove to be a method for dating potsherds, in which the baked clay has trapped electrons; these are released for measurement by sudden and intense heating under controlled conditions. The visible light rays emitted during heating are known as thermoluminescence. Thermoluminescence can also be applied to burnt flint artifacts of much greater age.
- Electron spin resonance and uranium series dating are also experimental chronometric methods that date sites between a million and 50,000 years old.
- Fission-track dating is done by measuring the uranium content of many minerals and volcanic glasses and examining the fission tracks left in the material by fragmentation of massive concentrations of energy-charged particles. It can be applied in sites between a million and 100,000 years old, where volcanic rocks are found in human-occupied levels.
- Dendrochronology (tree-ring dating) provides an accurate chronology for about two thousand years of southwestern prehistory and can be used on sites as early as 8000 B.C. in Europe. Dendrochronologists count the annual growth rings in trees such as the bristlecone pine and correlate them into long sequences of growth years that are joined to a master chronology. Wooden beams and other archaeological wood fragments are correlated with this master chronology to provide accurate dates for pueblos and other sites.
- Historical records and calendars developed by such people as the ancient Egyptians and the Maya are of immense value for dating their literate civilizations. A great deal of valuable chronological information can also be obtained from objects of known age, such as clay pipes or coins. But, again, these objects are confined to the most recent periods of human history.

GUIDE TO FURTHER READING

Aitken, M. J. *Science-based Dating in Archaeology.* New York: Longmans, 1990. An introduction to scientific dating methods for the general reader.

Leute, Ulrich. *Archaeometry.* Weinheim, West Germany: VCH, 1987. A useful summary of dating techniques and science in archaeology. Quite technical in orientation.

Michels, J. W. *Dating Methods in Archaeology.* Orlando, Fla.: Academic Press, 1973. Probably the most widely read book on dating presently available. A good follow-up to this chapter.

RECOVERING ARCHAEOLOGICAL DATA

A mere hole in the ground, which of all sights is perhaps the least vivid and dramatic, is enough to grip their attention for hours at a time.

P. G. Wodehouse
A Damsel in Distress

Archaeology is the only branch of anthropology where we kill our informants in the process of studying them.

Kent V. Flannery
"The Golden Marshalltown"

Part Four deals with the ways in which archaeologists acquire data in the field. As we stressed earlier, acquiring such data depends on a sound research design and on formulating specific hypotheses before reconnaissance, site survey, or excavation can begin. Our knowledge of the past is limited by preservation in the ground and also by our own methods for recovering data. Chapters 9 and 10 describe some of the fundamental principles and processes of archaeological fieldwork, as well as some of the many special problems encountered by archaeologists in the field. And rather than draw on a single case study, I have chosen to give many examples, relying on your instructors to use examples derived from their own experience.

9

FINDING AND ASSESSING ARCHAEOLOGICAL SITES

Until fairly recently, archaeologists paid relatively little attention to the techniques for locating archaeological sites and interpreting them without actual excavation. A new emphasis on regional archaeological studies, innovative remote-sensing techniques, and, above all, the urgent need to save and record sites before they are destroyed by twentieth-century development has changed all of this. In the pages that follow, we review some of the archaeologist's techniques for locating and studying archaeological sites without digging them.

Two basic processes are involved in locating archaeological sites:

Archaeological survey, which is the systematic attempt to locate, identify, and record the distribution of archaeological sites on the ground and against the natural geographic and environmental background.

Site assessment, which is the collecting of surface data and evaluating of each site's archaeological significance.

Both these methods are nonintrusive, in the sense that they do not destroy archaeological context. Archaeological excavation (Chapter 10) involves the investigation of the site by means of actual digging. With so many sites being destroyed today, this is now the strategy of last resort.

FINDING ARCHAEOLOGICAL SITES

The competent field-worker can identify archaeological sites with an ease born of experience that can astound the lay onlooker. I remember being astonished when, on a survey in the Zambezi Valley in Central Africa in 1959, my senior and very experienced colleague stopped suddenly and picked up half a stone flake from a gravel bed covered with Stone Age artifacts. "This is the other half of a flake I found here in 1938," he told me. I flatly disbelieved him. But he was right. We located the original in the local museum collections, and the two halves were reunited. My colleague's archaeological memory was astounding, but it was also a result of long experience with local conditions.

Let us examine some key indicators of archaeological sites:

• Conspicuous earthworks, stone ruins, or other surface features are among the most obvious indicators. Good examples are the Adena and Hopewell burial mounds of the Ohio Valley, the pueblos of the American Southwest, and the fortified *pa,* or defensive earthworks, built by the Maori in New Zealand. One of the most extensive settlement surveys ever undertaken was that in the Basin of Mexico in the 1960s and 1970s. It was designed to locate every surviving site in the area and to establish relationships among them (Sanders and others, 1979).

- Vegetational cover is a useful indicator, for grass may grow more lushly on areas where the subsoil has been disturbed or the nitrogen content of the soil is greater. Conversely, many California shell middens are covered with stunted vegetation because of the artifact-filled, alkaline soil, which contrasts sharply with the surrounding green grass at the end of the rainy season. Sometimes specific types of trees or brush are associated with archaeological sites. One is the breadnut, or *ramon,* tree, which was once cultivated by the Maya. These trees are still common near ancient sites and have been used as guides in locating many archaeological sites.

- Soil discolorations are a sign of archaeological sites. In many cases, the dark, organic sods of long-abandoned villages show up in plowed land as dark zones, often associated with potsherds and other artifacts. Burrowing animals living in such areas leave telltale traces in the form of organic earth and artifacts, which their activities bring to the surface.

- Surface finds of artifacts, broken bones, and other materials may show up in dry areas as dense concentrations of debris that stand out from the surrounding ground. In some cases, wind erosion may remove the soil mantling the artifacts and leave them exposed on the surface.

CHANCE DISCOVERIES

Whole chapters of the past have been exposed by accidental discoveries of sites, spectacular artifacts, or skeletons. Plowing, peat cutting, road making, and other day-to-day activities have been a fruitful source of archaeological discoveries. Industrial activity, highway construction, airport expansion, and other destructive actions of twentieth-century humanity have unearthed countless archaeological sites, many of which have to be investigated hurriedly before the bulldozers remove all traces. Deep plowing, highway construction, and urban renewal are bitter enemies of the past. Yet dramatic discoveries have resulted from our despoiling of the environment.

The excavation for Mexico City's Metro (subway) provided a unique opportunity for accidental discoveries of archaeological sites. The shallow tunneling, which extended more than 26 miles (42 km) under the city, yielded a wealth of archaeological material. Mexico City is built on the site of Tenochtitlán, the capital city of the Aztecs. Tenochtitlán, destroyed by the Spanish under Hernando Cortés in 1521, was a wonderful city whose markets rivaled those of most major Spanish cities in size. Little remains of Tenochtitlán on the surface today, but the contractors for the Metro found more than 40 tons of pottery, 380 burials, and even a small temple dedicated to the Aztec god of the wind, Ehecatl-Quetzalcoatl (Figure 9.1). The temple is now preserved on its original site in the Pino Suárez station of the Metro system, part of an exhibit commemorating Mexico City's ancestor. The tunneling operations, happily, were under the constant supervision of a large group of archaeologists. The archaeologists were empowered to halt

FIGURE 9.1   The temple of Ehecatl-Quetzalcoatl, the god of wind and the feathered serpent, found during the excavations for the Pino Suárez subway station, Mexico City.

digging whenever an archaeological find of importance was made. As a result, many newfound sculptures and artifacts were saved from destruction for the national collections (R. F. Townsend, 1992). Subsequently, another accidental discovery of a ceremonial stone depicting the sun led to the uncovering and excavation of the Temple of the Sun and Rain gods of the Aztecs, Huitzilopochtli and Tlaloc, which lay in the heart of the Aztec capital.

Hydroelectric schemes and flood control programs in North America and elsewhere have destroyed thousands upon thousands of archaeological sites without a trace—and have accelerated the discovery of others. Some of these projects have stimulated much intensive surveying. The Aswan Dam scheme in Nubia provided a rare opportunity for intensive investigation of Pleistocene geology and Stone Age sites in the area to be flooded by Lake Nasser (Wendorf and others, 1968). Nearer to home, the flood control schemes initiated by the Tennessee River Valley Authority and by the Army Corps of Engineers elsewhere in the agriculturally rich South have led to many river basin surveys, while highway surveys have sometimes yielded rich dividends (for example, see Bareis and Porter, 1984).

Nature itself sometimes uncovers sites for us, which may then be located by a sharp-eyed archaeologist looking for natural exposures of likely geological strata. Erosion, flooding, tidal waves, low lake levels, earthquakes, and wind action can all lead to exposure of archaeological sites. One of the most famous sites to be exposed in this manner is Olduvai Gorge in Tanzania, a great gash in the Serengeti Plains where nature, by earth movement, has sliced through hundreds of feet of Pleistocene lake bed to expose numerous site locations of early humans.

In 1957 wind erosion exposed what appeared to be five piles of bison bones in an arroyo near the town of Kit Carson in southeastern Colorado (Wheat, 1972). Some projectile points were found with the bones. The bone bed, known as the

FIGURE 9.2   A layer of bison bones from the Olsen-Chubbuck site in Colorado, a Paleo-Indian kill site found by a cowboy.

Olsen-Chubbuck site, lay in a filled bison trail, of a type that crisscrossed the plains in early frontier days (Figure 9.2). The remains of nearly 200 bison came from the arroyo, but only some were fully dismembered. Clearly, the arroyo was a trap into which the beasts had been stampeded. (Bison have a keen sense of smell but poor vision; a lumbering herd of these gregarious beasts can be readily stampeded into an abrupt declivity, and the leaders have no option but to plunge into the gully and be immobilized or disabled by the weight of those behind them.) So vivid a reconstruction of the Paleo-Indians' hunt could be made that the excavators were even able to guess at the direction of the wind on the day of the stampede. The vivid traces of this hunt of 8,500 years ago were buried in the arroyo by nature and exposed again in our time to be discovered by the vigilant eye of an amateur archaeologist.

FIELD SURVEY

Famous archaeological sites like the Parthenon have never been lost (Figure 1.7). The Acropolis at Athens was remembered even when Athens itself had become an obscure Medieval village. The temples of ancient Egyptian Thebes were famous as long ago as Roman times and have never vanished from historical consciousness. Other sites, such as Homeric Troy, were celebrated in Classical literature, but its precise location at Hissarlik in northwestern Turkey only came to light with Heinreich Schliemann's excavations in 1871.

Of course, most of the world's archaeological sites are far less conspicuous than the Parthenon, and unlike Troy, they have no historical records to testify to their existence. The early antiquarians discovered sites primarily by locating burial mounds, stone structures, hill forts, and other conspicuous traces of prehistoric human works on the European landscape. The tells of the Near East, occupied by generation after generation of city dwellers, were easily recognized by early travelers, and the temples and monuments of ancient Egypt have attracted antiquarian and plunderer alike for many centuries. New World archaeological sites like Teotihuacán were described by some of the first conquistadors. Maya sites were vividly cataloged by John Lloyd Stephens and Frederick Catherwood in the mid-nineteenth century (Figure 9.3) (Fagan, 1985).

Site survey did not become a serious part of archaeology until field archaeologists began to realize that people had lived their lives against the back-

FIGURE 9.3   Copán in Honduras, a conspicuous archaeological site found by the Spanish in 1576 and made known by Stephens and Catherwood in the nineteenth century. This photograph shows the reconstructed ball court.

ground of an ever-changing natural landscape, modified both by climatic and other ecological changes and by human activities. Before World War I, archaeologists J. P. Williams Freeman and O. G. S. Crawford, among others, traced Roman roads and ancient field systems in Britain, walking and bicycling over the countryside in search of known and unknown sites. In Bolivia and Peru, Max Uhle, a German, was among those who pioneered systematic field survey in the New World.

Most early archaeological survey sought individual sites for eventual excavation. But as archaeologists have grown more intent on studying variability in the archaeological record, they have come to deal with entire regions rather than individual sites. The objectives of survey also have partly shifted. Although archaeologists still search for sites to excavate, most do so within an entirely different theoretical framework. Those following the more traditional approaches tend to think of a survey area as a group of sites rather than a unit of space in which prehistoric peoples lived. Thus the modern regional survey is more properly defined as "some specified unit of space within which archaeological sites and other relevant variables are tabulated" (Dunnell and Dancey, 1983). This approach makes surface surveying a much more important component of archaeological investigation than ever before. For example, in recent years archaeologists have paid special attention to what they call "off-site" areas, places with a low density of artifacts. Some of these locations may not, indeed, qualify as sites. But such areas are of vital importance, especially when studying hunter-gatherers or herders, who enjoyed a highly mobile lifeway and left few traces behind them. Off-site evidence can include scatters of artifacts, ancient plow marks, and even entire field systems that can only be spotted from telltale traces visible in aerial photographs. At Céide Fields in northwestern Ireland, more than 5,000 acres (2,023 ha) of field systems dating to about 5000 B.C. are still preserved, and they are as revealing about the society that created them as their houses and settlements.

Before considering the surface survey, let us examine the more traditional survey methods.

APPROACHES TO ARCHAEOLOGICAL SURVEY

Most archaeological sites are discovered by careful field surveying and thorough examination of the countryside for both conspicuous and inconspicuous traces of the past (Willey, 1953). A survey can vary from searching a city lot for historic structures or a tiny river valley with a few rock shelters in its walls to a large-scale survey of an entire river basin or water-catchment area—a project that would take several years to complete. For all these, the theoretical ideal is the same: to recover all traces of ancient settlement in the survey area. Often a survey intended to recover all or nearly all sites in a region is called a *complete survey* or *comprehensive survey*.

Archaeological sites manifest themselves in many ways: in the form of tells, which are mounds of occupation debris; middens, which are mounds of food remains and occupation debris; or conspicuous caves or temples. But many others are far less easily located, perhaps displaying no more than a small scatter of stone tools or a patch of discolored soil. Still other sites leave no traces of their presence above the ground and may come to light only when the subsoil is disturbed, like the temple of Ehecatl-Quetzalcoatl, found during excavation of Mexico City's Metro line (Figure 9.1). Thus it can be seen that no surface survey, however thorough and however sophisticated its remote-sensing devices, will achieve complete coverage. The key to effective archaeological surveying lies in proper research designs and in rigorous sampling techniques to provide a reliable basis of probability for extending the findings of the survey from a sample zone to a wider region.

The comprehensiveness of any survey is affected by other factors, too. Many surveys are carried out in intensively populated areas or on private farmland. Some landowners may refuse access to their lands. To their credit, most farmers or landlords do not. Indeed, owners may recall past discoveries on their land, hitherto unsuspected by archaeologists. Inaccessibility can be further complicated by such factors as dense vegetation, crops, and floodwaters. In many parts of Mexico and California, the obvious months for site surveys are at the end of the dry season, when the vegetation is dry or even burned off. But in lush, lowland floodplains, such as those of the American South, large tracts of the survey area may be totally inaccessible all year, except to shovel testing and controlled surface collecting of known sites. Only the most conspicuous sites, like mounds, show up under such conditions. And, of course, thousands of sites are buried under tract housing and parking lots, or countless huge earth-moving operations that have radically altered the landscape.

A great deal depends, too, on the intensity of the survey in the field. The survey area can be traversed by automobile, horseback, mule, camel, bicycle, or—most effectively—foot. Footwork is important, for it enables the archaeologist to acquire an eye for topography and the relationships of human settlement to the landscape.

Michael Schiffer of the University of Arizona identifies four basic types of intensive ground survey (Schiffer and House, 1976):

1. Conspicuous and accessible sites are located by superficial survey, such as that by Catherwood and Stephens with Maya sites in the Yucatán in the 1840s (Figure 1.1b). The investigator visits only very conspicuous and accessible sites of great size and considerable fame.

2. In the next level of survey, assisted by local informants such as landowners, relatively conspicuous sites at accessible locations are discovered. This approach was used frequently in the 1930s for the classic river basin surveys in the lower Mississippi Valley. It can be very effective, but it gives a rather narrow view of the archaeological sites in an area.

3. Limited-area survey involves door-to-door inquiries, supported by actual substantiation of claims that a site exists by checking the report on the ground. This type of survey, with its built-in system of verification, may yield more comprehensive information on sites. But it still does not give the most critical information of all, data on the ratios of one site type to another, nor does it assess the percentage of accessible sites that have been found.

4. In the last type, the foot survey, a party of archaeologists covers an entire area by walking over it, perhaps with a set interval between members of the party. This is about the most rigorous method of survey, but it does work. When Paul Martin and Fred Plog surveyed 5.2 square miles (13.5 sq. km) of the Hay Hollow Valley in east-central Arizona in 1967, they supervised a

team of eight people who walked back and forth over small portions of the area (Martin and Plog, 1973). Each worker was 30 feet (9 m) from the next, their pathways carefully laid out with compass and stakes. Two hundred and fifty sites were recorded by this survey, at the cost of 30 person-days per square mile. One would think every site would have been recorded. Yet two entirely new sites were discovered in the same area in 1969 and 1971, prehistoric irrigation canals were spotted by an expert on some aerial photographs, and some sandstone quarry sites were also found.

As we have said, the chances of any archaeological survey recording every site in even a small area are remote. Obviously, though, total survey of an area is desirable, and sometimes nearly total coverage can be achieved by combining remote sensing and ground survey. William Sanders and his colleagues carried out a long-term archaeological survey of the Basin of Mexico in which they elected to try locating every site in the area over many seasons of fieldwork. At the end of the project, Sanders argued that this approach was far more effective than any sampling of the area, for it gave a much clearer picture of site variability on the ground (Sanders and others, 1979). Undoubtedly he is right, if one has the time and the money. In these days of limited budgets and short-term archaeological contracts dictated by impending site destruction, the archaeologist has turned to both remote sensing and statistical sampling to achieve goals of the survey.

SAMPLING IN ARCHAEOLOGICAL SURVEY

Partly because regional studies have become more fashionable and partly because of the growing demands of cultural resource management, archaeologists have become deeply interested in economical methods for collecting survey data. Many of them have sought refuge in statistical sampling methods. Statistical sampling theory occupies an important place in archaeological research, and some statistical training is now integral to every professional's training.

Sampling is an enormous and complex subject which cannot be discussed in detail here. But systematic and carefully controlled sampling of archaeological data is essential if we are to rely heavily, as we do, on statistical approaches in the reconstruction of past lifeways and cultural process. If we are interested in past adaptations to environmental conditions, we must systematically sample many types of sites in each environmental zone, not merely those that look important or seem likely to yield spectacular finds. Sampling techniques enable us to ensure a statistically reliable basis of archaeological data from which we can make generalizations about our research data. (For more details, see Mueller, 1975; Nance, 1983.)

Archaeologists generally use *probabilistic sampling,* a means of relating small samples of data in mathematical ways to much larger populations. A classic example is the public opinion poll, which uses a tiny sample, say 1,500 people, to draw more general conclusions on major political issues. In archaeology, probability sampling improves the chance that the conclusions reached on the basis of the sample are relatively reliable. The outcome depends, of course, on very carefully drawn research designs and precisely defined sample units.

Three basic probability sampling schemes are common in archaeological survey and excavation:

1. *Simple random sampling* determines the sample size and the area to be sampled, then randomly selects the number of units required with a table of numbers, numbers being assigned to a grid drawn over the survey area or site. This approach treats all samples as absolutely equal, a useful approach when surveying an unknown area or site.
2. *Systematic sampling* is a refinement of simple random sampling, which chooses one unit at random, then selects others at equal intervals from the first one. This is useful for studying artifact patterning on a surface site.
3. *Stratified sampling* is used when sample units are not uniform. The population is divided into separate groups, or strata, which reflect the observed range of variation within the strata chosen, like, for example, ecological zones, occupation layers, artifact classes, and so on. Such units permit intensive sampling of some units and less detailed work on others.

Random sampling is the most common sampling strategy used in survey and excavation.

Few modern archaeological surveys fail to make use of sampling, for archaeologists are only too aware that many site distributions reflect the distribution of archaeologists rather than an unbiased sampling of the archaeological record. This bias applies particularly in densely vegetated areas such as the Mesoamerican and Amazonian rain forests, where the cover is so thick that even new roads are in constant danger of being overgrown. It is no coincidence that most archaeological sites found in rain forests are near well-trodden roads and tracks. The early archaeologists located sites by following narrow paths through the forest cut by chicleros, local people who collected resin from forest trees and guided researchers to sites. Even today, archaeologists can pass right through the middle of a large site in the forest or within a few feet of a huge pyramid and see nothing (Chartkoff, 1978). Sophisticated sampling techniques will transform survey techniques beyond recognition in the coming years, even if they never completely supersede the traditional task of the archaeologist: investigating archaeological sites on the ground.

REMOTE SENSING

Increasingly, archaeologists are relying on technology and elaborate instrumentation to help them discover the past. Some archaeologists are beginning to talk about "nondestructive archaeology," the analysis of archaeological phenomena without excavations or collecting of artifacts, both of which destroy the archaeological record. The major methods in this approach are generally labeled *remote sensing* (Scollar and others, 1990). These techniques include aerial photography, various magnetic prospecting methods, and side-scan radar.

AERIAL PHOTOGRAPHY

Aerial photography gives an unrivaled overhead view of the past. Sites can be photographed obliquely or vertically, at different seasons or times of day, and from many directions. Numerous sites that have left almost no surface traces on the ground have come to light through the all-embracing eye of the air photograph (D. N. Riley, 1987). Thousands of hitherto unknown sites have been plotted on maps. Whole field systems and roadways have been incorporated into panoramas of prehistoric or Roman landscapes in Italy and North Africa, and well-known sites such as Stonehenge and the many Mesoamerican and South American temples have been photographed in the context of their landscapes (Figure 9.4).

SHADOW SITES   Many earthworks and other complex structures have been leveled by plow or erosion, but their reduced topography shows up clearly from the air. The rising or setting sun can set off long shadows, emphasizing the relief of almost-vanished banks or ditches, so that the features of the site stand out in the oblique light.

CROP AND SOIL MARKS   These are found in areas where the subsoil is suitable for revealing differences in soil color and in the richness of crop growth on a particular soil (Figure 9.5). Such marks cannot be detected easily on the surface, but under favorable circumstances they can be seen clearly from the air. The principle on which the crop mark is based is that the growth and color of a crop are mainly determined by the amount of moisture the plant can derive from the soil and the subsoil. If the soil depth has been increased by digging features, such as pits and ditches, and then filling them in or by heaping up additional earth to form

FIGURE 9.4   Oblique aerial photograph of the stone circles at Avebury in southern Britain, built around 2000 B.C. The aerial perspective places the circles in a wider context of earthworks and landscape.

FIGURE 9.5   A crop mark site, a series of enclosures, from Thorpe, Huntingdonshire, England. Under favorable circumstances, such marks can be seen clearly from the air.

artificial banks or mounds, crops growing over such abandoned structures are tall and well nourished. The converse is true where topsoil has been removed and the infertile subsoil is near the surface, or where impenetrable surfaces, such as paved streets, are below ground level and crops are stunted. Thus a dark crop mark can be taken for a ditch or pit, and a lighter line will define a more substantial structure. Soil marks result from plowing soil from such features as banks and show up as a color lighter than that of the darker, deeper soil around them.

EXAMPLES OF AERIAL PHOTOGRAPHY   A classic application of air photography was provided by Gordon Willey, who used a standard Peruvian Air Force mosaic of cultivated valley bottoms and margins of the Virú Valley in northern coastal Peru to survey changing settlement patterns there (Willey, 1953). Employing these photographs as the basis for a master site map of the valley, Willey was able to plot many archaeological features. Three hundred and fifteen sites in the Virú Valley were located, many of them stone buildings, walls, or terraces that showed up quite well on the mosaics. Some much less conspicuous sites were also spotted, among them midden heaps without stone walls, refuse mounds that appeared as low hillocks on the photographs, and small, pyramidal mounds of insignificant proportions. The aerial photographs enabled Willey and his team to pinpoint many sites before going out in the field. The result was the fascinating story of shifting settlement patterns in Virú over many thousands of years, a classic of its kind.

Aerial surveys have been used effectively in many areas, especially to plot prehistoric and later occupation directly onto maps. This approach was used at Chaco Canyon, New Mexico, where a prehistoric road system was plotted, using both side-scan radar and aerial photographs (Sever and Wiseman, 1985).

Most aerial photographs are taken with black-and-white film, which gives definition superior to that of color film and is much cheaper to buy and reproduce than color. The wide range of filters that can be used with black-and-white give the photographer great versatility in the field. Infrared film, which has three layers sensitized to green, red, and infrared, detects reflected solar radiation at the near end of the electromagnetic spectrum, some of which is invisible to the human eye. The different reflections from cultural and natural features are translated by the film into distinctive "false" colors. Bedrock comes up blue on infrared film, but vigorous grass growth on alluvial plains shows up bright red. Experiments at the famous Snaketown site in the American Southwest, a great Hohokam Indian pueblo, trade center, and ceremonial center, did not show up new cultural features, but tonal contrasts within a color indicated various cultural components. Vigorous plant growth showing up red on infrared photographs has been used to track shallow subsurface water sources where springs were used by prehistoric peoples (Harp, 1978).

NONPHOTOGRAPHIC METHODS

Archaeological sites can be detected from the air, even from space, by nonphotographic techniques as well. But aerial photography is the last of the "do-it-yourself" types of remote sensing, a technique whose cost is within the reach of even a modest archaeological expedition. Aerial sensor imagery, using aircraft, satellites, and even manned spacecraft, involves instrumentation that is astronomically expensive by archaeological standards. Thus these exciting techniques are only occasionally used, and then only when the collaboration of NASA and interested experts can be enlisted.

AIRCRAFT-BORNE SENSOR IMAGERY   Aircraft-borne instrumentation of several types can be used to record images of the electromagnetic radiation that is reflected or emitted from the earth's surface. A multispectral scanner, for example, measures the radiance of the earth's surface along a scan line perpendicular to the aircraft's line of flight. A two-dimensional image is processed digitally. Multispectral scanners are ideal for mapping vegetation and for monitoring bodies of water when more complete data are needed than can be obtained from aerial photographs. Thermal infrared line scanners were originally used for military night survey but now have many applications in the environmental sciences. The line scanners have thermal devices that record an image on photographic film. The temperature data obtained from such scans is combined with aerial photographs to reveal tiny thermal patterns that may indicate different crop uses, the distribution of range animals, or variations in soil moisture and groundwater, both ancient and modern.

SIDEWAYS-LOOKING AIRBORNE RADAR (SLAR)   This technique senses the terrain to either side of an aircraft's track. It does this by sending out long pulses of electromagnetic radiation. The radar then records the strength and time of the pulse return to detect objects and their range from the aircraft. SLAR has great potential for archaeology because it is not dependent on sunlight. The flying aircraft enables the observer to track the pulse lines in the form of images, no matter what obscures the ground. The SLAR images are normally interpreted visually, using radar mosaics or stereo pairs of images, as well as digital image processors. SLAR was originally used for oil exploration, geology, and geomorphology, in applications that could justify its high cost. It is useful for mapping surface soil moisture distributions, something that has great potential for the study of ancient roads such as the Silk Route between China and the West and ancient Angkor (Figure 9.6).

SLAR can show where many changes in topography have taken place or the subsoil of large sites has been disturbed. It can also be applied to underwater sites to locate wrecks on the sea floor. So far, applications of this exciting technology to the past have been few and far between, but experiments in the Mesoamerican lowlands have hinted that SLAR may be able to identify buildings beneath dense rain forest canopy. Scans of the Maya lowlands have shown that areas of wet-season swamp often have irregular grids of gray lines in them, multitudes of ladder, lattice, and curvilinear patterns. These have been compared to known ancient canal systems and are thought to represent long-forgotten large-scale irrigation schemes (Adams and others, 1981). The investigators believe that nearly all swamp edges in the Petén, the rain forest lowlands of northern Guatemala, once were extensively canalized for agriculture and communication purposes. They may have provided food supplies for much denser populations than today's.

The field testing of data from this remote-sensing technique has hardly begun. But surface investigations at Pulltrouser Swamp in northern Belize have shown that Maya farmers exploited the edges of seasonally flooded swamps between 200 B.C. and A.D. 850. A rising population of farmers brought under cultivation more than 740 acres (300 ha) of raised field plots, linked with interconnecting canals. These fields were hoed, mulched, and planted with maize, amaranth, and perhaps cotton (Turner and Harrison, 1983).

The space shuttle Columbia used an imaging radar system to bounce radar signals off the surfaces of the world's major deserts in 1981. This experiment was designed to study the history of the earth's aridity, not archaeology, but it identified bedrock valleys in the limestone up to 20 feet (6 m) under overlying sand sheets in the eastern Sahara Desert. Such identifications were possible because of the arid deposits. Wetter soils do not permit such deep access, for the water table blocks the radar eye completely. All remote sensing is useless unless checked on the ground, so a team of geologists, including archaeologist C. Vance Haynes of the University of Arizona, journeyed far into the desert to investigate the long-hidden water courses. About the only people to work this terrain were the British army in World War II and Egyptian oil companies. The oil companies kindly arranged for a skip loader to be transported into the desert. To Haynes's astonishment, the skip-loader trenches yielded some 200,000-year-old stone axes, dramatic and unexpected proof that early Stone Age hunter-gatherers had lived in the heart of the Sahara when the

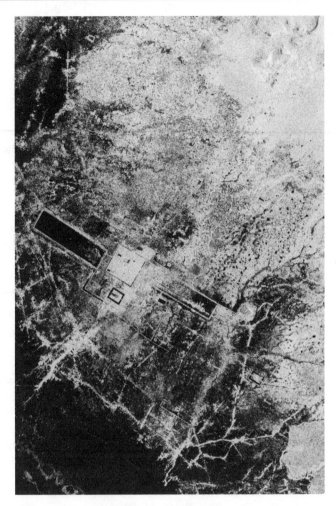

FIGURE 9.6 A Spaceborne Imaging Radar-C/X-band Synthetic Aperture Radar photograph of the city of Angkor, Cambodia, taken from the space shuttle *Endeavour* on September 30, 1994. The image shows an area about 34 miles by 53 miles (55 by 85 km). The principal complex, Angkor Wat, is the rectangle at lower right, surrounded by a dark line, which is a reservoir. Cambodia's great central lake, the Tonle Sap, lies at lower right. A network of ancient and modern roads can also be seen. The data from these images are being used to establish why the site was abandoned in the fifteenth century A.D., and to map the vast system of canals, reservoirs, and other works built during the city's heyday.

landscape was more hospitable than it is today. The Haynes find is of cardinal importance, for African archaeologists now believe that the Sahara was a vital catalyst in early human history that effectively sealed off both archaic and modern Africans from the rest of the Ice Age world for many millennia.

The most accurate space images of all are, of course, in the closely guarded hands of the military. Despite the veil of secrecy, some astonishingly clear black and white satellite photographs have proved a bounty to geologists who are expert in analyzing subtle tone, texture, and light reflections given off by rock formations on earth. Herein lies a remarkable bonus for archaeology, for potential hominid fossil beds in Ethiopia and other parts of East Africa can be detected from shuttle images. Only a few years ago, paleoanthropologists like the Leakeys and Don Johanson could spend months on end combing hundreds of square miles of potentially fossil-bearing landscape just to locate promising deposits. Recently John Fleagle of the State University of New York at Stony Brook used shuttle photographs to investigate fossil beds in the Fejeji region of the Ethiopian Rift Valley. He returned some months later with some 3.7-million-year-old hominid teeth from one of the earliest *Australopithecus* yet discovered. Ethiopian archaeologists are now using images from space to develop an inventory of potential fossil deposits in their country.

SATELLITE SENSOR IMAGERY   This method is well known for its military applications, but earth resources technology satellites, both manned and unmanned, have proved extremely valuable for environmental monitoring. The most famous of these satellites are the LANDSAT series, which scan the earth with readers that record the intensity of reflected light and infrared radiation from the earth's surface. The data from scanning operations are converted electronically into photographic images and from these into mosaic maps. Normally, however, these maps are taken at a scale of about 1:1,000,000, far too imprecise for anything but the most general archaeological surveys. The first LANDSAT images could detect images about 200 feet (61 m) wide. The pyramids and plazas of Teotihuacán in the Valley of Mexico might appear on such a map, but certainly not the types of minute archaeological distribution information that the average survey seeks. The latest images pick up features only 90 feet wide, while the French SPOT satellites can work to within 60 feet (18 m). In their latest generations, both have great potential for archaeological use. Both are expensive, especially when complex imaging processing equipment is required. At a cost of up to $3,000 an image or even more, only the most well-heeled researchers can make free use of this revolutionary technology—and few archaeologists have access to this kind of money. The LANDSAT imagery offers an integrated view of a large region and is made up of light reflected from many components of the earth: soil, vegetation, topography, and so on. Computer-enhanced LANDSAT images can be used to construct environmental cover maps of large survey regions that are a superb backdrop for both aerial and ground survey for archaeological resources.

ASSESSING ARCHAEOLOGICAL SITES

In these days of wholesale destruction of archaeological sites through industrial activity, deep plowing, and illegal excavation, archaeologists do all they can to avoid disturbing subsurface levels. This, and the need for management of archaeological resources of all kinds (Chapter 20), makes the assessment of archaeological sites a critical process. Assessment involves recording of location, controlled surface collection and investigation, and, in some cases, subsurface detection using electronic and other methods.

RECORDING SITES

Studies of changing settlement distributions plotted against environmental data are now of major importance, as they provide significant information on changing human exploitation of the landscape (Chapter 15). Thus, recording the precise geographic location of the archaeological phenomena revealed by a survey is a high priority. On a small-scale survey, site data come almost entirely from actual fieldwork. With larger regional investigations, and extensive cultural resource management projects, especially in the western United States, remote sensing and geographic information systems are used to record and manage archaeological sites (see Chapter 20). Except for rainfall patterns, all the environmental information required for many surveys can be plotted with information obtained from aerial and satellite maps. Although large archaeological sites such as road systems or major cities can be located on aerial photographs, very small phenomena such as scattered artifacts or cattle enclosures are generally impossible to find on even the most detailed maps. Aerial photographs can be used, however, to mark the locations of any archaeological phenomena once they have been located on the ground. It is not enough, however, just to plot a site on a good map and record its precise latitude, longitude, and map grid reference. Special forms are used to record the location of the site, as well as information about surface features, the landowner, potential threats to the site, and so on. Every site in the United States is given a name and a number. Sites in Santa Barbara County, California, for example, are given the prefix CA-SBa- and are numbered sequentially.

So many sites are now known in North America that most states and many large archaeological projects have set up computer data banks containing comprehensive information about site distributions and characteristics. Arkansas, for example, has a statewide computer bank that is in constant use for decisions on conservation and management.

MAPS

Maps are a convenient way of storing large quantities of archaeological information. Mapping specialists, called cartographers, have developed many effective and dramatic ways of communicating information graphically, devices that are very useful inclusions in archaeological reports (Ebert, 1984) (Figure 9.7).

TOPOGRAPHIC MAPS   The distributions of archaeological sites are plotted on large-scale topographic maps that relate the ancient settlements to the basic features of the natural landscape (Figure 9.7, left). This master base map can be overlaid with plots that show vegetational cover—either prehistoric or modern— and soil types, and even prehistoric trade routes.

PLANIMETRIC MAPS   These are commonly used to record details of archaeological sites. They relate different archaeological features to each other and contain no topographic information (Figure 9.7, right).

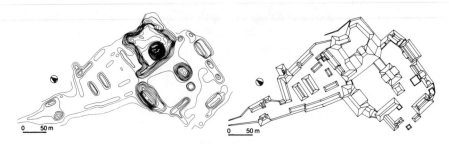

FIGURE 9.7   Examples of archaeological maps. Left: a topographic map that shows the relationship between sites and the landscape. Right: a planimetric map showing the features of a site. Both are of Nohmul, a Maya ceremonial center.

SITE PLANS   These are specially prepared maps made by archaeologists to record the horizontal provenance of artifacts, food residues, and features. Site plans are keyed to topographic and other surveys from a carefully selected point (datum point), such as a survey beacon or a landmark that appears on a large-scale map. This datum point provides a reference from which a grid of squares can be laid out over the area of the site, normally open-ended so that it can be extended to cover more ground if necessary. A site grid is critical for recording surface finds and during excavation for use in three-dimensional recording.

GEOGRAPHIC INFORMATION SYSTEMS (GIS)

More and more survey and site data are now entered into geographic information systems (GIS). Computer-aided mapping came into being during the 1970s as a means of presenting cartographic information rapidly and accurately. Geographic Information Systems go beyond mapping. They are computer-aided systems for the collection, storage, retrieval, analysis, and presentation of spatial data of all kinds (Gaffney and Stancic, 1991). GIS incorporates computer-aided mapping, computerized data bases, and statistical packages, and is best thought of as a computer data base with mapping capabilities. It also has the ability to generate new information based on the data within it. GIS is really a distinct technology, based on recent developments in cartography and many other disciplines, with enormous potential for the study of site distributions and spatial problems in archaeology, especially of artifacts, settlements, and cultures distributed over a landscape (Kvamme, 1989).

GIS data comes from digitizing maps and from remote-sensing devices such as LANDSAT satellites, as well as manual entries on a computer keyboard. Sophisticated software packages allow the acquisition, processing, analysis, and presentation of data of many kinds. From the archaeological perspective, GIS has the advantage of allowing the manipulation of large amounts of data, which is especially useful for solving complex settlement analysis problems (Chapter 15). Satellites acquire environmental and topographic information; the archaeological data can be added to the same data base. Analyses that once took years can be done in minutes, even seconds. Until the advent of GIS, most archaeological surveys and

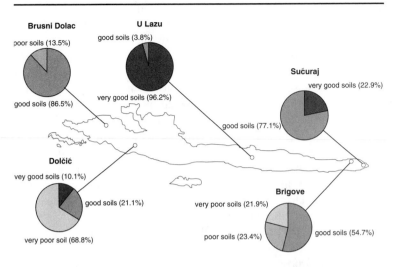

FIGURE 9.8   Roman sites on Hvar with pie charts illustrating the proportions of soil types within catchment areas derived from GIS analysis.

settlement studies were confined to the site itself. Now the archaeologist can move away from the narrow confines of the site and examine, for example, the environmental potential of areas where no sites have been found—as a way of assessing the overall distribution of sites within the environment.

GIS is still new to archaeology and good examples of its application are rare. Vincent Gaffney and Zoran Stancic (1991) used GIS for a regional survey of the island of Hvar off the Adriatic coast. They created an environmental data base for the island by covering it with a grid of 66-foot (20 m) square pixels, for a total of 3.8 million pixels. Then they entered modern data on elevation, soils, geology, and microclimate. In the field, they visited and recorded every known archaeological site on the island from early farming villages to post-Roman settlements, entering the data into a computer data base. They then combined this data base with the GIS data for a series of studies on the extent of site territories, analysis of land use within the same territories, and on the factors that affected site location. For instance, they were able to show that Roman villas were located near good agricultural soils (Figure 9.8). GIS also allows archaeologists to model different environmental scenarios and to study such problems as the ways in which different settlements controlled valuable land.

The Italian archaeologists responsible for Roman Pompeii, overwhelmed by an eruption of Vesuvius on August 24, A.D. 79, have used GIS technology to capture and interpret life in the town as it was 2,000 years ago, employing a computerized data base of material excavated since 1862. They used an IBM computer to digitize archaeological maps and local terrain, to integrally link visual representations of the artifacts to both the detailed descriptions of each find from the city and to the locations in which they were found. The thousands of computerized pictures of specific artifacts are linked to the maps to provide detailed insights into individual houses, rooms, and walls, the places where the finds were excavated. This "Neapolis" system, with its 50 gigabytes of detailed information about Pompeii, can be used to study such topics as the relationships between lifestyle and distribution of wealth, the spread of fashions and trends, or to correlate fresco motifs on house walls from one end of the town to the other. In this instance, GIS is used to understand relationships not readily perceived by the human mind, the myriad interconnections that tie works of art, buildings, and individual artifacts to an entire culture and community.

The most comprehensive North American GIS project is the National Archaeological Archive, described in more detail in Chapter 20. It provides American archaeologists with access not only to archaeological site distribution data from all parts of the United States, but with the ability to consult a bibliographic data base and to review site distribution data against a background of topographic, climatic, and other information, even seasonal changes. The Arkansas Archaeological Survey is already using this data base in its field research (Chapter 15, Sabo and others, 1990).

The primary purpose of many remote-sensing surveys is to map concentrations of sites and, on larger projects, to identify where maximal efforts in ground surveying and excavation should be concentrated. This decision requires not only remote-sensing data but a comprehensive record of all sites known from the survey area as well.

ASSESSMENT: SURFACE INVESTIGATIONS

The artifacts and other archaeological finds discovered on the surface of a site are a potentially vital source of information about the people who once lived there. Surface collection has these objectives:

- To gather representative samples of artifacts from the surface of the site to establish the age of the area and the various periods of occupation.
- To establish the types of activity that took place on the site.
- To gather information on the areas of the site that were most densely occupied and that might be most productive for either total or sample excavation.
- To locate major structures that lie, for the most part, below the surface.

Many archaeologists distrust surface collection, arguing that artifacts are easily destroyed on the surface and can be displaced from their original positions by many factors. But this viewpoint neglects a truth: all archaeological deposits, however deep, were once surface deposits, subject to many of the same destructive processes as those outcropping on the surface today (Dunnell and Dancey, 1983). With the increased emphasis on regional surveys and settlement archaeology in recent years, many field-workers have demonstrated that surface deposits can provide much information on artifact distributions and other phenomena also found underground, provided, of course, that they have not been subjected to catastrophic industrial activity, strip mining, or other drastic modifications.

Like buried deposits, surface levels contain abundant information about artifact patternings if one can separate cultural patterns from those caused by formation processes that have occurred since the site was abandoned. The same influences affect both surface and buried deposits: natural weathering, erosion, rainfall, and human activity for years, which may result in the pulverizing of potsherds, stone tools, and bone fragments. But surface data have two major advantages: they are a body of information that can be obtained on a regional scale, not site by site, and the cost of obtaining the data is but a fraction of that for excavation. Increasingly, archaeologists are thinking of surface data as primary archaeological information essential to understanding regional prehistories (Lewarch and O'Brien, 1981).

There are various ways of collecting artifacts from the surface of a site, but the process is always carefully controlled. Controlled surface collection sometimes involves meticulous recording of all finds, using a grid laid out over the surface of the site, an approach especially effective on plowed fields. Experiments have shown that even more than a century of cultivation will scatter artifacts over no more than a radius of 20 feet (6 m). This relatively small "halo" area makes total collection feasible, especially for small hunter-gatherer settlements.

When dealing with a well-known area or with sites containing distinctive artifacts, it is possible to collect only diagnostic artifacts, items such as potsherds, stone artifacts, or other characteristic finds that are easily classified and identified. These key finds may enable the archaelolgist to assess what periods of occupation are represented at the site. Under these, and indeed all, circumstances, surface collections are carefully controlled, in such a way that the provenance of the finds is plotted on a map at the time of collection.

A common controlled surface collection method involves random sampling. Because total collection is impossible on sites of any size where surface finds are abundant, some type of sampling technique is used to obtain a valid random sample of the surface artifacts. One oft-used random-sampling approach involves laying out a grid of squares on the surface of the site and then collecting everything found in randomly selected units. Once such a "controlled collection" has been made, the rest of the site is covered for highly diagnostic artifacts. Rigorous sampling techniques are essential to obtain even a minimal sample of finds at the individual site level. Surface collection and sampling are often combined with small test-pit excavations to get preliminary data on stratigraphic information.

Evidence of the activities of a region's inhabitants can be obtained from surface collections, but only when the relationship between remains found on the surface and those found below the ground is clearly understood. Sometimes the surface finds may accurately reflect site content; at other times they may not. This problem is compounded not only by natural erosion and other factors but also by the depth of the occupation deposits on the site. Obviously, almost no finds from the lowest levels of a 30-foot-deep (9 m) village mound will lie on the surface today, unless erosion, human activity, or animal burrows bring deeply buried artifacts to the surface (McManamon, 1984).

Finally, very small test trenches, called "shovel units," or sampling with augers are methods commonly used when time is short, especially on sites located on cultural resource management (CRM) surveys.

With shallow sites, such as Teotihuacán and many prehistoric settlements in the American West, it is a reasonable assumption that the artifacts on the surface accurately reflect those slightly below the surface (Millon, 1973). This assumption provides a basis for studying activities from surface finds. Any conclusions derived from surface collections, however, have to be verified by subsequent excavation.

SITE SURVEY

Archaeological surveys are designed to solve specific research problems and find sites. Once sites are located, they are surveyed carefully, with these objectives in mind:

- To collect and record information on subsurface features, such as walls, buildings, and fortifications, traces of which may be detected on the surface. Such features may include ancient roads, agricultural systems, and earthworks, which are first detected from the air and then investigated on the ground.
- To collect and record information on artifacts and other finds lying on the surface of the site.
- To use both of these categories of data to test hypotheses about the age, significance, and function of the site.

TEOTIHUACÁN

Site surveys can be as complex as those covering large areas. Perhaps the largest site survey project ever undertaken was the Teotihuacán Mapping Project directed by George Cowgill and René Millon. Teotihuacán lies northeast of Mexico City and is one of the great tourist attractions of the Americas. This great pre-Columbian city flourished from about 250 B.C. until A.D. 700. Up to 150,000 people lived in Teotihuacán at the peak of its prosperity. Huge pyramids and temples, giant plazas, and an enormous market formed the core of the well-organized and well-planned city (Figure 16.7). The houses of the priests and nobles lay along the main avenues; the artisans and common people lived in crowded compounds of apartments and courtyards (Millon, 1973).

Cowgill and Millon realized that the only effective way to study the city was to make a comprehensive map of all of the precincts; without it they would never have been able to study how Teotihuacán grew so huge. Fortunately, the streets and buildings lay close to the surface, unlike the vast city mounds of the Near East, where only excavation yields settlement information.

The mapping project began with a detailed ground survey, conducted with the aid of aerial photographs and large-scale survey maps. The field data were collected on 147 map data sheets of 500-meter squares at a scale of 1:2,000. Intensive mapping and surface surveys, including surface collections of artifacts, were then conducted systematically within the 8-square-mile (20 sq. km) limits of the ancient city defined by the preliminary survey. Ultimately, the architectural interpretations of the surface features within each 1,640-foot (500 m) square were overprinted on the base map of the site. These architectural interpretations were based on graphic data and surface data collected on special forms and through artifact collections, photographs, and drawings. Extensive use of sophisticated sampling techniques and quantitative methods was essential for successful completion of the map.

By the end of the project more than 5,000 structures and activity areas had been recorded within the city limits. The Teotihuacán maps do not, of course, convey to us the incredible majesty of this remarkable city, but they do provide, for the first time, a comprehensive view of a teeming, multifaceted community with vast public buildings, plazas, and avenues, and thousands of small apartments and courtyards, which formed individual households and pottery, figurine, and obsidian workshops, among the many diverse structures in the city. The survey also revealed that the city had been expanded over the centuries according to a comprehensive master plan. (For more on Teotihuacán, see Chapter 15.)

Site survey has the great advantage of being much cheaper than excavation, provided that the methods used are based on explicit research designs. Many of the most exciting recent studies of cultural process and changing settlement patterns have depended heavily on archaeological survey and site survey. The large-scale field surveys around the Maya city of Copán have used remote sensing, field survey, and obsidian hydration dating to record changing settlement patterns before and during the collapse of Maya civilization (Freter, 1993). The data from the survey show a concentration of population in the urban core during the height of Classic Maya civilization, then a rapid, followed by a slowing, dispersal into rural communities causing the environment to become overexploited at the time of the collapse.

SUBSURFACE DETECTION

Every archaeologist dreams of a way of exploring sites without the labor of excavating them! Subsurface detection methods are new to archaeology, many of them originally developed for oil or geological prospecting (A. Clark, 1990; Weymouth, 1986). Most are expensive; some are very time-consuming. But their application can sometimes save many weeks of expensive excavation and, on occasion, aid in formulating an accurate research design before a dig begins.

NONMECHANICAL DETECTION

BOWSING   In this low-tech, nonmechanical method, the surface of the site is thumped with a suitable heavy pounder. The earth resonates in different ways, so much so that a practiced ear can detect the distinctive sound of a buried ditch or a subsurface stone wall. Bowsing, more an art than a geophysical method, really works—with practice. The author has used it on several occasions to detect buried walls.

THE AUGER, OR CORE BORER   This is a tool used to bore through subsurface deposits to find the depth and consistency of archaeological deposits lying beneath the surface. This technique has its value during an excavation, but it has the obvious disadvantage that the probe may destroy valuable artifacts. Augers were used quite successfully at the Ozette site in Washington to establish the depth of midden deposits (Kirk, 1974). Some specialized augers are used to lift pollen samples. Augers with a camera attached to a periscope head are also used to investigate the interiors of Etruscan tombs (Figure 9.9). The periscope is inserted through a small hole in the roof of the tomb to inspect the interior. If the contents are undisturbed, excavation proceeds. But if tomb robbers have emptied the chamber, many hours of labor have been saved.

FIGURE 9.9   A periscope being used to investigate an Etruscan tomb.

MECHANICAL DETECTION

Three types of mechanical detection are resistivity survey, magnetic survey, and pulse radar.

RESISTIVITY SURVEY   The electrical resistivity of the soil provides some clues to subsurface features on archaeological sites (Carr, 1982; Leute, 1987). Different soils vary in their ability to conduct electricity, mainly because the deposits have moisture containing mineral salts in solution. For example, clay soils provide the least resistance to current flow, sandy soils much more. A resistivity survey meter can be used to measure the variations in the resistance of the ground to an electric current. Stone walls or hard pavements obviously retain less dampness than a deep pit filled with soft earth or a large ditch that has silted up. These differences can be measured accurately so that disturbed ground, stone walls, and other subsurface features can be detected by systematic survey. To survey a site, all that is needed is the meter, which is attached to four or five probes. A grid of strings is laid over the site, and the readings taken from the probes are plotted as contour lines. These show the areas of equal resistance and the presence of features such as ditches and walls (Figure 9.10). This method was, for example, employed to identify subsurface features at the Late Woodland and Early Historic Howorth-Nelson site in southwestern Pennsylvania (Adovasio and Carlisle, 1988; see Chapter 20).

MAGNETIC SURVEY   Magnetic location is used to find buried features such as iron objects, fired clay furnaces, pottery kilns, hearths, and pits filled with rubbish or softer soil (Leute, 1987). The principle is simple: any mass of clay heated to

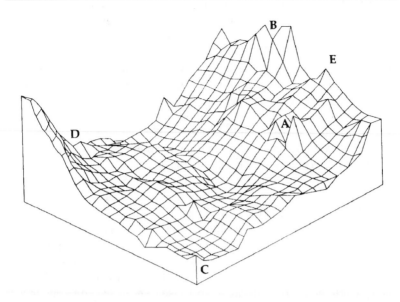

FIGURE 9.10   A three-dimensional computer plot of a resistivity survey at the Maya village at Cerén, San Salvador. The anomalies resulting from different electrical resistance show up as sharp peaks (A to E), of which A and B have been investigated and shown to be prehistoric structures.

about 700° C and then cooled acquires a weak magnetism. Rocks, boulders, and soil will also acquire magnetism if iron oxides are present when they are heated. When the remanent magnetism of fired clay or of other materials in a pit or similar feature is measured, it will give a reading different from that of the intensity of the earth's magnetic field normally obtained from undisturbed soils. The proton magnetometer is the instrument most commonly used to magnetically detect archaeological features. A site is surveyed by laying out 50-foot-square (15 sq. m) units, each of them divided into a grid of 5-foot (1.5 m) squares. The measurement is taken with a staff, to which are attached two small bottles filled with water or alcohol enclosed in electric coils. The magnetic intensity is measured by recording the behavior of the protons in the hydrogen atoms in the bottle's contents. The magnetometer itself amplifies the weak signals from the electrical coils. Features are traced by taking closely spaced measurements over areas where anomalies in the magnetic readings are found. Computers record the field data and convert them into a display on a TV screen or a printout. Sophisticated software allows the operator to screen out nonarchaeological variations in soil magnetism.

Magnetic detection has been used successfully to record pits, walls, and other features in the middle of large forts or fortified towns, where total excavation of a site is clearly uneconomical. This method has been used widely in Europe and on Olmec pyramids at La Venta, Mexico, but it is subject to some error because of such modern features as barbed wire fences, electric trains, and power cables (Kaczor and Weymouth, 1981).

PULSE RADAR   The pulse induction meter applies pulses of magnetic field to the soil from a transmitter coil. This instrument is very sensitive to metals and can be used to find pottery and metal objects and graves containing such objects. A soil conductivity meter can be used to detect subsoil features by measuring changes in the conductivity of the soil. Anomalies spotted by the instrument can be plotted with good accuracy, and pits as small as 12 inches (30 cm) in diameter and 4 inches (10 cm) deep have been located. Individual metal objects can also be detected using this method, which holds great promise for the future.

The application of radar and other electronic devices is proliferating in archaeology. Ken Weeks and a team of fellow Egyptologists have embarked on a long-term project to map all of the royal tombs in Thebes's Valley of the Kings. They are using a hot-air balloon, X rays, and sonic detectors to map subterranean features and hidden chambers in royal tombs; they have recently located a large tomb which once housed Ramesses II's sons.

The excavations at the Maya village of Cerén in San Salvador offer an instructive example of coordinated use of geophysical methods to locate subsurface features (Sheets, 1992). The site was buried under up to 16 feet (5 m) of volcanic ash and was first located by a chance bulldozer cut. Obviously, it was uneconomical to bulldoze large areas, so Payson Sheets called in geophysicist Hartmut Spetzler, who analyzed the properties of the volcanic ash at Cerén, and of the adobe buildings buried beneath it. There were considerable differences in porosity and density between the ash and the adobe, so he recommended deploying a portable seismograph, a ground-penetrating radar, and a resistivity meter.

The survey started with the seismograph, which records shock waves passing through the earth. Instead of the usual dynamite, Sheets struck a steel plate set in the soil with a hammer, recording the resulting waves with a set of 12 sensitive microphones. Buried hut floors conducted shock waves faster than the surrounding ash, and the seismograph did indeed locate some structures, but, designed as it was for detecting huge geological anomalies, the results were somewhat haphazard. Sheets now turned to ground-penetrating radar, using an instrument developed for studying permafrost melting along the Alaska Oil Pipeline. Instead of attaching it to a pickup truck, he enlisted the services of an ox cart, which eliminated all background vibration. The ox-cart driver simply drove slowly and steadily along a carefully marked straight line (Figure 9.11). The machine itself sent microwave energy deep into the soil and detected it as it was reflected back. The subsurface stratigraphy was recorded on special paper and revealed some strong reflectors, some of which turned out to be the clay surfaces of hut floors covered by ash.

Using a drill rig, Sheets then tested some of the anomalies. Some were the result of eroded and redeposited volcanic ash. Others were large structures, but the radar was unable to detect smaller features, although it may be able to do so when the data are digitized and the original ground surface is mapped.

Resistivity surveys over Cerén recorded the resistance of subsurface deposits to electricity. Sheets expected that house floors would conduct electricity better than the surrounding ash, for they are constructed of dense, fired clay. His researchers recorded measurements along a grid over the site and fed the data into a laptop computer. The three-dimensional software revealed interesting

FIGURE 9.11 Ground-penetrating radar slung behind an ox cart being used at Cerén, San Salvador.

double-peaked anomalies, which, when tested with a drill rig, turned out to be large prehistoric structures (Figure 9.10).

Thus a combination of geophysical methods provided an effective and economic way to locate subsurface features at Cerén, at a fraction of what it would have cost to bulldoze away acres of ashy overburden.

SUMMARY

- Two processes are involved in locating archaeological sites: survey and site assessment.
- Many archaeological sites are discovered by accident, industrial activity, modern agriculture, or natural happenings, such as floods and earthquakes.
- Many famous archaeological sites, such as the Parthenon, have never been lost to human knowledge. But other, less conspicuous locations are found only by planned ground survey. Archaeological sites manifest themselves in many ways, such as in the form of mounds, middens, caves, and rock shelters. Many more are much less conspicuous and are located only by soil discolorations or surface finds.
- Ground survey is done at one of several levels of intensity, ranging from general surveys leading to location of only the largest sites down to precise foot

surveys aimed at covering an entire area in detail. Even these are not totally effective, and all survey is, at best, a major sampling of the research area.

• In most cases, total survey is impracticable, and so archaeologists rely on probabilistic sampling methods to obtain unbiased samples of the research area.

• Key indicators of archaeological sites include conspicuous above-ground features, vegetational coverage, soil colors, and surface finds.

• A battery of new survey techniques involves aerial photography and remote sensing. Photographs taken from the air can be used to locate sites spread over huge areas. Pioneer efforts have been made with side-scan aerial radar and scanner imagery.

• Site assessment involves mapping, controlled surface collection, and subsurface detection methods designed to assess the significance of the site without intrusive excavation.

• Controlled surface collection is designed to collect and record artifacts and other surface finds. These categories of data are used to test hypotheses about the age, significance, and function of the site.

• Surface collections may be made by gathering every artifact on the surface of the site, by selecting for diagnostic artifacts, or by random sampling. Surface collections are used to establish the activities that took place on the site, to locate major structures, and to gather information about the most densely occupied areas of the site.

• Geographic Information Systems (GIS) technology offers great potential as a way of mapping archaeological data and analyzing it in a wider environmental context.

• Subsurface features are often detected with subsurface radar, and also resistivity surveys, which measure the differences in electrical resistivity of the soil between disturbed and undisturbed areas. Proton magnetometers are used to locate iron objects, fired clay furnaces, and other features.

GUIDE TO FURTHER READING

Gaffney, Vincent, and Zoran Stancic. *GIS Approaches to Regional Analysis: A Case Study of the Island of Hvar*. Ljubljana: Znanstveni institut Filozofske fakultete, 1991. An exemplary case study in the use of Geographic Information Systems in archaeology. It is also readable!

Millon, René. *The Teotihuacán Map: Urbanization at Teotihuacán, Mexico*, vol. 1. Austin: University of Texas Press, 1973. A prime example of a complicated survey and mapping project.

Mueller, James A., ed. *Sampling in Archaeology*. Tucson: University of Arizona Press, 1975. Useful essays on problems in field survey sampling, for the advanced reader.

Sanders, William T., Jeffrey R. Parsons, and Robert S. Santley. *The Basin of Mexico: Ecological Processes in the Evolution of a Civilization*. Orlando, Fla.: Academic Press, 1979. The best description of a long-term survey project and of survey problems.

10

ARCHAEOLOGICAL EXCAVATION

E xcavation! The very word conjures up romantic images of lost civilizations and royal burials, of long days in the sun digging up inscriptions and gold coins. Yet, though the image remains, the techniques of modern excavation are far less romantic than they are rigorous, requiring long training in practical field techniques. Unlike reconnaissance and surface survey, excavations recover data from beneath the surface of the ground—where conditions for preservation are best, and accurate information on provenance, context, and association can be recovered intact. In this chapter we discuss some of the basic principles of archaeological excavation: the organization, planning, and execution of a scientific dig.

ORGANIZING ARCHAEOLOGICAL EXCAVATIONS

The twentieth century has witnessed a total transformation of archaeology, from treasure hunting and curiosity to scientific investigation and problem-oriented excavation (Figure 10.1). Today's excavation is limited by ever-rising costs, by the need to minimize damage to the archaeological record, and by the sheer complexity of the data that can now be recovered from a site. Some of the more elaborate sites are dug by teams of specialists with very little unskilled help. Others are staffed by volunteer laborers, interested amateurs, and students who gain practical experience in all aspects of excavation, from using a shovel to recording a complicated stratigraphic profile.

The director of a modern archaeological field expedition needs skills beyond those of a competent archaeologist. He or she also must be able to fill the roles of accountant, politician, doctor, mechanic, personnel manager, and even cook. On a large dig, though manual labor may not be the director's responsibility, logistic problems are compounded, and he or she will head a large excavation team of site supervisors, artists, photographers, and numerous minor functionaries (Dancey, 1981; Joukowsky, 1981). Above all, the field director has to be the leader of a multidisciplinary team of specialist field-workers.

MULTIDISCIPLINARY RESEARCH TEAMS

Modern archaeology is so complex that all excavation projects now require multidisciplinary teams of archaeologists, botanists, geologists, zoologists, and other

FIGURE 10.1   General Augustus Lane Fox Pitt-Rivers (1827–1900) was the father of modern archaeological excavation. His excavations, like this one on a burial mound at Wor Barrow, Cranborne Chase, in southern England, were remarkable for their careful organization, precision, and attention to even minute details.

specialists who work together on closely integrated research problems, such as the origins of food production. The team approach is particularly important where environmental problems are most pressing, where the excavations and research seek the relationships between human cultures and the rest of the ecosystem.

A good interdisciplinary or multidisciplinary study is based on an integrated research design bringing a closely supervised team of specialists together to test carefully formulated hypotheses against data collected by all of them. Notice that we say "data collected by all of them." An effective multidisciplinary archaeological team must be just that—a team whose combined findings are used to test specific hypotheses.

Multidisciplinary research teams have been employed with great success at early hominid sites in East Turkana, Kenya, where geologists provided the background environmental data; zoologists, the identifications and interpretations of fossil animals found in the sites; and archaeologists, the data on surviving cultural remains, while physical anthropologists studied the human remains found in the 2- to 2.5-million-year-old sites. This approach is logical, but it is rarely carried to its logical extreme, where the experts would design their research together, share an integrated field mission, and communicate daily about their findings and research problems (Isaac and Isaac, 1989).

The criteria, then, for selecting members of multidisciplinary research teams include academic skills, the ability to communicate with people in other disciplines, highly specific specialist qualifications, and, above all, a willingness to work closely with a group of scholars who are committed to solving common problems. Such people are hard to find, and thus truly effective interdisciplinary research teams are few and far between. More loosely knit team approaches in which each member of a group pursues his or her own research but contributes to more general overall goals are far more common.

EXCAVATION STAFF

Large, elaborate excavations that take several seasons to complete are staffed by a director and other specialist experts and by several technicians as well. Among the technicians are these:

Site supervisors. Skilled excavators are responsible for excavating trenches and recording specific locations. The large-scale digs of Medieval York in northern England are divided into localities, each with a skilled excavator who supervises the volunteers doing the actual digging.

Recording experts. Some very large excavations will have a full-time surveyor, who does nothing but draw and record the stratigraphic profiles and structures found in the dig. Expert archaeological artists and photographers are in great demand and will make thousands of slides and black-and-white prints during even a short season. Their task is to create a complete record of the excavation from beginning to end (Adkins and Adkins, 1989; Dorrell, 1994).

Artifact and small-finds staff. Even a small excavation can yield a flood of artifacts and floral and faunal remains that can overwhelm the staff of a dig. A basic laboratory staff to bag the finds and wash, rough-sort, and mark them for eventual transport to the laboratory is essential on any but the smallest excavation. Some knowledge of preservation techniques is essential as well. Most excavations, such as that at the Maya city of Copán, Honduras, now use computers to handle their finds.

Foremen. Paid foremen can become skilled archaeological excavators in their own right, but their primary responsibility is managing paid laborers, especially on overseas excavations. Some devote their entire working lives to archaeology. Sir Leonard Woolley worked with the same foreman, Sheikh Hamoudi, from 1912 to 1941. Hamoudi, who became almost a part of Woolley's family, was famous for his invective and for his sensitivity to the moods of the workers.

In these days of rising costs and limited budgets, most excavations are conducted on a comparatively small scale. A team of students or paid laborers works under the overall supervision of the director and perhaps one or two assistants; the assistants may be graduate students with some technical training in archaeological fieldwork who can take some of the routine tasks from the director's shoulders, allowing him or her to concentrate on general supervision and interpretative problems. But on many sites, the director will not only be in charge of the research and arrangements for the excavation but will also personally supervise all trenches excavated. On that one person, therefore, devolve the tasks of recording, photography, drawing, measurement, and supervision of labor. The director may also take a turn at recovery of fragile burials and other delicate objects that cannot be entrusted to students or workers; he or she is also responsible for maintaining the excavation diaries and find notebooks, storage and marking of artifacts, and the logistics of packing finds and shipping them to the laboratory.

So varied are the skills of the excavator that much of a professional archaeologist's training in the field is obtained as a graduate student working at routine tasks and gaining experience in the methods of excavating and site survey under experienced supervision. For the director, such students provide not only useful supervisory labor but also an admirable hone upon which to try out favorite theories and discuss in ruthless detail the interpretation of the site. Opportunities to gain excavation experience are always open, and notices of digs can be found on many college and university bulletin boards. You can also obtain information on field schools from the Society for American Archaeology's Field School Catalog, or by watching issues of *Archaeology Magazine* for field opportunities. The camaraderie and happiness of a well-run, student-oriented excavation is one of the most worthwhile experiences of archaeology.

PLANNING AN EXCAVATION

Excavation is the culminating step in the investigation of an archaeological site. It recovers from the earth data obtainable in no other way (Barker, 1995; Dancey, 1981). Like historical archives, the soil of an archaeological site is a document whose pages must be deciphered, translated, and interpreted before they can be used to write an accurate account of prehistory.

Excavation is destruction—the archaeological deposits so carefully dissected during any dig are destroyed forever and their contents removed. Here, again, there is a radical difference between archaeology and the sciences and history. A scientist can readily re-create the conditions for a basic experiment; the historian can return to the archives to reevaluate the complex events in a politician's life. But all that we have after an excavation are the finds from the trenches, the untouched portions of the site, and the photographs, notes, and drawings that record the excavator's observations for posterity. Thus accurate recording and observation are overwhelmingly vital in the day-to-day work of archaeologists, not only for the sake of accuracy in their own research but also because they are creating an archive of archaeological information that may be consulted by others. Archaeological sites are nonrenewable resources. Thus, unfocused excavation is useless, for the manageable and significant observations are buried in a mass of irrelevant trivia. Any excavation must be conducted from a sound research design intended to solve specific and well-defined problems.

RESEARCH DESIGNS

As archaeology becomes more explicitly scientific and more sophisticated, much more specific research designs are essential (Figure 10.2). Lewis Binford (1964), who wrote about the need for sound research design in archaeological research, argues that archaeologists have no explicit criteria for selecting "important" sites. Excavations are traditionally conducted on larger sites, on sites that look more productive, on sites threatened by development, or on those nearest to roads. These criteria bear no resemblance to the goal that is actually required, which is

FIGURE 10.2   An organized horizontal-grid excavation on the Iron Age hill fort at Danebury, England. The Danebury research was carried out over many years, its research designs constantly modified.

acquiring representative and unbiased data to answer a particular problem—a problem whose limits are ultimately defined by available money and time. Unbiased data, which do not reflect the investigator's idiosyncrasies, can properly yield statistical estimates of the culture from which the samples were drawn. This kind of information requires explicit sampling procedures, to select a few sites from an area to excavate and also to control reliability of the information by using probability and statistics.

Excavation costs are so great that problem-oriented digging is now the rule rather than the exception, with the laboratory work forming part of the continuing evaluation of the research problem. The large piles of finds and records accumulated at the end of even a small field season contain a bewildering array of interdigitating facts that the researcher must evaluate and reevaluate as inquiry proceeds—by constantly arranging propositions and hypotheses, correlating observations, and reevaluating interpretations of the archaeological evidence. Finds and plans are the basis of the researcher's strategy and affect fieldwork plans for the future, the basis for constant reevaluation of research objectives.

The need for sound planning and design is even more acute in ecological research in archaeology, in which archaeologists try to understand changes in human culture in relation to human environmental systems. Let us take the example of the Koster excavation in Illinois, one of the largest and most complex digs ever undertaken in North America.

THE KOSTER SITE

In the lower Illinois Valley lies the site, a deep accumulation of 26 prehistoric occupation layers extending from about 10,000 years ago to around A.D. 1100 to 1200 (Struever and Holton, 1979). The wealth of material at Koster first came to light in 1968 and has been the subject of extremely large-scale excavation. The dig involved collaboration by three archaeologists and six specialists from such other disciplines as zoology and botany, as well as use of a computer laboratory (Figure 10.3). Even superficial examination of the site showed that a very careful research design was needed, both to maximize use of funds and to ensure adequate control of data. In developing the Koster research design, James Brown and Stuart Struever (1973) were well aware of the numerous, complex variables that had to be controlled and the need to define carefully their sampling procedure and the size of the collecting units.

They faced a number of formidable difficulties. Thirteen of the Koster cultural horizons are isolated from their neighbors by a zone of sterile slopewash soil, which makes it possible to treat each as a separate problem in excavation and analysis—as if it were an individual site—although, in fact, the 13 are stratified one above another. Because the whole site is more than 30 feet (9 m) deep,

FIGURE 10.3   General view of the Koster excavations in southern Illinois.

the logistical problems were formidable, as in all large-scale excavations. One possible strategy would have been to sink test pits, obtain samples from each level, and list diagnostic artifacts and cultural items. But this approach, though cheaper and commonly used, is quite inadequate to the systems model the excavators drew up to study the origins of cultivation in the area and cultural change in the lower Illinois Valley. Large-scale excavations were needed to uncover each living surface so that the excavators could not only understand what the living zones within each occupation were like but also, after studying in detail the sequence of differences in activities, make statements about the processes of cultural change.

From the large scale of the excavations, Brown and Struever saw the need for immediate feedback from the data flow from the site during the excavation. Changes in the excavation method would no doubt be needed during the season's fieldwork to ensure that maximum information was obtained. To accomplish this flexibility, both excavation and data-gathering activities were combined into a data flow system (Figure 10.4) to ensure feedback to the excavators that would be as close to instantaneous as possible. The categories of data—animal bones, artifacts, vegetable remains—were processed in the field, and the information from the analyses was then fed by remote access terminal to a computer in Evanston, Illinois, many miles away. Pollen and soil samples were sent directly to specialist laboratories for analysis. The effects of the data flow system are highly beneficial. The tiresome analysis of artifacts and food residues is completed on the site, and the data are available to the excavators in the field in a few days, instead of months later, as is usual. The research design can be modified in the field at short notice, with ready consultation between the team members in the field. A combination of instant data retrieval; comprehensive and meticulous collecting methods involving, among other things, flotation methods (see Chapter 13); and a systems approach to both excavation strategy and research planning have made

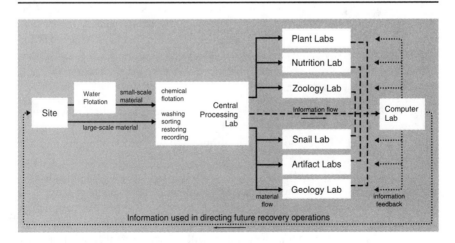

FIGURE 10.4   Data flow system of the Koster site.

the Koster project an interesting example of effectively used research design in archaeology.

In many projects, excavation is only part of the overall research design. As a method, it should be used sparingly, for the end result is always destruction of a site (Barker, 1986).

TYPES OF EXCAVATION

Archaeological excavation is designed to acquire as much raw data as possible with available financial and other resources. Its ultimate objective is to produce a three-dimensional record of an archaeological site, in which the various artifacts, structures, and other finds are placed in their correct provenance and context in time and space.

TOTAL AND SELECTIVE EXCAVATION

Total excavation of a site has the advantage of being comprehensive, but it is expensive and is undesirable because it leaves none of the site intact for excavation at a later date with, perhaps, more advanced techniques. *Selective excavation* is much more common. Many prehistoric sites are simply too large for total excavation and can only be tested selectively, using sampling methods or carefully placed trenches. Selective excavation is used to obtain stratigraphic and chronological data as well as samples of pottery, stone tools, and animal bones. From this evidence, the archaeologist can decide whether or not to undertake further excavation.

VERTICAL AND HORIZONTAL EXCAVATION

Invariably, vertical excavation is selective digging, uncovering a limited area on a site for the purpose of recovering specific information. Most vertical excavations are probes of deep archaeological deposits, their real objective being to reveal the chronological sequence at a site. Horizontal excavation is used to expose contemporaneous settlement over a larger area. *However, it should be stressed that all excavation strategies are based on decisions made as an excavation, and a research design, unfold.* The illustrations in this, and other texts for that matter, invariably show completed excavations. Thus, an archaeologist may legitimately switch from test pits to horizontal or vertical excavation, or back again, during even a short dig.

VERTICAL EXCAVATION TEST PITS   Sometimes given the French name *sondages,* are a frequently used form of vertical excavation. They consist of small trenches just large enough to accommodate one or two diggers and are designed to penetrate to the lower strata of a site to establish the extent of archaeological deposits (Figure 10.5). Test pits are dug to obtain samples of artifacts from lower layers, and this method may be supplemented by augers or borers.

Test pits are a preliminary to large-scale excavation, for the information they reveal is limited, at best. Some archaeologists will use them only outside the main area of a site, on the grounds that they will destroy critical strata. But carefully placed test pits can provide valuable insights into the stratigraphy and artifact content of a site before larger-scale excavation begins.

FIGURE 10.5   A line of test pits at Quirigua, a Maya ceremonial center,
laid out at 49.2-foot (15 m) intervals and aligned with the site grid.

Test pits are also used to obtain samples from different areas of sites, such as
shell middens, where dense concentrations of artifacts are found throughout the
deposits. In such cases, test pits are excavated on a grid pattern, positioning of the
pits being determined by statistical sampling or by a regular pattern such as alter-
nate squares.

Vertical trenches are much larger, deeper cuttings used to establish such
phenomena as sequences of building operations, histories of complex earthworks, and long cultural sequences in deep caves (Figure 10.6). Vertical trenches
have been widely used to excavate early village sites in the Near East (Moore,
1983). They may also be used to obtain a cross-section of a site threatened by
destruction or to examine outlying structures near a village or a cemetery that has
been dug on a large scale. Vertical excavations of this kind are almost always dug
in the expectation that the most important information to come from them will be
the record of layers in the walls of the trenches and the finds from them. But
clearly, the amount of information to be obtained from such cuttings is of limited
value compared to that from a larger excavation.

HORIZONTAL (AREA) EXCAVATION   Horizontal, or area, excavation is
done on a much larger scale than vertical excavation and is as close to total
excavation as archaeology can get. An area dig implies covering wide areas to
recover building plans or the layout of entire settlements, even historic gardens

FIGURE 10.6   A classic example of vertical excavation from Sir Mortimer Wheeler's excavations at Maiden Castle, Dorset, England. The recording posts on either side of the cutting and the worker in the trench give an idea of the scale of the dig.

(Figure 10.7; Figure 10.20). The only sites that almost invariably are totally excavated are very small hunting camps, isolated huts, and burial mounds.

A good example of horizontal excavation comes from St. Augustine, Florida (Deagan, 1983; Milanich and Milbrath, 1989). St. Augustine was founded on the east coast of Florida by the Spanish conquistador Pedro Menéndez de Avilés in 1565. Sixteenth-century St. Augustine was plagued with floods, fire, and hurricanes and was plundered by Sir Francis Drake in 1586. He destroyed the town, which was a military presidio and mission designed to protect Spanish treasure

FIGURE 10.7   Horizontal excavation of an open area: an Iroquois long-house at the Howlet Hill site, Onondaga, New York. The small stakes mark the house's wall posts; hearths and roof supports are found inside the house.

fleets passing through the Florida Straits. In 1702, St. Augustine was attacked by the British. The inhabitants took refuge in the Castillo de San Marcos (which still stands). The siege lasted six weeks before the attackers retreated, after burning the wooden buildings of the town to the ground. This time the colonists replaced them with masonry buildings as the town expanded in the first half of the eighteenth century.

Kathleen Deagan and a team of archaeologists have investigated eighteenth-century and earlier St. Augustine on a systematic basis since 1977, combining historic preservation with archaeological excavation. Excavating the eighteenth-century town is a difficult process on many accounts, partly because the entire archaeological deposit for three centuries is only about 3 feet (0.9 m) deep at the most, and it has been much disturbed. The excavators have cleared and recorded dozens of barrel-lined wells. They have also used horizontal excavations to uncover the foundations of eighteenth-century houses built of tabby, a cementlike substance of oyster shells, lime, and sand. The foundations of oyster shell or tabby were laid in footing trenches in the shape of the intended house (Figure 10.8). Then the walls were added. The tabby floor soon wore out, so another layer of earth was added and a new floor poured on top. Since the deposits outside the house had been disturbed, the artifacts from the foundations and floors were of great importance. And selective, horizontal excavation was the best way to uncover them.

FIGURE 10.8 Horizontal excavation at St. Augustine, Florida, showing oyster-shell house footings from an early eighteenth-century building.

The problems with horizontal digs are exactly the same as those with any
excavation: stratigraphic control and accurate measurement. Area excavations
imply exposure of large, open areas of ground to a depth of several feet. A
complex network of walls or postholes may lie within the area to be investigated.
Each feature relates to other structures, a relationship that must be carefully
recorded so that the site can be interpreted correctly, especially if several periods
of occupation are involved. If the entire area is uncovered, it is obviously difficult
to measure the position of the structures in the middle of the trench, far from the
walls at the excavation's edge. To achieve better control of measurement and
recording, it is better to use a system that gives a network of vertical stratigraphic
sections across the area to be excavated. This work is often done by laying out a
grid of square or rectangular excavation units, with walls several yards thick
between each square (see Figure 10.9). Such areas may average 12 feet (3.6 m)
square or larger. As the figure shows, this system allows stratigraphic control of
large areas. Large-scale excavation with grids is extremely expensive and time-
consuming. It is also difficult to use where the ground is irregular, but it has been
employed with great success at many excavations, being used to uncover structures, town plans, and fortifications. Many area digs are "open excavations," in
which large tracts of a site are exposed layer by layer without a grid (Figure 10.2).
    Stripping off overlying areas with no archaeological significance to expose
buried subsurface features is another type of large-scale excavation. Stripping is

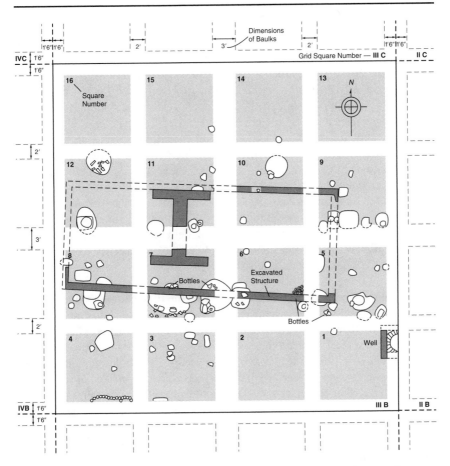

FIGURE 10.9 A horizontal-grid excavation showing the layout of squares relative to an excavated structure at Colonial Williamsburg, Virginia.

especially useful when a site is buried only a short distance below the surface and the structures are preserved in the form of postholes and other discolorations in the soil.

Horizontal excavation depends, of course, on precise stratigraphic control. It is normally combined with vertical trenches, which provide the information necessary for accurately peeling off successive horizontal layers.

TOOLS OF THE TRADE

Every archaeological site poses different technical problems, not the least of which is deciding what types of tools will be used to excavate them. The choice of digging tools radically affects the excavation as a whole. The following are some of the options.

Earth-moving equipment is often used to remove the sterile overburden covering large areas of a site or when speed of excavation is vital. Backhoes are sometimes used to cut crude test pits when sites are threatened by immediate destruction. The use of mechanical equipment is always limited, however, for such devices are highly destructive of fragile archaeological remains.

Spades, shovels, mattocks, picks, and forks are used for loosening and moving large amounts of soil. The traditional archaeological symbol is the spade, which has a flat back and a straight edge and is used for cleaning walls. Shovels, with their scooplike shape, are used for piling up earth in a trench preparatory to its being examined; they have innumerable applications in cleaning straight edges and tidying trenches, and they are the principal working tool of the archaeologist where much ground is to be uncovered.

Tools for loosening soil are the mattock, the pick, and the fork. The mattock and the pick may be considered together because they are variants on the same type of tool; when used with care, they are a delicate gauge of soil texture, an indication used often in larger sites. The traditional Near Eastern excavation used teams of pickmen, shovelers, and basket carriers to remove the soil and dump it off the site.

The most common archaeological tool is the diamond-shaped trowel, its straight edges and tip having innumerable uses: it can ease soil from a delicate specimen; the edges can scrape a feature in sandy soil into higher relief; and as a weapon of stratigraphic recording, it can trace a scarcely visible stratum line or barely discernible feature. It is also used for clearing postholes and other minor work, so much so that it is rarely out of a digger's hand on smaller sites.

Brushes are among the most useful tools, especially for dry sites. The most commonly used is the household brush, which has fairly coarse bristles that can be held by the handle or the bristles. Wielded with short strokes, it effectively cleans objects found in dry and preferably hard soil. The excavator uses various paintbrushes for more delicate jobs. The one-inch or half-inch domestic paintbrush has wide application in cleaning animal bones and coarser specimens. Fine camelhair artists' brushes are best for most delicate bones, beads, and fragile ironwork.

Small tools, some improvised on the site, aid in clearing delicate finds. Six-inch nails may be filed to a point and used for delicate cleaning jobs on bones and other fragile artifacts. The needle is another tool used to clear soil from such delicate parts of skeletons as the eye sockets and cheekbones. One of the most useful digging tools is the dental pick, available in a bewildering variety of shapes.

Screens are essential tools because many finds, such as coins, glass beads, shells, small tacks, nails, and other artifacts, are minuscule. Most deposits from sites where small artifacts are likely to occur are laboriously sifted through fine screens with openings of one-quarter to one-eighth inch or smaller. Flotation techniques are also widely used (see Chapter 13).

Surveying tools normally include lines or metal tapes, plumb bobs, string, spirit levels, drawing boards, drawing instruments, a plane table, and a surveyor's level and compass—all essential for accurate recording of site plans and sections for setting up the archaeological archive. Increasingly, field-workers use laser surveying equipment tied into a laptop computer, a technology which enables the production of three-dimensional plans, even architectural renderings of buildings.

Storage containers are vital on any excavation to pack and transport the finds to the laboratory, as well as to store them permanently. Paper and plastic bags are essential for pottery, animal bones, and other small finds; vegetal remains and other special items may require much more delicate packaging. Cardboard cartons, supermarket bags, even large oil drums can be used for storing finds.

This by no means exhausts the list of equipment at the archaeologist's disposal, for much depends on conditions in the field and the type of finds encountered.

THE PROCESS OF ARCHAEOLOGICAL EXCAVATION

The description of excavation that follows can be applied, generally, to any archaeological site. Realize, however, that very few digs are conducted under ideal conditions, with unlimited time, adequate funds, and superb facilities.

The excavator's aim should be to explain the origin of every layer and feature encountered in the site, whether natural or humanly made. It is not enough just to excavate and describe the site; one must also explain how the site was formed. This process is achieved by removing the superimposed layers of the site one by one. In so doing, the archaeologist records the full details of each layer and its contents as they are excavated. The process of archaeological excavation involves deciding where to dig, the actual digging, recording of the evidence contained in the excavation, and interpretation of the site and the processes by which it was formed.

DECIDING WHERE TO DIG

All archaeological excavation begins with making a precise surface survey and an accurate topographic map of the site. A grid is then laid out over the site (see Chapter 9). The surface survey and the collections of artifacts made as part of it determine the working hypotheses that the archaeologist uses as a basis for deciding where to dig.

The first decision to be made is whether to carry out a total or a selective excavation. This decision depends on the size of the site, its possible imminent destruction, the hypotheses to be tested, and the time and money available. Most excavations are selective. Anyone contemplating a selective dig is faced with choosing the areas of the site to be dug. The choice can be clear-cut and nonprobabilistic, or it can be based on complex sampling approaches. A selective excavation to determine the age of one of the stone uprights at Stonehenge obviously will be at the foot of the stones. But excavation of a shell midden with no surface features may be determined by sampling and selection of random grid squares that are excavated to obtain artifact samples.

In many cases, an excavation can involve both probabilistic and nonprobabilistic choices. For the Maya ceremonial center at Tikal in Guatemala (Figure 15.2), the archaeologists were eager to learn something about the hundreds of mounds that lay in the hinterland around the main ceremonial precincts (M. D. Coe, 1993). These extended at least 6 miles (10 km) from the center of the site and were identified along four strips of carefully surveyed ground, extending out from Tikal. Because, obviously, excavation of every mound and structure identified on the surface was impossible, a test-pit program was designed to collect random samples of datable pottery so that the chronological span of the occupation could be established. By using a well-designed sampling strategy, the investigators were able to select about one hundred mound structures for testing and obtain the data they sought.

The choice of where to dig can also be determined by logistical considerations, such as access to the trench, which can present problems in small caves; by the time and funds available; or, regrettably often, by the imminent destruction of part of a site that is close to industrial activity or road construction. Ideally, though, the archaeologist will dig where the results will be maximal and the chances of acquiring data to test working hypotheses are best.

The location of some excavations may be established by test digging. When Richard MacNeish (1978) surveyed the Tehuacán Valley in Mexico, he tested 39 sites with vertical trenches and selected 11 of them for more extensive excavation. The sites chosen were those from which MacNeish felt he could obtain maximal information on different chronological periods. This strategy was successful. The excavations enabled him to trace the early history of domesticated maize (see Chapter 13).

STRATIGRAPHY AND SECTIONS

The actual mechanics of archaeological excavation are best learned in the field. There is an art in the skillful use of the trowel, brush, and other implements to clear archaeological deposits (Barker, 1986). Stripping off layers exposed in a trench requires a sensitive eye for changing soil colors and textures, especially when excavating postholes and other features, and a few hours of practical experience are worth thousands of words of instructional text. Figures 10.16 through 10.20 will give some idea of the practical problems (E. C. Harris, 1989).

We touched briefly on archaeological stratigraphy in Chapter 7, where we said that the basis of all excavation is the properly recorded and interpreted stratigraphic profile (Wheeler, 1954). A section through a site gives a picture of the accumulated soils and occupation levels that constitute the ancient and modern history of the locality. Obviously, anyone recording stratigraphy needs to know as much about the history of the natural processes that the site has undergone since abandonment as about the formation of the ancient site itself (Stein, 1987). The soils that cover the archaeological finds have undergone transformations that radically affect the ways in which artifacts are preserved or moved around in the soil. Burrowing animals, later human activity, erosion, wind action, grazing cattle—all can modify superimposed layers in drastic ways (Schiffer, 1987).

Archaeological stratigraphy is usually much more complicated than geological layering, for the phenomena observed are much more localized and the effects of human behavior tend to be intensive and often involve constant reuse of the same location (Villa and Courtin, 1983). Subsequent activity can radically alter the context of artifacts, structures, and other finds. A village site can be leveled and then reoccupied by a new community that digs the foundations of its structures into the lower levels and sometimes even reuses the building materials of earlier generations. Postholes and storage pits, as well as burials, are sunk deep into older strata; their presence can be detected only by changes in soil color or the artifact content.

Here are some factors to be taken into account when interpreting stratigraphy (E. C. Harris, 1989):

- Human activities at the times in the past when the site was occupied and the effects, if any, on earlier occupations.
- Human activities, such as plowing and industrial activity, *subsequent* to final abandonment of the site (Wood and Johnson, 1978).
- Natural processes of deposition and erosion at the time of prehistoric occupation. Cave sites were often abandoned at times when the walls were shattered by frost and fragments of the rock face were showering down on the interior (Courty and others, 1993).
- Natural phenomena that have modified the stratigraphy after abandonment of the site (floods, tree uprooting, animal burrowing).

Interpreting archaeological stratigraphy involves reconstructing the depositional history of the site and then interpreting the significance of the natural and occupation levels observed. This analysis means distinguishing between types of human activity; between deposits that result from rubbish accumulation, architectural remains, and storage pits; and between activity areas and other artifact patterns.

Philip Barker, an English archaeologist and expert excavator, advocates a combined horizontal and vertical excavation for recording archaeological stratigraphy (Figure 10.6). He points out that a vertical profile gives a view of stratigraphy in the vertical plane only (Barker, 1995). Many important features appear in the section as a fine line and are decipherable only in the horizontal plane. The principal purpose of a stratigraphic profile is to record the information for posterity so that later observers have an accurate impression of how it was formed. Because stratigraphy demonstrates relationships—among sites and structures, artifacts, and natural layers—Barker advocates cumulative recording of stratigraphy, which enables the archaeologist to record layers in section and in plan at the same time. Such recording requires extremely skillful excavation. Various modifications of this technique are used in both Europe and North America.

All archaeological stratigraphy is three-dimensional; that is to say, it involves observations in both the vertical and horizontal planes. The ultimate objective of archaeological excavation is to record the three-dimensional relationships throughout a site, for these are the relationships that provide the provenance.

ARCHAEOLOGICAL RECORDING

Notebooks, or computer files, are an important part of record keeping. An archaeologist maintains a number of notebooks throughout the excavation, including the site diary or daybook. In this large notebook, he or she records all events at the site—the amount of work done, the daily schedule, the number of people on the digging team, and any labor problems that may arise. Dimensions of all sites and trenches are recorded. Any interpretations or ideas on the interpretations, even those considered and then discarded, are meticulously recorded in this book or on the computer file. Important finds and significant stratigraphic details are also noted carefully, as is much apparently insignificant information that may later prove to be vital in the laboratory. The site diary purports to be a complete record of the procedures and proceedings of the excavation. It is more than just an aid to the fallible memory of the excavator; it is a permanent record of the dig for future generations of scientists who may return to the site to amplify the original findings. For this reason, site records need to be recorded on archivally stable paper.

Site plans may vary from a simple contour plan for a burial mound or occupation midden to a complex plan of an entire prehistoric town or of a complicated series of structures (Barker, 1995). Accurate plans are important, for they provide a record not only of the site's features but also of the measurement recording grid set up prior to excavation to provide a framework for the trenching. The advent of computer aided mapping (CAD) programs and computers has made the production of accurate plans much easier in expert hands. For example, Douglas Gann (1994) has produced a three-dimensional AutoCad map of Homol'ovi Pueblo near Winslow, Arizona, which is a far more vivid reconstruction of the 150-room pueblo than any two-dimensional map. Combined with animations made with visualization software, this enables someone unfamiliar with the site to envisage what it must have been like when in use (Gann, 1994). Classical archaeologists working at Corinth have used a laser theodolite to map the ancient city. The survey has provided the first accurate spatial record of human occupation on the site from Neolithic to Byzantine times. Corinth was laid waste by the Roman general Mummius in 146 B.C., and refounded as a Roman colony by Julius Caesar in 44 B.C. The laser survey has enabled the archaeologists to reconstruct the division of the site into plots for military veterans ordered by the Romans after the destruction of the city at the end of the second century B.C.

Stratigraphic records can be drawn in a vertical plane, or they can be drawn axonometrically using axes. Any form of stratigraphic record is complex and requires not only skill in drawing but also considerable interpretive ability. The difficulty of recording varies with the site's complexity and with its stratigraphic conditions. Often, the different occupation levels, or geological events, are clearly delineated in the stratigraphic sections. On other sites, the layers may be much more complex and less visible, especially in drier climates where the soil's aridity has leached out colors. Some archaeologists have used scaled photographs or surveying instruments to record sections, the latter being essential with large sections, like those through city ramparts.

Three-dimensional recording is the recording of artifacts and structures in time and space. The provenance of archaeological finds is recorded with reference to the site grid (Figure 10.10). Three-dimensional recording is carried out with a surveyor's level, or with tapes and plumb bobs. It assumes particular importance on sites where artifacts are recorded in their original

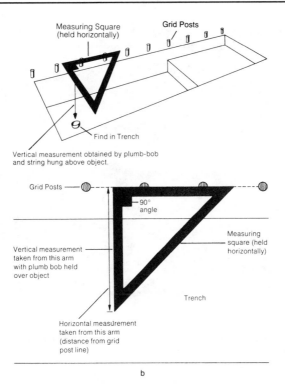

FIGURE 10.10   Three-dimensional recording the traditional way. (top) Using a measuring square. (bottom) A close view of the square from above. A horizontal measurement is taken along the edge, perpendicular to the grid post line; the vertical measurement, from that arm with a plumb bob. Electronic instruments are now commonly used for three-dimensional recording.

positions or on those where different periods in the construction of a building are being sorted out.

High technology is adding new accuracy to three-dimensional recording. By using theodolites equipped with laser beams, an excavation team can cut recording times dramatically. Harold Dibble has used the laser surveying device with great success at the La Quina Middle Palaeolithic rock shelter in southwestern France. He estimates that the device cuts recording time by 50 percent and increases accuracy by 300 to 500 percent. A small microprocessor wired to the surveyor's tool records the measurement data, eliminating handwriting. Later, back in camp, the small field computer unloads its data into a personal computer that processes the measurements and produces a color-coded diagram of the day's work. The resulting map can be analyzed in a few minutes. Dibble is also experimenting with digitized graphics to analyze and record actual artifacts (Dibble, 1987).

FIGURE 10.11   Meticulous recording of an excavation at Boomplaas Cave in South Africa, where the researchers were recovering dozens of transitory Stone Age occupation horizons and fragile environmental data. The excavation removed tiny layers of deposit, recording the positions of individual artifacts with the aid of a grid suspended from the cave roof.

Grids, units, forms, and labels are the backbone of all recording efforts. Site grids are normally laid out with painted pegs and strings stretched over the trenches when recording is necessary. Small-scale recording of complex features may involve using an even smaller grid that covers but one square of the entire site grid.

At Boomplaas Cave in South Africa, Hilary Deacon used a precise grid laid out using the cave roof to record the position of minute artifacts, features, and environmental data (Figure 10.11) (Deacon, 1979). Similar grids have been erected over underwater wrecks in the Mediterranean (Bass, 1966), although laser recording is gradually replacing this technique. The various squares in the grid and the levels of the site are designated by grid numbers (Figure 10.11), which provide the means for identifying the location of finds, as well as a basis for recording them. The labels attached to each bag or marked on the find bear the grid square numbers, which are then recorded in the site notebook.

ANALYSIS, INTERPRETATION, AND PUBLICATION

The process of archaeological excavation itself ends with filling in the trenches and transporting the finds and site records to the laboratory. The archaeologist retires from the field with a complete record of the excavations and with the data needed to test the hypotheses that were formulated before going into the field. But with this step, the job is far from finished; in fact, the work has hardly begun. The next stage in the research process is analyzing the finds, a topic covered in Chapters 13–15. Once the analysis is completed, interpretation of the site can begin (see Chapters 18–19).

In these days of high printing costs, it is impossible to publish the finds from any but the smallest sites in complete detail. Fortunately, many data retrieval systems enable us to store data on CD-ROM and microfilm so that they will be available to the specialists who need them.

Beyond publication, the archaeologist has two final obligations. The first is to place the finds and site records in a convenient repository where they will be safe and readily accessible to later generations. The second is to make the results available to a general audience as well as fellow professionals.

SPECIAL EXCAVATION PROBLEMS

Not all excavation consists of sifting through shell mounds or uncovering huge palaces. A great deal of archaeological fieldwork is dull and monotonous, but occasionally archaeologists face unexpected and exciting challenges that require special excavation techniques. Imagine being confronted with a royal grave, such as that of Tutankhamun, which took Howard Carter nearly ten years to excavate, or with the incredible complexities of the burials of the Lords of Sipán. In both sites, the excavators had to find special techniques for dealing with these fragile discoveries.

Let us examine some of the most common problems in excavation.

FRAGILE OBJECTS

Narratives of nineteenth-century excavation abound with accounts of spectacular and delicate discoveries that crumbled to dust on exposure to the air. Regrettably, similar discoveries are still made today, but many spectacular recoveries of fragile artifacts have been made. In almost every find, the archaeologist responsible has had to use great ingenuity, often with limited preservation materials on hand.

Leonard Woolley faced very difficult recovery problems when he excavated the Royal Cemetery at Ur-of-the-Chaldees in the 1920s (Woolley, 1954). In one place, he recovered an offering stand of wood, gold, and silver, portraying a he-goat with his front legs on the branches of a thicket, by pouring paraffin wax over the scattered remains. Later, he rebuilt the stand in the laboratory and restored it to a close approximation of the original.

Conservation of archaeological finds has become a highly specialized field of endeavor (Plenderleith and Werner, 1973) which covers every form of find, from textiles to leather, human skin, and basketry. Many conservation efforts, like those used to preserve the Danish bog corpses, can take years to complete (Glob, 1969). One of the largest conservation efforts was mounted at Ozette, Washington, where the sheer volume of waterlogged wooden artifacts threatened to overwhelm the excavators. The finds that needed treatment ranged from tiny fishhooks to entire planks. A large conservation laboratory was set up in Neah

Bay, where the finds were processed after transportation from the site. Many objects were left to soak in polyethylene glycol to replace the water that had penetrated into the wood cells, a treatment that takes years for large objects. The results of this major conservation effort can be seen in the Neah Bay Museum, where many of the artifacts are preserved (Kirk, 1974).

BURIALS

Human remains have been encountered either as isolated finds or in the midst of a settlement site. Some projects are devoted to excavating an entire cemetery. In all cases in which graves are excavated, the burial and its associated grave, funerary furniture, and ornamentation are considered as a single excavation unit or grave lot.

Excavation of burials is a difficult and routine task that must be performed with care because of the delicacy and often bad state of the bones. The record of the bones' position and the placement of the grave goods and body orna-ments is as important as the association of the burial, for the archaeological objective is reconstructing burial customs as much as establishing chronology (J. E. Anderson, 1969). Although the Maya lords of Mesoamerica were some-times buried under great pyramids, as at Palenque, where the Lord Pacal lay under the Temple of the Inscriptions, most burials are normally located by means of a simple surface feature, such as a gravestone or a pile of stones, or through an accidental discovery during excavation. Once the grave outline has been found, the skeleton is carefully exposed from above. The first part of the skeleton to be identified will probably be the skull or one of the limb bones. The main outline of the burial is then traced before the delicate backbone, feet, and finger bones are uncovered. The greatest care is taken not to displace the bones or any of the orna-ments or grave goods that surround them (Stirland, 1987). Normally, the under-surfaces of the bones are left in the soil so that the skeleton may be recorded photographically before removal (Figure 10.12). Either the burial is removed bone by bone, or it is removed as a single unit to the laboratory, where it is cleaned at leisure. This technique is expensive and is used only when a skeleton is of outstanding scientific importance.

Some burials are deposited in funerary chambers so elaborate that the contents of the tomb may reveal information not only on the funeral rites but also, as in the Sumerian royal burials at Ur, on the social order of the royal court (Chapter 16).

The great royal tombs of the Shang civilization of northern China are an example of complex tombs, where careful excavation made possible recording of many chariot features that otherwise would have been lost (Chang, 1980). The shaft, axle, and lower parts of the chariot wheels were visible only as discolored areas in the ground.

Excavation of American Indian burials has generated furious political controversy in recent years, with native groups arguing that it is both illegal and unethical to dig up even the prehistoric dead. Reburial and repatriation legislation now restricts the excavation of ancient burials. Many collections are now being returned to their historic owners for reburial (Powell and others, 1993). (See also Chapter 19.) In some states, like California, it is now illegal to disturb ancient Native American burial grounds (D. Anderson, 1985).

FIGURE 10.12 A Classic Maya collective tomb at Gualan in the Motagua Valley of Guatemala. Note the clean excavation, the carefully brushed skeletons, and the stone lining of the tomb.

Human skeletons are a valuable source of information on prehistoric populations. The bones can be used to identify the sex and age of a burial, as well as to study ancient diseases. A whole series of new techniques are revolutionizing studies of prehistoric diet, and even DNA (Chapman and others, 1981; Stirland, 1987).

STRUCTURES AND PITS

Open excavations are normally used to uncover structures of considerable size (Barker, 1995). Grids allow stratigraphic control over the building site, especially over the study of successive occupation stages. Many such structures may have been built of perishable materials like wood or matting. Wooden houses are normally recognized by the postholes of the wall timbers and,

FIGURE 10.13 Mud-brick structures are especially hard to excavate, for the brick is often virtually indistinguishable from the surrounding soil. Here archaeologists uncover the mud-brick foundations of the Oval Temple at Khafaje, Iraq, c. 2500 B.C.

sometimes, foundation trenches. Clay walls collapse into a pile when a hut is burned or falls down; thus the wall clay may bear impressions of matting, sticks, or thatch. Stone and mud-brick structures are often better preserved, especially if mortar was used, although sometimes the stone has been removed by later builders, and only foundation trenches remain (Figure 10.13). Stratigraphic cross sections across walls give an insight into the structure's history. The dating of most stone structures is complicated, especially when successive rebuilding or occupation of the building is involved (Figure 10.14).

Some of the most spectacular buildings in the archaeological record leave few traces on the surface. Figure 10.7 shows an Iroquois longhouse that was

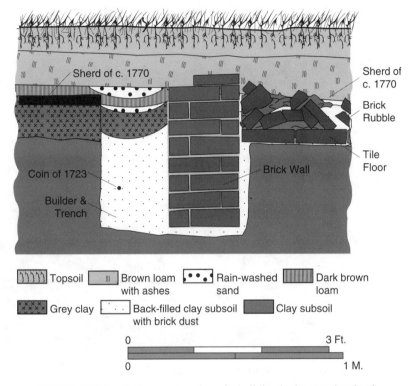

FIGURE 10.14 Dating construction of a building by its associated artifacts. The brick wall was built in a foundation trench that was filled with
brick dust and clay. Someone dropped a coin dating to 1723 into the clay
as the trench was being filled. Obviously, then, the building of which the
wall forms a part dates to no earlier than 1723.

identified purely from subsurface markings in the soil. Numerous longhouses
from early farming sites in Europe have been identified in the same way.

The pueblos of the American Southwest offer another type of problem in
excavation. The many rooms of the pueblos contain complicated deposits full of
occupation debris and many artifacts (Figure 10.15). Such assemblages can be
used to identify the activities carried out in different spaces.

Storage and rubbish pits are commonly found on archaeological sites and
may reach several meters in depth (Figure 10.16). Their contents furnish important information on dietary habits, data gleaned from food residues or caches of
seeds. Trash pits are even more informative. Garbage pits and privies at Colonial
Williamsburg have yielded a host of esoteric finds, including wax seals from
documents that were used as toilet tissue (Noël Hume, 1969). Some historic pits
can be dated from military buttons and other finds.

Storage and trash pits are normally identified by circular discolorations in
the soil. The contents are then cross-sectioned, and the associated finds are
analyzed as an associated unit (Figure 10.16). Large pits, which may contain

FIGURE 10.15   The Cliff Palace at Mesa Verde, Colorado, an Anasazi pueblo from the northern Southwest.

thousands of seeds and other informative materials, are excavated with particular care.

Postholes are normally associated with houses and other such structures. The posts they once contained were buried in holes that were dug larger than the base of the post itself. Once the structure was abandoned, the post might be left to rot, might be removed, or might be cut off. The traces each of these outcomes leaves in the ground differ sharply and can be identified with careful excavation. Sometimes it is possible to find fragments of the post or of the charcoal from its burning, which enable archaeologists to identify the type of wood used.

Each archaeological site offers challenges to the investigator, including preservation, recording, or interpretation. Though individual methods may vary from site to site and from area to area, the fundamental objective is the same—recovering and recording data from below the ground as systematically and scientifically as possible.

Figures 10.17 through 10.20 constitute a picture essay on archaeological excavation. The pictures illustrate the great variety of excavation problems encountered by archaeologists around the world.

FIGURE 10.16   A double storage pit at Maiden Castle, Dorset, England, that was cut into the chalk subsoil.

SUMMARY

- Excavation is a primary way in which archaeologists acquire subsurface data about the past. Modern archaeologists tend to carry out as little excavation as possible, however, because digging archaeological sites destroys a finite resource—the archaeological record.
- Modern excavations are often conducted by multidisciplinary research teams made up of specialists from several disciplines, who work together on a carefully formulated research design.

FIGURE 10.17   Excavation at the FxJj50 site, Koobi Fora, Kenya. This is an early hominid site, a scatter of broken animal bones and stone artifacts more than 2 million years old.

- All archaeological excavation is destruction of a finite resource. Accurate methods for planning, recording, and observation are essential.
- The Koster site in Illinois, where the excavators devised a sophisticated data flow system to keep their research design up-to-date, illustrates the essential research design.
- Sites can be excavated totally or, as is more common, selectively. Vertical excavation is used to test stratigraphy and to make deep probes of archaeological deposits. Test pits, often combined with various sampling methods, are dug to give an overall impression of an unexcavated site before major digging begins. Horizontal or area excavation is used to uncover far wider areas and especially to excavate site layouts and buildings.
- The process of archaeological excavation begins with a precise site survey and establishment of a site recording grid. A research design is formulated, and hypotheses are developed for testing. Placement of trenches is determined by locating likely areas or by sampling methods. Excavation involves not only digging but also recording of stratigraphy and the proveniences of finds, as well as observations of the processes that led to the site's formation.
- Careful stratigraphic observation in three dimensions is the basis of all good excavation and is used to demonstrate relationships among layers and between layers and artifacts.

FIGURE 10.18   Galatea Bay shell midden, North Island, New Zealand.
An exemplary excavation through the midden (a dump of remains and occupation debris, including shells, fish bones, ash, and occasional artifacts).
Sampling is often used to dig such sites (Shawcross, 1967; Terrell, 1967).

- Excavation is followed by analysis and interpretation and, finally, publication of the finds to provide a permanent record of the work carried out.
- Among the special excavation problems we discussed were the recovery of fragile objects and human skeletons and the digging of postholes and structures.

GUIDE TO FURTHER READING

Barker, Philip. *Understanding Archaeological Excavation*. London: Batsford, 1986. An expert guide to excavation. Strong British orientation.

Bray, Tamara L., and Killion, Thomas W., eds. *Reckoning with the Dead: The Larsen Bay Repatriation and the Smithsonian Institution*. Washington D.C.: Smithsonian Institution Press, 1994. An absolutely superb discussion of a

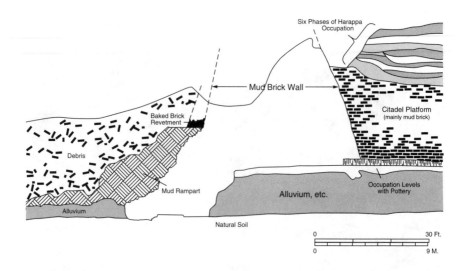

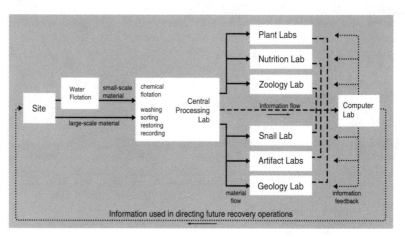

FIGURE 10.19 City mounds and other mound sites (Rosen, 1986). (top) Stratigraphic profile through the ramparts of the ancient city of Harappa in the Indus Valley, Pakistan. (bottom) Photograph of the actual excavation, a deep probe into the depths of the city's citadel. Vertical excavation provided the history of the defenses. The right of the top illustration is the back of the back of this picture.

controversial case study in repatriation, which includes valuable information on the Native American perspective.

Dancey, W. S. *Archaeological Field Methods: An Introduction.* Minneapolis: Burgess, 1981. An excellent brief survey of American fieldwork approaches.

Frankel, David. *Remains to Be Seen.* Melbourne, Australia: Longman Cheshire, 1991. A simple manual of Australian archaeology that is crammed with helpful insights about archaeological methods in general; for the beginning reader. Excellent illustrations.

FIGURE 10.20   The ultimate in horizontal excavation: King Henry VIII's Privy Garden at Hampton Court, England, has been restored after archaeological excavations by Brian Dix of Northamptonshire Archaeology located the outlines of flower beds and other features.

Joukowsky, Martha. *Complete Manual of Field Archaeology.* Englewood Cliffs, N.J.: Prentice Hall, 1981. A comprehensive survey of excavation methods in both New World and Old World contexts. Recommended for general reading.

Wheeler, R. E. M. *Archaeology from the Earth.* Oxford: Clarendon Press, 1954. An archaeological classic that describes excavation on a grand scale with verve and elegance. A must for every archaeologist's bookshelf, if only for its common-sense information.

ANALYZING THE PAST

ARTIFACTS AND TECHNOLOGY

Intelligence . . . is the faculty of making artificial objects, especially tools to make tools.

Henry Bergson
L'Evolution Créatrice, 1907

Part Five begins our exploration of archaeology's ultimate objectives: constructing culture history, reconstructing past lifeways, and studying cultural process. Upon returning from the field, we begin by sorting the data that come from the excavation into categories. From there we concentrate on artifacts and prehistoric technology. We outline the basic principles of archaeological classification and examine the ways in which ancient peoples used organic and inorganic raw materials. Proper understanding of technology, its uses, and its limitations is an essential preliminary to any discussion of prehistoric lifeways and culture change in the past.

11

IDENTIFYING AND CLASSIFYING DATA

Once fieldwork is over, the archaeologist confronts an enormous task: organizing, analyzing, and interpreting the data. This chapter describes the processes of identifying and classifying artifacts.

Artifact analysis starts in the field alongside excavation—processing and organizing the finds so that they can be analyzed and interpreted. At the same time, the excavator keeps an eye on the data flowing from the trenches and plans further excavation to obtain larger samples, if they are required.

These first stages in processing newly excavated archaeological data are entirely routine. Most excavations maintain some form of field laboratory. It is here that the major site records are kept and developed, stratigraphic profile drawings are kept up to date, and radiocarbon samples and other special finds are packed for examination by specialists. A small team staffs the field laboratory. They ensure that all finds are cleaned, processed promptly, packed carefully, and labeled and recorded precisely. A successful laboratory operation allows the director of the excavation to evaluate the available data daily, even hourly. It is here, too, that basic conservation work is carried out, reassembling fragmented pots, hardening bones with chemicals, or stabilizing fragile objects. Computers play an important role in the field laboratory, for they are used to code vast quantities of information for later use.

CLASSIFYING ARTIFACTS

Our attitude toward life and our surroundings involves constant classification and sorting of massive quantities of data. We classify types of eating utensils: knives, forks, and spoons—each type has a different use and is kept in a separate compartment in the drawer. We group roads according to their surface, finish, and size. A station wagon is classified separately from a truck. In addition to classifying artifacts, lifestyles, and cultures, we make choices among them. If we are eating soup, we choose to use a spoon. Some people eat rice with a fork, some use chopsticks or their fingers, and others have decided that a spoon is more suitable. A variety of choices is available, the final decision often being dictated by cultural custom rather than by functional pragmatism.

All people classify, because doing so is a requirement for abstract thought and language. But everyday classes are not often best for archaeological purposes. In our daily life we habitually use classification as a tool for our lifestyle. Like the computer, however, it should be a servant rather than a master. Sometimes our classifications of good and bad—those based on color of skin or on our definitions of what is moral or immoral—are made and then adhered to as binding principles of life without ever being questioned or modified, no matter how much our circumstances may change. The dogmatism and rigidity that result from these attitudes are as dangerous in archaeology as they are in daily life. In archaeology, classification is a research tool, a means for ordering data. All classifications used by archaeologists follow directly from the problems they are studying. Let us say that our prehistorian is studying changes in pottery designs over a 500-year period in the Southwest. The classification he or she uses will follow not only from what other people have done but also from the problems being studied. How and even what you classify stems directly from the research questions asked of the data. Because the objectives of classifications may change according to the problems being investigated, archaeologists must be sensitive to the need for revising their classifications when circumstances require it.

TAXONOMY AND SYSTEMATICS

Taxonomy is the name given to the system of classifying concepts, materials, objects, and phenomena used in many sciences, including archaeology. The taxonomies of biology, botany, geology, and some other disciplines can be highly sophisticated. Some are very rigid systems that were created in the nineteenth and early twentieth centuries, and many are now outgrown. In contrast, archaeology has built its own taxonomy of specialist terminologies and concepts quite haphazardly. Universal comparisons and classifications have been a virtual impossibility. British archaeologists refer to *cultures,* North American scholars refer to *phases,* and the French to *civilizations.* Each term has basically the same meaning, but the subtle differences stem from cultural traditions and from different field situations (Dunnell, 1986b).

Systematics is essentially a way of creating units that can be used to categorize things as a basis for explaining archaeological or other phenomena (Dunnell, 1971). It is a means of creating units of classification within a scientific discipline. Biologists classify human beings within a hierarchy of classification developed by Carl Linnaeus in the eighteenth century. It begins with the kingdom *Animalia,* the phylum *Chordata* (animals with notochords and gill slits), the subphylum *Vertebrata* (animals with backbones), the class *Mammalia,* the subclass *Eutheria,* the order *Primates,* the suborder *Hominoidea* (apes and hominidae), the family *Hominidae,* the genus *Homo,* the species *sapiens,* and, finally, the subspecies *sapiens.* This hierarchy is gradually refined down until only *Homo sapiens sapiens* remains in its own taxonomic niche. The biological classification just described is based on each form having common progenitors or just similarities. It consists of empirically defined units arranged in the form of a hierarchy. Each element in the hierarchy is defined and related to the others. Classification in archaeology is a matter of using a classification closely related to the problem being studied.

OBJECTIVES OF CLASSIFICATION

As we have stated, classification in archaeology depends on the problem being studied. Four major objectives can be identified, however:

1. *Organizing data into manageable units.* This step is part of the preliminary data-processing operation, and it commonly involves separating finds on the basis of raw material (stone, bone, and so on) or artifacts from food remains. This preliminary ordering allows much more detailed classification later on.

2. *Describing types.* By identifying the individual features (attributes) of hundreds of artifacts, or clusters of artifacts, the archaeologist can group them, by common attributes, into relatively few types. These types represent patterns of separate associations of attributes. Such types are economical ways of describing large numbers of artifacts. Which attributes are chosen depends on the purpose of the typology.

   Artifact types (sometimes called archaeological types) are based on criteria set up by archaeologists as a convenient way of studying ancient tool kits and technology. They are a useful scientific device that provides a manageable way of classifying small and large collections of prehistoric tools and the by-products from manufacturing them.

3. *Identifying relationships between types.* Describing types provides a hierarchy, which orders the relationships between artifacts. These stem, in part, from the use of a variety of raw materials, manufacturing techniques, and functions.

   These three objectives are much used in culture-historical research. Processual archaeologists may use classification for a fourth:

4. *Studying assemblage variability in the archaeological record.* These studies are often combined with middle-range research on dynamic, living cultural systems (see Chapter 14).

   Archaeological classifications are artificial formulations based on criteria set up by archaeologists. These classificatory systems, however, do not necessarily coincide with those developed by the people who made the original artifacts (Willey and Phillips, 1958; Dunnell, 1986b).

TYPOLOGY

Typology is a system of classification based on the construction of types. It is a search for patterns among either objects or the variables that define these objects, a search that has taken on added meaning and complexity as archaeologists have begun to use computer technology and sophisticated statistical methods. This kind of typology is totally different from arbitrarily dividing up the objects and variables. I remember sitting in a Cambridge archaeological laboratory many years ago and learning the basics of stone tool classification. Our instructor laid out a series of Acheulian hand axes in front of us, magnificent specimens from the gravels of the Thames River (Figure 2.4). He divided them into different categories. "These are pointed axes, these ovates (oval-shaped), these ovates with twisted edges, these linguate, with tongue-shaped ends," he declared. One of us pointed out that some of the axes in the "pointed" category were far from ideal examples of the form; in fact, one or two were distinctly oval. "They are pointed hand axes," pronounced our instructor firmly, brooking no disagreement. The arbitrariness of his classifications was just like that used by a stamp collector classifying postage stamps. It was as if prehistoric hand axes were all standardized productions turned out by an impersonal stone-flaking machine. Lost was the opportunity to examine the underlying patterns of human design and behavior, which is what interests archaeologists more than mere classification.

Typology enables archaeologists to construct arbitrarily defined units of analysis that apply to two or more samples of artifacts, so that these samples can be compared objectively. These samples can come from different sites, or from separate levels of the same site. Typology is classification to permit comparison, an opportunity to examine underlying patterns of human design and behavior (W. Adams and E. Adams, 1991; J. A. Brown, 1982). The value of typology is that it enables you to compare what has been found at two sites or in different levels of the same site. Typology, as James Deetz (1967) puts it, has one main aim: "classification which permits comparison. . . . Such a comparison allows the archaeologist to align his assemblage with others in time and space." Let us look over a group of archaeologists' shoulders as they sort through a large pile of potsherds, from one occupation level, on the laboratory table.

First the sherds are separated by decoration or lack of it, paste, temper, firing methods, and vessel shape. Once the undecorated or shapeless potsherds have been counted and weighed, they are put to one side, unless they have some special significance. Then the remaining sherds are examined individually and divided into types, according to the features they display. Soon a number of piles are on the table: one consists of sherds painted with black designs; a second, red-painted fragments; a third, a group of plain sherds that come from shallow platters. Once the preliminary sort is completed, the archaeologists look over each pile in turn. They have already identified three broad types in the pottery collection. But when they examine the first pile more closely, they find that the black-painted sherds can be divided into several smaller groupings: one with square, black panels; another with diamond designs; and a third with black-dotted decoration. The other two major piles also yield several subtypes. Eventually, the original three types become nine as the archaeologists study the collection in minute detail, identifying dozens—if not hundreds—of attributes, conspicuous and inconspicuous, stylistic or dimensional, even some based on chemical analyses. These data are programmed into a computer in preparing for the quantitative analyses that will help sort out discrete types and variations among them. This is the process of typology, classifying artifacts so that one type can be compared with another. Obviously, the nine types from this one site can be compared with other arbitrary types found during laboratory sorting of collections from nearby sites.

For accurate and meaningful comparisons to be made, rigorous definitions of analytical types are needed, to define not only the "norm" of the artifact type but also its approximate range of variation, at either end of which one type becomes one of two others. Conventional analytical definitions are usually couched in terms of one or more attributes that indicate how the artifact was made, the shape, the decoration, or some other feature that the maker wanted the finished product to display. These definitions are set up following carefully defined technological differences, often bolstered by measurements or statistical clusterings of attributes. Most often, the average artifact, rather than the variation between individual examples, is the ultimate objective of the definition. A classifier who finds a group, or even an individual artifact, that deviates at all conspicuously from the norm often erects a new analytical type. "Splitters" tend to proliferate types, and "lumpers" do the opposite. The whole operation is more or less objective (Dunnell, 1971).

TYPES

All of us have feelings and reactions about any artifact, whether it is a magnificent wooden helmet from the Pacific Northwest coast (Figure 11.1), or a simple acorn pounder from the southern California interior. Our immediate instinct is to look at and classify these and other prehistoric artifacts from our own cultural standpoint. That is, of course, what prehistoric peoples did as well. The owners of the tools archaeologists study classified them into groups for themselves, each one having a definite role in their society. We assign different roles in eating to a knife, a fork, and a spoon. Knives cut meat; steak knives are used in eating steaks. The prehistoric

FIGURE 11.1   Tlingit carved ceremonial wooden helmet from the Pacific Northwest coast, a "natural" type, classified as such when found in an archaeological context. This artifact would obviously be classified as a helmet from the perspective of our cultural experience. (Height, 9 inches; width, 10 inches [23/25cm])

arrowhead is employed in the chase; one type of missile head is used to hunt deer, another to shoot birds, and so on. The use of an artifact may be determined not only by convenience and practical considerations but also by custom or regulation. The light-barbed spearheads used by some Australian hunting bands to catch fish are too fragile for dispatching a kangaroo; the special barbs permit the impaled fish to be lifted out of the water. Pots are made by women in most African and American Indian societies, which have division of labor by sex; each has formed complicated customs, regulations, or taboos, which, functional considerations apart, categorize clay pots into different types with varying uses and rules in the culture (Figure 11.2).

FIGURE 11.2   A Chumash parching tray. A good example of the difficulties in archaeological classification. This finely crafted basket was
made by the Chumash Indians of southern California (Deetz, 1967). It
was made by weaving plant fibers. The design was formed in the maker's
mind by several factors, most important of which is the tremendous reservoir of cultural experience that the Chumash have learned, generation by
generation, over the several thousand years that they have lived in southern California. The designs of their baskets are almost unconscious and
relate to the feeling that such and such a form and color are "correct" and
traditionally acceptable. But there are more pragmatic and complex
reasons, too, including the flat, circular shape that enables the user to
roast seeds by tossing them with red embers.
    Each attribute of the basket has a good reason for its presence—
whether traditional, innovative, functional, or imposed by the technology
used to make it. The band of decoration around the rim is a feature of the
decorative tradition of the Chumash and occurs on most of their baskets. It
has a rich red-brown color from the species of reed used to make it. The
steplike decoration was dictated by the sewing and weaving techniques, but
the diamond pattern is unique, the innovative stamp of one weaver, which
might or might not be adopted by other craftspeople in later generations.
The problem for the archaeologist is to measure the variations in human
artifacts and to establish the causes behind, and directions of, change—and
to find what these variations can be used to measure. This fine parching tray
is a warning that variations in human artifacts are both complex and subtle.

Furthermore, each society has its own conception of what a particular artifact should look like. Americans have generally preferred larger cars, Europeans
small ones. These preferences reflect not only pragmatic considerations of road
width and longer distances in the New World but also differing attitudes toward
traveling and, for many Americans, a preoccupation with prestige manifested in
gold-leaf lettering and custom colors, hubcabs, and style. The steering wheel is
on the left, and the car is equipped with turn signals and seat belts by law. In
other words, we know what we want and expect an automobile to look like, even
though minor design details change—as do the length of women's skirts and the
width of men's ties.

Archaeologists have to devise archaeological types that are appropriate to
the research problems they are tackling, an extremely difficult task. In archaeology, a type is a grouping of artifacts created for comparison with other groups.
This grouping may or may not coincide with the actual tool types designated by
the original makers. A good example comes from the world-famous Olduvai
Gorge site in East Africa, where Louis and Mary Leakey excavated a series of
cache sites used by very early humans, *Homo habilis*. Mary Leakey studied the
stone tools and grouped them in the "Oldowan tradition," a tradition characterized by jagged-edged chopping tools and flakes (M. D. Leakey, 1971). She
based her classifications on close examination of the artifacts, and an assumption that the first human tool kit was based on crude stone choppers soon
became archaeological dogma. Recently, Nicholas Toth of Indiana University
has taken a radically different approach to classifying Oldowan artifacts (Toth
and Schick, 1993). He has spent many hours not only studying and classifying
the original artifacts, but also learning Oldowan technology for himself, replicating hundreds of artifacts made by *Homo habilis* 2 million years ago. His
controlled experiments have shown that *Homo habilis* was not using chopping
tools at all. The primeval stone workers were more interested in the sharp-edged
flakes they knocked off lumps of lava, for cutting and butchering the game meat
they scavenged from predator kills. The "chopping tools" were, in fact, just
cores or the end product of knocking flakes off convenient lumps of lava.
Controlled experiments like Toth's provide useful insights into how prehistoric
peoples manufactured the tools they needed. Toth and other experts are now
trying to study the telltale patterns of edge wear on the cutting edges of
Oldowan flakes, for the polish, striations, and micro-flake scars left by working,
for example, fresh bone as opposed to hide or wood are highly distinctive. With
controlled experimentation and careful examination of edge wear, they hope to
achieve a closer marriage between the ways in which the first humans used
stone tools and the classifications devised by the archaeologist hundreds of
thousands of years later.

Everyone agrees that a type is based on clusters of similar attributes or on
clusters of objects. Although patterns of attributes may be fairly easy to identify,
how do archaeologists know what is a type and what is not? Should they try to
reproduce the categories of pot that the makers themselves conceived? Or
should they just go ahead and create "archaeological" types designed purely for
analytical purposes? Herein lies the hub of the controversy about types in
archaeology.

The archaeologist constructs typologies based on the reoccurrence of formal patterns of physical features of artifacts. Many of these formal types have restricted distributions in space and time, which suggest they represent distinctive "styles" of construction and/or tasks that were carried out in the culture to which they belong. For example, the so-called Chavín art style was widespread over much of coastal and highland Peru after 900 B.C. The jaguar, snake, and human forms of this art are highly characteristic, and mark the spread of a distinctive iconography over a large area of the Andean region. Chavín art, and the characteristic styles associated with it, had a specific role in Peruvian society of the time (Figure 17.2).

Archaeologists tend to use four "types of types," described briefly here, which, in practice, are rarely separated one from another, for experts tend to draw this kind of information from more general classifications of artifacts (Steward, 1955) (Figure 11.3).

DESCRIPTIVE Descriptive types are the most elementary, with descriptions based solely on the form of the artifact—physical or external properties. The descriptive type is used when the use or cultural significance of the object or practice is unknown. For example, the excavations at Snaketown in Arizona

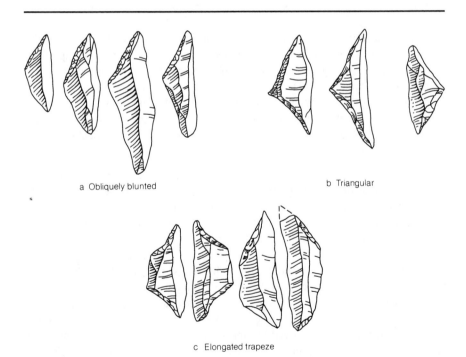

a Obliquely blunted

b Triangular

c Elongated trapeze

FIGURE 11.3 Some 9,000-year-old stone artifacts from Star Carr, England (actual size). You can classify these by descriptive type as geometric stone tools, by chronological type as Mesolithic microliths, Star Carr forms, and by functional type as microlithic arrowhead barbs.

revealed a "large basin-like depression," a mysterious feature that also turned up at other Hohokam sites in the Southwest. This descriptive type was subsequently proven to be a ball court, and so the noncommittal descriptive classification was abandoned in favor of a functional one that defined the structure's role in Hohokam culture. Descriptive types are commonly used for artifacts from early prehistory, when functional interpretations are much harder to reach (Figure 2.4). For instance, the famous prehistoric stone circles found throughout Britain are usually classified as just that, because we have no idea what their purpose was, except for a general impression that they had a ritual and symbolic function.

CHRONOLOGICAL   Chronological types are defined by form, but are time markers. They are types with chronological significance. Like descriptive types, they are part of a culture's inventory as reflected in the archaeological record, but are widely used to distinguish chronological differences. For example, on the Great Plains of North America, Clovis and Folsom points were used for short periods of prehistoric time, the former for about five centuries from about 9500 to 9000 B.C. Projectile points have long been used as chronological markers in North American archaeology. Chronological types are defined in terms of attributes that show change over time. The archaeologist compares artifacts known to be of different ages. Certain attributes are observed to be different, so he or she uses them to define the types.

The great Egyptologist Flinders Petrie used chronological types when he studied the pre-Dynastic jars from Diospolis Parva on the Nile (Chapter 7). Chronological types figure prominently in Southwestern archaeology and were used by Alfred Kidder (1924) in his classic excavations at Pecos. Such types have the disadvantage that they are often hard for an archaeologist other than their originator to duplicate owing to poor definitions of different types, except under favorable conditions or by archaeologists who have received identical extensive training (Sackett, 1977).

FUNCTIONAL   Functional types are based on cultural use or role in their user's culture rather than on outward form or chronological position. The same artifacts can be treated as of the functional type or the descriptive one. You can classify an assemblage in broad categories: "wood," "bone," "stone," and so on. But equally well, you may adopt a functional classification: "weapons," "clothing," "food preparation," and so on.

Ideally, functional types should reflect the precise roles and functional classifications made by the members of the society from which they came. Needless to say, such an objective is very difficult to achieve because of incomplete preservation and lack of written records. We have no means of visualizing the complex roles that some artifacts achieved in prehistoric society. Although in some cases obvious functional roles, such as that of an arrowhead for hunting or warfare or of a pot for carrying water, can be correctly established in the laboratory, functional classifications are necessarily restricted and limited. Let us consider a Scandinavian flint dagger (Figure 11.4)—a beautifully made, pressure-flaked tool, a copy of the bronze daggers so fashionable at the time in central Europe. This tool has been classified by generations of archaeologists as a dagger, by

FIGURE 11.4   A pressure-flaked Scandinavian flint dagger. (After Oakley; one-half actual size)

implication a weapon of war and defense, worn by Scandinavian farmers who still had no metal and made a slavish imitation of a more advanced metal tool. This instinctive designation may seem obvious, but we really do not know whether our functional classification is correct. Does use-wear on the blade show a dagger was actually used in warfare and for personal defense? Was it a weapon, or was it purely an object of prestige for the owner, perhaps with some religious function?

STYLISTIC   Stylistic types are best exemplified by items such as clothing, because style is often used to convey information through public display. The Aztecs of central Mexico lived in a ranked society in which everyone's dress was carefully regulated by sumptuary laws (Anawalt, 1981). Thus a glance at the noble in the marketplace could reveal not only his rank but also the number of prisoners he had taken in battle and many other subtle distinctions. Even the gods had their own regalia and costumes that reflected their roles in the pantheon (Figure 11.5)

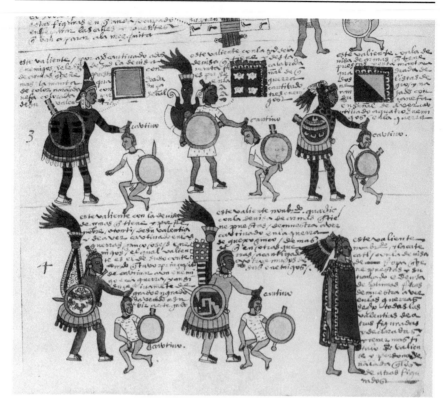

FIGURE 11.5   Aztec warriors in their elaborate uniforms with their captives. The Aztecs had strict sumptuary laws, which governed the uniform of each grade of warrior. (From the *Codex Mendoza*)

(R. F. Townsend, 1992). Stylistic types may have a structure entirely different from that of functional ones. They are not used often in archaeological classification, except when historical records are available (Conkey and Hastorf, 1990; Plog, 1983).

PROCESSES OF ARCHAEOLOGICAL CLASSIFICATION

As we have emphasized, archaeological classification is the ordering of data on the basis of shared characteristics. But how do archaeologists go about this process, and what procedures do they use to do so (Dunnell, 1986b)?

Traditionally, classification has been based on the archaeologist's "concept of types," subject of one of the great controversies in archaeology. On a formal level, a type can be defined as "a group or class of items that is internally cohesive and separated from other groups by one or more discontinuities" (Whallon and Brown, 1982). Until the late 1950s, almost all archaeological classification was qualitative, based to a great extent on instinct and experience rather than on numerical methods or empirical testing. The new perspectives on the archaeological record that emerged in the 1960s coincided with a new generation of quantitative techniques that bear on the traditional problem of archaeological classification, techniques that are revolutionizing typology. (For a comprehensive discussion, see Shennan, 1988.)

QUANTITATIVE METHODS

The concept of quantitative methods has great breadth in archaeology. It refers not only to the standard techniques of statistical analysis and inference that readily come to mind but also to various techniques of numerical analysis and numerical manipulation, as well as graphical techniques for displaying data so that the patterns in the data are more readily apparent. Modern archaeology relies heavily on all manner of quantitative methods. In fact, quantitative methods are now central to archaeology in that the descriptive and explanatory power inherent in those methods and the carefully structured reasoning behind the methods provide us with very powerful tools for answering such fundamental questions as "How old is it?" "Where does it come from?" and "What was it used for?"

An understanding of the process of applying quantitative methods to archaeological problems and a basic level of computer literacy are fundamental skills for all modern archaeologists. Quantitative methods are no longer the sole province of the specialist but rather are fundamental tools employed by all archaeologists at some level. There are certainly some cases where very specialized data require arcane analyses and approach requiring specialist expertise (Shennan, 1988; Thomas, 1989). In general, however, some very sophisticated techniques are performed almost routinely by most practicing archaeologists today. There are three fundamental issues in applying quantitative methods to archaeological problems. The first is realizing when quantitative methods can aid in resolving a problem. The second is being familiar enough with various techniques and their underlying assumptions to know which techniques are appropriate to specific kinds of archaeological problems. Finally, the third issue revolves around being familiar enough with the data, the methods, and general anthropological theory to formulate a reasonable interpretation of the analytical results that has meaning in terms of the ultimate topic of archaeology—human behavior.

Quantitative methods are valuable in archaeology in three broad areas: data exploration and characterization, data description, and hypothesis testing or confirmation. It is important to keep in mind the distinction between descriptive techniques and confirmatory or inferential techniques. The former term applies to economic methods of describing sets of data in ways that are useful to other researchers and preserve the inherent structure of the data. The latter refers to methods aimed at inferring the characteristics of an unobservable population on the basis of the characteristics of a sample taken from that population and providing some guide as to the reliability of the inference.

EXPLORATION   In recent years, a new suite of analytical tools has been added to the archaeologist's repertoire. These tools rely on a slightly different way of thinking about archaeological data, as well as new ways of looking at the data. Collectively known as exploratory data analysis (EDA), these techniques have been specifically designed to aid in detecting patterns and deviations in sets of data by relying heavily on visual displays of data rather than on summary statistics and statistical significance tests. Two basic principles lie behind these techniques. First, the fastest, most sophisticated pattern recognition hardware and software known are the human eye and brain. To the extent that large quantities of data can be reorganized and presented in a graphical rather than numerical form, the researcher can more readily detect patterns and deviations in the data that may have important implications for the problem at hand. The proliferation of microcomputers and minicomputers with graphics capabilities in the 1980s dramatically accelerated the development and acceptance of these techniques among archaeologists and other scientists. The second principle is a basic assumption about the structure of data sets. In EDA parlance, a set of observations can be divided into a general pattern, sometimes called the "smooth," and deviations from that pattern, the "rough." The smooth is important for understanding the general distribution of the data and the phenomena responsible for the observed regularity. The rough is important for potentially pointing out either unique events or perturbations in the normal operation of the system.

These techniques for analyzing data have a very compelling application in archaeology, particularly in the area of typology, where the ultimate goal of the analysis is to identify regular patterns in the artifactual data that may reveal patterning in the human behavior that produced or distributed the artifacts. EDA is useful for reducing masses of data to some kind of observable order, usually in the form of frequency distributions, to obtain an initial impression of the rough and the smooth. This may be achieved through any number of graphical devices, including bar charts, histograms, frequency curves, box plots, and stem-and-leaf plots. These can give the researcher valuable insights into the structure of the data, point up possible relationships between variables, and suggest appropriate techniques for later descriptive or confirmatory analysis (for an excellent discussion of EDA, see Shennan, 1988).

DESCRIPTION Descriptive statistics aid in the economical presentation of facets of the archaeological record. These techniques provide a means for organizing and quantifying archaeological data in a manner that facilitates objective comparison while preserving the inherent structure of the data. Descriptive statistics provides archaeologists with an economical way of indicating the numbers and kinds of artifacts found at a site or the dimensions of artifacts and the degree of variation in those dimensions. It provides a means of taking masses of data stored in computer data bases and summarizing them into a readily digestible form. Today, descriptive statistics are often employed on-site as an aid to excavation or survey. The basic data are often collected and entered into a computer data base in the field laboratory on a daily basis. Those data can then be quickly summarized using basic descriptive techniques to indicate differences in the frequency of artifacts between excavation areas or levels or to indicate emergent patterns in survey data that can then be used to refine field techniques and strategies. Descriptive statistics generally involves summarizing sets of data using very straightforward measures of the structure of the data. These include such things as measures of central tendency (mean, median, mode) and measures of dispersion (standard deviation, spread, range), as well as basic graphical devices such as bar graphs, histograms, and line graphs. In archaeology, the ultimate goal of descriptive statistics is to organize data into a more manageable form in order to facilitate comparison and indicate patterning. It is one of the oldest and simplest sets of techniques of quantitative analysis for archaeologists and remains one of the most frequently used because of its simplicity and its power. In innumerable archaeological problems, basic descriptive statistics are all that is required to characterize the data adequately and to provide meaningful interpretive information on the problem.

HYPOTHESIS TESTING (CONFIRMATION)   Confirmatory or inferential statistics are designed to allow the researcher to make informed inferences about the characteristics of a population or the relationship between variables on the basis of data collected from a sample of the population of interest. All the various confirmatory techniques provide a summary statistic that indicates how reliable the inference is likely to be. Archaeologists are concerned with making inferences about the past on the basis of patterns and relationships evident in the archaeological record. However, because the relationship between the observable phenomena (the archaeological record) and the unobservable phenomena of real interest (past human behavior) is often a very imperfect one, archaeologists need to know how reliable their inferences are. Since we cannot go back in a time machine to see for ourselves whether our inferences are good, we must rely on mathematics and the known laws of probability to give us an indication of the reliability of our inferences. As Stephen Shennan (1988) puts it, "The area where mathematics meets the messier parts of the real world is usually statistics." The tricky part about employing any of the various univariate and multivariate techniques of inferential statistics is that the test statistic (Student's t, F test, chi square, etc.) is only measuring the reliability of the *mathematical relationship* between variables in a data set, between a sample and its presumed population, or among data sets. How inferences about these mathematical relationships are interpreted in terms of the actualities of the archaeological record or human behavior depends on the archaeologist. Those interpretations can only be judged with reference to the archaeologist's understanding of the data, the technique employed and its assumptions and limitations, a coherent body of theory about the archaeological record and human behavior, and common sense.

In the final analysis, quantitative methods enable archaeologists to organize their artifact and other data in intelligent, efficient, and replicable ways, allowing them to view the data more clearly and objectively as they work toward the goal of discerning patterns that relate to past human behavior. These techniques also allow archaeologists to evaluate objectively the reliability of their inferences from small samples to larger populations of archaeological entities, as well as inferences about the interrelations among variables. To the extent that these techniques are applied to attribute and object pattern recognition, they are extremely valuable aids to artifact classification.

Quantitative methods have been applied to two contrasting approaches to artifact classification, both of which were in use before the advent of computers and statistical methods in archaeology: attribute analysis and object clustering.

ATTRIBUTE ANALYSIS   Attribute analysis emphasizes combinations of attributes that distinguish and isolate one artifact type from another. The physical characteristics or features of significance used to distinguish one artifact from another are known as attributes (Whallon and Brown, 1982). As archaeologists work out their typologies, they find themselves examining hundreds of individual fragments, each of which bears several distinctive attributes (Figure 11.6). Every commonplace artifact we use can be examined by its attributes. The familiar glass beer mug has a curved handle that extends from near the lip to the base, often fluted sides, a straight, rounded rim, and dimensions that are set by the amount of beer it is intended to contain. It is manufactured of clear, relatively thick glass (the thickness can be defined by precise measurement). You can find numerous attributes on any human artifact, be it a diamond ring or a prehistoric pot. For example, a collection of 50 potsherds lying on a laboratory table may bear black-painted designs, while eight have red panels on the neck, 10 are shallow bowls, and so on. An individual potsherd may come from a vessel made of bright red clay mixed with powdered sea shells so that the clay would fire better. It may come from a pot with a thick rim made by applying a rolled circle of clay before firing, and a crisscross design cut into the wet clay with a sharp knife during manufacture. Each of the many individual features is an attribute, most of which are obvious enough. Only a critically selected few of these attributes, however, will be used in classifying the artifacts. (If all were used, then no classification would be possible: each artifact would be an individual object identified by an infinite number of attributes.) Thus, the archaeologist works with only those attributes considered most appropriate for the classificatory task at hand.

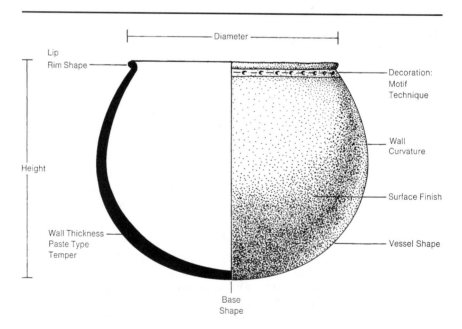

FIGURE 11.6   Some common attributes of a clay vessel. Specific attributes that could be listed for this pot are concave shoulder, dot-and-drag decoration, mica temper, round base, and thickness of wall at base.

A number of broad groups of attributes are in common use:

- *Formal attributes* are such features as the shape of the artifact, its measurable dimensions, and its components. Usually they are fairly obvious.
- *Stylistic attributes* involve decoration, color, surface finish, and so on (Sackett, 1977, 1982).
- *Technological attributes* cover the material used to make an artifact and the way it was made.

The selection of attributes normally proceeds through a close examination of a collection of artifacts. EDA techniques can be very useful in helping to determine which attributes provide the most diagnostic discrimination. A group of potsherds can be divided into different decorative styles based on shapes, surfaces, and colors. The selected attributes are then hand-recorded, and a series of artifact types is erected from them. The definition of the type here can depend on the order in which the attributes are examined (Figure 11.6) and on the researcher's decision as to which are important.

Statistical typologies are derived from attribute clusters, usually coded on a computer, which are then used to divide the artifact collection into categories defined by statistically derived attribute clusters. James Sackett (1966) used this approach on 32,000-year-old Aurignacian end scrapers from Upper Palaeolithic sites in southwestern France, and found that the extent and location of trimming on the edges and the angle between the two longer sides were important variables that may have defined classes of artifacts used for different purposes.

OBJECT CLUSTERING   The object clustering approach to classification begins with a series of so-called operational taxonomic units (OTUs), usually artifacts (Cowgill, 1982). The archaeologist calculates the similarities between all possible pairs of objects, using similarity coefficients. On the basis of similarity scores, the analyst can then link the OTUs into a hierarchical structure, which ranges all the way from complete uniqueness of all artifacts (an unanalyzed collection) to complete unity, when all OTUs are in the same cluster. In contrast to attribute approaches, object clustering uses attributes to assess the *similarity* between objects, not associations (Cowgill, 1982, describes the differences between the two approaches). Object clustering classifications are based on a quantitative approach known as cluster analysis, a form of numerical taxonomy.

Each approach to classification supplies different information about the very structure of archaeological data, all of which are valuable. In a sense, the approaches are descriptions of the structure in archaeological data, based, in their quantitative guises, on a greater concern for techniques for discovering variations in artifacts than on the actual selection of attributes for comparison. At present there is still little theoretical justification for selecting the attributes that are used to classify artifacts or to cluster them. Certainly as far as stone tools are concerned, it is likely that classifications based on function and technology will become more widespread as a result of highly precise research into such phenomena as edge wear on modern artifacts. This provides a basis for testing hypotheses about tool use in the past and a firm foundation for classifications based on actual human behavior.

ASSEMBLAGES AND PATTERNS

Culture history in archaeology is based on classification of artifacts and assemblages, defined as associations of artifacts that are thought to be contemporary. This was the approach espoused by V. Gordon Childe in the 1930s and 1940s and was also popular in North America. "We find certain types of remains . . . constantly recurring together," Childe (1925) wrote: "Such a complex of regularly associated traits we shall term . . . a 'culture.' We may assume that such a complex is the material expression of what would today be called a 'people.'" This assumption was virtually archaeological law until the 1950s, when a number of prehistorians began using statistical methods to look at assemblages of artifacts.

These earlier archaeologists had assumed a steady, almost inevitable progression of human culture through the ages. They assumed that artifact assemblages with recurring patterns were merely traces of contemporary cultural "species" that extended far back into antiquity. This "organic" view of culture history regarded assemblages of artifacts as distinct categories, like organic species that did not modify their form from one context to the next (Sackett, 1981). The argument went on to assume that a specific cultural tradition leads to only one characteristic type of industry in the archaeological record that is circumscribed in time and space.

WHAT DO ASSEMBLAGES AND PATTERNINGS MEAN?

The "organic" view of the past is a highly organized scheme, rather like the Medieval "Chain of Being" in early biology, in which every living thing had its place in the general scheme of things.

American archaeologists have generally preferred a more "cultural" perspective, making considerable use of data on artifacts and other cultural traits known to have been used by living societies in North America. The observation of these data has shown that there is a strong correlation between the distributions of distinctive cultural forms and different environments. For example, plank houses and an elaborate canoe technology are characteristic of the peoples of the Pacific Northwest coast, where readily split cedar and other trees flourished in abundance. In contrast, desert peoples in the Great Basin lived in much more transitory settlements of brush shelters and houses, using a highly portable tool kit adapted to a mobile desert lifeway. It is all very well to say that such correlations were true of historic times, but what about earlier prehistory? Can one say that artifact assemblages from the Great Basin dating to 5,000 years ago reflect similar adaptations, similar social groups? Were conditions different in the past from today—can one use modern artifact patternings as a basis for interpreting ancient behavior?

Observations of living societies, such as Lewis Binford's research on the Nunamiut caribou hunters in Alaska, have shown that it may not be possible to distinguish among ethnic and cultural groups from artifact assemblages alone (Binford, 1978, 1983a). Thus the role of classification in archaeology is shifting away from organic viewpoints that view artifacts and cultures as finite in time and space to new means of problem-oriented classification that concentrate not just on individual tools but on entire assemblages and their patterns in archaeological sites. In other words, classification alone is meaningless, unless the classifications are interpreted in terms of other data. This is where middle-range theory comes in (Chapter 14).

Artifact classifications are still carried out, for the most part, using approaches meant for reconstructing culture history, formulations of time and space that owe much to functional classifications of artifacts based on common sense. Robert Dunnell (1978) points out that relatively few new classificatory concepts are relevant to the new interest in processual archaeology. In classifying artifacts, archaeologists have usually made use of functional units or stylistic types on the basis of their historical significance through time. Archaeologists have adopted inductive, statistical procedures (Spaulding, 1953; Doran and Hodson, 1975) that are technically more rigorous and of great use within an assemblage but less applicable on a wider canvas. Thus the same classificatory units have remained in use, while archaeologists pay lip service to newer approaches. As Dunnell (1986b) points out, the question of questions is a simple one: Can style be explained within a scientific and evolutionary framework, using laws of cultural change? So far, such a theoretical framework does not exist.

SUMMARY

- The first stage in laboratory analysis is processing field data into a form that will enable one to analyze and interpret them. The finds are also inventoried during this stage.
- Classifying artifacts in archaeology is somewhat different from our day-to-day classification of the objects around us.
- Two systems of classification are taxonomy and systematics. Taxonomy is a classification system of concepts and terms used by many sciences, archaeology among them. Systematics is a way of creating units that can be used to categorize things as a basis for explaining archaeological or other phenomena. It is a means of creating units of classification within a scientific discipline.
- The objectives of archaeological classification are to organize data into manageable units, to describe types, and to identify relationships among types.
- Archaeological types are groupings of artifacts created for comparisons with other groups. These groupings may or may not coincide with the actual tool types designed by the manufacturers.
- Types are based on clusters of attributes. There are four "types of types" commonly used today:

    1. *Descriptive types* are based on the form of the artifacts, using physical or external properties.
    2. *Chronological types* are defined by form but are time markers.
    3. *Functional types* are based on cultural use or role rather than outward form or chronological position.
    4. *Stylistic types* use changing styles for classification purposes.

- Archaeological classification begins with identifying artifact attributes, the characteristics that distinguish one artifact from another. Formal attributes are such features as the shape of an artifact, and technological attributes include the materials used to make an artifact and manufacturing methods. Attributes can be selected by closely examining a collection of artifacts, or they can be derived statistically.

- Statistically based classifications are now in common use, based on quantitative analyses, including the use of exploratory data analysis (EDA). Attribute-based and object-cluster classifications are two major approaches now based on quantitative methods.
- Culture history in archaeology is based on classification of artifacts and assemblages, defined as associations of artifacts that are thought to be contemporary. This "organic" view of culture history has been replaced by a more "cultural" viewpoint in which environment and culture play important roles.

GUIDE TO FURTHER READING

The literature on archaeological classification is both complex and enormous. I strongly advise you to obtain expert advice before delving into even key references. Here, however, are some useful starting points.

Cowgill, George L. "Clusters of Objects and Associations between Variables: Two Approaches to Archaeological Classification," in Robert A. Whallon and James A. Brown, eds., *Essays in Archaeological Typology,* pp. 30–55. Evanston, Ill.: Center for American Archaeology, 1982. An excellent comparison of attribute-based and object cluster-based classifications in archaeology.

Dunnell, R. C. "Methodological Issues in Americanist Artifact Classification," *Advances in Archaeological Method and Theory* 9 (1986): 149–208. A specialist essay on artifact classification that summarizes the major controversies surrounding the subject.

Dunnell, R. C. *Systematics in Prehistory.* New York: Free Press, 1971. A highly technical introduction to systematic classification in archaeology.

Shennan, Stephen. *Quantifying Archaeology.* Orlando, Fla.: Academic Press, 1988. A superb introduction to quantitative archaeology for the advanced student. Includes simple exercises.

Thomas, David Hurst. *Refiguring Anthropology.* Prospect Heights, Ill.: Waveland Press, 1989. A widely used basic text on quantitative approaches.

12

TECHNOLOGY AND ARTIFACTS

The technological achievements of humanity over the past 3 million years of cultural evolution have been both impressive and terrifying. Today we can land an astronaut on the moon, transplant human hearts, and build sophisticated computers. Yet in the final analysis, our contemporary armory of lasers, atomic bombs, household appliances, and every conceivable artifact designed for a multitude of specialized needs has evolved in a direct, albeit branching, way from the first simple tools made by the earliest human beings. In this chapter we examine some of the main technologies used by prehistoric people to adapt to, and extend their use of, their natural environments and look at some of the ways in which archaeologists study them (Cotterell and Kamminga, 1989).

STONE

Bone, plant fiber, wood, and some kinds of rock have been the primary raw materials for human technology for most of human existence. Metallurgy is but a recent development, and stone tools have provided the foundation for classification of many prehistoric cultures since scientific archaeology began. The raw material itself has set severe limits on people's technological achievements for much of their history, and the evolution of stoneworking over the millions of years during which it has been practiced has been infinitely slow. Nonetheless, people eventually exploited almost every possibility afforded by suitable rocks for making implements.

WORKING STONE

The manufacture of stone tools is what is called a "reductive (or subtractive) technology," for stone is acquired, then shaped by removing flakes until the desired form is achieved. Obviously, the more complex the artifact, the more reduction is required (Swanson, 1975). Basically, the process of tool manufacture is linear. The stoneworker acquires the raw material, prepares a lump of stone (the core), then carries out the initial reduction by removing a series of flakes. These flakes are then trimmed and shaped further depending on the artifact required. Later, after use, a tool may be resharpened or modified for further use.

PRINCIPLES OF MANUFACTURE   The making of stone tools depends on conchoidal fracturing. The simplest way of producing a stone that will cut or chop, surely the basic tool produced by prehistoric people, is simply to break off a piece and use the resulting sharp edge. But to make a tool that has a more specialized use or can be employed for several purposes requires a slightly more sophisticated flaking technique. First, an angular fragment or smooth pebble of suitable rock can be brought to the desired shape by systematically flaking it with another stone. The flakes removed from this core, or lump, are then primarily waste products, whereas the core becomes the implement that is the intentional end product of the tool-maker. Furthermore, the flakes struck from the core can themselves be used as sharp-edged knives, or they can be further modified to make other artifacts. From this simple beginning, many complex stone industries have evolved, the earliest tools being simple—many of them virtually indistinguishable from naturally fractured rock (Crabtree, 1972a).

Generally, Stone Age people and other makers of stone tools chose flint, obsidian, and other hard, homogeneous rocks from which to fashion their artifacts. All these rocks break in a systematic or predictable way, like glass. The effect is similar to that of a hole in a window produced by a BB gun. A sharp blow by percussion or pressure directed vertically at a point on the surface of a suitable stone dislodges a flake, with its apex at the point where the hammer hit the stone. This results in a conchoidal fracture (Figure 12.1). When a blow is directed at a stone slab obliquely from the edge, however, and the break occurs conchoidally, a flake is detached. The fractured face of the flake has a characteristic shape, with a bulge extending from the surface of the piece outward down the side. This is known as the bulb of percussion (or force); there is a corresponding hollow or flake scar on the core from which the flake has been detached. The bulb of percussion is readily recognized, as Figure 12.2 shows, not only by the bulge itself but also from the concentric rings that radiate from the center of the impact point, widening gradually away from it. Such deliberate human-made fractures are quite different from those produced by such natural means as frost, extreme heat or cold, water action, or stones falling from a cliff and fracturing boulders below. In these types the rock sometimes breaks in a similar manner, but most of the flake scars are irregular, and instead of concentric rings and a bulb of percussion, often a rough depressed area is left on the surface with concentric rings formed around it.

Distinguishing human-worked from naturally fractured stones requires long experience with stone tool manufacture, especially when handling very early human artifacts. Our earliest ancestors used the simplest of hard hammer percussion techniques, removing two or three sharp-edged flakes from lava pebbles (Figure 12.3). Several famous controversies have raged over alleged "artifacts" found in Lower Pleistocene deposits in Europe and Africa that are contemporary with periods when hominids were already flourishing elsewhere. Under such circumstances, the only sure identification of human-fractured stone implements is to find them in association with fossil human remains and broken animal bones, preferably on living sites.

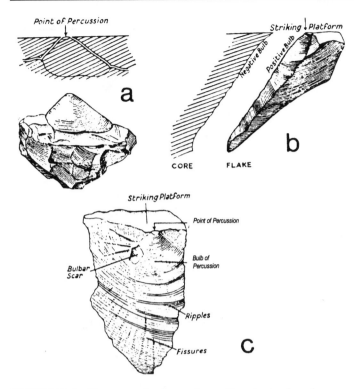

FIGURE 12.1 How stone fractures when a blow is struck on homogeneous types of rock: (a) When a blow is struck, a core of percussion is formed by the shock waves rippling through the stone. (b) A flake is formed when the block (or core) is hit at the edge and the stone fractures along the edge of the ripple. (c) Features of a struck flake.

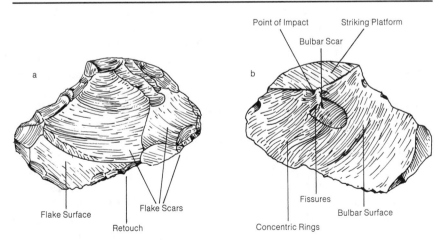

FIGURE 12.2 The components of a flake tool: (a) flake surface; (b) bulbar surface.

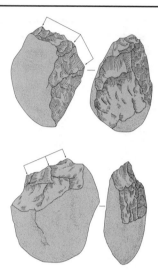

FIGURE 12.3   These cores from Olduvai Gorge, Tanzania, are some of the earliest human tool forms. Arrows show the working edges. (Three-fifths actual size)

METHODS   Figures 12.4 through 12.7 show some of the major stone-flaking methods prehistoric peoples used. The simplest and earliest was direct fracturing of the stone with a hammerstone (Figure 12.4). After thousands of years, people began to make tools flaked on both surfaces, such as Acheulian hand axes (Figure 12.5). As time went on, the stoneworkers began to use bone, "soft" antler, or wood hammers to trim the edges of their hand axes. The hand ax of 150,000 years ago had a symmetrical shape; sharp, tough working edges; and a beautiful finish.

As people became more skillful and specialized, such as the hunter-gatherers of about 100,000 years ago, they developed stone technologies producing arti-facts for highly specific purposes. They shaped special cores that were carefully prepared to provide one flake or two of a standard size and shape (Figure 12.6). About 35,000 years ago, some stoneworkers developed a new technology based on preparing cylindrical cores from which long, parallel-sided blades were removed by indirect percussion with a punch and hammerstone (Figure 12.7). These regular blanks were then trimmed into knives, scraping tools, and other specialized artifacts (Figure 12.8). Blade technology was so successful that it spread all over the world. It has been shown to be highly efficient. Controlled experiments resulted in 6 percent of the raw material being left on one exhausted blade core; 91 percent of it formed 83 usable blades (Sheets and Muto, 1972).

Once blades had been removed from their cores, they were trimmed into shape using a variety of techniques. In some, the blade's side was pressure-flaked with an antler or a piece of wood to sharpen or blunt it. Sometimes the flake would be pressed against another stone, a bone, or a piece of wood to produce a steep, stepped edge or a notch (Figure 12.8a and b).

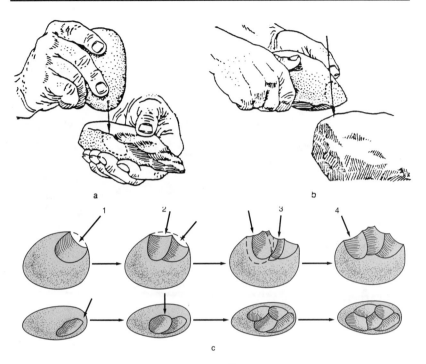

FIGURE 12.4   The earliest stoneworking techniques: (a) Using a hammerstone. (b) A variant on the hammerstone, striking a core against a stone block, the so-called anvil technique. (c) The earliest stone tools were made by a simple method. The top row shows the side view: First, two flakes were struck off (1 and 2); second, the stone was turned over, and two more flakes were removed (3); third, a fifth flake completed the useful life of the core (4). The bottom row shows the process from above.

Pressure flaking became so refined that it became the most common technique of later prehistory, especially in the New World (Figure 12.8c and d). The stoneworker used a small billet of wood or antler pressed against the working edge to exert pressure in a limited direction and remove a fine, thin, parallel-sided flake. This formed one of many flake scars that eventually covered most of the implement's surfaces. Pressure flaking facilitates the production of many standardized tools with extremely effective working edges in a comparatively short time.

In the Near East, Europe, and many parts of Africa and southern and eastern Asia, small blades were fashioned into minute arrowheads, barbs, and adzes, known as *microliths*, often made using a characteristic notching technique (Figure 11.3). A variant of this technique also evolved in arctic America and Australia, where small cores were produced to manufacture diminutive microblades or bladelets.

The blade technologies of later times could produce far more tools per pound of material than earlier methods. Later Stone Age peoples ground and polished

FIGURE 12.5 An Acheulian hand ax from Wolvercote, Oxford, England, with finely trimmed edges made with a bone hammer. (Approximate length, 5 inches [13 cm])

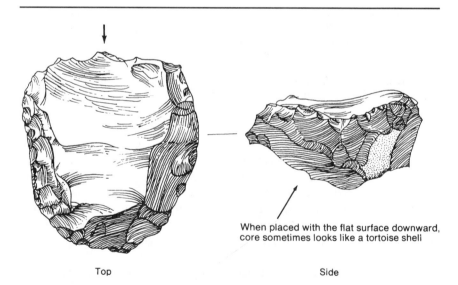

When placed with the flat surface downward, core sometimes looks like a tortoise shell

Top   Side

FIGURE 12.6 A special core shaped to produce one thin flake. Arrow indicates where flake was removed. Archaeologists call these Levallois cores, so named after a suburb of Paris, France, where such cores were first discovered. (One-half actual size)

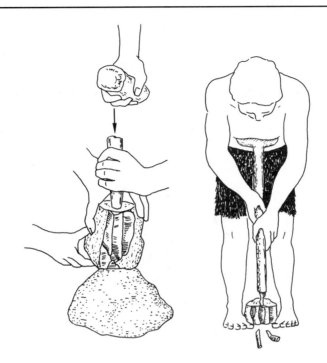

FIGURE 12.7   Two uses of the blade technique, employing a punch.

stone when they needed a sharp and highly durable blade. They shaped the edges
by rough flaking and then laboriously polished and ground them against a coarser
rock, such as sandstone, to produce a sharp, tough working edge. Modern experiments have demonstrated the greater effectiveness of polished stone axes in
felling forest trees, the toughened working edge taking longer to blunt than that
of a flaked ax (W. H. Townsend, 1969). Polished stone axes became important in
many early farming societies, especially in Europe, Asia, Mesoamerica, and parts
of temperate North America. They were used in New Guinea as early as 28,000
years ago and in Melanesia and Polynesia for the manufacture of canoes, which
were essential for fishing and trade (White and O'Connell, 1982).

Expert stoneworkers still fashion artifacts to this day, especially gunflints for
use in flintlock muskets. Gunflint manufacture was a flourishing industry in
Britain and France into the twentieth century and is still practiced in Angola,
Africa, where flintlock muskets are still in use for hunting.

STONE TOOL ANALYSIS

LITHIC ANALYSIS   Early attempts at stone tool analysis used finished tools,
or "type fossils," which were thought to be representative of different human
cultures. This type-fossil approach was abandoned gradually as more sophisticated typological methods came into use, methods that named well-defined artifact types according to their shape, dimensions, and assumed use, such as the

Acheulian hand ax (Figure 12.5) and the Mousterian side scraper (Figure 12.8a). This approach led, like the type-fossil concept before it, to searches for perfect, "typical" artifacts. Many functional labels such as "projectile point" remain in use in modern stone tool studies, but they are no longer thought of as anything more than a generalized description of the form of an artifact. Functional analyses of this type have achieved great refinement in western Europe, where many

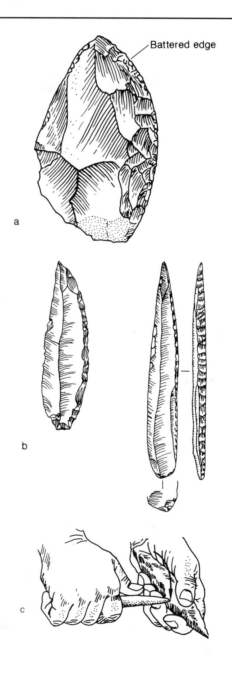

Battered edge

a

b

c

(continued)

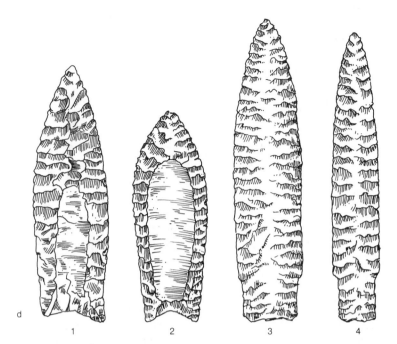

FIGURE 12.8   Some methods of trimming stone tools: (a) steep retouch by battering, on a Mousterian, Middle Paleolithic, side scraper. (One-half actual size) (b) Specialized blade tools made by pressing and sharpening the edges. These are backed blades used as spearpoints about 22,000 years ago. (Actual size) (c) The pressure-flaking technique. (d) Paleo-Indian pressure-flaked points: (1) Clovis point, (2) Folsom point, (3) Scottsbluff point, (4) Eden point. (All actual size; used with permission of McGraw-Hill Book Company and Thames and Hudson, Ltd.)

varieties of Stone Age tools are to be found (Bordaz, 1970; Bordes, 1968). As with other artifact forms, recent classifications have a sophisticated concern with analyses based on attributes chosen for their ability to throw light on manufacturing technology or function.

In recent years, the focus of lithic analysis has shifted dramatically away from a preoccupation with finished tools to a broader concern with prehistoric lithic technology in a context of human behavior. Modern studies of stone technology rely on a combination of several approaches, which focus as much on the processes of manufacture of artifacts as they do on the artifacts themselves.

DEBITAGE ANALYSIS   The making of any stone artifact is the result of a reduction sequence, a series of steps that begins with the selection of a core of fine-grained rock and ends with the completion of a finished artifact. Reconstructing these reduction sequences is one way in which archaeologists achieve an understanding of artifact manufacturing processes in prehistory.

Prehistoric stone tool manufacture can be reconstructed in several ways, for the clues lie in abandoned cores, in flake scars, in striking platforms, in the dimensions of flakes and blades, and even in the obvious and not-so-obvious mistakes made by ancient artisans. For example, a blow struck at the wrong point on a Levallois core can shatter the core in distinctive ways easily recognized by someone familiar with lithic technology. Most steps in stone tool manufacture can be recognized by studying finished artifacts, cores, and, above all, the debris, often called debitage, left behind by the stoneworker. By close examination of debitage, an expert lithic technologist can separate primary flakes, flakes resulting from the rough blocking out of the core, from the finer flakes that were removed as the artisan prepared the striking platform on the top or sides of the core. Then there are the flakes that all this preparatory work was aimed at—the artifact blanks struck from the core. Finally, there are the fine retouching flakes that turn the blank into the finished projectile point, scraper, or whatever other implement was needed (Sullivan and Rozen, 1985).

Some of the most productive analyses of artifact manufacturing processes have come from meticulous combinations of debitage analysis with experimental replications of early technology. Nicholas Toth spent months replicating very early hominid technology as used at Olduvai Gorge, Tanzania, more than 1.75 million years ago. He compared his own cores and debitage with the originals and was not only able to show that the flakes removed from the cores were more important than the cores themselves, often called chopping tools, but that some of the world's very early stone toolmakers were left-handed as well (Toth and Schick, 1993).

LITHIC EXPERIMENTATION   Archaeologists have experimented with the making of stone tools since the mid-nineteenth century. Today many archaeological laboratories ring to the sound of people trying to make stone tools and replicate ancient technology—and cutting their fingers in the process (Flenniken, 1984). Experimental work began with general attempts to compare the stone toolmaking methods of living peoples like the Australian Aborigines with those of prehistoric cultures. Modern experimenters have drawn on both experimentation and ethnographic observation to work out prehistoric techniques (Swanson, 1975). Recent research has focused on reconstructing reduction sequences and also on quarry sites, both as part of efforts to reconstruct prehistoric trade in obsidian and other rocks that can be traced back to their source (Chapter 16) (Torrence, 1986), and in attempts to achieve closer understanding of the relationships between human behavior and lithic technology (Ericson and Purdy, 1984). There is another side to experimental lithic technology as well. Obsidian flake and blade edges are so sharp that they are widely used by modern eye surgeons, on the grounds that such cutting tools are superior to modern steel!

PETROLOGICAL ANALYSES   Petrological analyses have been applied with great success to the rocks from which stone tools are made, especially ground stone axes in Europe. Petrology is the study of rocks (Greek, *petros* = "stone"). A thin section of the ax is prepared and examined under a microscope. The minerals in the rock can then be identified and compared with samples from quarry sites (Ericson and Purdy, 1984). British archaeologists have had remarkable success with this approach and have identified more than 20 sources of ax blade stone (Bradley and Edmonds, 1993). Spectrographic analysis of distinctive trace elements in obsidian has yielded remarkable results in the Near East and Mesoamerica, where this distinctive volcanic rock was traded widely from several quarry centers (Torrence, 1986) (Chapter 16).

REFITTING   Watch someone making stone tools and you will find that they are sitting in the middle of a pile of ever-accumulating debris—chips, flakes, abandoned cores, and discarded hammerstones. Prehistoric stoneworkers produced the same sort of debris—hundreds, if not thousands, of small waste fragments, by-products of toolmaking that are buried on archaeological sites of all ages. Vital information on prehistoric lithic technology comes from careful excavation of all the debitage from a place where a prehistoric artisan worked, then trying to fit the pieces together one by one, to reconstruct the procedures used. Refitting taxes the patience of even the most even-tempered archaeologist but can yield remarkable results. At the 9,000-year-old Meer II site in northern Belgium, Daniel Cahen and Lawrence Keeley (1980) combined edge-wear analysis with refitting to reconstruct a fascinating scenario. They used the evidence from three borers that were turned counterclockwise to show that a right-handed artisan walked away from the settlement and made some tools, using some prepared blanks and cores he brought with him. Later a left-handed artisan came and sat next to him, bringing a previously prepared core, from which he proceeded to strike some blanks that he turned into tools. Reconstruction in this sort of fine detail is often impossible, but it has the advantage that the artifact pattern revealed in the archaeological record can be interpreted with extreme precision because the refitting shows that no modification has affected the evidence displayed in the archaeological record.

Sometimes lithic specialists trace the movement of individual fragments or cores horizontally across a site, a process that requires even more patience than simple refitting. This procedure is of great value in reconstructing the functions of different locations in, say, a rock shelter site, where a stoneworker might make tools in one place, then carry a core to a nearby hearth and fashion another blade for a quite different process. This approach works well on Folsom Paleo-Indian sites on the Great Plains, where individual flakes have been refitted to their cores after having been excavated from locations as much as 12 feet (3.6 m) away.

USE-WEAR ANALYSIS   Use-wear analysis involves both microscopic examination of artifact working edges and actual experiments using stone tools, in an effort to interpret telltale scratches and edge luster resulting from their use (Hayden, 1979; Keeley, 1980). Many researchers have experimented with both low- and high-power magnification and are now able to distinguish with considerable confidence between the wear polishes associated with different materials like wood, bone, and hide (Phillips, 1988). The approach is now reliable enough to allow one to state whether a tool was used to slice wood, cut up vegetables, or strip meat from bones, but relatively few archaeologists are trained in using the microscopes and photographic techniques required for analyzing wear. Cahen and Keeley's study (1980) of stone tools from the Meer II site in Belgium showed that two people had used the tools they made to bore and grave fragments of bone. In instances like this, tool-wear analysis offers exciting opportunities for studying the behavior of individual stoneworkers thousands of years ago.

There are many examples of distinctive microwear patterns, among them polishes that can be identified with high-powered microscopes. One instance is the flint sickle blade used for harvesting wild or domesticated grasses, which often shows a gloss caused by the silica in the grass stems.

Patrick Vaughan (1985) completed a use-wear analysis of an 18,000-year-old Magdalenian stone tool assemblage from Cassegros in southwestern France. The edges of a 532-item sample of the stone artifacts were cleaned with medicinal alcohol or other chemicals, then examined under a 280-power metallurgical microscope. Twenty-five variables relating to use wear were coded on a computer and analyzed statistically—with fascinating results. Tools displaying the characteristic use-wear patterns associated with working dry hide were common inside the cave. So were stone artifacts whose edges had worked harder materials like wood; Vaughan believes they were used to make wooden racks, frames, pegs, and other devices used to stretch and deflesh or dehair skins. Stone tools may also have been used to fashion antler, bone, and wood implements used to prepare fresh hides, for, interestingly enough, the Cassegros stone tools show few signs of fresh-hide as opposed to dry-hide use wear. Vaughan speculates that Cassegros was a hide-processing station used in the fall, when reindeer hunters pursue their quarry for hides.

Marvin Kay of the University of Arkansas is using three-dimensional Nomarski optics (Figure 12.9). This enables him to examine artifact surfaces with different colors of polarized light, to focus on polishes and on microscopic striations that result not only from hafting projectile points, but from the impact on the head when it strikes an animal. It also has other uses such as butchery and woodworking. Kay compares the use wear on prehistoric artifacts to different use patterns resulting from modern experiments with artifact replicas against elephants and other animals. He has found, for example, that Clovis points from North America display minute scratches near the base that result from the head absorbing the shock of impact during the hunt. Not only that, but there are clear signs that many of them were used, then reshaped and used again, often serving as knives after their usefulness as points was over. Kay's methodology is so sophisticated that he can even detect planing effects on tough stone like quartzite, the planing resulting from use of the artifact for butchery. This exciting research will, one day, allow archaeologists to develop histories of individual artifacts as part of a larger-scale analysis of activities on archaeological sites.

Another approach studies organic residues, the trace elements of debris from use adhering to tool edges. In particular, biochemical and immunological studies of blood residues have proved fruitful even on artifacts more than 1,200 years old. The Head-Smashed-In Buffalo Jump in southwestern Alberta was used by prehistoric hunters for more than 5,500 years (Brink and Dawe, 1989). Many projectile points lie among the bones at the site and it is a reasonable supposition that they were used for killing buffalo. By using a 5 percent solution of ammonia, possible residues were extracted from buffalo bones and associated soil samples, then analyzed using the crossover electrophoresis method, in which they were compared to antisera from ten animals, selected as the most likely game in the area. Buffalo antisera yielded a positive reaction from the artifact residues, even on samples more than 5,000 years old. Although it will never be possible to

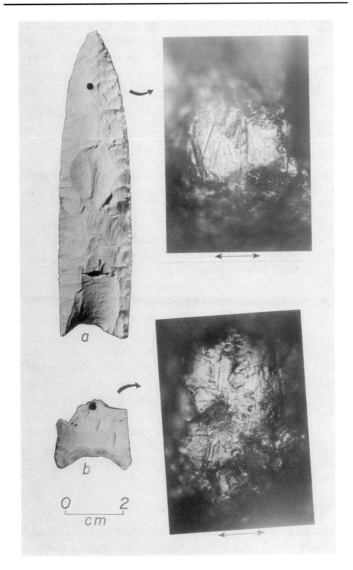

FIGURE 12.9   Microwear on two Clovis points from two big-game kill sites in North America. (a) Kimmswick: striations are oriented only to the longitudinal axis of the point and originate at its tip. These are due to impact and carcass penetration. (b) Lang-Geruson site: striations show a more complex pattern of tool use—longitudinally oriented striations are due to impact, intersecting horizontal and oblique striations to subsequent use as a butchering tool or knife. (magnified 200 times, arrowed scale bars are 0.1 mm)

achieve 100 percent identification, the Head-Smashed-In samples produced a 29 percent rate, which is comparable to results obtained from other sites.

The important thing about lithic analysis is not just the study of the implements themselves; it is understanding of what the implements mean in terms of human behavior. And the new, multifaceted approaches to lithic analysis offer a real chance that methods like edge-wear analysis will provide definitive ways of classifying stone tools in terms of their original functions.

CLAY (CERAMICS)

Objects made of clay are among the most imperishable of all archaeological finds, but pottery is a relatively recent innovation. From the very earliest times, people used animal skins, bark trays, ostrich eggshells, and wild gourds for carrying loads beyond the immediate surroundings of their settlements. Such informal vessels were ideal for hunter-gatherers, who were constantly on the move. Pottery appeared before 6000 B.C. at such early agricultural settlements in the Near East as Çatal Höyük, Jarmo, and Jericho (Moore, 1985). In contrast, in Japan pottery was made by hunter-gatherers as early as 8000 B.C. (Akazawa and Aikens, 1986). The inhabitants of the Tehuacán Valley in highland Mexico began cultivating crops before the first pottery appeared in North America in about 2500 B.C. (B. D. Smith, 1994).

The invention of pottery seems to have coincided with the beginnings of more lasting settlement. Fired clay receptacles have the advantage of being both durable and long-lived. We can assume that the first clay vessels were used for domestic purposes: for cooking, carrying water, and storing food. They soon assumed more specialized roles in salt making, in ceremonial activities, and as oil lamps and burial urns. Broken ceramic vessels are among the most common archaeological finds. Their shape, style, and form have provided the foundations for thousands of archaeological analyses (Olin and Franklin, 1982; Orton and others, 1993); Rice, 1987).

POTTERY TECHNOLOGY

Modern industrial potters turn out dinnerware pieces by the millions, using mass-production methods and automated technology. Prehistoric artisans created each of their pieces individually, using the simplest of technology but attaining astonishing skill in shaping and adorning their vessels.

The clay used in potmaking was invariably selected with the utmost care; often it was even traded over considerable distances. The consistency of the clay is critical; it is pounded meticulously and mixed with water to make it entirely even in texture. By careful kneading, the potter removes the air bubbles and makes the clay as plastic as possible, allowing it to be molded into shape as the pot is built up. When the clay is fired, it loses its water content and can crack, so the potter adds a temper to the clay, a substance that helps reduce shrinkage and cracking. Although some pot clays contain a suitable temper in their natural state, potmakers commonly added many other materials like fine sand, powdered shell, or even mica as artificial temper.

Potmaking (ceramics) is a highly skilled art, with three major methods:

1. *Coil.* The vessel is built up with long coils or wedges of clay that are shaped and joined together with a mixture of clay and water (Figure 12.10). Sometimes the pot is built up from a lump of clay. Hand methods were common wherever potmaking was a part-time activity satisfying local needs.

2. *Mold.* The vessel is made from a lump of clay that is either pressed into a concave mold or placed over the top of a convex shape. Molding techniques were used to make large numbers of vessels of the same size and shape, as well as figurines, fishing net weights, and spindle whorls. Sometimes several molds were used to make the different parts of a vessel.

3. *Potter's wheel.* Wheel-made pots came into wide use after the invention of the potter's wheel in Mesopotamia about 5,000 years ago. The vessel is formed from a lump of clay rotating on a platform turned by the potter's hands or feet. The wheel method has the advantage of speed and standardization and was used to mass-produce thousands of similar vessels, such as the bright red Roman Samian ware (Shepard, 1971). Wheel-made pots can sometimes be identified by the parallel rotation marks on their interior surface.

Surface finishes provided a pleasing appearance and also improved the durability of the vessel in day-to-day use. Exterior burnishing and glazing made

FIGURE 12.10   Pueblo Indian woman making pots using the coil method.

vessels watertight or nearly so. The potter smoothed the exterior surface of the pot with wet hands. Often a wet clay solution, known as a slip, was applied to the smooth surface. Brightly colored slips were often used and formed painted decorations on the vessel (Figure 12.11). In later times, glazes came into use in some areas. A glaze is a form of slip that turns to a glasslike finish during high-temperature firing. When a slip was not applied, the vessel was allowed to dry slowly until the external surface was almost like leather in texture. Many utilitarian vessels were decorated with incised or stamped decorations, using shells, combs, stamps, and other tools. Some ceremonial pots were even modeled into human effigies or given decorations imitating the cords used to suspend the pot from the roof (Figure 12.12).

The firing of clay objects requires careful judgment on the part of the potter. Most early pottery was fired over open hearths. The vessels were covered with fast-burning wood, whose ash would fall around the vessels and bake them evenly over a few hours. Far higher temperatures were attained in special ovens, known as kilns, which would not only bake the clay and remove its plasticity but also dissolve carbons and iron compounds. Kilns were used for firing vessels at high temperatures and also for glazing, when two firings were needed. Once fired, the pots were allowed to cool slowly, and small cracks were repaired before they were ready for use.

FIGURE 12.11   A painted Zuni pot of the 1880s. (Height, 9 3/4 inches [25 cm])

FIGURE 12.12   A spouted Moche bottle from Peru bearing a portrait of a man.

The making of clay vessels was circumscribed by all manner of social and other variables. Archaeological literature is rich in descriptions of potmaking techniques among people all over the world. Unfortunately, however, few of these studies go beyond technology and processes of manufacture. They may tell us something about the division of labor in making pots, but they reveal little about the potters' status in their own society, their artistic attitudes, or changing ceramic fashions. In many societies, pottery has a well-defined economic role, and the training of potters is long and elaborate. The analysis of ceramics in archaeology must, however, depend on an understanding of the cultural influences that lie behind the variations in pottery in the archaeological record (Rice, 1984, 1987; Vitelli, 1993). Although recent research has focused on the significance of the variations, it also deals with the role of the individual potter (Krause, 1985).

CERAMIC ANALYSIS

An enormous expenditure of archaeological energy has gone into ceramic analysis, and a sophisticated literature covers the common analytical methods (Olin and Franklin, 1982; Rice, 1987; Shepard, 1971).

Analogy and Experiment   Controlled experiments to replicate prehistoric ceramic technology have been undertaken to acquire data on firing temperatures, properties of tempers, and glazing techniques (Coles, 1973; Shepard, 1971). Ethnographic analogy has been a fruitful source of basic information on potters and their techniques, and the direct historical approach traces modern pottery styles back to the prehistoric past.

Form and Function Analysis   Two features of prehistoric pottery are immediately obvious when we examine a collection of vessels: shape and decoration. Generations of archaeologists have used ethnographic analogy to assign specific functions to different vessel forms. Bowls are commonly used for cooking and eating, but globular vessels are most suitable for storing liquids. Sometimes associations of clay vessels and other artifacts, such as cooking utensils, leave no doubt as to their function. But such instances are rare, and archaeologists usually must rely on analysis of the vessel's form to infer its function.

Form analysis depends on the common assumption that the shape of a vessel directly reflects its function. This assumption, which is based on ethnographic analogies, can be dangerous, for many intangibles affect the function of pottery. Intangibles include the properties of the clay used, the technological devices available, and perhaps most important, the cultural values that constrain not only the technology but also the uses and fashions of the vessels. Changes in vessel form can sometimes reflect a change in economic activities, but the economic evidence must be complete before such conclusions can be drawn. The functional distinction between utilitarian (Figure 11.6) and ceremonial vessels (Figure 12.12) is one of the most evident, but it must be supported by vessel form and also by direct association.

Form analysis is based on careful classification of clusters of different vessel shapes. These shapes can be derived from complete vessels or from potsherds that preserve the rim and shoulder profiles of the vessel. It is possible to reconstruct the pot form from these pieces by projecting measurements of diameter and vessel height. Such analyses produce broad categories of vessel form that are capable of considerable refinement (Sabloff, 1975).

Stylistic Analysis   This form of analysis is much more commonly used, for it concentrates not on the form and function of the vessel but on the decorative styles used by the potters. These are assumed to be independent of functional considerations and so to reflect more accurately the cultural choices made by the makers. In areas like the American Southwest, pottery styles have been used to trace cultural variations over thousands of years.

Even a cursory glance at pottery reports from different parts of the world will show you that archaeologists have used dozens of different stylistic classifications to study their potsherds. Only in recent years have people tried to standardize stylistic classifications, using clusters of easily recognized attributes to produce hierarchies of types, varieties, and modes.

With this approach, small numbers of distinctive attributes from different pottery assemblages are recorded. These attributes commonly appear in associated sets of features that provide the basis for erecting types and varieties of pottery styles, which are assumed to represent the social system behind the pots studied. For instance, Attic and Corinthian pottery from Greece reflect standardized styles which can be dated accurately. Although a variety may represent only the activities of one family of potters, a type can represent the work of several villages or an entire community. Thus, goes the argument, standardized pottery types reflect a fairly rigid social system that prescribes what pottery styles are used, but less formal designs are characteristic of a less restrictive society. James Gifford studied the ceramics from Barton Ramie in the Belize Valley and traced the development of Maya pottery from 800 B.C. onward. He argued that the highly localized styles of earlier times reflected a much more flexible social system than in the Late Preclassic period, after 300 B.C., when pottery designs were standardized over large areas and were controlled, perhaps by rigid cultural values (Gifford, 1976).

Gifford's analysis is based on behavioral assumptions that have yet to be tested. Can one really assume that pottery styles reflect social behavior? The answer must await the day when many more standardized typologies from different areas of the world are available.

Technological Analysis   The more elaborate, computer-generated classifications of today reveal that many of the archaeologist's classificatory cornerstones, such as pottery temper, are in fact subject to complex behavioral and environmental factors rather than being the simple barometers of human behavior they were once thought to be. For example, Marian Saffer found that classifications developed for pottery from the Georgia coast in the Southeastern United States were based on simple criteria, among them tempers of sand, grit, and ground-up potsherds. There appeared to be little variation in the style and decoration in Georgia coastal pottery for 2,000 years. As a result, archaeologists used variations in temper as criteria for distinguishing new cultures and phases. Saffer used clay samples from the islands and the mainland, as well as many decorative and stylistic attributes, together with a sophisticated computer analysis to show that variations in temper could be correlated with the qualities of different potting clays. Thus variations in temper are due not only to cultural factors but to environmental conditions as well (Rice, 1984).

Technological analyses of pottery focus on the fabric and paste in potting clays, and relate ceramic vessels to locally available resources (Bronitsky, 1986). These also provide useful, statistically based yardsticks for interpreting variability between different pottery forms and for developing much more sophisticated pottery classifications. Furthermore, the current interest in regional studies of prehistoric cultures and in trade and exchange encourages the analysis of pottery clays as a means of tracing centers of ceramic manufacture. Throughout later prehistory, clay vessels were major trade commodities, not only for their own qualities but also because they were convenient receptacles for such products as olive oil, wine, or salt. For example, Tell el Amarna in Egypt was founded by the heretic ancient Egyptian king Akhenaten in 1348 B.C. and only occupied until his death 15 years later. It is famous for its fine artworks and the immortal head of Queen Nefertiti, and for its diplomatic correspondence. Egyptologist Flinders Petrie found more than 1,300 Mycenaean potsherds in rubbish dumps from the palace and nearby noble residences. Most of them were from containers used to carry imported, scented oils, which were traded widely from the Aegean across the eastern Mediterranean at the time. By using neutron activation analysis of 37 elements in the clays used to make these vessels, and comparing them with samples taken from Mycenaean vessels discovered in Greece, German scientists have pinpointed their original place of production as a major pottery workshop in the Mycenae-Berbati region of the eastern Peloponnese in mainland Greece, a remarkable piece of archaeological detective work now being expanded with computer data bases (Mommsen and others, 1992).

Numerous other procedures yield valuable information on ancient ceramics, including X-ray diffraction studies and ceramic petrology. These approaches can be used in combination to study what can be called "ceramic ecology," the interaction of resources, local knowledge, and style that ultimately leads to a finished clay vessel (Stimmell and others, 1982). For instance, Mississippian pottery, manufactured in the Southern and Southeastern United States between A.D. 800 and 1500, was fired to a temperature between 800°C and 900°C. The Mississippians used crushed shell to temper their pots, so their vessels should not vitrify at these temperatures. But they did, and scanning electron microscope photographs revealed that the potters may have added salt to their raw clay, perhaps even tasting the clay during manufacture to see if it was correctly mixed. Mississippian settlement was concentrated in valley bottoms, where the potters used clays heavy in montmorillonite, adding crushed shell to it, so that they could work it more easily. This created another problem, that of poor firing. So the potters added salt to improve the firing qualities. However, salt was available in relatively few locations, so a complex trading system in this newly vital commodity developed.

Technological analyses of pottery offer useful ways to amplify manufacturing data obtained from archaeological sources and ethnographic analogy (D. E. Arnold, 1988). Even the sediment found inside ancient pots can be examined spectrographically, and sometimes identified, as was the case with a wine storage jar from Iran dating to 4000 B.C. (Biers and McGovern, 1990).

METALS AND METALLURGY

The study of metallurgy and metals found in archaeological sites is limited both by the state of preservation and by our knowledge of prehistoric metallurgy as a whole (Muhly and Wertime, 1980; Tylecote, 1992). Preservation of metal tools in archaeological horizons depends entirely on the soil's acidity. In some circumstances, iron tools are preserved perfectly and can be studied in great detail; in other cases, soil acids have reduced the iron to a rusty mass that is almost entirely useless. Copper, silver, and gold normally survive somewhat better.

Metals first became familiar to people in the form of rocks in their environment. Properties of metal-bearing rocks—color, luster, and weight—made them attractive for use in the natural state. Eventually, people realized that heat made such stone as flint and chert easier to work. When this knowledge was applied to metallic rocks, stoneworkers discovered that native copper and other metals could be formed into tools by a sequence of hammering and heating. Of the 70 or so metallic elements on earth, only eight—iron, copper, arsenic, tin, silver, gold, lead, and mercury—were worked before the eighteenth century A.D. Properties of these metals that were important to ancient metalworkers were, among others, color, luster, reflecting abilities (for mirrors), acoustic quality, ease of casting and welding, and degrees of hardness, strength, and malleability. Metal that was easily recycled had obvious advantages.

We know much about ancient metallurgy because prehistoric artifacts preserve traces of their thermal and mechanical history in their metallic microstructure. This structure can be studied under an optical microscope. Each grain of the metal is a crystal that forms as the metal solidifies. The shape and size of the grains can reveal whether alloys were used and indicate the cooling conditions and the type of mold used. At first, prehistoric metallurgists used "pure" metals, which could be worked easily but produced only soft tools. Then they discovered how to alloy each of these metals with a second one to produce stronger, harder objects with lower melting points. The basic data for studying prehistoric alloys come from phase diagrams, which relate temperature and alloy composition, showing the relative solubility of metals when combined with other metals. Phase diagrams were developed under controlled conditions in a laboratory and tend to reflect ideal conditions. By examining the object under an optical microscope, researchers can often spot differences in chemical composition, such as the cored, treelike structure that is characteristic of cast copper-tin alloys. Metals contain insoluble particles that can give clues to the smelting procedures and types of ores used. An energy-dispersive X-ray spectrometer and a scanning electron microscope are used to identify the particles. This impressive battery of analytical techniques has enabled archaeologists to study how 6,000 years of experimentation took humanity from simple manipulation of rocks to the production of steel in about 1000 B.C. The record of these millennia is read in the lenses of the microscope, and reveals the triumphs and frustrations of the ancient smith.

COPPER

The earliest metal tools were made by cold-hammering copper into simple artifacts. Such objects were fairly common in Near Eastern villages by 6000 B.C. Eventually, some people began to melt the copper. They may have achieved sufficiently high temperatures with established methods used to fire pottery in clay kilns. The copper was usually melted or smelted into shapes and ingots within the furnace hearth itself. Copper metallurgy was widespread by about 4000 B.C. (Muhly, 1980). European smiths were working copper in the Balkans as early as 3500 B.C. (Coles and Harding, 1979). In contrast to high-quality stone and iron, copper ores are rare and concentrated in well-defined regions. The metal was normally, but not invariably, alloyed with tin, which is even rarer. In the New World, copper-working was well-developed among the Aztecs and the Inca. The archaic peoples of Lake Superior exploited the native deposits of copper ore on the southern shores of the lake, and the metal was widely traded and cold-hammered into artifacts from Archaic to Woodland times (Figure 12.13).

BRONZE

The real explosion—it was nothing less—in copper metallurgy took place midway through the fourth millennium B.C., when Near Eastern smiths discovered that they could improve the properties of copper by alloying it with a second metal such as arsenic, lead, or tin (Coles and Harding, 1979). Perhaps the first alloys came about when smiths tried to produce different colors and textures in ornaments. But they soon realized the advantages of tin, zinc, and other alloys that led to stronger, harder, and more easily worked artifacts. There is reason to

FIGURE 12.13 Mississippian copper repoussé plate of a human head, perhaps a portrait.

believe that they experimented with the proportions of tin for some time, but most early bronzes contain about 5 to 10 percent (10 percent is the optimum for hardness). An extraordinary development in metallurgical technology occurred during the third millennium B.C., perhaps in part resulting from the evolution of writing (Muhly, 1980). By 2500 B.C., practically every type of metallurgical phenomenon except hardening of steel was known and used regularly. The use of tin alloying may have stimulated much trading activity, for the metal is relatively rare, especially in the Near East. Bronze-working was developed to a high pitch in northern China after 2000 B.C. (Chang, 1984).

GOLD

Gold-decked burials fascinate many people, but in fact they are rare finds in archaeological excavations. Gold did, however, have a vital part in prestige and ornament in many prehistoric societies. It is not without reason that Tutankhamun is sometimes described as the "Golden Pharaoh": his grave was rich in spectacular gold finds (Reeves, 1990). The burials of Moche lords of A.D 400 under an adobe platform at Sipán, on the northern coast of Peru, revealed the remarkable wealth of this desert civilization. One shroud-wrapped warrior-priest wore a pair of gold eyes, a gold nose, and a gold chin-and-neck visor; his head was lying on a gold, saucerlike headrest (Figure 1.2). Hundreds of minute gold and turquoise beads adorned the Lord of Sipan, who wore 16 gold disks as large as silver dollars on his chest. There were gold-and-feather headdresses and intricate ear ornaments, one of a warrior with a movable club (Alva and Donnan, 1993). The Chimú peoples of coastal Peru were master goldsmiths of pre-Columbian Latin America (Figure 12.14). The Aztecs and the Inca also were talented goldsmiths whose magnificent products were shipped off to Europe and melted down for royal treasuries in the sixteenth century (Hosler, 1995).

Gold is a metal that rarely forms compounds in its natural state. It was collected in this form, or in grains gathered by crushing quartz and concentrating the fine gold by washing. The melting point of gold is about the same as that of copper, so no elaborate technology was needed. Gold is easily hammered into thin sheets without annealing—heating and cooling of metal to make it less brittle. Prehistoric smiths frequently used such sheets to sheath wooden objects such as statuettes. They also cast gold and used appliqué techniques, as well as alloying it with silver and other ores. Gold was worked in the Near East almost as early as copper, and it was soon associated with royal prestige. The metal was widely traded in dust, ornament, and bead form in many parts of the New World and the Old.

IRON

Bronze Age smiths certainly knew about iron. It was a curiosity, of little apparent use. They knew where to find the ore and how to fashion iron objects by hammering and heating. But the crucial process in iron production is carburization, in which iron is converted into steel. The result is a much harder object, far tougher than bronze tools. To carburize an iron object, it is heated in close contact with charcoal for a considerable period of time. The solubility of carbon in iron is very low at room temperature but increases dramatically at temperatures above 910°C, which could easily be achieved with charcoal and a good Bronze Age bellows. It

FIGURE 12.14   Gold beaker with repoussé (hammered into relief from reverse side) decoration and turquoise inlay, attributed to Chimú gold-smiths of coastal Peru. (About two-thirds actual size)

was this technological development that led to the widespread adoption of iron technologies in the eastern Mediterranean area at least by 1000 B.C. (Muhly and Wertime, 1980).

Iron tools are found occasionally in some sites as early as 3000 B.C., but widespread smelting does not seem to have begun until the second millennium B.C. Use of iron was sporadic at first, for objects made of the metal were still curiosities. Iron tools were not common until around 1200 B.C., when the first weapons made of it appear in eastern Mediterranean tombs. The new metal was slow to catch on, partly because of the difficulty of smelting it. Its widespread adoption may coincide with a period of disruption in eastern Mediterranean trade routes as a result of the collapse of several major kingdoms, among them that of the Hittites, after 1200 B.C. Deprived of tin, the smiths turned to a much more readily available substitute—iron. It was soon in use even for utilitarian tools and was first established on a large scale in continental Europe in the seventh century B.C. by the Hallstatt peoples (Collis, 1984). In earlier times iron had a comparatively limited economic role, most artifacts being slavish copies of bronze tools before the metal's full potential was realized. Weapons such as swords and spears were the first artifacts to be modified to make use of the new material. Specialized ironworking tools, such as tongs, as well as woodworking artifacts, began to be used as soon as the qualities of iron were recognized.

Iron ore is much more abundant in the natural state than copper ore. It is readily obtainable from surface outcrops and bog deposits. Once its potential was realized, it became much more widely used, and stone and bronze were relegated to subsidiary, often ornamental, uses.

The influence of iron was immense, for it made available abundant supplies of tough cutting edges for agriculture. With iron tools, clearing forests became easier, and people achieved even greater mastery over their environment. Ironworking profoundly influenced the development of literate civilizations. Some people, such as the Australian Aborigines and the pre-Columbian Americans, never developed iron metallurgy.

METAL TECHNOLOGIES

Copper technology began with the cold-hammering of the ore into simple artifacts. Copper smelting may have originated in the accidental melting of some copper ore in a domestic hearth or oven. In smelting, the ore is melted at a high temperature in a small kiln and the molten metal is allowed to trickle down through the charcoal fuel into a vessel at the base of the furnace. The copper is further reduced at a high temperature, then cooled slowly and hammered into shape. This annealing adds strength to the metal. Molten copper was poured into molds and cast into widely varied shapes.

Copper ores were obtained from weathered surface outcrops, but the best material came from subsurface ores, which were mined by expert diggers. Copper mines were in many parts of the Old World and provide a fruitful field for the student of metallurgy to investigate. The most elaborate European workings were in the Tyrol and Salzburg areas, where many oval workings were entered by a shaft from above (Champion and others, 1984). At Mitterburg, Austria, the miners drove shafts into the hillside with bronze picks and extracted the copper using elaborate fire-setting techniques. Many early copper workings have been found in southern Africa, where the miners followed surface lodes under the ground (Figure 12.15) (Bisson, 1977). Fortunately, the traditional Central African processes of copper smelting have been recorded. The ore was placed in a small furnace with alternating layers of charcoal and smelted for several hours at high heat maintained with goatskin bellows. After each firing, the furnace was destroyed and the molten copper dripped onto the top of a sand-filled pot buried under the fire. Bronze technology depended on alloying, the mingling of small quantities of such substances as arsenic and tin with copper. With its lower melting point, bronze soon superseded copper for much metalwork. Some of the most sophisticated bronze-working was created

FIGURE 12.15   Excavation in a prehistoric copper mine at Kansanshi, Zambia, Central Africa. The miners followed outcrops of copper ore deep into the ground with narrow shafts, the earth fillings of which yielded both radiocarbon samples and artifacts abandoned by the miners.

by Chinese smiths, who cast elaborate legged cauldrons and smaller vessels with distinctive shapes and decoration in clay molds (Figure 12.16).

Ironworking is a much more elaborate technology that requires a melting temperature of at least 1537°C. Prehistoric smiths normally used an elaborate furnace filled with alternating layers of charcoal and iron ore that was maintained at a high temperature for many hours with a bellows. A single firing often yielded

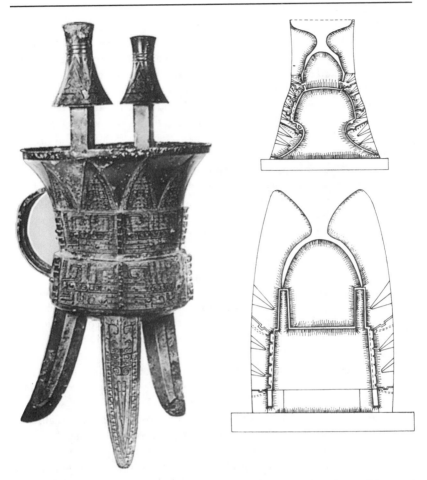

FIGURE 12.16   Shang ceremonial bronze vessel from about the twelfth century B.C., and diagrams of clay molds for casting such vessels.

only a spongy lump of iron, called a bloom, which then had to be forged and hammered into artifacts. It took some time for the metallurgists to learn that they could strengthen working edges by quenching the tool in cold water. This process gave greater strength, but it also made the tool brittle. The tempering process, reheating the blade to a temperature below 727°C, restored the strength. Iron technology was so slow in developing that it remained basically unchanged from about 600 B.C. until Medieval times (Piggott, 1985).

ANALYSIS OF METAL ARTIFACTS

Typological Analyses   In Europe, metal tools have been analyzed for typology since the early nineteenth century. Stylistic changes in bronze brooches, swords, axes, and iron artifacts were very sensitive to fashion and to changing trading patterns. As a result, the evolution of bronze pins or iron slashing swords, for example, can be traced across Europe, with small design changes providing both relative dating and occasional insights into the lifeways of the people using them (Champion and others, 1984). In many ways, such studies are similar in intent to those carried out with stone implements or potsherds.

Technological Analyses In many respects, technological analyses are more important than the study of finished artifacts. Many of the most important questions relating to prehistoric metallurgy involve manufacturing techniques. Technological studies start with ethnographic analogies and actual reconstructions of prehistoric metallurgical processes. Chemists study iron and copper slag and residues from excavated furnaces. Microscopic examination of metal structure and ores yields valuable information not only on the metal and its constituents and alloys but also on the methods used to produce the finished tool. The ultimate objective of the technological analyses is to reconstruct the entire process of metal tool production, from the mining of the ore to the production of the finished artifact.

BONE

Bone as a material for toolmaking probably dates to the very beginnings of human history, but the earliest artifacts apparently consisted of little more than fragments of fractured animal bone used for purposes that could not be fulfilled by wood or stone implements (M. D. Leakey, 1973).

The earliest standardized bone tools date from later prehistoric times. Splinters of bone were sharpened and used as points in many societies, but bone and antler artifacts were especially favored by the Upper Paleolithic peoples of southwestern France from 30,000 to 12,000 years ago and by postglacial hunter-gatherers in Scandinavia (Bordes, 1968). In both the Old World and the New, later bone implements were ground and scraped from long bones, hardened in the fire, and polished with beeswax to produce arrowheads, spearpoints, needles, and other artifacts. Bone was also carved and engraved, especially during Upper Paleolithic times in western Europe, as was reindeer antler (Bahn and Vertut, 1988).

Deer antler was an even more important material than bone for some later hunter-gatherers. Fully grown deer antler is particularly suitable for making barbed or simple harpoons and spearpoints. Bone and antler were much used in prehistoric times for harpoons for fishing and for conventional hunting. Numerous harpoons are found in Magdalenian sites in western Europe (Figure 12.17) and in Eskimo settlements in the Arctic, where they form a valuable index of cultural development, analogous to that of pottery in the American Southwest (Dumond, 1987).

The humble bone or ivory needle may have been a revolutionary artifact in prehistory, for it enabled humans to manufacture layered, tailored clothing. Such garments were essential for colonizing periglacial latitudes of the Old World, an event that occurred at least 25,000 years ago (Fagan, 1991).

BONE TOOL ANALYSIS

In the Arctic, where bone and ivory are critical materials, elaborate typological studies have been made of the stylistic and functional changes in such diverse items as harpoons and the winged ivory objects fastened to the butts of harpoons

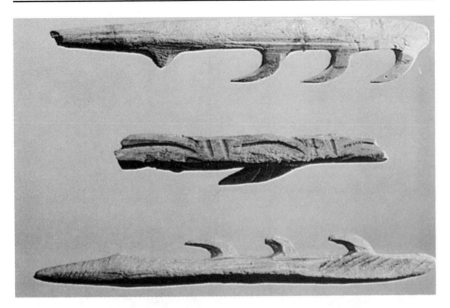

FIGURE 12.17   Magdalenian antler harpoons from France, about 15,000 years old. (About two-thirds actual size)

(Figure 12.18). Other artifacts include picks made of walrus tusk and snow shovels and wedges of ivory and bone, as well as drills and domestic utensils. Studying such a range of bone artifacts is complicated by the elaborate and variable engraved designs applied to some, but H. B. Collins and others have been able to trace the development of the harpoon of the Northern Maritime Eskimo, from the elaborate types of the Okvik and Old Bering Sea phases to the simpler forms characteristic of the Punuk phase and the modern Eskimo weapons (Fitzhugh, 1988).

Functional Analysis   In some areas, such as the Arctic and southern Africa, contemporary ethnographic accounts can be used for fruitful analogies with prehistoric tools. There are, however, dangers to this approach. Although no one can seriously doubt the functional classification of the Old Bering Sea harpoon socket in Figure 12.18, a classification based firmly in analogies, the situation is more complex for the remote past. The Magdalenian peoples who lived in southwestern France 18,000 years ago made extensive use of bone and antler to produce a wide range of artifacts, ranging from spear throwers to harpoons and thong straighteners. While we are probably right in assuming that spear throwers and harpoons were used in the chase, the Magdalenians flourished too far back in the past for us to have any confidence in closer ethnographic analogies (Chapter 14).

Technological Analysis   The simplest bone technologies involved splitting and flaking bones. Fine points were produced by polishing slivers of bone against grinding surfaces. The Magdalenians used fine lengths of reindeer antler, which

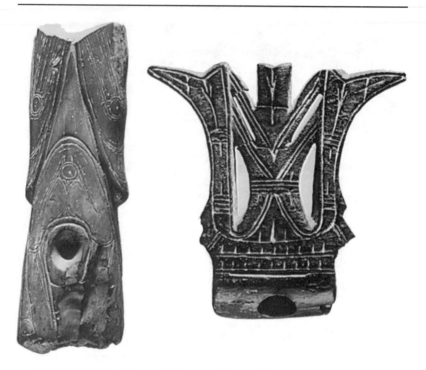

FIGURE 12.18   Bone and ivory artifacts. Left: Harpoon socket piece, Old Bering Sea style (3.7 inches [9.5 cm] long). Right: Turreted ivory object of the Punuk phase (2.7 inches [7 cm] wide). (From the University of Alaska Museum, used by permission)

they removed from the beam by grooving through the hard outer core of the antler with stone burins or engraving tools. It is no coincidence that their material culture included a wide range of scraping and graving tools (R. White, 1986).

WOOD

Nonhuman primates sometimes use sticks to obtain grubs, or for other purposes, so it is logical to assume that since the earliest times, humans also may have used sticks. Wood implements form a major part of many modern hunter-gatherer tool kits; occasional tantalizing glimpses of prehistoric wood artifacts have come down to us where preservation conditions have been favorable. One of the earliest is a fire-hardened spearpoint found in the Clacton Channel, England, which dates to the Holstein interglacial, thought to be around 150,000 B.P. (J. G. D. Clark, 1970). Numerous wood artifacts, as well as basketry, have come from dry sites in western North America (Fagan, 1995b).

The Ozette prehistoric village on the Olympia Peninsula in Washington was buried by a prehistoric landslide that covered up not only several wood long-houses but also many domestic artifacts, baskets, boxes, and other fine wooden tools. The waterlogged conditions preserved fibers and delicate halibut fishhooks complete with their bindings. Richard Daugherty's most important wooden find was a ritual whale fin carved in cedar wood, decorated with 700 sea otter teeth (Figure 12.19) (Kirk, 1974).

WOOD TECHNOLOGY AND ANALYSIS

The manufacture of wood tools involves such well-understood mechanical processes as cutting, whittling, scraping, planing, carving, and polishing. Fire was often used to harden sharpened spearpoints, and oil and paint imparted a fine sheen and appearance to all kinds of wood artifacts. On the rare occasions when wood artifacts are preserved, important clues to their manufacture can be obtained by closely examining the objects themselves. Unfinished tools are very useful, especially handles and weapons that have been blocked out but not finished (Coles and Coles, 1986). Even more revealing are wood fragments from abandoned buildings, fortifications, and even track walkways. Microscopic analysis of wood fragments and charcoal can provide information on the woods used to build houses, canoes, and other such objects. On very rare occasions, stone projectile heads and axes have been recovered in both waterlogged and dry conditions in which their wood handles and shafts have survived, together with the thongs used to bind stone to wood. The Ozette excavations yielded complete

FIGURE 12.19   A whale fin carved from cedar wood and inlaid with more than 700 sea otter teeth, found at Ozette, Washington. The teeth at the base are set in the design of a mythical bird with a whale in its talons.

house planks and even some wood boxes that had been assembled by skillful grooving and bending of planks (Kirk, 1974).

In many instances, the only clues to the use of wood come from stone artifacts, such as spokeshaves and scrapers used to work it, or from stone ax blades and other tools that were once mounted in wood handles. Only the form of the artifact and occasional ethnographic analogies allow researchers to reconstruct the nature of the perishable mount that once made the artifact an effective tool.

Wood was probably the most important raw material available to our ancestors. The thousands upon thousands of ground stone axes in the archaeological record all once had wood handles. Wood was used for house building, fortifications, fuel, canoes, and containers. Most skilled woodworking societies used the simplest technology to produce both utilitarian and ceremonial objects. They used fire and the ringing of bark to fell trees, stone wedges to split logs, and shells and stones to scrape spear shafts.

BASKETRY AND TEXTILES

Basket production was one of the oldest crafts (Adovasio and Gunn, 1977). Basketry includes such items as containers, matting, bags, and a wide range of fiber objects. Textiles are found in many later, dry sites, and they are well preserved along the Peruvian coast (Moseley, 1992).

Some scholars believe that basketry and textiles are among the most sensitive artifacts for the archaeologist to work with, culturally speaking, on the grounds that people lived in much more intimate association with baskets and textiles than with clay vessels, stone tools, or houses. Furthermore, even small fragments of basketry and textiles display remarkable idiosyncrasies of individual manufacture.

In a remarkable experiment, Dale Croes and Jonathan Davis (1977) used a computer mapping program to study the baskets made by several families occupying a large house at the waterlogged Ozette site in Washington. They compiled a computer plot of the distribution of basket types and found that basketry activities were concentrated near the walls of the house. Using the computer, they then plotted and compared different attributes throughout the structure. The clusters that resulted from these analyses were used to show that basketry styles differed from family to family within the group who lived in the house. This is highly experimental research, but it does show the great potential for computer-aided studies of basketry and other artifacts. When preserved, baskets are amenable to the same kinds of functional and stylistic analyses as other artifacts.

Patricia Anawalt is a textile expert who has spent many years studying pre-Columbian garments depicted on Mexican Indian codices. This research has enabled her to work out some of the complicated sumptuary rules that governed military uniforms and other clothing. For example, the lengths, material, and decoration of Aztec men's cloaks were regulated precisely by the state (Figure 11.5). Even the type of knot was specified (Anawalt, 1981).

The dry climate of the Peruvian coast has preserved the wardrobes of Paracas nobles buried between 600 and 150 B.C. Paracas rulers wore mantles, tunics, ponchos, skirts, loincloths, and headpieces. These garments were embroidered with rows of brightly colored anthropomorphic, zoomorphic, and composite figures

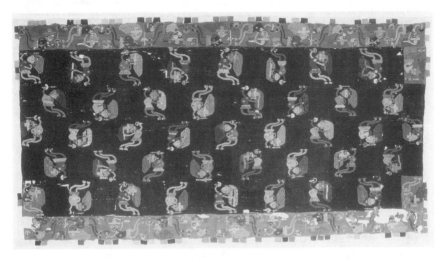

FIGURE 12.20   Cotton funerary textile from the Paracas Peninsula, Peru, dating to c. 300 B.C.

(Figure 12.20). Interpreting the iconographic patterns that appear on these ancient garments tells us something of Paracas religious and social customs (Paul and Turpin, 1986). One of the important functions of a Paracas ruler was to mediate between people and the supernatural forces that influenced and determined life's events. Many of the rulers' garments were adorned with shaman figures, showing that the wearer had a special relationship to the supernatural (Anton, 1988).

It is easy for archaeologists to become preoccupied with technology and artifacts, but the potential is great for insights into prehistoric society and subsistence from such research, provided that the ultimate objective is to study people rather than inanimate objects.

SUMMARY

- One of the main inorganic materials used by prehistoric people was stone, especially hard, homogeneous rock, which fractures according to the conchoidal principle.
- We described the basic techniques for manufacturing stone tools, starting with the stone-on-stone technique, the cylinder-hammer method, and the prepared cores used to produce blanks for Middle Paleolithic artifacts. Blade technology came into use about 45,000 years ago.
- Lithic experimentation and ethnoarchaeology have leading roles in the study of stone technologies; edge-wear and petrological studies throw light on the trade in raw materials and the uses to which tools were put.
- Ceramics (clay objects) are a major preoccupation of archaeologists and date to the last 10,000 years of prehistory. We described the process of pottery manufacture, the various methods used, and the surface finishes employed.

- Ceramic analysis proceeds by analogy and experiment, research in which controlled experiments with firing and the properties of clay have had leading parts. The vessels themselves are studied through form and functional analyses. Many archaeologists prefer to use stylistic analyses. Clusters of attributes are used now, also, in attempts to standardize stylistic classifications.
- Prehistoric metallurgy is a phenomenon of the past 6,000 years. We described the basic properties of copper, bronze, gold, and iron and some of the cultural contexts in which metallurgy developed. Typological and technological analyses are used to study prehistoric metallurgy.
- Bone tools are thought to be among the earliest of all artifacts. They are important in some areas, particularly the Arctic, as indicators of typological change. The functional analysis of bone tools is somewhat easier than that of stone tools or ceramics, for the uses of bone objects are often easier to determine.
- The manufacture of wood tools involves well-understood mechanical processes, such as cutting and whittling, and these can often be identified even from unfinished artifacts. Stone artifacts and other materials have been found mounted in wood handles, and this provides insights into the uses of composite artifacts.
- Basketry and textiles offer unique opportunities for studying individual idiosyncrasies in the archaeological record; they also provide useful chronological markers.

GUIDE TO FURTHER READING

Arnold, Dean E. *Ceramic Theory and Cultural Process*. Cambridge: Cambridge University Press, 1985. A well-written and closely argued discourse on ceramic ecology.

Crabtree, Don E. *An Introduction to Flintworking*. Pocatello: Idaho State Museum, 1972. The best simple account of basic lithic technology ever written, by an expert with a lifetime of experience. Valuable glossary and clear illustrations.

Hosler, Dorothy. *The Sounds and Colors of Power*. Cambridge, Mass.: MIT Press, 1995. An authoritative study of metallurgy in the Americas. For the advanced reader.

Keeley, Lawrence H. *Experimental Determination of Stone Tool Uses*. Chicago: University of Chicago Press, 1980. An especially valuable monograph on use wear and stone tools.

Muhly, James D., and Theodore Wertime, eds. *The Coming of the Age of Iron*. New Haven, Conn.: Yale University Press, 1980. Essays on early metallurgy, ranging more widely than just ironworking.

Rice, Prudence M. *Pottery Analysis: A Sourcebook*. Chicago: University of Chicago Press, 1987. An excellent reference book for anyone interested in ceramics.

Shepard, Anna O. *Ceramics for the Archaeologist*, 2d ed. Washington, D.C.: Smithsonian Institution, 1971. The definitive work on ceramics in the New World. Technical and informative.

PART 6

RECONSTRUCTING PAST LIFEWAYS

And I prophesied as I was commanded; and as I prophesied, there was a noise, and behold, a rattling; and the bones
came together, bone to its bone. And as I looked, there were
sinews on them, and flesh had come upon them, and skin
had covered them.

Ezekiel 37:10

In Part Six we discuss how archaeologists study the ways in which people
have solved the problems of making a living and adapting to their environment. Chapter 13 describes the analysis of food remains, animal bones,
vegetable foods, and evidence of prehistoric diet. Archaeologists rely very heavily on ethnographic analogies for interpreting prehistoric subsistence and past
lifeways. In Chapter 14 we examine some of the latest work in experimental
archaeology and ethnoarchaeology, approaches that involve both controlled
experiments and observations in the field. Human settlements changed radically
through prehistory. In Chapter 15 we examine the ways in which archaeologists
study ancient settlement patterns, with special reference to recent research in
Mesoamerica. We give special attention to methods for reconstructing ancient
environments. Trade, social organization, and religious beliefs are the topics of
Chapter 16, which makes the point that much information on these subjects can
be obtained through careful research design and meticulous analysis of field
data. The study of prehistoric lifeways is an essential preliminary to interpretation of culture change, discussed in Part Seven.

—13—

SUBSISTENCE AND DIET

As we saw earlier, archaeologists have long considered humans and their culture as merely one element in a complex ecosystem. The study of prehistoric subsistence, then, has developed hand in hand with attempts to understand the complex interrelationships between the way people make their living and their environment. Chapter 13 examines some of the many ways in which archaeologists study ancient subsistence in an ecological context.

EVIDENCE FOR SUBSISTENCE

Evidence for ancient subsistence comes from many sources:

- *Environmental data.* Background data on the natural environment are a prerequisite for studying subsistence. Such data can include information on such things as animal distributions, ancient and modern flora, and soils—a range of potential resources to be exploited.
- *Faunal remains.* Animal bones are a major source of information on hunting practices and domestic animals. The identification and interpretation of such finds depends on detailed knowledge of mammalian anatomy, as well as ethnographic data relating to butchery practices.
- *Plant remains.* These can include both wild and domestic species, obtained using flotation methods or from carbonized contexts. Such materials are less frequently preserved in the archaeological record than animal bones. Sometimes pollen analysis will throw light on prehistoric agriculture and collecting habits.
- *Human bones.* Stable carbon isotopes of skeletal collagen from human bones provide vital information on ancient diets, anatomical anomalies, ancient diseases and dietary stress.
- *Feces (coprolites).* These yield tiny fragments of ecofacts and pollen grains and are preserved in dry caves. They are vital evidence for reconstructing prehistoric diet in both animals, and in our context, humans.
- *Artifacts.* The picture of human subsistence yielded by artifacts can be limited because of poor preservation. Many critical artifacts used in the chase or for gardening and food preparation were made from perishable materials, such as basketry, wood, or fiber.

• *Prehistoric art.* Artists sometimes depicted scenes of the chase, fishing, and food gathering.

ANIMAL BONES (ZOOARCHAEOLOGY)

Zooarchaeology is the study of animal bones found in the archaeological record. Its goal is to reconstruct the environment and behavior of ancient peoples to the extent that animal remains allow (Klein and Cruz-Uribe, 1984). Although some zoologists have specialized in the study of animal bones from archaeological sites, most zooarchaeologists either have a background in paleontology or in the study of prehistoric faunas (faunal analysis). (For general discussions, see Binford, 1981b; Brewer, 1992; S. J. M. Davis, 1987. A series of case studies appears in Crabtree and Ryan, 1991.)

TAPHONOMY

The word taphonomy (Greek, *taphnos,* "tomb"; *nomos,* "law") is used to describe the processes that operate on organic remains, after the organism dies, to form fossil deposits (Lyman, 1994; Shipman, 1981). Simply put, it is the study of the transition of animal remains from the biosphere to the lithosphere.

A fossil fauna goes through several stages as it passes from the biosphere into the hands of the archaeologist. The bones originally come from what scientists call the "life assemblage," the community of live animals in their natural proportions. The animals that are killed or die of natural causes become the "deposited assemblage," the carcasses or portions of carcasses that come to rest in a site. The "fossil assemblage" consists of the animal parts that survive in a site until excavation or collection by a scientist. The "sample assemblage," however, is what reaches the laboratory, the part of the fossil assemblage that is actually excavated or collected (Klein and Cruz-Uribe, 1984). Anyone carrying out faunal analysis must solve two problems: the statistical problem of estimating the characteristics of a fossil assemblage from a sample, and the taphonomic problem of inferring the nature of the deposited assemblage from the fossil one.

Taphonomy involves two related avenues of investigation. The first is actual observation of recently dead organic remains as they are transformed gradually into fossils; the other is the study of fossil remains in the light of this evidence. This field of investigation came into fashion during the 1960s and 1970s, when archaeologists became interested in the meaning of animal bone scatters at such early sites as Olduvai Gorge in East Africa and especially in the celebrated *Australopithecus* caves of South Africa (Shipman and Rose, 1983).

In the 1950s, South African anatomist Raymond Dart (1957) had studied the fragmentary bones from the South African caves and argued that the bone fragments had been broken systematically by *Australopithecus,* an early hominid. *Australopithecus,* he argued, had not used stone for tools but had relied on an "osteodontokeratic" culture of bone, tooth, and horn to satisfy daily needs. Dart's research was based on little more than study of the bones alone and on the assumption that the caves were typical inhabitable caverns rather than refuges. Then biologist C. K. Brain (1981) questioned Dart's assumptions with long-term observations of bone fractures made by nonhuman primates. He showed that the uninhabitable caves were filled with the remains of hyena kills and that the bone fractures were not the result of human toolmaking. Brain also pointed out that different skeletal parts had different preservation qualities—that some more delicate bones might vanish sooner than, say, robust limb bones.

Many questions about the processes that transform living organisms into "archaeological" bones remain unanswered, despite some research into such topics as ways in which bones can be transported and disarticulated by both carnivores and natural agents such as water. For example, experiments with captive hyenas have shown that they first choose backbones and hip bones, which they usually destroy completely. Limb bone ends are often hewed off, while shafts are often intact. These experiments are of importance because they tell us that the early hominid bone caches at Olduvai Gorge were picked over by hyenas after their human owners had departed, a process that led to the destruction of many body parts, thereby making it impossible to tell whether the hominids had selectively transported some parts of animal kill and not others (Marean and others, 1992). Humans disarticulate animals with tools long before the carcasses are dispersed by natural phenomena or by carnivores, so their systematic activities are at least a baseline for examining patterns of damage on archaeological bones. Interpretation of prehistoric living floors and kill sites has to be undertaken with great care, for the apparent patterns of bones and artifacts on such a prehistoric land surface represent not only human activity but complex and little-understood natural processes as well.

Many zooarchaeologists worry that interpretations of bone assemblages from archaeological sites will never reconstruct the actual living population environment. However, Klein and Cruz-Uribe (1984) believe that viable paleoecological reconstructions can be made when several fossil assemblages can be compared using statistical measures, provided that both the quality of bone preservation and the sedimentary conditions of the bones at each location are similar. Each situation must be assessed with great care.

SORTING AND IDENTIFICATION

Faunal remains are usually fragmentary, coming from dismembered carcasses butchered either at the archaeological site or at the hunting grounds. To some degree, how much of the carcass is carried back to camp depends on the animal's size. Small deer may be taken back whole, slung from the shoulder. Hunter-gatherers sometimes camped at the site of the kill of a large animal, where they ate parts of the carcass and dried parts for later use. Almost invariably, however, the bones found in occupation sites have been broken to splinters. Every piece of usable meat was stripped from the bones; sinews were made into thongs, and the skin was formed into clothing, containers, or sometimes housing. Even the entrails were eaten. Limb bones were split for their delicious marrow; some bones were made into such tools as harpoon heads, arrow tips, or mattocks (Figure 13.1).

It would be a mistake to assume that the fragmentary bones found in an archaeological deposit will give you either an accurate count of the number of animals killed by the inhabitants or accurate insights into the environment at the

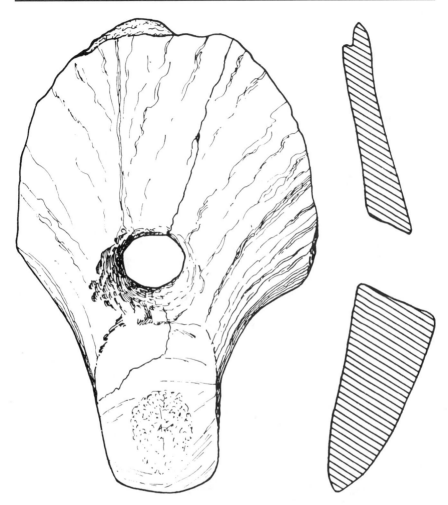

FIGURE 13.1   Elk antler mattock from Star Carr, England. (Two-thirds actual size)

time of occupation (Grayson, 1984). The fragmentary bones found in an archaeological deposit have been subjected to many diverse processes since their deposition. Taphonomic processes often result in major changes in buried bone, perhaps even destroying the bones of smaller animals though not of larger ones. Then there are human factors: people may carry in some game from far away, yet kill all of their goats at the village. We have no means of knowing what spiritual role some animals possessed in ancient societies or of studying taboos and other prohibitions that may have caused certain animals to be hunted and others to be ignored. Nor, as we have already pointed out, have we any means of knowing precisely what the relative frequencies of different animal species were in the prehistoric environment. Certainly researchers cannot use animal bones from archaeological sites for this purpose. The difference between what one might call the "actual animal" and the "archaeological animal" identified by the archaeologist is always unknown (S. J. M. Davis, 1987; Grayson, 1981). The archaeological animal consists of a scatter of broken bones that have been shattered by a butcher, then subjected to hundreds or thousands of years of gradual deterioration in the soil (Figure 13.2).

Most bone identification is done by direct comparison with bones of known species. It is fairly simple and easily learned by anyone with sharp eyes (S. J. M. Davis, 1987). But only a small proportion of the bones in a collection are complete enough for this purpose. The drawing of a dog in Figure 13.3 illustrates a typical mammalian skeleton. Small skull fragments, vertebrae, ribs, scapulae, and pelvic bones are normally of little use in differentiating a domestic animal from a wild one or one species of antelope from another. Upper and lower jaws and their dentition, individual teeth, the bony cores of horns, and sometimes the articular surfaces of long bones are easy to identify. Teeth are identified by comparing the cusp patterns on their surfaces with those on comparative collections carefully taken from the site area (Figure 13.4). In some parts of the world, the articular ends of long bones can be used as well, especially in such regions as the Near East or parts of North America, where the indigenous mammalian fauna is somewhat restricted. It is even possible to distinguish the fragmentary long bones of domestic stock from those of wild animals of the same size in the Near East, provided that the collections are large enough and the comparative material is sufficiently complete and representative of all ages of individuals and of variations in size from male to female. But in other areas, such as sub-Saharan Africa, the indigenous fauna is so rich and varied, with such small variations in skeletal anatomy, that only horn cores or teeth can help distinguish between species of antelope and separate domestic stock from game animals. Even the dentition is confusing, for the cusp patterns of buffalo and domestic cattle are remarkably similar, often distinguishable only by the smaller size of the latter. Experts disagree as to what constitutes identifiability of bone, so it is best to think in terms of levels of identifiability rather than simply to reject many fragments out of hand. For example, you can sometimes identify a fragment as coming from a medium-sized carnivore even if you have no way of telling that it is from a wolf.

The identification stage of a bone analysis is the most important, for several fundamental questions need answering: Are domestic and wild species present? If so, what are the proportions of each group? What types of domestic stock did the inhabitants keep? Did they have any hunting preferences that are reflected in the proportions of game animals found in the occupation levels? Are any wild species characteristic of vegetational associations no longer found in the area today?

COMPARING BONE ASSEMBLAGES

Zooarchaeologists Richard Klein and Kathryn Cruz-Uribe (1984) describe measures of taxonomic abundance for assessing whether differences between assemblages are real or the result of biased collecting or other factors. They also use the same measures to make estimates of the relative abundance of different species. The number of identified specimens (NISP) is a count of the

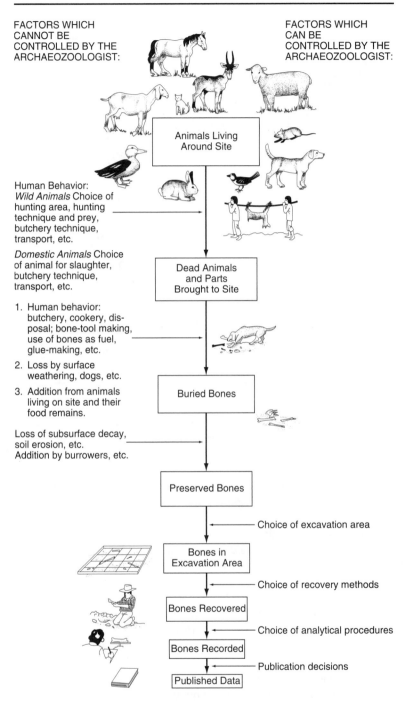

FACTORS WHICH
CANNOT BE
CONTROLLED BY THE
ARCHAEOZOOLOGIST:

FACTORS WHICH
CAN BE
CONTROLLED BY THE
ARCHAEOZOOLOGIST:

Animals Living
Around Site

Human Behavior:
Wild Animals Choice of
hunting area, hunting
technique and prey,
butchery technique,
transport, etc.

Domestic Animals Choice
of animal for slaughter,
butchery technique,
transport, etc.

Dead Animals
and Parts
Brought to Site

1. Human behavior:
   butchery, cookery, disposal; bone-tool making,
   use of bones as fuel,
   glue-making, etc.

2. Loss by surface
   weathering, dogs, etc.

3. Addition from animals
   living on site and their
   food remains.

Buried Bones

Loss of subsurface decay,
soil erosion, etc.
Addition by burrowers, etc.

Preserved Bones

Choice of excavation area

Bones in
Excavation Area

Choice of recovery methods

Bones Recovered

Choice of analytical procedures

Bones Recorded

Publication decisions

Published Data

FIGURE 13.2   Analysis of bones from the archaeological record. This
figure shows some of the factors that affect the data. Factors that the
archaeologist cannot control are on the left; those that the archaeologist
can control are on the right.

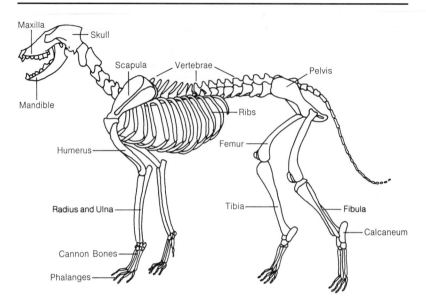

FIGURE 13.3   Skeleton of a dog, showing the most important body parts from the osteological viewpoint.

number of bones or bone fragments from each species in a bone sample. This measure has obvious disadvantages, especially since it can overemphasize the importance of one species that has more bones than another or has carcasses that were butchered more thoroughly than those of other species. Both human activities like butchering and natural processes like weathering can affect the NISP as well. The NISP does have a certain value, especially when used in conjunction with an estimate of the minimum number of individuals from which the identified bones have come. The minimum number of individuals (MNI) is a count of the number of individuals necessary to account for all the identifiable bones. This count is smaller than the NISP and is often based on careful counts of such individual body parts as heel bones. The MNI overcomes many limitations of the NISP because it is a more accurate estimate of the actual number of animals present. However, everything depends on the experts using the same method of calculating the MNI—which they often do not (Grayson, 1984).

The NISP and MNI together permit us to estimate the number of animals present in a bone sample, but they are highly imperfect ways of measuring abundance of animals in an archaeological sample, let alone of providing a means for relating the bone materials to a living animal population in the past. Klein and Cruz-Uribe have developed sophisticated computer programs to overcome some of the limitations of NISP and MNI, programs that lay out the basic information that is vital for intersample comparisons.

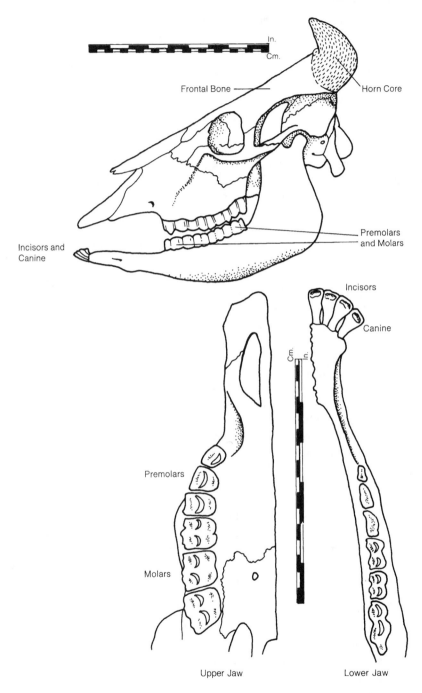

FIGURE 13.4   The skull and mandible of a domestic ox, showing important osteological features. (One-fourth actual size)

SPECIES ABUNDANCE AND CULTURAL CHANGE

Climatic rather than cultural change was probably responsible for most long-term shifts in animal species abundance in the Ice Age. Some shifts must reflect human activity, changes in the way in which people exploited other animals (Klein and Cruz-Uribe, 1984). These changes are, however, very difficult to distinguish from environmental changes.

One of the few places where it has been possible to document such changes is in South Africa. Richard Klein has studied large faunal samples from two coastal caves in the Cape Province. The Klasies River cave was occupied by Middle Stone Age hunter-gatherers between about 130,000 and 95,000 years ago, during a period of warmer climate, and thereafter until about 70,000 years ago, when the weather had become much cooler. The seashore was close to the cave during the earlier, warmer millennia. Numerous mollusks, seal bones, and penguin remains tell us much about Middle Stone Age diet in the cave. Seabirds and fish are rare. Eland, a large antelope, is the most common large mammal, more than twice as common as the Cape buffalo. The rest of the land mammals are species common in the area during modern historic times.

In contrast, the Nelson's Bay cave nearby contains evidence of later Stone Age occupation, dating to after 20,000 years ago, much of it at a time when the sea was some miles from the cave, during the coldest part of the last Ice Age glaciation. Bones of flying seabirds and fish are abundant in this cave, whereas eland are only a third as common as buffalo.

Klein points out that tool kits are quite different in the two caves. The Middle Stone Age people of the Klasies River cave used large flake tools and spears. In contrast, the later Nelson's Bay hunters had bows and arrows and a rich tool kit of small stone tools and bone artifacts, many of them for specialized purposes such as fowling and fishing. These innovations allowed Late Stone Age hunters to kill dangerous or more elusive species with greater frequency. Thus, the reason that the Middle Stone Age people took more eland was not that eland were more abundant in earlier times but that more elusive creatures were captured less frequently. There is every indication that the Klasies people were less advanced behaviorally (Klein and Cruz-Uribe, 1984).

Klein combines some other faunal evidence with his mammalian and climatic data. The Klasies River site contains larger tortoise and limpet remains, as if these creatures were permitted to grow to a larger size than in later times. This implies less pressure on the tortoise and shellfish populations from a smaller human population before technologically more advanced people arrived.

GAME ANIMALS

Though the listing of game animals and their habits gives an insight into hunting practices, in many cases the content of the faunal list gains particular significance when we seek to explain why the hunters concentrated on certain species and apparently ignored others.

TABOOS   Dominance by one game species can result from economic necessity, convenience, or it can simply be a matter of cultural preference. Many societies restrict hunting of particular animals or consumption of certain game meat to one or the other sex. The !Kung San of the Dobe area of Botswana have complicated personal and age- and sex-specific taboos on eating mammals (R. B. Lee, 1979). No one can eat all 29 game animals regularly taken by the San; indeed, no two individuals will have the same set of taboos. Some mammals can be eaten by everyone, but with restrictions on what part they may eat. Ritual curers will set personal dietary restrictions on other animals; no one eats primates and certain carnivores. Such complicated taboos are repeated with innumerable variations in other hunter-gatherer and agricultural societies and have undoubtedly affected the proportions of game animals found in archaeological sites.

Examples of specialized hunting are common, even if the reasons for the attention given to one or more species are rarely explained. The specialized big-game hunting economies of the Plains Indians are well-known (Frison, 1978). Another factor is overhunting, or the gradual extinction of a favorite species (Grayson, 1980). One well-known example is *Bos primigenius* (Figure 13.5), the European aurochs or wild ox, which was a major quarry of Upper Paleolithic hunters in western Europe and was still hunted in postglacial times and after food production began (Kurtén, 1968). The last aurochs died in a Polish park in 1627. We know from illustrations and contemporary descriptions what these massive animals looked like. The bulls were large, up to 6 1/2 feet (2 m) at the shoulder, and often had very long horns. The male coat was black with a white stripe along the back and white curly hair between the horns. Through careful, long-term breeding and selecting for the physical features of the aurochs, German and Polish biologists have "reconstituted" these beasts successfully. Reconstituted aurochs are fierce, temperamental, and extremely agile if allowed to run wild. The German experiments have provided a far more convincing reconstruction of a most formidable Pleistocene mammal than could any number of skeletal reconstructions or artists' impressions.

CHANGES IN HUNTING ACTIVITIES   Hunting activities have changed drastically in recent times. Richard Lee (1979) records how the older members of the San state say that in earlier times there were more game animals and a bigger hunting population in the central interior of Botswana. Their forefathers used to hunt in large groups, killing buffalo, giraffe, and elephants. Today, their descendants have a predominantly gathering economy, supplemented by the meat of 29 mammals, mostly those whose carcasses have a relatively high meat yield. Hunting is a common pursuit, the warthog being the most important source of meat, together with small game. This change in hunting habits results directly from the importation of Victorian rifles and from early hunting safaris, which decimated the wonderful African fauna within three generations.

SEASONAL OCCUPATION

Many prehistoric hunter-gatherers and farmers, like their modern counterparts, lived their lives in regular, seasonal cycles in which subsistence activities changed according to the seasons of the year. The Pacific Northwest Indians congregated near salmon rivers when the summer runs upstream took place. They would catch thousands of salmon and dry them for consumption during the winter months. The early dry season in central Africa brings into season an

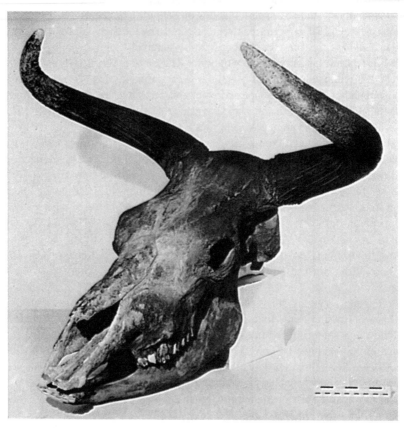

FIGURE 13.5   *Bos primigenius.*(top) A *Bos primigenius* skull from Cambridgeshire, England. (bottom) The aurochs as depicted by S. von Herbenstain in 1549.

abundance of wild fruit, which formed an important part of early farmers' diet 1,500 years ago. How do archaeologists study seasonal activities and reconstruct the "economic seasons" of the year (Jochim, 1979)? Every aspect of prehistoric life was affected by seasonal movements. The Northwest Indians enjoyed a complex ceremonial life during the sedentary winter months. The settlement pattern of the Khoi Khoi pastoralists of the Cape of Good Hope changed radically between dry and wet seasons (Elphick, 1977). During the dry months they would congregate at the few permanent water holes and near perennial rivers. When the rains came, the cattle herders spread out over the neighboring arid lands, watering their herds in the standing waters left by rainstorms.

How do archaeologists study seasonality? A variety of approaches have been used with some success (Monks, 1981). The simplest method uses bones or plant remains. To illustrate this technique, in one case bird bones were used to establish that a San Francisco Bay site was visited about June 28, when cormorants were young (Howard, 1929). The presence of cod bones in early Norwegian fishing sites indicates that they were occupied during the winter and early spring. This type of analysis is fine, provided that the habits of the animals or of the plants being examined are well-known or have not changed through time. Some plants are available for much of the year but are edible only during a few short weeks.

Knowledge about the ecology of both animals and plants is essential, for the "scheduling" of resource exploitation, though perhaps not explicit, was certainly a major factor in the evolution of cultural systems. Some species such as deer are relatively insensitive to seasonal changes, but people sometimes exploited them in different ways at different times of the year. The Coast Salish of the Pacific Northwest took bucks in the spring and does in the fall (Monks, 1981).

Then there are physiological events in an animal's life that an archaeologist can use to establish seasonal occupation. During the fifteenth century A.D., a group of Plains hunters regularly took bison near a water hole at Garnsey, New Mexico (Speth, 1983). John Speth analyzed the body parts at the kill site and discovered that the hunters had a strong preference for male beasts during the spring, the season at which the hunts took place. The butchers had abandoned body parts with a low meat yield like skulls and upper neck bones. In contrast, bones that yielded a great deal of meat, marrow, or grease were underrepresented at Garnsey. Many more high-utility bones like these were taken from males than females. Speth believes that the hunters concentrated on males because their meat had a higher fat content and they were in better condition than females after the winter months.

Growth patterns in animal bones can sometimes yield clues on seasonal occupation. The epiphyses at the ends of limb bones are slowly joined to the main bones by ossification as an animal ages. This approach can certainly give some clues as to the general age of an animal population in, say, a hunting camp, but such variables as nutrition, even castration in domesticated animals, can affect the rate of fusion. Some species, such as ducks, mature much faster than others, such as deer. Clearly, knowledge of the different ages at which epiphyses fuse is essential to this approach.

Everyone knows that teeth erupt from upper and lower jaws as one grows into adulthood, often causing problems with wisdom teeth in people. Teeth are such durable animal remains that many archaeologists have tried to use them to age game and domestic animal populations. It is easy enough to study tooth eruption from complete or even fragmentary upper and lower jaws, and it has been done with domesticated sheep, goats, and wild deer. Again, factors of nutrition, even domestication, can affect eruption rates, and the rate at which teeth wear can vary dramatically between one population and another (Monks, 1981).

In some cases, too, archaeologists have used reindeer and deer antlers to study seasonal occupations. The males of the deer family shed their antlers after the fall breeding season. By studying the antlers in the site and the migration habits of red deer, scientists believe that a 10,000-year-old hunting camp at Star Carr in northeast England was occupied from May to September (Legge and Rowley-Conwy, 1988).

Interpretation of seasonal occupation depends heavily on ethnographic analogies. One classic example is wild wheat. Botanist Gordon Hillman has studied the gathering of wild wheat in the Near East and has shown that the collectors must schedule their collecting activities very precisely if they are to gather the harvest before the ears fall off the stems or the grain is consumed by birds and other animals (Hillman and Davis, 1990). It is reasonable to assume that the same precise scheduling was essential during prehistoric times, an analogy that has enabled Near Eastern archaeologists to interpret seasonal occupations on sites in Syria and elsewhere.

Seasonality is still a surprisingly neglected subject in the archaeological literature, but it has great potential. By studying not only large mammals and obvious plant remains but also tiny mollusks and even fish bones and fish scales, it may be possible to narrow the window of seasonal occupation at many sites to surprisingly tight limits.

DOMESTIC ANIMALS

Nearly all domestic animals originated from a wild species with an inclination to be sociable, facilitating an association with humans (Clutton-Brock, 1981). Domestic animals did not all originate in the same part of the world; they were domesticated in their natural area of distribution in the wild. Scholars have assumed that domestication of wild animals takes place when a certain level of cultural achievement is reached. Domestication everywhere seems to begin when a growing population needs a more regular food supply to feed larger groups of people; domestication is dependent on such conditions and is a prerequisite for further population growth.

Wild animals lack many characteristics that are valuable in their domestic counterparts. Thus wild sheep have hairy coats, but their wool is not the type produced by domestic sheep, which is suitable for spinning; aurochs, ancestors of the domestic ox, and wild goats produce sufficient milk for their young, but not in the quantities so important to humans. Considerable changes have taken place during domestication, as people develop characteristics in their animals that often render them unfit for survival in the wild.

The history of domestic species is based on fragmentary animal bones found in the deposits of innumerable caves, rock shelters, and open sites (Clutton-Brock and Grigson, 1985; Clutton-Brock, 1989). Osteological studies of wild and domesticated animals are inhibited both by fragmentation of the bones in most sites and by the much greater range of sexual and growth variation in domestic populations than in wild ones (S. J. M. Davis, 1987). Nevertheless, a number of sites have produced evidence of gradual osteological change toward domesticated animals. If the bones of the wild species of some prehistoric domesticated animals are compared with those of the domestic animals throughout time, the range of size variations first increases, and eventually selection in favor of smaller animals and less variation in size appears. This transition is fluid, however, and it is difficult to identify wild or domestic individuals from single bones or small collections.

The bones of domestic animals demonstrate that a high degree of adaptability is inherent in wild animals. People have found it necessary to change the size and qualities of animals according to their needs, with corresponding effects on their skeletal remains. Different breeds of cattle, sheep, and other domestic animals have been developed since the beginning of domestication.

SLAUGHTERING AND BUTCHERY

Some insights into peoples' exploitation of wild and domestic animals can be obtained by studying not only animal bones themselves but also their frequency and distribution in the ground. As Lewis Binford (1978) points out, however, the problem is not to record distributions and frequencies alone but to establish what they mean in terms of human behavior. His studies of caribou hunting and exploitation by the Nunamiut Eskimo of Alaska have provided a mass of data on the ways in which people exploit animals and are directly relevant to interpretation of faunal remains (see Chapter 14).

Sex, Age, and Slaughter Patterns Clearly, determining the sex of an animal and the age at which it was killed may provide a way of studying the hunting or stock-raising habits of the people who did the slaughtering. Archaeologists have used a variety of methods for establishing sex and age from fragmentary bones (S. J. M. Davis, 1987).

In many mammal species, males and females vary considerably in size and build. For example, male horses have canine teeth, but females usually lack them. In humans, the female pelvis is very different from that of the male in order to accommodate the birth canal. We can estimate the proportions of males and females in sites like the Garnsey bison kill by comparing the ratio of male to female body parts; in this case the differences between male and female beasts are known. Such analyses are much harder when less is known of size differences or when bones are very fragmentary. Zooarchaeologists use a variety of bone measurements to distinguish sex, but such approaches are fraught with statistical and practical difficulties; they work best on complete bones. Even then, it may only be possible to identify different measurement distributions that may or may not reflect differences between the sexes.

How old were these cattle when they were slaughtered? Did the inhabitants concentrate on immature wild goats rather than on fully grown ones? These are the kinds of questions that are of importance on many sites. To answer them, researchers must establish the age of the animals in the faunal sample at death.

The skeletal parts most commonly used to determine the age of an animal at death are teeth and the epiphyses at the ends of limb bones. In almost all mammals, bones where the epiphyses are unfused come from younger animals. This enables us to construct two age classes: immature and fully grown. If we know the ages at which epiphyses fuse, as is sometimes the case in species like domestic cattle, we can add additional classes. Unfortunately, epiphyseal fusing is too coarse a method to provide the kind of data that archaeologists need.

Fortunately, teeth and upper or lower jaws provide a more accurate way of establishing animal age. Teeth provide an almost continuous guide to the age of an individual from birth to old age. Complete upper and lower jaws allow us to study immature and mature teeth as they erupt, so we can identify not only the proportion of young animals but the very old animals as well.

Individual teeth can also be a mine of information on animal age. Some biologists are using growth rings on teeth, but this method is still highly experimental. A far more promising approach measures the height of tooth crowns. Richard Klein, an expert on African bones, has measured crown heights on Stone Age mammal teeth found at the Klasies River and Nelson's Bay caves in the Cape Province of South Africa. Taken as two groups, the teeth measurements probably give interesting general impressions of the hunting habits of Middle and Late Stone Age peoples in this area (Klein, 1977). Klein compared the mortality distributions from the Cape buffalo and other large and medium-sized species to mortality curves from modern mammal populations. He identified two basic distributions (Klein and Cruz-Uribe, 1983):

The catastrophic age profile is stable in size and structure and has progressively fewer older individuals. This is the normal distribution for living ungulate populations (Figure 13.6, left) and is that normally found in mass game kills achieved by driving herds into swamps or over cliffs.

The attritional age profile (Figure 13.6, right) shows an underrepresentation of prime-age animals relative to their abundance in living populations, but young and old are overrepresented. This profile is thought to result from scavenging or simple spear hunting.

Klein found that the Cape buffalo age distributions from both sites were close to those observed for modern buffalo killed by lions, where both young and old males are vulnerable to attack because they are isolated from the large herds of formidable prime animals. Thus, he argued, the Stone Age hunters at both caves enjoyed a lasting, stable relationship with their prey populations of buffalo. The distributions for eland and bastard hartebeest (smaller, gregarious antelopes) were much more similar to the catastrophic profile. Klein speculates that they were similar because these species were hunted in large game drives, like the bison on the Great Plains. Thus entire populations would be killed at one time.

Age distributions can reflect all kinds of other activities as well. The Star Carr site in northeastern England contains no young red deer. Most of the animals were 3 to 4 years old, inexperienced subadults killed as they were leaving their mothers (Legge and Rowley-Conwy, 1988).

Hunting and slaughter patterns are subject to all manner of subtle variables, many of which are described by Lewis Binford (1978, 1981b). While studying hunting practices among the Nunamiut Eskimo of Alaska, he found that the

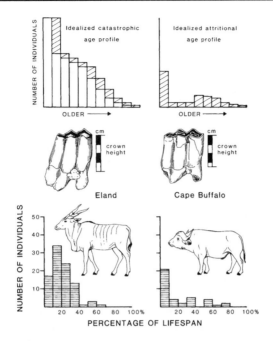

FIGURE 13.6   Idealized mortality data based on molar crowns of two common South African mammals, the eland and the Cape buffalo: (left) idealized catastrophic age profile; (right) idealized attritional age profile.

hunters butchered animals as part of a much broader subsistence strategy. The Nunamiut rely heavily on stored meat for most of the year and thus orient their hunting practices toward storage objectives, as well as many other considerations. In the fall, they may hunt caribou calves to obtain skins for winter clothing, and the heads and tongues of these animals provide the meat for the people who process the skins. Binford stresses that it is difficult to interpret slaughter patterns without closely understanding the cultural systems of which hunting was a part.

Domestic animals are a controllable meat supply and subject to quite different selection criteria. In more advanced agricultural societies, cattle or horses might be kept until old age for draught purposes, surplus males being castrated and females being retained until they stopped lactating or were of no further use for breeding or plowing. Even if riding or work animals were not kept, the problem of surplus males persists. This surplus is an abundant source of prime meat, and these animals were often slaughtered in early adulthood. Cattle stood for wealth in many traditional societies, as they do in some today; and they were slaughtered on such special occasions as funerals or weddings. The herd surplus was consumed in this manner, and the owner's obligations were satisfied.

Butchery   The fragmentary bones in an occupation level are the end product of the killing, cutting up, and consumption of domestic or wild animals. To understand the butchery process, the articulation of animal bones must be examined in the levels where they are found, or a close study must be made of fragmentary body parts. The Olsen-Chubbock kill site in Colorado yielded evidence of a slaughtered bison herd. The hunters camped beside their kill, removing the skin and meat from a carcass and perhaps drying some surplus meat for later consumption. The butchering tools used by the skinners are found in direct association with the bones, so the excavations preserve the moment of butchery for posterity (Wheat, 1972).

Interpreting butchery techniques is a complicated matter, for many variables affect the way in which carcasses were dismembered. The Nunamiut relied heavily on stored meat, and the way they dismembered a caribou varied according to storage needs, meat yield of different body parts, and proximity of the base camp. The animal's size may affect the number of bones found at a base site: goats, chickens, or small deer could have been carried to the village as complete carcasses, but of larger beasts often only small portions were brought in. Sometimes animals with high meat yield were consumed where they were killed and every scrap of flesh and entrails utilized. Even using the NISP and MNI indices, interpretation is difficult.

Once again, the problem is to establish the meaning of archaeological distributions in terms of human behavior. Just how complicated this is in the context of butchery can be appreciated from Binford's comment (1978) that the Nunamiut criteria for selecting meat for consumption are the amount of usable meat, the time required to process it, and the quality of the flesh. The only way to interpret archaeological distributions is with a detailed understanding of the cultural systems that generated them (see Chapter 14).

VEGETAL REMAINS

Foraging, the gathering of wild vegetable foods, was a staple of the prehistoric world from the earliest times up to the moment when people first began to cultivate the soil some 10,000 years ago. Unfortunately, the foods that were collected or cultivated are very hard to find in the archaeological record, so our knowledge of prehistoric foraging and the early history of food crops is very incomplete (Hawkes, 1983). Seeds, fruits, grasses, and leaves are among the most fragile of organic materials and do not survive long unless they are carbonized or preserved under very wet or arid conditions. Fortunately, new flotation methods and AMS radiocarbon dating techniques (Chapter 8) are yielding a wealth of new information.

CARBONIZED AND UNBURNED SEEDS

These are normally found in cooking pots, in midden deposits, or among the ashes of hearths, where they were dropped by accident. Though the preservation conditions are not ideal, researchers can identify domestic and wild plant species from such discoveries (Pearsall, 1989; B. D. Smith, 1994). Much early evidence for cereal cultivation in the Near East comes from carbonized seeds. Many more unburned vegetable remains occur in waterlogged sites and in dry caves. A Stone Age campsite at Gwisho hot springs in central Zambia, on the edge of a tract of savannah woodland rich in vegetal foods, contained quantities of seeds and fruit preserved by the high water table in the spring (Fagan and Van Noten, 1971). Ten thousand identifiable vegetal fragments came from the occupation levels at Gwisho, many of them from six species eaten by southern African hunters, a remarkable continuity of subsistence patterns over more than 4,000 years.

The extremely dry conditions of the North American desert West and of the Peruvian coast have preserved thousands of seeds, as well as human coprolites that contain a wealth of vegetal material. Hogup cave in Utah was occupied as early as 7000 B.C. From about 6400 to 1200 B.C., the inhabitants relied so heavily on pickleweed seeds in their diet that the early deposits are literally golden with the chaff threshed from them (Aikens, 1970; Madsen and O'Connell, 1982). After 1200 B.C., deposits of pickleweed and the milling stones used to process it decline rapidly. An abrupt rise in the nearby Great Salt Lake may have drowned the marsh where the seed was collected, so the cave was only visited by hunting parties.

Four 19,000- to 17,000-year-old hunter-gatherer camps at the Wadi Kubbaniya site in the Egyptian desert have yielded remarkable collections of charred plant foods, some apparently roasted seeds preserved in human infant feces. The inhabitants brought back more than 20 types of food plant. The most common were nutgrass tubers, which are easily collected by the ton with simple digging sticks and are used as famine food when crops fail in West Africa and India today. Indeed, harvesting the wild tubers each year fosters new growth. When cooked to make it nontoxic, nutgrass can serve as a staple, and may, in fact, have fulfilled such a purpose at Wadi Kubbaniya (Wendorf and others, 1980).

TEHUACÁN

The Tehuacán Valley in the state of Puebla, Mexico, has provided a record of continuous human occupation, from the earliest times to the Spanish conquest, and a unique chronicle of early maize cultivation (Byers, 1967; MacNeish, 1970). Early inhabitants of the valley lived mainly by hunting rabbits, birds, and turtles. Later, about 6700–5000 B.C., their successors subsisted mostly on wild plants such as beans and amaranth. These people were seasonally mobile hunter-gatherers who eventually added the deliberate cultivation of plants to their seasonal round without making radical changes in their lifeways. The dry valley caves document a gradual shift from wild-plant foraging to an almost total dependence on cultivated crops, including maize and beans. And within a few centuries of full domestication of maize, the people had moved into permanent village settlements anchored to their fields.

The wild ancestor of maize was an indigenous grass, teosinte (*Zea mays* subsp. *parviglumis*), which still grows in Central America. Botanists now believe that both maize and beans were domesticated from identifiable wild ancestors in the Guadalajara region, some 155 miles (250 km) west of the Tehuacán Valley, where both teosinte and a population cluster of wild beans still flourish (B. D. Smith, 1994). Richard MacNeish has excavated more than a dozen sites in Tehuacán, five of which contained the remains of ancient corn; 80,000 wild-plant remains and 25,000 specimens of corn came from the sites. Early maize cobs came from the lowest occupation level in San Marcos cave, dried ears no more than three-quarters of an inch (20 mm) long. This was fully domesticated maize, incapable of dispersing its kernels naturally, as wild plants do to regenerate. The mature plants would have stood about 4 feet (1.2 m) high with one to five ear-bearing lateral branches,

FIGURE 13.7   The evolution of maize. The various stages in the transformation from teosinte to maize. The earliest teosinte form is (a), the stabilized maize phenotype (e). The harvesting process increased the condensation of teosinte branches and led to the husks becoming the enclosures for corn ears. (After Galinat, 1985)

each plant producing ten to fifteen small corn ears (Figure 13.7). Originally, MacNeish estimated their age at between 7,000 and 5,500 years ago, but recent AMS radiocarbon dates on actual cobs from San Marcos and Coxcatlán caves only date to as early as 4,700 to 4,600 years ago (about 2700 B.C.), a thousand years or so later than originally thought.

FLOTATION RECOVERY

Flotation techniques have been employed systemically to recover seeds in recent years. The method uses water or chemicals to free the seeds, which are often of microscopic size, from the fine earth or occupation residue that masks them; the

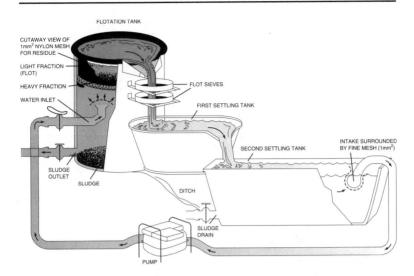

FIGURE 13.8   Model of a water flotation device, for recovering plant remains using recycled water, developed by botanist Gordon Hillman. The lightest remains float to the surface and are caught in float sieves. The heavier material sinks and is caught in light nylon mesh.

vegetal remains usually float and the residue sinks. Although this technique enables us to recover seeds from many sites where it was impossible before, by no means can it be applied universally, for its effectiveness depends on soil conditions. Using flotation, Stuart Struever and his colleagues recovered more than 36,000 fragments of carbonized hickory nut shell from ovens, hearths, and storage-refuse pits in the Apple Creek site in the lower Illinois Valley. This settlement also yielded 4,200 fragments of acorn shell, as well as more than 2,000 other seeds from at least three species. Few cultivated seeds were found, indicating that the inhabitants relied on hickory nuts and acorns for much of their vegetable diet (B. D. Smith, 1992).

Flotation has revolutionized the study of prehistoric vegetal remains. The methods used are being refined as more experience is gained with them under varied field conditions. A number of ingenious machines have been developed to carry out large-scale flotation (Figure 13.8). The sample of earth is poured into the screened container and agitated by the water pouring into the screen. The light plant remains and other fine materials float on the water and are carried out of the container by a sluiceway that leads to fine mesh screens, where the finds are caught, wrapped in fine cloth, and preserved for the botanists to study. The heavy sludge, in the meantime, sinks to the bottom of the container inside the oil drum.

Flotation is rewriting the early history of farming in all parts of the world, partly because it yields much larger samples of domestic and wild seeds to work with. Andrew Moore used flotation with great efficiency on the Stone Age farming village at Abu Hureyra on the Euphrates River in Syria. He acquired 712 seed samples from soil deposits that comprised a bulk of more than 132 U.S. gallons

(500 liters). Each sample contained as many as 500 seeds from over 150 plant taxa, many of them edible. By dissecting these large samples, botanist Gordon Hillman was able to document the retreat of oak forests in the region, and the changes in plant gathering which accompanied environmental change. He showed how Abu Hureyra was in the grip of a prolonged drought in about 8500 B.C. At first the people turned to drought-resistant small-seeded grasses. Then they abandoned Abu Hureyra, probably moving to places close to permanent water, where experiments with the cultivation of cereal crops began. As more favorable conditions returned in about 7700 B.C., a farming settlement appeared at Abu Hureyra, based on the cultivation of emmer, einkorn, and barley, staple cereal crops that were rotated with pulses like lentils, vetches, and chick-peas. But they still supplemented their diet by collecting significant quantities of wild vegetable foods (Moore, 1985). They lived in the same place for a long period of time because they rotated their crops and used a simple fallow system that allowed exhausted fields to recover before being replanted.

GRAIN IMPRESSIONS

Apart from the seeds themselves, which reveal what the food plants were, grain impressions in the walls of clay vessels or adobe brick help to uncover the history of agriculture or gathering. The microscopic casts of grains that adhered to the wet clay of a pot while it was being made are preserved in the firing and can be identified with a microscope. Numerous grain impressions have been found in European handmade pottery from the end of the Stone Age (Figure 13.9). Grain impressions have been studied in the Near East and the western Sahara; some related work on adobe bricks has been carried out in the Western United States.

PALYNOLOGY

The study of pollen has been an extremely valuable tool for analyzing European forest clearance (Figure 13.10). About 4000 B.C., the components of high forest—oak, ash, beech, and elm—simultaneously declined, while the pollen of grasses increased sharply in northern Europe. At many locations, charcoal layers underlie the zone where forest trees declined. The increase in grass pollen was also associated with the appearance of several cultivation weeds, including *Plantago,* which is associated with cereal agriculture in Europe and went with European farmers throughout the world, even to North America. The tree cover vanished as a direct result of farming activity—humanity's first major imprint on the environment. Similar pollen curves have been plotted from data gathered elsewhere in Europe.

The Chilean wine palm (*Jubaia chilensis*) is the largest in the world, growing to a height of at least 65 feet (20 m). The tree yields a valuable sap to make honey or potent wine, while the nuts have a prized oily kernel. At the time of its first settlement by Polynesian voyagers in the eighth or ninth century A.D., Easter Island in the south Pacific supported forests of wine palms. Pollen diagrams from the island show how deforestation and depletion of the environment through burning and cutting destroyed the palm forests, diminished water supplies, and cut the people off from the outside world by destroying the timber used for offshore canoes (Bahn, 1992).

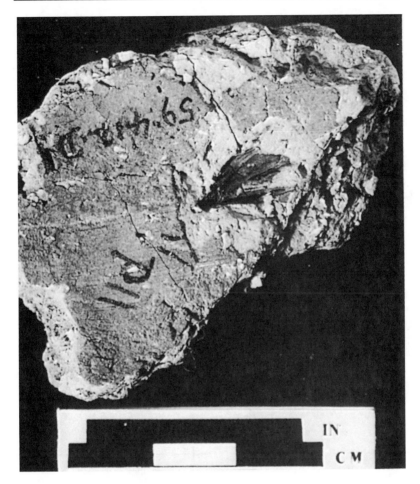

FIGURE 13.9 A grain impression from a Neolithic pot at Hurst Fen, Cambridgeshire, England.

PLANT PHYTOLITH ANALYSIS

Opal phytoliths, minute particles of silica from plant cells, are created from hydrated silica dissolved in groundwater that is absorbed through a plant's roots and carried through its vascular system (Rovner, 1983; Piperno, 1988). Silica production is continuous throughout the growth of a plant. Phytolith samples are collected in much the same way as pollen samples, then studied by identifying individual species. Most research in the field has been with grasses, so the archaeological applications are obvious, especially in the study of prehistoric agriculture.

Archaeological applications of phytolith research have hardly begun, but the method shows promise. Anna Roosevelt used phytolith analysis on sites in the Orinoco River Valley of Venezuela. She found that the percentages of grass

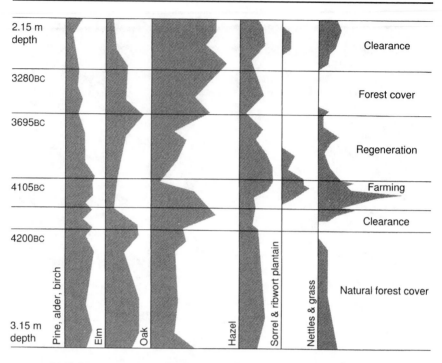

FIGURE 13.10   Pollen diagram from northern Ireland that documents the impact of farmers on the prehistoric landscape. About 4150 B.C., tree pollen counts fall dramatically, as farmers first clear the forest. At the same time, grasses and field weeds take over. Subsequently, the farmers abandon their fields and the forest regenerates before being cleared again after 3280 B.C.

phytoliths increased dramatically at the very moment when maize was introduced to the area, as indicated by carbon 13 and carbon 12 analysis of skeletal material and actual seeds. Deborah Pearsall and Dolores Piperno have developed a complex formula for distinguishing between phytolith samples produced by modern maize and those produced by wild grasses (Pearsall and Piperno, 1990). They analyzed soil samples from radiocarbon sites in coastal Ecuador and found phytolith evidence for the presence of maize in layers radiocarbon-dated to as early as 8,000 to 7,000 years ago. When these results were first announced, they seemed in broad agreement with the earlier chronology for maize at Tehuacán. But AMS dating of actual Mexican cobs has shortened the time frame considerably. There are no cobs in the Ecuadorian sites, and the average size of wild and possible domesticated phytoliths was tiny. Thus Pearsall and Piperno's results are somewhat controversial (B. D. Smith, 1994).

Phytolith analysis has many potential applications in archaeology in the study of diet, through the use of coprolites and even phytoliths embedded in jawbones, but research is still in its infancy. It is likely to become as important as palynology in the years to come.

INTERPRETING EVIDENCE

No matter how effective the recovery techniques used for vegetal remains, the picture of either food gathering or agriculture is bound to be incomplete. A look at modern hunter-gatherers reveals the problem (R. B. Lee, 1979). The !Kung San of the Kalahari in southern Africa are classic hunter-gatherers who appear in every book on ethnography. Many early writers on hunter-gatherers assumed that the !Kung relied on game alone and lived in perennial starvation that was relieved periodically by meat-eating orgies. In fact, nothing could be further from the truth. Much subsistence activity of the San and other hunter-gatherers is conducted by the women, who gather wild vegetable foods that comprise a substantial part of their diet. Many early observers were naturally preoccupied with hunting techniques and more spectacular subsistence activities, for in former times many people pursued larger game, often cooperating with other bands in the chase.

Today, vegetable foods have a leading part in the San diet and have presumably increased in importance as the large game herds have diminished. The San know of at least 85 species of edible fruit, seeds, and plants; of this enormous subsistence base, they eat regularly only some 9 species, especially the *bauhinia*. In a famine year or when prime vegetable food sources are exhausted, they turn to other species, having an excellent cushion of edible food to fall back on when their conventional diet staple is scarce. Theoretically, therefore, the San can never starve, even if food is scarce at times. Their territory, of course, is delineated in part by available sources of vegetable foods as well as by water supplies; its frontiers in many cases represent a day's walking distance to the gathering grounds and back to the base camp.

AGRICULTURE AND DOMESTIC AND WILD ANIMALS

Very few subsistence-farming peoples have ever relied on agricultural products or their herds alone to provide them with food year-round. Hunting, fishing, and gathering have always supplemented the diet, and in famine years or times of epidemic the people have fallen back on the natural resources of their environment for survival.

Since food production has led to increased population densities, however, famine often ensues because the resource base of wild foods for farmers is smaller than that which may have supported a smaller hunter-gatherer population in comfort (Scudder, 1962). Even in times of plenty, most food producers rely on game for some of their meat, judged from the bones of wild animals in faunal collections where cattle and small stock are also present. The proportions of domestic and wild species in such a collection are important in assessing the roles of hunting and pastoralism in the economy. If such figures are based on how many individuals are represented in the collection or on some sound formulas, the results can be revealing, especially when a series of collections is available from a cultural sequence extending over several hundred years.

The changeover from hunting and gathering to full-fledged agriculture and animal domestication took place remarkably rapidly in many places, as evidenced, for example, at the Abu Hureyra site.

FIGURE 13.11   Abu Hureyra, Syria.

ABU HUREYRA

Just how important an influence domesticated animals had on prehistoric horticulture and agriculture is well documented at the Abu Hureyra settlement (Moore, 1989). The first village of pit houses with reed roofs was built in about 9500 B.C. and flourished for 500 years. The climate was damper and warmer than today. Abu Hureyra lay in well-wooded steppe, where animals and wild cereals were abundant. The hamlet lay close to woodland and open country, and also to the fertile river floodplain where wild cereal grasses could be harvested. Each spring, Abu Hureyra's hunters preyed on thousands of migrating Persian gazelle, which moved northward with the changing season (Figure 13.11). They killed thousands of them and dried the meat for later use (Legge and Rowley-Conwy, 1987).With such a favorable location, Abu Hureyra increased in size to 300 to 400 people, until a long drought cycle and perhaps deforestation due to heavy firewood consumption caused abandonment of the settlement. About 7700 B.C. another village rose on the same site. This was a much larger village that grew to cover nearly 30 acres (12 ha). At first the inhabitants still hunted gazelle intensively. Then, about 7000 B.C., within the span of a generation or so, they switched over to herding domesticated sheep and goats and to growing cereal crops. Visitors to the village would have found themselves wandering through a closely knit community of rectangular, one-story, mud-brick houses, joined by narrow lanes and courtyards.

Andrew Moore's very thorough excavations show us that each gradual or rapid change in the subsistence pattern or environment of Abu Hureyra instituted by humans led to a complicated chain reaction affecting every sector of the inhabitants' culture.

The rate of herd growth is affected by many factors, among them endemic stock disease, nutrient qualities of grazing grass, availability of water supplies, and in some areas, distribution of the dreaded tsetse fly, carrier of trypanosomiasis, which is fatal to cattle and harmful to humans. Similar factors also affect the growth rate of domestic stock because the size of cattle or smaller stock can vary widely from one environment to another.

BIRDS, FISH, AND MOLLUSKS

BIRDS

Bird bones have been sadly neglected in archaeology, although some early investigators did realize their significance. In 1902 the famous Peruvianist Max Uhle dug a large Native American mound at Emeryville on the eastern shores of San Francisco Bay. The site was excavated again in 1926, and Hildegarde Howard studied a large collection of bird remains from the dig. Her report (1929) illustrates the potential importance of bird faunas in archaeology. She found that water birds were the predominant species, especially ducks, geese, and cormorants, and that land birds distinctive of hill country were absent. All the geese were winter visitors, mostly found in the bay area between January and April of each year. The cormorant bones were nearly all immature, suggesting that the Indians had been robbing cormorant rookeries; most of the cormorant bones equaled an adult bird's in size, but ossification was less complete, equivalent to that in modern birds about 5 to 6 weeks old. Howard examined rookery records and estimated that a date of June 28 each year would be the approximate time when the rookeries could be raided. Thus, from the evidence she concluded that the Emeryville mound was occupied during both the winter and the early summer, and probably all year.

Bird hunting has often been a sideline in the struggle for subsistence. In many societies, boys have hunted winged prey with bow and arrows while training for hunting larger game. A specialized bird-hunting kit is found in several cultures, among them the postglacial hunter-gatherer cultures of northern Europe. Though bows and spears were used in the chase, snaring was obviously practiced regularly. The birds found in some African hunting and farming sites are almost invariably species like guinea fowl, which fly rarely and are easily snared. No traces of the snares have been found in excavations, for they would have been made of perishable materials. Surprisingly little has been written on prehistoric fowling, perhaps because bird bones are fragile and present tricky identification problems (Avery and Underhill, 1986; Gilbert and others, 1985; Klein and Cruz-Uribe, 1984).

FISH

Fishing, like fowling, became increasingly important as people began to specialize in different and distinctive economies, and as their environmental adaptations became more sophisticated and their technological abilities improved. Evidence for this activity comes from both artifacts and fish bones (Colley, 1990; Wheeler and Jones, 1989).

Freshwater and ocean fish can be caught in various ways. Nets, basket traps, and dams were methods in wide use from 10,000 years ago on, but their remains rarely survive in the archaeological record except in dry sites or waterlogged deposits (Petersen and others, 1984). Basket fish traps have been found in Danish peat bogs, dating to the Atlantic vegetational period (J. G. D. Clark, 1975). The ancient Egyptians employed somewhat similar traps, depicted in Old Kingdom tomb paintings (2575–2134 B.C.). Nets remain the most popular fishing device and were used in northern Europe in postglacial times, too. A larger fish weir, constructed of vertical sticks 4 to 16 feet (1.2 to 4.9 m) long and sharpened at one end with a stone ax, enclosed an area of 2 acres (0.8 ha) at Boylston Street, Boston. The weir was built about 2500 B.C. and was probably the work of coastal Archaic people. Such traps were evidently widely used along the Atlantic Coast, built in estuary areas where tidal currents were strong. In the Boston weir, brush and flexible withies—twigs or branches—were placed between the stakes; fish were diverted into the enclosure by "leaders," also made of brush, leading to the trap mouth. Some days' work must have been necessary to build this weir, which provided an almost inexhaustible food supply for its designers.

Fishhooks, harpoons, and barbed spearheads are frequent finds in lakeside or riverside encampments. The earliest fishhooks had no barbs, but they did have a U-shaped profile (Figure 13.12). Postglacial hunting peoples, such as the Maglemose folk of Denmark, used such artifacts in the seventh millennium B.C., in all probability to hunt the pike, a prized freshwater fish in prehistoric times (J. G. D. Clark, 1975).

FIGURE 13.12   Bone fishhooks of the Maglemose culture in northern Europe. (After J. G. D. Clark; two-thirds actual size)

Artifacts alone tell us little about the role of fish in the prehistoric economy or about the fishing techniques of prehistoric peoples. Did they fish all year or only when salmon were running? Did they concentrate on bottom fish or rely on stranded whales for protein? Such questions can be answered only by examining the fish bones themselves—or actual fish scales. Perhaps the most effective method of collecting fish remains is to take samples from each level, an approach advocated by Richard Casteel, who found that this was one-ninth as time-consuming as normal collection methods. Furthermore, he succeeded in identifying 30 percent more fish types from his column samples. He used this approach at the Glenrose Cannery site on the Fraser River Delta in British Columbia, where salmon and sturgeon were taken for thousands of years, from at least 5,700 years ago (Casteel, 1976; Matson, 1981).

The Chumash Indians of southern California were remarkably skillful fishermen, venturing far offshore in frameless plank canoes and fishing with hook and line, basket, net, and harpoon. Their piscatory skill is reflected in the archaeological sites of Century Ranch, Los Angeles, where the bones of such deep-sea fish as the albacore and oceanic skipjack were found, together with the remains of large deep-water rockfish that live near the sea bottom in water too deep to be fished from the shore (C. King and others, 1968). Five other species normally occurring offshore, including the barracuda, were found in the same midden. The bones of shallow-water fish, among them the leopard shark and the California halibut, were discovered in the same sites, indicating that both surf fishing and canoe fishing in estuaries with hook and line, basket, or net were also practiced. The degree to which a community depends on fishing can be impressive. Lakeside or seaside fishing encampments tend to be occupied longer than hunting camps, for the food supply, especially when combined with collection of shellfish, is both reliable and nourishing.

MOLLUSKS

Shellfish from seashores, lakes, or rivers formed an important part of the prehistoric diet for many thousands of years (Waselkov, 1987). The identification of the mollusks in shell middens is a matter for expert conchologists, who possess a mine of information on the edibility and seasons of shellfish.

Freshwater mollusks were important to many Archaic bands living in the southeastern United States, but because each mollusk in itself has limited food value, the amount of mollusks needed to feed even a small band of about 25 people must have been enormous. It has been calculated that such a band would need between 1,900 and 2,250 mussels from the Meramec River each day, and a colossal accumulation of between 57,000 and 67,000 each month (Parmalee and Klippel, 1974). A group of 100 persons would need at least 3 tons of mussels each month. Confronted with such figures, no one can believe that mollusks were the staple diet of any prehistoric peoples. Rather, they were a valuable supplemental food at times of scarcity during the year or a source of variety in a staple diet of fish, game, or vegetable foods (Waselkov, 1987).

When freshwater or seawater mollusks were collected, the collectors soon accumulated huge piles of shells at strategic places on the coast or on the shores of lakes, near rocky outcrops or tidal pools where mollusks were commonly found (Meehan, 1982). Modern midden analysis involves systematic sampling of the deposits and counting and weighing of the various constituents of the soil. The proportions of different shells are readily calculated, and their size, which sometimes changes through time, is easily measured. California shell middens have long been the subject of intensive research, with the changes in frequency of mollusks projected against ecological changes in the site areas.

The La Jolla culture middens of La Batiquitos Lagoon in San Diego are a notable example of such analysis. Claude N. Warren (R. M. Crabtree, 1963) took column samples from one shell mound and found that the remains of five species of shellfish were the dominant elements in the molluscan diet of the inhabitants. The changes in the major species of shellfish were then calculated for each excavated level. They found that *Mytilus,* the bay mussel, was the most common in the lower levels, and was gradually replaced by *Chione,* the Venus shell, and *Pecten,* the scallop, both of which assumed greater importance in the later phases of the site's occupation, which has been radiocarbon-dated from the fifth to the second millennia B.C. Warren found that *Ostrea,* the oyster, a species characteristic of a rocky coast, was also most common in the lower levels, indicating that the San Diego shore was rocky beach at that time, with extensive colonies of shellfish. By about 6,300 years ago La Batiquitos Lagoon was silted to the extent that it was ecologically more suitable for *Pecten* than the rock-loving *Mytilus.* Soon afterward, however, the lagoons became so silted that even *Pecten* and *Chione* could no longer support a large population dependent on shellfish. The inhabitants then had to move elsewhere. Similar investigations elsewhere in California have also shown the great potential of mollusks in the study of prehistoric ecology.

Many peoples collected mollusks seasonally, but it is difficult to identify such practices from the archaeological record. Growth bands in mollusk shells have been used to measure seasonality, but the most promising approach is to measure the oxygen-isotopic ratio of its shell carbonate, which is a function of the water temperature (Lightfoot and Cerrato, 1988). Using a mass spectrometer, you can measure the oxygen 18 composition at the edge of a shell, obtaining the temperature of the water at the time of the mollusk's death. It is difficult to obtain actual temperature readings, but you can gain an idea of seasonal fluctuations, thereby establishing whether a mollusk was taken in winter or summer (Deith, 1983; Killingley, 1981).

Both freshwater and seawater shells had ornamental roles as well. Favored species were traded over great distances in North America. Millions of *Mercenaria* and *Busycon* shells were turned into wampum belts in New England in early Colonial times. *Spondylus gaederopus,* a mussel native to the Black Sea, the Sea of Marmara, and the Aegean, was widely distributed as far north and west as Poland and the Rhineland by European farmers in the fifth millennium B.C. The *Conus* shell, common on the East African coast, was widely traded, finding its way into the African interior and becoming a traditional perquisite of chieftainly prestige. The nineteenth-century missionary and explorer David Livingstone records that, on his visit to Chief Shinte in western Zambia in 1855, the going price for two *Conus* shells at that time was a slave; for five, a tusk of elephant ivory (Figure 13.13).

FIGURE 13.13   Ingombe Ilede, Zambia, Central Africa: burial with *Conus* shells, dating to around the fifteenth century A.D. The shells, objects of great prestige, are around the neck and numbered 1 to 4.

SUBSISTENCE DATA FROM ROCK ART

Rock art is a major source of information on economic activities. Upper Paleolithic cave art in southwestern France depicts dozens of mammal species, perhaps meant to represent large, meaty animals that were economically (and symbolically) valuable (Bahn and Vertut, 1988).

Much more detailed information comes from southern Africa. Some years ago, African archaeologist J. Desmond Clark published an account of Late Stone Age hunting and gathering practices in southern Africa in which he drew heavily on the rock art of Zimbabwe and South Africa. The paintings depict the chase, weapons, collecting, and camp life. Clark remarked, "In the rock art there is preserved an invaluable record of the people's hunting methods, the different

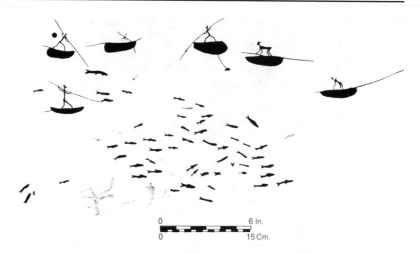

FIGURE 13.14   A rock painting depicting a fishing scene from Lesotho, southern Africa.

kinds of weapons and domestic equipment they used, their customs and cere-monies" (J. D. Clark, 1959).

The rock paintings of Natal, South Africa, provide fascinating information on fishing practices and the boats associated with them. Patricia Vinnecombe (1960) recorded a fishing scene in the Tsoelike River rock shelter in Lesotho, southern Africa (Figure 13.14). The fishermen, armed with long spears, are massed in boats, apparently cornering a shoal of fish that are swimming around in confusion. Some boats have lines under their hulls that may represent anchors; the fish cannot be identified with certainty, but they may be freshwater catfish or yellowfish. Another famous scene from the Cape Province of South Africa depicts a group of ostriches feeding peacefully; among them lurks a hunter wearing an ostrich skin, his legs and bow protruding beneath the belly of an apparently harmless bird. Such vignettes of prehistoric hunting life add insight into data obtained from the food residues recov-ered from caves and rock shelters, but the actual interpretation of the art is subject to many sophisticated variables, among them the symbolic meaning of the paintings (see Lewis-Williams, 1981; Lewis-Williams and Loubser, 1986).

Not only rock art but even pottery can throw light on prehistoric subsistence. The Mimbres culture developed in southwestern New Mexico in the late first millennium A.D., and is famous for its black-on-white painted pottery that was produced mainly between A.D. 950 and 1150 in some 20 villages along the Mimbres River. The potters depicted humans, other mammals, birds, reptiles, fish, insects, and mythical creatures. About 11 percent of the images are fish, many of them species that can be identified as being native to the Gulf of California, more than 450 miles away. Both the distribution of modern fish species and the marine mollusks found in Mimbres villages strongly suggest that the people had visited the ocean, perhaps to collect marine shells for making beads (Figure 13.15) (Jett and Moyle, 1986).

FIGURE 13.15   Mimbres painted bowl depicting a man spearing a large
fish, sometimes interpreted as a whale.

PREHISTORIC DIET

The ultimate objective of economic archaeology is not only to establish how
people obtained their food but also to reconstruct their actual diet. Dietary reconstruction is difficult, mainly because of incomplete economic information. Yet
the problems involved are fundamental. What proportion of the diet was meat?
How diverse were dietary sources? Did the principal sources of diet change from
season to season? To what extent did the people rely on food from neighboring
areas? Was food stored? What limitations or restrictions did technology or society place on diet? All these questions lie behind any inquiry into prehistoric
subsistence (Gilbert and others, 1985).

Diet (what is eaten) and nutrition (the ability of a diet to maintain the body in its
environment) must be studied in close conjunction, for they are quite distinct from
subsistence, the actual process of obtaining resources. The baseline for any study of
prehistoric diet and nutrition must be surveys of modern hunter-gatherers, subsistence cultivators, and pastoralists. Unfortunately, however, lack of agreement among

dietary experts is so widespread that it is difficult to estimate the caloric needs of prehistoric peoples. So many cultural, medical, and physiological factors must be weighed, even in modern situations, that research of prehistoric nutrition and food consumption will often be little more than inspired guesswork. Despite such recovery methods as flotation, it is still impossible to assess the intake of vitamins, minerals, and milk products in prehistoric diets. Nor do we have adequate data on the waste of food during preparation and storage or on the effects of different cooking techniques. Archaeological data can only indicate some of the foods eaten by prehistoric communities and show, at least qualitatively, how important some of them were generally. We are far from being able to ascribe precise food value to animal and plant remains, as would be demanded for precise studies of diet and nutrition.

SOURCES OF DATA ON DIET AND NUTRITION

There are only a few sources of data on prehistoric diet and nutrition, and these are subject to serious limitations. Human skeletal remains can sometimes provide evidence of ancient malnutrition and other dietary conditions (Huss-Ashmore and others, 1982; Larsen, 1987). For example, the parish church of Rothwell in Britain's Midlands has a massive bone crypt that houses the remains of more than 20,000 people disinterred from the graveyard when the church was expanded in the thirteenth century A.D., as well as skeletons from a nearby sixteenth-century hospice. A preliminary study of some of the bones has shown that many of these Medieval and later people suffered from malnutrition, as well as from arthritis, tuberculosis, and other infections. Fractures were also common (Shackley, 1985).

Physical anthropologist Jane Buikstra has studied diet and health among the prehistoric populations of the lower Illinois Valley. As early as 5500 B.C., the inhabitants of this area began harvesting hickory and other nuts on an ever-larger scale. Nuts provided a high-quality food resource, but to support large numbers of people, they had to be harvested over large areas. As time went on, the growing population of the valley turned more and more to wild seeds, especially oily ones like marsh elder that were high in protein and a concentrated source of food energy. In time, they actually cultivated marsh elder as well as sunflowers, whose seeds had equivalent food value. They supplemented the oily species with starchy seeds like knotweed that were highly dependable and easily stored. In the last half of the first millennium A.D., the starchy seeds gave way to cultivated maize. By this time there was considerable competition for game and other wild-animal foods, and Illinois Valley populations may have ranged as high as 40,000 people. As much more complex social organization and regional trade evolved, Buikstra observes that dental diseases became much more common and tuberculosis spread among the dense village populations. The introduction of maize appears to have coincided with a deterioration in child health, too. However, the effects of intensification of food production on prehistoric diet and health are still little understood (Buikstra, 1984; Cook, 1984).

One useful technique involves identifying types of plant foods from the isotopic analysis of prehistoric bone and hair (De Niro, 1987). By using the ratio between two stable carbon isotopes—carbon 12 and carbon 13 in animal tissue—researchers can establish the diet of the organism. Research on controlled animal populations has shown that as carbon is passed along the food chain, the carbon composition of animals continues to reflect the relative isotopic composition of their diet. Carbon is metabolized in plants through three major pathways: C^3, C^4, and Crassulacean acid metabolism. The plants that make up the diet of animals have distinct carbon 13 values. Maize, for example, is a C^4 plant. In contrast, most indigenous temperate flora in North America is composed of C^3 varieties. Thus a population that shifts its diet from wild vegetable foods to maize will also experience a shift in dietary isotopic values. Because carbon 13 and carbon 12 values do not change after death, you can study archaeological carbon from food remains, soil humus, and skeletal remains to gain insight into ancient diet.

This approach is of great importance to archaeologists studying dietary patterns, especially when combined with information from other sources. For example, excellent organic preservation at the Windover burial grounds in eastern Florida allowed a team of researchers to combine an archaeobotanical analysis with bone-collagen stable isotope and nitrogen-isotopic studies of human skeletal remains. They were interested in the degree of reliance on marine as opposed to terrestrial food resources among the people buried at Windover between about 6000 and 5000 B.C. A comparison of nitrogen-isotopic values from human bone collagen at Windover with coastal sites shows that the inhabitants of the former made little use of marine resources. Many C^3 plants were part of the Windover diet, with duck and catfish, with intermediate C^3/C^4 values also significant. The plant remains, such as elderberry, from the site included virtually all C^3 plants, confirming the isotopic data and data from well-preserved stomach contents. The research team believe they have evidence for seasonal foraging based on wild plant foods and freshwater and estuarine resources over a long period of time (Tuross and others, 1994).

A detailed bone chemistry analysis of adult burials from Grasshopper Pueblo in east-central Arizona shows the great potential of this approach. Joseph Ezzo (1993) was able to show that between A.D. 1275 and 1325 males had greater access to meat and cultivated plants, while females had greater access to wild plants. Between 1325 and 1400, both men and women ate virtually the same diet, one in which meat and wild plant foods were less important. This may have resulted from a combination of social and environmental factors: increased population, drought cycles, or use of marginal farming land, which compelled the Grasshopper people to live on agricultural products. The people responded to food stress by increasing storage capacity, reducing household size, and eventually by moving away.

The stable carbon isotope method is not restricted to use with agriculture; it has been applied with success to measure the reliance on marine species of prehistoric Northwest Coast populations in British Columbia (Chisholm and others, 1983). Forty-eight samples from prehistoric human skeletons from 15 sites along the coast revealed a dietary reliance of about 90 percent on marine sources, a figure much higher than crude ethnographic estimates. The same data suggest that there has been little dietary change along the British Columbia coast for the past 5,000 years, which is hardly surprising, given the rich maritime resources of the shoreline.

Isotopic and elemental analyses of prehistoric skeletons have been useful as a way of studying the origin and spread of maize in the New World, by using stable carbon isotopes of skeletal collagen, and as a way of detecting the consumption of marine foods. There remain important potential avenues of inquiry. Can one, for example, establish the importance of meat in early hominid diets? The debate about the uses and limitations of the technique continues, but research proceeds slowly, owing to the complex, multidisciplinary nature of the inquiry (Sillen and others, 1989).

Concentrations of strontium, a stable mineral component of bone as opposed to calcium, can be used to measure the contribution of plants to diet. For instance, it has been shown that prehistoric people in the eastern Mediterranean ate much the same proportions of meat and plant foods from 100,000 years ago up to the end of the Ice Age. Then there was a significant shift toward the consumption of plant foods. At Chalcatzingo, an Olmec site in Mexico, strontium analysis has shown that the elite, buried with valuable jade ornaments, had a lower strontium level, for they ate more meat, compared with commoners who consumed very little (Schoeninger, 1979).

Stomach contents and feces provide unrivaled momentary insights into meals eaten by individual members of a prehistoric society. Dietary reconstructions based on these sources, however, suffer from the disadvantage that they are rare and represent but one person's food intake. Furthermore, some foods are more rapidly digested than others. But even these insights are better than no data at all. The stomach of Tollund Man, who was executed around the time of Christ, contained the remains of a finely ground meal made from barley, linseed, and several wild grasses; no meat was found in the stomach contents (Glob, 1969).

Many American scholars have studied coprolites (human droppings) from dry caves in the United States and Mexico (Figure 13.16). Such researches include analyses of microscopic food remains found in the feces, and also of pollen, phytoliths, and parasites (Reinhard and Bryant, 1992). Over the past 20 years, researchers in southwest Texas have obtained coprolite evidence for a basically stable hunter-gatherer diet over 9,000 years of hunting and gathering in this arid region. Dry conditions in coastal Peru have also provided valuable information on changing diet along the Pacific Coast.

Recent coprolite studies in North America have analyzed pollen grains found in human feces. Fifty-four samples from Glen Canyon in Utah showed that the pollen ingested by their owners could yield valuable information on plants eaten, seasonal occupation, and even the medicinal use of juniper stem tea (Bryant, 1974). Vaughn Bryant analyzed coprolite pollen from a site near the mouth of the Pecos River in southwestern Texas. He found that the inhabitants of the site between 800 B.C. and A.D. 500 spent the spring and summer months at this locality. During their stay they ate many vegetable foods, including several flowers. One danger of using pollen grains is that of contamination from the background pollen "rain" that is always with us. But Bryant was able to show that all but two of the species represented in the pollen were local plants. In all these instances, too, valuable insights were obtained into minor details of prehistoric diet, as well as into intestinal parasites that were commonplace among peoples living on a diet of game meat that was often slightly rotten ("high") (Horne, 1985).

Basically, information on prehistoric diets comes from the analysis and identification procedures described in this chapter. Because the ultimate objective is explaining how people lived in the past, new theoretical frameworks, systematic use of ethnographic analogy, and quantitative methods will, it is hoped, intensify research on the dietary requirements of prehistoric peoples.

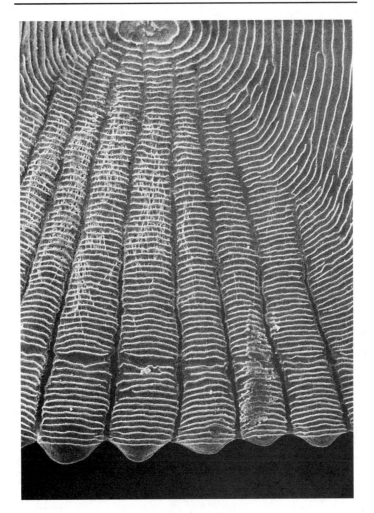

FIGURE 13.16   Fish scale found in a human coprolite.

SUMMARY

- Archaeologists rely on many sources to reconstruct prehistoric subsistence methods. These include environmental data, animal bones, vegetal remains, human feces, artifacts, and prehistoric art.
- Zooarchaeology involves the study of animal bones. Bone identification is carried out by direct comparison between modern and ancient bones.
- Game animal remains can give insights into prehistoric hunting practices. The proportions of animals present can be affected by cultural taboos, the relative meat yields of different species, and hunting preferences. Overhunting and extinction can also affect the numbers of animals in a site.

- Early domesticated animals are very difficult to distinguish from their wild ancestors. Domestication alters both the characteristics of an animal and its bone structure.
- Slaughtering and butchery practices can be derived from the frequency and distribution of animal bones in the ground. Teeth can be used to establish the age of animals slaughtered, but hunting and slaughter patterns are subject to all manner of subtle variables, including convenience and season of the year. Understanding the cultural systems of which the food remains are a part is essential for interpreting slaughter and butchery patterns.
- Carbonized and unburned vegetable remains are recovered from hearths and pits, often using a flotation method to separate seeds from the matrix around them. Dry sites, such as the rock shelters and camps in the Tehuacán Valley of Mexico, provide abundant evidence for early crop domestication. Grain impressions on European pots are studied to reconstruct prehistoric agriculture in the Old World. Danish archaeologists have used pollen analysis to study forest clearance in temperate zones during early farming times.
- Bird bones provide valuable information on seasonal occupation; fish remains reflect specialized coastal adaptations that became common in later prehistoric times. Hooks, nets, and other artifacts, as well as fish remains themselves, provide insights into both coastal and offshore fishing practices.
- Freshwater and saltwater mollusks were both consumed as food and traded over enormous distances as prestigious luxuries or ornaments.
- Prehistoric diet and nutrition must be studied together, for they are distinct from subsistence, which is the actual process of obtaining food. It is difficult to estimate the caloric needs of modern peoples, let alone those of prehistoric groups. Archaeological data can indicate only some of the foods eaten by prehistoric communities and show their importance in general. But this is far from ascribing their true caloric importance to prehistoric peoples.
- Human skeletal remains, stomach contents, and feces are the few direct sources available to us of information on prehistoric diet. The information they yield is limited, at best.

GUIDE TO FURTHER READING

Binford, Lewis R. *Bones: Ancient Men and Modern Myths*. Orlando, Fla.: Academic Press, 1981. A provocative essay on animal bones, concentrating both on ethnographic analogy and faunal analysis.

Davis, Simon J. M. *The Archaeology of Animals*. London: Batsford, 1987. A superbly illustrated, definitive book on zooarchaeology for beginners. Strongly recommended; comprehensive.

Klein, Richard G., and Kathryn Cruz-Uribe. *The Analysis of Animal Bones from Archaeological Sites*. Chicago: University of Chicago Press, 1984. The authors describe statistical approaches to faunal analysis. A book for more advanced readers.

Pearsall, Deborah. *Paleoethnobotany: A Handbook of Procedures*. Orlando, Fla.: Academic Press, 1989. A useful introduction to this complex subject.

Smith, Bruce D. *The Emergence of Agriculture*. New York: Scientific American Library, 1994. A superb introduction to this complex subject for the lay person.

14

ANALOGY, MIDDLE-RANGE THEORY, AND THE LIVING PAST

So far, we have considered the processes of archaeological research—data acquisition, analysis, and interpretation. It is now time to look more closely at the tools that archaeologists use to bridge the gap between the world of the past and the archaeological record of the present: analogy, middle-range theory, ethnoarchaeology, and experimental archaeology.

EARLY COMPARISONS

For well over a century anthropologists have been working among non-Western peoples. They have recovered a mass of information of great interpretative value, much of it still buried in museum storerooms and archives. For their part, archaeologists have long recognized the value of comparisons between prehistoric and modern cultures. In Chapter 2 we discussed the evolutionists of the late nineteenth century, who considered living tribes to be good examples of successive stages of development in culture history. Each stage of cultural development was correlated with a stage of technology, a form of the family, a kind of religious belief, and a type of political control that could be observed in some living group of people. Thus the Australian Aborigines, the Eskimo, and the San, who retained a hunter-gatherer way of life, manufactured stone tools, and had no knowledge of metallurgy, were considered to be living representatives of Paleolithic peoples. Many early investigators thought that the most primitive Stone Age peoples were matriarchal, had no government, and believed in numerous spirits. They believed it was perfectly in order to turn to the literature on Eskimo, or other living gatherers, for the "correct" interpretation of artifacts in the archaeological record.

ANALOGY

Analogy is a process of reasoning that assumes that if objects have some similar attributes, they will share other similarities as well. It involves using a known, identifiable phenomenon to identify unknown ones of broadly similar type. It implies that a particular relationship exists between two or more phenomena because the same relationship may be observed in a similar situation. Our abilities to reason by analogy are often tested in aptitude examinations by such questions as this: "A fish is to water as a bird is to: (a) a tree, (b) a house, (c) air, (d) grass seed." Obviously, if we grasp the relationship between fish and water, we will have no trouble completing the question. Analogy in archaeology involves inferring that the relationships among various traces of human activity in the archaeological record are the same as or similar to those of similar phenomena found among modern "primitive" peoples. Analogies in archaeology only suggest what modern human behavior is capable of and what the boundaries of prehistoric behavior might have been. Researchers can use them to generate hypotheses that can then be tested by real archaeological data.

Archaeologists use analogy on many levels. In a simple one, a researcher infers that small, pointed pieces of stone are projectile points because there are ethnographic records of peoples making small, pointed pieces of stone for the tips of lances or arrows. People often make use of an ethnographic name, such as arrowhead, as a label for an artifact. In doing so, they are assuming that their artifact type, which they recognize by attributes whose presence cannot be explained by natural processes, is identical in form to other, known arrowheads used by the people who made the kind of artifact in question (Figure 14.1). But this simple analogy is a far cry from claiming similarities—or analogies—between the ways in which the prehistoric culture referred to used the arrowhead and the ways in which a living society uses it. To do the latter is to assume that the relationship between the form and the function of the artifact has remained static through the ages. If you explain the past simply by analogy with the present, you are assuming that nothing new has been learned by many generations of people, and that the past was not much—if any—different from the present.

Many archaeologists make use of analogies based on the technology, style, and function of cultures as they are defined archaeologically. J. G. D. Clark (1952) wrote an economic prehistory of Europe in which he made systematic and judicious use of analogy to interpret such artifacts as freshwater fish spears that were still common in historical European folk culture. This type of analogy is secure enough, as are those about small, pointed pieces of stone claimed to be arrowheads (Wylie, 1985). Enough of these have been found embedded in the bones of animals and people for us to safely acknowledge that such tools were most likely projectile points. Still, we have no way of knowing if the points were part of ritual activity as well as the hunt. Similarly, archaeologists will have information about how houses were constructed and what they looked like, what plants were grown and how these were prepared for food, and perhaps some facts on grave furniture. But they will not know what the people who lived at this site thought a proper house should look like, which relatives would be invited to help build a house, what spirits were responsible for making crops grow, who in the house customarily prepared the food, or whether the people believed in life after death. Most analogies drawn from the ideas and beliefs of present-day people are probably inadequate.

Archaeologists develop analogies in many ways. One approach is direct historical analogy, using the simple principle of working from the known to the unknown. In archaeological problems, the known is the living people with

FIGURE 14.1 Eskimo demonstrating a sinew-backed bow and an ivory-tipped arrow at Chicago's Columbian Exposition in 1893. Archaeologists often make use of an ethnographic name, such as arrowhead, assuming that their artifact is identical to arrowheads used by the people who made the artifact. This is a simple example of an archaeological analogy.

written records of their way of life, and the unknown is their ancestors for whom we have no written records. Text-aided analogies involve using written records to interpret archaeological data. Ivor Noël Hume, working at the Colonial settlement on Martin's Hundred, Virginia, found some short strands of gold and silver wire in the cellar filling of one of the houses. Each was as thick as a sewing thread, the kind of wire used in the early seventeenth century for decorating clothing. Noël Hume turned to historical records for analogies. He found European paintings showing military captains wearing clothes adorned with gold and silver wire, and a resolution of the Virginia governor and his council in 1621 forbidding "any but ye Council & heads of hundreds to wear gold in their cloaths" (Noël Hume, 1982). Using this and other historical analogies, he was able to identify the owner of the house as William Harewood, a member of the council and the head of Martin's Hundred.

Then there are analogies for settlements occupied by peoples who themselves had no knowledge of writing but who were contemporary with literate societies. Their customs or affiliations may be mentioned in the written records of their literate neighbors. The Iron Age inhabitants of Maiden Castle in Dorset, England, though illiterate themselves, were subdued by the legions of a thoroughly literate Roman Empire; the conquerors left numerous traces of their campaigns, both in documentary records and in the archaeological record. Sir Mortimer Wheeler's classic 1943 account of the siege of Maiden Castle in the first century A.D. owes much to the Roman records of the conquest (Figure 14.2; Figure 6.5).

According to the proponents of the direct historical approach, confidence in interpretation of past lifeways diminishes as we move from historic to prehistoric times. Analogies to living peoples become less and less secure as we grow remote from written records. Nevertheless, many archaeologists have taken a functionalist approach to analogy.

FIGURE 14.2   Aerial photograph of Maiden Castle, Dorset, England, stormed by the Romans in A.D. 43, an event described through excavation and analogy by Sir Mortimer Wheeler.

Functionalist ethnographies integrate various aspects of culture with one another and with the adaptation of the culture as a whole to its environment. Functionalism stresses the notion that cultures are not made up of random selections of traits but that cultural traits are integrated in various ways and influence each other in fairly predictable ways. Much of processual archaeology, with its emphasis on adaptation and cultural systems, falls under the general title of functionalist archaeology. Functionalist thinking is evident in the way in which many archaeologists select analogies from the ethnographic data to help them interpret their archaeological finds. Because several ethnologically known cultures might provide reasonable analogies, functionally oriented scholars suggest selecting the ones that most resemble the archaeological culture in subsistence, technology, and environment—and are least removed from the archaeological culture in time and space.

We might want to know about the role of sandal making among the Great Basin Indians of 6,000 years ago. Were sandals produced by men, women, individuals on their own initiative, or formal groups working together? If we consider sandal making an aspect of technology, we might turn to the ethnographic literature on Australian and San material culture, in which sandals are sometimes featured. Among both the San and the Australian Aborigines, domestic tasks are generally done by women working alone or with one or two helpers. The analogy might lead us to argue that sandal making was regarded as a domestic task by Great Basin people and carried out by women who usually worked alone. Conversely, weaving is men's work among the Pueblo Indians and is carried out in special ceremonial rooms; because much ritual performed there today reflects very ancient Pueblo Indian practices, we might be led to infer by analogy that the Great Basin people of 6,000 years ago did not regard weaving as domestic work, so it was carried out by men. No matter what alternative we chose, we probably would not have much confidence in our choice.

The selection of possibly appropriate analogies from the ethnographic literature is increasingly being seen as only the first step toward interpretation. Once several analogies are chosen, the implications of each are explicitly stated and then are tested against the archaeological data. In our example of sandal making among Great Basin peoples, the ethnographic literature provided conflicting analogies. If we want to gain confidence in selecting one analogy over the other, we must state explicitly the implications each would have for the archaeological data and then examine the latter again in the light of each implication. If sandal making were a domestic task done by women working alone, we might expect to find the raw materials for sandal manufacture associated with tools that more surely represent women's work, such as grinding stones for food preparation. We might also expect to find tools for sandal making (such as awls and scrapers for preparing fiber) among the debris of more domestic sites. We could anticipate that women working alone might introduce more variation into the finished product than might be done in products made by group effort or by individuals working in the company of other specialists. A contrasting list of implications for the possibility that men produced sandals could also be made, and both sets could be tested against the archaeological data.

Devising test implications is not an easy task. To find a measure for the amount of variation in a finished product that one would expect under specific production conditions requires sophisticated measurements, various statistical tests, and often experimentation among groups of people. Archaeologists willing to make the effort entailed in this approach, however, have found that they are able to discover more about ancient societies than was previously thought possible. Reasoning by analogy is, of course, an important part of this process, but it is only one step in the archaeologist's task. Analogies provide the material from which test implications are drawn; they are not ends in themselves. Thus, analogy is not necessarily misleading, provided that the right criteria and research strategies are used to strengthen and evaluate inferences made from ethnographic and other analogies (Wylie, 1985).

A great deal of archaeological analogy is based on the assumption that because an artifact is used in a specific way today, it was used in that way millennia earlier. The great contribution of the processual archaeologists has been not in their search for general laws but in their insistence that independent data should be used to test and verify conclusions from surveys, excavations, and laboratory analyses. The basic objective in using hypotheses and deductions—the scientific method, if you will—is not to formulate laws but to explore the relationship between past and present. This relationship is assumed to have two parts. The first is that the past is dead and knowable only through the present. The second is that accurate knowledge of the past is essential to understanding the present (Leone, 1982). Lewis Binford (1983a) has argued that conventional analogy based on guesses or hunches constitutes projection of the present into the past. By turning these guesses into testable hypotheses associated with theory, the projections into the past can be sorted out according to their match against evidence that might represent their presence in the past. In other words, how do the images of the past we create match up against reality?

Whatever one's approach to archaeology, the leading problem in archaeological analogy is to let the present serve the past. Many archaeologists try to achieve this end with three interlocking approaches that help them to study the past by using the present:

1. *Middle-range theory:* methods, theories, and ideas from the present that can be applied to any time period and anywhere in the world to explain what we have discovered, excavated, or analyzed from the past.
2. *Ethnoarchaeology:* the study of living societies to aid in understanding and interpreting the archaeological record.
3. *Experimental archaeology:* controlled, modern experiments with ancient technologies and material culture that can serve as a basis for interpreting the past.

MIDDLE-RANGE THEORY

The sociological term "middle-range theory" is used to characterize the body of theory that is emerging as archaeologists develop methods of inference that bridge the gap between what actually happened in the past and the archaeological record of today, which is our chronicle of ancient times (Binford, 1977).

Middle-range theory is based on the notion that the archaeological record is a static and contemporary phenomenon—what survives today of the once-dynamic past. As Binford (1983b) wrote in one of his notebooks: "The archaeological record is contemporary; it exists with me today and any observation I make about it is a contemporary observation." How can researchers make inferences about the past unless they know "the necessary and determinant linkages between dynamic causes and static consequences"? The dynamic elements of the past are long gone. Binford (1981b) and others have been searching for "Rosetta stones. . . that permit the accurate conversion from observation on statics to statement about dynamics."

Middle-range theory begins with three fundamental assumptions:

1. The archaeological record is a static contemporary phenomenon—static information preserved in structured arrangements of matter.
2. Once energy ceased to power the cultural system preserved in the archaeological record, a static condition was achieved. Thus the contents of the archaeological record are a complex mechanical system, created both by long-dead human interaction and by subsequent mechanical forces and formation processes (Chapter 4) (Schiffer, 1987).
3. To understand and explain the past, we must comprehend the relationship between static, material properties common to both past and present and the long-extinct dynamic properties of the past.

According to Binford, middle-range theory provides theory to explain the transformation from past cultural dynamic to present physical residues. It helps reconstruct a long-defunct cultural system by aiding in reconstructions based on appropriate interpretation of the archaeological record. In contrast, general theory seeks to provide a basis for interpreting and explaining a succession of cultural systems, showing how they changed over time, again based on archaeological evidence read across the consecutive cultures. General theory builds on information obtained through middle-range theory.

Middle-range theory is often described as "actualistic" because it studies the coincidence of both the static and the dynamic in cultural systems in the only time frame in which it can be achieved—the present. It provides the conceptual tools for explaining artifact patterns and other material phenomena from the archaeological record. Michael Schiffer (1987) argues, in contrast, that the subject matter of archaeology is the relationship between human behavior and material culture in all times and places. Binford (1981a, 1981b) considers the archaeological record to be static and material, containing no direct information on the subject whatsoever. (For a critique, see Raab and Goodyear, 1984; Trigger, 1995.)

ETHNOARCHAEOLOGY

Middle-range research is important to archaeology, whether one believes that this research is meant to specify the relationships between behavior and material remains or to understand the determinants of patterning and structural properties of the archaeological record. It is conducted by studying living systems (ethnoarchaeology) and/or by using historical documents or controlled experiments.

Ethnoarchaeology is the study of living societies to aid in understanding and interpreting the archaeological record. By living in, say, an Eskimo hunting camp and observing the activities of its occupants, the archaeologist hopes to record archaeologically observable patterns, knowing what activities brought them into existence. Sometimes historical documents can be used to amplify observations in the field. Archaeologists have actually lived on San campsites, then gone back later and recorded the scatter of artifacts on them or excavated them (Yellen, 1977). The earliest ethnoarchaeological work focused on specific artifact patternings and on studies of hunter-gatherer encampments that might provide ways of interpreting the very earliest human sites at Olduvai Gorge and elsewhere. But a major focus of later work has been to develop archaeological methods of inference that bridge the gap between past and present (Cameron and Tomka, 1993).

Ethnoarchaeology is a form of ethnography that has a strongly materialist bias (Gould, 1978). Many archaeologists regard it as simply a mass of observed data on human behavior from which they can draw up suitable hypotheses to compare with the finds from their excavations and laboratory analyses. This interpretation is totally wrong, for in fact ethnoarchaeological research deals with dynamic processes in the modern world (Layton, 1994).

ETHNOARCHAEOLOGY AMONG THE SAN AND THE HADZA

Most, but by no means all, ethnoarchaeological research has been among hunter-gatherers, especially those perceived as having ancestry among earlier, prehistoric peoples (Gamble and Boismer, 1991). Both the San of southern Africa's Kalahari desert and the Australian Aborigines fall into this category.

Anthropologist Richard Lee (1979) has spent many years studying the human ecology of the !Kung San of the Kalahari and has accumulated a mass of information of use to archaeologists. Archaeologist John Yellen (1977) worked with Lee, collecting data on house and camp arrangements, hearth locations, census information, and bone refuse. Yellen pointed out that a San camp develops through conscious acts, such as the construction of windbreaks and hearths, as well as through such incidental deeds as the discarding of refuse and manufacturing debris (Figure 14.3). He recognized communal areas in the campsites, often in the middle of the settlement, that belonged to no one in particular, and family areas focused on hearths that belonged to individual families. The communal activities of the camp members, such as dancing and the first distribution of meat, took place in the open spaces that belonged to no one family. Such activities leave few traces in the archaeological record. Cooking and food processing as well as manufacturing of artifacts normally take place around family hearths. Yellen points out some interesting variations on this pattern: manufacturing activities taking place at one hearth will sometimes involve people from other families; large skins will normally be pegged out for treatment away from main living areas because of vermin and carnivores. The San study showed it is dangerous to assume that activities with the greatest archaeological visibility, such as preparing meat or cracking nuts, take place in special places. The activity

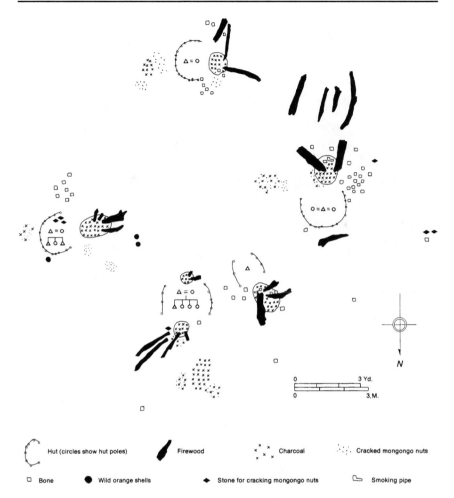

FIGURE 14.3 A San camp in Botswana, southern Africa, as plotted by John Yellen to show the layout of activity areas and artifacts. (After Lee, 1979)

patterning at San campsites relates, for the most part, directly to family groups. Hypothetically, Yellen argues, it should be possible to use artifact clusters through time to study the development and evolution of such social structures.

Since 1984, archaeologist James O'Connell and his research team have recorded more than 70 incidents of large mammal butchery by Hadza hunter-gatherers in East Africa (Figure 14.4). The Hadza hunt animals when they encounter them and also ambush them from specially built blinds near water holes in the late dry season (Figure 3.1). They are very determined hunters, tracking their wounded prey for hours, even days. They also scavenge meat from predator kills at every opportunity. O'Connell records kill rates for a single camp

FIGURE 14.4   Ethnoarchaeology among the Hadza. Recording details
of a hunter's kill.

of 70 to 80 large animals a year, or about one for 40 to 60 man-days of foraging,
with scavenging accounting for about 15 to 20 percent of the total. The
researchers were mainly interested in time allocation, food choice, and food sharing activities, so they routinely recorded site location, distance from residential
bases, method of acquiring the prey, carcass condition, details of the butchery,
and the sexes and ages of the people involved. In addition, they collected
comprehensive "archaeological" data from each location, where possible, including the positions of broken bones and abandoned artifacts.

The Hadza research yielded a mass of basic ethnoarchaeological data that
casts serious doubt on many of the assumptions made by archaeologists about
hunter-gatherer kill sites. O'Connell's team found that 75 to 80 percent of the
Hadza's large mammal prey were underrepresented in their bone samples, by
virtue of the people's hunting and butchering practices. Furthermore, most prehistoric kill sites have been excavated on a small scale, whereas many Hadza butchery sites occupy a large area, through which the hunters scatter the bones, often to
find shade in which to work. Sometimes, too, bones from different animals are
left in separate locations. The disarticulation of animal bones follows a similar
pattern, whether carnivores or humans are involved—the limbs first, then the
backbone, with differences being more the result of individual animal anatomy
than deliberate cultural choice. The Hadza findings cast doubt on many interpretations of animal butchery, and highlight the vital importance of ethnoarchaeology
and middle-range theory (O'Connell and others, 1992).

LITHIC TECHNOLOGY AMONG THE HIGHLAND MAYA

Although ethnoarchaeological investigations have tended to focus on hunter-gatherers, there are numerous instances of fascinating research on more complex societies, even our own. A major long-term study of modern urban garbage in Tucson, Arizona, for example, is based on the latest archaeological methods and research designs (Rathje and Murphy, 1992). The project is designed to investigate the relationships between resource management, urban demography, and social and economic stratification in a modern context, where some control data from interviews and other perspectives are available to amplify an archaeological study of a type that might be conducted at an ancient urban center. The Tucson garbage study has produced remarkable results, showing widely different patterns of resource management from one segment of the city's population to another, with the middle class being the most wasteful.

In an example of immediate relevance to archaeology, when Brian Hayden was examining Maya stone tools of the postconquest Colonial period from sites once occupied by a minor Maya group known as the Coxoh, near the Mexico-Guatemala border, he discovered that some present-day Maya-speaking communities in the area still made and used stone artifacts. Even after four-and-a-half centuries of European contact, a few people were making *metates* (grinders) in the traditional way, and simple stone tools still fulfilled many basic functions. There were no living Coxoh populations for direct historic comparisons, so the archaeologists studied stone tool technology among the most closely related groups they could find (Hayden, 1987).

The objectives of the project were to "record and understand the conception, life, death, and discard of lithic artifacts (or their substitutes)." The investigators combined descriptive research with highly exploratory, new theoretical approaches based on design analysis theory, among other things. The research was broad-based, concerned with the properties of the stone collected for tool manufacture, the efficiency of stone technology, and the evolution of the forms of stone tools as they were used and reused. The researchers looked closely at patterns of waste deposition and site-formation processes and at the social and economic positions of stoneworking artisans. They were able to work closely with a 50-year-old specialist *metate* maker named Ramon Ramos Rosario, one of the few full-time specialists still working. Since his lands cannot support his family, Ramon makes his living manufacturing *manos* (pounders) and *metates* and selling them over a wide area of western Guatemala. He can sell more widely today because of improved public transport. In earlier years, he and other specialists would sell locally. Hayden followed Ramon through the entire manufacturing process, from the selection of the material to the final surface smoothing of the artifact. Time and motion studies showed that it took this expert two and a half days to rough out and smooth a *metate* blank using only stone tools, and four-and-a-half to five-and-a-half days to finish both a *metate* and a *mano*. Finally, Hayden examined the characteristics of the picks used to chip and peck the rock as if they were archaeological finds, combining these studies with use-wear analysis. Hayden seriated the picks on the basis of the intensity of edge-wear development as a way of estimating the relative length of use of comparable tools. He compared his results to prehistoric artifacts and was able to show that many blunt-edged Maya celts in archaeological sites, tools that were of no use for woodworking, were probably used by women to repeck (roughen) used *manos* and *metates*.

The study also threw interesting light on site-formation processes. For example, the stoneworker removes as much waste material from the *metate* blank at the quarry as possible to save weight. At the same time, he carefully conserves the stone tools used in roughing out blanks, caching them at the quarry and resharpening them to prolong their life. Observations like this, combined with specific environmental conditions, could one day provide a body of what Hayden calls "robust" middle-range theory.

The importance of the Maya lithic study is that it demonstrates the power and potential of a many-sided approach to ethnoarchaeology, using data from the dynamic present to evaluate archaeological evidence from the static archaeological record (Hayden, 1987).

NUNAMIUT ESKIMO

Lewis Binford and his students undertook ethnoarchaeological studies to help begin construction of middle-range theory. He decided to study the Nunamiut Eskimo of Alaska, 80 percent of whose subsistence comes from hunting caribou. His aims were to find out as much as he could about "all aspects of the procurement, processing, and consumption strategies of the Nunamiut Eskimo and relate these behaviors directly to their faunal consequences" (Binford, 1978). He chose to concentrate on animal bones rather than on artifacts because, although the bones were not human-manufactured, the patterns of their use were the result of cultural activity.

The Nunamiut depend more heavily on meat than any other known hunter-gatherers. Indeed, Binford estimates that each adult eats around a cup and a half of vegetable foods a year, supplemented by the partially digested stomach contents of caribou. In an environment that has a growing season of only 22 days, the Eskimo rely on stored food entirely for eight-and-a-half months a year and partly for an additional month and a half. Fresh meat is freely available for only two months a year. Binford soon realized that the strategies the Eskimo used to feed themselves were based not only on game distributions but on other considerations as well. With such a heavy reliance on stored food, the problem of bulk was always important. Was it easier to move people to where fresh meat was available or to carry the meat back to a base camp where precious stored food was kept? It is no coincidence that the Nunamiut move around most in late summer and early fall, when stored foods are at their lowest levels. The Nunamiut's way of life involved complicated and interacting decisions related to the distribution of food resources at different seasons, the storage potential of different animals and of different parts of an animal, and the logistics of procuring, carrying, and storing meat.

By close study, not only of the Nunamiut's annual round of activities but also of their butchery and storage strategies, Binford was able to develop indices that measured, in exhaustive detail, the utility of different body parts of caribou and to describe the butchering techniques, distribution of body parts, and methods of food preparation used. He showed that the people have an intimate knowledge of caribou anatomy with regard to meat yield, storage potential, and consumption needs—relative to the logistical, storage, and social needs of the moment. The field study also included analysis of 42 archaeologically known locations that dated to earlier times.

The Nunamiut adaptation depended on long-term storage strategies that were keyed to two aggressive periods of caribou hunting, in spring and fall. That the Nunamiut were able to hunt the caribou twice a year was linked to the topography in their homeland, which lies close to the borders of both summer and winter caribou feeding ranges (Figure 14.5). The movement of the people was

FIGURE 14.5   The Mask site, a Nunamiut Eskimo hunting stand: (top) the hunting stand in its environmental setting; (bottom) caribou remains at the stand.

keyed to seasonal game movements and to storage and other needs. Fall hunting was directed toward calves, whose skins were used to make winter clothing. Small, mobile parties of Nunamiut would pursue them, knowing that their prey would yield not only skins but also the added bonus of heads and tongues to feed the people who processed the skins. Without taking account of this fact, the Nunamiut would have been unable to maintain a viable cultural system.

What is the importance of the Nunamiut research? First, it provides a mass of empirical data on human exploitation of animals that is applicable not only to the Nunamiut and other caribou hunters but also to the interpretation of different types of archaeological sites in many parts of the world. Binford showed how local any cultural adaptation is—that the Nunamiut depended on interacting topographic, climatic, logistical, and other realities. The result is considerable variation in archaeological sites and in artifact frequencies and forms.

"There is an unrelenting demonstration that the Nunamiut behave rationally in their treatment of animal foods," Binford (1978) writes. "This rationality is facilitated by a truly remarkable knowledge of animal anatomy. It is facilitated by an outlook that is future-oriented. . . . The Eskimo are pragmatic, they are empiricists, and they are very skeptical of statements as to the 'right' way to do something."

Such ethnoarchaeological studies show that archaeologists can no longer assume that all variability in the archaeological record is directly related to cultural similarity and difference. They have profoundly affected archaeological studies of prehistoric hunter-gatherers, both of the earliest hominids and in more recently occupied areas such as the Great Basin (O'Connell, 1975). Ethnoarchaeology has led to such fundamental cross-cultural statements of possible predictive value as "optimal foraging strategy" (Chapter 15). So far, the main influence of middle-range theory and ethnoarchaeology has been on the archaeology of hunter-gatherers (but see Longacre, 1991; Longacre and Stark, 1992). Harriet Blitzer's long-term study of eighteenth- and nineteenth-century Greek jars (*pithoi*) has important implications for the study of ancient Aegean trade (Blitzer, 1990).

STRUCTURES AND SYMBOLS

Ian Hodder (1982b) has taken a somewhat different structural and symbolic tack in ethnoarchaeological studies of farming and hunter-gatherer societies in tropical Africa. He studied the Nuba farmers of the Sudan and the Lozi of western Zambia, among other peoples. "Symbols are actively involved in social strategies," he writes. Every society, he believes, has a set of general conceptual principles that form a "structure" that runs through each society. Structuralism has long been debated in anthropology but is new to archaeology. Under this approach, Hodder would have archaeologists looking for the principles and concepts that played a part in all social and ecological actions in individual ancient societies, a structure that affected the patterning of the material culture found in the archaeological record. There is little actual difference between the structure of the Binford and Hodder approaches (Kosso, 1991). Middle-range theories relate the empirical to the real, as do Hodder's structuring principles, themselves middle-range theories. Where the two schools of thought differ is in their styles of analysis. More science-based approaches rely more heavily on statistics and numerical data, focusing on behavior rather than its meaning, and on cross-cultural laws more than cultural patterns. For most archaeologists ethnoarchaeology is a way of raising analogical consciousness, of sensitizing them to the dimensions of variability and the richness of the relationship between human beings and their artifacts. But, combined with experimental archaeology, and integrating history and science, it can be a valuable way of approaching the realities of the past, which are often hard to discern from the archaeological record alone (David, 1992; Hammersley, 1992).

EXPERIMENTAL ARCHAEOLOGY

Controlled experiments with the dynamics of material culture can be fruitful sources of data to test middle-range theory. Experimental archaeology began in Europe during the eighteenth century, when people tried to blow the spectacular bronze horns recovered from peat bogs in Scandinavia and Britain. One ardent experimenter, Dr. Robert Ball of Dublin, Ireland, blew an Irish horn so hard that he was able to produce "a deep bass note, resembling the bellowing of a bull." Sadly, a subsequent experiment with a trumpet caused him to burst a blood vessel, and he died several days later (Coles, 1973). Dr. Ball is the only recorded casualty of experimental archaeology. It was not until the early years of this century that experimental archaeology took on more immediate relevance. One reason that it did was the capture and observation of Ishi, one of the last California Indians to follow a traditional way of life.

ISHI

Ishi, the last "wild" Yahi Indian, was captured near Oroville, California, in 1913 (Kroeber, 1965). Fortunately, the story of his capture came to the notice of University of California anthropologists Alfred Kroeber and Thomas Waterman. They managed to assume responsibility for Ishi, who resided at the University Museum at Berkeley for four-and-a-half years before he died of tuberculosis. Ishi became a local attraction, a living museum exhibit who brought hundreds of visitors to the campus. But he was far more than an exhibit; he proved to be a mine of information about the hunter-gatherer way of life and about the simple technology that the Yahi had enjoyed. Kroeber, Waterman, and a doctor named Saxon Pope from the University of California Medical School accompanied Ishi to his homeland and observed him as he stalked game and used his bow and snares. They acquired a mass of vital anthropological and linguistic information that would otherwise have been lost forever. Pope, an archery expert, not only apprenticed himself to Ishi but also spent years studying bows and arrows in the museum collections. He subsequently published a monograph on the subject, which did much to make archery the popular sport it is today (Pope, 1923).

STONE TECHNOLOGY

Ishi left a wonderful legacy to archaeologists, a mass of data that made people realize just how ignorant we were about prehistoric technologies. Only the sketchiest historical accounts of stoneworking and other craft activities survive in the records of early explorers. Some of the Spanish friars, notably Juan de Torquemada, saw Indian stoneworkers flaking obsidian knives. In 1615 he described how the Indians would take a stick and press it against a stone core with their "breast." "With the force of the stick there flies off a knife," he wrote. But until recently, no one knew just how pressure flaking, as it is called, was done.

It was an Idaho rancher named Don Crabtree who worked out some of the ways in which the Paleo-Indians had made the beautiful Folsom projectile points found on the Plains. He experimented for more than 40 years and was able to describe no fewer than 11 methods of reproducing the "flute" at the base of the artifact (D. E. Crabtree, 1972b). Eventually, he came across Torquemada's account of pressure flaking and used a chest punch to remove flakes from the base of unfinished points gripped in a vise on the ground. The result was points that were almost indistinguishable from the prehistoric artifacts. Many others have followed in Crabtree's footsteps and have successfully replicated almost every kind of stone artifact made by pre-Columbian Indians.

Does the production of an exact replica mean, in fact, that modern experimentation has recovered the original technique? The answer, of course, is that we can never be certain. Lithic expert Jeff Flenniken has replicated dozens of Paleo-Indian projectile points and argues that many of the different "types" identified by Plains archaeologists are in fact simply heads that have been modified for reuse after they have broken in use. By reducing an existing head, he argues, the Paleo-Indian artisan produced a different but convenient shape that did the job to be done just as well as the original. The same reduction process might lead the worker to the same shape again and again, but he certainly did not design it that way (Flenniken, 1984). David Hurst Thomas (1986), a Great Basin specialist, disagrees. He argues that modern stoneworkers must not interpret prehistoric artifacts in terms of their own experience, for to do so ignores the vast chronological gap that separates us from prehistoric times. Thomas believes that a strictly technological approach to stone tool experimentation restricts the questions to be asked about lithic technology. Lithic experimentation is a valuable approach to the past, but only if combined with other approaches, such as retrofitting or edge-wear analysis.

CRITERIA FOR EXPERIMENTAL ARCHAEOLOGY

Experimental archaeology can rarely provide conclusive answers. It can merely provide some insights into the methods and techniques perhaps used in prehistory, for many of the behaviors involved in, say, prehistoric agriculture have left no tangible traces in the archaeological record. But some general rules must be applied to all experimental archaeology. First, the materials used in the experiment must be those available locally to the prehistoric society one is studying. Second, the methods must conform with the society's technological abilities. Obviously, modern technology must not be allowed to interfere with the experiment. Experiments with a prehistoric plow must be conducted with a plowshare made correctly, with careful reference to the direction of wood grain, the shape and method of manufacture of working edges, and all other specifications. If the plow is drawn by a tractor, the experiment's efficiency will be radically affected;

thus, for accuracy, you will need a pair of trained oxen. The results of the experiment must be replicable and consist of tests that lead to suggested conclusions.

SOME EXAMPLES OF EXPERIMENTAL ARCHAEOLOGY

One of the best-known instances of experimental archaeology is the Kon Tiki expedition, on which Thor Heyerdahl attempted to prove that Polynesia had been settled by adventurous Peruvians who sailed rafts across thousands of miles of ocean (Heyerdahl, 1950). He did succeed in reaching Polynesia, and his expedition showed that long ocean voyages in rafts were possible; but he did not prove that the Peruvians settled Polynesia.

Most experimental archaeology is far more limited in scope, often involving experiments with spears or bows against animal targets and the like (Odell and Cowan, 1986). Many experiments have been done on clearance of forests in Europe and elsewhere. Stone axes have been surprisingly effective at clearing woodland, one Danish experiment yielding estimates that a man could clear one-half acre of forest in a week. Tree ringing and fire have been shown to be effective tree-felling techniques in West Africa and Mesoamerica. Experiments with agriculture over eight or more years have been conducted in the southern Maya lowlands and in Mesa Verde National Park. The latter experiment lasted 17 years. Two and one-half acres of heavy red clay soil were cultivated and planted with maize, beans, and other small crops. Good crop yields were obtained in all but two of the 17 years, when drought killed the young crop. The test revealed how important careful crop rotation is to preserving the land's carrying capacity.

HOUSING EXPERIMENTS Houses of poles and thatch, logs, or hut clay normally survive in the form of postholes, foundation trenches, or collapsed rubble. Unfortunately, traces of the roof and information on wall and roof heights are usually lacking. But this absence has not deterred experimenters from building replicas of Mississippian houses in Tennessee, using excavated floor plans associated with charred poles, thatching grass, and wall-clay fragments (Nash, 1968). Two types of houses dating to A.D. 1000–1600, were rebuilt. One of these was a "small pole" type with slender poles bent over to form an inverted, basket-like rectangular structure with clay plaster on the exterior. Later houses were given long walls, which supported steep, peaked roofs. In this, as in many other instances, many details of the rafter and roof design are probably lost forever.

BUTSER HILL, ENGLAND An ambitious long-term experimental archaeology project flourishes at Butser Hill in southern England, where Peter Reynolds has reconstructed a communal Iron Age round house dating to about 300 B.C. (Figure 14.6). The house is built of hazel rods and a binding mixture of clay, earth, animal hair, and hay. This is part of a much larger experimental project that is exploring every aspect of Iron Age life. Reynolds and other members of the Butser team have grown prehistoric cereals using Iron Age technology, kept a selection of livestock that resembled prehistoric breeds, and even stored grain in subterranean storage pits. The project is concerned not only with how individual aspects of Iron Age subsistence operated, but also with how they fitted together. Some fascinating results have come from the Butser experiment; for instance, Reynolds found that wheat yields were far higher than had been expected and

FIGURE 14.6   A reconstructed Iron Age hut at Butser Hill, England.

that grain could be stored underground for long periods without rotting. The Butser experiment provides valuable information that can be used for calculating prehistoric crop yields and land carrying capacities (P. J. Reynolds, 1979).

OVERTON DOWN   One of the longest experiments in archaeological interpretation is that of the Overton Down earthwork in England, which will last as long as 128 years. In 1960 the British Association for the Advancement of Science built the experimental earthwork at Overton Down, Wiltshire (Jewell and Dimbleby, 1966). The earthwork and its associated ditch were built on chalk subsoil, with profiles approximating those of prehistoric monuments. Archaeological materials including textiles, leather, wood, animal and human bones, and pottery were buried within and on the earthwork. The Overton Down earthwork was built partly with modern picks, shovels, and hatchets and partly with red deer antlers and ox shoulder blades in an attempt to establish relative work rates for different technologies. The difference was about 1.3:1.0 in favor of modern tools, mostly because modern shovels were more efficient. Overton Down was then abandoned, but small and very precise excavations of the ditch and bank were to take place at intervals of 2, 4, 8, 16, 32, 64, and 128 years. The digs were to be used to check the decay and attrition of the earthwork and the silting of the ditch over a lengthening period. The project will yield priceless information of great use for interpreting archaeological sites of a similar type on chalk soils.

Such types of controlled, long-term experiments will give archaeologists the objective data they need to understand the static archaeological record as studied in the dynamic present. They will help us evaluate our ideas about the past, and in answering the question of questions, not "what happened?" but "why?"

SUMMARY

- Ethnographic analogy helps in ascribing meaning to the prehistoric past. Analogy itself is a form of reasoning that assumes that if objects have some similar attributes, they will share other similarities as well. It involves using a known, identifiable phenomenon to identify unknown ones of a broadly similar type.
- Most simple analogies are based on technology, style, and function of artifacts, as they are defined archaeologically. Such analogies, however, based as they are on people's beliefs, can be unreliable.
- Direct historical analogies and comparisons made with the aid of texts are common, but meaningful analogies for American and Paleolithic sites are much harder to achieve. One approach has been to devise test implications, using several analogies. This technique is based on the functional approach assuming that cultures are not made up of random traits but are integrated in various ways. Thus analogies are made between recent and prehistoric societies with closely similar general characteristics.
- Middle-range research is carried out on living societies, using ethnoarchaeology, experimental archaeology, and historical documents. It is designed to create a body of middle-range theory, objective theoretical devices for forging a link between the dynamic living systems of today and the static archaeological record of the past.
- Ethnoarchaeology is ethnographic archaeology with a strongly materialist bias. Archaeologists engage in ethnoarchaeology as part of middle-range research in attempts to make meaningful interpretations of artifact patterns in the archaeological record.
- Experimental archaeology seeks to replicate prehistoric technology and lifeways under carefully controlled conditions. As such, it is a form of archaeological analogy. Experiments have been conducted on every aspect of prehistoric culture, from lithics to housing. Archaeology by experiment provides insights into the methods and techniques used by prehistoric cultures.

GUIDE TO FURTHER READING

Aldenderfer, Mark, ed. *Quantitative Research in Archaeology: Progress and Prospects.* Newberry Park, Calif.: Sage Publications, 1987. Essays that survey major issues in quantitative archaeology. For the more advanced reader.

Binford, Lewis R. *Nunamiut Ethnoarchaeology.* Orlando, Fla.: Academic Press, 1978. A descriptive monograph about ethnoarchaeology among caribou hunters. A must for the serious student.

Binford, Lewis R. *In Pursuit of the Past.* New York: Thames and Hudson, 1983. An account of living archaeology and middle-range theory for a more general audience. Strongly recommended for beginners.

Coles, John M. *Archaeology by Experiment.* London: Heinemann, 1973. An introduction to experimental archaeology with numerous examples, mainly from the Old World.

Gould, Richard A. *Living Archaeology*. Cambridge: Cambridge University Press, 1980. A wide-ranging discussion of ethnoarchaeology that covers both method and theory.

Hodder, Ian, ed. *Symbols in Action*. Cambridge: Cambridge University Press, 1982. Ethnoarchaeological studies in tropical Africa that are used to support a structural and symbolic approach to archaeology.

Yellen, John E. *Archaeological Approaches to the Present: Models for Predicting the Past*. Orlando, Fla.: Academic Press, 1977. Ethnoarchaeology among the San of the Kalahari. A technical work with broad implications.

15

SETTLEMENT ARCHAEOLOGY AND SPATIAL ANALYSIS

So far we have examined the ways in which archaeologists study artifacts and prehistoric subsistence and the various technologies that people developed to adapt to their environments. We also glanced briefly at some methods used to reconstruct the prehistoric environment itself. In this chapter we examine some of the ways in which archaeologists have studied changing settlement patterns in prehistoric times.

SETTLEMENT ARCHAEOLOGY AND SETTLEMENT PATTERNS

SETTLEMENT ARCHAEOLOGY   The study of changing human settlement patterns is part of the analysis of adaptive interactions between people and their external environment, both natural and cultural (Chang, 1968).

Settlement patterns, the layout of human settlements on the landscape, are the result of relationships between people who decided, on the basis of practical, political, economic, and social considerations, to place their houses, settlements, and religious structures where they did. Thus settlement archaeology offers the archaeologist a chance to examine not only relationships between different communities but trading networks, exploitation, and social organization as well. The study of settlement patterns involves examining the degree to which human settlement reflects a society and its technology's adaptation to a specific environment.

DETERMINANTS OF SETTLEMENT PATTERNS

Settlement patterns are determined by many factors related to the environment, economic practices, and technological skills. Inherited cultural patterns and established networks of human behavior have an impelling influence on settlement patterns in some societies. The distribution of San camps in the Kalahari desert depends on the availability of water supplies and vegetable foods, and ancient Maya centers in Mexico were laid out in segments dictated by political and religious considerations.

Village layout may be determined by the need to protect one's herds against animal predators or war parties. Other settlements may be strung out at regular intervals along an important trade artery, such as a river. Even the positioning of individual houses is dictated by a complex variety of social, economic, and even personal factors that can defy explanation.

The determinants of settlement patterns operate on at least three levels, each formed by factors that differ in quality or degree from the ones that shape other levels (Trigger, 1968b).

1. *Building or structure.* Houses, household clusters, and activity areas are minimal units of archaeological analysis.
2. *Communities.* The arrangement of structures within a single group constitutes a community. The term community is defined as a "maximal group of persons who normally reside in face-to-face association" (Murdock, 1949).
3. *Distribution of communities.* The density and distribution of communities, whatever their size, is determined to a considerable extent by the natural resources in their environment and by the economy, nutritional requirements, and technological level of the population, as well as by social and religious constraints.

A critical part of settlement archaeology is understanding the factors that interact to determine a settlement pattern at any of these three levels. These factors can best be understood by analogy with modern societies (see Chapter 14). The ultimate objective of the exercise is to study prehistoric settlement systems as an aspect of the whole picture of a prehistoric society. In this connection, "off-site" features like field systems are of great importance (Chapter 9).

STRUCTURES AND COMMUNITIES

STRUCTURES

Human dwelling places occur in an infinite range of sizes and types, from the crude windbreak of the Tasmanian Aborigine to the magnificent palaces of England's King Henry VIII. Temples, fortifications, and even cattle pens are all forms of standardized structures. Domestic architecture may be standardized, or it may vary according to strict guidelines dictated by a number of factors. The study of individual structures can be approached from several standpoints.

Form and material are among the major determinants of house design. For example, 15,000 years ago the late Ice Age hunters of the western Russian plains lived in semisubterranean dwellings with roofs made of skins and mammoth bones and with interior hearths (Soffer, 1985). Theirs was a treeless, arctic environment, where protection from icy-cold winds was vital. The people made use of the only abundant raw materials available to them—the bones and skins of the huge mammoths they hunted. In contrast, the Tonga peoples of the Middle Zambezi Valley in Central Africa, where the midday temperature is often over 100° F, and the nights are hot most of the year, spend more of their lives in the shade of their pole-and-mud huts than they do inside them. Their dwellings, therefore, have thatched roofs that project far from the walls to form large and shady verandas (B. Reynolds, 1967). People living in damp, cool conditions lived in settlements with multipurpose dwellings (Figure 15.1).

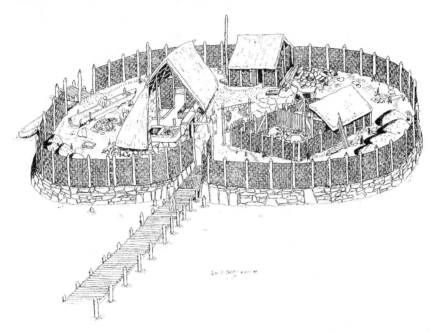

FIGURE 15.1   Adaptation to cool, damp conditions. A superb artist's reconstruction of a Neolithic house and associated structures from a small settlement at Loch Olabhat, Hebrides, Scotland. A wooden causeway leads through a narrow entrance. The house is at left, cut away to show the hearth inside. The artist has conveyed the excavators' uncertainty about the function of the structure to the right with masterly ambiguity.

The raw materials used to build a structure affect not only its form but also its preservation in the archaeological record. Unfired mud brick was used throughout the Near East for house building, and it is still employed today. Once a house is abandoned, the unmaintained brick melts and reverts to clay. It took archaeologists generations to learn how to recover traces of mud-brick houses from their matrix (Lloyd, 1963). As we saw in Chapter 10, wooden structures often leave no trace in the soil except, perhaps, postholes or foundation trenches.

Function radically affects house design, too. The earliest human beings lived in temporary brush shelters that reflected their mobile lifestyle and the fact that the nights were rarely cold. More sedentary communities, such as those of subsistence farmers in the Near East, built houses that combined a need for shelter with a need for storage and cooking facilities for each family.

Social and political organization can affect the design of structures also, for the size and layout of a dwelling can reflect the family organization of the occupants, as well as their social standing. A polygamous family may live in a house with several kitchen areas, each owned by a different wife. Sometimes, with controlled use of anthropological data, particular house types in the archaeological record can be related to specific forms of family organization. Within one

house, a family unit can be distinguished only by interpreting the use of the artifacts found in it in order to identify different rooms, especially cooking areas.

Many societies developed special architectural styles and structures that were
associated with political or religious activities or with leadership. Classic Maya
temples, exemplified by the pyramids at Tikal (Figure 15.2), provide an excellent
instance of such structures (Sabloff, 1989). The plazas and pyramids were
designed to create a sense of awe. Artisans' houses can be identified by distinctive
artifact clusters, such as the potters' workshops found by James Mellaart (1975) at
the early town of Hacilar in Turkey, dating to about 5300 B.C.

RECOVERING HOUSES AND HOUSEHOLDS

Evidence for individual houses and households is obtained by carefully excavating
features, household clusters, and activity sets in the archaeological record. In many
societies, limited economic opportunities and even distribution of wealth resulted
in standardized floor plans (Bermannr, 1994; Netting and others, 1984). Such
houses, which served as shelters for their occupants, provide the archaeologist,
centuries afterward, with convenient analytic units, as long as the house remains
isolated from surrounding occupation debris. The variations between houses may
reflect a variation between families in subsistence activities, social status, manufacturing activity, wealth, and so on (Douglas and Kramer, 1992).

EARLY MESOAMERICAN HOUSES   Between 1350 and 850 B.C., the one-
room, thatched wattle-and-daub house became the most common dwelling type
in Early Formative Mesoamerican villages. In the Valley of Oaxaca, Early
Formative houses were generally rectangular. The floors were sand-covered and

FIGURE 15.2   Temple 1 at Tikal, Guatemala, which dates to about A.D.
700, an example of a ceremonial structure.

dug out from the subsoil, and the thatched roof was supported by pine posts. The puddled clay walls were smoothed and sometimes whitewashed (Flannery, 1976; Flannery and Marcus, 1983).

HOUSE CONTENTS   In studying such houses, Kent Flannery and his colleagues distinguished carefully among the households themselves; the household unit of associated features, such as storage pits and graves; and the various activity areas sometimes associated with them (Flannery and Marcus, 1983; Winter, 1976). Many of the houses were swept clean before abandonment, but several contained accumulations of debris that included not only potsherds and bone tools but food remains as well. Marcus Winter broke down the house contents into at least five possible activities, including sewing and basketry (needles), cooking and food consumption (pots and food remains), and cutting and scraping (stone tools). He plotted the house contents (Figure 15.3) in an attempt to distinguish the craft activities of the family that occupied each dwelling.

The Oaxacan *household units* included bell-shaped storage pits large enough to hold a metric ton of maize; some of them contained maize pollen and grinders. Human burials were associated with some houses, perhaps those of the family, but archaeologists were unable to prove this. The Oaxacan household units also included various types of ovens, refuse middens, and drainage ditches (Figure 15.4).

ACTIVITY SETS   **Activity sets** are sets of artifacts associated with specific activities, such as a bow and arrow with hunting. Twenty-two household clusters found in the Oaxaca project were analyzed for traces of activity sets that would indicate specialist activities. Food procurement, preparation, and food storage activities were common to all households; these were identified by grindstone fragments, storage pits, jars, and food remains. Every household chipped local stone and made baskets; but there were also signs of specialist activities. One large pit at Tierras Largas contained large quantities of pressure-flaking debris, while other household clusters yielded no such fine debitage. Perhaps this household boasted a part-time specialist who made fine stone artifacts for others.

The Oaxacan study offered some potential for identifying division of labor within a household and artifacts used by children rather than adults. Unfortunately, the excavated samples were too small for definitive study, but Figure 15.5, from Evon Vogt's classic study of the Maya of Zinacantán in Chiapas, shows some of the long-term possibilities (For discussion of this issue, see Gero and Conkey, 1991; Kent, 1984; Vogt, 1967; Wilk, 1991).

COMMUNITIES

Many variables act to determine the layout of communities, both large and small (Figure 15.6).

ENVIRONMENT AND ECONOMY   These two factors limit the size and permanence of a settlement because the ability to gather and store food is as important as the technology necessary to transport and process it into edible form. Environment and economy are vital because they determine whether a community lives in one place permanently or must shift camp at regular intervals

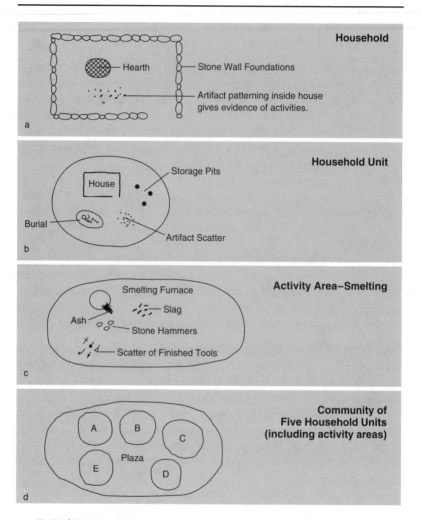

FIGURE 15.3 Various spatial units used by archaeologists in studying human settlement: (a) household; (b) household unit; (c) activity area; (d) community.

during the year. Preliterate `Ubaid farmers in Mesopotamia (c. 4500 B.C.) relied on simple irrigation agriculture. Because they had no need to move in order to achieve a stable subsistence cycle, they lived at the same location for centuries, forming large tells (Redman, 1978a).

SOCIAL AND POLITICAL FACTORS   These are also strong determinants, even in simple societies. Family and kinship considerations are important in camps and small villages. State-organized societies reserved special precincts for ceremonial centers, palaces, and official buildings where the business of the state was conducted (see Figure 15.2). Whole sectors of towns were sometimes

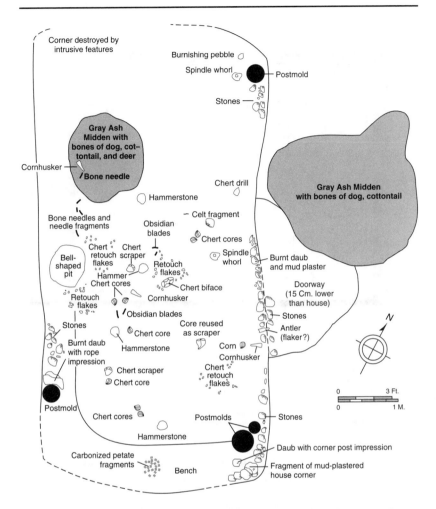

FIGURE 15.4   Plan of a house at Tierras Largas, Oaxaca, from around 900 B.C., with selected artifacts plotted on the floor.

reserved for minority religious groups or foreign traders living under the protection of the local ruler. These quarters may be reflected in the archaeological record by exotic objects, unusual architecture, or religious objects. At the trading port of Kilwa on the Tanzanian coast, the sultan lived in a magnificent palace, a special precinct with its own mosque. The fine artifacts in the palace are not duplicated in any numbers elsewhere in the site, where a cosmopolitan population of Arabs and Africans lived and traded (Chittick, 1974).

STUDYING A COMMUNITY: TEOTIHUACÁN, MEXICO

The behavior of a complete community, insofar as it can be discerned as having a pattern, is reflected in its artifact grouping, and in the characteristic settlement

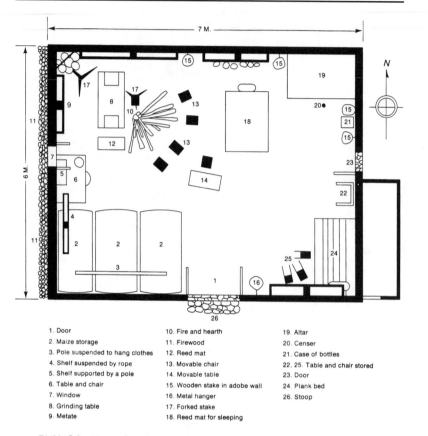

1. Door
2. Maize storage
3. Pole suspended to hang clothes
4. Shelf suspended by rope
5. Shelf supported by a pole
6. Table and chair
7. Window
8. Grinding table
9. Metate
10. Fire and hearth
11. Firewood
12. Reed mat
13. Movable chair
14. Movable table
15. Wooden stake in adobe wall
16. Metal hanger
17. Forked stake
18. Reed mat for sleeping
19. Altar
20. Censer
21. Case of bottles
22, 25. Table and chair stored
23. Door
24. Plank bed
26. Stoop

FIGURE 15.5 Modern highland Maya house from Zinacantán, Chiapas, Mexico, conceptually divided into male and female spaces.

pattern of the location as a whole—house design and layout and the distribution of household clusters and activity areas. The archaeologist uses site survey and selective excavation, as well as sampling techniques, to look for systematic and statistical associations of settlement attributes—in the same way as for artifact attributes—that may reflect a grouping of social units.

The most ambitious settlement pattern study of a community ever undertaken, which was really a study of many communities, was George Cowgill and René Millon's survey of the city of Teotihuacán in the Valley of Mexico, which flourished from around 250 B.C. to A.D. 700 (Millon, 1973, 1981). Their objective was to examine the changing settlement pattern of the urban complex during the vital period when the city was growing rapidly. How large was the population? How did it come into being? What was the social composition of the city, and how was it organized (Berrin and Pasztory, 1993)?

Cowgill and Millon spent years mapping and sampling the city (see Chapter 9). They found that it was built in four quadrants, following a master plan that was adhered to for centuries. The basic cruciform layout was estab-

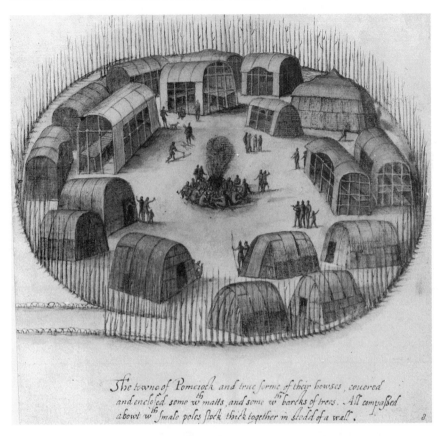

FIGURE 15.6 Example of a community: Algonquian village in North Carolina, sketched by John White in 1585.

lished very early, when the great Street of the Dead (Figure 15.7) was laid out. The oldest part of the city lies in the northern quadrant, where most of the city's craftspeople lived. It contains many more structures than the southern quadrants, where exceptionally fertile soils, ideal for irrigation agriculture, are located. The archaeologists found that the city spread southward from the northern quadrant and that it was organized into neighborhoods, or barrios, groups of apartment compounds separated from one another. Teotihuacán's population may have reached a peak of more than 150,000 people in A.D. 600. More than 2,000 compounds contained thousands of standardized, one-story apartments sharing courtyards and temples with their neighbors. Some of these compounds contained large concentrations of obsidian flakes or potters' artifacts and were identified as specialist precincts or groups of workshops.

There were foreign traders' quarters, too. One Oaxacan barrio seems to have flourished in the western part of the city, a compound where Oaxacan pottery and artifacts were common. The percentage of Oaxacan wares was very high in this

FIGURE 15.7   The Pyramid of the Sun at Teotihuacán, Mexico. The
Street of the Dead runs in front of the Pyramid.

area compared with other precincts. Millon hypothesizes that there may have
been an Oaxacan quarter in Teotihuacán for centuries.

A major objective of the Teotihuacán research is to understand the diverse
internal workings of this remarkable city as a going organization throughout its
long history. This result can be won only by comprehensive surveys that rely
heavily on samples of artifact patterns and analyses of house contents and entire
neighborhoods conducted all over this enormous site (Cowgill and others, 1984).

ANALYSIS OF SMALLER COMMUNITIES

Communities much smaller than Teotihuacán can be investigated somewhat
more easily, but large amounts of archaeological data are still involved. Early
Formative villages in the Valley of Oaxaca were investigated to test a number of
hypotheses about the relationships among parts of the settlement. Were the
villages subdivided into a number of barrios, which are still an organizational
unit in modern Indian communities that have well-defined communal and ceremonial responsibilities (Flannery, 1976; Flannery and Marcus, 1983)? By studying artifact patterns and inventories, the archaeologists found traces of at least
four residential wards at San José Mogote, each separated from its neighbors by
an erosion gully where the trash was dumped. This larger village displayed some
different craft specializations among the wards.

Artifact distributions are notoriously unreliable for identifying human
activities. Gerald Oetelaar (1993) has studied site structure at the Bridges, a

late Mississippian site in southern Illinois occupied between A.D. 1100 and 1300. He applied a research model that subdivides small settlements into four major activity zones: a communal front region for public activities; family front and back regions for domestic tasks, entertainment, and messy tasks; and a communal back region (Figure 15.8). The diverse activities in these various regions generate different debris, the model providing an analytical framework for inferring the organization and use of space at the site, when large areas of ground are exposed, as they were at Bridges. Oetelaar argues that the model shows long-term stability at the settlement, the large communal areas depicting a degree of collaboration among different families, perhaps at planting and harvest seasons. Models like this may allow researchers to study the interactions among households within the confines of a single site, and also enable the identification of specific activities at individual settlements within a larger settlement pattern.

POPULATION ESTIMATES FOR COMMUNITIES

How does one estimate community populations? Obviously, as in the Algonquian historical villages (see Figure 15.6), written records can sometimes provide a fairly accurate estimate. Modern censuses of villages and towns, however, are of only marginal use, for many variables affect even nineteenth-century population densities relative to those of prehistoric times. Some investigators have attempted to estimate population sizes with mathematical formulas that allocate so much living space to each individual and each family. But again, one is dealing with so many intangible variables, such as social restrictions, that it is difficult to be accurate. Estimates of the rates at which people accumulate refuse middens over long periods have also been used to calculate population size (Zubrow, 1976), but this method has the same serious disadvantages as the others mentioned. About the only reliable estimates of population are based on the number of households at any one moment in a community's history. Millon's guesses about Teotihuacán's population are based on such house counts. Using samples of early Mesoamerican villages, Joyce Marcus (1976) showed that perhaps 90 percent were small hamlets with from one to 10 or 12 households and up to 60 people. But some villages were much larger than this average. The contemporary Olmec site of San Lorenzo in Veracruz may have housed as many as 1,200 people. Thus you can see that this method, too, is far from accurate (see De Roche, 1983).

Community population estimates are important because they can give insights into the maximum size a settlement can achieve. What, for example, was the maximum size that early Mesoamerican hamlets and villages could reach before further growth was impossible? Characteristically, societies that were not organized into large states tended to live in small villages, which frequently split off from one another as further growth at the mother settlement was cut off. This process is straightforward enough, and in Formative Mesoamerica many villages split off in just this manner. But others, such as the Olmec settlement at San Lorenzo, were able to grow larger and still remain viable settlements. Why was this growth possible? The search for explanations of evolving settlement patterns takes us to a broader area of research, the layout of communities against the background of their natural environment (Hietala, 1984).

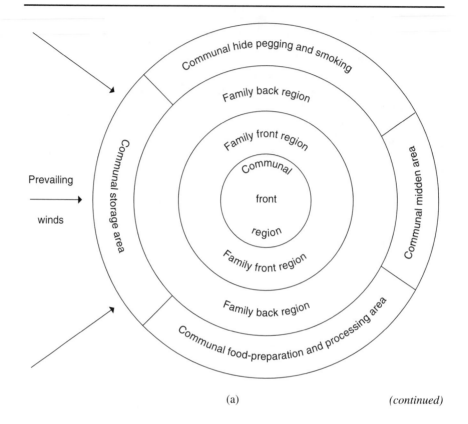

(a)   *(continued)*

RECONSTRUCTING THE NATURAL ENVIRONMENT

The density and distribution of communities, whatever their size, are determined to a considerable extent by the natural resources of the region in which they flourish, and by cultural factors. The requirements of hunter-gatherers, for example, differ from those of agriculturalists, and those of cattle herders are different from both. In Africa, the distribution of cattle is determined by zones of tsetse fly-infested country, for the insect's bite is fatal to stock and dangerous to humans. Pastoral populations tend to concentrate their settlements in grassland areas that are free from these flies, and where good fodder and abundant standing water are available (Clark and Brandt, 1984).

The settlement patterns of agricultural populations are determined by equally critical factors. For example, in the case of the Mississippian chiefdoms of the Savannah River basin region in the southeastern United States, rainfall patterns and storage capabilities were of paramount importance (D. G. Anderson and others, 1995). Tree rings from living and subfossil bald cypress logs provided a chronology for 800 years on the Atlantic coastal plain. Bald cypress are highly sensitive to rainfall and temperature fluctuations, which allowed the researchers to compile indices of drought severity, hours of

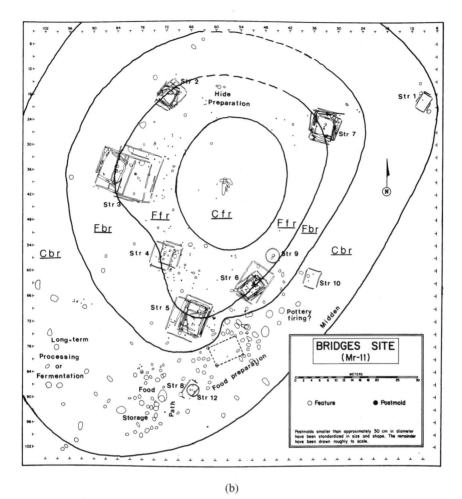

(b)

FIGURE 15.8   Site structure. (a) A hypothetical model showing a possible arrangement of work spaces in a small settlement. (b) A plan of the Bridges site, showing activity zones plotted over archaeological finds (Cfr = community forward region, and so on).

sunshine, and amount of rain per growing season from A.D. 1005 to 1600, the period of Mississippian occupation of the Savannah River valley. These figures were then compared with estimates of the agricultural reserves available to local farmers, derived from ethnohistorical records, historical accounts, and archaeological observations of storage facilities. Anderson and his colleagues were able to plot periods of above- and below-average rainfall, and showed that Mississippian populations were able to maintain a year's reserve grain supply for three-quarters of the period between A.D. 1005 and 1600. When drought did occur, there was enough surplus to give people time to switch to other food sources. Settlement patterns changed considerably during these six centuries, in part because of climatic change, but also because of political rivalries and other historical factors. During the sixteenth century, for instance, the

Savannah River peoples were caught between two powerful and competing neighboring chiefdoms. At a time of drought and stress, the smaller population of the Basin and its leaders were at a disadvantage when compared with their neighbors. In time, the Savannah chiefdoms collapsed, and the people either died out or moved elsewhere.

The dynamics of human behavior are closely tied to those of the natural environment: the dynamics of such resources as soils, plants, and animals. The changes and patterns of behavior in these resources are just as variable as those of human populations, and they condition the way in which people plan their hunting and gathering activities and plant their crops. Increasingly, archaeologists are becoming involved not only with cultural ecology but also with modern ecological research on feeding activities, energy inputs and outputs, and data on the ways in which modern populations use natural resources (Hardesty, 1977).

A viable concept of environment that an archaeologist can adopt is that it must be considered a dynamic factor in the analysis of archaeological context (Butzer, 1982). Archaeology has a four-dimensional spatial and temporal context that consists of both a cultural and a noncultural environment. The ultimate goal of environmental archaeology is to understand the relationship between culture and environment. The immediate goal of environmental archaeology is to define the characteristics and processes of the biophysical environment. This environment is the matrix for the interaction that occurs between socioeconomic systems and the natural environment. Another objective is to understand the human ecosystem, which is defined by the interaction between the environmental and human systems. Archaeological sites, or distributions of them, are part of the human ecosystem, a useful conceptual framework for examining such interactions.

Butzer (1982) considers environmental archaeology to have five major themes, themes common to geography and biology as well but especially important in the study of prehistoric human ecology:

1. *Spatial patterning,* both of natural and human phenomena, is amenable to spatial analysis.
2. *The size and scale* of both environmental and human phenomena can be measured, also through spatial analysis.
3. *The complexity* of both environments and human communities can vary greatly and must be defined and delimited.
4. *The interaction of human and nonhuman communities* is unavoidable in any complex environment where the distribution of resources is uneven. These communities interact internally and with one another, as well as with the nonliving environment, and interaction takes place on many levels and at changing or unequal rates.
5. *Equilibrium* between human societies and their environments is an ideal that is almost never achieved. Thanks to constant negative feedback resulting from both internal and external processes and inputs, they are in a continual state of environmental readjustment.

ENVIRONMENTAL SYSTEMS

Environmental systems provide the spatial and temporal frameworks within which human societies flourish. These are some key ecological concepts.

Human societies are part of the **biosphere,** which encompasses all of the earth's living organisms interacting with the physical environment. The biosphere is organized both vertically and horizontally, with genes and cells at the base and organisms, populations, and communities above them. The community, all of the biological populations in an area, functions together with the nonliving environment in an **ecosystem.**

Every ecosystem is maintained by the regulation of trophic levels (vertical food chains) and by patterns of energy flow (Figure 15.9). The complexities of even modern ecosystems make them difficult to study empirically; prehistoric

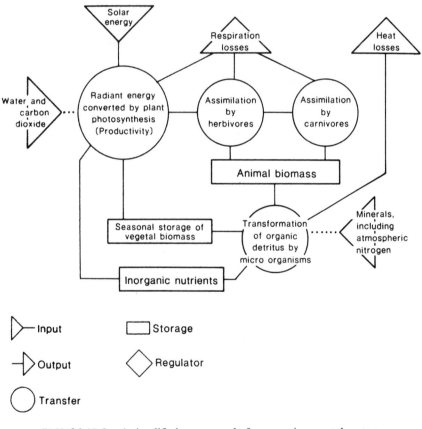

FIGURE 15.9   A simplified energy cycle for an environmental system. (After Butzer, 1982)

ones are impossible to reconstruct. But the broad conceptual framework of the ecosystem serves as a very useful research tool for archaeologists.

Human ecosystems differ from other biological ecosystems in many ways. Information, technology, and social organization all have much greater roles. Human beings, both as individuals and as groups, have unique capacities for matching resources with specific objectives. They not only think objectively about such matching but also transform the natural environment to meet their objectives. As Figure 15.10 shows, value systems and goal orientation are important to human ecosystems, as are group attitudes and decision-making institutions, especially in more complex societies. Any attempt to reconstruct prehistoric environments must take account not only of environmental resources and constraints but also of the ways in which human beings used resources and intervened in the environment and changed it.

GEOARCHAEOLOGY AND OTHER APPROACHES

Archaeological research using the methods and concepts of the early sciences, or **geoarchaeology,** is a cornerstone of environmental reconstruction (Butzer, 1982). This is a far wider enterprise than mere geology; it is deeply enmeshed in the planning and execution of both surveys and excavations and encompasses at least five major approaches:

1. Geochemical, electromagnetic, and other remote-sensing techniques to locate sites and features (Chapter 9).

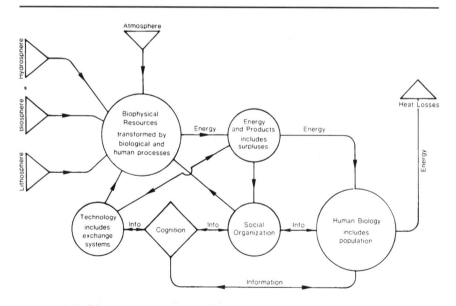

FIGURE 15.10   A much-simplified energy cycle for a human ecosystem. This chart does not include provisions for storage of food and other resources. (After Butzer, 1982)

2. Studies of site-formation processes and of the spatial context of a site within its habitat (Chapter 4).
3. Development of methods for differentiating cultural from natural features. This distinction includes disturbances due to biological, geological, and pedological processes since sites were occupied.
4. Relative and chronometric dating to establish chronological contexts both in and outside a site (Chapters 5 and 6).
5. Reconstructing the ancient landscape using a variety of paleogeographic and biological methods. These include pollen analysis and phytolith studies (Chapters 5 and 13).

Until recently, geoarchaeology was little more than a battery of techniques, many of them either developed and used by nonarchaeologists or used as a sideline. This was an ineffective approach, for nonarchaeologists have little appreciation of prehistoric human activities. People are geomorphic agents, just like the wind. Accidentally or deliberately, they carry inorganic and organic materials to their homes. They remove rubbish, make tools, build houses, abandon tools. All these mineral and organic materials are subjected to all manner of mechanical and biochemical processes during occupation and after the site is occupied. The controlling geomorphic system at a site, whatever its size, is made up not only of natural elements but of a vital cultural component as well. The geoarchaeologist is involved with archaeological investigations from the very beginning and deals not only with formation of sites and with the changes they underwent during occupation, but also with what happened to them after abandonment.

In the field, the geoarchaeologist is part of the multidisciplinary research team, recording vertical profiles within the excavation and in special pits close by, to obtain information on soil sediment sequences (Butzer, 1982). At the same time, he or she takes soil samples for pollen and sediment analyses and relates the site to its landscape by topographic survey. Working closely with survey archaeologists, geoarchaeologists locate sites and other cultural features on the natural landscape using aerial photographs, satellite images, and even geophysical prospecting on individual sites. As part of this process, they examine dozens of natural geological exposures, where they study the stratigraphic and sedimentary history of the entire region as a wider context for the sites found within it. The ultimate objective is to identify not only the microenvironment of the site but also that of the region as a whole—to establish ecological and spatial frameworks for the socioeconomic and settlement patterns that are revealed by archaeological excavations and surveys (Figure 15.11). Geoarchaeology is an integral part of the settlement archaeology process, even if many of its research procedures are the province of specialists (for example, Brochier and others, 1992).

In addition to geoarchaeology, both animal bones and paleobotanical finds can yield important information on prehistoric environments, especially if combined with other approaches. Pollen analysis has proved useful for this purpose and has sometimes provided reconstructions of the surroundings of prehistoric sites, as well as measures of the effects of human activities such as agriculture on the natural vegetation (Dimbleby, 1985). For example, thousands

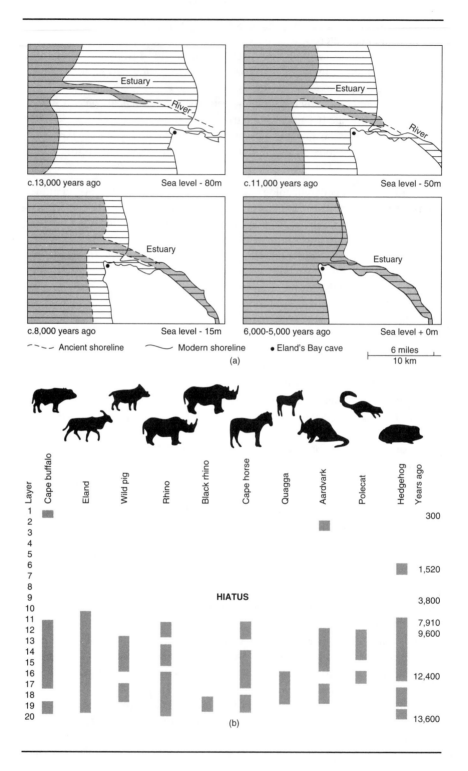

c.13,000 years ago   Sea level - 80m

c.11,000 years ago   Sea level - 50m

c.8,000 years ago   Sea level - 15m

6,000-5,000 years ago   Sea level + 0m

- - - Ancient shoreline   ~~~ Modern shoreline   • Eland's Bay cave

6 miles / 10 km

(a)

(b)

FIGURE 15.11   An example of sophisticated environmental reconstruction. Eland's Bay cave in the Cape Province of South Africa lies near the mouth of the Verlorenvlei estuary, which opens into the south Atlantic Ocean. A multidisciplinary research study of the cave has shown how the inhabitants adapted to rising sea levels at the end of the Ice Age. (a) Rising sea levels after 13,000 years ago gradually reduced the extent of the coastal shelf and its grassland. The cave was 7.5 miles (12 km) from the ocean 13,000 years ago. The inhabitants took few fish or shellfish, for the coast was more than two hours' walk away. After 9,000 years ago, the Atlantic was less than 1.25 miles (2 km) distant. Grassland animals disappeared and marine foods became common. (b) Decline in numbers of grassland animals at Eland's Bay, 13,000 to 300 years ago.

of tiny pollen grains and waterlogged wood fragments found in the deposits of the 10,000-year-old hunter-gatherer site at Star Carr, England, showed that the occupants had thrown down a tiny birch platform in some lakeside reeds. The site was surrounded by birch trees that came down to the water's edge. Some pine and willow trees grew nearby, and water plants and fungi were common (Legge and Rowley-Conwy, 1988).

INVENTORYING ENVIRONMENTAL RESOURCES

Cultural adaptation to any environment can be understood only in the context of two categories of data: the ancient environment and resources available therein, and the technology of the culture being studied. Once these data are on hand, the archaeologist can proceed to establish which subsistence and economic options the people chose, given the available resources and their technological ability to exploit them.

It is easy enough to make an inventory of the natural resources available in any area, but it is not sufficient merely to list them, for it is the ways in which they can be exploited—the seasons of availability of vegetable foods, the migration patterns of game, the months when salmon runs take place—and not just the resources themselves that are significant. These many variables, to say nothing of soil distributions, rainfall patterns, and distributions of valuable raw materials, determine the critical element of a settlement pattern—the carrying capacity of the land.

Carrying capacity is the number and density of people that any tract of land can support. It is a flexible statistic that can be affected by factors other than those of the available resources in an area. People can alter the carrying capacity of their land by taking up agriculture or by cultivating a new crop that needs deeper plowing and thus exhausts the land faster. The introduction of fertilizer can enable people to settle permanently in one village because their lands are kept fertile through artificial means.

Prehistoric carrying capacities are difficult to establish, except with carefully controlled experimental data, such as those obtained for Southwestern agriculture and Maya cultivation (see Chapter 14). Attempts have been made to measure the amount of meat available to prehistoric hunters in the Mississippi Valley (B. D. Smith, 1974), and it has been clear for some time that Classic Maya populations were much larger than those that could be supported from the felling and burning of trees to make forest gardens. One problem has been that earlier settlement models were far too simple to accommodate the complexity of the data. Recent research has concentrated on resource inventories, systems models, and even computer simulation of the variables that affect carrying capacity (Hodder, 1978).

One approach that has been tried is **site-catchment analysis,** which is difficult to apply under modern conditions when the environment is greatly modified. It is based on the assumption that every human settlement has a catchment area around it. This is a zone of domestic and wild resources within easy walking distance of the settlement. The !Kung San of the Kalahari in southern Africa are unlikely to forage much farther from their base camps than 6 miles (10 km), a comfortable day's walking distance. The fundamental assumption, then, is simple: the farther the resources in an area are from a site, the less likely they are to be exploited. Site-catchment studies are used as a way of making empirical statements about the sources or origin of materials recovered in archaeological sites (Bailey, 1981; Roper, 1979). Two key concepts are important.

The economic catchment area of a site is the area from which the food resources consumed by the inhabitants are obtained. Such areas vary in size and shape according to the resources exploited, the site function, and the lifeway of its inhabitants. Clearly, the accuracy with which the economic catchment area can be defined will depend on the precision with which one can identify food remains in the site itself.

The site-exploitation territory is quite different; it is the potential area rather than the actual territory from which food resources may be obtained. This theoretical territory is assumed to have been used regularly for subsistence by the site inhabitants. Its boundaries are defined by "least cost" principles, by the maximum radii of the distances that people are willing to cover on foot. Much depends on the nature of the resources and how they are exploited. For example, in two hours' walking time a person can cover about 6 miles (10 km)—a reasonable distance to travel for some purposes. But a much smaller radius of half a mile (1 km) is useful when analyzing farming economies where land is exploited very intensively, for it is the most economical use of labor to cultivate land close to the village. The boundaries of such radii are based on assumptions about normal human behavior and on examination of the economic potential of resources lying with them. Thus this type of site-catchment analysis is little more than a statement of what was potentially available to the site inhabitants.

Site-catchment analysis involves examining both the economic catchment area and the site-exploitation territory as a way of assessing the relationship between what was *potentially* available in the environment and what was actually exploited. Typically, variations in the economic potential of a site-catchment area are compared with variations in patterns of data from the site itself. As we saw in Chapter 9, geographic information systems analysis offers great potential for the study of site catchments, for it allows the archaeologist to overlay such features as topography, hill slopes, soil distributions, and the like onto site catchments and site-distribution territories.

George Sabo and his colleagues of the Arkansas Archaeological Survey have used GIS very effectively to study the catchment area of the Dirst site in the Buffalo River Valley of northern Arkansas. Dirst was occupied intermittently from as early as 10,000 years ago, and was a major Late Woodland settlement between A.D. 600 and 900. During these centuries, the inhabitants lived off of deer hunting, fishing, and foraging. They also planted some maize and native plants like little barley and maygrass. Frederick Limp and Pamela Smith used a GIS approach to develop an evaluation of the Dirst environment, using the Geographic Resources Analysis Support System (GRASS), the GIS system used by the National Park Service (Limp and Smith, 1990). By overlaying different GIS data layers, they were able to show that the Dirst settlement lay on a north-west-facing slope of 2 degrees. It lay in oak-pine vegetation, on a soil of marginal agricultural potential. Limp then proceeded to make two site-catchment analyses of the site. The first was a traditional one, using concentric rings, based on the assumption that travel was equally feasible in all directions. It was obvious that this simplistic approach was inappropriate, for the Buffalo River Valley walls are very steep in places. So Limp (1990) used a set of criteria such as landscape gradient to refine the analysis. Obviously, in terms of effort, the "cost" of climb-ing steep slopes is much higher than that of, say, walking along a valley-bottom trail. The result was a very irregular catchment area that reflected the relative ease with which one could move up and down the river valley and nearby valleys to the northwest, which offered easy routes to the neighboring uplands.

GIS data enabled Limp to evaluate the relative occurrence of potential resources within variable catchments around the site. He concluded that the Dirst settlement was well situated to take advantage of floodplain areas, both for their agricultural potential and for the abundance of game and plants in the same "low cost" zones. Interestingly, there were other site locations where the Dirst people would have had better access to fertile soils, but then they would not have been close to easy routes to the uplands. In other words, access to a variety of environ-mental zones and their various resources was more important than any particular resource close at hand, a finding that explains why many Arkansas societies of 1,500 years ago were able to maintain sedentary settlements, despite being dependent on seasonal food resources.

The Dirst investigation provides a remarkable example of the potential of GIS analysis in site-catchment research, for it is now possible to introduce numerous factors, such as, for example, river level, into the catchment investiga-tion, adding a high degree of realism to this form of settlement archaeology.

This approach helps with a major problem in settlement archaeology—defining variations in activities at different sites and testing hypotheses about how sites were linked. An interesting example of this approach comes from work by Kent Flannery and others in the Valley of Oaxaca, Mexico. They focused on individual sites where rigorously analyzed data from households and communities were available for comparison (Flannery, 1976; Flannery and Marcus, 1983). At San José Mogote, a village occupied between 1150 and 850 B.C., Flannery wanted to know from how far away the villagers obtained their animal and plant resources. He tested the various resources: those from within the village (turkeys, stored maize, edible fruit); those from the river, half a mile (1 km) away (reeds, sand, mud turtles); those on the high alluvium, within 1 to 3 miles (2 to 5 km) (maize and other crops); those on the piedmont, up to 3 miles (5 km) away (seasonal vegetable foods); and those in the mountains, 3 to 9 miles (5 to 15 km) distant (hut timbers, game, and firewood). Mineral resources—essentials such as salt, chert, and pottery clay—were obtained from 2 to 31 miles (3 to 50 km) away. Pacific marine shells, freshwater mussels, jadeite, and other exotic substances and objects came from distant regions, perhaps as far as 125 miles (200 km) away.

San José Mogote thus needed circles with a radius of less than 3 miles (5 km) to satisfy its basic agricultural needs, 3 miles (5 km) to supply basic minerals and seasonal wild vegetable foods, and 9 miles (15 km) for game meat and construction materials. Exotic trade materials and ceremonial life required occasional collecting trips of up to 31 miles (50 km) from the settlement and some of even greater distances. When Flannery plotted San José Mogote catchment areas relative to those of the neighboring Early Formative villages, he found that the innermost circles of 1 to 3 miles (2 to 5 km) of one village did not overlap those of any other village, but that wider circles did, as the exclusive possession of catchment areas was progressively reduced. Once the 31-mile (50 km) ring was reached, all of the villages of Oaxaca shared a common catchment area. Seasonal campsites were placed at strategic points on the outer rings, places where hut timbers, game, and trade materials were collected, perhaps by three or four villages sharing the same area. Such temporary camps were annexes to the main villages, providing more ready access to resources, which were, in their way, as important as those in the inner rings.

The San José Mogote study was carried out before the days of GIS, but it shows the general potential of sophisticated catchment analysis.

SITE DISTRIBUTIONS AND INTERACTIONS

The distribution of natural resources in the environment was but one determinant of settlement patterns. As human societies became more complex, so did the interactions between them, and these interactions were reflected in evolving settlement patterns. The study of entire settlement patterns brings into play a number of basic research methods that require large quantities of archaeological data.

DISTRIBUTION MAPS

The distribution map, which plots site distributions against the environmental background, has been used by archaeologists for a long time. Such maps, and the settlement patterns plotted on them, are normally derived from aerial photographs and ground reconnaissance. As such, they are subject to several obvious sources of error, among them the location of archaeologists in the field, site destruction by modern construction, and the difficulties of dating sites without excavation. Obviously, such impressionistic interpretations are far too superficial. Ultimately, the objective is not only to describe the distribution or settlement pattern itself, but to look as well at the factors that generated the settlement pattern in the first place. These factors cannot be deduced from archaeological evidence alone, but they can be deduced by computer simulations or statistical techniques of probability.

SPATIAL ANALYSIS

Any attempt to analyze a settlement pattern must begin with development of a site typology. Such a classification should provide objective criteria for separating sites on the basis of size, function, and other features. Archaeologists in the Valley of Mexico, for example, use a local classification that distinguishes between primary and secondary regional centers, nucleated and dispersed villages, hamlets, camps, and residences, on the basis of population size, architecture, and other specific criteria. Each of these site types has a relationship to the others; the sites form a constellation that makes up a settlement pattern on a local, regional, or even continental level. And the precise definitions of site types—ceremonial centers, villages, and so on—supply us with an explicit administrative hierarchy, a series of successive levels of settlement that organizes our patterns of dots on the map hierarchically (Figure 15.12). This hierarchy raises a fundamental question: What were the rules that shaped it on the landscape?

SITE-DISTRIBUTION ANALYSES

Our thinking about site hierarchies, settlement spacing, and hypothetical rules of settlement patterning depends on accurate distribution information and, even more importantly, on our evaluation of the significance of the various clusters of sites that can be discerned on the map. Are these clusterings accidental, the result of deliberate human planning, or due to modern factors?

A number of statistical techniques can be used to analyze site distributions, most of them borrowed from geographers. David Thomas used a method called

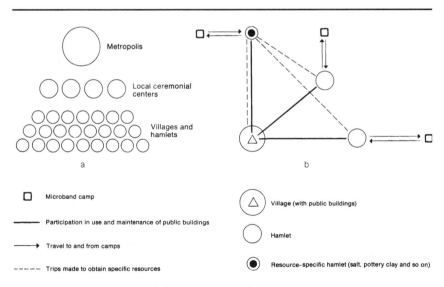

FIGURE 15.12   (a) A hypothetical population pyramid of archaeological site types. (b) A simplified diagram showing possible and hypothetical interactions among various Early Formative settlement types in the Valley of Oaxaca.

cluster analysis to study socioeconomic patterns in the Great Basin, where he found striking differences in site distributions. He discovered that "harvesting village and rabbit-driving implements are in a clumped distribution, while hunting artifacts tend to be distributed over piñon-juniper and upper sagebrush-grass zones." He was able to compare the theoretical distributions of the artifacts with his observed patterns (Thomas, 1983a). Other approaches include point-pattern analysis, in which site distributions are plotted on a grid and tested for nonrandom patterning (Figure 15.13). The nearest-neighbor statistic of the geographers is another (Earle, 1976). All these techniques require sophisticated statistical manipulations and data of meticulous quality to be effective (Stark and Young, 1981).

One essential ingredient for understanding settlement patterns is knowledge of how site hierarchies came into being and of the intensity of interaction between the inhabitants of each site type. One useful concept for this end is central-place theory.

CENTRAL-PLACE THEORY

Central-place theory, first developed by the German geographer Walter Christaller (1933) in a study of southern German communities, is a series of statements about the relationship among settlement systems. Christaller stated that "if the population distribution and its purchasing power, as well as the topography, its resources, and transport facilities, are all uniform, then all central places providing similar services, performing similar functions, and serving areas of equal size, will be spaced at an equal distance from one another."

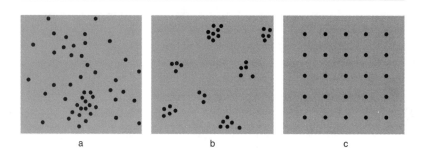

a   b   c

FIGURE 15.13   Three possible models for archaeological distributions: (a) A random distribution, with the points scattered without pattern. All points have an equal probability of being located at any given place on what is assumed to be a featureless landscape. (b) Clusters of points, representing artifacts or sites grouped in clumps. Distribution in clumps can occur when people are attracted toward a valuable resource, or when a village, for example, generates new settlements that are located nearby. An extreme example is, of course, a distribution in which everyone is located at the same point. (c) A spaced distribution, which has the sites or artifacts at more or less regular intervals. Here, people are spaced at regular intervals because they are competing with one another for resources or in some other way.

After this general definition, Christaller went on to develop a hierarchy of central places, which divided groups of centers of decreasing size and facilities into various hierarchical groups. In these hierarchies it was assumed that there were fewer large places than small ones, the large places providing the widest range of services possible. Not only did the largest places perform the services of the smaller ones, but they also performed central functions that distinguish them from their lesser neighbors.

The simple Christaller model has been modified by later research to allow the size of a service area to vary with the size of the central place that services it. Under this arrangement, the central-place function of Teotihuacán, for example, affects a much larger area than that serviced by smaller centers lying within, say, 20 miles (32 km) of the city (Blanton, 1978). The latter merely duplicate services available at Teotihuacán and are less likely to develop close to the city than they are to develop close to one another. Behind these modifications is the assumption that the location of any form of center will be determined, at least in part, by convenience to its clients. It will be located where it can be reached with minimal effort. Ideally, a single service center that provides multiple services to a surrounding population situated on a flat plain will service a circular area, with the center located in the middle. But when there are several types of central place, each fulfilling different functions within a region, the most logical shape of the service territory will be a hexagon.

The hexagon is a theoretical configuration, to be sure, but it does reflect the essential regularity of service areas. This shape of territory minimizes the distance to the centers from the boundaries of the area and keeps population movement to a minimum (Figure 15.14). This model has been tested using southern English market towns, which were spaced 4 to 6 miles (6 to 10 km) apart in Medieval times, a convenient day's journey by cart from the surrounding rural villages. Indeed, a twelfth-century law expressly forbade placement of markets closer than 6 miles (10 km) apart. This spacing cannot be claimed as a universal law, for many factors, such as terrain or population density, can still act on even the seemingly most regular patterns. In 2800 B.C., Sumerian towns and villages in the Diyala area of southern Iraq were placed unevenly to locate them near the best water transport networks rather than purely to maximize the use of fertile land.

Central-place theory's main use to archaeologists is as a descriptive device for regional settlement patterns. The central-place model provides a means of suggesting hypotheses about what economic moves and organizational decisions were needed. These can then be tested against field data. In addition, the notion of a hierarchy of central places serving areas of different sizes—that is, in an interlocking relationship in space—is vital to archaeology (see Trombold, 1992).

SOCIOECOLOGICAL MODELS

The formal methods of spatial analysis archaeologists use are little more than general perspectives, part of a wider examination of archaeological sites considering the spaced resources available to their inhabitants and the constraints placed on them by such variables as perception, information, and technology (Butzer, 1982).

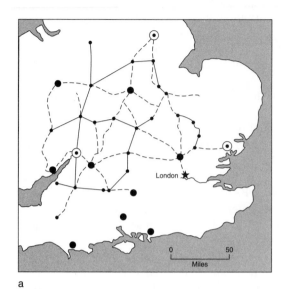

KEY

●   Capital

⊙   Colony

·   Lesser walled town

- - - -   Road

———   Boundary of tributary areas

a

b

FIGURE 15.14   Map of Romano-British settlement in southern Britain during the third century A.D.: (a) the site hierarchy plotted on a conventional map; (b) the hexagonal lattice erected over the hierarchy.

HUNTER-GATHERER SITES

A large and complex literature surrounds living and prehistoric hunter-gatherers (Bettinger, 1991). The implicit models used by archaeologists to describe the spatial behavior of hunter-gatherers have a distinct evolutionary undertone. The assumption seems to be that human beings progressed from a simple, unspecialized, freewheeling way of life to a more and more specialized existence circumscribed within a scheduled annual round. This led, eventually, to a farming life with more lasting settlement. The chronicle of North American prehistory seems to bear out this general scenario, for the earliest Paleo-Indian and Archaic societies were adapted to a highly mobile lifeway. During Middle and Late Archaic times, and certainly after 2000 B.C., hunter-gatherer societies living in areas of relatively abundant and seasonally predictable food resources, such as the bottomlands of the Midwest and some coastal areas such as the Pacific Northwest, evolved a more sedentary settlement pattern. This had them residing at one location for many months of the year, sometimes even year-round. In the Midwest, rising population densities and resource shortages apparently led to the deliberate cultivation of some native plants such as goosefoot to amplify wild sources. Maize agriculture did not take hold in the Eastern Woodlands of North America until the past 2,000 years, or perhaps somewhat earlier (B. D. Smith, 1994; Fern and Liu, 1995).

Karl Butzer (1982) made another assumption when he studied the Lower Paleolithic Acheulian sites of Ambrona and Torralba in central Spain. He argued that early hunter-gatherers shared the ability of large grazing animals like elephants to adopt different feeding habits and seasonal movements according to the abundance of resources through the year. Ambrona and Torralba lie along the only low-altitude mountain pass dividing the plains of Castile. This was the route through which large mammals migrated in spring and fall, from winter to summer pastures and back again. The Acheulians preyed on these migrating beasts. During other seasons of the year, they spread over the neighboring country in temporary camps near water and constantly moving herds (Figure 15.15). This settlement pattern is suggested not only by site distributions but also by such phenomena as migratory bird bones in the archaeological deposits. It is, of course, possible that the Acheulians were scavenging elephants that died after becoming enmired in swampy ground.

This Spanish example suggest that the movements of hunter-gatherers were related to different ways of exploiting local resources that can be detected in the archaeological record. The first requirement in establishing spatial and temporal variables is to find the span of time during which individual sites were used. They can be ephemeral, occupied for a few hours or days; temporary, used for several days or weeks; seasonal; or semipermanent. Functional and social considerations affect the duration of occupation, too, but these cannot always be inferred from the archaeological record. Armed with these data, you can prepare "mobility models" for hunter-gatherers, samples of which are shown in Figure 15.16.

EARLY ARCHAIC SETTLEMENT ON THE ATLANTIC SLOPE The large-scale cultural resource management surveys and test excavations of recent years have led to many important regional studies of prehistoric culture, not just in North America but throughout the world. Many of these describe relatively small

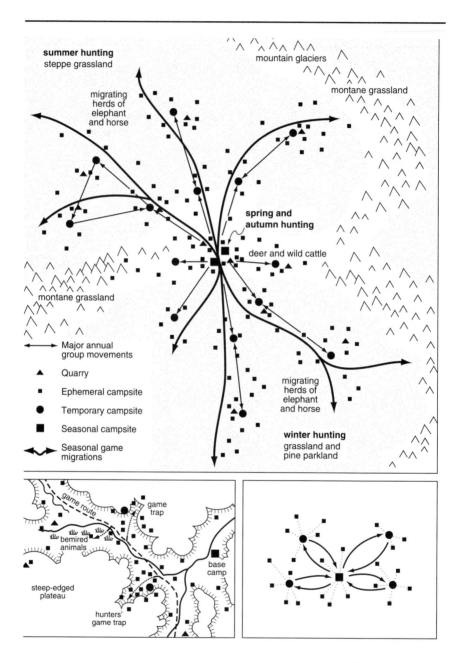

FIGURE 15.15 A seasonal mobility model for Acheulian hunter-gatherers in central Spain, based in part on data from Torralba and Ambrona. During spring and fall, the hunters preyed on herds migrating through the mountain passes (map at lower left). In summer and winter, the hunters divided into smaller groups and lived in temporary sites near water, animal herds, and stone outcrops. (After Butzer, 1982)

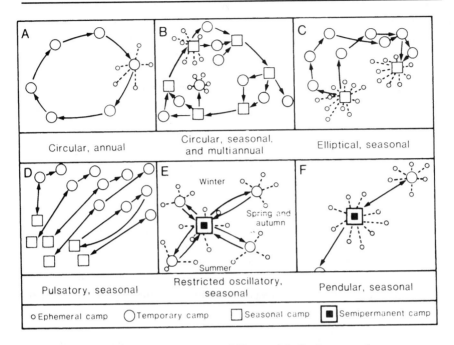

FIGURE 15.16   Hypothetical mobility models for hunter-gatherers. (a) Seasonal camps on a semirandom annual circular movement. (b) Seasonal aggregation and dispersal to optimize use of scattered, less-predictable resources. Over the years, the pattern will be roughly circular. (c) Elliptical nomadic pattern, such as one might find along a perennial river, with the inhabitants moving out into less well-watered areas during the rainy season. (d) Pulsatory seasonal movement, as might occur when lowland herders venture into the highlands at certain seasons of the year. (e) Oscillatory pattern, in which people use one base at certain times of the year, then disperse outward at other seasons. This is the Ambrona-Torralba model. (f) Pendular model, which might apply when people were experimenting with crops and were living in one place for much of the year, dispersing at others; it can be likened to a seasonal pendulum effect. (After Butzer, 1982)

hunter-gatherer populations using models derived from general ecological and anthropological theory derived by ethnoarchaeological research.

David Anderson and Glen Hanson's (1988) study of Early Archaic settlement in the Savannah River Valley of the Southeastern United States is an excellent example of a regional research project carried out with a sophisticated theoretical underpinning combined with widespread surveying and careful excavation. Modern ecological research has established that clear relations exist between the distribution of resources within an environment and the foraging strategies of the animals that live in it. In ecosystems with patchily distributed resources, animals tend to forage for specific resources, whereas they tend to be more eclectic in their foraging when resources are evenly distributed throughout the landscape. By the same token, hunter-gatherer populations tend to be less mobile, to collect and store food in environments with patchy resources, whereas in more uniform environments they tend to forage over the landscape, moving frequently. This phenomenon led Anderson and Hanson to predict that as homogeneous hardwood forest spread over the southeastern Atlantic slope at the very end of the Ice Age some 10,000 years ago, Early Archaic human populations would tend to adopt increasingly mobile foraging adaptations over the same region.

Ecological theory, based, among other things, on research into blackbird nesting behavior, also suggested that during the winters, when plant foods were relatively scarce in this woodland environment and deer were concentrated in larger groups, Early Archaic populations would tend to live in more sedentary base camps, dispersing into more mobile, widely distributed camps during the plentiful warmer months.

Anderson and Hanson developed a general biocultural model of Early Archaic settlement on the southern Atlantic Coast of North America that reflected both general ecological theory and the character of the regional archaeological record. They hypothesized that Early Archaic bands living in this area used warmer, well-provisioned base camps on the warmer coastal plain during the winter. These settlements were located within river drainages, close to raw material sources, and placed according to the availability of food resources, including deer, which tended to move in larger groups during the winter. In early spring the deer dispersed and edible plant resources appeared over much of the landscape, first at the warmer coast, then inland. The people now moved out into small, regularly spaced camps, their distribution reflecting the fairly even distribution of food resources. To some extent, the bands were "tethered" to raw material sources, which were irregularly distributed over the landscape. They foraged over the Upper Coastal Plain and the Piedmont (Figure 15.17) during the summer. Come fall, the bands moved downstream, probably choosing base camp locations that were different from the year before, for resources at those locations were probably still depleted. Anderson and Hanson used estimates derived from site surveys and excavations to argue that between 50 and 150 people lived in each neighboring drainage at the beginning of the Early Archaic, a figure that rose over the centuries, resulting in decreases in annual ranges as bands fissioned into new groups that occupied smaller territories.

The settlement pattern of Early Archaic bands over the South Atlantic Slope reflected the northwest-to-southeast flow of most major drainages there from the Appalachian Mountains to the Atlantic. Anderson and Hanson believe that to maintain a viable equilibrium population, bands from three to five drainages had to be in regular contact. They maintained networks both through the movements of individuals and through regular gatherings, probably in the fall, reflected by major sites located midway between winter and summer foraging grounds. The two archaeologists argue that there was a South Atlantic macroband of between 500 and 1,000 people, perhaps made up of as many as eight separate groups living in contiguous drainages. Other such macrobands may have lived on all sides of the region, those to the south and west separated from the South Atlantic Slope by natural geographic barriers. This important regional study argues that Early Archaic adaptations in this area, like many other prehistoric hunter-gatherer adaptations, were conditioned not only by the local environment but also by biological interaction between different groups, population spacing, and restraints of information exchange between neighboring groups.

AGRICULTURAL SETTLEMENTS

The clustering and patterning of agricultural settlements are affected by cultural and environmental factors combined. The following are some key variables.

Distribution of economic resources such as different types of land with separate uses for grazing, cultivation, and so on, is critical. Soil distributions are also vital, for different depths, textures, and subsoils can impose severe limitations on grazing and other uses. The earliest European farmers concentrated on well-drained, easily dug soils because they lacked the heavy plows that enabled cultivators to turn over heavier clay soils. The distribution of game and vegetable food resources is also vital.

Available technology, land clearance techniques, available transport or draft animals, crop types exploited, and other such factors within the site itself are critical. So is the socioeconomic organization that schedules planting and harvest, determines who works with whom, and copes with the obligations among members of the community. Wide-ranging symbolic and social values also place their imprint on settlement patterns, for they determine not only perceptions of resources but also attitudes toward the environment as well as toward one's neighbors.

Topography influences the placement of agricultural sites in relation to their neighbors, affects direction of trade routes, and encourages or inhibits communication. The ancient Egyptians depended on the Nile for transportation and water; their modern successors do so still. The same topography can profoundly affect the ways in which agricultural settlement fills in areas that were not settled at first, for spacing of new communities will be affected by location of the original settlements with their continuing needs for land. Defense, too, can radically affect agricultural site distributions. Everyone may elect to live on hilltops, simply to guard against surprise attack.

Trade networks play a leading role in the emergence of central places, such as great cities like the Aztec capital of Tenochtitlán, which attracted trade from all over Mesoamerica (R. F. Townsend, 1992). Originally a settlement pattern based on trade may be determined in part by environment or social considerations, but eventually a vertical hierarchy of sites may grow, as technological, demographic, social, and religious forces come into play. Eventually, as society becomes more complex, site networks may be modified by overriding religious or political considerations. This change happened in colonial Mexico, where the incoming Spanish authorities resettled thousands of Indians into small towns that were under the direct control of the central government.

Agricultural settlements on any scale are affected by so many environmental, economic, social, and other factors that simple propositions like those developed for hunter-gatherers are untenable. Any approach to the study of agricultural settlements must emphasize not only the distribution patterns, so critical in interpreting hunter-gatherer subsistence patterns, but also the interactions between sites that made them occur, for agricultural settlements were far more dependent on one another than those of hunter-gatherers.

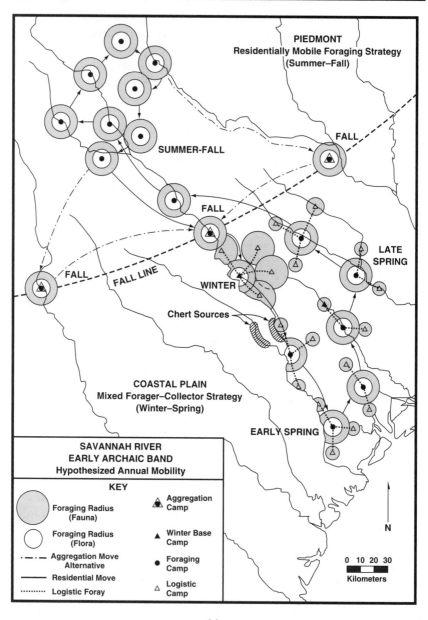

(a)   (continued)

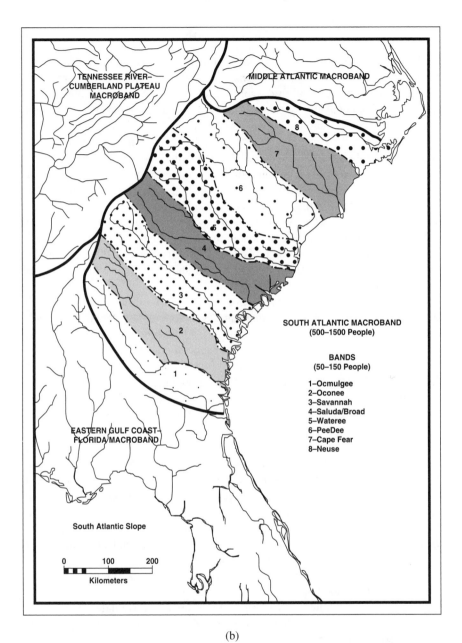

TENNESSEE RIVER–
CUMBERLAND PLATEAU
MACROBAND

MIDDLE ATLANTIC MACROBAND

8

7

6

5

4

3

2

1

SOUTH ATLANTIC MACROBAND
(500–1500 People)

BANDS
(50–150 People)

1–Ocmulgee
2–Oconee
3–Savannah
4–Saluda/Broad
5–Wateree
6–PeeDee
7–Cape Fear
8–Neuse

EASTERN GULF COAST–
FLORIDA MACROBAND

South Atlantic Slope

0   100   200
Kilometers

(b)

FIGURE 15.17   Anderson and Hanson's (1988) hypothesized model of
Early Archaic settlement on the southern Atlantic Coast of North
America: (a) model of seasonal mobility; (b) model of Early Archaic
band-macroband distribution over the region.

POPULATION

Settlement patterns evolve in response to three broad variables: environmental change, alterations in population density, and interaction among people. One major factor in the later cultural evolution of humanity has undoubtedly been rapidly growing population densities. Many of the classic arguments of archaeology have revolved around the role of population growth in the origins of agriculture, urban life, and civilization. Unfortunately, however, as mentioned previously, estimating population densities is a task fraught with difficulty.

Methods based on food consumption in Europe and on shell middens in the Western United States have been used to calculate populations of hunter-gatherer camps. A clever though mainly theoretical calculation, but one that may give a reasonable estimate of general population size, was made by a group of California archaeologists, who estimated that about 30 people occupied what is now the Scripps estate in southern California between about 5500 and 3500 B.C. They based their estimates on the amount of shell refuse and the number of grindstones found there.

Cemeteries and burial grounds have been used to estimate population also, but this evidence has the disadvantage that it is seldom representative of the population as a whole. Most cemeteries are used for a long time and represent a cumulative population rather than the number of people living at a given moment.

Most demographic figures from large geographic areas are clearly little more than guesses. One estimate places the average population of the early Sumerian states in Mesopotamia at about 17,000 people (Redman, 1978); another puts the Late Glacial population of Britain at about 10,000 (J. G. D. Clark, 1975).

POPULATION GROWTH

Although accurate population estimates, settlement by settlement, are obviously of great interest, especially if one assumes that the growing size of a village represents a growing population, the consequences of population growth and decline are even more important. Population is a key element in the cultural process, for there is a clear cause-and-effect relationship between population and the potential carrying capacity and productivity of agricultural land. Competition and cooperation between communities may result from a shortage of resources engendered by population growth, and these interactions may in turn affect both settlement patterns and population density (Hassan, 1981).

The classic hypothesis on world population was formulated by Thomas Robert Malthus late in the eighteenth century. Malthus believed that humankind's reproductive capacity far exceeds available food supplies; in other words, people must compete for the necessities of life. Competition causes famine, war, and misery. The Malthusian thesis has so dominated archaeological thinking for generations that many scholars believed that the capacity of land and other resources, as well as that of technology, places limits on population growth.

The Malthusian viewpoint was challenged by economist Ester Boserup (1965), who stated the thesis that population growth should be treated as a quite independent variable when studying technological and cultural change. "As population grows," she argued, more people per unit of land are faced with the necessity of providing more food per trait of land, and they are able to do this by intensifying their relationship with the land—technology—moving from hunting and gathering through stages of cultivation with ever-shorter fallow periods up to the final stage of intensification, which is multi-cropping with no fallowing.

She went on to argue that people intensify their agricultural efforts only when forced by population pressure to do so. The implication is that more intensive land use is accompanied by parallel intensification of other aspects of culture and society (Spooner, 1972).

Boserup's theoretical viewpoint highlights population as another variable in settlement archaeology. Nowhere has this been shown more dramatically than at the Maya city of Copán, where a large-scale settlement survey has examined more than 52 square miles (135 sq. km) around the urban core (Freter, 1994). This project was modeled after the famous Basin of Mexico survey (Sanders and others, 1979), where efforts were concentrated on the areas most suitable for human settlement. A combination of aerial photographs and foot survey recorded more than 1,425 archaeological sites in the Copán Valley, and researchers mapped and surface-collected each one of them. Two hundred and fifty-two sites were test-pitted and all sites were classified in a hierarchy of simple to complex, those tested being selected on the basis of statistical sampling methods. The survey revealed an urban core, a densely occupied area surrounding the core, and a rural region with a much lower settlement density. By using obsidian hydration dating on obsidian samples (Chapter 8), the investigators were able to date the sampled sites quite precisely and reconstruct the demography of the Copán Valley.

Between A.D. 550 and 700, the Copán state expanded rapidly, with most of the population concentrated in the core and immediate periphery zones. There was only a small, scattered rural population. Between 700 and 850, the Copán Valley reached its greatest sociopolitical complexity, with a rapid population increase to between 20,000 and 25,000 people. These figures, calculated from site size, suggest the local population was doubling every 80 to 100 years, with about 80 percent of the people living within the core and immediate periphery. Rural settlement expanded outward along the valley floor, but was still relatively scattered. But now people were farming foothill areas, as the population density of the urban core reached over 8,000 people per 0.3 sq. mile (1 sq. km), with the periphery housing about 500 people per 0.3 sq. mile (1 sq. km). Some 82 percent of the population lived in relatively humble dwellings, an indication of the extreme stratification of Copán society. Then, after A.D. 850, depopulation occurred, as Copán's ruling dynasty ended in 822. The urban core and periphery zones lost about half their population after 850, while the rural population increased by almost 20 percent. Small regional settlements replaced the scattered villages of earlier times, a response to cumulative deforestation, overexploitation of even marginal agricultural soils, and sheet erosion near the capital. After 1150, the Copán Valley population had fallen to between 2,000 and 5,000 people.

The Copán research, like that of Robert Adams on early Mesopotamian settlements (1974), clearly demonstrates the complex economic and social variables that could affect population growth in prehistory. Much of the time, settlement archaeology involves hypothesizing about intangibles, those aspects of human society that are never preserved in the archaeological record. But as Chapter 16 shows, much of our understanding of cultural evolution and changing settlement patterns comes from the insights we can obtain into the interactions between different communities reflected in their trading, social, and religious practices.

SUMMARY

- Settlement archaeology, the study of changing human settlement patterns, is part of the analysis of adaptive interactions between people and their environment.
- Settlement patterns are determined by many factors, among them the environment, economic practices, and technological skills. Learned cultural skills and established networks of human behavior also affect settlement, as do practical political considerations, population growth, and social organization.
- Bruce Trigger defines three levels of settlement: the building or structure, the arrangement of structures within individual communities, and the distribution of communities across the landscape.
- Single structures can be studied from the perspective of form and material or from a functional viewpoint. Social and political institutions also affect the design of individual houses.
- A community is a maximal group of people that normally resides in face-to-face associations. The layout of communities is much affected by political and social considerations. The archaeologist looks for clusters of settlement attributes that may indicate a grouping of social units.
- Estimates of population are very difficult to obtain from even comprehensive archaeological data—there simply are too many intangible variables that affect the archaeological record.
- Prehistoric environmental data are obtained both from Pleistocene geology and from animal bones, especially those of small mammals. Pollen analysis is one of the most effective methods of reconstructing ancient environments.
- Site-catchment analysis is a method used to inventory resources within range of prehistoric sites. It is a study of the relationships between technology and available natural resources.
- Site-distribution maps are used to study prehistoric settlement patterns; these are analyzed using rigorous, objective criteria, which take into account sampling errors and other variables. The objective of such analyses is to establish the factors that governed human settlement in prehistoric times.
- Spatial analyses in archaeology make use of a variety of techniques developed by geographers. They include central-place theory and cluster analysis.
- Population estimates for prehistoric sites have been made using subjective guesswork, mathematical formulas, and sophisticated estimates of the carrying capacity of the land. Such estimates are rarely precise.

• Population growth was a major factor in later prehistory. Most archaeologists agree with Thomas Robert Malthus that humanity's reproductive capacity far exceeds available food supplies. But Ester Boserup and her colleagues disagree, arguing that people intensify their food-gathering or production efforts in the face of rising population. This controversy highlights the need for archaeologists to examine the many intangible variables that affect cultural change over long periods of prehistoric time.

GUIDE TO FURTHER READING

Bettinger, Robert L. *Hunter-Gatherers: Archaeological and Evolutionary Theory.* New York: Plenum Press, 1991. An excellent synthesis of hunter-gatherer studies from an evolutionary perspective.

Butzer, Karl W. *Archaeology as Human Ecology.* Cambridge: Cambridge University Press, 1982. An authoritative description of basic environmental and spatial concepts in archaeology. Strongly recommended as a starting point.

Flannery, Kent V., ed. *The Early Mesoamerican Village.* Orlando, Fla.: Academic Press, 1976. A modern classic, a study by a team of Michigan archaeologists of settlement patterns in the Valley of Oaxaca. Enlivened by some hypothetical but highly entertaining debates between fictitious archaeologists of different theoretical viewpoints.

Hietala, H., ed. *Intersite Spatial Analysis in Archaeology.* Cambridge: Cambridge University Press, 1984. Essays on relationships between sites in the archaeological record.

Sanders, William T., Jeffrey R. Parsons, and Robert S. Santley. *The Basin of Mexico: Ecological Processes in the Evolution of a Civilization,* 2 vols. Orlando, Fla.: Academic Press, 1979. A settlement-ecological study that gives an admirable impression of the state-of-the-art research in this field.

16

EXCHANGE, SOCIAL ORGANIZATION, AND RELIGIOUS LIFE

So far, we have focused on the analysis of artifacts and ancient technology, on settlement, subsistence and the interpretation of the archaeological record. Chapter 16 moves a stage further and uses the material remains of the past to study the ways in which ancient societies interacted with one another. Two related questions are of fundamental importance. How can we study prehistoric social organization, and how can we use surviving artifacts to study ancient religious beliefs?

EXCHANGE SYSTEMS

Many Americans drive Japanese cars. French teenagers like the taste of hamburgers. Pacific Islanders crave Mexican-made television sets. We live in an international world, where economic ties link nations many thousands of miles apart. As anthropologist Eric Wolf has pointed out (1984), human societies throughout the world have become part of a vast web of economic interconnectedness which developed during the European Age of Discovery after A.D. 1500. But the ultimate roots of our modern-day global economic system date back more than 5,000 years, to the dramatic growth of long-distance trade which preceded the appearance of the world's first civilizations in the Near East. But exchange and trade were part of human life long before the Sumerians and ancient Egyptians. Black Sea shells appear in late Ice Age hunting encampments deep in the Ukraine at least 18,000 years ago. The Paleo-Indians of the Great Plains exchanged fine-grained toolmaking stone over long distances as early as 9000 B.C. Few human societies are completely self-sufficient, for they depend on others for resources outside their own territories. And, as the need for raw materials, or for prestigious ornaments, increased, so did the tentacles of exchange and trade between neighbors near and far. This trade often had powerful political or symbolic overtones, conducted under the guise of formal gift-giving or as part of complex exchange rituals.

Exchange and trade have been defined as the "mutually appropriative movement of goods between hands" (Renfrew, 1975). People make trade connections and the **exchange systems** that handle trade goods when they need to acquire goods and services that are not available to them within their own site-catchment area. The movement of goods need not be over any great distance, and it can operate internally, within a society, or externally, across cultural boundaries—within interaction spheres. Both exchange and trade always involve two elements: the goods and commodities being exchanged and the people doing the exchanging. Thus any form of trading activity implies both procurement and handling of tools and raw materials and some form of social system that provides the people-to-people relationships within which the trade flourishes. Not only raw materials and finished objects but also ideas and information passed along trade routes.

Conventionally, exchange and trade are recognized in the archaeological record by the discovery of objects exotic to the material culture or economy of the host society. For instance, glass was never manufactured in sub-Saharan Africa, yet imported glass beads are widespread in archaeological sites of the first millennium A.D. (Connah, 1987). Until recently, such objects were recognized almost entirely on the basis of style and design—the appearance of distinctive pottery forms far from their known point of origin, and so on. Sometimes exotics such as gold, amber, turquoise, or marine shells, commodities whose general area of origin was known, provided evidence of long-distance exchanges. Late Archaic and Woodland peoples in the North American Southeast used native copper from outcrops near Lake Superior and conch shells from the Gulf Coast, both commodities of known origin (Baugh and Ericson, 1994).

In the early days of archaeology, such exotica were deemed sufficient to identify trade, even what were loosely called "influences" or even "invasions." The assumptions made about the nature of human interactions were very limited and never precise (Torrence, 1986). Today, however, studies of prehistoric exchange are far more sophisticated, owing to two major developments. The first is a new focus throughout archaeology on the cultural process and on regional studies. The second is the development of a wide range of scientific techniques that are capable of describing the composition of certain types of raw material and even of identifying their sources with great precision (see below).

TYPES OF EXCHANGE AND TRADE

Exchange can be internal, within a society, or external, with other groups. Internal distribution of artifacts and commodities is commonplace even in the least complex societies. Much internal exchange is gift-giving. Perhaps the most famous example is that of the *kula* ring of Melanesia in the southwestern Pacific. An elaborate network of gift exchanges passes shell necklaces in one direction, arm shells in the other. They are passed as ceremonial gifts from one individual to another, in gift partnerships that endure for decades. These gift exchanges enjoy great prestige, yet serve as a framework for the regular exchange of foodstuffs and other more day-to-day commodities. With all gift exchange, much depends on the types of commodities being exchanged. In the case of the *kula* ring, precious seashell ornaments pass between individuals of higher status; foodstuffs are a more common form of transaction involving many individuals and families. And of course, not only objects but also information can be exchanged, which may lead to technological innovation or social change.

Gift-giving is a common medium of exchange and trade in societies that are relatively self-supporting. The exchange of gifts is designed primarily to reinforce a social relationship between both individuals and groups. The gifts serve as gestures that place obligations on both parties. This form of exchange is common in New Guinea and the Pacific, and was widespread in Africa during the past 2,000 years, as well as in the ancient Americas. Gift-giving and bartering formed a basic trading mechanism for millennia, a simple means of exchanging basic commodities. But this sporadic interaction between individuals and communities reduced peoples' self-sufficiency and eventually made them part of a larger society whose members were no longer so self-sufficient and who depended on one another for basic commodities and also for social purposes.

Reciprocity, the mutual exchange of goods between two individuals or groups, is at the heart of much gift-giving and barter trade. It can happen year after year at the same place, which can be as humble as someone's house. Such central places become the focus of gift-giving and trade. When a village becomes involved in both the production of trade goods and their exchange with other communities, it will probably become an even more important center, a place to which people will travel to trade.

Redistribution of trade goods throughout a culture requires some form of organization to ensure that the redistribution is equitable. A redistributive mechanism may be controlled by a chief, a religious leader, or some form of management organization. Such an organization might control production of copper ornaments, or it might simply control distribution and delivery of trade objects. Considerable social organization is needed for the collection, storage, and redistribution of grain and other commodities. The chief, whose position is perhaps reinforced by religious power, has a serious responsibility to his community that can extend over several villages, as his lines of redistribution stretch out through people of lesser rank to the individual villager. A chief will negotiate exchanges with other chiefs, substituting the regulatory elements of reciprocal trading for a redistributive economy in which less trading in exotic materials is carried out by individual households.

Prehistoric exchange was an important variable that developed in conjunction with sociopolitical organization. In many areas, external trade proceeded from simple reciprocal exchange to the more complex redistribution of goods under a redistributor. In other words, trading is closely tied to growing social and political complexity, although it does not necessarily imply the special production of exotic artifacts specifically for exchange.

The term *markets* (at a higher level than redistribution) covers both places and particular styles of trading. The administration and organization encourages people to set aside one place for trading and to establish relatively stable prices for staple commodities. This stability does not mean regulated prices, but some regulation is needed in a network of markets in which commodities from an area of abundant supplies are sold to one with strong demand for the same materials. The mechanisms of the exchange relationship particularly require some regulation. Markets are normally associated with more complex societies. No literate civilization ever developed without strong central places, where trading activities were regulated and monopolies developed over both sources of materials and trade routes themselves.

Successful market trading required predictable supplies of basic commodities and adequate policing of trade routes. It is significant that most early Mesopotamian and Egyptian trade was riverine, where policing was easier. With the great caravan routes opened, the political and military issues— tribute, control of trade routes, and tolls—became paramount. The caravan, predating the great empires, was a form of organized trading that kept to carefully defined routes set up and maintained by state authorities. The travelers moved along these set routes, looking neither left nor right, bent only on delivering and exchanging imports and exports. These caravans were a far cry from the huge economic complex that accompanied Alexander the Great's army across Asia or the Grand Mogul's annual summer progress from the heat in Delhi to the mountains, which moved a half-million people, including the entire Delhi bazaar.

THE STUDY OF SOURCES

Obtaining evidence of long-distance trade involves far more sophisticated inquiry than merely plotting the distribution of distinctive artifacts hundreds of miles away from their place of manufacture. Much current research involves identifying the sources of raw materials. By far the most significant of these materials is obsidian, volcanic glass that is ideal for fabricating stone tools, ornaments, and in Mesoamerica, highly polished mirrors (Figure 16.1). In the 1960s, Colin Renfrew and others used spectrographic analysis to identify no fewer than 12 early farming villages that had obtained obsidian from the Ciftlik area of central Turkey (Renfrew and others, 1966). This pioneer study showed that 80 percent of the chipped stone in villages within 186 miles (300 km) of Ciftlik was obsidian. Outside this "supply zone," the percentages of obsidian dropped away sharply with distance, to 5 percent in a Syrian village and 0.1 percent in the Jordan Valley. If these calculations were correct, each village was passing about half its imported obsidian further down the line (Figure 16.2). Renfrew and his colleagues have identified no fewer than nine Neolithic and Early Bronze Age obsidian "interaction zones" between Sardinia and Mesopotamia, each of them linked to well-defined sources of supply (Torrence, 1986).

In Mesoamerica, many scholars have attempted to trace the trade routes over which obsidian traveled from highlands to lowlands. The use of source data enables researchers to conceive of exchange on a regional basis, an approach used with success at Copán and combined with obsidian hydration dating to trace changes in obsidian trade networks (Freter, 1993). Today, archaeologists regard exchange as "a form of interaction such that a system of interrelations operates on a regional level" (Torrence, 1986). Nowadays, the ultimate research goal is to identify the exchange mechanisms that distributed the obsidian within each interaction zone. Thus the data requirements have changed. No longer is it sufficient to know the approximate source of a raw material or an artifact. Sources must be pinpointed accurately, and distributions of traded goods or commodities must be

FIGURE 16.1   Obsidian mirror from Mesoamerica, reflecting a figurine.

quantified precisely. Such data provide the groundwork for studies of trade. However, it remains to translate these distributions and the source data into characterizations of human behavior.

Most obsidian studies have concentrated on the use of the rock and the amount of it traded from settlement to settlement. Future studies will have to monitor exchange by taking analogies from ethnohistorical and historical studies of quarrying and trade, and by developing new ways of inferring behavior from the archaeological record. Chipped stone is useful in this regard, for one can reconstruct the reduction strategies used to produce traded raw material and finished artifacts and thereby gain insights into efficiency of production and other such facets of human behavior. Prehistoric quarries, such as those in Greece, Mesoamerica, and Australia, are potentially valuable sources of information on the exchange of exotic materials. Torrence (1986) based her ideas on an innova-

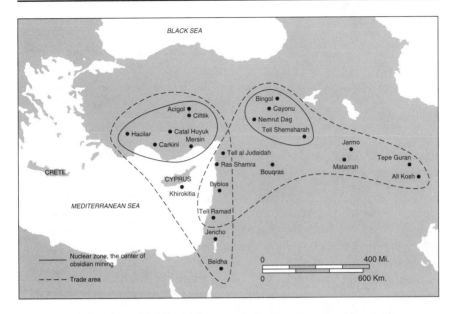

FIGURE 16.2 Obsidian trade routes in the Near East. Sourcing studies reveal that early farming communities in Cyprus, Anatolia, and the Levant obtained their obsidian from two sources in central Anatolia. Meanwhile, villages like Jarmo in the Zagros mountains of Iran and Ali Kosh far to the southeast relied on sources in Armenia, western Anatolia. Settlements like Çatal Höyük in Anatolia were so close to obsidian sources that they probably collected their own. More than 80 percent of their stone artifacts are made of the material, while obsidian tools are much rarer down the line, the further one travels from a source.

tive study of Aegean obsidian trade, finding that the exchange was noncommercial and noncompetitive: the prehistoric knappers visited quarries and prepared material for exchange with minimal concern for economical use of the raw material. On the island of Melos, for example, the visitors simply quarried what they wanted and left. There is no evidence of specialized production. During early farming times, obsidian mining may have been a seasonal occupation, but during the Bronze Age it became a specialized occupation requiring special voyages to Melos and other quarries. The reason for the shift is unknown. Perhaps it was connected to a rising demand that outstripped the yield from seasonal visits.

Sourcing studies are sometimes called **characterization studies,** as they involve petrology and other approaches for identifying the characteristic properties of the distinctive raw materials used to fashion, say, stone axes. One should stress the word "distinctive," for the essence of these methods is that one be able to identify the specific source with great accuracy. For example, obsidian from Lipari Island off Sicily was traded over a wide area of the central Mediterranean, an obsidian with highly specific characteristics that show it came from Lipari and nowhere else.

Isotopic chemistry has been highly effective in studying metal sources. For example, the isotopic composition of lead depends on the geological age of the ore source. Lead mines were few and far between in antiquity. Provided their location is known, it is possible to study lead sources in bronze artifacts, and also those of silver, for the latter is extracted from lead ores. This technique has been used to distinguish between Classical Greek silver coins made from mainland Laurion ore and those manufactured with metal from the Aegean island of Siphnos and other locations.

STUDYING EXCHANGE NETWORKS

Merely studying the distribution of artifacts gives one a grossly inadequate picture of ancient trade. For example, there may or may not be a physical marketplace; it is the state of affairs surrounding the trade that forms the focus of the trading system and the mechanisms by which trade interacts with other parts of the culture (Figure 16.3) (Sabloff and Lamberg-Karlovsky, 1975). The archaeological finds of exotic materials, even when sourced, are the material expressions of complex, interdependent factors. These factors include the need for goods—which prompts a search for supplies. The supplies themselves represent production beyond local needs and are created to satisfy external demands. Other factors are the logistics of transportation and the extent of the trading network, as well as the social and political environment. With all these variables, no one aspect of trade can be viewed as an overriding cause of cultural change or of evolution in trading practices.

THE ULUBURUN SHIP

Shipwrecks offer unique opportunities to study ancient trade, for each ship on the sea bed is a sealed capsule, its cargo a mirror of trading conditions at the time.

FIGURE 16.3   Much long-distance trade was in ceremonial and prestigious objects like this beautifully carved Maya metate, used for grinding corn and other foodstuffs. Such artifacts were widely traded in the Mesoamerican lowlands 1,500 years ago. (Courtesy Museum of Fine Arts, Boston)

George Bass and Cemal Pulak's excavation of the Bronze Age ship at Uluburun off southern Turkey has yielded a mine of information on the commercial world of the eastern Mediterranean in the fourteenth century B.C. (Bass and others, 1989; summary in Fagan, 1995a). The heavily laden ship was sailing westward from the eastern Mediterranean when it was shattered on the jagged rocks of Uluburun. It sank in 151 feet (48 m) of water. Bass and Pulak have plotted the exact position of every timber, every item of the ship's equipment and cargo as they lift artifacts from the sea bed. They have recovered an extraordinary portrait of eastern Mediterranean trade more than 3,000 years ago.

The Uluburun ship was laden with 6 tons of copper ingots, probably mined in Cyprus, and with tin ingots and artifacts (Figure 16.4). The tin may have come

FIGURE 16.4 Excavating the Uluburun shipwreck off southern Turkey. This Bronze Age ship's cargo is a mine of information on eastern Mediterranean trading at the height of Mycenaean civilization in Greece.

from southern Turkey. Canaanite jars from Palestine or Syria held olives, glass beads, and resin from the terebinth tree, used in religious rituals. The ship's hold contained Baltic amber that probably reached the Mediterranean overland, ebony-like wood from Africa, elephant and hippopotamus ivory, and ostrich eggshells from North Africa or Syria. Egyptian, Levantine, and Mycenaean daggers, swords, spearheads and woodworking tools lay aboard, and also sets of weights, some fashioned in animal forms. There were costly glass ingots, Mesopotamian cylinder seals, a Mycenaean seal stone, even a gold cup and parts of a tortoiseshell lute. The ship carried Egyptian scarabs, dozens of fishing weights, fishhooks, and 23 stone anchors, vital when anchoring in windy coves. Even the thorny burnet shrub used to pack the cargo was preserved.

By using find distributions from land sites and a variety of sourcing techniques, Bass and Pulak have reconstructed the anonymous skipper's last journey. They believe he started his voyage on the Levant coast, sailed north up the coast, crossed to Cyprus, then coasted along the southern Turkish shore. The ship called at ports large and small on its way west, along a well-traveled route that took advantage of changing seasonal winds, to Crete, some Aegean islands, and perhaps to the Greek mainland. The skipper had traversed this route many times, but on this occasion his luck ran out and he lost his ship, the cargo, and perhaps his life on Uluburun's pitiless rocks. From the archaeological perspective, the Uluburun shipwreck is a godsend, for it allows researchers to fill in many details of an elaborate trade network that linked the eastern Mediterranean with Egypt, the Aegean, and Greece more than 3,300 years ago. Bass and Pulak suspect that the Uluburun ship may have been carrying an unusually valuable cargo, but the owners remain a mystery.

The study of prehistoric trade is a vital source of information on social organization and the ways in which societies became more complex. Trade itself developed a great complexity, in both goods traded and in the interactions of people involved. Colin Renfrew (1975) identified no fewer than ten types of interaction between people that can result from exchange and trading, ranging from simple contact between individuals to trading by professional traders, such as the pochteca of the Maya and the Aztec, who sometimes acted as spies (Figure 16.5) (R. F. Townsend, 1992).

SOCIAL ORGANIZATION

Traditionally, archaeologists have regarded the more intangible aspects of human society, such as religious and social organization, as particularly difficult to infer from archaeological data. Many minor differences between prehistoric peoples—speech, religion, and social organization among them—are, it is true, seldom obvious in the archaeological record. Traditional definitions of culture help us to recognize differences only when they are detectable in the data obtained by excavation, analysis, and induction. But an approach that sees human cultures in archaeology as sociocultural systems enables us to think of social and religious factors as vital subsystems in regulating cultural change. These intangibles can be reconstructed, at least partially, by studying artifact patterns and stylistic changes in material culture. Many archaeologists have pointed out that material culture is

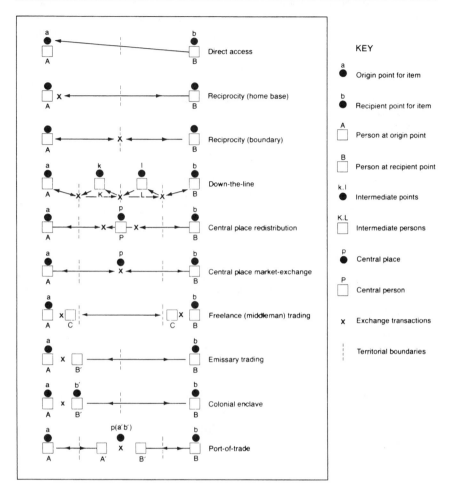

FIGURE 16.5   The ten ways in which prehistoric trade can operate, as determined by Colin Renfrew (1975). The diagram illustrates the wide variety of means by which trade goods are exchanged, each of which has specific implications for settlement patterns. The arrows show the direction of trading relationships.

extremely sensitive to changes in ideology, as reflected in stylistic changes in such items as New England Colonial tombstones (Deetz, 1967) (Figure 7.13). As we saw in Chapter 15, other archaeologists disagree with this notion.

Research into prehistoric social organization is concerned with two basic questions: the size or scale of the society, and how it was organized.

STAGES OF SOCIAL ORGANIZATION

Questions of social scale are important, for they enable the archaeologist to examine not only the complexity of individual societies but the ways in which they interact with others. Archaeologists look at social organization in prehistory with the aid of general conceptual schemes drawn up by anthropologists. Such schemes are particularly important when examining human cultural evolution. Anthropologist Elman Service, in his classic *Primitive Social Organization* (1971), has defined several broad levels of sociocultural evolution, which have provided a general framework for tracing the evolution of human social organization from the first simple, primitive family structures of the earliest hunter-gatherers to the highly complex state-organized societies of the early civilizations.

All theories of cultural evolution are based on the premise that human societies have changed over long periods of time and that the general trend throughout prehistory has been toward a greater complexity of human culture and social institutions. Service divided human societies into bands, tribes, chiefdoms, and states, a classification that has won wide acceptance but is much criticized for its arbitrary rigidity. Since this is a complex and controversial issue, many archaeologists prefer a broader grouping, into which Service's categories fall.

PRESTATE SOCIETIES

Prestate societies are societies on a small scale, based on the community, band, or village. They vary greatly in their degree of political integration, and can be divided into three categories:

1. *Bands* are autonomous and self-sufficient groups that usually consist of only a few families. They are egalitarian, with leadership coming from the experience and personal qualities of particular individuals rather than from political power.
2. *Tribes* are egalitarian like bands, but with a greater level of social and cultural complexity. They have developed kin-based mechanisms to accommodate more sedentary living, to redistribute food, and to organize some communal services. Some more complex hunter-gatherer societies, including the Pacific Northwest groups, can be classified as tribal; most were associated with village farming. In egalitarian societies, public opinion plays a major role in decision making.
3. *Chiefdoms* are societies headed by individuals with unusual ritual, political, or entrepreneurial skills and are often hard to distinguish from tribes. Society is still kin-based, but more hierarchical, with power concentrated in the hands of powerful kin leaders. Chiefdoms tend to have higher population densities and to display the first signs of social ranking, reflected in more elaborate material possessions. The degree of elaboration varied greatly and depended on many factors, including the distribution of population over the landscape. Tahitian chiefs presided over powerful, constantly quarreling chiefdoms, frequently waging ferocious wars against their neighbors. The elaborate Mississippian chiefdoms of the American Midwest and South flourished during the early second millennium A.D., maintaining extensive trade networks and ritual contacts over long distances.

The term "chiefdom" is highly controversial and varies greatly in its definition (Earle, 1991; Yoffee, 1993). Current thinking considers it basically a political unit, in which local autonomy at the village or band level has given way to a form of authority where a paramount chief controls a number of settlements. Chiefdoms organize regional populations, and their form of social stratification and social inequality is less than that of early states, to which they are an alternative trajectory of social development.

STATE-ORGANIZED SOCIETIES

State-organized societies operate on a large scale, with centralized social and political organization, class stratification, and intensive agriculture. They have complex political structures, many permanent government institutions, and firm notions of social inequality.

A state-organized society is governed by a full-fledged ruling class whose privileges and powers are bolstered by a hierarchical secular and religious bureaucracy, at least a rudimentary system of justice, and a system of ranked classes of nobility, warriors, traders, priests, bureaucrats, peasants, and perhaps slaves. The ruler enjoys great wealth and is often regarded as semidivine. Egyptian pharaohs were divine monarchs with absolute powers. Ownership of land and administration of state religion were vested in their hands. The pharaohs ruled by centuries of legal precedent, through an elaborate hierarchy of bureaucrats whose principal officials represented practically hereditary dynasties (Kemp, 1989). Many state societies, such as those of the Maya and the Inka, were organized along rigid lines, with strict classes of nobles, craftsmen, and others. Only the most extraordinary act of military skill or religious devotion would allow a few lucky people entry into the highest classes of society (R. F. Townsend, 1992). All the people knew exactly where they stood in society, even slaves. State-organized societies were the foundation of the early civilizations of the Near East, China, and the Americas; indeed, they were precursors of the Classical civilizations of Greece and Rome.

SOCIAL ORGANIZATION IN THE ARCHAEOLOGICAL RECORD

The archaeological evidence that bears directly on prehistoric social organization comes from several sources, each of which can give us insights into the general level of social organization of a prehistoric society and into much more specific social details as well. Archaeologists study three important phenomena: the emergence and existence of social ranking (social distinctions between individuals as revealed in the archaeological record), relationships between individuals, households, communities, and the wider society, and social diversity (ethnicity).

SOCIAL RANKING

The Aztec rulers and nobles of Mexico, a tiny minority, commanded the loyalty of millions of commoners, as did other rulers of early state-organized societies. One fundamental question in world prehistory surrounds the identification of the emergence of greater social complexity and social ranking in the archaeological record, of societies more centralized than the egalitarian hunter-gatherer cultures of earlier times.

A variety of approaches provide insights into social ranking. Clearly, material evidence for great wealth, such as hoards of buried gold ornaments or fine drinking vessels, suggests some form of ranking that concentrated wealth in a few hands. So do elaborate palaces and public buildings, like Mycenaean palaces in Greece or Sumerian temples in Mesopotamia. As was the case with great Maya ceremonial centers like Tikal and Palenque in Mesoamerica, many such structures were built as important symbolic statements of political, social, and religious power. Tikal, for example, is a symbolic model of the Maya spiritual world, complete with sacred mountains, trees, and caves (Figure 15.2). Perhaps the most elaborate example of such a structure is the Khmer temple at Angkor Wat, Cambodia, a stunning depiction of the Buddhist world built at enormous expense at the behest of divine kings over a 40-year period in about A.D. 1400 (Figure 16.6).

Many such monuments, like, for example, the Temple of the Sun God Amun at Karnak, Egypt, were adorned with paintings and statues of great pharaohs, often in the presence of the gods. Accompanying hieroglyphs and small details of royal costume provide constant, symbolic reminders of royal power and divinely given authority.

FIGURE 16.6   Angkor Wat, Cambodia. This magnificent structure is awesome testimony to the ability of the rulers of early state-organized societies to command the labor of thousands of their subjects. Angkor is a symbolic depiction of the sacred world, adorned with thousands of carvings.

Evidence of social ranking can sometimes be inferred from buildings and community layout. Teotihuacán shows every sign of having been an elaborately planned city, with special precincts for markets and craftspeople, and the houses of the leading priests and nobles near the Street of the Dead, which bisected the city (Figure 16.7). In instances like this, it is easy enough to identify the houses belonging to each class in the society, both by their architecture and by the distinctive artifacts found in them.

Some civilizations seem to have regulated the houses occupied by the various classes of society with almost stultifying monotony. A classic example is the Harappan civilization of the Indus Valley in Pakistan. Both Harappa and Mohenjodaro were dominated by great citadels, with rectangular grids of monotonous workers' houses surrounding them. Special quarters of the city were reserved for craftspeople and for storage. In these and many other cases, researchers can study the relationships between different segments of society by examining the spacing between the structures in the site.

Human burials are the most important source of information about prehistoric social organization and ranking (Brown, 1971). The actual disposal of the corpse is really a minimal part of the sequence of mortuary practice in a society. Funerary rites are a ritual of passage and are usually reflected not only in the position of the body in the grave but also in the ornaments and grave furniture that accompany it. The contents of a grave, whether spectacular or extremely simple, are useful barometers of social ranking. For instance, the

FIGURE 16.7   The Street of the Dead at Teotihuacán. The residences of the elite lay on either side of this wide, imposing avenue.

FIGURE 16.8   The Pyramid of Khufu (Cheops), Giza, Egypt.

Egyptian pharaoh Khufu expended vast resources on building his pyramid and mortuary temple at Giza (Figure 16.8). Thousands of laborers moved more than 2.3 million limestone blocks weighing between 1.5 and 2.5 tons to build his pyramid alone during his 23-year reign. The Egyptian pyramids were built by a highly centralized state over a period of little more than a century, at great expense of labor, food, and materials. Then, suddenly, these same resources were diverted away to other works, and to the provinces, as if there were major changes in the nature of Egyptian society and government (Kemp, 1989). Archaeologists are still trying to puzzle out the social and political implications of this shift.

Sometimes the differing status of burials may indicate that a society was rigidly ranked. When Leonard Woolley excavated the Early Dynastic royal burials of Ur-of-the-Chaldees in Mesopotamia (Figure 16.9), he found a great cemetery

FIGURE 16.9   The Royal Cemetery at Ur in southern Iraq, excavated by Sir Leonard Woolley.

containing 1,850 graves (Woolley, 1943). Sixteen of them stood out by virtue of their remarkable grave furniture. The royal tombs were sunk into the earlier levels of the mound, and a sepulcher consisting of several rooms was erected in the middle of a huge pit. The royal corpses were decked out in a cascade of gold and semiprecious stone ornaments, gold and silver ornaments were placed next to the biers, and several attendants were slaughtered to accompany the dead. Once the royal sepulcher was closed, the entire court filed into the grave pit, drank poison, and lay down to die in correct order of protocol. Woolley was able to identify the different rankings of the courtiers from their ornaments. In contrast to all this luxury, the average person was buried in a matting roll or a humble coffin.

In burials like this, pharaohs' graves, and even burials of Iron Age chieftains in Europe, the ranking of society is obvious. But what about less affluent societies in which differences in rank and social status are often more muted? It is very important for archaeologists to be able to recognize such inequalities, for the degree of social ranking is often a measure of the size and complexity of a society. Very often, too, rank appears when centuries-old ties of kin and family are being replaced by rulers who preside over much more elaborate social systems. Brown (1981) points out that such variables as age, sex, personal ability, personality, and even circumstances of death can affect the way in which one is buried. The evidence for ranking comes not only from grave furniture and insignia of rank deposited with the deceased but also from the positions of graves in a settlement or cemetery and even from symbolic distinctions that are hard to find in the archaeological record (O'Shea, 1984). Generally, however, the greater and more secure a ruler's authority becomes, the more effort and wealth is expended on burial. This lavishness may also extend to immediate relatives and friends (Chapman and others, 1981).

The Mississippian ceremonial center at Moundville, Alabama, was in its heyday in the thirteenth and fourteenth centuries A.D. More than 20 mounds topped by temples and elite residences lay inside a wooden palisade covering 370 acres (150 ha) on the banks of the Black Warrior River. More than 3,000 burials have been excavated at Moundville. Archaeologist Chris Peebles combined a pottery seriation of vessels found with a sample of the burials with a cluster analysis of more than 2,000 graves as a means of grouping them by social rank. Peebles found that the highest-ranking people were buried in or near the earthen mounds with elaborate grave furniture, including copper artifacts. A second group had fewer grave goods and were not buried in mounds, while the lowest-ranking people were buried at the edge of the site with almost no grave furniture (Peebles, 1987). Peebles also developed a social hierarchy for Moundville that was headed by seven burials, all of them males (Figure 16.10).

RELIGION AND RITUAL

An anonymous archaeologist wrote cynically that "religion is the last resort of troubled excavators." At one time, archaeologists ascribed any artifact or structure with even vaguely religious associations to a category broadly named "ritual." In many famous instances, the religious associations of an artifact or a structure can be determined readily enough. The Pyramid of the Sun at Teotihuacán is clearly a structure of religious significance; so are the Temple of Amun at Karnak in Egypt and the famous stone circles at Stonehenge in England (Chippendale, 1983) (Figure 2.2). The "Venus" figurines of the European Upper Paleolithic have been widely interpreted as fertility symbols or commemorations of womanhood, and later human figures have received similar interpretations, but the ritual associations of such objects are still in doubt (Figure 16.11) (Bahn and Vertut, 1988). In southern Africa, rock paintings of eland hunts created by prehistoric hunter-gatherers have been shown to have deep symbolic meaning to the artists (Lewis-Williams, 1981). Burial mutilations, oral tradition, and even astronomy have been used to infer religious activities from archaeological data.

RELIGION AND BURIALS

The traditional archaeological evidence for religious rituals has come from burials. The first human beings to deliberately bury their dead were the Neanderthal peoples of 70,000 years ago. The bodies of Neanderthal families have been found in French caves, such as La Ferrassie, buried in shallow pits, the skeletons covered with the red ocher powder that was scattered over their corpses.

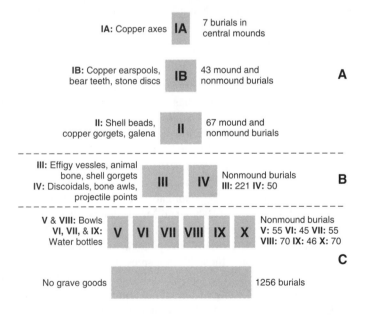

IA: Copper axes | **IA** | 7 burials in central mounds

IB: Copper earspools, bear teeth, stone discs | **IB** | 43 mound and nonmound burials | **A**

II: Shell beads, copper gorgets, galena | **II** | 67 mound and nonmound burials

III: Effigy vessels, animal bone, shell gorgets
IV: Discoidals, bone awls, projectile points | **III** **IV** | Nonmound burials III: 221 IV: 50 | **B**

V & VIII: Bowls
VI, VII, & IX: Water bottles | **V VI VII VIII IX X** | Nonmound burials V: 55 VI: 45 VII: 55 VIII: 70 IX: 46 X: 70 | **C**

No grave goods | | 1256 burials

FIGURE 16.10 Moundville, Alabama: (top) General view; (bottom) Peeble's pyramidlike social hierarchy of Moundville burials, based on analysis of more than 2,000 graves. Artifacts listed against each category are grave goods found with individual skeletons.

FIGURE 16.11   A Venus figurine from Dolní Věstonice, Czech Republic.

There are clear signs that highly organized religions were a feature of many of the more complex prehistoric societies. To verify this, we need only mention the Chavín and Olmec art styles and religious beliefs that spread widely in Peru and Mesoamerica just before the emergence of state-organized societies. Such organized religions can be detected by the patterning of characteristic art objects or other artifacts clearly associated with religious rituals or by the appearance of public temples or ceremonial centers in small villages and towns (Figure 16.12). The ceremonial centers of the Mesopotamians were towering ziggurats that gave rise to the legend of the Tower of Babel, and Maya centers consisted of pyramids and other large structures grouped around huge open plazas. The ceremonial center became a focus for a group of independent settlements, "the sanctified terrain where were manifested those hierophanies that guaranteed the seasonal renewal of cyclic time, and where the splendor, potency, and wealth of their rulers symbolized the well being of the whole community" (Wheatley, 1971). According to Mircea Eliade (1954), the ceremonial center ensured the continuity of cultural traditions; the religious and moral models of society were laid down in sacred canons recited in temples in reassuring chants passed from generation to generation.

The distinctive religious art and architecture of Teotihuacán reflects such interest in cultural continuity and ritual; so do the cult objects of the Hopewell and the endless religious friezes and inscriptions of the ancient Egyptians. Maya calendars, too, are convincing evidence that the priests of one generation

FIGURE 16.12   A ceremonial Olmec ax head, depicting a god who combines the features of a man and a jaguar. His head is stylized, with flamelike eyelashes and a drooping mouth. Such art objects were symbolic renderings of complex Olmec religious beliefs connected with shamanism, the relationship with the spiritual world, and with the powerful, versatile jaguar, symbol of power and kingship. (One-half actual size)

considered it their responsibility to ensure the continuity of religion for future generations.

RELIGIOUS SYSTEMS

Religious beliefs have often linked large areas of the world into gigantic spheres of common cosmology and ritual practices, even if the many peoples unified under a common religious banner enjoy widely disparate governmental, societal, and economic institutions. The distribution of Christianity and Islam make one realize the importance of religion as an integrative force. Thousands of prehistoric societies were linked by common beliefs and cosmologies, which are reflected in the archaeological record by common artistic traditions, temple and ceremonial-center architecture, wall paintings, and even trade in cult objects. For example, in the Midwest the Hopewell religious cult, with its preoccupation with ceremonial burial, spread far beyond its Ohio heartland. And in southern Africa, the ceremonial centers at Mapungubwe and Great Zimbabwe are associated with the rainmaking beliefs and ancestor cults of the Shona peoples (Connah, 1987).

We can learn a great deal more about prehistoric cosmology and religion when ethnohistorical or written sources are available; witness Lawrence Sullivan's remarkable study (1989) of indigenous ancient and modern Latin American religions. Some of the beliefs he discusses are mirrored in Andean art, architecture, and textile designs (Stone-Miller, 1995), but serious archaeological studies which combine material evidence with other sources are still rare. David Friedel and Linda Schele's work on Maya cosmology is a fine example of this type of research. They have studied Maya images and hieroglyphs for years and have used changes in them to trace changes in the meaning of symbols associated with political power (Schele and Friedel, 1990, 1993). For example, the religious symbolism of the late Preclassic was based on the passage of Venus as morning and evening star with the rising and setting of the sun. The people of any Maya community could identify and verify their cosmos simply by observing the sky.

As time went on, Maya cosmology was expanded and elaborated. The names of late Preclassic rulers were not recorded publicly. Perhaps such permanent verification on public monuments was not yet deemed necessary. Classic rulers followed a quite different strategy. They legitimized their rule through genealogies, public ceremonies, and monuments—much Classic Maya art was erected as part of this process of legitimizing rulers, who claimed identity with gods in the Maya cosmos.

Friedel and Schele (1987) believe that the metaphor of the twin ancestors— Venus and the sun—provided a potent image for lateral blood ties between lineages, communities, and everyone who believed in the same myths. Since twins are of the same womb and blood, so the Maya are all of common ancestry and blood. This Maya research shows that archaeologists should never think of religion and ritual in isolation but rather as integral to social organization, economic life, and political systems. The ideas and beliefs, the core of all religions, are reflected in many aspects of human life, especially in art and architecture. Every society has its own model of how the world is put together, its own ultimate beliefs. These sacred propositions are interpreted for the faithful through a body of theology and rituals associated with it. The rituals are more or less standardized, religious acts often repeated at regular times of the year—harvests, plantings, and other key times. Others are performed when needed: marriages, funerals, and the like. Some societies, such as those of the ancient Egyptians and the Maya, made regular calendars to time religious events and astronomical cycles. These regular ceremonies performed important functions not only in integrating society but also in such activities as redistributing food, controlling popu-

lation through infanticide, and dispersing surplus male cattle in the form of ritu-
ally accumulated wealth. Religious experiences are predominantly emotional,
often supernatural and awe-inspiring. Each aspect of religion—sacred propositions, ritual, experience—supports the others. A religion will operate through
sanctified attitudes, values, and messages, an ethic that adds a sacred blessing,
derived from the ultimate sacred propositions of the society, to elicit predictable
responses from the people. Such predictability, sparked by directives from some
central religious authority, ensures orderly operation of society. In time, as in
Mesopotamia, that authority can become secular as well. The institutions and
individuals associated with these messages can become sanctified, for they are
associated with the sacred propositions that lie at the heart of the society's
beliefs. As societies became more complex, so did the need for a stable framework to administer the needs of the many increasingly specialized subgroups that
made up society as a whole.

There are signs that, by 3000 B.C. in Egypt and Mesopotamia and between
1150 and 850 B.C. in Mesoamerica, administrative authority had become more
institutionalized, dealing with all manner of social and economic problems, such as
new rankings in society (reflected in burials), specialists' communities and households of specialists in each village, and an increased need for predictable social
behavior and mutual interdependence. It is during these periods that the first of the
more elaborate public buildings appear in the Near East and, independently, in
Mexico, temples and monumental works that reflect not only the involvement of
individual communities but also that of other villages without ceremonial structures of their own (Figure 16.13). The emergence of such ceremonial buildings and,

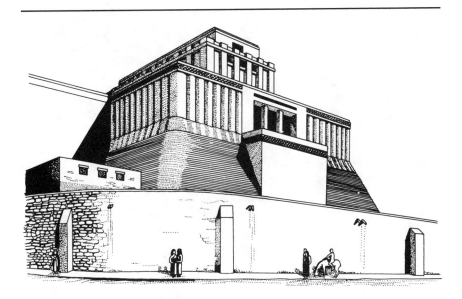

FIGURE 16.13   Reconstruction of the mud-brick ziggurat at Erech,
southern Iraq, one of the earliest public buildings in the world.

presumably, administrative centers had, as we showed earlier, a major effect on the hierarchies and spacing of settlements. Thus, in a sense, a circular relationship links the ultimate sacred beliefs and rituals of a society with the processes of social and environmental change that act on them. The link between administrative policy and belief is in ritual and the sanctified message.

Religious beliefs are intangible, and survive only in the form of temples, ritual paraphernalia, and art. Viewed in isolation, the study of ancient religion seems a hopeless task, if archaeological finds are the only source of information available. But if we view religion and ritual as integral in a society, closely tied to all other aspects of its activities, there is some hope that we may be able to look at ritual and religious artifacts in the context of a society as a whole.

FORMATIVE OAXACA

The presence or absence of distinctive ritual artifacts or buildings in a site or a society may be significant. In Formative Oaxaca, public buildings appear

FIGURE 16.14   Four figurines grouped deliberately to form a scene, found buried beneath an Early Formative house at San José Mogote, Oaxaca, Mexico.

between 1400 and 1150 B.C., many of them oriented 8 degrees west of north and built on adobe and earth platforms (Flannery, 1976). Rare conch-shell trumpets and turtle-shell drums traded from the coastal lowlands were apparently used in public ceremonies in such buildings. Clay figurines of dancers wearing costumes and masks that make them look like fantastic creatures and animals, as well as pottery masks, are also signs of communal ritual (Figure 16.14). The personal ritual of self-mutilation by bloodletting was widespread in early Mesoamerica. The Spanish described how the Aztec nobles would gash themselves with knives or with fish and stingray spines in acts of mutilation that were penances before the gods, imposed by religion. A few stingray spines have come from Middle Formative villages, probably traded into the far interior for the specific use of community leaders. Marine fish spines have been found in public buildings, houses, and even refuse heaps of the Early Formative. Flannery suggests that bloodletting fish spines were kept and used at home, and that they were also used in public buildings. The ritual artifacts in the Oaxacan villages enabled Flannery and his colleagues to identify three levels of religious ceremony: personal bloodletting; dances run by sodalities, which cut across household lines; and public rituals in ceremonial buildings, involving a region wider than one village.

The study of prehistoric religion depends heavily on the study of sacred artifacts and temples and on careful research design. The most effective way to study such intangibles as social organization or religious beliefs and rituals is to consider them as integral to a society, closely tied to all other aspects of its activities.

SUMMARY

- Human subsistence is based on natural resources and on exploitation of the environment, whether or not people produce food. Trade may have had its beginnings when people moved to a new territory where a previously available raw material was no longer abundant. Much early trade probably took the form of gift exchanges and the bartering of food and other commodities between neighboring settlements. The pattern of trade was established by the distance between settlements and available sources of raw materials.
- Trade is normally recognized in the archaeological record by the discovery of objects exotic to the material culture of the economy of the host society. Prehistoric trade networks are studied by examining the distributions of such objects and the sources of raw materials used to make artifacts.
- Trading activity is closely tied to growing complexity in social and political organization among prehistoric peoples. It is not enough simply to identify trading activity in the archaeological record; researchers must also understand the exchange processes that lay behind the trading.
- Trade cannot be studied except by referring to the cultural systems of which it was a part. One example is the Uluburun shipwreck off southern Turkey, which revealed the complexity of eastern Mediterranean trading in the fourteenth century B.C.
- Redistribution of trade objects through a society is often controlled politically by chiefs and other leaders. We used obsidian trading in Mesoamerica

to show how such redistribution mechanisms can be studied in the archaeological record.

- Social organization is difficult to study from archaeological evidence, although a systematic view of human culture makes it possible to examine it as one variable among the many that affect cultural change.

- Archaeologists distinguish between prestate and state-organized societies, the latter characterized by social stratification, centralized political and social organization, and intensive agriculture.

- Social organization can be studied in the archaeological record by using burials and associated grave furniture, as at Ur in Mesopotamia, and by using structures or artifact patterns.

- Religion has traditionally been studied through burials, burial rites, and sacred buildings. Organized religions were a feature of many of the more complex prehistoric societies, and there were often centers of elaborate ceremonial areas that were a focus for state-organized societies. The rituals that ensured the continuity of religious belief are reflected in architecture and art. The presence or absence of sacred artifacts in the archaeological record may reveal valuable information on prehistoric religion, provided that research designs are carefully made.

GUIDE TO FURTHER READING

Chapman, Robert, Ian Kinnes, and Klavs Randsborg, eds. *The Archaeology of Death.* Cambridge: Cambridge University Press, 1981. A series of essays on the interpretation of mortuary practices. Somewhat outdated, but still useful.

Earle, Timothy K., ed. *Chiefdoms: Power, Economy, and Ideology.* Cambridge: Cambridge University Press, 1991. This volume discusses the concept of chiefdoms in prehistory, with case studies.

Earle, Timothy K., and Jonathan E. Ericson, eds. *Exchange Systems in Prehistory.* Orlando, Fla.: Academic Press, 1977. Articles dealing with method and theory in the study of prehistoric trade. For the more advanced reader.

Sabloff, Jeremy A., and C. C. Lamberg-Karlovsky, eds. *Early Civilization and Trade.* Albuquerque: University of New Mexico Press, 1975. Conference papers that cover a wide range of problems in the study of prehistoric trade. Strong on theory and actual case studies.

Schele, Linda, and David Friedel. *A Forest of Kings.* New York: William Morrow, 1990. A popular account of Maya civilization that is a mine of information on religion, iconography, and social ranking. Engrossing and readable.

Schele, Linda, and Mary Miller. *The Blood of Kings,* 2d ed. New York: Thames and Hudson, 1992. Excellent work on attitudes and beliefs of the Maya.

Sullivan, Lawrence. *Icanchu's Drum.* New York: Free Press, 1989. Sullivan's study of ancient and modern Latin American indigenous religions is a remarkable monograph that should be read by every archaeologist.

17

THE ARCHAEOLOGY OF
PEOPLE AND GROUPS

A rchaeology is the science of material things, a discipline which is one of the few ways in which one can study cultural change in human societies over long periods of time. The processual archaeology of the last quarter-century has been much concerned with studying ancient lifeways and the processes of cultural change. Many of these studies are highly technical and somewhat impersonal, in the sense that they are concerned with broad processes of cultural change, with multilinear evolution, and with ancient societies as somewhat anonymous entities. Of course prehistoric archaeology will never study the deeds of known individuals, for there are no historical records to chronicle their doings, and the archaeological record is simply too coarse-grained to zero in on any smaller social units than a family or a tiny group. But there are moments when the archaeologist can glimpse an individual household from a scatter of artifacts by a hearth, or study the interaction of a small, often historically anonymous group with others in a society. Such opportunities and the sophisticated data recovery methods of modern archaeology have caused many archaeologists to turn from studies of cultural process to research of people and small groups. A new focus on gender has resulted in some important studies of changing male/female roles and of gender inequalities in ancient societies, two avenues of inquiry which have been the subject of intense discussion in recent years. Chapter 17 is about the archaeology of gender and of small groups, about new research in archaeology concerned not with general processes, but with peoples' interactions with one another at a daily level.

The relationships between individuals and their own households, communities, and society at large are expressed in all manner of tangible and intangible ways. As we saw in Chapter 16, there are relationships between people and communities that are expressed through gift exchanges, as well as through kin ties and reciprocal obligation. Then there are the issues of division of labor, of ever-changing roles of men and women from one generation to the next. Many such relationships are intangible, in the sense that they cannot be identified readily in the archaeological record, except in indirect ways. Theoretically, at any rate, distinctive artifact patterns within houses, other structures, household clusters, and communities should provide data on relationships between people and other communities (for settlement archaeology, see Chapter 15).

To carry out such research involves drawing not only on artifact studies, but, if possible, on ethnoarchaeological and historical sources, too. For example, during the 1960s, Southwestern archaeologists studying pueblo rooms and their contents assumed that all households were self-sufficient in their pottery needs and use. But ethnoarchaeological research among the Kalinga people of the Philippines has shown that at least half the pots used in the two major study villages were not made by resident potters. Archaeologically, one can hypothesize that household pottery inventories in pottery-making communities should exhibit a low variability with respect to the number of producers in a given household. Alternatively, diverse ceramic assemblages would be characteristic of households in a society that consumes pots but does not make them. There would be more producers with wares circulating in society. Data from Kalinga villages appear to support this hypothesis. The researchers also found that patterns of social affiliation among producing and consuming communities were reflected in patterns of material consumption. Kin ties, for example, have a profound effect on the numbers of vessels made by individual potters in different communities.

The Kalinga inquiries have important implications for studying kin and social ties. They suggest that perhaps some form of village-based specialization in potmaking flourished in many Southwestern pueblos. So differences in pottery assemblages may, in fact, reflect differences in consuming and producing communities and the intricate kin ties that linked pueblo communities near and far over many generations (Longacre, 1991; Longacre and Stark, 1992).

At present, the most promising studies of social relationships have come from historic sites, where written records can be used to amplify the archaeological record (Orser and Fagan, 1995; Scott, 1994). The same is true of the study of gender.

ENGENDERING ARCHAEOLOGY

During the past 20 years, the social sciences and the study of history have been transformed by feminist scholarship, but archaeology has lagged behind, although such thought has figured in interpretations of such topics as the origins of the sexual division of labor and changing gender relations. Only recently have archaeologists started to frame gender-related questions, taking advantage of an emerging body of feminist theory in other disciplines (Classen, 1991; Conkey and Gero, 1996; Gero and Conkey, 1991). One fundamental goal of such research is the analysis of gender relations, as well as the study of gender as a historical process. Such inquiries are of importance, not only in identifying and correcting gender bias in archaeological inquiry, but also in "finding" women in archaeological contexts and identifying their participation in what are loosely called "gender roles." In other words, archaeologists need to reframe the ways in which they think about gender and social relations.

Fundamental to any feminist archaeology is the assumption that gender is socially and culturally constructed, the recognition that gender roles and relations are set up and acquire meaning in culturally and historically meaningful ways. Under this approach, gender is a vital part of human social relations and is an important issue of history and prehistory. This also means that the expression of gender has varied greatly from society to society and through time, for it illustrates ways in which roles and relationships are socially constructed, something that archaeologists, given the evidence available to them, can study most readily in relation to matters of production and the material world. Such research offers opportunities to study the productive roles and contributions of women to prehistoric societies, and to examine ways in which social roles were played out in ancient social systems, in daily life, and in the spiritual realm. The engendering of archaeology, then, is an attempt to "frame an archaeology of gender, to reclaim women and men in non-sexist ways in prehistory" (Gero and Conkey, 1991). This goes much further than merely attempting to ascribe gender to different elements of the archaeological record, such as pots or projectile points. Nor is it merely a matter of developing new methods to achieve linkages between artifacts and men or women.

The archaeology of gender involves far more than male and female activities. It deals with the ideology of gender, roles, gender relations—all the ways in which gender interacts with all aspects of human social life. In other words, it is using a wide diversity of archaeological methods and approaches to find out how gender "works" in ancient societies, to unravel its cultural meanings. To engender the past means focusing not on major material achievements or paleoenvironments, but on another fundamental issue—interpersonal relations and the social dynamics of everyday activity. These are the activities that take up most of peoples' lives, that led to the accumulation of so much of the archaeological record—potmaking and stone artifact manufacture, gardening and preparing meals, building houses and making clothing. But gender extends much further than such mundane activities. It impacts on trade, on craft specialization, on state formation, architecture, religion, and ritual. As such, its study is a fundamental part of modern archaeology (for theoretical arguments, see Wylie, 1991).

The new generation of gender research is taking archaeology in fresh directions. Art styles and representations were one powerful way in which struggles for political power were worked out in many ancient societies. Rosemary Joyce (1993) uncovered a pair of cached Maya figurines in the central platform of a small residential group at the Terminal Classic Maya site of Cerro Palenque, Honduras (Figure 17.1). The two finely made figurines had been buried upright in small pits east and west of an exotic stone slab. The eastern figurine was a male wearing a bird-feather costume, a helmet, and carrying a conch shell trumpet. The western figure was a woman in an ankle-length skirt. Her breasts were bare, her left hand raised, and she balanced a necked, handled jar on her head. Joyce believes the pair represent a duality of interdependent household members, a symbolic placement on either side of a family shrine. She studied other figurines in Classic Maya and lower central American societies, especially those buried under house floors, identifying a "significant thematic dichotomy associated with gender," the women often represented as mothers and those responsible for providing food. In monumental architecture, too, ritual is enacted through the shared actions of men and women, but the unique gestures of each imply different roles. Gender imagery in such art and in painted ceramic vessels associates women with the transformation of raw material (clay, textiles) into finished artifacts, with the labor of grinding grain and preparing food. Classic Maya public art showed elite men and women

FIGURE 17.1 Maya figurines from Cerro Palenque, Honduras.

collaborating in ritual activities. However, in highly stratified Maya society, ceramic images challenged any assumptions that the elite exercised completely centralized control; their depictions of men and women reminded everyone that extended households could be economically independent of such control. Joyce's researches unfolded in an area outside the Maya heartland, where the integrity of the household was not a political issue. Thus, Joyce argues, the status of women, as shown in her Cerro Palenque figurines, was more stable than in a more stratified society where the traditional values of the family and women's roles as food producers were downplayed in the face of powerful ritual messages.

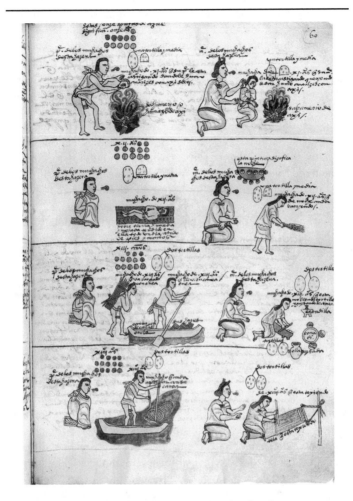

FIGURE 17.2   An Aztec woman teaches her daughter how to weave.

"The good middle-aged woman [is] a skilled weaver, a weaver of designs, an artisan, a good cook, a preparer of good food." Thus did Franciscan friar Bernardino de Sahagun's Aztec informants describe a noblewoman's role in Mexican civilization before the Spanish conquest (Figure 17.2). But this description is grossly misleading and simplistic, for it ignores the links between weaving, cooking, and child-rearing (to mention only a few women's tasks) and the wider society in which the women lived (Brumfiel, 1991). For instance, the population of the Valley of Mexico rose tenfold during the four centuries before the conquest, a striking testimony to the success of the Aztec household economy. Women wove textiles and the capes that were the badges of social status in Aztec society. Their woven products were vital to the enormous tribute system on which Aztec civilization depended. Cotton mantles even served as a form of currency. Cloth was a primary way of organizing the ebb and flow of goods and services that sustained the state. Elizabeth Brumfiel uses archaeological evidence to refine this general picture. She shows that the women living in the Aztec capital, Tenochtitlán, turned away from weaving to cultivation of swamp gardens and the salting of fish, while weaving to satisfy tribute needs was still the dominant activity at a distance from the city. Here the burden of tribute production fell on female heads. In the city, men and women often labored away from home on food production and other activities, a shift also reflected in a change from wet foods like stews to tortillas and other dried foods that were easily carried to a work site elsewhere. Brumfiel shows that the Aztec household and the roles of women were much more varied than those attributed to them by Sahagun's informants. Furthermore, the skills of cooking and weaving were important political tools, ways of maintaining social and political control. Thus, she argues, the idealization of these skills in both Aztec folklore and schooling developed because women were makers of both valuable goods and of people. It was they who assured the continuity of Aztec kin groups. The simplistic view of Aztec life of Sahagun's informants reflected contemporary ideology, but masked the dynamic and highly adaptive role that women played in this remarkable civilization.

Clothing and ornamentation are another fruitful avenue of inquiry; witness Michelle Marcus's study of "lion pins" from Hansalu, Iran, an important trading city of 1100 to 800 B.C., which lay on caravan routes which linked the Assyrian empire with Urartu and Elam (Marcus, 1994). Marcus's pins came from an unsettled period when Urartu and Assyria were competing with one another. Hansalu was finally destroyed by fire following an Urartian invasion of about 800 B.C. The Marcus study focused on sexed burials with garment and shroud pins, the latter being attached to women's shrouds only. She found that early Mesopotamian literature gives symbolic meaning to women's pins, as if they marked different stages of the female life cycle (girl, married woman, and mother). They may also have symbolized the importance of a man as actor or witness. The women of Hasalu lived during a period of political uncertainty and military insecurity. The authorities may have promoted an ideology of military security which sometimes took precedence over rules of gender difference. Thus, Marcus argues, women's pins were widely distributed and were extremely long, so they could double as symbolic messages and also as means of defense if the need arose. The Hasalu pins are a reflection of personal adornment as a way of constructing and reinforcing social ideologies in ancient societies.

The engendering of archaeology is an exciting development, one that will transform our interpretations of human prehistory beyond recognition in coming years. At present, however, gender studies are still in their infancy, and based, for the most part, on extrapolations from ethnoarchaeological and ethnological data. This kind of direct historical approach can be useful. For example, it can be argued that it was women, with their detailed knowledge of botany derived from thousands of years of plant foraging, who first deliberately cultivated native seeds such as sunflowers and sumpweed in eastern North America at least 3,000 years ago (Watson and Kennedy, 1991).

In such a study, Christine Hastorf (1991, 1992) has used food remains to study changing gender relations in pre-Hispanic Sausa society in the Andes. The Sausa are maize and potato farmers who live in highland Peru's northern Mantaro Valley. Before the Inka took control in about A.D. 1460, the Sausa lived in local population groups of several thousand people. Their conquerors, anxious to increase maize production, dispersed them into small village settlements. Hastorf was interested in the changing social dynamics resulting from the Inka conquest. How did women's social position change as a result of the new conditions? She approached this fundamental question not by marshaling subjective evidence, but by using two different approaches: the distribution of food remains in excavated settlements compared with those in modern house compounds, and dietary evidence obtained by stable isotope analyses of male and female skeletons from ancient Sausa villages.

Hastorf, an expert on native plants, believes modern studies of Sausa houses show a relationship between the distribution of plant remains in dwellings and compounds and the behavior of men and women in those households. In modern Andean households, women are responsible for food preparation and storage. Moreover, in households with male heads, she found the most diverse plant forms in kitchen areas, and fewer crop seeds elsewhere in the compound where other activities took place. In contrast, a household with a female head had concentrations of crop seeds not only in the kitchen area but on the patio, as if there were different constraints acting on preparation and food consumption.

Next, Hastorf plotted the distribution of crop seeds in pre-Hispanic compounds. The pre-Inka structures date from a time when maize was less common and of great sacred value. The inhabitants of every dwelling used and consumed a wide range of plant foods, including potatoes and many legumes. Maize occurred mostly in patio areas. It was here, Hastorf argues, that such communal activities as making beer, a commodity that was a vital part of ritual, social, and political meetings, took place. A later, Inka-period compound yielded fewer potatoes and much more maize. Here the processing of corn was more concentrated, with little burning of corn, as if more of it was consumed as beer. Hastorf wonders if the dense and restricted distribution of maize in the later compound might reflect more intensified processing of corn by women. They were now living under Inka policies that sought a constant rise in maize production, regular taxation in the form of labor and produce, and, therefore, more restricted, intensified roles for women in support of male activities.

Hastorf now turned her attention to male and female skeletons found in the compounds. She studied the stable isotopes in bone collagen extracted from Sausa skeletons. She found pre-Inka diets were the same for men and women, mainly consisting of quinoa and tubers, with some maize. These similar values suggest that beer was shared between men and women. Then the Inka entered Sausa society. The 21 skeletons (12 males, nine females) from these centuries reveal a higher consumption of maize, but half the male diets were much richer in maize than those of the women. Hastorf believes this reflects changed social conditions under Inka rule. The women were processing much more maize into beer, which was consumed not by everyone, but by a relatively small proportion of the males in the community. Furthermore, most men were eating more meat than women. The dietary differences reflect a changed political climate in which the Sausa, once small groups, were now incorporated into a larger political sphere that depended on men becoming involved in far more gatherings, rituals, and obligatory tasks, when beer was consumed. The women worked harder, but their position outside the home was more restricted under the Inka regime. The Inka state depended on the obligatory *mit'a* tax, levied on male household heads. The most common *mit'a* tasks were agriculture and military service, performed by men, who were fed "meat and maize and cornbeer." *Mit'a* tasks separated men and women physically, politically, and symbolically. Archaeological evidence, gathered from two sources, tends to confirm this, documents the changes in women's position in Sausa society, and makes men and women visible in the archaeological record.

Only rarely does the archaeological record give absolutely unambiguous evidence of the division of labor. The Abu Hureyra village in Syria is one of the earliest farming settlements in the world. Here, biological anthropologist Theya Molleson (1989) examined the skeletons of the villages, finding ample evidence of work injuries. She also observed malformations of the toes, knees, and lower vertebrae in the skeletons of all the adult women, a condition almost certainly due to hours of grinding grain on their knees. This is some of the earliest evidence for the division of labor in human history.

A small farming village lies in now-drained marshlands north of the Danube River at Opovo in what was once Yugoslavia. A late Neolithic hamlet of rectangular, thatched houses of the Vinca culture flourished in this far-from-favorable agricultural environment between 4400 and 4000 B.C. Traditional interpretations of the site stated that all the dwellings were destroyed by fire at the end of the occupation. But Ruth Tringham and her Yugoslav colleagues have changed the focus of their investigations from a community-wide study to research into individual dwellings and their fate. They have discovered that the houses were, almost certainly, burnt down individually at the end of what Tringham calls "the household cycle" (Tringham, 1994). Instead of merely investigating the foundations of the dwellings *under* the collapsed fire debris, they dissected the rubble and discovered that each fire was confined to an individual house. The entire research project was oriented toward individual households, the resources within them, and the gender relationships therein. Tringham's research was designed not necessarily to search for the surviving material remains of gender roles, but to "produce a visibility of gender when visualizing the human social actors in and around the built environment of the past" (Tringham, 1994). She assumed the archaeologist was an "active mediator . . . limiting and encouraging the reader to view, visualize, imagine, and participate in the interpretation of the built environment of the past." Thus, she argues, the passive view of the past obtained from material culture becomes an active arena for studying the tensions of gender relations and interactions between individuals. Tringham originally used a processualist approach in excavating Opovo, but her feminist interpretations assume that every aspect of material culture is endowed with some kind of significance for the original occupants. "Feminist archaeology means writing the archaeology of *people*," she writes. She makes them social actors with individual biographies, genders, and personalities. Each of these actors viewed the place she studied differently, with perspectives colored by age, gender, power, and life history. So her challenge was to present these multiple perceptions at different scales. She did so by studying the houses as having *life histories* rather than *use-lives,* in order to write a biography of individual places.

Under more traditional interpretations, Tringham would have explained the founding of Opovo as part of a process of dispersal of settlement aimed at maintaining kin-based domestic groups as units of social and economic organization. This tiny hamlet of no more than 10 households had only a marginal part to play in this larger process. In her feminist interpretation, she argues that the founding of this village in a marginal farming area where red-deer hunting was always important had major implications for the division of labor within the community. Each household had a different history of social relations with its neighbors, with kin in other communities. Thus, to write the history of Opovo is to write an intertwined biography of individual households and their members, using an interplay between different levels of archaeological analysis, everything from entire regions to individual lives.

Tringham approaches this task by using data collected using a processualist approach, then combining this data and her field notes on the excavation of an individual house with what she calls "plausible scenarios" developed from the data. For example:

A SCENARIO:

"She watched the house burn. . . . He had died.
He's strung up in the tree now, safe. Now it's time to kill the house. . .
So much ash! . . . It's choking me. Now it swirls around. It stings my eyes. . .
I used to be happy down at the bottom of this well. So quiet, so cool. . . ."

FROM THE FIELD NOTES:

"July 25 1989: Underneath rubble well-fill is a lense of dense grey clay that probably represents primary deposition of well muck. Excavate this to the sterile loess bottom of pit/well. *Now* I can understand what's going on! In originally digging the pit (6,000 years ago), the underlying loess was left as a spiral ramp winding from its lowest point at the southern end of the pit. . . Into this pit there appear to be steps cut. . . you could climb down with your bucket to the water of the well, which lay. . . in the bottom 1 meter of this 3-meter deep pit" (Tringham, 1994).

Tringham's Opovo research uses narratives and visual imagery to introduce the "actors," some of the men and women who lived in this particular house over several generations. As the scenario unfolds, they interact with one other, as individuals, as young and old, as men and women, as they move within and without a dwelling which was burnt, its well then filled with still-warm rubble. This is archaeology conducted not at a "macroscale," as most processual investigations are, but at a microlevel, where the archaeologist interprets domestic social acts within single dwellings, where individuals were actors. This research, and much other feminist archaeology, is a logical extension of sound approaches that have reconstructed general trends, structures, and patterns of the archaeological record. The archaeologist acts as an active mediator of the remote past in a new generation of researches, which promise to be controversial, provocative, and fascinating.

The engendering of archaeology is long overdue, and will affect not only basic research but also the ways in which we write about the past. As the Hastorf example shows, the research that studies gender will be a marriage of new approaches, often involving what Tringham (1994) calls "interpretative dialectical interplay between material remains, comparative historical or ethnographic observation, and imagined actors" with high-tech science and well established methods of archaeological research. This will give us the potential to go far beyond the material, to probe the subjective and the gender-driven, even, as Hastorf shows, the ways in which women (and men, for that matter) adapt to changing circumstances. This kind of meticulous, incredibly detailed research, with its concern for the changing dynamics of ancient society, offers great promise for the future.

ETHNICITY AND INEQUALITY

Feminist archaeology concerns itself with male/female roles and social inequality, which is also becoming a major topic of concern in archaeology.

For the most part, archaeologists have focused their attentions on two broad topics. Culture historians have described long-lasting cultural traditions in many parts of the world, while cultural ecologists and advocates of processual archaeology have studied the ever-changing relationships between human societies and their natural environments. In recent years, however, a small number of scholars have used archaeology's unique perspective to study ethnic diversity and what is sometimes called "the archaeology of inequality" (McGuire and Paynter, 1991): the ways in which people have exercised economic and social power over others. This is a reaction against approaches that minimize the importance of social power and assume that ancient societies enjoyed a high degree of cultural uniformity. In fact, many archaeological studies have shown that cultural change can occur very rapidly, at times at a speed that is well within the limits of human memory, as it does in our society (Sanders and others, 1979). Nor should one minimize the importance of social power in the appearance of early states, like those of the Maya or Aztecs (R. F. Townsend, 1992). Despite a few studies that are now focusing on the importance of social ranking and the political power of kings and nobles, almost no archaeologists have studied the phenomenon of resistance to overwhelming social and political power and the archaeology of ethnic minorities.

Elites have used many tactics to exercise power over others, everything from gentle persuasion to divine kingship, precedent, economic monopolies, and naked force. Perhaps most important of all are the ideologies of domination. The ancient Maya lords built great ceremonial centers with towering pyramids and vast plazas that were symbolic models of the sacred landscape, of the Maya universe. Their pyramids were sacred mountains, the sites of sacred openings that were the threshold to the spiritual world of the ancestors. It was here that the ruler went into a shamanistic trance, communicating with the gods and ancestors in lavish public ceremonies. Everything validated the complex relationship between the living and the dead, between the ruler and the commoner, displayed in lavish, pointed metaphors that confirmed the divine power of the supreme lords (Schele and Friedel, 1990).

Archaeologist Mark Leone (1984) has even used eighteenth-century land-scaping in Annapolis, Maryland, to show how a crisis of confidence in an exist-ing social order resulted in an ambitious example of public display. William Paca, a wealthy landowner, lawyer, and governor of Maryland, was a fervent believer in individual liberty. He signed the Declaration of Independence, with its strong emphasis on individual liberty, while living in a slave-owning Colonial society. Paca lived a life of contradictions, which he expressed in the powerful, symbolic layout of his garden (Figure 17.3) with its paths, terraces, and plantings, all care-fully calculated to bolster their owner's civil and social authority, which he also expressed in the law. Some scholars have criticized Leone's interpretation on the grounds that Paca used well-established traditions of landscape construction in

FIGURE 17.3   William Paca's garden in eighteenth-century Annapolis, Maryland. The outlines of the garden were established by archaeological investigation; the terraces and plantings are conjectural.

his garden. These were not necessarily a reflection of ideology, but they may have played a role in Paca's long-term social aspirations (Hodder, 1986).

Political and social power are extremely heterogenous phenomena which are exercised in many forms. From the archaeologist's point of view, it is fascinating that one can use material objects like pottery to study how people negotiated their social positions and resisted the submergence of their own culture (Beaudry and others, 1991; Orser and Fagan, 1995). Artifacts offer a unique way of examining the history of the many communities that kept no written records, but expressed their diverse feelings and cultures through the specific artifacts and commodities that they purchased and used.

Promising studies of such resistance are coming from the South, where the earliest Africans to reach North America brought their own notions of religion, ritual, and supernatural power to their new homes. "The guinea negroes had sometimes a small inclosure for their god house," wrote one Florida plantation owner in 1839. Historical records rarely refer to such shrines, but archaeologists have found blue beads and other charms at many slave sites in the North American Southeast. At the Garrison and Kingsmill plantations in Maryland and Virginia, engraved pewter spoons bear motifs remarkably similar to those executed by African-Americans living in Suriname in South America. Bakongo-style marks from Central Africa have come from bowls found in other southern sites (Ferguson, 1992). Everything points to people who arrived in North America with cultural values and a world view radically different from those of their masters. Slave plantations were part of very complex, much wider networks that linked planters to other planters, planters to slaves, slaves to slaves on other plantations. It is significant that slaves within these harsh, oppressive, and racist environments were able to maintain important elements of their own culture. Despite such conditions, African-Americans maintained their own beliefs and culture, which they melded over the generations with new ideas and material innovations from their new environment. They believed that their culture, their way of living—everything from cuisine to belief systems—was the best way.

African spiritual beliefs in all their variety were highly flexible, and were often responses to outside influences, whether political, religious, or economic. Thus, existing spiritual beliefs adapted readily to the new American environment, adopting new artifacts or modifying existing ones over the generations. For example, archaeologists working at Thomas Jefferson's Monticello estate have recovered crystals, pierced coins, and other ritual artifacts from Mulberry Row, where his slaves resided. Traditional practitioners were operating in a hostile environment, so they were careful to disguise their activities. At the Levi Jordan cotton and sugar plantation in south Texas, archaeologists Kenneth Brown and Doreen Cooper have excavated a cabin occupied by an African-American healer-magician. The cabin yielded animal bones, iron spikes, and other artifacts that were part of the paraphernalia of a traditional West African healer. But, as Brown and Cooper point out (1990), the same simple artifacts had other uses, too, so much so that an outside observer would not suspect that their owner was engaged in traditional medicine. To the African-American workers on the plantation, the same objects had an entirely different symbolic meaning that was not revealed to outsiders. For this reason, none of the healer's tools-in-trade bore any telltale symbolic decoration that might reveal their true purpose. African archaeologists and historians have pointed out that the sheer diversity of West African cultures makes it foolhardy to make direct comparisons between African-American and African artifacts. But the survival of African beliefs and culture in African-American society is well-documented as a general phenomenon and has persisted into recent times.

All these finds suggest that African-Americans maintained their own distinctive culture in the face of repressive slavery. They were disfranchised from white people in their own villages and slave quarters, to the point that their masters and mistresses may well have been more like parts of their environment than key players in their social lives (Orser and Fagan, 1995). In South Carolina and Georgia, slaves even spoke a distinctive African-American language. Children growing up in this culture used material objects like earthen bowls that were made by members of this culture, and heard stories of magic and religious chants that were important ways of establishing African-American identity, of maintaining ideological power and molding values. While many slaves may not have resisted their inferior, white-bestowed social status on a day-to-day basis, they ignored European-American culture in favor of their own and rejected an ideology that rationalized their enslavement.

Leland Ferguson (1991, 1992) has documented this resistance in South Carolina, where, in 1740, blacks outnumbered whites by almost 2 to 1, and one-half of that majority was African-born. Here, as elsewhere along the south Atlantic coast, African women arrived with a knowledge of potmaking that they used to fashion domestic wares in their new homes. Their distinctive unglazed earthenware products occur in slave quarters, on plantations, and in cities (Figure 17.4). Once considered Native American pots that had been traded to slaves, these wares were the product of complex demographic and cultural forces that resulted from interactions between blacks and whites, and between both of them and Native Americans. Ferguson undertook a study of this "Colono Ware" from the Southeast, focusing on complete vessels recovered from all manner of locations, including slave quarters, free Native American villages, plantations, and missions. He found that what he calls the "container environment" of South Carolina consisted of wood, basketry, and earthenware manufactures broadly similar to those of the slaves' African homeland. Not only that, but the bowls and other vessels mirrored basic eating habits in Africa, for they were used for preparing and serving carbohydrate porridges with a vegetable or meat relish on the side. Ferguson believes that African-American eating habits were quite similar to those of West Africa and radically different from those of the European-Americans around them. Colono Ware is remarkably similar over a large area, made by people living in an ethnic environment where reciprocal relationships with one another were of vital importance, and where there were strong ties to ancestral African culture. It was, Ferguson says, an unconscious resistance to slavery and the plantation system. The development of southern culture, he concludes, was a long process of quasipolitical negotiation. It is exciting that one can use archaeology to look at the early stages of this complex process of negotiation from both sides.

FIGURE 17.4 Colono Ware.

Another fascinating chronicle of ethnic resistance comes from an archaeolog-ical investigation of the route taken by a small group of Northern Cheyenne when they broke out of Fort Robinson, Nebraska, on January 9, 1879. They fought a running battle with the garrison, across the White River, up some bluffs, and into open country, where it took the military 11 days to capture them. This much is beyond controversy, but the route that the Cheyenne took out of the river valley is disputed (McDonald and others, 1991). According to military accounts, the escap-ing party moved up an exposed sandstone ridge to reach the bluffs. This exposed route was illogical, indeed foolhardy, for there was a full moon. Cheyenne oral traditions insist on another route to the bluffs through a well-protected drainage that offered excellent cover from pursuing riflemen. Archaeologists from the University of South Dakota Archaeology Laboratory investigated the escape routes with the collaboration of local Cheyenne representatives. They used random shovel testing and metal detectors to search for spent bullets in three areas—two drainages and the exposed ridge mentioned in military accounts. The survey recovered no bullets from the exposed ridge, but did find them in the drainages, thereby confirming the oral account of the Cheyenne Outbreak. This may seem like a footnote to modern history, but it is important to remember that the Outbreak has become a classic story of the American West in white eyes, immortalized by John Ford's movie *Cheyenne Autumn*. This film tells the story from the victors' perspective, and is a form of moral tale of the Old West. Now oral tradition and archaeology have shattered part of the myth, telling the story from the Indian perspective in circumstances where science has helped fashion a mosaic of the recent past that is the historical truth rather than a myth.

The most compelling studies of ethnic minorities, of resistance to social domination, at present come from the United States, from historical sites where written records amplify the archaeological record in important ways. As so often happens, methodology developed on historical sites will ultimately be applied to prehistoric situations. What, for example, was the position of Oaxacan merchants living at Teotihuacán in A.D. 600? Were they treated differently from citizens of the city? Does their material culture reflect carefully orchestrated responses to the dominant culture around them? What was the lifeway of slaves and workers in Egypt? How did their relationships with their noble masters change through, say, the New Kingdom? Archaeology, with its rich potential for studying the mundane and the trivial, the minutest details of daily life, is an unrivaled tool for the dispassionate study of social inequality and ethnicity.

SUMMARY

- A new generation of archaeological research is turning away from impersonal cultural processes toward the study of people and small groups. Such research marries modern archaeological data recovery methods with new interpretative approaches that consider the archaeologist as an "active mediator" of the archaeological record of the past.
- The archaeology of gender is assuming increasing importance as a means of identifying changing male-female roles in the past, and of studying individuals in prehistory. These researches involve detailed studies of grave furniture, studies of female pathology, which reflects such activities as constant grain grinding, and extrapolations of material data into hypothetical scenarios of changing gender relations.
- Ethnicity and social inequality have been studied by archaeologists working with African-American and other sites in North America. Such researches involve identifying distinctive artifacts that reflect African religious beliefs and material signs of silent resistance to the dominant culture.

GUIDE TO FURTHER READING

Bacus, Elizabeth A., and others. *A Gendered Past: A Critical Bibliography of Gender in Archaeology*. Ann Arbor: University Museum of Anthropology, Technical report 25, 1993. An invaluable, annotated bibliography of gender in archaeology.

Ferguson, Leland. *Uncommon Ground.* Washington D.C.: Smithsonian Institution Press, 1992. An exemplary study of African-American culture in the archaeological record.

Gero, J. M., and M. W. Conkey. *Engendering Archaeology.* Oxford: Blackwell 1991. An influential series of essays on gender in archaeology.

Orser, Charles E., and Brian M. Fagan. *Historical Archaeology.* New York: HarperCollins, 1995. A basic text on historical archaeology with numerous examples of studies of social conditions and social inequality with archaeological data.

PART 7

INTERPRETING CULTURE CHANGE IN THE PAST

Is it too late for salvation? If not, please let me have the analytical expertise of the New Archaeology—and the humility and common sense of the Old.

Kent V. Flannery
The Early Mesoamerican Village, 1976

There may be rigorous ways to approach cognitive questions about archaeology. At the same time. . . such cognitive approaches can only be used when conditions are appropriate; that is, when the body of supporting data is sufficiently rich. When it is not so rich, cognitive archaeology becomes little more than speculation, a kind of bungee jump into the Land of Fantasy.

Kent V. Flannery and Joyce Marcus
Cognitive Archaeology, 1993

Part Seven shows what an amazing battery of powerful analytical tools is being brought to bear on archaeological interpretation. Archaeology is in the throes of a quantum jump in analytical sophistication, in which the work of mathematicians, statisticians, and scientists has a leading part. As Colin Renfrew (1979) observed, archaeologists are "replacing anecdote by analysis."

18

CONSTRUCTING CULTURE HISTORY

T he reconstruction of culture history has been a major preoccupation of archaeologists from the early years of the twentieth century. Culture history itself describes human cultures in the past, and it is based on chronological and spatial ordering of archaeological data. In contrast, the study of cultural process has been a phenomenon of recent decades. This chapter describes the culture-historical approach and some of the ways in which archaeologists approach the study of culture change.

THE CULTURE-HISTORICAL METHOD

The study of culture history is based on two fundamental principles. One is *descriptive (inductive) research methods,* the development of generalizations about a research problem that are based on numerous specific observations (see Chapter 5); the other is a *normative view of culture,* which is based on the notion that abstract rules govern what the culture considers normal behavior. The normative view is a descriptive approach to culture; it can be used to describe culture during one time period or throughout time. Archaeologists base it on the assumption that surviving artifacts, such as potsherds, display stylistic and other changes that represent the changing norms of human behavior over time.

Most archaeological interpretation in the New and Old World has been based on normative models. The culture-historical approach has resulted in a descriptive outline of prehistory in time and space for much of the world. The interpretation of culture-historical data is based on simple analogies from historical and ethnographic data, far simpler than those envisaged by archaeologists studying living societies today (Chapter 14). Within its limitations, culture-historical reconstruction is a useful organizational tool that has added some descriptive order to human prehistory.

CONSTRUCTING CULTURE HISTORY

All culture-history research is based on descriptive methods that acquire specific data, from one or many archaeological sites, which are not only accumulated but also subjected to a gradual synthesis that leads to generalizations based on the data. The sequence of research begins with identifying a research area, using reconnaissance and surface surveys. These surveys yield a mass of surface collections, which allow the researcher to develop at least a tentative chronological sequence for the area, based on attributes and artifact types seriated according to the principles outlined in Chapter 12. The research continues with carefully selected excavations designed to test the validity of the sequence and to refine and expand it as well. Although the excavations may be meant, ultimately, to recover structures and village layouts, their primary goals are always stratigraphic—observing and recording occupation layers and developing relative and absolute chronologies. The data from the excavations are then analyzed and classified and used to refine the preliminary classifications and chronologies put together before digging began.

This data base consists of artifacts, structures, food remains, and other information. The process of classification involves analyzing all these categories of data. Artifacts and structures are the primary interest of culture historians, for they provide a sensitive barometer for studying technological and cultural change throughout time and space. Often, artifacts and structures are divided into complexes, chronological subdivisions of artifact forms, such as stone tools, pottery, and bone objects, each of which can be used to chronicle an aspect of technological and cultural change. Some artifact complexes, such as pottery, are more sensitive than others, and these are the ones that are used for correlating cultural sequences with one another. Archaeologists have developed arbitrary time-space units to aid them in this process.

SYNTHESIS: ARCHAEOLOGICAL UNITS

The basis of all culture-historical reconstruction is the precise and carefully described site chronology. The synthesis of these chronologies beyond the confines of one site or local area involves not only repeating the same descriptive processes at other sites, but also constantly refining the original cultural sequence from the original excavations. The synthesis is cumulative, for some new excavations may yield cultural materials that are not represented in the early digs. It is here that the techniques of seriation and cross-dating come into play. This is, of course, an entirely descriptive exercise that yields no explanations whatsoever. It is a site-oriented procedure, too, very different from the regional surveys that have dominated archaeological research in recent years.

The **archaeological units** used to aid the synthesis form an arbitrary, hierarchical classification for this purpose. They represent the combining of the formal content of a site or sites with its distribution in time and space. Three occupation levels in a Utah cave each have distinctive artifact assemblages that have been sorted into types. Occupation levels at a dozen nearby sites contain examples of these three assemblages. What arbitrary units can we use to help us compare these various sites and occupation levels with their different contents? What arbitrary units will assist us in studying cultural change as well? The archaeological units used most widely in the Americas are those developed by Gordon Willey and Philip Phillips (1958); we describe some of these here.

COMPONENTS AND PHASES

The basis of culture history is the local chronological sequence, whether at one site or many. Once chronological types are identified, they are studied closely to see how they cluster to reflect the cultural chronology of the site as a whole. It is here that researchers use the first in the hierarchy of archaeological units, components.

Components are the physically bounded positions of a site that contain a distinct assemblage, which serves to distinguish the culture of the inhabitants of a particular land. An occupation site like Martin's Hundred, Virginia, will consist of a single component, but a settlement occupied at three different times will contain three distinct components. Each may belong to a separate cultural phase. The Koster site in Illinois is an excellent example of a multicomponent site, with its various layers representing different components separated by sterile layers of soil (Struever and Holton, 1979).

"Cultural homogeneity" is, of course, an intangible, so the definition of a component depends very much on stratigraphic observation and on the archaeologist's observational skills. Some cave sites in southwestern France contain many occupation levels separated by sterile layers. These can, of course, be isolated stratigraphically and grouped on the basis of shared chronological types like antler harpoons or side scrapers. In other sites, as in San Cristóbal in the Great Basin, the midden deposits were so churned up that the various components had to be separated by quantitative artifact analysis rather than stratigraphic observation (Thomas, 1988).

Components occur at one location. To produce a regional chronology, archaeologists must synthesize them with components from other sites, using the next analytical step, phases.

Phases are cultural units represented by like components on different sites or at different levels of the same site, although always within a well-defined chronological bracket (Willey and Phillips, 1958). The characteristic assemblage of artifacts of the phase may be found over hundreds of miles within the area covered by a local sequence. Many archaeologists use the term *culture* in the same sense as *phase*. Both are concepts designed to assist in ordering artifacts in time and space. Phases or cultures usually are named after a key site where characteristic artifacts are found. The *Magdalenian* culture of 16,000 years ago, for example, is named after the southwest French rock shelter of La Madeleine, where the antler harpoons and other artifacts so characteristic of this culture are found.

Thomas (1983a, 1988) uses the Gatecliff shelter in Nevada to show how components and phases mesh. He found five components at the site, each defined by chronological types. As long as he was excavating just one site, this procedure was fine. But he wanted to compare the Gatecliff findings with those from other excavated sites in central Nevada. He found that a number of these sites contained late components with artifacts like projectile points and Shoshone pottery similar to those found in equivalent stratigraphic contexts at

Gatecliff. He brought together the components from Gatecliff and the other sites into a phase, which he named Yellow Blade. This period dates from about A.D. 1300 to 1850, the moment of European contact. The phase term applies not only to Gatecliff but to the entire region. It is the basic unit of area synthesis. Some phases are but a few years long; others span centuries, even millennia. All the phase really does is break up long, continuous periods of prehistoric time into discrete chronological and spatial units, each with its own specific artifacts. The Gatecliff site was occupied for about 8,000 years, divided by chronological types into five components stacked one upon the other. Each of these components has its own dates and characteristic artifacts. The components can be compared to those from other sites and used to build up a regional chronology. The phase enables us to establish regional contemporaneity. At first a phase may embrace, as the Yellow Blade phase does, 500 years or more. But as research proceeds, chronologies become more refined, and as artifact classifications become finer, the original phase may be broken down even further into more and more chronologically precise subphases.

REGIONS AND CULTURE AREAS
Culture-historical synthesis involves working with much larger areas in time and space than those covered by phases or local sequences. The two major divisions are archaeological regions and culture areas.

Archaeological regions are normally defined by natural geographic boundaries. They may also be defined, however, by a heavy concentration of archaeological sites. Normally, a region will display some cultural homogeneity. Examples are the Santa Barbara Channel region and the Valley of Oaxaca in Mexico.

Culture areas define much larger tracts of land, and they often coincide with the broad ethnographic culture areas identified by early anthropologists. Many areas tend to coincide with the various physiographic divisions of the world. The southwestern United States is one such area, as it is defined in part by its history of research and in part by cultural and environmental associations that lasted more than 2,000 years. Such large areas can be divided into subareas, where differences within the culture of an area are sufficiently distinctive to separate one subarea from another. Gordon Willey (1966) divided the Southwest into the Anasazi, Hohokam, and Mogollon subareas, among others (Figure 18.1). But area implies nothing more than a very general and widespread cultural homogeneity. Within any large area, societies will adapt to new circumstances, some evolving more quickly than others, and enjoy quite different economies.

STAGES, PERIODS, HORIZONS, AND TRADITIONS
New World archaeologists have two units that synthesize archaeological data over wide areas: horizons and traditions.

1. *Horizons* link a number of phases in neighboring areas that have rather general cultural patterns in common. In some parts of the world, an all-embracing religious cult may transcend cultural boundaries and spread over an enormous area. Such cults are often associated with characteristic religious artifacts or art styles that can be identified in phases hundreds of miles

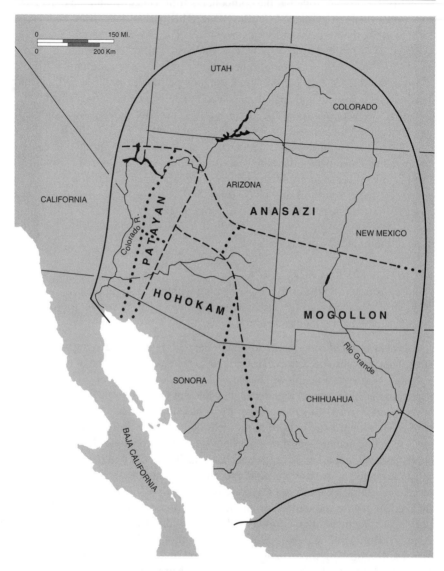

FIGURE 18.1 Archaeological regions and subareas in the North American Southwest. (After Willey)

apart—in well-defined chronological contexts. The Chavín art style of coastal Peru, for example, was associated with distinctive religious beliefs and rituals shared by many Peruvian societies in the highlands and lowlands between 900 and 200 B.C. (Moseley, 1992). This commonality of belief is manifested in the archaeological record by Chavín art, a style that stresses exotic, jaguar-like motifs; hence the use of the term Early Horizon (Figure 18.2).

FIGURE 18.2 Chavín carving on a pillar in the temple interior at Chavín de Huantar, Peru. The Chavín art style formed one of the bases for identifying the Early Horizon in Peruvian prehistory.

2. The term *tradition* has widespread application in archaeology. It is used to describe an artifact type, assemblages of tools, architectural styles, economic practices, or art styles that last much longer than one phase or even the duration of a horizon. The toolmaking tradition, for example, may continue in use while the many cultures that share it develop in entirely different ways. Tradition implies a degree of cultural continuity, even if shifts in cultural adaptation have taken place in the meantime. A good example of such a tradition is the so-called Arctic Small Tool tradition of Alaska, which originated at least as early as 4000 B.C. (Dumond, 1987). The small tools made by these hunter-gatherers were so effective that they continued in use until recent times and led to the modern Eskimo cultures of the Far North.

INTERPRETATION

The interpretation of culture history depends on analogy and descriptive cultural models, which are used to identify the variables that are in operation when culture change takes place. These models are used to account for changes in the archaeological record. This record, however, does not invariably show a smooth and orderly chronicle of culture change. A seriated pottery sequence from six sites may display the sudden arrival of a new ware that is radically different from others in the sequence. An entirely new artifact inventory may suddenly appear in components at eight sites, while the tool kits of earlier centuries rapidly vanish. The economy of sites in a local sequence may change completely within 50 years as the plow comes into use in the locality. Such changes are readily observed in the thousands of local sequences found in the archaeological record. But how did these changes come about? What processes of cultural change were at work to cause major and minor alterations in the archaeological record? A number of descriptive models have been formulated to characterize culture change: some of these are cultural models, others noncultural; several involve internal change, others external influence.

CULTURAL MODELS

The widely used models of culture change in archaeology are inevitable variation, cultural selection, and the three classic processes—invention, diffusion, and migration (Trigger, 1968a).

INEVITABLE VARIATION   This is somewhat similar to the well-known biological phenomenon of genetic drift. As people learn the behavior patterns of their society, inevitably some minor differences in learned behavior will appear from generation to generation; although minor in themselves, these differences accumulate over a long time, especially if the populations are isolated. Today we live in a far more complex society than people did even 30 years ago. The "snowball effect" of inevitable variation and slow-moving cultural evolution can be detected in dozens of prehistoric societies. For instance, the great variation in Acheulian hand ax technology throughout Europe and Africa between 100,000 and 150,000 years ago can be explained in part by the effects of inevitable variation.

Inevitable variation is often the result of isolation, of a very low density of humans per square mile. It should not be confused with broad trends in prehistory that developed over long periods of time. The increasingly complex burial rituals that developed in the Adena and Hopewell cultures of the American Midwest between 500 B.C. and A.D. 300 probably resulted from trends toward greater complexity in religious beliefs and rituals as well as in political and economic organization over a long period of time—not from isolation (Fagan, 1995). Inevitable variation is also quite different from what happens when a society recognizes that certain culture changes or inventions may be advantageous. Presumably, for example, many hunter-gatherer societies deliberately took up the cultivation of the soil once they saw the advantages it gave neighboring peoples who had already adopted the new economies.

CULTURAL SELECTION   This concept is somewhat analogous to that of natural selection in biological evolution. It is the notion that human cultures accept or reject new traits—technological, economic, or intangible—on the basis of whether they are advantageous to society as a whole. Cultural selection results in cumulative cultural change, and it operates within the prevailing values of the society. This condition tends to make it harder for a society to accept social change as opposed to technological advances, which are less circumscribed by restrictive values. The state-organized societies in Mesopotamia and Mexico resulted from centuries of gradual social evolution, where centralized political and religious authority was perceived to be advantageous.

INVENTION   The first of the three classic processes that contribute to culture change involves creating a new idea and transforming it—in archaeological contexts—into an artifact or other tangible innovation. Unfortunately, many inventions, such as new religions or ideas, leave little tangible trace in the archaeological record. An invention implies either the modifying of an old idea or series of ideas or the creation of a completely new concept; it may come about by accident or by intentional research. The atom was split by long and patient investigation, with the ultimate objective of fragmentation; fire was probably the result of an accident. Inventions spread, and if they are sufficiently important, they spread widely and rapidly. The microchip is in almost universal use because it is an effective advance in electronic technology; plows had an equally dramatic effect on agriculture in prehistoric Europe. How inventions spread has been studied extensively by archaeologists and anthropologists, for the quality of inventiveness is an essential part of the human genius, as our society defines it.

In the early study of prehistory, people assumed that metallurgy and other major innovations were invented in only one place, a notion that led to the great diffusionist theories of a half-century ago (Figure 18.3). But as people have come to understand the importance of environment and adaptation in prehistory, they have realized that many inventions have been made in several parts of the world, where identical adaptive processes occurred. Agriculture is known to have developed independently in the Near East, south Asia, China, Mesoamerica, and Peru.

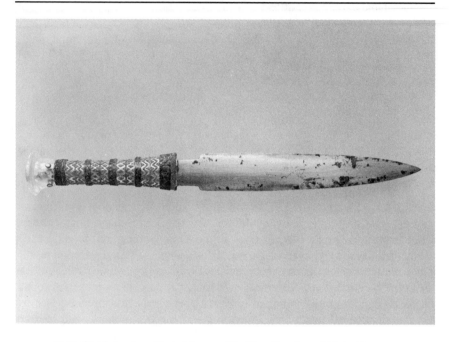

FIGURE 18.3   Iron-bladed dagger of the Egyptian pharaoh Tutankhamun, 1323 B.C. The weapon was probably made of native hammered iron. The Egyptians tried, without success, to obtain iron tools from the Hittites in distant Anatolia after hearing of the revolutionary new metal.

DIFFUSION   This model is defined as the processes by which new ideas or cultural traits spread from one person to another or from one group to another, often over long distances. Much modern research on diffusion is about how innovations that are new to the recipients spread to other areas. Diffusion can proceed through such diverse mechanisms as trade, warfare, frequent visits between neighboring communities, and migrations of entire communities. A key issue here is the formal or informal mechanisms of contact between the members of separate groups that account for the spread and acceptance of a new idea.

Just how are patterned stylistic trait distributions diffused from one area to another? The subject is rich in controversy and invalid assumptions (D. D. Davis, 1983). The growing popularity of evolutionary explanations in recent years has led to wholesale rejections of diffusion as a way of interpreting the past, so much so that archaeologists have tended to neglect it. Diffusion is, however, assuming new importance as large bodies of regional data are produced by large-scale cultural resource management surveys in such areas as the San Juan Basin and Great Basin.

Current archaeological thinking about diffusion stems from pioneer work by early anthropologists Franz Boas, Alfred Kroeber, and their contemporaries. They were interested in diffusion but argued that the symbolic value or prestige of a culture trait was a major factor in determining whether it was accepted and diffused to other societies. Archaeologists borrowed some of this thinking in the 1930s, but found it impossible to establish the social context of culture traits from the archaeological record alone. They therefore assumed that acceptance of culture traits was directly proportional to the frequency with which people learned about an innovation. This simplistic approach, which often talked of culture "contact" instead of diffusion, collapsed in the face of more sophisticated archaeological and ethnographic studies showing that knowledge of an innovation did not necessarily mean that it would be adopted (Schiffer, 1979). A classic example occurs among the Aborigines of northern Australia, who are well aware of agriculture among their neighbors but remain hunter-gatherers themselves.

Diffusion research of this simplistic type is still found among some archaeologists, including those who study possible transatlantic and transpacific contacts between Old World and New (Riley, 1971). Were European or African crops diffused to the Americas? The researchers interested in this kind of topic concentrate not so much as they should on the social context of the innovations as on the archaeological criteria for establishing diffusion in the archaeological record. Let us look at this sort of approach to diffusion more closely. Figure 18.4 diagrams a culture trait in space and time. Let us say that a new type of painted pot is invented in a village in about A.D. 1400. The advantages of this new pot are so great that villagers 10 miles (16 km) away learn about the vessel at a beer party five years later; within 10 years their potters are making similar receptacles. In a short time the pot form is found not only in one village but in three within a 10-mile (16 km) radius. By 1450 the pot form is so widely used that dozens of villages within a 50-mile (80 km) circle of the original settlement are making the same vessels. Plotting this development on paper yields the cone effect shown in Figure 18.4; that is the principle applied by culture historians looking at diffusion.

Under this topic, several criteria must be satisfied before researchers can decide whether a series of artifacts in archaeological sites distant from one another are related in a historically meaningful way. First, the traits or objects must be sufficiently similar in design and typological attributes to indicate that they probably have a common origin. Second, it must be shown that the traits did not result from convergent evolution. The earlier development of the trait, perhaps as general as a form of architecture or the use of a domestic animal, must be carefully traced in both cultures. Third, distributions of the surviving traits must be carefully studied, as well as those of their antecedents. The only acceptable evidence for diffusion of a trait is a series of sites that show, when plotted on a map, continuous distribution for the trait or, perhaps, a route along which it spread. Accurate chronological control is essential, with a time gradient from either end of the distribution or one from the middle. For many traits, the archaeological criteria may be difficult to establish; indeed, they are rarely satisfied, but the importance of reliable evidence is obvious. Theoretical speculations are all very well, but they may result in completely false conclusions, sometimes supported by uncritical use of scanty archaeological evidence (R. H. Thompson, 1956).

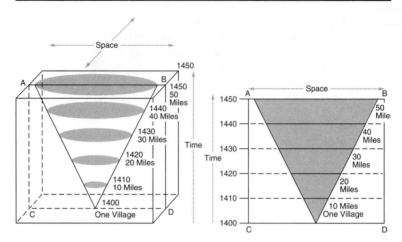

FIGURE 18.4   The spread of a culture trait in time and space: the cone effect.

Instances of diffusion in prehistory are legion. There are innumerable cases in which ideas or new technologies have spread widely from their place of origin, although none are as grandiose as Thor Heyerdahl's attempts to prove that the Egyptians colonized Mesoamerica. A well-documented instance is the religion of the Adena and Hopewell peoples of the Midwest, who held beliefs associated with death that spread far beyond the relatively narrow confines of the Midwest. Religious beliefs are expressed in the form of distinctive rituals, which for the Adena and Hopewell involved extensive earthworks and mound building. Such monuments are found outside the Adena and Hopewell heartlands, as are the cult objects associated with Hopewell ritual (Figure 18.5).

During the 1960s and 1970s, the move away from normative explanations led to research into a number of basic assumptions about diffusion. Ethnoarchaeological studies of pottery making have shown just how important informal communication between potters is in spreading technological and stylistic changes (Longacre, 1991). Some basic research into the role of artifact style in reinforcing social identity and solidarity is important because it identifies factors that may have accelerated or prevented adoption of culture traits. Despite these efforts and a large body of diffusion research in other social sciences, many archaeologists are deeply suspicious of diffusion research, partly because a body of archaeological theory on the subject still does not exist (D. D. Davis, 1983).

Much of the unpopularity of diffusion stems from archaeologists using the term wrongly. Diffusion itself is not a cause of the spread or adoption of culture traits; it is a way of referring to a set of phenomena that have been caused by a wide range of cultural factors. To say that bronze sword-making diffused from one society to another is merely to describe what happened. It does not describe how the spread occurred. Under the culture-history title, diffusion has been in-

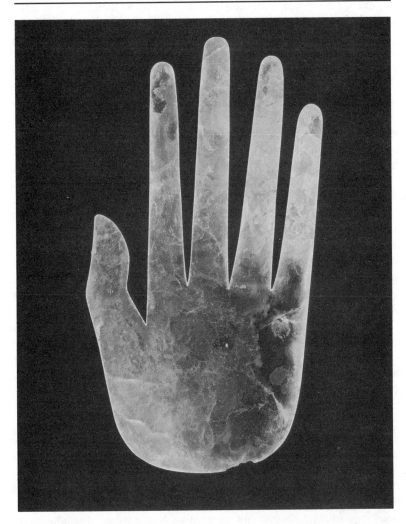

FIGURE 18.5   A Hopewell artisan cut this human hand from a sheet of mica about 2,000 years ago. It was found in an Ohio burial mound with the body of its owner, who lived 370 miles (595 km) from the nearest mica source. An example of the consequence of the diffusion of religious beliefs, this hand probably had powerful shamanistic associations in Hopewell society.

voked as a satisfactory explanation for distribution patterns of culture traits when, in fact, the factors behind the diffusion are still unexplained.

MIGRATION   Migration as an explanatory concept suffers from many of the same disadvantages as diffusion. But this type of cultural change involves movement of entire populations, both large and small. Migration can be peaceful, or it can be the result of deliberate aggression, ending in invasion and conquest.

In every case, people deliberately decide to expand their sphere of influence into new areas. English settlers moved to the North American continent, taking their own culture and society with them; the Spanish conquistadors occupied Mexico. Such population movements result not only in diffusion of ideas but also in a mass shift of people, accompanied by extensive social and cultural changes.

For migration to be recognized in the archaeological record, one would need to find local sequences where the phases show a complete disruption of earlier cultural patterns by an intrusive new phase—not just of one tool type, or even several. Of course, some elements in earlier cultural traditions might survive and become an acculturated part of the peoples' new culture. Perhaps the classic instance of migration in world prehistory is that of the Polynesians, who settled the remote islands of the Pacific by deliberately voyaging from archipelago to archipelago (Finney, 1994). Each time, the islands were discovered through an act of deliberate exploration, by voyagers who set out with every intention of returning. Hawaii, Easter Island, and Tahiti were first settled by deliberate colonization that was perforce a migration of a small number of people to a new, uninhabited land mass. The kind of total population movement, or in some cases, population replacement, that occurs with mass migrations of this type is rare in human prehistory. It will be reflected in the archaeological record either by totally new components and phases of artifacts, or by skeletal evidence.

A second type of migration, on a much smaller scale, occurs when a small number of foreigners moves into another region and settles there as an organized group. A group of Oaxacans may have done just that at Teotihuacán in the Valley of Mexico (Millon, 1973). They settled in their own special precinct of the city, tentatively identified by a concentration of Oaxacan potsherds and ornaments. The Oaxacan enclave lasted for centuries.

There are other forms of migration, too. Slaves and artisans wander as unorganized migrants. Artisans are an important source of diffusion of techniques and ideas. This type of unorganized migration is difficult to discern in the form of culture traits, for the individual migrant leaves little behind except, perhaps, some specialist artifacts, as bronze-working migrant artisans did in prehistoric Europe. Finally, there are great warrior migrations, such as those of the eastern nomads in temperate Europe and the warlike Nguni tribes of southern Africa. Each of these warrior bands swept over an indigenous, sedentary population, causing widespread disruption and population shifts. But within a few generations, the warrior newcomers had adopted the sedentary way of life of their neighbors and were virtually indistinguishable from them. Such migrations leave few traces in archaeological sites.

NONCULTURAL MODELS

Cultural change triggered by such noncultural factors as alterations in the natural environment is an integral part of culture history. The most recent research in archaeology has focused heavily on specific details of the relationship between the environment and prehistoric cultures. The complex models growing from this research show that earlier models invoking such mechanisms as diffusion were far too general to explain these complex and ever-changing environment-culture relationships.

Reconstruction of culture history is a very difficult and complex descriptive process that depends on the availability of large amounts of basic data to be effective. In itself, inductive research of the type involved in culture history takes little account of the role of artifacts in the whole cultural system. As we shall see in Chapter 19, explanation of cultural process requires far more complex models based on quite a different approach to archaeology.

SUMMARY

- The study of culture history is based on descriptive research methods and on a normative view of culture, which assumes that abstract rules govern what a given culture considers to be normal behavior.
- The process of constructing culture history begins with identifying a research area using reconnaissance and surface surveys. These efforts yield at least a tentative chronological sequence for the area, which is based on attributes and artifact types that have been seriated in their correct order. Then carefully selected excavations are made to test, refine, and expand the sequence. The data are then analyzed and classified. Artifacts and structures are used as sensitive barometers of cultural change; they are divided into complexes, each of which is used to chronicle one aspect of technological and cultural change.
- The process of synthesis in culture history is based on constructing precise chronological sequences. Expanding these chronologies beyond one site or occupation layer is a cumulative process in which seriation and cross-dating have key roles.
- A series of arbitrary archaeological units are used to aid in this synthesis. Local chronological sequences lie at the core of all culture-historical research. These are based on *phases,* which are cultural units in a local sequence that possess culture traits sufficient to distinguish them from all other phases. Normally, the boundaries of a phase are set arbitrarily. The term *component* describes a single manifestation of a phase at a single site.
- Archaeological regions are normally defined by natural geographic boundaries, but culture areas are much larger and coincide with major ethnographic culture areas; the American Southwest is an example.
- *Horizons* link a number of phases in neighboring areas, containing rather general cultural patterns, which are often distinguished by characteristic art styles, such as the Chavín of Peru. The term *tradition* describes a lasting artifact type— assemblages of tools, architectural styles, and so on that last much longer than a phase or even a horizon.
- The interpretation of culture history depends on analogy and descriptive cultural models that are used to identify variables that operate when culture change takes place.
- Some commonly accepted descriptive models of cultural change are inevitable variation, cultural selection, invention, diffusion, and migration. These in themselves, however, do not describe the factors that led to cultural change in the first place.

GUIDE TO FURTHER READING

Binford, L. R. *In Pursuit of the Past*. New York: Thames and Hudson, 1983. An essay on approaches to archaeology that is critical of the culture-history approach.

Rouse, Irving. *Introduction to Prehistory: A Systematic Approach*. New York: McGraw-Hill, 1972. A basic account, which is widely quoted, of archaeological units at the synthetic level.

Willey, Gordon R., and Philip Phillips. *Method and Theory in American Archaeology*. Chicago: University of Chicago Press, 1958. Often described as the culture historian's bible, this is a fundamental source on the methods of culture history, an essential part of the training of every professional archaeologist.

19

EXPLAINING THE PAST

E xplanation of culture change in the past, of cultural process, has been a major preoccupation of archaeologists for the past 30 years. This chapter examines processual archaeology and new approaches to archaeology that reflect a new direction for our study of the past.

PROCESSUAL ARCHAEOLOGY

Processual archaeology, defined in Chapter 6, provides a vehicle for closely examining the cultural process and a viable means of searching for explanations of culture change in prehistory (Wylie, 1988). It is based on the scientific method. It employs research design, formulation of explicit research hypotheses through induction from which specific results can be deduced, and testing of these results against new data. Its methods are cumulative; that is, initial hypotheses are designed that propose a working model to explain culture change. These hypotheses are tested against new data, and some are discarded, while others are tested again and again until the factors that affect culture change are isolated in highly specific form. The synthesized archaeological data are interpreted on the basis of successive generations of working hypotheses that are tested many times.

The processual approach is firmly based on culture history and data obtained from earlier studies. It has to be, for the chronological and spatial frameworks for prehistory come from descriptive methods developed over many years of arduous fieldwork and analysis. The difference between the descriptive and processual approaches lies in the orientation of the research. Processual archaeologists rely on the scientific method to formulate testable hypotheses and proceed to the gathering of new data to test them. The early days of processual archaeology were marked by furious academic controversy, not only between culture historians and those espousing processual methodology but also between proponents of different approaches to the study of cultural process (Meltzer and others, 1986). Two methods are commonly espoused: the deductive-nomological approach and the systems-ecological approach (Flannery, 1968).

DEDUCTIVE-NOMOLOGICAL APPROACH

Archaeologists who use this approach are firmly committed to a highly formal, scientific methodology, based on the work of Carl Hempel and other philosophers of science (Watson and others, 1984). Nomology is the study of general laws; a deductive-nomological approach is based on the philosophy of logical positivism. This philosophy considers the world to be composed of observable phenomena that act in an orderly way. It views the world as governed by general laws that can be identified by rigorous research methods. In other words, the world can be explained by predicting when a set of phenomena that indicate that a particular law is in operation will occur.

In archaeology, these general laws are derived from anthropology and other social sciences. Laws have been formulated about the relationships between human cultures and the environment, about ecological adaptation, and about cultural evolution (Sahlins and Service, 1960). Most of them are so generalized, however, that it is difficult to test them with specific data. Nevertheless, some archaeologists believe that archaeological data can be used to formulate and test hypotheses that identify the general and universal laws governing cultural processes.

At the heart of this approach to processual archaeology is the notion that there actually are general laws that govern human behavior. Proponents of the deductive-nomological approach also assume that formal scientific experiments, which can be repeated and can produce predictable results, can be used to identify instances when a particular law is in operation. Their explanations of cultural change are based on the predictability of these results. In other words, the hypothesis that allows accurate prediction of phenomena in one area, under circumstances similar to those elsewhere, is the one that can be justified as the best explanation.

The trouble is that archaeology is just not that sort of science. The deductive-nomological approach came to archaeology late in the 1960s, when to become a science was a desirable goal for archaeology. Physics had a theoretical rigor that was attractive to people who wanted more scientific rigor in archaeology. But physics has an essentially metaphysical and abstract conception of reality that is quite different from that of archaeology, which concentrates on change through time (Dunnell, 1982). The highly specific methods applied to physics and other hard sciences are far less applicable to archaeological data, which are governed mainly by intangible variables such as values and beliefs. Deductive-nomological research is extremely valuable for the study of the past, provided that realistic account is taken of the uniqueness of archaeological data. If there is one scientific discipline that archaeology lies closest to, it is biology, for biologists are struggling with many similar theoretical problems connected with change (Dunnell, 1982).

SYSTEMS-ECOLOGICAL APPROACH

The second and more common processual approach deals with the ways in which cultural systems function, both internally and in relation to external factors such as the natural environment. It involves three basic models of cultural change: systems models, which are based on general systems theory; cultural ecology, which provides complicated models of the interactions between human cultures and their environments; and multilinear cultural evolution, which combines both systems approaches and cultural ecology in a theory of the cumulative evolution of culture over long periods through complex adaptations to the environment (Gibbon, 1984).

General systems theory was first constructed in the sciences in the 1950s. It is a body of theoretical concepts that provides a way of searching for "general relationships" in the empirical world. A system is defined as "a whole which functions as a whole by virtue of the interdependence of its parts" (Rapoport, 1968). Systems theory has been widely applied in physics and other hard sciences, where relationships between parts of a system can be defined with great precision. It has obvious appeal to archaeologists, for its believers assume that any organization, however simple or complex, can be studied as a system of interrelated concepts (Salmon, 1982). A change in one of these components will trigger reactions in many of the other parts. The notion of cultural systems, which was described in Chapter 6, is derived, in part, from systems theory.

The advantage of systems theory is that it frees researchers from having to look at only one agent of cultural change, such as irrigation or diffusion, allowing them to focus instead on regulatory mechanisms and on the relationships between various components of a cultural system and the system as a whole and its environment. The systems approach is valuable to archaeology as it is to the study of ecology—as a general concept. But we must keep in mind that the data used to test the hypotheses derived to validate this model are acquired by the same methods used to acquire valuable culture-historical information.

CULTURAL ECOLOGY

As we saw in Chapter 6, processual archaeology relies on the concepts of systems theory and on the study of cultural ecology (Gibbon, 1984). Cultural ecology is a way of obtaining a total picture of how human populations adapt to and transform their environments. These environments include not only the natural landscape but also vegetational and animal populations as well as other cultures.

Cultural ecologists see human cultures as subsystems interacting with other subsystems, all forming part of a total ecosystem with three major subsystems: human culture, the biotic community, and the physical environment. Thus the key to the cultural process lies in understanding the interactive relationships among the various subsystems. William Sanders and Barbara Price have pointed out that every biological and physical environment presents problems for human use (Sanders and Price, 1968). Furthermore, the human response to different environments will be different and distinctive. Although the possibilities for human adaptation to an environment are almost unlimited, the number of probable adaptations to a specific environment is limited. Thus communities with very different cultures may occupy the same or similar environments, and the level of technological achievement and effectiveness of the hunting-gathering or food-producing economy involved naturally affects their responses in other aspects of culture. Some environments are inherently less productive than others, a factor that can limit population growth as well as other cultural responses.

The adaptation of any population is achieved primarily through effective subsistence strategies and technological artifices, but social organization and religious beliefs are important in ensuring cooperative exploitation of the environment as well as technological cooperation. Religious life provided an integrating force in many societies, not least among them the Egyptians and Mayans. Human cultures are as dynamic as all other components of an ecological system, and any human culture can be thought of as what Sanders and Price (1968) call "a complex of techniques adaptive to the problems of survival in a particular geographical region." Human culture is, ecologically speaking, a way in which human beings compete successfully with animals, plants, and other human beings. Sanders and Price point out that "the product of plant and animal evolution is more effective utilization of the landscape in competition with individuals of the same and other species. This effectiveness is usually expressed in population growth, and this growth can therefore be taken as a measure of success in a given area at a given point."

There are obvious difficulties in studying the interactions between people and their environment, especially when preservation conditions limit the artifacts and other data available for study. Fortunately, however, artifacts and other elements of the technological subsystem often survive. Because technology is a primary way in which different cultures adapt to their environment, detailed models of technological subsystems allow archaeologists to obtain a relatively comprehensive picture of the cultural system as a whole. It is in research of this type that the storage capacity of the computer has come into play. Cultural-ecological studies depend for their effectiveness on enormous quantities of basic data. Once these data are stored on the computer, researchers can use simulation techniques to model possible cultural outcomes by inserting hypothetical variables into the surviving cultural system. The techniques are somewhat like those used for business forecasting, but they are still in a highly experimental stage.

MULTILINEAR CULTURAL EVOLUTION

Multilinear evolutionary theory recognizes that there are many evolutionary tracks, from simple to complex, the differences resulting from individual adaptive solutions (Steward, 1955). Despite these variations, some broad evolutionary developmental stages can be recognized in the world's societies. The four-stage evolutionary classification of bands, tribes, chiefdoms, and state-organized societies was described in Chapter 16 (Service, 1971). These highly flexible stages are defined with reference to social complexity, subsistence strategy, and population size. None of them is rigidly defined, for multilinear evolutionary theory recognizes that cultural adaptations are complex processes that are fine-tuned to local conditions, with long-term, cumulative effects.

Multilinear cultural evolution, then, is the vital integrative force that brings systems theory and cultural ecology together into a closely knit, highly flexible way of studying and explaining the cultural process (Sanders and Webster, 1978).

Theoretical approaches are meaningless unless they are tested against actual field data. The models of processual archaeology have been applied successfully to many small-scale problems. They have provided new means of studying major developments in world prehistory, such as the origins of literate civilization in the Near East some 5,000 years ago (Figure 19.1).

POSTPROCESSUAL ARCHAEOLOGY

Archaeology is based on the optimistic, Modernist belief that knowledge about human societies has accumulated gradually through rational inquiry modeled on the hard sciences and mathematics. This notion of cumulative science and knowledge is vital to understanding the convoluted history of archaeological theory since the 1960s.

In the 1960s and 1970s, archaeologists were talking about a "new archaeology," a revolutionary approach to the past that promised to overcome the many limitations of the archaeological record. In fact, this "new" archaeology, usually called "processual archaeology", has failed to deliver on many of its promises. Processual archaeology has emphasized subsistence and settlement patterns, animal bones, plant remains, and ancient population distributions, topics covered extensively in this book. Its many practitioners embraced methodological rigor and interpreted the past in terms of cultural systems, with a strong emphasis on material objects. Many of its once "new" tenets are part of today's mainstream archaeology. Back in the 1960s, Lewis Binford and others believed that processual archaeology would allow researchers to investigate all aspects of human experience, including intangibles such as beliefs (Binford and Binford, 1968). But very soon, the focus tended toward ecology and subsistence, to the point that some processualists referred to investigations of the intangible as "palaeopsychology" (Binford, 1987).

Inevitably, there was a reaction against this materialist approach, which seemed to dehumanize the past in a quest for processes of cultural change. Many processual archaeologists dismissed religion, ideology, and human ideas as marginal to the central enterprise of studying subsistence and settlement. But during the late 1970s and 1980s, more researchers began thinking about the entire spectrum of human behavior—the development and expression of human consciousness, religion and belief, symbolism and iconography, as part of a more holistic archeology. Thus was born **postprocessual archaeology,** a sometimes violent antidote to its predecessor, in general terms a reaction against the relatively anonymous, processual approach, which emphasized cultural processes over people and individuals.

We live in fractious times, in societies riven by factional disputes, special interest groups, and accusations of racism and "political correctness." The violent passions raised by postprocessual archaeology are a reflection both of Western society being in transition, and of a discipline made up of a loose patchwork of dozens of often arcane specialties. Hardly surprisingly, postprocessual archaeology is a loosely defined term which covers several often aggressively expressed intellectual developments, which often parallel the "postmodernist" schools of

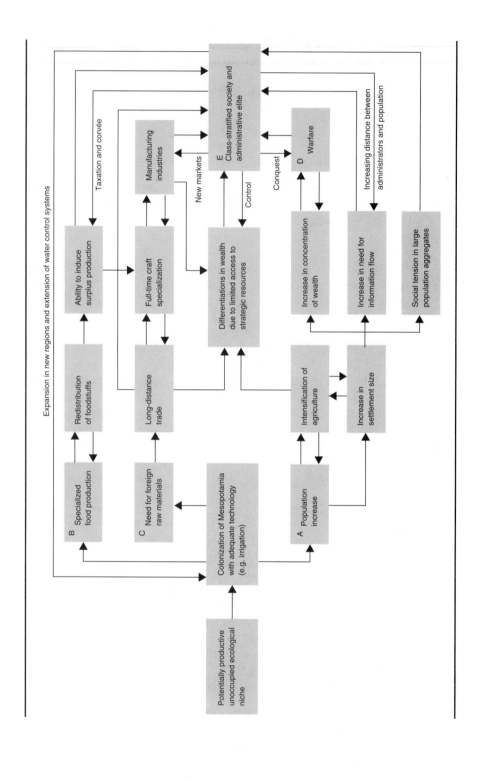

FIGURE 19.1   The processual approach: the origins of literate civilization in the Near East. A processual, systems-ecological approach argues that the rise of civilization was the result of a series of interacting and cumulative processes triggered by favorable cultural and ecological conditions. These continued to develop cumulatively as a result of continual positive feedback, as the diagram shows. The process began with establishment of agricultural communities in the Mesopotamian delta before 5000 B.C. These settlements triggered three processes: steady population growth in the delta, increased specialization in food production, and heightened demand for imported raw materials. Each of these processes set off feedback reactions that became more and more complex as time went on. As the diagram shows, it is possible to develop a highly complex, multicausal model for emergence of Mesopotamian civilization that is based on logical, interlocking hypotheses. The problem is to test this model and its many hypotheses in the field, something that requires the development not only of rigorous methodologies for identifying the variables in the archaeological record, but also of comparative studies of these variables in regions where civilization emerged and where it did not, and also in societies that flourished immediately before this development.

thought in literature and anthropology (Hodder, 1986; Shanks and Tilley, 1987a, 1987b). In a scathing analysis of postpreprocessual archaeology, John Bintcliff (1991) points out that what appears to be a subdiscipline of archaeology, archaeological theory, has unfolded not in a cumulative manner, but by a process of almost total renewal every ten years or so. In each case, the leading proponents of the new approach write off the previous paradigm as useless and introduce new concepts, often derived from attractive theoretical approaches developed in other disciplines and not in archaeology itself. Postprocessualism is no exception, representing a long period of theoretical instability in the 1970s and 1980s, which saw some archaeologists, notably British scholar Ian Hodder, turning to spatial analysis, then structuralism and postmodernism. Almost without exception, the new approaches arrive within archaeology via what Bintcliff (1991) calls "a novel bibliography of intellectual traditions likely to be esoteric and unpalatable to their predecessors—who 'write themselves out' of the debate by failing to read the new sacred texts." Very often, their original authors in, say, sociology, have never thought about archaeology in their lives! With such constant renewal going on, there is often very little debate or even dialog between people who adhere to or have developed new theoretical approaches. Very often, their predecessors are too busy testing their own laboriously developed approaches in the field.

For all its constantly shifting paradigms, postprocessual archaeology has made three positive and important contributions:

1. First, meaning is more important than materialism. No longer can archaeologists interpret the past in terms of purely ecological, technological, and other material considerations. Culture is interactive. In other words, people are actors who create, manipulate, and remake the world they live in.

2. Second, archaeologists must critically examine their social responsibilities, looking beyond their specialties to the broader aims of the discipline and to issues of moral and emotional involvement with the past in contemporary society. How does the public interact with the past?
3. Third, there are many perspectives on ancient society that have been neglected, among them those of women, ethnic minorities, and those who are often called "the people without history," anonymous, often illiterate commoners.

John Bintcliff (1991) described postprocessual archaeology rather extravagantly as a "rampant monster," best understood by reading the original postmodernist authors (in other disciplines) and the perceptive and often powerful critiques their works evoked (see also Yoffee and Sherratt, 1993). But, as we shall see below, some of its approaches offer promise when combined with the best of processual archaeology, with its empirical data collection, rigorous data description, and meticulous analyses of archaeological sites and their ecological contexts. In the final analysis, archaeological research will always be a cumulative process that continues to unfold from one generation to the next. It is this belief that has led to the emergence of cognitive archaeology, described later in the chapter.

FUNCTIONALISM AND STRUCTURAL ARCHAEOLOGY

Functionalism, the notion that a social institution within a society has a function in fulfilling all the needs of a social organism, is a concept that has been integral to much anthropological thinking since late in the nineteenth century. Hodder (1982a) uses the analogy of the stomach, which fulfills a function for the human body as a whole. Thus functionalists assess any aspect of a society according to its contribution to the total working of society. Functionalism has long been a controversial topic among anthropologists, but it is inextricable from the notions of systems and cultural systems, concepts that are fundamental tenets of processual archaeology. As Renfrew (1975) points out, to examine connections among cultural subsystems is to look at ancient society through a functionalist perspective. Systems are seen as in equilibrium or disequilibrium, populated by human beings who, as individuals, are minimally important. It is within this context that ethnoarchaeology and concepts like middle-range theory have become fashionable. Prehistoric institutions were rational in dealing with their environments, archaeologists of this persuasion assume.

There is much more to culture than functions and activities. Behind functioning and doing there is a structure and content that must be partly understood on its own terms, with its own logic and coherence. This applies as much to refuse distributions and "the economy" as it does to burial, pot decoration and art. Structure in an archaeological context is defined by Ian Hodder (1982a) not as a set of relationships between components of a cultural system (a way in which it could be used interchangeably with "system"), but as "the codes and rules according to which observed systems of interrelations are produced." Hodder argues that many studies of areas like the Peruvian coast or the American Southwest have explained the structure of human societies in terms of social functions and adaptive values. But they also hint that there is more to culture than observable relationships and functional utility. Hodder writes of a set of rules, a code, as it were, that he likens to those operating in chess or Monopoly, which are followed as people go about the business of survival, adaptation, and making a living.

Structural archaeology is an attempt to get at the active, social manipulation of symbols, at objects as they are perceived by their owners—not merely at their use. Hodder studied the Nuba agriculturalists of the Sudan and showed that all aspects of their material culture, including burial customs, settlement patterns, and artifact styles, could be understood in the context of a set of rules that perpetuated their beliefs in "purity, boundedness, and categorization" (Hodder, 1982b). Thus Nuba society is the result of structured, symbolizing behavior and has fundamental utility. But it also has a logic of its own, which generated the material culture that is observed by the archaeologist. Structural archaeologists believe that although functionalist analyses can yield information on the underlying codes, explanations for them must be based not on function but on the logic behind them.

What structural archaeology is basically concerned with is the identification of the "idea of complex dimensions" (Leone, 1986). There are few examples of in-depth research that reveal such a structure. David Friedel and Linda Schele's (1987) research on Maya iconography (Chapter 16) is one possible example, although the authors do not describe their study as a structural approach. They do show how ritual life, shrines, and temple structures helped shape people's lives. In other words, people think order into their world by using "central, powerful, and pliable symbols" (Leone, 1986).

Structural archaeology arose through frustration with the problems and limitations of spatial analysis (Chapter 15), in which one confronts head-on the difficulties and frustrations of interpreting spatial patterns and the variables that affected their distribution. The concept is all very well in theory, but few archaeological studies have yet provided convincing accounts of the relationships between the "codes" and social and ecological organization.

To some extent, structural archaeology is an extension of the functionalist approach of processualists in that it reconsiders many of the basic issues about culture, ideology, and structure that worried earlier archaeologists just as much as their successors. It is part of a fundamental, long-term shift in archaeology, as it begins to be a cultural and historical discipline that has the potential not only to contribute to our understanding of the past but also to contribute some highly original ideas to humanity's thinking about itself (Hodder, 1984, 1995; Leone, 1986).

CRITICAL ARCHAEOLOGY

People are like actors, interacting with their culture. This concept is the major difference in approach between archaeologists using a materialist approach to the past and those who are concerned with symbolic meaning, structure, and the "rules" that once governed society.

Critical archaeology concerns itself with the patterns behind material culture. What are the links between large and diverse series of apparently unrelated artifacts? These artifacts manifest the changes in people's minds as time went on. The classic research is that of James Deetz (1983) on New England tombstones, which we described in Chapter 7. Deetz chronicles how housing and artifacts, as well as tombstone styles, changed as society became more individualist and the face-to-face community withered. For example, the impersonal, private urn-and-willow gravestone design replaced the earlier death's-heads and cherubs, which had portrayed a human aspect of each individual and related that individual to the community of which he or she had once been a part. This study drew on historical research into folk housing and may prove to be a highly effective technique for use on historic sites.

Critical archaeology assumes that since archaeologists are actors in contemporary culture, they must have some active impact on our society (Shanks and Tilley, 1987a). Our reconstructions of the past have a social function, just as astronomy did in Maya civilization. Thus archaeology may be more than a neutral, objective science. By engaging in critical analysis, an archaeologist can explore the relationship between a reconstruction of the past and the ideology that helped create that reconstruction. One extreme is the Marxist view of archaeology, which states that all knowledge is class-based, so archaeology composes history for class purposes (Spriggs, 1984). Much critical archaeology focuses on understanding the pasts of people who have been "denied" a history—women, blacks, the Third World, and so on. In other words, we should be concerned with the cultural roots of our work (Shanks and Tilley, 1987a, 1987b). In a sense, this approach to archaeology reproaches current archaeological practice and demands that archaeologists be socially and politically responsible in their research. Many archaeologists object to this thesis because of its strong critical and moral undertones, which, they feel, undermine basic method and theory in the discipline (Bintcliff, 1991).

Critical archaeology produces studies that assume a political and economic relationship between the past and interpretations of the past made today. This past can be interpreted archaeologically to provide insights into the impact of that relationship. The research has two steps, well-documented by Russell Handsman's research in western Connecticut (1981). He studied New England urban villages that appeared around 1800, communities "marked by an increase in the disparity of the distribution of wealth between many villages." The landscape changed from one of isolated farmsteads and occasional nuclear settlements to one of much larger villages. Analyzing artifacts found in a Canaan, Connecticut, tavern midden dating to between 1750 and 1850, Handsman argues that the homogeneous ceramics, glass vessels, and other objects of the earlier layers show an unchanging, homogeneous way of life. But after 1800 the artifacts become more individualized and fine-grained, as if individual wealth and status had become more important.

What are we to make of this research? Handsman shows that Canaan was constructed to provide a way in which the new, industrial elite could, by creating village communities, ground themselves and their great variations in wealth in an earlier farming era with different values. He has given Canaan's early history an economic and political context through archaeological research. His critical approach establishes that Canaan came into being as a way of disguising the switch to an industrial society. He argues that New England society used settlement pattern and architecture to avoid knowledge of shifting family values and relations, new property rules, and wage relations. Research like this can contribute to a greater consciousness of modern society.

Critical archaeology developed as a reaction to the feeling that modern archaeology has become too dehumanized, too divorced from its "proper role" in modern society—that it has no cultural context (Shanks and Tilley, 1987a, 1987b). In a sense, this is a process of archaeologists becoming more critical of their own place in the unfolding intellectual development of Western scholarship (Trigger, 1984a, 1989). As Ruth Tringham puts it (1994), we are "active mediators" of the past (Chapter 17).

COGNITIVE ARCHAEOLOGY

The *Oxford English Dictionary,* the ultimate arbiter of the English language, even for Americans, defines cognition as "the action or faculty of knowing taken in its widest sense, including sensation, perception, conception, etc." From an archaeological perspective, the term **cognitive archaeology** covers the whole spectrum of human behavior, especially religion and belief, but also the development and expression of human consciousness. Since the very early days of archaeology, researchers have been concerned with ancient religion, belief, and expression, the subject matter of cognitive archaeology, what has sometimes been called the "archaeology of mind." How can one define cognitive archaeology? Is it possible to study human cognition from the material remains of the archaeological record, even if we cannot afford to ignore it? Some of the best minds in archaeology are debating these questions and attempting to create a "cognitive-processual" approach, with a new framework for archaeology drawing on both old and new models and methods. This is an important exercise, because the archaeology of the 1990s is built on solid scientific foundations, not hermeneutics, interpretive approaches which allow insight to play a key role. This is the approach used by those who believe ancient civilizations lie under Antarctic ice or that astronauts from outer space founded Maya civilization (Chapter 1). Cognitive-processualists never claim they can establish *what* people thought, but they can give insights into *how* they thought (Renfrew, 1993; Skibo and others, 1995).

Cognitive archaeology covers all of the human past, but can be divided into two broad areas of concern. One involves the study of the cognitive facilities of early hominids and archaic humans, the relationships between toolmaking and cognitive abilities, the origins of language, and the social contexts of early human behavior (Barkow and others, 1992; Donald, 1991; Gibson and Ingold, 1993). The other covers the past 40,000 years and the cognitive aspects of such major developments as the origins of food production and civilization. Renfrew (1993) considers the challenge for cognitive archaeology to be establishing how the formation of symbolic systems in, say, the Near East or Pre-Formative Mesoamerica, molded and conditioned later cultural developments, such as, for example, Maya civilization. He considers humans to use symbols in about six ways: in design and planning; for measurement and social relations, the latter using symbols to structure and regulate interpersonal behavior; and for representation and mediating between the human and supernatural worlds (Renfrew, 1994). He also believes the reason that cognitive archaeology has been neglected is that it lacks a coherent methodology. This methodology may emerge from the convergence of such diverse fields as cognitive psychology, artificial intelligence, computer simulation, and cognitive archaeology itself. But this convergence, and the potential intellectual leap forward that might result, will not occur until archaeologists interested in human cognition develop a rigorous and explicit methodology that will substitute for many of the simplistic generalizations that masquerade under the label of postprocessual archaeology.

Kent Flannery and Joyce Marcus (1993) have long been interested in cognition, but in the same context as Renfrew, as part of an effort to make mainstream archaeology more holistic. Their earliest work was an attempt to understand ancient Zapotec subsistence behavior in Mexico's Valley of Oaxaca by taking into account what early Spanish accounts told of local Indian cosmology. They believe this kind of approach, which makes use of critically analyzed historical documents and other sources, to be productive, as opposed to the inspired speculation so common in the 1980s. Flannery and Marcus (1993) consider cognitive archaeology not to be the study of epiphenomena, but "the study of all those aspects of ancient culture that are the product of the ancient mind." This includes cosmology, religion, ideology, iconography, and all forms of human intellectual and symbolic behavior. They also firmly state that effective cognitive archaeology depends on rigorous research methods. Thus, it can only be used when the body of supporting data is rich (Sullivan, 1989). Otherwise, it becomes "little more than speculation, a kind of bungee jump into the Land of Fantasy." In practical terms, and for obvious reasons, cognitive archaeology is usually most effective when historical records are available to amplify the archaeological record, as they are working with archaeological evidence and Maya inscriptions (Schele and Friedel, 1990).

Under this approach, cognitive archaeology has considerable limitations. All cultures have a theory of the universe in which they live. Their cosmology, like that of Western civilization, which is based on modern astronomy, constitutes a theory of the origin of the universe, defines space and time, and can provide a structure for religion and ideology. Many cultures, among them ancient Greek and Maya, envisage a cosmos inhabited by supernatural beings, another link to religious beliefs. Although cosmology can have a strong influence on both settlement and subsistence, as, for example, in cases where certain aspects of the environment, like pristine forest, may be held sacred, it is difficult if not impossible to reconstruct cosmology from animal and plant remains alone.

Religious beliefs provide ethics and values, often within the framework of a quest for the values of an ideal life. A well-defined worldview links cosmology and religion, the latter providing the rituals and practices which help the worshiper attain the ideal. Clearly, these ethics and values can have a powerful effect on human behavior, even on such pragmatic areas of life as obtaining food and trading. Religion can be a powerful catalyst for social and political change, as was the case, for example, when Buddhist merchants brought their religion to southeast Asia and changed the course of history by providing the spiritual inspiration for a series of brilliant kingdoms, like those of the Khmer (Figure 16.6) (Wheatley, 1975). Flannery and Marcus (1993) believe that one approach to reconstructing ancient religions is to construct models from ethnohistoric sources, then to isolate temples, artifacts, art styles, and other cultural elements which can be identified archaeologically. These are studied in their cultural context, and the observed archaeological remains are compared with the model from ethnohistoric documents (see also Chapter 16).

"Ideology is a product of society and politics, a body of doctrine, myth, and symbolism associated with a social movement, an institution, class, or group of individuals, often with reference to some political or cultural plan, along with the strategies for putting the doctrine into operation" (Flannery and Marcus, 1993). For example, any archaeologist concerned with the appearance of ranked, as opposed to egalitarian societies is studying fundamental changes in ideology, simply because egalitarian societies tend to have leveling mechanisms which prevent one individual or group from attaining superior rank. Again, these changes can only be documented through judicious use of historical analogies and artifacts. In the Valley of Oaxaca, many village farming communities func-tioned without any apparent ranking between 1400 and 1150 B.C. Between 1150 and 850 B.C., the first artistic depictions of supernatural lineage ancestors appear; some may represent the earth, others sky, in the form of lightning or a fire serpent. Some form of hereditary social ranking seems to accompany the new art (Flannery and Marcus, 1993). Then the Zapotec state came into being, with a powerful elite ruling from Monte Alban, a tiny minority associated with depic-tions of sky and lightning, while earth and earthquake symbols fade into obscu-rity. It is as if those who rose to prominence were associated with lightning's descendants, in an ideological shift in which hereditary social inequality is condoned for the first time. Such a shift is well-documented among the Kachin hill people of highland Burma (Leach, 1954).

Iconography offers another fertile avenue for cognitive archaeology; it is the "analysis of the way ancient peoples represented religious, political, ideological, or cosmological objects or concepts in their art" (Flannery and Marcus, 1993). Again, ethnohistory and history provide vital background for the interpretation of the archaeological record, for without such information one is engaged in little more than guesswork. Such studies, based very often on intuition and "aesthetic sense," reflect the author's personality more than reality.

Flannery and Marcus (1993) quote Olga Linares' little known study (1977) of high-status cemeteries in central Panama as an excellent example of a rigorous approach to ancient ideology. Using sixteenth-century Spanish eyewitness accounts of local Panamanian chiefdoms engaged in constant warfare and raiding, and detailed information on local animal species, Linares studied graves and the associ-ated flamboyant polychrome vessels found in them. They were open pots designed to be seen from above, where mourners could see the animal motifs painted upon them. Sometimes, apparently, the pots were so valuable that they were exhumed from one grave and put in another. Ethnohistorical accounts mention that the highly competitive chiefs vied constantly for leadership and prestige, painting and tattoo-ing their bodies with badges of rank and bravery. Each group of warriors wore different symbols that associated them with their leader. They went to their graves with helmets, weapons, other military paraphernalia, and painted pottery. Linares noticed that the art styles rarely depicted plants, but rather many animal species, motifs that commemorated qualities of aggression and bravery. Crocodiles, large felines, sharks, stingrays, scorpions, and even poisonous snakes were the animals that were dangerous, and therefore symbols of bravery. They often appeared on clay vessels, and sometimes parts of their bodies, like shark's teeth and stingray spines, were buried with the dead. In contrast, prey species and animals with soft parts like, say, monkeys, were largely ignored by the artists. Thus, the cognitive world of the Panamanian chiefdoms used carefully selected animals to communicate the qualities most admired in chiefs and warriors.

Such researches are highly effective, if they use established analytical techniques and draw on information from many sources. Cognitive archaeology reaches a high degree of refinement when document-aided, as is the case with the Aztec civilization of Mexico, or the Inka of the Andes. But earlier societies, like, for instance, the first farming societies of the Near East, with their female figures and plastered human skulls, offer much greater challenges. It is all too easy to call each female figure a "fertility figurine" and to talk of ancient mother goddesses, when there is, in fact, no scientific basis for such conclusions.

Cognitive archaeology is no shortcut, but an approach to cosmology, religion, ideology, and iconography based on rigorous analysis and data from many sources. It is a theoretical perspective which offers enormous promise for the future, but it falls far short of reconstructing entire ideologies from the orientation of a building or a single carving.

WHAT LIES AHEAD: EVOLUTION AND THE ARCHAEOLOGY OF CONSTRAINTS

EVOLUTIONARY APPROACHES

Where does the future lie? The answer can only be that archaeologists are uncertain. Clearly, both evolutionary theory and ecology will be important in the study of cultural change and the birth of complex societies. New approaches subsumed under the label of cognitive archaeology will combine the most effective perspectives and methods of processual and postprocessual archaeology. At the same time, many archaeologists find evolutionary theory useful, so one future direction of archaeological theory will lie in reconsidering the applications of evolutionary theory to our discipline. As Steven Mithen (1989) points out, *Homo sapiens sapiens* is a cultural animal, our capacity for culture a product of evolution in which natural selection played an important part. What is crucial for archaeologists is whether these same evolutionary processes had any consequences for the nature of human behavior. In other words, is culture independent of its biological roots and thus irrelevant to the study of human behavior?

Some postprocessualists, with their strong criticisms of functionalism, seem to imply that culture is independent of biology. Thus evolutionary theory is irrelevant as a way of understanding human behavior (Shanks and Tilley, 1987b). An alternative viewpoint supports the idea that natural selection produced culture by conferring some reproductive advantage on its bearers. Thus thought and action were channeled by natural selection in directions that were adaptive for an evolving Homo Sapiens Sapiens.

The legacy of this is a tendency for humans to think and act in certain ways and not in others. The result is a strong tendency toward conformity in thought and action among very diverse human societies with very different institutions and beliefs. Archaeologists of this persuasion maintain that natural selection has constrained human thought and action, that the way in which people behave can be understood by understanding the constraints placed on the human mind by its long evolutionary heritage. It should be remembered, however, that the environment in which the human mind evolved is very different from that in which we live today and in which we have lived for many thousands of years. We must carry out research "armed with humility in the face of the complexity of human cognitive functioning and social systems" (Hinde, 1987; see also O'Brien and Holland, 1992).

The rich diversity of human society results from the interaction between universal psychological propensities of humankind and the unique circumstances that cause each individual to adapt to different social, ecological, and historical situations. It is the interaction between universals and individual adaptation that is important. Neither alone can explain the great differences and similarities between ancient or modern societies. Thus the most useful evolutionary perspective in archaeology, concerned as it is with change through time, is one that focuses on individuals who are constantly adjusting their behavior as their social and physical environments change. These same individuals are people capable of creative thinking, a uniquely human characteristic. There are, of course, limits on human knowledge—problems we cannot cope with, processes of comprehension that are beyond us, mistakes we can make through mental confusion. These limits place a premium on cooperation between individuals in the solving of problems, such as finding a way to kill large numbers of bison at one time.

Under this emerging rubric, evolutionary approaches in archaeology will be more concerned with "active individuals endowed with common psychological propensities to think and act in certain ways rather than others, taking decisions in ecological, social, and historical contexts which are unique to themselves" (Mithen, 1989). In this respect, cognitive archaeology and evolutionary approaches have much in common.

CONSTRAINTS

Archaeology is a curious social science, since archaeologists are "unable either to observe human behavior or to learn about human thoughts at first hand from their primary data," writes Bruce Trigger (1991). Therein lies the crux of current theoretical debates. Trigger and others believe that the processual approach may lend a better understanding of what archaeologists know, but this is useless without a better comprehension of what human behavior produced the archaeological record (Wylie, 1988).

Today, many archaeologists believe there was much greater variation in human behavior than processual archaeologists have allowed for. In other words, human behavior is less orderly than many cultural evolutionists would like us to believe, yet not entirely random, as some postprocessual scholars assume. There are sufficient regularities in cultural developments in different regions, such as, for example, in the development of agriculture and village life in the Near East and Mesoamerica, to suggest that recurrent operations of cause and effect result in the evolution of similar forms of behavior in widely separated areas. There is much we do not know about the nature of cultural and social systems. Does a change in one subsystem affect all others, as many archaeologists assume? It is by no means certain that this is the case. Unfortunately, while materialist approaches tell us much about ancient life and how economy and material culture influenced political, social, and intellectual life, we still have inadequate knowledge of the constraints that influence human behavior. Bruce Trigger has urged archaeologists to read the works of the French philosopher Jean-Paul Sartre, who spent his lifetime trying to understand the relationships between individual human beings as decision-makers and their social context. Thus, he says (1991), we should view human behavior as "the product of interaction between the ability of individual human beings to foresee at least some of the consequences of what they do and the sorts of constraints on human behavior, both physical and imagined, that such calculations must take into account."

Processual archaeologists have made important studies of the ecological, technological, and economic constraints that act on human societies. Two such examples are research on changes in settlement patterns in the Basin of Mexico, (Sanders and others, 1979) and the rise of Mesopotamian civilization (Flannery, 1972). But many noneconomic and nonecological factors also influence human behavior. So do actual physical limitations of the human body and the nature of our brains. So instead of saying that the environment was responsible for cultural change, one can argue that it constrained human behavior (Fish and Kowalewski, 1990). Finally, general systems research has shown convincingly that there are relatively few alternative ways to process information and make decisions. This limits the number of social and political organizations that are viable for human societies. For instance, decision-making by consensus, so typical of small-scale societies, works well only in groups of about 300 people or fewer. Some form of coercion is essential when more than 1,500 people live in the same group. In general terms, the larger the scale of the society, the more complex and bureaucratized are the institutions that regulate it. There are a limited number of viable social and political structures that human societies can adopt, which accounts for the striking similarities in general organization between, say, Sumerian and Maya civilization in different corners of the world.

Internal constraints also operate on our behavior. These include knowledge, beliefs, values, and other culturally conditioned habits, all of them different in each culture. Yet some of them are shared by cultures flourishing thousands of miles apart. For instance, two widely separated cultures may develop bronze metallurgy, which is based on a common body of technological know-how, but the cultural context of that knowledge is radically different, as it was, say, in the Shang civilization of China and in Moche culture in coastal Peru. Some symbols, like the common practice of elevating chiefs or kings on a dais, or associations between rulers and the sun, have developed in many places. That does not mean that they are connected, as early diffusionists would have argued; they are simply more or less uniform operations of the human mind.

According to this perspective, human cultures are historical phenomena shaped by both external and internal constraints. This counters the Darwinian argument that new human concepts are like genes, the products of purely random processes that create the highly variable raw material upon which a cultural equivalent of natural selection operates. This somewhat biological view of culture change suggests that cultural selection automatically favors the most adaptive ideas, by ensuring that those cultures that adopt them survive. Our ability to use our imaginations, to make calculated decisions, plays a significant part in streamlining any form of innovation. Our culture has a store of ideas and social values that channel and restrict innovation. Although many processualists deny it, cultural traditions do play a major role in constraining social change. As Karl Marx once wrote: "human beings make their own history. . . not under circumstances chosen by themselves. . . but directly encountered, given, and transmitted from the past." In other words, information transmitted from one generation to the next provides most of the knowledge an individual has to deal with ecological and social realities. Each generation reworks this information and its accompanying cultural constraints to reflect the realities of their own circumstances, a process that transformed human societies and at times led to new social institutions (Bender, 1990).

Cultural traditions provide guidance for coping with the environment, a force that can operate against innovation, and a body of intellectual information that changes constantly from one generation to the next. They are as important as ecological factors in influencing human behavior. Under this approach, the individual is the one who has perception, who takes steps to make changes. Thus external and internal constraints on human behavior are equally important and complement each other throughout human history. Ecological and other external factors can be culturally mediated, but they operate independently of human actions, which makes them susceptible to understanding in terms of evolutionary theory and other such generalizations. Cultural traditions, the internal constraints, are far more idiosyncratic, far more haphazard. This makes it difficult to impose evolutionary order on human history, for, despite external constraints, much cultural change is contingent on ever-changing circumstances. Human culture's open-ended capacity for further elaboration creates a need for order to make its diversity understandable. Under this controversial argument, by studying individual cultural traditions, archaeologists can explain the distinctive features of cultures in ways that evolutionists and cultural ecologists can never hope to.

Trigger believes that archaeologists should try to explain the past in terms of constraints. There are those of a natural order, such as environment, technology, and limitations placed on social organization by the cultural system. Such general factors can best be explained through applications of middle-range theory and ethnoarchaeological data. This research should be combined with inquiries into cultural meanings, using refinements of the direct historical method that employ documents, archaeology, linguistics, and oral traditions to provide cultural meaning for the generalizations of middle-range theory. Archaeological understandings of all the constraints that have shaped ancient societies will vary considerably from one culture to another. While the direct historical method can take us back many millennia, there are many societies, like, for example, those of the European Cro-Magnons of 20,000 years ago, that will always be known to us mainly from the perspective of external constraints. This does not mean, of course, that archaeologists despair of ever understanding the behavior of very early human societies. It is simply that they have a lively perception of the limitations of archaeological data. At the same time, they are striving to make archaeology more human-centered than the kind of impersonal science that characterized much of earlier processual archaeology.

The debate over a new, more human-centered archaeology has barely begun, but we can predict that more holistic approaches to the past will replace the somewhat polarized viewpoints so characteristic of the discipline today (Yoffee and Sherratt, 1993; Trigger, 1995; Ucko, 1995).

SUMMARY

- The processual approach is based firmly on culture history and on data obtained from inductive research. The differences between it and the inductive approach lie in the orientation of the research, which is deductive rather than inductive.

- Processual archaeologists who use the deductive-nomological approach are committed to a highly formal, scientific methodology based on the study of general laws and the work of philosophers of science. They consider the world to be composed of observable phenomena that act in an orderly way. In other words, the world can be explained by predicting when a set of phenomena that indicate a particular law is in operation will occur. But many archaeologists reject the assumption that such general laws exist and believe that the highly specific, deductive scientific methods of physics and other sciences are inappropriate for archaeological data. They do, however, recognize the value of deductive research.

- Most processual archaeology embraces a systems-ecological approach that deals with the ways in which cultural systems function, both internally and in relation to external factors, such as the environment. This approach is based on general systems theory, cultural ecology, and multilinear cultural evolution.

- The systems approach provides a way of looking at the relationships of various traits within a cultural system. Archaeologists deal with open systems that are regulated, at least in part, by external stimuli. In cultural systems, these stimuli are the elements in the environment. The regulatory mechanisms that govern the system keep it in equilibrium and sometimes trigger further cultural change through positive feedback.

- Cultural ecologists see human cultures as subsystems interacting with other subsystems, all of which are part of a total ecosystem. Under this rubric, human culture is, ecologically speaking, a way in which human beings compete successfully with plants, animals, and other human beings.

- Multilinear cultural evolution recognizes that cultural adaptations are complex processes, fine-tuned to local conditions, with long-term cumulative effects. The multicausal models of processual archaeology resulting from the systems-ecological approach require development of new, rigorous methodologies for data collection, and comparative studies of cultural variables in the archaeological record.

- Postprocessual archaeology is a reaction against the evolutionary and functionalist approaches and takes several forms. Structural archaeology tries to analyze the patterns of human culture and their transformations, while critical archaeology concerns itself with the patterns behind material culture and with the contemporary context of archaeological research.
- Cognitive archaeology, the "archaeology of mind," is a synthesis of processual and postprocessual archaeology that uses rigorous scientific methods and analogy to reconstruct the intangibles of ancient human societies.
- Evolutionary theory based on the interaction between individual adaptations and common behavioral characteristics of all humans is useful for studying long-term cultural change. It involves developing new methodologies focused on examining social adaptations, as well as subsistence and adaptations to the natural environment.
- Some archaeologists are now trying to explain the past in terms of environmental and cultural constraints, a synthesis of several theoretical approaches. This is part of an attempt to make archaeology more human-centered and less a study of impersonal cultural processes.

GUIDE TO FURTHER READING

Binford, Lewis R. *In Pursuit of the Past.* New York: Thames and Hudson, 1983. An essay on the archaeological record and archaeological interpretation that chronicles the development of processual archaeology.

Mithen, Steven. "Evolutionary Theory and Postprocessual Archaeology," *Antiquity* 63 (1989): 483–494. An eloquent, closely argued statement on evolutionary archaeology.

Renfrew, Colin, and others. "What is Cognitive Archaeology?" *Cambridge Archaeological Journal* 3 (1993) (2): 247–270. A series of essays on the emerging approach called "cognitive archaeology." Invaluable as a thoughtful analysis of current theory.

Trigger, Bruce G. "Distinguished Lecture in Archaeology: Constraint and Freedom," *American Anthropologist* 93 (3) (1991): 551–569. A thoughtful essay on the current status of archaeological theory by a master of the craft.

Watson, Patti Jo, Steven A. Le Blanc, and Charles L. Redman. *Archaeological Explanation: The Scientific Method in Archaeology,* 2d ed. New York: Columbia University Press, 1984. A book that describes processual archaeology in a methodological context. For the advanced reader.

8

CULTURAL RESOURCE MANAGEMENT

These great towns and temples and buildings rising from the water, all made of stone, seemed like an enchanted vision. . . Indeed some of our soldiers asked whether it was not all a dream. . . I stood looking at it, and thought no land like it would ever be discovered in the whole world. . . But today all that I then saw is overthrown and destroyed; nothing is left standing.

Bernal Díaz del Castillo on Aztec
Tenochtitlán, A.D. 1519
The Conquest of New Spain

We have now completed our journey through the complexities of contemporary archaeology, a journey that should leave you with some insights into the processes of archaeological research. Our discussion of contemporary archaeology would be incomplete, however, without considering cultural resource management, one of the most pressing and complex aspects of the discipline. A major crisis confronts archaeologists: destruction of finite resources. In the two chapters that follow we survey the problems of managing the world's archaeological resources and look at the various ways in which you can become involved in archaeology, both as a pastime and as a professional career.

20

MANAGING THE PAST AND PUBLIC ARCHAEOLOGY

A ll archaeological excavation and surface collection is destruction: the destruction of a finite resource. Although archaeologists themselves have destroyed thousands of sites in their research, far more damage has resulted from looting, treasure hunting, and modern agricultural and industrial activity (Fowler, 1982). The emerging crisis is rapidly turning archaeology from an academic discipline into a profession. Chapter 20 explores how archaeologists are trying to control such destruction through legislation and the management of finite cultural resources.[1]

The inexorable destruction of archaeological sites has accelerated rapidly since the 1960s. Deep plowing, freeway construction, water control schemes, strip mining, and unprecedented urban development have all played havoc with the archaeological record. In many areas the situation has reached crisis proportions. It is estimated that less than 5 percent of the 1850s archaeological resource base in Los Angeles County is still undisturbed. Charles McGimsey estimated in 1972 that at least 25 percent of the sites that existed in Arkansas in 1750 had been destroyed by agricultural and other land use, to say nothing of looters, in the previous 10 years. Archaeologists in Britain, worried about the wanton destruction of archaeological sites by industrial development and by treasure hunters using metal detectors, have formed an organization named Rescue (Figure 20.1) that helps fight to save key sites and to prevent looting (Rahtz, 1974). Perhaps the most famous example of "rescue" archaeology was the international effort, sponsored by UNESCO, that resulted in moving the Abu Simbel temples in Egypt from the banks of the Nile behind the Aswan High Dam to a new site clear of the rising waters of Lake Nasser. The Aswan project also resulted in the discovery of hundreds of additional sites in the area to be flooded (Macquilty, 1965).

---

[1] This chapter is concerned entirely with cultural resource management in North America, where most of our readership resides. Unfortunately, space precludes discussion of similar problems in other countries like Canada and Britain; in Japan, very different problems are encountered. Interested readers are referred to Henry Cleere's edited volume, *Archaeological Heritage Management in the Modern World* (1989). See Prott and O'Keefe, 1984.

Tomorrow maybe too late.

Rescue

Trust for British Archaeology. Central Office, 25 The Tything, Worcester, Worcs. Tel: Worcester 20651

FIGURE 20.1   Rescue speaks for itself: "Tomorrow may be too late."

Many archaeological activities come under the title *cultural resource management* (CRM). Because much of this work is done under contract to government agencies or private companies, it is sometimes called contract archaeology, to distinguish it from the actual management of the cultural resources.

Cultural resources are the human-made and natural physical features associated with human activity. They are unique and nonrenewable and can include sites, structures, and artifacts significant in history or prehistory. Cultural resource management (CRM) is the application of management skills to preserve important parts of our cultural heritage, both historic and prehistoric, for the benefit of the public today and in the future. The concept of cultural resource management came into being in the mid-1970s, but stemmed from long anxiety on the part of archaeologists and others over the destruction of archaeological sites and historic buildings (Figure 20.2).

ANTIQUITIES LEGISLATION

People have worried about the destruction of archaeological sites for a long time. There were, for example, loud outcries as long ago as 1801, when Lord Elgin removed the stunning marbles that now bear his name from the

FIGURE 20.2   The Great Serpent Mound in Ohio, an early example of archaeological conservation. This remarkable monument, a depiction of a serpent devouring a burial mound, was saved by the efforts of Harvard archaeologist Frederick Putnam and a group of Boston women in 1886. In recent years, the mound was again saved from development by concerted efforts of local archaeologists.

Parthenon and bore them away to London (Bracken, 1975). The Greek government is still trying to get them back. The first formal preservation of America's past began with the passage of the Antiquities Act of 1906, primarily aimed at controlling a lucrative trade in painted pueblo pots from the Southwest. This extended some protection to archaeological sites on land owned or controlled by the United States government. There matters remained until the 1940s, when widespread archaeological surveys in areas threatened by federal dam projects yielded a mass of information on site distributions and key cultural sequences before the sites where they occurred vanished forever under human-made lakes (Fowler, 1986).

Since World War II, an accelerating destruction of archaeological sites throughout North America has resulted in a jigsaw pattern of complicated legislation that serves as a framework for cultural resource management activity. This legislation is now so complex that we can do little more than summarize the key provisions of each act since 1960 in Box 20.1.

BOX 20.1

SOME ANTIQUITIES LEGISLATION IN THE UNITED STATES, 1960–1992

This is a summary of some of the key features of federal antiquities legislation, which built on the Historic Sites Act of 1935. This baseline act gave the National Park Service a broad mandate to identify, protect, and preserve cultural properties. It also meant that the federal government acknowledged broad responsibility for archaeological and historic sites on and off federally owned land.

It should be noted that numerous state and Native American tribal laws amplify and complicate this already complex legislative picture. We can summarize only the most basic provisions of each federal act in the space available.

RESERVOIR SALVAGE ACT OF 1960

This act authorized archaeologists to dig and salvage sites that were in danger of destruction. It was a last-ditch measure, but it did make possible some important surveys, as well as many rough-and-ready salvage operations literally under the blade of oncoming bulldozers (Figure 20.3).

HISTORIC PRESERVATION ACT OF 1966

This act set up a national framework for historic preservation, requiring the federal government to establish a nationwide system for identifying, protecting, and rehabilitating what are commonly called "historic places." The act called for the establishment of the National Register of Historic Places (a "historic place" could include prehistoric and historic archaeological sites) and required federal agencies to protect Register properties when development projects were planned.

NATIONAL ENVIRONMENTAL POLICY ACT OF 1969 (NEPA)

The NEPA laid down a comprehensive policy for government land-use planning and resource management. It required federal agencies to weigh environmental, historical, and cultural values whenever federally owned land is modified or private land is modified with federal funds. The idea was that the nature, extent, and significance of archaeological resources should be inventoried, on the assumption that this information would affect land-use planning in the future. This made it a requirement that such surveys be made. It was an attempt to develop a sensible federal policy on archaeological and historic preservation. It ordered all

FIGURE 20.3 (top) Much late 20th century CRM work unfolds in urban settings, a step ahead of developers. (bottom) Underwater archaeologists battle constantly against unauthorized looting of ancient shipwrecks, which only enjoy limited protection against disturbance.

federal agencies to take the lead in historic preservation and to locate properties that might qualify for the National Register. They were also to develop programs to contribute to protection of important historic properties on nonfederal lands.

NEPA and Executive Order 11593 developed requirements that made it essential for archaeologists to prepare and maintain extremely comprehensive information on archaeological resources on state, federal, and privately owned land. This would enable them to assess, at short notice, the potential effects of development on these resources. In addition, the states had begun to develop historic preservation programs of their own, each headed by a state historic preservation officer, as required by the Historic Preservation Act of 1966.

ARCHAEOLOGICAL RESOURCES PROTECTION ACT OF 1979 (ARPA)

The ARPA gave more stringent protection to archaeological sites over 100 years old on federal land. People removing archaeological materials from federal lands without a permit are committing a felony; they can be fined up to $10,000 and sentenced to a year in prison. The penalties rise sharply when more valuable finds are involved. This legislation is aimed at commercial vandals; it does not forbid individuals from removing arrowheads "located on the surface of the ground." Unfortunately, it gives no protection to archaeological resources on privately owned land.

Amendments to ARPA in recent years have tightened the definition of what constitutes an "archaeological resource" and have legislated far more severe penalties for violations of the original law.

ABANDONED SHIPWRECKS ACT OF 1988

This act extended protection to shipwrecks and defined ownership of abandoned vessels in state and federal waters more clearly. It is an important weapon in the fight against unauthorized looting of shipwrecks, looting that all too often masquerades as "underwater archaeology."

For a long time, federal legislation was concerned for the most part with site preservation as opposed to protection and management. This has changed. In particular, the National Environmental Policy Act of 1969 (NEPA) developed requirements that made it essential for archaeologists to prepare and maintain extremely comprehensive information on archaeological resources on state, federal, and privately owned land. This would enable them to assess, at short notice, the potential effects of development on these resources. In addition, states have developed historic preservation programs of their own, each headed by a state historic preservation officer, as required by the National Historic Preservation Act of 1966. The result of all these changes was a dramatic explosion of archaeological effort, much of it contracted by government agencies as well as private companies. It has also resulted in the emergence of cultural resource management as a sophisticated phenomenon, its practice surrounded by an elaborate framework of laws, regulations, and statutes, not only at the federal and state levels but also at the county, city, and Native American tribe levels. Much of this new effort is designed to amplify federal legislation and to adapt it to local conditions. Such local laws have become essential, to deal both with looting and vandalism and also with such issues as repatriation of Native American skeletons and an explosion of destructive urban development throughout North America (Hutt and others, 1993; Smith and Ehrenhard, 1991; see also *Federal Archaeology,* 7(3), 1993).

Underlying this jigsaw of legislation is one fundamental difference between United States law and that, for example, of many European nations. In many countries, antiquities are considered the property of the state, whereas American law is ambiguous. This is because the Fifth Amendment to the Constitution forbids the seizure of private property for public use without just compensation. Private property is almost sacrosanct, and over the years, archaeological resources on private land have come to be thought of as part of that land and therefore the private property of the owner.

While many landowners take the preservation of archaeological resources on their land very seriously, others regard sites as sources of income. The damage done to such sites by pothunters has been incalculable. Often they lease sites for large sums of money and move in quite openly with earth-moving machinery and other sophisticated equipment. The objective is simple—to recover as many valuable artifacts as possible. This nefarious practice continues to this day: witness a recent case at Slack Farm, Kentucky, where an undisturbed Late Mississippian riverside cemetery and settlement were leased by a landowner to a group of pothunters. They dug for weeks before the state police moved in; the site was left looking like a battlefield (Figure 1.5) (Fagan, 1991).

The Slack Farm incident highlights the financial incentives for looters. As the legal and official pressure on looters and pothunters intensifies, prices in the auction room and on the illegal market go up. More and more sites on private and public land are being mined secretly for profit. Among the pieces most in demand are the beautifully painted Mimbres ceramics from the valley of that name in New Mexico (Figure 13.17). Almost all major Mimbres sites, including those on federal and state land, have been ravaged in recent years, many with backhoes. The pace of damage is accelerating rapidly. Between 1980 and 1987, no less than 560 archaeological sites in the Four Corners area of the Southwest alone were looted or vandalized. Many of the artifacts found in them turned up on the open market.

It is in the West that the most extensive damage has been done, for the stunning basketry and pottery of Southwest Native Americans has attracted collectors and dealers for more than a century. One Anasazi basket alone went for $152,000 in a London auction room some years ago, while a Mississippian stone ax was sold in New Orleans for $150,000. Even relatively prosaic vessels are worth several hundred dollars, so there is a flourishing commercial, but underground, trade, which is probably a network of well-connected operators. Their work may not lead to fabulous profits, but does yield enough to keep the enterprise alive. That is not to say that the Midwest and East are immune, as the tragic Slack Farm incident reminds us. The situation is eerily like that of the drug trade. A crackdown in the field leads to higher prices—and in the case of American Indian artifacts, there are plenty of wealthy private collectors at home and overseas who care nothing about ethics. Native Americans have long fought against such activities, which they regard as sacrilege and the theft of their native patrimony, as little more than common greed. Today, archaeologists and Native Americans are developing an uneasy alliance against a common enemy—the looter.

There have been some successful prosecutions under the Archaeological Resources Protection Act. The 2,000-year-old GE Mound is a Middle Woodland Hopewell mound at the Mt. Vernon site in southern Indiana (Munson and others, 1995). Artifacts from the mound came to light in 1988, during road-making operations for an adjacent construction project monitored by a professional archaeologist. Subsequently, looters entered General Electric's property, digging and removing artifacts from the mound without the company's permission. Following anonymous tips, authorities established that looting had taken place with scientific test excavation. While GE installed fences and motion detectors on-site, the U.S. Department of Justice became involved when the chief of the Miami Nation of Indiana expressed concern that the looted artifacts might be sold in other states. One Indiana man was soon arrested and agreed to cooperate with authorities. Subsequently, many of the artifacts were recovered. A two-and-a-half year investigation led to the conviction of five men for ARPA violations. The ringleader, Arthur Gerber, a commercial photographer from Tell City, Indiana, pleaded guilty to three counts of purchase and transport of unlawfully removed artifacts from the GE Mound, of illegal transport, and unlawful commercial sale. He plea-bargained a fine of $5,000, a sentence of 12 months in prison on each count, and three years of supervised release during which he could not purchase, barter, or excavate archaeological resources, or attend artifact shows. Two vehicles used in the looting were confiscated and he agreed to return all GE Mound artifacts in his possession. Four associates were also convicted of lesser offenses. The recovered artifacts included copper axes, breastplates and other artifacts, more than 2,000 bifaces, freshwater pearls, fragments of wooden and leather objects, and cloth. In court, Gerber and his supporting witnesses claimed they were doing "recovery archaeology," when, in fact, they were using shovels and picks to unearth very delicate, exceptionally well-preserved artifacts. The judge told the defendant he was "stealing history," and that he had been doing so for 25 years. Gerber's attorneys appealed the case as far as the U.S. Supreme Court, but the appeal was denied.

The GE Mound case unfolded against a background of shifts in public opinion toward protecting local sites against looters. But many collectors raised the issue of individual rights on private land, lobbying for changes in federal and state legislation. Once the case was closed, the artifacts were reburied, following intense controversy, which revealed widely differing perspectives on reburial and archaeological research practices among archaeologists. To some members of Indiana's Native American Council, the reburied artifacts were a symbol to establish political power and personal prestige while promoting Native American beliefs in heritage rights and spiritual journeys. The entire GE Mound case epitomizes the extraordinary complexity of obtaining convictions in looting cases, and of disposing of the looted artifacts in an environment in which many special interests are involved (for a valuable discussion, see Munson and others, 1995). The convictions may have had the effect of convincing some collectors that their activities are socially unacceptable.

MANAGING THE ARCHAEOLOGICAL RECORD

Cultural resource management, and the archaeological research that goes with it, is but one component of a much larger enterprise—the study of the effects of human activity on the total landscape (Adovasio and Carlisle, 1988). It is part of a much larger concern for the fragile ecology of North America, and the finite archaeological record is only part of the context in which decisions are made about projects that affect the landscape (Fowler, 1986). As we have learned more about ecology, scientists have come to realize that archaeological resources are part of the "public wealth" (Knudson, 1986). Recent legislation, especially the NEPA, reflects this realization, as do the explicitly ecological approaches of archaeological research in recent years. Indeed, the NEPA provided the legal framework for environmental impact statements, the studies required for all major federal and state projects that can affect human life on earth. In this way, the NEPA may well override the notion of private ownership of archaeological sites.

A morass of laws and regulations at all levels and a growing body of legal opinions and court decisions provide an elaborate framework for long-term cultural resource management in American archaeology. This compliance process on even a medium-sized federal project is an attempt to see that cultural resources threatened by the project are properly managed—recorded, evaluated, protected, or, if necessary, salvaged (Fowler, 1986). Conflicting interests and regulations can lead to unforeseen problems, as, for example, when the local Native Americans insisted that the Chimney Rock Mesa skeletons in Colorado, disturbed by vandals, be reburied. The archaeologists wanted to conserve and study the human remains, but they were overruled by the federal land manager on legal grounds.

The procedure of identification and management in the compliance process has three phases:

1. An overview of cultural resources in an area is compiled, ideally consisting of a description of the environment and the ethnographic background, a history of previous research, and a description of the known culture history of the area. Then the authors assess the research potential of the area, identify important research problems, and make management recommendations.

2. An archaeological assessment report involves further inventory and assessment, including reexamination of known sites and surveys for new ones. These reports are especially important for areas where substantial modification of the land is likely to take place as a result of strip mining, dam building, and other such developments. The finished document discusses known cultural resources in the area and recommends additional research needed to evaluate their significance, to determine their eligibility for the National Register of Historic Places, and to establish suitable mitigation measures to

protect them. The assessment report often forms a preliminary environmental impact report on the area.

3. A management plan proposes measures for protecting, preserving, interpreting, and using cultural resources. This is a formal part of the final environmental impact report. To be effective, a management plan should be regarded as a constantly evolving document, maintained and changed as archaeologists continue to manage and monitor the area.

The compliance process, even on simple projects, can be a nightmare, involving the archaeologist as it does in both recommending management strategies and conducting delicate negotiations with several government agencies at once. One of the most interesting examples of a management plan in action is that for the San Juan Basin in the Four Corners area of the American Southwest.

The San Juan Basin has been occupied since around 10000 B.C. Not only Anglos and Spanish-Americans but also several Pueblo groups and Navajo, Apache, and Ute live in the region, which has been subjected to extensive energy development, including strip mining. Still more exploration and mining are planned. Not only that, but large numbers of people will start depending on the area for recreation—and archaeological sites are part of that recreation. At least seven federal, state, and local agencies have some CRM jurisdiction in the area, and several of them have joined in a cooperative management effort. The National Park Service carried out a preliminary assessment study in 1980. At the time, a data base was compiled that contained more than 15,000 sites, with 15 categories of information on each one. An additional 4,000 entries made up a survey file (Plog and Wait, 1982). At the time, it was estimated that this now-inactive data base contained about 70 percent of the known sites in the San Juan Basin. The data base was conceived of as a management tool, with categories of information in it limited to those considered to management potential.

The compliance process involves both federal and state agencies in other management duties as well. They have the responsibility for protecting sites against vandalism, a major problem in some areas. Then the value of each individual resource must be assessed, either on account of its scientific value, established within the context of a valid research design, or because it merits preservation *in situ*. Agencies must also consider how a site can be utilized for the public good. This responsibility means interpreting it for the public, who may either visit the location, as they do at, say, Mesa Verde, or learn about it through books, television programs, popular articles, and so on.

The main goal of cultural resource management in the United States has been preserving sites and artifacts for the information they have yielded or may yield. Experts in the field have confronted a number of management problems:

- Because archaeological sites are a nonrenewable resource, which of them should be saved for future research rather than being investigated now?
- Should data from sites acquired for conservation and planning be used for pure research as well?
- How is the significance of archaeological resources to be established for legal compliance purposes?

MANAGEMENT PROBLEMS

CONSERVATION

Obviously, the basic ethics of archaeology demand that as many sites as possible be preserved. Under ideal circumstances, the sites are not threatened by development, and the investigator can develop a research design based on purely scientific considerations. However, many other variables—budget, the public interest, possible design alternatives in the development project, and mitigation costs, to mention only a few—come into play when sites are threatened by imminent destruction. Then there is the problem of "secondary impacts," when unexpected spin-offs of the main project destroy resources outside the main project area. Don Fowler (1982) cites the monstrous MX missile project in the Great Basin, which would have affected archaeological resources in no fewer than 23 valleys in the region. Although the project primarily would have affected sites in the lowlands, the archaeologists pointed out that most of the sites lay in the foothills and uplands nearby. These would have been affected disastrously by secondary activities such as seismic testing, survey work, and the sheer numbers of construction workers and military personnel brought into the area during the MX project. Whether effective ways of mitigating these secondary impacts would have been possible is questionable. Few, if any, agencies consider such impacts, but they are often critical to archaeologists.

MANAGEMENT VERSUS ACADEMIC RESEARCH

The apparent conflict between resource management on the one hand and academic research in archaeology on the other comes down to a dilemma. Most CRM contracts involve collecting or developing scientifically useful data from a highly specific area, such as the site of an oil-drilling pad or the sites of pylons along a hundred-mile power line. Are such activities meaningful if not tied to other cultural resources in the region? Though compliance requirements may be satisfied, scholarly needs often most emphatically are not (T. F. King, 1983). Although the Historic Preservation Act requires each state to have a plan as a mechanism for management overviews of individual projects, only around half have allocated funds to create such plans.

One reason for the conflict between contract archaeology, with its emphasis on compliance and management, and academic archaeology, which concentrates on basic research, is that most contracting parties assume that archaeology is a descriptive science. Certainly the traditional methods of archaeological research have been inductive. That is, they assume that sufficient facts can eventually be collected to provide enough data for synthesis and inference from the data. Of course, inductive research is useful, especially in the sort of general exploratory work that is carried out in many large survey areas, such as the Cache River Valley in Arkansas (Schiffer and House, 1976). Until recently, most contracting agencies thought of archaeology as a discipline able to conduct piecemeal research. They assumed that the results from each small project would somehow eventually become part of a grand, final synthesis. And until recently, the laws all related to specific projects. This type of archaeology was, in fact, attractive to people with some command of excavation techniques whose final objective was to produce a descriptive site report. Sites or areas were preselected by such criteria as imminence of destruction or availability of salvage funds.

In fact, the 1970s saw much archaeological research become deductive, and archaeologists were now viewing fieldwork and excavation as activities to be carried out only when a specific problem needed solving or a hypothesis needed testing. To these scholars, salvage archaeology for its own sake was an entirely inconsistent activity that simply did not mesh with the specific-problem orientation of deductive research. There has been a dangerous and often unthinking tendency to segment archaeology into two broad camps—the academic, deductive researchers taking on specific problems on one side, and the contract archaeologists involved with salvage, management, and compliance on the other. This insidious distinction is, of course, a gross simplification, for many distinguished academic archaeologists are deeply involved in cultural resource management. Thus there is often constant feedback between emerging archaeological theory and methodology and the realities of contract work, which is always funded on a project-by-project basis and never in a wider, say, regional, context. And in the final analysis, major cultural resource management projects are funded at a far higher level than even the most ambitious academic project—not only for survey and excavation but for analysis and, sometimes, for publication as well (Adovasio and Carlisle, 1988).

Can management and research needs be reconciled? Many CRM projects are small-scale operations, involving no more than a small plot of urban land or a simple inventory of a few acres. Such projects are usually undertaken by freelance archaeologists, as are many of the test excavations required for more significant sites. The reports on these operations are usually of relatively limited circulation and are basically descriptive, even if they are conducted within a sound intellectual context. With large-scale projects of regional or even broader scope, the marriage between management and research needs is much closer.

In recent years, many CRM projects have involved massive archaeological operations and the expenditure of millions of dollars in survey and excavation. The Texas-California pipeline, the Dolores Project in Colorado, and the Black Mesa project in the Southwest (Gumerman, 1984) have all yielded important methodological contributions and sometimes major theoretical perceptions. Most of these projects are conducted by larger private companies that specialize in environmental impact work or by CRM organizations with close ties to academic institutions. For instance, the Institute of Archaeology and Anthropology at the University of South Carolina has developed an elaborate archaeological organization with strong academic ties to the university that carries out major CRM projects in an academic setting. With their excellent technical resources and large project budgets, they are able to conduct detailed research and fine-grained field and laboratory investigations that are beyond the budgetary scope of all purely academic research projects.

Virtually all federal and state agencies have strict requirements for the analysis and reporting of any archaeological data recovered from CRM projects. Such analysis is, of course, very expensive, and it is certain that significant advances in knowledge about the human past will come from major and well-funded CRM projects like the large-scale excavations and surveys conducted as part of the space shuttle launch-pad construction operations at Vandenberg Air Force Base in California (Glasgow, 1996).

As Adovasio and Carlisle (1988) point out, CRM archaeology is the only viable way to identify and document rapidly vanishing archaeological resources in North America. It is also a primary means of assembling large bodies of basic archaeological data, the very kinds of data required to fulfill one of archaeology's major objectives—the explanation of cultural processes. Furthermore, CRM activities are also a primary way of gathering culture-historical data, not only chronological sequences but also detailed records of individual sites and their environments.

"Nowhere else in contemporary archaeology can the methodological and theoretical challenges raised by the 'new archaeology' be realized with greater clarity than in CRM work," write Adovasio and Carlisle (1988). As they point out, this is not only a matter of economic realities but also one of perceiving the opportunity to make major intellectual advances in archaeology while still meeting the requirements of individual contracts. No one can claim that all CRM work is good archaeology, but "good archaeology stands the best chance of answering the questions upon which reasonable management decisions about cultural resources depend."

In short, CRM archaeology offers unique opportunities for archaeologists to test and refine basic operational theories in the field. It provides unusual opportunities to refine existing models of ancient human behavior and to develop new ones. In the 1990s, CRM archaeology, especially when conducted on a large scale, offers unique opportunities for answering basic questions about the prehistoric past. The challenge is to grasp these opportunities and to exploit them to the fullest (Figure 20.4).

RESEARCH DESIGNS

In the context of contract archaeology, the research design is best described as a "frame of reference"—in which basic assumptions, research goals, hypotheses, methodologies, and operating procedures are laid out (Fowler, 1982). Ideally, there should be a hierarchy of research designs. The Historic Preservation Act of 1966 required all states to prepare historic preservation plans. In 1976 the secretary of the interior developed regulations formulating these plans under professional supervision. The surveys, still incomplete, are to include nominations for the National Register of Historic Places, plus inventories and predictions of where all forms of cultural resources may exist.

States are, of course, political rather than cultural entities, so the best overall research designs are those for regions, whether defined topographically, ecologically, or culturally. A good example of a region is the San Juan Basin in the Four Corners area of the Southwest.

Fowler (1982) lists six key elements for a successful research design:

1. A description of the resource base—an outline of current knowledge about the area and its culture history.
2. A statement of the implications of previous research, combined with a statement of basic assumptions and of the investigators' theoretical approach, whether ecological, materialist, or some other.

FIGURE 20.4   CRM excavation goes on year-round. Excavations at the Howorth-Nelson site in southwestern Pennsylvania carried on through the cold winter months, under a heated inflatable shelter. (Courtesy, Society for Pennsylvania Archaeology)

3. A statement of general areas of research interest, including both general and specific problems to be worked on. These questions are the basis for specific hypotheses and related test implications.
4. A description of the kinds of data needed to complete the research design, and specifics on maintaining the quality of the data and on the standards of data required.
5. A formulation of investigative strategies to acquire data of the quality needed. The vital element here is sampling strategies that reflect the realities of time, contract requirements, available funding, and size of the research area.
6. For specific project design, a statement of operating procedures from preliminary fieldwork to completion of the final report must be specified.

Research designs may be laid out in many ways, but the critical point is that they must be dynamic, ever-changing statements—not rigid dogma, but state-of-the-art designs that keep up with new methodological advances and changing circumstances in the field and out of it. A large-scale CRM research design is far more than a plan for archaeological research; it is a management document, an administrative manifesto, and a quality-control manual in the bargain. The administrative and legal skills required of a contract archaeologist are much further-ranging than anything envisaged by an academic researcher.

STRATEGIES OF CRM RESEARCH

With CRM now the dominant force in archaeological fieldwork in North America, the problem of ensuring quality research is of major concern. Two basic strategies are used in CRM work:

1. The conservation approach regards preservation and protection of the archaeological record for humanistic and scientific purposes as the first priority (Lipe, 1970). This is a relatively theory-free and descriptive approach in which management decisions are based on a representative sample of resources in an area.
2. The problem-oriented approach regards CRM as part of contemporary archaeology with all its sophisticated theoretical apparatuses for studying and evaluating the past. In other words, the researcher relies on contemporary knowledge, belief, and concepts in archaeology to make management judgments about the content of the archaeological record in the future (Dunnell, 1985).

The debate about which of these approaches is the most appropriate rages at a high technical level. Much of the argument centers on the conflicting interests of management and pure research. Is one justified in using statistical models that predict the distribution of archaeological sites as a basis for deciding which areas are to be flooded and which are not? Could not one's predictions be so false that they might leave our descendants with a completely skewed archaeological record?

For all the debate about conflicting approaches, and, to be frank, a good deal of dubious research, CRM has brought extensive methodological benefits to basic research, among them a much greater emphasis on prehistoric settlement patterns, sampling procedures, computer applications, and, above all, remote sensing. The San Juan Basin project and others are excellent examples of how sophisticated research designs and theoretical constructs are blended into a multitude of small contract projects. Unfortunately, some agencies and contractors are even today quietly accepting second-rate reports and claiming that even minimal surveys are fulfilling both the requirements and the spirit of the law. Work of such poor quality has led the Society for Professional Archaeologists to prepare ethical guidelines and certification procedures for archaeologists. These steps have helped mitigate the problem of quality somewhat. But the problem is so large and the amount of activity so great that the only long-term solution to the crisis of quality lies in a close relationship between the goals and research techniques of sophisticated scientific archaeology on the one hand and the realities and demands of cultural management and contract archaeology on the other (Dunnell, 1984.)

The crisis of quality has taken a new twist in recent years. Proliferating contract archaeology and CRM have caused an explosion not only of raw data but also of publications and reports on completed projects. The essence of publishing archaeological data is, of course, to make them available to as wide an audience of archaeologists as needs access to them. This distribution is achieved through many books and national or international journals, and even through regional periodicals such as *Plains Anthropologist*. But many contract archaeology reports are either restricted-circulation documents buried in the files of government agencies or private companies or, at best, photocopied publications that have a severely limited circulation—the so-called "grey literature." One authority has estimated that there are about 200,000 grey literature reports in existence, with an additional 10,000 to 20,000 reports accruing annually (McManamon, 1992). Sometimes within months they are forgotten, even destroyed, and the vital data in them are as good as lost to science.

The problem of failure to publish is enormous. Ironically, now that awareness about destruction of the archaeological record is greater than ever, the results of much of this anxiety are being buried, almost as effectively as if they had been destroyed, in inaccessible or temporary publications. Fortunately, electronic media such as CD-ROM have great potential for the future. There is also the National Archaeological Data Base, an on-line system that contains almost 15,000 records of archaeological reports. Any archaeologist with a telephone line or an electronic mail system can now access the data base, which also provides comprehensive site distribution from many states and background environmental information, some of it even seasonal, through the Geographic Resources Analysis Support System (GRASS), the GIS system used by the National Park Service. The National Archaeological Data Base is managed by the Center for Advanced Spatial Technology at the University of Arkansas, Fayetteville. This powerful resource is an invaluable tool for North American archaeologists of all specialties and is mirrored by others being developed in other countries, notably Denmark. The National Archaeological Data Base is really a data base of data bases. It is a system that allows managers to acquire information on everything from county-level site data to progress on reburial and repatriation of burials.

Then there is the issue of what is called *curation,* the careful management of artifacts and other data recovered in the course of CRM activities. The National Park Service, for example, has issued regulations for the curation of federal collections, as required under amendments to existing legislation. But curation is expensive, and the costs of providing permanent conservation and storage are prohibitive. Many museums and other designated repositories are grappling with seemingly insurmountable curation problems for the mountains of archaeological finds that pour in from CRM projects. There are simply not enough funds to pay the real costs of curation.

PROTECTION AND THE PUBLIC

Although expenditures on contract archaeology may no longer be at the levels of the late 1970s, arguments rage about the worth of even a tenth of such expenditure. Though one can argue that knowledge in itself is valuable and is worth spending money on, one must show at least something for the money beyond an abundance of technical and often inaccessible reports. To begin with, one must convince people that the sites are worth preserving. Archaeologists may wax lyrical about the scientific significance of a site within a specific research design, but the public is much more interested in sites with humanistic significance. Gettysburg has a supreme place in our national heritage, as does Mesa Verde. Both are visited by tens of thousands of people each year. The protection afforded by the National Register of Historic Places lists both sites in the "significant" category, a designation that provides a basis for management decisions about cultural resources.

Protection of archaeological sites proceeds through legislation, but until 1979 the United States had no laws forbidding the export of antiquities. The Archaeological Resources Protection Act of 1979 gives federal resource managers and prosecutors access to stringent criminal and civil penalties. These penalties have slowed the destruction of sites on public lands (Smith and Ehrenhard, 1991). The Abandoned Shipwreck Act of 1988 has finally extended a degree of protection to shipwrecks in U.S. waters, though not before incalculable damage was done by professional treasure hunters and amateur divers.

Legislation is not the only protective tool available to archaeologists. The power of eminent domain, zoning, easements, and even tax incentives are tools that may be used to protect cultural resources on private land.

The Archaeological Conservancy is a bright hope, a privately funded membership organization formed in the early 1980s to purchase threatened archaeological sites and manage them as permanent archaeological preserves on hundred-year management plans. The sites this organization has purchased include the Hopewell Mound group in Ohio; Savage Cave in Kentucky, a site with human occupation from Paleo-Indian to Mississippian times; and San Marcos Pueblo in New Mexico, a 2,000-room pueblo near Santa Fe. (You can join by writing to the Conservancy at 5301 Central Ave. NE Suite, 1218, Albuquerque, NM 87108.)

A great deal of the effectiveness in protecting archaeological sites depends on public attitudes toward the past. The basic question is easily stated: Is the public benefiting in practical ways from the expenditure of enormous funds on archaeology?

PUBLIC INVOLVEMENT

Many people think of archaeology as a luxury, and wonder how much taxpayer money is spent on cultural resource management. They are very ambivalent about protecting the past, let alone spending money on it. Yet thousands of other interested citizens have joined amateur archaeological societies in many parts of the country.

Ruthann Knudson, an expert on cultural resource management, points out (1986) that one problem revolves around the ownership of archaeological sites. Who actually owns them, the finds from them, and the records that detail the artifacts removed from them? Does the landowner have the right, or does a government agency? To put the question very simply, are archaeological sites and finds the property of individuals, or are they the property of the public, as represented by the state, and recognized as part of our common cultural heritage? The answer to this question is clear-cut in countries like Australia, where the Crown owns all archaeological sites, even those on private land—just like mineral rights (Cleere, 1989). Ownership of archaeological sites tends to be in the hands of the state in countries where there is a direct tie between the current occupiers of the land and the people who lived at the site in earlier times. The situation is very different in the United States, where the dominant political community has no genetic relationship to prehistoric America (Fowler, 1986; Trigger, 1986).

Furthermore, the right of private ownership of land was established in the American Bill of Rights, the so-called "taking" clause of the Fifth Amendment: "Nor shall private property be taken for public use without just compensation." Since archaeological sites were virtually unknown in the eighteenth century, ownership of them passed to individuals by default.

Today, the legal philosophy about the ownership of America's resources is beginning to change, even if case law on the subject has yet to develop. Increasingly, these resources are being recognized as part of the public wealth, so their treatment is a matter of public concern. This is implicit in much federal legislation since the 1950s and is being addressed much more specifically in recent planning laws affecting everything from forests to archaeological sites. As things stand now, current legislation is beginning to reflect the belief of major policymakers and the people who elected them that archaeological resources have public significance. In the long run, all of us, archaeologists or not, will be accountable for the proper treatment of archaeological resources, regardless of who owns them.

In recent years, massive efforts have gone into informing the public about archaeology, to the point that many archaeologists now talk of "public archaeology," a form of archaeology open and accessible to the public through television, state-sponsored "archaeology weeks," special museum displays, television, and many other avenues, including the Internet. This new outward-looking perspective is vital to the future conservation and preservation of the world's archaeological heritage. The new archaeological buzzword is "stewardship," the notion that we are stewards of a finite resource for the benefit of future generations. As David Poirier and Ken Feder put it (1995), an archaeologist is now "Scholar, Steward, Storyteller."

But there is still a long way to go. Although agencies like the Bureau of Land Management are now expending significant resources on public education, most CRM work has had little effect on public involvement in archaeology. A few projects provide excellent examples of how to reach a wider audience. A team of archaeologists in Annapolis has worked closely with historians and the local community to provide walking tours, lectures, and other educational programs that share with visitors to historic Annapolis the thinking of archaeologists about the past (Potter, 1994). In southern Labrador, archaeologist James Tuck and his research team from Memorial University in Newfoundland have worked closely with the community of Red Bay in developing public awareness of sixteenth-century whaling sites near the village (Tuck and Grenier, 1989).

WORKING WITH NATIVE AMERICANS

The American Indian Religious Freedom Act of 1978 states that it is "the policy of the United States to protect and preserve for Native Americans their inherent freedom to believe, express, and exercise the traditional religions of the American Indian. . . including but not limited to access to sites, use and possession of sacred objects and the freedom to worship through ceremonials and traditional rites" (Fowler, 1982). The act guarantees access to sacred sites, requires federal agencies to adjust management policies to reflect its provisions, and recognizes the existence of sacred sites. This legislation is profoundly affecting American archaeology, for it often involves consulting with tribal and religious leaders if religious sites are to be disturbed.

Most archaeologists have thought of themselves as objective observers of the past or as favorably inclined toward Native Americans. But as Bruce Trigger points out (1986), many archaeologists have been influenced by popular stereotypes of indigenous peoples. Only recently have they become aware of the social significance of their studies. They have also realized that archaeology can no longer be undertaken independent of society. In recent years, for example, Native Americans in many parts of the country have protested strongly about archaeological excavations and surveys in sacred areas in many parts of the West and the Southwest. Recent legislation has given them considerable say in the conduct of CRM on public lands, and they have reacted strongly to development projects destined for sacred, privately owned lands as well. Some groups, like the Hopi, Navajo, and Zuni of the Southwest, are now working closely with archaeologists, using their own archaeological units (Anyon and Ferguson, 1995).

WORKING TOGETHER: THE HOPI EXAMPLE   The Hopi tribe's Cultural Preservation Office has used existing historic preservation legislation as a way of ensuring input on management decisions about archaeological sites on their reservations and in adjacent areas.

The Hopi are trying to participate in the decision-making process as it affects their ancestral sites. Their tribe-funded Cultural Preservation Office includes a tribal archaeologist, project archaeologists, a transcriber, and Hopi research specialists. Its mandate is to preserve the "spiritual and cultural essence of the Hopi, encompassing . . . archaeology, ethnology, recovery of stolen sacred artifacts, farming, and the preservation of the Hopi language" (T. J. Ferguson and others, 1995). As far as archaeology and ethnology are concerned, the Cultural Preservation Office is developing appropriate ways for villages, clans, and religious societies to participate in ongoing research activities. Since clan histories are ritual knowledge, rarely shared with members of other clans, let alone non-Indians, involvement of Hopi elders, the guardians of sacred knowledge, is vital. The Cultural Preservation Office works closely with an advisory group of representatives from each Hopi community, from clans, priesthoods, and religious societies, people who possess vital information for the management of cultural resources. The consultation process is very time-consuming, but essential to overcoming the suspicions many Hopi have of archaeologists and other Western scientists. For example, the Hopi have stated that their participation in the compliance process does not mean that they endorse a specific project or development. Their interest is in protecting as many sites as possible, not in facilitating their destruction. They will never condone the destruction of a site, but they will recommend mitigation through scientific study, on the grounds that a written report of an ancient site is better than no record at all, so that their memory is not lost forever.

The Hopi definition of a site worth preserving is far more wide-reaching. In legal terms, they, and other Native American groups, define every ancestral archaeological site as a traditional cultural property to be protected and left alone. The same term "traditional cultural property" is applied to shrines, sacred sites, springs, quarries, and prehistoric land forms with place names commemorating prehistoric or historic events. Thus, archaeological sites play a central role in the transmission and retention of Hopi culture. Sites can be associated with broad patterns of Hopi history such as clan migrations, and with ancestors significant in the Hopi past—places with the potential to yield valuable historical information.

In practical terms, this broad definition, which many archaeologists now accept, raises interesting problems. For example, the Hopi want sites registered in the state archaeological data bases, but they want to keep the location of certain cultural properties a secret. Both the archaeologists and the Hopi are working to develop accurate ways of defining sites while respecting these concerns.

While many Native Americans are interested in preserving sites, they are not interested in archaeology as such. But the Hopi are interested in archaeology, in how archaeologists collect data, and how they analyze it. Some elders want to compare archaeological findings with their own system of knowledge. Ferguson and others (1995) point out that points of agreement between archaeological and traditional data are often explained in the context of Hopi ritual knowledge. For instance, Hopi prophecies of a time when even the ash left by the ancestors will be used to prove their claims have been connected to the flotation methods used to dissect ancient hearths. Many archaeologists use the Hopi for developing ethnographic analogies to earlier peoples like the Anasazi. But they have done so inconsistently, and without the kind of intellectual rigor demanded by the complexities of Hopi understanding of the ancient cultures of the Southwest.

"The Hopi want to be treated as peers in archaeological research so that their knowledge, values, and beliefs are respected in the same way that archaeologists respect one another when they differ in research methods or interpretations," write Ferguson and his colleagues (1995). They do not want to censor ideas or impose research designs on archaeologists. But they believe that not all information should be divulged, and that not all information is suitable for direct tribal involvement. Hopi standards as to what constitutes legitimate research are slowly evolving, as all parties involved become more familiar with one another, and as archaeology itself evolves. At the same time, tribal members may feel new needs to acquire information about their past. Says Vernon Masayesva, Hopi tribal chairman: "When we talk about cultural preservation, it's not just because we want to save something, I think it's because we don't want to forget who we are as Hopis. . . . You will never know who you are unless you know where you came from. You never know where you are going unless you understand where you have been" (T. J. Ferguson and others, 1995). (For another example, see Ravensloot, 1993.)

THE REPATRIATION ISSUE   Many Indian communities are incensed by the excavation of prehistoric burials and have pushed for laws forbidding such activity and compelling reburial or repatriation of excavated skeletons. Their activist policies and a growing public awareness of the complex issues involved led to passage of the Native American Grave Protection and Repatriation Act of 1990 (Powell and others, 1993).

The 1990 act establishes two main requirements. First, all federal agencies and museums receiving federal funds are required to inventory their holdings of Native American human remains and associated funerary objects. They must also develop written summaries for funerary objects not found in graves, sacred objects, and what are called "objects of cultural patrimony" that are in the collections they control. This inventorying process, which will take years to complete, also requires that agencies and museums establish, as best they can, whether their individual holdings have cultural affiliation, or, in the case of skeletons, lineal descendants with living Native American groups. If they do establish such relationships, then they are required to notify the relevant Native American organization about the existence of the materials, and to offer to repatriate them. Even if they have no cultural affiliation with museum holdings, or disagree with the museum's identifications, a group can still request repatriation.

The second requirement protects all Native American graves and other cultural objects found within archaeological sites on federal and tribal land. This requirement encourages the in-situ preservation of archaeological sites, or at least those parts of them that contain graves. It also requires anyone carrying out archaeological investigation on federal and tribal lands to consult with affiliated or potentially affiliated Native Americans concerning the treatment and disposition of any finds, whether made during formal investigations or by accident. The Repatriation Act also stipulates that illegal trafficking in human remains or cultural objects may result in criminal penalties, authorizes the secretary of the interior to set up a grant program to assist museums and Native American tribes in complying with the law, and authorizes the development of regulations to administer the provisions of the Act in consultation with a national review committee.

The Native American Grave Protection and Repatriation Act will have a profound effect on the way in which American archaeologists go about their business, for it mandates a level of consultation and concern for Native American rights that is far greater than has been the norm in the United States. This is quite apart from the scientific impact on the study of ancient Native American populations. The Native American Rights Fund estimates that there may be as many as 600,000 Native American human skeletons in museums, historical societies, universities, and private collections. There are some 18,500 in the Smithsonian Institution alone (for a complex case involving the Smithsonian, see Bray and Killion, 1994).

The signing of the 1990 act came after years of controversy that pitted, and still pits, Native Americans against scientists. The archaeologists and anthropologists point out that revolutionary new research techniques are beginning to yield a mine of new information about prehistoric North Americans. To rebury the data base for such research would deprive science, and future generations of Americans, of a vital resource, they argue. Others, including some archaeologists, respond that this is an ethical and moral issue, and that such considerations should outweigh any potential scientific gains. While the Smithsonian will examine each repatriation application on a case-by-case basis, many states are considering repatriation legislation and the extension of further protection to prehistoric sites; however, they have no jurisdiction over federal lands. Many museums, universities, and other institutions are adopting specific repatriation policies, and the Society for American Archaeology has drawn up a statement that defines the complex dimensions of the problem—not that these efforts are doing much to dampen emotions on both sides of the issue.

The Native Americans feel deeply about repatriation for many complex reasons, if nothing else because they are concerned about preserving old traditions and values as a way of addressing current social ills. The scientists, for their part, are afraid that they will lose their data base, which, from their perspective, is an intellectual crime.

There will be no quick resolution of the repatriation issue, however promptly and sensitively archaeologists and their institutions respond to Native American concerns and comply with the provisions of the 1990 act. Many of the issues are inchoate, of great moral importance and sensitivity, and address basic questions about the morality of all archaeological research. Only one thing is certain—no archaeologist in North America, and probably elsewhere, will be able to excavate a prehistoric or historic burial without the most careful and sensitive preparation. This involves working closely with native peoples in ways that archaeologists have not imagined until recently. Nothing but good can come of this.

American archaeologists have long regarded their work as a way of studying ancient American Indian lifeways, but the Indians themselves have displayed little interest in archaeology. As Fowler (1982) points out, Western intellectual traditions regard scholarly research as beneficial to the public. Other societies have entirely different cultural values, prohibiting desecration of sacred sites through study by outsiders, even if this activity adds to the common knowledge of the outside world (Johnson and others, 1977). American archaeologists now must forge a working partnership with Native Americans. The influence of this change on archaeology remains to be seen, but it is certain to be profound.

The repatriation issue has international overtones, for native groups outside North America, notably the Australian Aborigines, have striven for strict control of burial excavations. Increasingly, archaeologists and native peoples are working together to hammer out long-term agreements, or at a minimum statements of principle, to cover repatriations and burial excavations. On the international front, the executive committee of the World Archaeological Congress has adopted an accord that calls on archaeologists to be sensitive to the concerns of indigenous peoples. Named the Vermillion Accord, after the town of Vermillion, South Dakota, where it was drafted, the statement calls for respect both for the dead and for the wishes of their descendants, as well as for the scientific research value of human remains. It establishes the principle that agreement on the disposition of human remains be established on the basis of mutual respect for the legitimate concerns for the correct burial of ancestors as well as those of science and education.

The fundamental conflicts between Native American cultural values and religious beliefs and Western science will be very difficult to resolve, a task that will continue far into the future. But archaeologists and Native Americans have a common concern for the preservation of archaeological sites for future generations, both as the settlements and shrines of the ancestors and as a finite scientific archive. Collaboration between native peoples and archaeologists involves far more than management and mitigation. It involves profound respect and sensitivity toward the values and expectations of others in the interests of the long-term public good.

The problems of CRM are a leading issue in contemporary archaeology and will never disappear. All archaeologists are managers of a finite resource, which is banked in various ways—in the ground, within the pages of a report, or by finds and records in a museum storeroom. We as a nation have two alternatives for the future: either collect and interpret information about our cultural resources in a useful manner as an activity that contributes to the public good, or take the easy way out and abandon the archaeological record to extinction.

SUMMARY

- In this chapter we surveyed the destruction of archaeological sites in the United States and outlined some of the federal legislation designed to protect antiquities.
- The 1960s saw the development of the concept of cultural resource management, overall strategies for conservation priorities and management of a finite resource, the archaeological record. New federal legislation, notably the National Environmental Policy Act of 1969 and the Archaeological Resources Protection Act of 1979, laid down regulations for land use and resource policies and also defined archaeological resources as any artifact more than a century old. The Native American Grave Protection and Repatriation Act of 1990 protects Native American graves on federal and tribal lands and requires museums and government agencies to inventory their holdings and to offer to repatriate those with direct affiliations with living groups.
- Much CRM activity is on a small scale. However, larger-scale projects often provide opportunities for major archaeological excavations and surveys that have important bearing on the development of archaeological methods and theories. CRM is having an increasingly important impact on the future direction of American archaeology, on account of both its large budgets and its unique opportunities for large-scale field and laboratory research. There are two basic approaches to cultural resource management: a conservation approach that is basically descriptive, and a problem-oriented one that uses the latest methods of contemporary archaeology to make management decisions about the past. These approaches are the subject of much controversy.
- In recent years, Native American groups have demanded that many Indian skeletons in public and private collections be returned to them, a movement that culminated in the passing of the 1990 act. This controversy has pitted native peoples against scientists not only in North America but in other parts of the world as well. In the future, American archaeologists will have to work closely with Native American communities when excavating sites where burials are likely to be found.

GUIDE TO FURTHER READING

Contract archaeologists and resource managers are still wrestling with the basic issues of their work and have yet to generate an extensive methodological and theoretical literature. Many of the best field reports are, for all intents and purposes, inaccessible to the general reader. Listed here are useful signpost publications to a complicated literature.

Cleere, Henry, ed. *Archaeological Heritage Management in the Modern World.* London: Unwin-Hyman, 1989. A series of essays on CRM in different countries under radically different governments. A fascinating comparative exercise.

Fowler, Don D. "Cultural Resources Management," *Advances in Archaeological Method and Theory* 5 (1982): 1–50. A superb essay on the basic issues of CRM in the early 1980s. Recommended also for its clear exposition and comprehensive references.

Fowler, Don D. "Conserving American Archaeological Resources," in David J. Meltzer, Don D. Fowler, and Jeremy A. Sabloff, eds., *American Archaeology Past and Future,* pp. 135–162. Washington, D.C.: Smithsonian Institution Press, 1986. An excellent account of conservation in North America.

Green, Ernestine, ed. *Ethics and Values in Archaeology.* New York: Free Press, 1984. A series of essays on the ethics of studying the past, with a strong emphasis on cultural resource management.

Smith, G. S., and J. E. Ehrenhard, eds. *Protecting the Past.* Boca Raton, Fla.: CRC Press, 1991. An edited volume that covers a wide spectrum of conservation and management problems.

——21——
ARCHAEOLOGY AND YOU

W**e have two final questions to answer: How can I become an archaeologist? And even if I do not become one, what are my responsibilities as
an informed citizen?

ARCHAEOLOGY AS A PROFESSION

Professional archaeologists are much more numerous than they were even a
generation ago, mostly because the discipline now has many more career tracks.
Archaeology has changed rapidly, from a purely academic discipline into a
profession, with archaeologists performing a multitude of management, conservation, and environmental tasks. Until recently, most American archaeologists
taught in universities and colleges and a few high schools. Once they also
headed archaeology departments of national, state, city, or local museums all
over the country or directed state archaeological surveys. But today, the majority of America's archaeologists work for the National Park Service, the Bureau
of Land Management, or other federal, state, or local agencies in many activities
that can be labeled loosely as cultural resource management. Others are employed by private firms undertaking environmental impact projects, both large
and small, or are in business on their own doing similar work. The specialties of
these archaeologists range from early Plains Indian settlement to historical sites
in New England, from theoretical models of early agriculture to computer simulations. Although most North American archaeologists now work on the
"applied" side of archaeology, a considerable number of academic archaeologists work abroad—in Africa, Europe, Mesoamerica, Peru, and even farther
afield.

But a word of warning! Jobs in archaeology, except those involved in
cultural resource management, are often hard to come by, even with a doctoral
degree.

QUALIFICATIONS

Most archaeological jobs, whether on a campus or in a museum, require an M.A.
degree, but most often a Ph.D. is needed. The doctorate is a research degree
requiring comprehensive seminar, course, and field training in graduate school
followed by a period of intensive fieldwork that in written form constitutes the

Ph.D. thesis. The average doctoral program takes between four and seven years to complete. The M.A. degree is normally completed in two or three years and provides broad, general training in the basic methods and theories of archaeology and world prehistory. In addition to this general knowledge, you will specialize in a local area or in cultural resource management. You may have to write a library thesis and obtain some digging experience as well. The M.A. does not give you as much access to research funds and opportunities as a Ph.D. However, you can do valuable work in cultural resource management or local archaeology.

Do not consider becoming a professional archaeologist unless you have these qualifications:

- An academic record well above average, with in-depth coverage of archaeology *and* anthropology. An A-minus grade point average is a minimal requirement for good graduate schools. Remember that archaeology is part of anthropology. Thus a sound training in general anthropology is essential.
- Some field experience on a dig or survey.
- Strong and meaningful support from at least two qualified archaeologists who are able to write letters for you.
- A strong motivation to become an archaeologist and, for the Ph.D., a specific research interest.
- The type of personality that thrives on hard work and some discomfort, a mass of detail, and long hours of routine laboratory work.
- The ability to face up to a very tight employment situation.
- An interest in teaching or in resource management.
- A moral commitment not to collect artifacts for profit or for personal gain.

GAINING DIGGING EXPERIENCE

Many people want to gain some digging experience, whether or not they intend to go to graduate school. The best way to learn is to take a course in field methods and then volunteer to dig for a time on a summer excavation. Details of these excavations are normally posted on anthropology department bulletin boards or at local museums. There are also endless possibilities for volunteer laboratory work during the academic year. The best way of all to get formal training in the field is to attend a university-sponsored field school and to obtain academic credit for your work. A good school gives you a far better grounding than an informal apprenticeship. General field schools are worthwhile because they combine excavation, laboratory analysis, and academic instruction into one intensive experience. And the camaraderie among participants in such digs can be memorable. Very often, attendance at a field school gives you a basic qualification that will help in getting summer work with a research institute or private contract firm.

Some people venture further and join an excavation overseas for several weeks. By contacting such organizations as the Council for British Archaeology in York, it is possible to obtain details of excavations in progress where volunteers are needed. (Very few digs, either in this country or overseas, pay you to be an excavator.) At the other end of the spectrum are package travel tours that take students to such places as Israel to dig and learn archaeology under close supervision. These can be expensive experiences, often of variable academic quality. Some of them are little more than "grades for labor" operations. Whatever type of dig you choose, an excavation experience is a good way of testing your commitment to archaeology.

UNDERGRADUATE DEGREE

With a B.A., it is possible to get a low-level job in archaeology as a field-worker or laboratory assistant. Someday, however, you probably will need further qualifications, and it is best to acquire these as soon as possible.

Most people who take a B.A. with a major in or emphasis on archaeology never become professionals. Nevertheless, they can enjoy the achievements and perspectives derived from archaeology for the rest of their lives. There are many ways to enjoy archaeology as a lay person. You can join a local archaeological society, participate in excavations and volunteer museum programs, and keep an eye on endangered sites in your neighborhood. Your background in archaeology will enable you to visit famous sites all over the world as an informed observer and to enjoy the achievements of prehistoric peoples to the fullest. I received a postcard mailed from Stonehenge by a former student: "Thank you for introducing me to archaeology," it read. "I enjoyed Stonehenge so much more after taking your course." His postcard made my day, for archaeology cannot survive without the involvement and interest of many people besides professional archaeologists. And as an interested lay person, you have responsibilities.

RESPONSIBILITIES TO THE PAST

Professional archaeologists have ethical responsibilities as members of a demanding profession (Lynott and Wylie, 1995). But everyone interested in archaeology has responsibilities, too. The world's archaeological sites are under attack from many sources: industrial development, mining, and agriculture, as well as treasure hunters, collectors, and professional tomb robbers. In these times of inflation, even modest antiquities fetch high prices on the antiquarian market. No government can hope to free the necessary funds to protect its antiquities adequately. And such countries as Egypt, Guatemala, and Mexico, with rich archaeological heritages, have almost overwhelming problems protecting even their well-known sites. As long as there is a demand for antiquities among collectors and we maintain our materialistic values about personal possessions, destruction of archaeological sites will continue unabated. Even the necessary legal controls to prevent destruction of archaeological sites are just barely in force in most parts of the world (McBryde, 1985; Layton, 1989).

Yet there is still hope, which stems from the enormous numbers of informed people who have gained an interest in archaeology from university and college courses or from chance encounters with archaeologists or the prehistoric past. If sufficient numbers of lay people can influence public behavior and attitudes toward archaeological sites and the morality of collecting, there is still hope that our descendants will have archaeological sites to study and enjoy.

Is there a future for the past? Yes, but only if we all help, not only by influencing other people's attitudes toward archaeology but also by obeying this simple code of ethics:

- Treat all archaeological sites and artifacts as a finite resource.
- Never dig an archaeological site.
- Never collect artifacts for yourself or buy and sell them for personal gain.
- Adhere to all federal, state, local, and tribal laws that affect the archaeological record.
- Report all accidental archaeological discoveries.
- Avoid disturbing any archaeological site, and respect the sanctity of all burial sites.

SUMMARY

- Career opportunities for professional archaeologists can be found in universities, colleges, museums, government service, and private businesses both in the United States and abroad. Most archaeological jobs require at least an M.A. and very often a Ph.D.
- Do not consider becoming a professional archaeologist unless you have an above-average academic record, some field experience, strong support from your professors, and a moral commitment not to collect artifacts for profit.
- Even people who have no intention of becoming professional archaeologists can gain digging experience by attending a field school or by digging overseas.
- Archaeology can give you insight into the past and the potential for involvement as an informed lay person. It will also enable you to enjoy the major archaeological sites of the world in a unique way and to aid in archaeologists' attempts to preserve the past.
- All of us have ethical responsibilities to the past: not to collect artifacts; to report new finds; and to obey federal, state, and tribal laws that protect archaeological sites. Unless we all take our responsibility to the past seriously, the past has no future.

GUIDE TO FURTHER READING

Lynott, Mark J., and Alison Wylie. *Ethics in American Archaeology: Challenges for the 1990s.* Washington D.C.: Society for American Archaeology, 1995. Very much a working document, this important volume lays out the fundamentals of archaeological ethics as a basis for discussion in the profession.

Messenger, Phyllis M., ed. *The Ethics of Collecting Cultural Property.* Albuquerque: University of New Mexico Press, 1989. Invaluable essays on the international trade in antiquities and the ethics behind the controversy.

SOME USEFUL ADDRESSES

Here are three addresses from which you can obtain information about archaeological activities and excavations that need volunteers:

Archaeological Institute of America
Box 1901, Kenmore Station
Boston, MA 02215

The institute publishes the Archaeological Fieldwork Opportunities Bulletin. Members receive *Archaeology Magazine*.

Society for American Archaeology
Railway Express Building
980 2nd Street NE Suite 12
Washington, DC 20002

Society members receive a *Bulletin* and *American Antiquity,* a more technical journal.
For excavation opportunities overseas, contact:

The Council for British Archaeology
Bowes Morrell House
111 Walmgate
York YO1 2UA
England

This admirable organization publishes a monthly *Calendar of Excavations,* which you can obtain by airmail subscription. It contains complete details of volunteer excavations in Britain and sometimes in other parts of the world.

Information on archaeological field schools can be obtained from fliers posted on university department bulletin boards and also from the Society for American Archaeology. The American Anthropological Association publishes a summer field school list annually.

GLOSSARY

This glossary is designed to give informal definitions of words and ideas in the text, particularly those that are theoretical. It is not a comprehensive dictionary of archaeology. Jargon is kept to a minimum, but a few technical expressions are inevitable. Terms such as adaptation and mutation, which are common in contexts other than archaeology, are not listed; a good dictionary will clarify these. Champion (1980) has published a good archaeological dictionary, Scarre (1988) an excellent atlas.

ABSOLUTE DATING   Dating in calendar years before the present; chronometric dating.

ACTIVITY AREA   A pattern of artifacts in a site indicating that a specific activity, such as stone toolmaking, took place.

ACTIVITY SET   A set of artifacts that reveals the activities of an individual.

ALLUVIUM   Geological deposit laid down by the action of a river or stream.

ANALOGY   A process of reasoning whereby two entities that share some similarities are assumed to share many others.

ANALYSIS   A stage of archaeological research that involves describing and classifying artifactual and nonartifactual data.

ANALYTICAL TYPE   Arbitrary groupings that an archaeologist defines for classifying manufactured artifacts. Analytical types consist of groups of attributes that define convenient types of artifacts for comparing sites in space and time. They do not necessarily coincide with actual tool types used by prehistoric people.

ANTHROPOLOGY   The study of humanity in the widest possible sense. Anthropology studies humanity from the earliest times up to the present; it includes cultural and physical anthropology and archaeology.

ANTIQUARIAN   Someone interested in the past who collects and digs up antiquities unscientifically, in contrast to the scientific archaeologist.

ARCHAEOLOGICAL CONTEXT   See Context.

ARCHAEOLOGICAL CULTURE   A group of assemblages representing the surviving remains of an extinct culture.

ARCHAEOLOGICAL DATA   Material recognized as significant as evidence by the archaeologist, and collected and recorded as part of the research. The four main classes of archaeological data are artifacts, features, structures, and food remains.

ARCHAEOLOGICAL RECONNAISSANCE Systematic attempts to locate, identify, and record the distribution of archaeological sites on the ground and against the natural geographic and environmental background.

ARCHAEOLOGICAL THEORY A body of theoretical concepts providing both a framework and a means for archaeologists to look beyond the facts and material objects for explanations of events that took place in prehistory.

ARCHAEOLOGICAL UNIT An arbitrary unit of classification set up by archaeologists to separate conveniently one grouping of artifacts in time and space from another.

ARCHAEOLOGIST Someone who studies the past using scientific methods, with the motive of recording and interpreting ancient cultures rather than collecting artifacts for profit or display.

ARCHAEOLOGY A special form of anthropology that studies extinct human societies using the material remains of their behavior. The objectives of archaeology are to construct culture history, reconstruct past lifeways, and study cultural process.

ARCHAEOMAGNETIC DATING Chronometric dating using magnetic alignments from buried features, such as pottery kilns, which can be compared to known fluctuations in the earth's magnetic field and produce a date in years.

ARCHAIC In the New World, a period when hunter-gatherers were exploiting a broad spectrum of resources and may have been experimenting with agriculture.

AREA EXCAVATION Excavation of a large, horizontal area, normally used to uncover houses and prehistoric settlement patterns.

ARTIFACT Any object manufactured or modified by human beings.

ASSEMBLAGE All the artifacts found at a site, including the sum of all subassemblages at the site.

ASSOCIATION The relationship between an artifact and other archaeological finds and a site level, or another artifact, structure, or feature in the site.

ASSYRIOLOGIST A student of the Assyrian civilization of Mesopotamia.

ATTRIBUTE A well-defined feature of an artifact that cannot be further subdivided. Archaeologists identify types of attributes, including form, style, and technology, in order to classify and interpret artifacts.

ATTRIBUTE ANALYSIS Analyzing artifacts using many of their features. Normally these attributes are studied statistically to produce clusters of attributes that can be used to identify statistical classes of artifacts.

ATTRITIONAL AGE PROFILE The distribution of ages in an animal population that results from selective hunting or predation.

AUGER A drill, either hand- or power-driven, used to probe subsurface deposits.

AUSTRALOPITHECUS Primate whose fossil remains have been found mainly in eastern and southern Africa. Thought to be closely related to the first human beings, who may indeed have evolved among *Australopithecines*.

BAND The simple form of human social organization that flourished for most of prehistory. Bands consist of a family or a series of families, normally with 20 to 50 people.

BATTLESHIP CURVE   A seriation graph formed by plotted points representing, for instance, the rise in popularity of an artifact, its period of maximum popularity, and its eventual decline.

BIOME   Major biotic landscapes in which distinctive plant and animal communities live in harmony together.

BIOSPHERE   All the earth's living organisms interacting with the physical environment.

BLADES   Parallel-sided stone flakes, normally removed from a carefully prepared core, often by means of a punch.

BOWSING   Technique for detecting buried features by thumping the ground and sensing the differences between compacted and undisturbed earth.

BULBAR SURFACE   The surface upon which the bulb of percussion occurs.

BULB OF PERCUSSION   The conelike effect caused by conchoidal fracture on siliceous rocks.

BURIN   A blade tool, flaked on one or both ends to form a small chisel or grooving tool.

CAMBIUM   A viscid substance under the bark of trees in which the annual growth of wood and bark takes place.

CARRYING CAPACITY   The number and density of people per square mile that a specified area of land can support, given a particular subsistence level.

CATASTROPHIC AGING PROFILE   Distribution of ages in an animal population as a result of death by natural causes.

CAUSES   In archaeology, events that force people to make decisions about how to deal with new situations.

CENTRAL-PLACE THEORY   A geographic theory applied to archaeology, stating that human settlements will space themselves evenly across a landscape as a function of the availability of natural resources and other factors. Eventually, these will evolve into a hierarchy of settlements of different size that depend on one another.

CERAMICS   Objects of fired clay.

CHARACTERIZATION STUDIES   The study of sources of raw materials used to make artifacts.

CHIEFDOM   A form of social organization, more complex than a tribal society, that has evolved some form of leadership structure and some mechanisms for distributing goods and services throughout the society. The chief who heads such a society and the specialists who work for the chief are supported by the voluntary contributions of the people.

CHRONOLOGICAL TYPES   Types defined by form that are time markers.

CHRONOMETRIC DATING   Dating in years before the present; absolute dating.

CLAN   A group of people from many lineages who live in one place and have a common line of descent—a kin grouping.

CLASS   A general group of artifacts, like "hand axes," which can be broken down into specific types, like "ovates," and so on.

CLASSIC   In Mesoamerica, the period of vigorous civilization characterized by numerous ceremonial centers and small states.

CLASSICAL ARCHAEOLOGIST   A student of the Classical civilizations of Greece and Rome.

CLASSIFICATION   The ordering of archaeological data into groups and classes, using various ordering systems.

CLOSED SYSTEM   A system that is internally self-regulating and receives no feedback from external sources; a good example is a household heating and cooling system.

CLUSTER ANALYSIS   The process of analyzing clusters of sites in space.

COGNITIVE ARCHAEOLOGY   The study of human intangibles using archaeological data.

COMMUNITY   In archaeology, the tangible remains of the activities of the maximum number of people who together occupy a settlement at any one period.

COMPLEX   In archaeology, a chronological subdivision of different artifact types, such as stone tools or pottery.

COMPONENT   An association of all the artifacts from one occupation level at a site.

CONCHOIDAL FRACTURE   A characteristic fracture pattern that occurs in siliceous rocks, such as obsidian and flint.

CONCHOLOGIST   One who studies shells.

CONSERVATION ARCHAEOLOGY   Another name for cultural resource management.

CONTEXT   The position of an archaeological find in time and space, established by measuring and assessing its associations, matrix, and provenance. The assessment includes study of what has happened to the find since it was buried in the ground.

COPROLITE   Excrement preserved by desiccation or fossilization.

CORE   In archaeology, a lump of stone from which human-struck flakes have been removed.

CORE BORER   A hollow tubelike instrument used to collect samples of soils, pollens, and other materials from below the surface.

CRANIAL   Of or pertaining to the skull (cranium).

CROP MARKS   Differential growth in crops and vegetational cover that reveals the outlines of archaeological sites from the air.

CROSS-DATING   Dating of sites by means of objects or associated artifacts of known age.

CULTURAL ANTHROPOLOGY   The aspects of anthropology focusing on cultural facets of human societies (a term widely used in the United States).

CULTURAL ECOLOGY   The study of the dynamic interactions between human societies and their environments. Under this approach, culture is the primary adaptive mechanism used by human societies.

CULTURAL EVOLUTION   A theory similar to that of biological evolution that argues that human cultures change gradually over time as a result of a number of cultural processes.

CULTURAL PROCESS A deductive approach to archaeological research that is designed to study the changes and interactions in cultural systems and the processes by which human cultures change throughout time. Processual archaeologists use both descriptive and explanatory models.

CULTURAL RESOURCES Human-made and natural physical features associated with human activity.

CULTURAL RESOURCE MANAGEMENT (CRM) The conservation and management of archaeological sites and artifacts as a means of protecting the past.

CULTURAL SELECTION The process that leads to the acceptance of some cultural traits and innovations that make a culture more adaptive to its environment; somewhat akin to natural selection in biological evolution.

CULTURAL SYSTEM A perspective on culture that views culture and its environment as a number of linked systems in which change occurs through a series of minor, linked variations in one or more of these systems.

CULTURAL TRADITION In archaeology, a distinctive tool kit or technology that lasts a long time, longer than the duration of one culture, at one locality or several localities.

CULTURAL TRANSFORMATIONS Changes in the archaeological record resulting from later human behavior, such as digging a rubbish pit into earlier levels.

CULTURE A set of designs for living that help mold human responses to different situations. Culture is our primary means of adapting to our environment. In archaeology, a culture is an arbitrary unit applied to similar assemblages of artifacts found at several sites, defined in a precise context of time and space.

CULTURE AREA An arbitrary geographic or research area in which general cultural homogeneity is found.

CULTURE HISTORY An approach to archaeology that assumes that artifacts can be used to build up a generalized picture of human culture and descriptive models in time and space, and that these can be interpreted.

CUMULATIVE RECORDING Excavating and recording a trench in three dimensions, using both horizontal and vertical observations to reconstruct events at the site.

CUNEIFORM The earliest known script from Mesopotamia, consisting of wedge-shaped markings (Latin, *cuneus,* "wedge").

CURATION Deliberate attempts by prehistoric peoples to preserve key artifacts and structures for posterity. Also used in a modern context to describe the careful management of artifacts and other data recovered in archaeological research.

CYBERNETICS General systems theory.

CYLINDER HAMMER TECHNIQUE Stone-flaking technique using a bone hammer that removes small, flat flakes from a core.

DATA UNIVERSE A defined area of archaeological investigation, bounded in time and space, often a geographic region or an archaeological site.

DATUM POINT A location from which all measurements on a site are made. The datum point is tied into local survey maps.

DEBITAGE   Waste by-products resulting from the manufacture of stone tools.

DEDUCTION   A process of reasoning that involves testing generalizations by generating hypotheses and trying them out with data. Deductive research is cumulative and involves constant refining of hypotheses. Contrasts with inductive approaches, which proceed from specific observations to general conclusions.

DEDUCTIVE-NOMOLOGICAL REASONING   A way of explaining observable phenomena by means of formal scientific methods, testing hypotheses generated from general laws governing human behavior. Some archaeologists believe that this is the appropriate way to explain cultural processes.

DEMOGRAPHY   The study of population.

DENDROCHRONOLOGY   Tree-ring chronology.

DESCRIPTIVE TYPES   Types based on the physical or external properties of an artifact.

DETRITUS   Debris or droppings.

DIFFUSION   The spread of a cultural trait from one area to another by means of contact among people.

DIRECT HISTORICAL ANALOGY   An analogy using historical records or historical ethnographic data.

DIRECT HISTORICAL APPROACH   The archaeological technique of working backward in time from historic sites of known age into earlier times.

DRIFT   A glacial deposit laid down by ice or water in glacial streams, lakes, or arctic oceans.

ECOFACTS   Archaeological finds that are of cultural significance but were not manufactured by humans, such as bones and vegetal remains. Not a commonly used term.

ECOSYSTEM   An environmental system maintained by the regulation of trophic levels (vertical food chains) and by patterns of energy flow.

ECOTONE   A transition zone between habitats.

EGYPTOLOGIST   A student of the cultures of Ancient Egypt.

EPIGRAPHER   One who studies inscriptions.

EPIPHYSIS   The articular end of a long bone, which fuses at adulthood.

ESCARPMENT   A hill range or cliff (a geological term).

ETHNOARCHAEOLOGY   Living archaeology, a form of ethnography that deals mainly with material remains. Archaeologists carry out living archaeology to document the relationships between human behavior and the patterns of artifacts and food remains in the archaeological record.

ETHNOGRAPHY   A descriptive study, normally an in-depth examination of a culture.

ETHNOHISTORY   Study of the past using non-Western, indigenous historical records and especially oral traditions.

ETHNOLOGY   A cross-cultural study of aspects of various cultures, usually based on theory.

EVOLUTIONARY ARCHAEOLOGY   An explanatory framework for the past that accounts for structure and change in the archaeological record.

EXCAVATION   The digging of archaeological sites, removing the matrix and observing the provenance and context of the finds therein, and recording them three-dimensionally.

EXCHANGE SYSTEM   A system for exchanging goods and services between individuals and communities.

EXOGAMY   A rule requiring marriage outside a social or cultural unit (endogamy means the opposite).

EXPERIMENTAL ARCHAEOLOGY   The use of carefully controlled modern experiments to provide data to aid in interpretation of the archaeological record.

EXTRASOMATIC   Outside the body.

FAIENCE   Glazed terra cotta.

FEATURE   An artifact such as a house or a storage pit that cannot be removed from a site; normally, it is recorded only.

FECES   Excrement.

FEEDBACK   A concept in archaeological applications of systems theory reflecting the continually changing relationship between cultural variables and their environment.

FIRE SETTING   Quarrying stone by using fire to shatter the outcrops of rock.

FISSION-TRACK DATING   Observing accumulations of radioactivity in glass and volcanic rocks to produce absolute dates.

FLAKE TOOLS   Stone tools made of flakes removed from cores.

FLOTATION   In archaeology, recovering plant remains by using water to separate seeds from their surrounding deposit.

FOCUS   Approximately equivalent to a phase.

FORM   The physical characteristics—size and shape or composition—of any archaeological find. Form is an essential part of attribute analysis.

FORM ANALYSIS   Analysis of artifacts based on the assumption that the shape of a pot or other tool directly reflects its function.

FORMATION PROCESSES   Human-caused or natural processes by which an archaeological site is modified during or after occupation and abandonment.

FORMATIVE   In Mesoamerica, the period when more complex societies and settlement patterns were coming into being; these led to the complex states of later times (contemporary with the rise of agriculture).

FORM TYPES   Artifact types based on the shape of an artifact.

FORMULATION   In archaeology, the process of making decisions about a research project as a preliminary to formal research design.

FOOT SURVEY   Archaeological reconnaissance on foot, often with a set interval between members of the survey team.

FULLER   A cloth maker.

FUNCTION   In an evolutionary context, the forms that directly affect the Darwinian fitness of the populations in which they occur.

FUNCTIONALISM   The notion that a social institution within a society has a function in fulfilling all the needs of a social organism.

FUNCTIONAL TYPE   Type based on cultural use or function rather than on outward form or chronological position.

GENERAL SYSTEMS THEORY   The notion that any organism or organization can be studied as a system broken down into many interacting subsystems or parts; sometimes called cybernetics.

GEOARCHAEOLOGY   Archaeological research using the methods and concepts of the earth sciences.

GEOCHRONOLOGY   Geological dating.

GLACIAL EUSTACY   The adjustments in sea levels and the earth's crust resulting from expansion and contraction of Pleistocene ice sheets.

GLAZE   A form of pottery slip with additives that cause the coating to vitrify in the kiln.

HABITAT   An area in the biome where different communities and populations flourish, each with specific locales.

HALF-LIFE   The time required for one-half of a radioactive isotope to decay into a stable element. Used as a basis for radiocarbon and other dating methods.

HEURISTIC   Serving to find out; a means of discovery.

HIEROGLYPHS   Ancient writing featuring pictographic or ideographic symbols; used in Egypt, Mesoamerica, and elsewhere.

HISTORICAL ARCHAEOLOGY   The study of archaeological sites in conjunction with historical records. Sometimes called historic sites archaeology.

HISTORIOGRAPHY   The process of studying history.

HISTORY   Study of the past through written records.

HOMINID   A member of the family Hominidae, represented today by one species, *Homo sapiens*.

HOMO ERECTUS   Human beings who evolved from Lower Pleistocene hominids. They possessed larger brains and made more elaborate stone tools than their predecessors and settled in much more extreme environments, as far apart as western Europe, Asia, and tropical Africa.

HOMOTAXIAL   Describing strata or cultures that have the same relationship to one another but are not necessarily contemporaneous.

HORIZON   A widely distributed set of culture traits and artifact assemblages whose distribution and chronology allow researchers to assume that they spread rapidly. Often, horizons are formed of artifacts that were associated with widespread, distinctive religious beliefs.

HORIZONTAL (AREA) EXCAVATION   Archaeological excavation designed to uncover large areas of a site, especially settlement layouts.

HOUSEHOLD UNIT   An arbitrary archaeological unit defining artifact patterns reflecting the activities that take place around a house and assumed to belong to one household.

HYDROLOGY   The scientific study of water, its properties, and its laws.

IDEOLOGY   The knowledge or beliefs developed by human societies as part of their cultural adaptation.

INDUCTION   Reasoning by which one proceeds from specific observations to general conclusions.

INDUSTRIAL ARCHAEOLOGY   The study of sites of the Industrial Revolution and later.

INDUSTRY   All the particular artifacts (bone, stone, wood) found at a site that were made at the same time by the same population.

INEVITABLE VARIATION   The notion that cultures change and vary with time, cumulatively. The reasons for these changes are little understood.

INORGANIC MATERIALS   Objects that are not part of the animal or vegetable kingdoms.

INTERPRETATION   The stage in research at which the results of archaeological analyses are synthesized and we attempt to explain their meaning.

INTERSTADIAL   A period of slightly warmer climate between two cold periods during a major glaciation.

KINSHIP   In anthropology, relationships between people that are based on real or imagined descent or, sometimes, on marriage. Kinship ties impose mutual obligations on all members of a kin group; these ties were at the core of most prehistoric societies.

KNAPPER   One who manufactures stone artifacts.

LEACHING   Water seeping through the soil and removing the soluble materials from it.

LEVALLOIS TECHNIQUE   Stoneworking technique that involves preparing a bun-shaped core from which one preshaped flake is removed.

LIMITED-AREA RECONNAISSANCE   Comprehensive door-to-door inquiries, supported by actual substantiation of claims that sites exist by checking on the ground. This method fails to give information on proportions of different sites in an area.

LINEAGE   A kinship that traces descent through either the male or female members.

LITHIC   Of or pertaining to stone.

LITHIC EXPERIMENTATION   Experimenting with the manufacture of stone tools. A useful analytical approach to the interpretation of prehistoric artifacts.

LOESS   Windblown glacial soil.

LOST-WAX TECHNIQUE   A method of bronze-working that employs a wax model of the object. The mold is assembled with wax in place of the artifact. The wax is then melted and replaced with molten bronze. The technique was much-used by the Shang bronze workers of China.

LOWER-LEVEL THEORY   A means of identifying site-formation processes.

MAGNETOMETER   A subsurface detection device that measures minor variations in the earth's magnetic field and locates archaeological features before excavation.

MATERIAL CULTURE   Technology and artifacts.

MATRIARCHAL   Characterized by family authority resting with the woman's family.

MATRILINEAL   Characterized by descent reckoned through the female line only.

MATRILOCAL   Characterized by married couples living with or near the wife's mother.

MATRIX   The surrounding deposit in which archaeological finds are situated.

MESOLITHIC   Rather dated name sometimes applied by Old World archaeologists to the period of transition between the Paleolithic and Neolithic eras. No precise economic or technological definition has been formulated.

MICA   A mineral that occurs in a glittering, scaly form, widely prized for ornament.

MIDDEN   A deposit of occupation debris, rubbish, or other by-products of human activity.

MIDDLE-RANGE THEORY   A way of seeking accurate means for identifying and measuring specified properties of past cultural systems.

MIDWESTERN TAXONOMIC SYSTEM   A system of archaeological units developed before World War II to organize artifacts and sites in North America; still in widespread use in modified form.

MITIGATION   In archaeology, measures taken to minimize destruction on archaeological sites.

MODEL   A theoretical reconstruction of a set of phenomena, devised to explain them better. Archaeological models can be descriptive or explanatory.

MODIFIED DIFFUSIONISM   A form of diffusionist theory, espoused by V. Gordon Childe and others, that allows for some local cultural evolution.

MONOTHEISTIC   Recognizing only one god.

MORAINE   A deposit of debris left by an advancing or retreating glacier.

MULTILINEAR CULTURAL EVOLUTION   A theory of cultural evolution that sees each human culture evolving in its own way through adaptation to diverse environments. Sometimes divided into four broad stages of evolving social organization (band, tribe, chiefdom, and state-organized society).

NATURAL TRANSFORMATIONS   Changes in the archaeological record resulting from natural phenomena that occur after the artifacts are deposited in the ground.

NATURAL TYPE   An archaeological type coinciding with an actual category recognized by the original toolmaker.

NEGATIVE FEEDBACK   A response to a system that lessens the chance of change.

NEOLITHIC   A dated Old World term referring to the period of the Stone Age when people were cultivating without metals.

NICHE   The physical space occupied by an organism, its functional role in the community, and how it is constrained by other species and external forces.

NORMATIVE VIEW   A view of human culture arguing that one can identify the abstract rules regulating a particular culture; a commonly used basis for studying archaeological cultures over time.

OBJECT CLUSTERING   An approach to typology based on clusters of human artifacts that are seen as specific classificatory types.

OBSIDIAN   Volcanic glass.

OBSIDIAN HYDRATION   A dating method that measures the thickness of the hydration layer in obsidian artifacts. The hydration layer is caused by absorption of water on exposed surfaces of the rock.

OPEN SYSTEM   In archaeology, cultural systems that interchange both energy and information with their environment.

ORAL TRADITION   Historical traditions, often genealogies, passed down from generation to generation by word of mouth.

ORDERING   In archaeology, the arranging of artifacts in logical classes and in chronological order.

ORGANIC MATERIALS   Materials such as bone, wood, horn, or hide that were once living organisms.

OSSIFICATION   The fusion of a limb bone with its articular end. Implies calcification of soft tissue into bonelike material.

OSTEOLOGIST   One who studies bones.

PALEOANTHROPOLOGIST   An archaeologist who studies the archaeology of the earliest human beings.

PALEOBOTANIST   One who studies prehistoric botany.

PALEOECOLOGY   The modern study of past ecology.

PALEOLITHIC   The Old Stone Age.

PALEONTOLOGY   The study of fossil (or ancient) bones.

PALYNOLOGY   Pollen analysis.

PATINATION   Natural weathering on the surface of rocks and artifacts.

PATRILINEAL   Characterized by descent reckoned through the male line only.

PATRILOCAL   Characterized by married couples living with or near the husband's father.

PATTERNS OF DISCARD   Remains left for investigation after natural destructive forces have affected artifacts and food remains abandoned by their original users.

PEDOLOGY   The scientific study of soil.

PERCEIVED ENVIRONMENT   The physical environment as perceived by a human society; does not coincide with the archaeologist's perception of the same phenomenon.

PERIGLACIAL   Surrounding a glacial area.

PERIOD   An archaeological unit defining a major stretch of prehistoric time; it contains several phases and pertains to a wide area.

PERMAFROST   Permanently frozen subsoil.

PETROLOGICAL ANALYSIS   Examining thin sections of stone artifacts to determine the provenance of the rock used to make them.

PETROLOGY   The study of rocks; in archaeology, analysis of trace elements and other characteristics of rocks used to make such artifacts as ax blades, which were traded over long distances.

PHASE   An archaeological unit defined by characteristic groupings of cultural traits that can be identified precisely in time and space. It lasts for a relatively short time and is found at one or more sites in a locality or region. Its cultural traits are clear enough to distinguish it from other phases.

PHYSICAL ANTHROPOLOGY   Basically, biological anthropology, which includes the study of fossil human beings, genetics, primates, and blood groups.

PLANIMETRIC MAPS   Maps used to record details of archaeological sites; they contain no topographic information.

PLEISTOCENE   The last major geological epoch, extending from about 2 million years ago until about 11,500 years ago. It is sometimes called the Quaternary or the Great Ice Age.

POPULATION   In sampling methods, the sum of sampling units selected within a data universe.

POSITIVE FEEDBACK   A system's response to external stimuli that leads to further change and reinforces it.

POSTCLASSIC   A stage in Mesoamerican prehistory during which militarism arose, such as that of the Aztec.

POSTPROCESSUAL ARCHAEOLOGY   Theoretical approaches that search for the meaning of the archaeological record, for the ideology and structure of ancient societies. A reaction to processual archaeology.

POTASSIUM-ARGON DATING   An absolute dating technique based on the decay rate of potassium 40, which becomes argon 40.

POTSHERD   A fragment of a clay vessel.

PRECLASSIC   See Formative.

PREHISTORY   The millennia of human history preceding written records. Prehistorians study prehistoric archaeology.

PRESSURE FLAKING   A stoneworking technique in which thin flakes are removed from a core or an artifact by applying hand or chest pressure.

PRIMARY CONTEXT   An undisturbed association, matrix, and provenance.

PRIME MOVERS   An early concept in the study of the origins of civilization, meaning a single, primary cause generating urban societies; many theorists considered irrigation a prime mover of Egyptian civilization.

PROBABILISTIC SAMPLING   Archaeological sampling based on formal statistical criteria. This method enables researchers to use probability statistics in analyzing data.

PROCESS   In archaeology, the cultural change that takes place as a result of interactions between a cultural system's elements and the system and its environment.

PROVENANCE   The position of an archaeological find in time and space, recorded three-dimensionally.

PROXIMAL   Describing the end of a bone nearest to the skeleton's center line; opposite to distal.

PULSE RADAR   Use of a pulse induction meter that applies pulses of magnetic field to the soil; this method can be used to find graves, metals, and pottery.

QUADRAT   A unit of spatial analysis used to divide an area into cells for analysis.

QUATERNARY   Geological time since the beginning of the Pleistocene up to recent times. The exact date of its commencement is uncertain, but it is more than 2 million years ago.

RADIOCARBON DATING   An absolute dating method based on measuring the decay rate of the carbon isotope, carbon 14, to stable nitrogen. The resulting dates are calibrated with tree-ring chronologies, from radiocarbon ages into dates in calendar years.

RANDOM SAMPLING   Sampling based on a totally random selection of sample units to be investigated.

RECIPROCITY   In archaeology, the exchange of goods between two parties.

REDISTRIBUTION   The dispersing of trade goods from a central place throughout a society, a complex process that was a critical part of the evolution of civilization.

REFITTING   The reassembling of stone debitage and cores to reconstruct ancient lithic technologies.

REGION   A geographically defined area in which ecological adaptations are basically similar.

RELATIVE CHRONOLOGY   A time scale developed by the law of superposition or artifact ordering.

REMOTE SENSING   Reconnaissance and site survey methods using such devices as aerial photography to detect subsurface features and sites.

RESEARCH DESIGN   A carefully formulated and systematic plan for executing archaeological research.

RESISTIVITY SURVEY   The measurement of differences in electrical conductivity in soils, used to detect buried features such as walls and ditches.

SAMPLE UNIT   An arbitrary or nonarbitrary unit of the data universe, used for sampling archaeological data.

SCANNER IMAGERY   A method of recording sites from the air using infrared radiation that is beyond the practical spectral response of photographic film. Useful for tracing prehistoric agricultural systems that have disturbed the topsoil over wide areas.

SCIENCE   A way of acquiring knowledge and understanding about the parts of the natural world that can be observed. A disciplined and highly ordered search for knowledge carried out systematically.

SEASONALITY   Seasonal occupation.

SECONDARY CONTEXT   A context of an archaeological find that has been disturbed by subsequent human activity or natural phenomena.

SELECTIVE EXCAVATION   Archaeological excavation of parts of a site using sampling methods or carefully placed trenches that do not uncover the entire site.

SERIATION   Methods used to place artifacts in chronological order; artifacts closely similar in form or style are placed close to one another.

SETTLEMENT PATTERN   Distribution of human settlement on the landscape and within archaeological communities.

SHADOW SITES   Archaeological sites identified from the air, where oblique light can show up reduced topography of sites invisible on the ground.

SITE   Any place where objects, features, or ecofacts manufactured or modified by human beings are found. A site can range from a living site to a quarry site, and it can be defined in functional and other ways.

SITE-CATCHMENT ANALYSIS   Inventorying natural resources within a given distance of a site.

SITE-FORMATION PROCESSES   Cultural and noncultural phenomena that act on the formation of the archaeological record.

SITE PLANS   Specially prepared maps for recording the horizontal provenance of artifacts, food remains, and features. They are keyed to topographic maps.

SITE SURVEY   The collection of surface data and evaluation of each site's archaeological significance.

SLIP   A fine, wet finish applied to the surface of a clay vessel prior to its firing and decoration.

SOCIAL ANTHROPOLOGY   The British equivalent of cultural anthropology, but emphasizing sociological factors.

SOCIOCULTURAL   Combining social and cultural factors.

SODALITY   A nonkinship organization within a society that cuts across kinship groups and lineages for specific purposes that add to the cohesiveness of that society.

SONDAGE   See Test Pit.

SPECTROGRAPHIC ANALYSIS   Chemical analysis that involves passing the light from a number of trace elements through a prism or diffraction grating that spreads out the wavelengths in a spectrum. This enables researchers to separate the emissions and identify different trace elements. A useful approach for studying metal objects and obsidian artifacts.

STAGE   A technological subdivision of prehistoric time that has little chronological meaning but denotes the level of technological achievement of societies within it, such as the Stone Age.

STELA (OR STELE)   A column or stone slab, often with an inscribed or sculptured surface.

STRATIFIED SAMPLING   A probabilistic sampling technique used to cluster and isolate sample units, when regular spacing is inappropriate for cultural reasons.

STRATIGRAPHY   Observation of the superimposed layers in an archaeological site.

STRATUM   A single-deposited or cultural level.

STRUCTURAL ARCHAEOLOGY   A theoretical approach to archaeology based on the assumption that codes and rules produce observed systems of relations in human culture.

STYLE   In an evolutionary context, a means of describing forms that do not have detectable selective values.

STYLISTIC ANALYSIS Artifact analysis that concentrates not only on form and function but also on the decorative styles used by the makers—a much-used approach to ceramic analysis.

STYLISTIC ATTRIBUTES Attributes based on stylistic features.

STYLISTIC TYPE Type based on stylistic distinctions.

SUBAREA The subdivision of an archaeological area, normally defined by geographic or cultural considerations.

SUBASSEMBLAGE An association of artifacts denoting a particular form of prehistoric activity practiced by a group of people.

SURFACE SURVEY The collecting of archaeological finds from sites with the objective of gathering representative samples of artifacts from the surface. Surface surveys also establish the types of activity on the site, locate major structures, and gather information on the most densely occupied areas of the site that could be most productive for total or sample excavation.

SYNTHESIS The assembling and analyzing of data preparatory to interpretation.

SYSTEMATICS In archaeology, procedures for creating sets of archaeological units derived from a logical system for a particular purpose.

SYSTEMATIC SAMPLING A refinement of random sampling in which one unit is chosen, then others at regular intervals from the first. Useful for studying artifact patterns.

TAPHONOMY The study of the processes by which animal bones and other fossil remains are transformed after deposition.

TAXONOMY An ordered set of operations that results in the subdividing of objects into ordered classifications.

TECHNOLOGICAL ANALYSIS The study of technological methods used to make an artifact.

TECHNOLOGICAL ATTRIBUTES (TECHNOLOGICAL TYPES) Attributes based on technological features of an object.

TECTONIC Referring to the earth's crust; a tectonic movement is an earthquake.

TELEHISTORIC SITES Sites far removed from written records; prehistoric sites.

TELL A mound; used to refer to archaeological sites of this type in the Near East.

TEMPER Coarse material such as sand or shell added to fine pot clay to make it bond during firing.

TEMPERING A process for hardening iron blades that involves heating and rapid cooling. Also, material added to potter's clay.

TEST PIT An excavation unit used to sample or probe a site before large-scale excavation or to check surface surveys.

THERMOLUMINESCENCE A chronometric dating method that measures the amount of light energy released by a baked clay object when heated rapidly. Gives an indication of the time elapsed since the object was last heated.

THREE-AGE SYSTEM A technological subdivision of the prehistoric past developed in 1806 for Old World prehistory.

TOPOGRAPHIC MAPS Maps that can be used to relate archaeological sites to basic features of the natural landscape.

TOTAL EXCAVATION Complete excavation of an archaeological site. Normally confined to smaller sites, such as burial mounds or campsites.

TRACE ELEMENTS Minute amounts of chemical elements found in rocks that emit characteristic wavelengths of light when heated to incandescence. Trace-element analysis is used to study the sources of obsidian and other materials traded over long distances.

TRADITION A persistent technological or cultural pattern identified by characteristic artifact forms. These persistent forms outlast a single phase and can occur over a wide area.

TRANSFORMATIONAL PROCESSES Processes that transform an abandoned prehistoric settlement into an archaeological site through the passage of time. These processes can be initiated by natural phenomena or human activity.

TRIBE A larger group of bands unified by sodalities and governed by a council of representatives from the bands, kin groups, or sodalities within it.

TRYPANOSOMIASIS Sleeping sickness.

TSETSE A fly that carries trypanosomiasis. Belts of tsetse-fly country in Africa prevent inhabitants from raising cattle.

TUFF Solidified volcanic ash.

TYPE In archaeology, a grouping of artifacts created for comparison with other groups. This grouping may or may not coincide with the actual tool types designed by the original manufacturers.

TYPE FOSSIL A tool characteristic of a particular "archaeological era," a dated concept borrowed from geology.

TYPOLOGY The classification of types.

UNAERATED Not exposed to the open air.

UNDERWATER ARCHAEOLOGY The study of archaeological sites and shipwrecks beneath the surface of the water.

UNIFORMITARIANISM The doctrine that the earth was formed by the same natural geological processes that are operating today.

UNILINEAR CULTURAL EVOLUTION A late nineteenth-century evolutionary theory envisaging all human societies as evolving along one track of cultural evolution, from simple hunting and gathering to literate civilization.

UNIT In archaeology, an artificial grouping used for describing artifacts.

USE-WEAR ANALYSIS Microscopic analysis of artifacts to detect signs of wear through use on their working edges.

VARVES Annual clay deposits made by retreating and melting glaciers. Used to measure recent Pleistocene geological events.

VERTICAL EXCAVATION Excavation undertaken to establish a chronological sequence, normally covering a limited area.

VOTIVE Intended as an offering as a result of a vow.

ZOOARCHAEOLOGY The study of animal remains in archaeology.

BIBLIOGRAPHY

T his bibliography is not intended as a comprehensive reference guide to method and theory in archaeology. Rather, it is a compilation of some sources used to compile this book and a cross section of important methodological and theoretical research. Readers interested in probing even more deeply into the literature should consult the guide to further reading at the end of each chapter. In order to keep the bibliography within manageable limits, I have tended to cite more general works, on the assumption that readers will use the references in these to delve more deeply into the literature.

Adams, R. E. W. 1975. "Stratigraphy," in T. R. Hester, R. F. Heizer, and J. A. Graham, eds., *Field Methods in Archaeology,* 6th ed., pp. 147–162. Palo Alto, Calif.: Mayfield.

Adams, R. E. W., and others. 1981. "Radar Mapping, Archaeology, and Ancient Maya Land Use," *Science* 213 (4515): 1457–1462.

Adams, R. M. 1974. *The Uruk Landscape.* Chicago: University of Chicago Press.

Adams, W. Y., and E. W. Adams. 1991. *Archaeological Typology and Practical Reality.* Cambridge: Cambridge University Press.

Adkins, Lesley, and Roy Adkins. 1989. *Archaeological Illustration.* Cambridge: Cambridge University Press.

Adovasio, J. M. 1979. *Basketry Technology: A Guide to Identification and Analysis.* Hawthorne, N.Y.: Aldine.

Adovasio, J. M., and J. D. Gunn. 1977. "Style, Basketry, and Basketmakers," in J. Hill and J. D. Gunn, eds., *The Individual in Prehistory,* pp. 137–154. Orlando, Fla.: Academic Press.

Adovasio, J. M., and R. C. Carlisle. 1988. "Some Thoughts on Cultural Resource Management Archaeology in the United States," *Antiquity* 62: 72–87.

Ahlstrom, Richard V. N., and others. 1991. "Evaluating Tree-Ring Interpretations at Walpi Pueblo, Arizona." *American Antiquity* 56 (4): 628–644.

Aikens, C. M. 1970. *Hogup Cave.* University of Utah Anthropological Papers, No. 93.

———. 1978. "The Far West," in J. D. Jennings, ed., *Ancient Native Americans,* 2d ed., pp. 131–182. New York: Freeman.

Aitken, M. J. 1984. *Thermoluminescence Dating.* London: Academic Press.

———. 1990. *Science-based Dating in Archaeology.* New York: Longmans.

Akazawa, T., and C. M. Aikens. 1986. *Prehistoric Hunter-Gatherers in Japan.* Tokyo: University Museum, Bulletin 27.

Aldenderfer, Mark, ed. 1987. *Quantitative Research in Archaeology: Progress and Prospects*. Newberry Park, Calif; Sage Publications, 1987.

Alexander, J. 1970. *The Directing of Archaeological Excavations*. New York: Humanities Press.

Allan, W. 1965. *The African Husbandman*. Edinburgh: Oliver and Boyd.

Alva, Walter, and Christopher Donnan. 1993. *Royal Tombs of Sipán*. Los Angeles: Fowler Museum of Cultural History, UCLA.

Ambler, J. R. 1984. "The Use and Abuse of Predictive Modeling in CRM," *American Archaeology* 4: 140–145.

Ammerman, A. J. 1981. "Surveys and Archaeological Research," *Annual Review of Anthropology* 10: 63–88.

Ammerman, A. J., and G. D. Schaffer. 1981. "Neolithic Settlement Patterns in Calabria," *Current Anthropology* 22: 430–432.

Anawalt, P. 1981. *Indian Clothing Before Cortés*. Norman: University of Oklahoma Press.

Anderson, Duane. 1985. "Reburial: Is It Reasonable?" *Archaeology* 38 (5): 48–51.

Anderson, D. G., and G. T. Hanson. 1988. "Early Archaic Settlement in the Southeastern United States," *American Antiquity* 53: 262–286.

———— and others. 1995. "Paleoclimate and the Potential Food Reserves of Mississippian Societies: A Case Study from the Savannah River Valley," *American Antiquity* 60 (2): 258–286.

Anderson, J. E. 1969. *The Human Skeleton: A Manual for Archaeologists*. Ottawa: National Museum of Canada.

Anton, F. 1988. *Ancient Peruvian Textiles*. London: Thames and Hudson.

Anyon, Roger, and T. J. Ferguson. 1995. "Cultural Resources Management at the Pueblo of Zuni, New Mexico, U.S.A." *Antiquity* 69: 913–930.

Arnold, B. 1992. "The Past as Propaganda," *Archaeology* 45 (4): 30–37.

Arnold, D. E. 1988. *Ceramic Theory and Cultural Process*. Cambridge: Cambridge University Press.

Arnold, P. J. 1991. *Domestic Ceramic Production and Spatial Organization*. Cambridge: Cambridge University Press.

Arriaza, Bernardo. 1995. "Chile's Chinchorro Mummies," *National Geographic Magazine* 103 (3): 68–88.

Asch, D. L. 1975. "On Sample Size Problems and the Uses of Nonprobabilistic Sampling," in J. A. Mueller, ed., *Sampling in Archaeology,* pp. 170–191. Orlando, Fla.: Academic Press.

Atkinson, R. J. C. 1957. "Worms and Weathering," *Antiquity* 31: 46–52.

————. 1969. "Moonshine on Stonehenge," *Antiquity* 43: 212–216.

Avery, G., and L. G. Underhill. 1986. "Seasonal Exploitation of Seabirds by Late Holocene Coastal Foragers," *Journal of Archaeological Science* 13: 339–360.

Bahn, Paul. *Easter Island Earth Island*. New York: Thames and Hudson, 1992.

Bahn, Paul, and J. Vertut. 1988. *Images of the Ice Age*. New York: Viking Penguin.

Bailey, G. N., ed. 1981. *Hunter-Gatherer Economy in Prehistory*. Cambridge: Cambridge University Press.

————. 1983. "Concepts of Time in Quaternary Prehistory," *Annual Review of Anthropology* 12: 165–192.

Bailey, G. N., M. R. Deith, and N. J. Shackleton. 1982. "Oxygen Isotope Analysis and Seasonality Determinants: Limits and Potential of a New Technique," *American Antiquity* 48: 390–398.

Baillie, M. G. L. 1982. *Tree-Ring Dating and Archaeology*. Chicago: University of Chicago Press.

Baker, C. M. 1978. "The Size Effect: An Explanation of Variability in Surface Artifact and Assemblage Content," *American Antiquity* 43: 288–293.

Bareis, C. F., and J. W. Porter, eds. 1984. *American Bottom Archaeology*. Urbana: University of Illinois Press.

Barfield, Lawrence. 1994. "The Iceman Revisited," *Antiquity* 68 (258): 10–26.

Barker, P. 1986. *Understanding Archaeological Excavation*. London: Batsford.

————. 1995. *Techniques of Archaeological Excavation*. New York: Humanities Press.

Barkow, J.H., and others, eds. 1992. *The Adapted Mind*. Oxford: Oxford University Press.

Bartel, B. 1982. "A Historical Review of Ethnological and Archaeological Analyses of Mortuary Practice," *Journal of Anthropological Archaeology* 1: 32–58.

Bass, G. F. 1966. *Archaeology Underwater*. London: Thames and Hudson.

————. 1970. *A History of Seafaring from Underwater Archaeology*. London: Thames and Hudson.

————, ed. 1988. *Ships and Shipwrecks of the Americas*. London: Thames and Hudson.

———— and others. 1984. "A Late Bronze Age Shipwreck at Kas, Turkey," *International Journal of Nautical Archaeology* 13 (4): 271–279.

————. 1989. "The Bronze Age Shipwreck at Ulu Burun: 1986 Campaign," *International Journal of Nautical Archaeology* 93: 1–29.

Baugh, Timothy G., and Jonathan E. Ericson, eds. 1994. *Prehistoric Exchange Systems in North America*. New York: Plenum.

Beattie, O., and J. Geiger. 1986. *Frozen in Time: The Fate of the Franklin Expedition*. London: Bloomsbury Publications.

Beaudry, M., and others. 1991. "Artifacts and Active Voices: Material Culture as Social Discourse," in R. McGuire and R. Paynter, eds., *The Archaeology of Inequality*. Oxford: Blackwell.

Becker, B. 1993. "An 11,000-year German pine and oak dendrochronology for radiocarbon calibration," *Radiocarbon* 35 (1): 201–213.

Bender, B. 1990. "The Dynamics of Nonhierarchical Societies," in Steadman Upham, ed., *The Evolution of Political Systems,* pp. 247–263. Cambridge: Cambridge University Press.

Bermannr, Marc. 1994. *Lukurmata: Household Archaeology in Prehispanic Bolivia*. Princeton, N.J.: Princeton University Press.

Bernal, Martin. 1987. *The Afroasiatic Roots of Classical Civilization.* New Brunswick, N.J.: Rutgers University Press.

Berrin, Kathleen, and Esther Pasztory. 1993. *Teotihuacán: Art from the City of the Gods*. New York: Thames and Hudson.

Berry, M. S. 1984. "Sampling and Predictive Modeling on Federal Lands in the West," *American Antiquity* 49: 842–853.

Bettinger, R. L. 1980. "Explanatory/Predictive Models of Hunter-Gatherer Adaptations," *Advances in Archaeological Method and Theory* 3: 189–256.

———. 1991. *Hunter-Gatherers: Archaeological and Evolutionary Theory.* New York: Plenum Press.

Biers, W. R., and P. E. McGovern, eds. 1990. *Organic Contents of Ancient Vessels: Materials Analysis and Archaeological Investigation.* Philadelphia: MASCA, University Museum.

Binford, L. R. 1962. "Archaeology as Anthropology," *American Antiquity* 28: 217–225.

———. 1964. "A Consideration of Archaeological Research Design," *American Antiquity* 29: 425–441.

———. 1968. "Archaeological Perspectives," in S. R. Binford and L. R. Binford, eds., *New Perspectives in Archaealogy,* pp. 5–32. Hawthorne, N.Y.: Aldine.

———. 1972. *An Archaeological Perspective.* New York: Seminar Press.

———, ed. 1977. *For Theory Building in Archaeology.* Orlando, Fla.: Academic Press.

———. 1978. *Nunamiut Ethnoarchaeology.* Orlando, Fla.: Academic Press.

———. 1980. "Willow Smoke and Dog's Tails: Hunter-Gatherer Settlement Systems and Archaeological Site Formation," *American Antiquity* 45: 4–20.

———. 1981a. "Behavioral Archaeology and the Pompeii Premise," *Journal of Anthropological Research* 37: 195–208.

———. 1981b. *Bones: Ancient Men and Modern Myths.* Orlando, Fla.: Academic Press.

———. 1983a. *In Pursuit of the Past.* New York: Thames and Hudson.

———. 1983b. *Working at Archaeology.* Orlando, Fla.: Academic Press.

———. 1984. "An Alyawara Day: Flour, Spiniflex Gum, and Shifting Perspectives," *Journal of Anthropological Research* 40: 157–257.

———. 1987. Data, relativism, and archaeological science," *Man* 22: 391–404.

———. 1989. *Debating Archaeology.* Orlando, Fla.: Academic Press.

Binford, L. R., and J. A. Sabloff. 1982. "Paradigms, Systematics, and Archaeology," *Journal of Anthropological Research* 38: 137–153.

Binford, S.R., and L.R. Binford, eds. 1968. *New Perspectives on Archaeology.* Chicago, Ill.: Aldine.

Bintcliff, J. 1991. "Post-modernism, rhetoric, and scholasticism at TAG: the current state of British archaeological theory." *Antiquity* 65 (247): 274–278.

Bisson, M. S. 1977. "Prehistoric Copper Mining in North West Zambia," *Archaeology* 29: 242–247.

Blanton, R. E. 1978. *Monte Alban: Settlement Patterns at the Ancient Zapotec Capital.* Orlando, Fla.: Academic Press.

Blitzer, Harriet. 1990. "ΚΟΡΩΝΑΙΚΑ: Storage-Jar Production and Trade in the Traditional Aegean," *Hesperia* 59: 675–711.

Bordaz, J. 1970. *Tools of the Old and New Stone Age.* Garden City, N.Y.: Natural History Press.

Bordes, F. 1968. *The Old Stone Age.* New York: McGraw-Hill.

Boserup, E. 1965. *Conditions of Agricultural Growth: The Economics of Agrarian Change Under Population Pressure.* Hawthorne, N.Y.: Aldine.

Bracken, C. P. 1975. *Antiquities Acquired*. Newton Abbott, England: David and Charles.

Bradley, R. 1990. *The Passage of Arms*. Cambridge: Cambridge University Press.

Bradley, Richard, and Mark Edmonds. 1993. *Interpreting the Axe Trade*. Cambridge: Cambridge University Press.

Braidwood, R. J., and Braidwood, L. S., eds. 1983. *Prehistoric Archaeology Along the Zagros Flanks*. Chicago: Oriental Institute.

Braidwood, R. J., and B. Howe. 1962. "Southwestern Asia Beyond the Lands of the Mediterranean Littoral," in R. J. Braidwood and G. R. Willey, eds., *Courses Toward Urban Life*, pp. 132–146. New York: Viking Penguin.

Brain, C. K. 1967. "Hottentot Food Remains and Their Bearing on the Interpretation of Fossil Bone Assemblages," *Scientific Papers of the Namib Desert Research Station* 32 (6): 1–7.

————. 1981. *The Hunters or the Hunted: An Introduction to African Cave Taphonomy*. Chicago: University of Chicago Press.

Bray, Tamara L. and Thomas W. Killion. 1994. *Reckoning with the Dead: The Larsen Bay Repatriation and the Smithsonian Institution*. Washington, D.C.: Smithsonian Institution Press.

Breiner, S. 1973. *Applications Manual for Portable Magnetometers*. Sunnyvale, Calif.: Geometrics.

Brewer, Douglas J. 1992. "Zooarchaeology: Method, Theory, and Goals," *Archaeological Method and Theory* 4: 195–244.

Brink, Jack, and Bob Dawe. 1989. "Final Report of the 1985 and 1986 Field Season at Head-Smashed-In Buffalo Jump, Alberta," *Archaeological Survey of Canada Manuscript Series* 16.

Brochier, Jacques, and others. 1992. "Shepherds and Sediments: Geoethnoarchaeology of Pastoral Sites," *Journal of Anthropological Archaeology* 11 (1): 47–102.

Bronitsky, G. 1986. "The Use of Materials Science Techniques in the Study of Pottery Construction and Use," *Advances in Archaeological Method and Theory* 10: 209–276.

Brown, J. A., ed. 1971. *Approaches to the Social Dimensions of Mortuary Practices*. Memoirs of the Society for American Archaeology, vol. 25.

————. 1981. "The Search for Rank in Prehistoric Burials," in R. Chapman, I. Kinnes, and K. Randsborg, eds., *The Archaeology of Death*, pp. 25–38. Cambridge: Cambridge University Press.

————. 1982. "On the Structure of Artifact Typologies," in R. A. Whallon and J. A. Brown, eds., *Essays on Archaeological Typology*, pp. 176–190. Evanston, Ill.: Center for American Archaeology.

Brown, J. A., and S. Struever. 1973. "The Organization of Archaeological Research: An Illinois Example," in C. L. Redman, ed., *Method and Theory in Current Archaeology*, pp. 261–280. New York: Wiley Interscience.

Brown, K. L., and D. C. Cooper. 1990. "Structural Continuity in an Afro-American Slave and Tenant Community," *Historical Archaeology* 24 (4): 7–19.

Brumfiel, E. O. 1991. "Weaving and Cooking: Women's Production in Aztec Mexico," in J. M. Gero and M. W. Conkey, eds., *Engendering Archaeology*, pp. 224–253. Oxford: Blackwell.

————, and T. K. Earle, eds. 1987. *Specialization, Exchange, and Complex Societies*. Cambridge: Cambridge University Press.

Bryant, V. M. 1974. "Prehistoric Diet in Southwest Texas: The Coprolite Evidence," *American Antiquity* 39: 407–420.

————, and R. G. Holloway. 1983. "The Role of Palynology in Archaeology," *Advances in Archaeological Method and Theory* 6: 191–224.

Buikstra, J. 1984. "The Lower Illinois River Region: A Prehistoric Context for the Study of Ancient Diet and Health," in M. N. Cohen and G. J. Armelagos, eds., *Paleopathology at the Origins of Agriculture,* pp. 217–236. Orlando, Fla.: Academic Press.

Burghardt, A. F. 1959. "The Location of Towns in the Central Lowland of the United States," *Annals of the Association of American Geographers* 49: 305–323.

Burleigh, R., and D. R. Brothwell. 1978. "Studies on Amerindian Dogs," *Journal of Archaeological Science* 5: 355–362.

Butzer, K. W. 1974. *Environment and Archaeology,* 3d ed. Hawthorne, N.Y.: Aldine.

————. 1982. *Archaeology as Human Ecology*. Cambridge: Cambridge University Press.

Byers, D. S., ed. 1967. *The Prehistory of the Tehuacán Valley*. Austin: University of Texas Press.

Cahen, D., and L. H. Keeley. 1980. "Not Less Than Two, Not More Than Three," *World Archaeology* 12: 166–180.

Campbell, B. G. 1985. *Humankind Emerging*, 4th ed. Boston: Little, Brown.

Campbell, J. B. 1977. *The Upper Paleolithic of Britain*. Oxford: Oxford University Press.

Cameron, Erine M., and Steve A. Tomka, eds. 1993. *Abandonment of Settlements and Regions: Ethnoarchaeological and Archaeological Approaches*. Cambridge: Cambridge University Press.

Cann, J. R., and A. C. Renfrew. 1964. "The Characterization of Obsidian and Its Application to the Mediterranean Region," *Proceedings of the Prehistoric Society* 30: 111–133.

Carr, C. 1982. *Handbook on Soil Resistivity*. Evanston, Ill.: Center for American Archaeology Press.

Carter, H., and others. 1923–1933. *The Tomb of Tutankhamun*. London: Cassell.

Casteel, R. W. 1976. *Fish Remains in Archaeology and Paleoenvironmental Studies*. Orlando, Fla.: Academic Press.

Ceci, L. 1984. "Shell Midden Deposits as Coastal Resources," *World Archaeology* 16: 62–74.

Ceram, C. W. 1953. *Gods, Graves, and Scholars*. New York: Knopf.

Champion, S. 1980. *A Dictionary of Terms and Techniques in Archaeology*. Oxford: Phaidon.

Champion, T., and others. 1984. *Prehistoric Europe*. Orlando, Fla.: Academic Press.

Chang, K. C., ed. 1968. *Settlement Archaeology*. Palo Alto, Calif.: National Press

————. 1980. *Shang Civilization*. New Haven: Yale University Press.

————. 1984. *The Archaeology of Ancient China,* 3d ed. New Haven, Conn.: Yale University Press.

Chapman, R., I. Kinnes, and K. Randsborg, eds. 1981. *The Archaeology of Death.* Cambridge: Cambridge University Press.

Chartkoff, J. L. 1978. "Transect Interval Sampling in Forests," *American Antiquity* 43: 46–53.

Charton, T. H. 1981. "Archaeology, Ethnohistory, and Ethnology: Interpretative Interfaces," *Advances in Archaeological Method and Theory* 4: 129–176.

Childe, V. G. 1925. *The Danube in Prehistory.* London: Routledge and Kegan Paul.

———. 1942. *What Happened in History.* Baltimore: Pelican.

———. 1956. *Piecing Together the Past.* London: Routledge and Kegan Paul.

———. 1958. "Retrospect," *Antiquity* 32: 69–74.

Chippendale, C. 1983. *Stonehenge Complete.* London: Thames and Hudson.

Chisholm, B. S., and others. 1983. "Marine and Terrestrial Protein in Prehistoric Diets on the British Columbia Coast," *Current Anthropology* 24: 396–398.

Chisholm, M. 1968. *Rural Settlement and Land Use.* London: Hutchinson.

Chittick, H. N. 1974. *Kilwa.* Nairobi: British Institute in Eastern Africa.

Christaller, W. 1933. *Die Zentralen Orte in Süddeutschland.* Jena, East Germany: Karl Zeiss.

Clark, A. 1990. *Seeing Beneath the Soil.* London: Batsford.

Clark, C. M. 1987. "Trouble at t'Mill: Industrial Archaeology in the 1980s," *Antiquity* 61: 169–179.

Clark, G. A. 1982. "Quantifying Archaeological Research," *Advances in Archaeological Method and Theory* 5: 217–274.

Clark, J. D. 1958. "The Natural Fracturing of Pebbles from the Batoka Gorge, Northern Rhodesia, and Its Bearing on the Kafuan Industries of Africa," *Proceedings of the Prehistoric Society* 24: 64–77.

———. 1959. *The Prehistory of Southern Africa.* Baltimore: Pelican.

———, and S. Brandt, eds. 1984. *From Hunters to Farming.* Berkeley: University of California Press.

Clark, J. G. D. 1952. *Prehistoric Europe: The Economic Basis.* Palo Alto, Calif.: Stanford University Press.

———. 1954. *Star Carr.* Cambridge: Cambridge University Press.

———. 1970. *Aspects of Prehistory.* Cambridge: Cambridge University Press.

———. 1975. *The Early Stone Age Settlement of Scandinavia.* Cambridge: Cambridge University Press.

———. 1978. *World Prehistory in New Perspective,* 3d ed. Cambridge: Cambridge University Press.

Clark, R. 1935. "The Flint Knapping Industry at Brandon," *Antiquity* 9: 38–56.

Clark, R. M. 1975. "A Calibration Curve for Radiocarbon Dates," *Antiquity* 49: 251–266.

Clarke, D. L. 1968. *Analytical Archaeology.* London: Methuen.

———, ed. 1977. *Spatial Archaeology.* Orlando, Fla.: Academic Press.

Clarke, J. E. 1982. "Manufacture of Mesoamerican Prismatic Blades: An Alternative Technique," *American Antiquity* 47: 355–375.

Classen, Cheryl, ed. 1991. *Exploring Gender Through Archaeology.* Madison, Wisc.: Prehistory Press.

Clay, R. B. 1976. "Typological Classification, Attribute Analysis, and Lithic Variability," *Journal of Field Archaeology* 3: 303–311.

Cleere, H., ed. 1989. *Archaeological Heritage Management in the Modern World.* London: Unwin-Hyman.

Clutton-Brock, J. 1981. *Domesticated Animals from Early Times.* Austin: University of Texas Press.

———. 1989. *The Walking Larder.* London: Unwin Hyman.

Clutton-Brock, J., and J. Grigson. 1985. *Early Herders and Their Flocks.* Oxford: British Archaeological Reports.

Coe, M. D. 1967. *Tikal: A Handbook of the Ancient Maya Ruins.* Philadelphia: University Museum.

———. 1984. *Mexico,* 2d ed. New York: Thames and Hudson.

———. 1993. *The Maya,* 3d ed. New York: Thames and Hudson.

———, and R. A. Diehl. 1980. *In the Land of the Olmec.* Austin: University of Texas Press.

Coe, W. 1982. *Introduction to the Archaeology of Tikal, Guatemala.* Philadelphia: University Museum, University of Pennsylvania.

Coles, B., and Coles, J. M. 1986. *Sweet Track to Glastonbury.* New York: Thames and Hudson.

———. 1989. *People of the Wetlands.* New York: Guild Publishing.

Coles, J. M. 1973. *Archaeology by Experiment.* London: Heinemann.

———. 1984. *The Archaeology of the Wetlands.* Cambridge: Cambridge University Press.

———, and A. F. Harding. 1979. *The Bronze Age in Europe.* London: Methuen.

———, and B. J. Orme. 1983. "Homo sapiens or Caster Fiber?" *Antiquity* 57: 95–102.

Colley, S. M. 1990. "The Analysis and Interpretation of Archaeological Fish Remains," *Archaeological Method and Theory* 2: 39–46.

Collis, J. 1984. *The European Iron Age.* London: Batsford.

Conkey, M. W., and J. Gero. 1996. "Archaeology and Gender." *Annual Review of Anthropology* 24.

Conkey, M. W., and C. Hastorf, eds. 1990. *The Uses of Style in Archaeology.* Cambridge: Cambridge University Press.

Connah, G. 1987. *African Civilizations.* Cambridge: Cambridge University Press.

Conrad, G. W., and A. A. Demarast. 1984. *Religion and Empire: The Dynamics of Aztec and Inca Expansion.* Cambridge: Cambridge University Press.

Cook, D. C. 1984. "Subsistence and Health in the Central Illinois Valley: Osteological Evidence," in M. N. Cohen and G. J. Armelagos, eds., *Paleopathology at the Origins of Agriculture,* pp. 237–270. Orlando, Fla.: Academic Press.

Cotterell, B., and J. Kamminga. 1989. *Mechanics of Pre-Industrial Technology.* Cambridge: Cambridge University Press.

Courty, Marie-Agnes, and others, eds. 1993. *Soils and Micromorphology in Archaeology.* Cambridge: Cambridge University Press.

Cowgill, G. L. 1982. "Clusters of Objects and Associations Between Variables: Two Approaches to Archaeological Classification," in R. A. Whallon and J. A. Brown, eds., *Essays in Archaeological Typology,* pp. 30–55. Evanston, Ill.: Center for American Archaeology.

———. 1986. "Archaeological Applications of Mathematical and Formal Methods," in D. J. Meltzer, D. D. Fowler, and J. A. Sabloff, eds., *American Archaeology Past and Future,* pp. 369–394. Washington, D.C.: Smithsonian Institution Press.

————, and others. 1984. "Spatial Analysis of Teotihuacán: A Mesoamerican Metropolis," in A. Hietala, ed., *Intrasite Spatial Analysis in Archaeology,* pp. 154–195. Cambridge: Cambridge University Press.

Crabtree, D. E. 1972a. *An Introduction to Flintworking.* Pocatello: Idaho State Museum.

————. 1972b. "A Stoneworker's Approach to Analysing and Replicating the Lindenmeier Folsom" *Tebiwa* 9: 3–39.

Crabtree, Pam J., and Kathleen, Ryan, eds. 1991. *Animal Use and Culture Change.* Philadelphia: University of Pennsylvania Museum.

Crabtree, R. M. 1963. "Archaeological Investigations at Batiquitos Lagoon, San Diego County," *California Archaeological Survey Annual Report*: 319–462.

Craddock, Paul T. 1995. *Early Metal Mining and Production.* Washington, D.C.: Smithsonian Institution Press.

Croes, Dale R. 1989. "Prehistoric Ethnicity on the Northwest Coast of North America: An Evaluation of Style in Basketry and Headgear." *Journal of Anthropological Archaeology* 8: 101–130.

————, and J. O. Davis. 1977. "Computer Mapping of Idiosyncratic Basketry Manufacturing Techniques in the Prehistoric Ozette House, Cape Alava, Washington," in J. N. Hill and J. D. Gunn, eds., *The Individual in Prehistory*, pp. 155–166. Orlando, Fla.: Academic Press.

Cronyn, J. M. 1990. *The Elements of Archaeological Conservation.* London: Routledge.

Culbert, T. P., ed. 1991. *Classic Maya Political History.* Santa Fe, N.M.: School of American Research.

Dalrymple, G. B., and M. A. Lamphere. 1970. *Potassium Argon Dating.* New York: Freeman.

Dancey, W. S. 1981. *Archaeological Field Methods: An Introduction.* Minneapolis, Minn.: Burgess.

Daniel, G. 1962. *The Idea of Prehistory.* London: Watts.

————, ed. 1967. *The Origins and Growth of Archaeology.* Baltimore, Md.: Pelican.

————. 1976. "Stone, Bronze, and Iron," in J. V. S. Megaw, ed., *To Illustrate the Monuments,* pp. 35–42. London: Thames and Hudson.

————. 1981. *A Short History of Archaeology.* New York: Thames and Hudson.

Däniken, E. von. 1970. *Chariots of the Gods?* New York: Bantam Books.

————. 1971. *Gods from Outer Space.* New York: Bantam Books.

Dart, R. A. 1957. *The Osteodontokeratic Culture of Australopithecus prometheus.* Pretoria, South Africa: Transvaal Museum.

Darwin, C. 1859. *On the Origin of Species.* London: John Murray.

David, Nicholas. 1992. "Integrating Ethnoarchaeology: A Subtle Realist Perspective," *Journal of Anthropological Archaeology* 11: 330–359.

Davis, D. D. 1983. "Investigating the Diffusion of Stylistic Innovation," *Advances in Archaeological Method and Theory* 6: 53–89.

Davis, S. J. M. 1987. *The Archaeology of Animals.* London: Batsford.

Deacon, Hilary. 1979. "Excavations at Boomplas Cave—a Sequence through the Upper Pleistocene and Holocene in South Africa," *World Archaeology* 10: 241–257.

Deagan, K. 1982. "Avenues of Inquiry in Historical Archaeology," *Advances in Archaeological Method and Theory* 5: 151–178.

————. 1983. *Spanish Saint Augustine: The Archaeology of a Colonial Creole Community*. Orlando, Fla.: Academic Press.

Dean, J. S. 1970. "Aspects of Tsegi Phase Soil Organization," in W. A. Longacre, ed., *Reconstructing Prehistoric Pueblo Societies*. Albuquerque: University of New Mexico Press.

Deetz, J. 1967. *Invitation to Archaeology*. Garden City, N.Y.: Natural History Press.

————. 1977. *In Small Things Forgotten*. Garden City, N.Y.: Anchor/Doubleday.

————. 1983. "Scientific Humanism and Humanist Science," *Geoscience and Man* 23: 27–34.

————. 1988. "American Historical Archaeology: Methods and Results," *Science* 239: 362–367.

Deith, M. R. 1983. "Molluscan Calendars," *Journal of Archaeological Science* 10: 423–440.

Dekin, A. 1987. "Sealed in Time," *National Geographic* (June): 824–836.

DeLoria, Vine, Jr. 1995. *Red Earth, White Lies*. New York: Scribner.

De Niro, M. J. 1987. "Stable Isotopy and Archaeology." *American Scientist* 75: 182–191.

De Perthes, B. 1841. *De la Création: Essai sur l'Origine et la Progression des Etres*. Abbeville, France.

De Roche, C. D. 1983. "Population Estimates from Settlement Area and Number of Residences," *Journal of Field Archaeology* 10: 187–192.

Dethlefsen, E., and J. Deetz. 1966. "Death's Heads, Cherubs, and Willow Trees: Experimental Archaeology in Colonial Cemeteries," *American Antiquity* 31: 502–510.

Deuel, L. 1969. *Flights into Yesterday*. London: Macdonald.

De Viro, B., and S. Epstein. 1978. "Dietary Analysis from 12C/13C Ratios of Carbonate and Collagen Fractions of Bone," *U.S. Geological Survey Open File Report,* 78–701: 90–91.

Dibble, H. 1987. "Penn Anthropologist Adapts Laser and Computers to Speed Archaeological Exploration," *SAA Bulletin* (March): 5.

Digby, B. 1926. *The Mammoth and Mammoth-Hunting in North-East Siberia*. London: Macmillan.

Dillehay, T. D., and D. J. Meltzer, eds. 1991. *The First Americans: Search and Research*. Boca Raton, Fla.: CRC Press.

Dimbleby, G. W. 1985. *The Palynology of Archaeological Sites*. London: Academic Press.

Donald, M. 1991. *Origins of the Modern Human Mind*. Cambridge, Mass.: Harvard University Press.

Doran, J. E. 1987. "Formal Methods and Archaeology," *Journal of Field Archaeology* 18: 21–37.

————, and F. R. Hodson. 1975. *Mathematics and Computers in Archaeology*. Cambridge, Mass.: Harvard University Press.

Dorrell, P. 1994. *Photography in Archaeology and Conservation*. 2d ed. Cambridge: Cambridge University Press.

Douglas, John E., and Carol Kramer, eds. 1992. "Interaction, Social Proximity, and Distance," *Journal of Anthropological Archaeology*. Special Issue 11 (2).

Dumond, Don E. 1977. "Science and Archaeology: When the Saints Go Marching In," *American Antiquity* 42: 33–49.

———. 1987. *The Eskimos and Aleuts,* 2d ed. London: Thames and Hudson.

Dunnell, R. C. 1970. "The Seriation Method and Its Evaluation," *American Antiquity* 35: 305–319.

———. 1971. *Systematics in Prehistory*. New York: Free Press.

———. 1978. "Style and Function: A Fundamental Dichotomy," *American Antiquity* 43: 192–202.

———. 1980. "Evolutionary Theory and Archaeology," *Advances in Archaeological Method and Theory* 3: 38–99.

———. 1982. "Science, Social Science, and Common Sense: The Agonizing Dilemma of Modern Archaeology," *Journal of Anthropological Research* 38: 1–25.

———. 1984. "The Americanist Literature for 1983: A Year of Contrasts and Challenges," *American Journal of Archaeology* 88: 489–513.

———. 1985. "Americanist Archaeology in 1984," *American Journal of Archaeology* 89: 585–611.

———. 1986a. "Five Decades of American Archaeology," in D. J. Meltzer, D. D. Fowler, and J. A. Sabloff, eds., *American Archaeology Past and Future,* pp. 23–52. Washington, D.C.: Smithsonian Institution Press.

———. 1986b. "Methodological Issues in Americanist Artifact Classification," *Advances in Archaeological Method and Theory* 10: 149–208.

———, and W. S. Dancey. 1983. "The Siteless Survey: A Regional Scale Data Collection," *Advances in Archaeological Method and Theory* 6: 267–288.

Earle, T. K. 1976. "A Nearest Neighbor Analysis of Two Formative Settlement Systems," in K. V. Flannery, ed., *The Early Mesoamerican Village*, pp. 196–224. Orlando, Fla.: Academic Press.

———, ed. 1991. *Chiefdoms: Power, Economy, and Ideology*. Cambridge: Cambridge University Press.

———, and J. E. Ericson, eds. 1977. *Exchange Systems in Prehistory*. Orlando, Fla.: Academic Press.

Eliade, M. 1954. *The Myth of the Eternal Return*. New York: Pantheon.

Elphick, Richard. 1977. *Kraal and Castle*. New Haven, Conn.: Yale University Press.

Erickson, C. L. 1992. "Applied Archaeology and Development: Archaeology's Potential Contribution to the Future." *Journal of the Steward Anthropological Society* 20 (1, 2): 1–16.

Ericson, J. E., and T. K. Earle, eds. 1982. *Contexts of Prehistoric Exchange*. Orlando, Fla.: Academic Press.

Ericson, J. E., and B. A. Purdy, eds. 1984. *Prehistoric Quarries and Lithic Production*. Cambridge: Cambridge University Press.

Evans, J. D. 1978. *An Introduction to Environmental Archaeology*. London: Paul Elek.

Evans, John. 1860. "On the Occurrence of Flint Implements in Undisturbed Beds of Gravel, Sand, and Clay," *Archaeologia* 38: 280–308.

Ezzo, Joseph A. 1993. "Dietary Change and Variability at Grasshopper Pueblo, Arizona," *Journal of Anthropological Archaeology* 11: 219–289.

Fagan, B. M. 1975. *The Rape of the Nile*. New York: Scribner. (Reprinted 1992.)

———. 1977. *Elusive Treasure*. New York: Scribner.

———. 1985. *The Adventure of Archaeology*. Washington, D.C.: National Geographic Society.

———. 1991. *The Journey from Eden*. London: Thames and Hudson.

———. 1995a. *Time Detectives*. New York: Simon and Schuster.

———. 1995b. *Ancient North America*. 2d ed. London: Thames and Hudson.

———. 1995c. *People of the Earth*. 8th ed. New York: HarperCollins.

———. 1995d. *Archaeology: A Brief Introduction*, 4th ed. New York: HarperCollins.

———. 1995e. *Snapshots of the Past*. Walnut Creet, Calif.: AltaMira Press.

———, and F. Van Noten. 1971. *The Hunter-Gatherers of Gwisho*. Tervuren, Belgium: Musée Royal de l'Afrique Centrale.

Feder, K. L. 1996. *Frauds, Myths, and Mysteries*. 2d ed. Mountain View, Calif.: Mayfield.

Ferguson, L. 1991. "Struggling with Pots in Colonial South Carolina," in R. McGuire and R. Paynter, eds., *The Archaeology of Inequality*, pp. 28–39. Oxford: Blackwell.

———. 1992. *Uncommon Ground*. Washington, D.C.: Smithsonian Institution Press.

Ferguson, T. J., and others. 1995. "Working Together: Hopi Oral History and Archaeology," *SAA Bulletin* 13 (2, 3): 12–15; 10–13.

Fern, Miriam L., and Kam-biu Liu. 1995. "Maize Pollen of 3500 B.P. from Southern Alabama," *American Antiquity* 60 (1): 109–117.

Finney, Ben. 1994. *A Voyage of Rediscovery: A Cultural Odyssey Through Polynesia*. Berkeley: University of California Press.

Fish, S. K., and S. A. Kowalewski, eds. 1990. *The Archaeology of Regions: A Case for Full-Coverage Survey*. Washington, D.C.: Smithsonian Institution Press.

Fitzhugh, W., ed. 1988. *Crossroads of Continents*. Washington, D.C.: Smithsonian Institution Press.

Fladmark, K. R. 1982. "Microdebitage Analysis: Initial Considerations," *Journal of Archaeological Science* 9: 205–220.

Flannery, K. V. 1968. "Archaeological Systems Theory and Early Mesoamerica," in B. J. Meggers, ed., *Anthropological Archaeology in the Americas*, pp. 67–87. Washington, D.C.: Anthropological Society of Washington.

———. 1972. "The Cultural Evolution of Civilizations," *Biennial Review of Ecology and Systematics*, 399–426.

———. 1973. "The Origins of Agriculture," *Biennial Review of Anthropology* 12: 271–310.

———, ed. 1976. *The Early Mesoamerican Village*. Orlando, Fla.: Academic Press.

———. 1982. "The Golden Marshalltown: A Parable for the Archaeology of the 1980s," *American Anthropologist* 84: 265–278.

Flannery, K. V., and J. Marcus, eds. 1983. *The Cloud People*. Orlando, Fla.: Academic Press.

———. 1993. "Cognitive Archaeology." *Cambridge Archaeological Journal* 3 (2): 260–267.

Flannery, K. V., and M. C. Winter. 1976. "Analyzing Village Activities," in K. V. Flannery, ed., *The Early Mesoamerican Village,* pp. 34–44. Orlando, Fla.: Academic Press.

Flannery, K. V., and others. 1989. *The Flocks of the Wamani.* Orlando, Fla.: Academic Press.

Fleischer, R. L. 1975. "Advances in Fission Track Dating," *World Archaeology* 7: 136–150.

Fleming, S. J. 1979. *Thermoluminescence Techniques in Archaeology.* Oxford: Clarendon Press.

Flenniken, J. J. 1984. "The Past, Present, and Future of Flintknapping: An Anthropological Perspective," *Annual Review of Anthropology* 13: 187–203.

Forbes, R. J. 1955–1958. *Studies in Ancient Technology.* The Hague, Netherlands: Brill.

Ford, R. I. 1979. "Paleoethnobotany in American Archaeology," *Advances in Archaeological Method and Theory* 2: 286–336.

———, ed. 1985. *Early Food Production in North America.* Ann Arbor: University of Michigan Museum of Anthropology.

Fowler, D. D. 1982. "Cultural Resources Management," *Advances in Archaeological Method and Theory* 5: 1–50.

———. 1986. "Conserving American Archaeological Resources," in D. J. Meltzer, D. D. Fowler, and J. A. Sabloff, eds., *American Archaeology Past and Future,* pp. 135–162. Washington, D.C.: Smithsonian Institution Press.

———. 1987. "Uses of the Past: Archaeology in the Service of the State," *American Antiquity* 52: 229–248.

Fox, Sir Cyril. 1932. *The Personality of Britain.* Cambridge: Cambridge University Press.

Frankel, D. 1991. *Remains to Be Seen.* Melbourne, Australia: Longman Cheshire.

Freter, AnnCorinne. 1993. "Obsidian-Hydration Dating: Its past, present, and future application in Mesoamerica." *Ancient Mesoamerica* 4: 285–303.

———. 1994. "The Classic Maya Collapse at Copán, Honduras: An Analysis of Maya Rural Settlement," In Glenn M. Schwartz and Steven E. Falconer, eds. *Archaeological Views from the Countryside.* Washington, D.C.: Smithsonian Institution Press, pp. 160–176.

Friedel, D. A., and J. A. Sabloff. 1984. *Cozumel: Late Maya Settlement Patterns.* Orlando, Fla.: Academic Press.

Friedel, D. A., and L. Schele. 1987. "Symbol and Power: A History of the Lowland Maya Cosmogram," in E. P. Benson and G. Griddin, eds. *Maya Iconography,* pp. 211–235. Princeton, N.J.: Princeton University Press.

Friedman, I., and F. Trembour. 1983. "Obsidian Hydration Update," *American Antiquity* 48: 544–547.

Frison, G. 1978. *Prehistoric Hunters of the High Plains.* Orlando, Fla.: Academic Press.

Fritts, H. C. 1976. *Tree Rings and Climate.* Orlando, Fla.: Academic Press.

Gaffney, V., and Z. Stancic. 1991. *GIS Approaches to Regional Analysis: A Case Study of the Island of Hvar.* Ljubljana: Znanstveni institut Filozofske fakultete.

Galinat, Walter. 1985. "Domestication and Diffusion of Maize," in Richard I. Ford, ed. *Prehistoric Food Production in North America,* pp. 245–278. Ann Arbor: University of Michigan Museum of Anthropology.

Gamble, Clive, and W.A. Boismier, eds. 1991. *Ethnoarchaeological Approaches to Mobile Campsites: Hunter-Gatherer and Pastoralist Case Studies.* Ann Arbor, Mich.: International Monographs in Prehistory.

Gann, Douglas. 1994. "Pompeii Forum Project Under Way," *CSA Newsletter* 7 (3): 6–10.

Garlake, P. 1973. *Great Zimbabwe.* London: Thames and Hudson.

Gero, J. M., and M. W. Conkey, eds. 1991. *Engendering Archaeology: Women and Prehistory.* Oxford: Blackwell.

Geyh, Mebus A., and Helmut Schleicher. 1990. *Absolute Age Detirminations: Physical and Chemical Dating Methods and Their Application.* Translated by R. Clark Newcomb. New York: Springer-Verlag.

Gibbon, G. 1984. *Anthropological Archaeology.* New York: Columbia University Press.

Gibson, Kathleen R., and Tim Ingold, eds. 1993. *Tools, Language, and Cognition in Human Evolution.* Cambridge: Cambridge University Press.

Gifford, J. C. 1976. *Prehistoric Pottery Analysis and the Ceramics of Barton Ramie in the Belize Valley.* Cambridge, Mass.: Peabody Museum, Harvard University.

Gilbert, R. I., and others, eds. 1985. *Analysis of Prehistoric Diet.* Orlando, Fla.: Academic Press.

Glassow, Michael A. 1996. *Purisimeño Chumash prehistory: Maritime Adaptations along the Southern California Coast.* Fort Worth, Texas: Harcourt Brace.

Glob, P. V. 1969. *The Bog People.* London: Faber and Faber.

Goodyear, A. C., L. M. Raab, and T. C. Klinger. 1978. "The Status of Archaeological Research Design in Cultural Resource Management," *American Antiquity* 43: 159–173.

Goudie, Andrew. 1992. *Environmental Change.* 2d ed. Oxford: Oxford University Press.

Gould, R. A., ed. 1978. *Explorations in Ethnoarchaeology.* Albuquerque: University of New Mexico Press.

———. 1980. *Living Archaeology.* Cambridge: Cambridge University Press.

———, ed. 1983. *Shipwreck Archaeology.* Albuquerque: University of New Mexico Press.

Gould, R. H., and M. B. Schiffer. 1981. *Modern Material Culture: The Archaeology of US.* Orlando, Fla.: Academic Press.

Gowlett, J. A. J. 1987. "The Archaeology of Radiocarbon Accelerator Dating," *Journal of World Prehistory* 1: 127–170.

Grayson, D. K. 1980. "Vicissitudes and Overkill: The Development of Explanations of Pleistocene Extinctions," *Advances in Archaeological Method and Theory* 3: 357–404.

———. 1981. "A Critical View of the Use of Archaeological Vertebrates in Paleoenvironmental Reconstruction," *Journal of Ethnobiology* 1: 28–38.

———. 1983. *The Establishment of Human Antiquity.* Orlando, Fla.: Academic Press.

———. 1984. *Quantitative Zooarchaeology.* Orlando, Fla.: Academic Press.

Guidon, N., and G. Delibrias. 1986. "Carbon 14 Dates Point to Man in the Americas 32,000 Years Ago," *Nature* 321: 769–771.

Gumerman, G. J. 1984. *A View from Black Mesa: The Changing Face of Archaeology.* Tucson: University of Arizona Press.

———, and R. C. Euler. 1976. *Papers on the Archaeology of Black Mesa, Arizona.* Carbondale: Southern Illinois University Press.

Hally, D. J. 1981. "Plant Preservation and the Content of Paleobotanical Samples: A Case Study," *American Antiquity* 46: 723–742.

Hammersley, M. 1992. *What's Wrong with Ethnography:* Methodological *Explorations.* London: Routledge.

Handsman, R. G. 1981. "Early Capitalism and the Center Village of Canaan, CT," *Artifacts* 9: 1–21.

Hancock, Graham. 1995. *Fingerprints of the Gods.* New York: Crown.

Hardesty, D. 1977. *Ecological Anthropology.* New York: Wiley.

———. 1980. "The Use of General Ecological Principles in Archaeology," *Advances in Archaeological Method and Theory* 3: 158–188.

Harp, E., Jr. 1978. *Photography for Archaeologists.* Orlando, Fla.: Academic Press.

Harrington, J. C. 1948. "Evidence of Manual Reckoning in the Cittie of Raleigh," *North Carolina Historical Review* 33: 1–8.

Harris, E. C. 1989. *Principles of Archaeological Stratigraphy,* 2d ed. Orlando, Fla.: Academic Press.

Harris, Marvin. 1968. *The Rise of Anthropological Theory.* New York: W. W. Crowell.

Harris, R.L. 1995. *The World of the Bible.* London and New York: Thames and Hudson.

Hassan, F. 1981. *Demographic Archaeology.* Orlando, Fla.: Academic Press.

Hastorf, C. 1991. "Gender, Space, and Food in Prehistory," in J. M. Gero and M. W. Conkey, eds., *Engendering Archaeology,* pp. 132–162. Oxford: Blackwell.

———. 1992. *Agriculture and the Onset of Inequality Before the Inka.* Cambridge: Cambridge University Press.

Hawkes, J. G. 1983. *The Diversity of Crop Plants.* Cambridge, Mass.: Harvard University Press.

Hayden, B., ed. 1979. *Lithic Wear Analysis.* Orlando, Fla.: Academic Press.

———, ed. 1987. *Lithic Studies Among the Contemporary Highland Maya.* Tucson: University of Arizona Press.

Hester, T. R., and R. F. Heizer. 1973. *Bibliography of Archaeology, Volume 1: Lithic Technology and Petrography.* Reading, Mass.: Addison-Wesley.

Hester, T. R., H. J. Shafer, and R. F. Heizer. 1987. *Field Methods in Archaeology.* Palo Alto, Calif.: Mayfield.

Heyerdahl, T. 1950. *The Kon-Tiki Expedition.* New York: Random House.

Hietala, H., ed. 1984. *Intersite Spatial Analysis in Archaeology.* Cambridge: Cambridge University Press.

Hill, J. N., ed. 1977. *Explanation of Prehistoric Change.* Albuquerque: University of New Mexico Press.

———, and J. D. Gunn, eds. 1977. *The Individual in Prehistory.* Orlando, Fla.: Academic Press.

Hillman, G. C., S. M. Colledge, and D. R. Harris. 1989. "Plant-Food Economy During the Epipalaeolithic Period at Tell Abu Hureyra, Syria: Dietary Diversity, Seasonality, and Modes of Exploitation," in D. R. Harris and G. C. Hillman, eds. *Foraging and Farming*, pp. 240–268. London: Unwin Hyman.

Hillman, G. C., and M. S. Davis. 1990. "Measured Domestication Rates in Wild Wheats and Barley Under Primitive Cultivation and Their Archaeological Implications," *Journal of World Prehistory* 4 (2): 157–222.

Hinde, R. 1987. *Individuals, Relationships, and Culture*. Cambridge: Cambridge University Press.

Hodder, I., ed. 1978. *Simulation Studies in Archaeology*. Cambridge: Cambridge University Press.

———, ed. 1982a. *Symbolic and Structural Archaeology*. Cambridge: Cambridge University Press.

———, ed. 1982b. *Symbols in Action*. Cambridge: Cambridge University Press.

———. 1984. *The Present Past*. New York: Pica.

———. 1986. *Reading the Past*. Cambridge: Cambridge University Press.

———. 1995. *Theory and Practice in Archaeology*. Cambridge: Cambridge University Press.

———, and C. Orton. 1976. *Spatial Analysis in Archaeology*. Cambridge: Cambridge University Press.

Hogg, A. H. A. 1980. *Surveying for Archaeologists and Other Professionals*. New York: St. Martin's Press.

Hole, F. 1984. "Analysis of Structure and Design in Prehistoric Ceramics," *World Archaeology* 16: 326–347.

———, K. V. Flannery, and J. A. Neely. 1969. *The Prehistory and Human Ecology of the Deh Luran Plain*. Ann Arbor: University of Michigan Museum of Anthropology.

———, and R. F. Heizer. 1973. *An Introduction to Prehistoric Archaeology*, 3d ed. Fort Worth: Holt, Rinehart and Winston.

Holly, G. A., and T. A. Del Bene. 1981. "An Evaluation of Keeley's Microwear Approach," *Journal of Archaeological Science* 8: 337–352.

Horne, P. D. 1985. "A Review of the Evidence of Human Endoplasm in the Pre-Columbian New World Through the Study of Coprolites," *Journal of Field Archaeology* 12: 299–310.

Hosler, Dorothy. 1995. *The Sounds and Colors of Power*. Cambridge, Mass.: MIT Press.

Howard, H. 1929. "The Avifauna of Emeryville Shellmound," *University of California Publications in Zoology* 23: 378–383.

Hudson, K. 1982. *World Industrial Archaeology*. Cambridge: Cambridge University Press.

Hutt, Sherry, and others. 1993. *Archaeological Resource Protection*. Washington, D.C.: National Trust for Historic Preservation.

Huss-Ashmore, R., A. H. Goodman, and G. J. Armegalos. 1982. "Nutritional Inference from Paleopathology," *Advances in Archaeological Method and Theory* 5: 395–476.

Huxley, T. 1863. *Man's Place in Nature*. London: Macmillan.

Ingersoll, D., J. E. Yellen, and W. Macdonald, eds. 1977. *Experimental Archaeology.* New York: Columbia University Press.

Isaac, G. L. 1983. "Review: Ancient Men and Modern Myths," *American Antiquity* 48: 416–419.

———, and B. Isaac. 1989. *The Archaeology of Human Origins.* Cambridge: Cambridge University Press.

Jarman, H. N., A. J. Legge, and J. A. Charles. 1972. "Retrieval of Plant Remains from Archaeological Sites by Froth Flotation," in E. S. Higgs, ed., *Essays in Economic Prehistory,* pp. 39–48. Cambridge: Cambridge University Press.

Jennings, J. D., ed. 1983. *Ancient Native Americans,* 2d ed. New York: Freeman.

Jett, S., and P. B. Moyle. 1986. "The Exotic Origins of Fishes Depicted in Prehistoric Mimbres Pottery from New Mexico," *American Antiquity* 51: 688–720.

Jewell, P. A., and G. W. Dimbleby. 1966. "The Experimental Earthwork at Overton Down, Wiltshire, England," *Proceedings of the Prehistoric Society* 32: 313–342.

Jochim, M. A. 1979. "Breaking Down the System: Recent Ecological Approaches in Archaeology," *Advances in Archaeological Method and Theory* 2: 77–119.

Johanson, D., and M. Edey. 1981. *Lucy.* New York: Simon and Schuster.

Johnson, E., and others. 1977. "Archaeology and Native Americans," in C. R. McGimsey and H. A. Davis, eds., *The Management of Archaeological Resources,* pp. 90–96. Washington, D.C.: Society for American Archaeology.

Johnson, L. 1968. *Item Seriation as an Aid for Elementary Scale and Cluster Analysis.* Eugene: University of Oregon.

Johnson, L. L. 1978. "A History of Flint Knapping Experimentation, 1838–1976," *Current Anthropology* 19: 337–372.

Jones, P. R. 1980. "Experimental Butchery with Modern Stone Tools and Its Relevance for Paleolithic Archaeology," *World Archaeology* 12: 153–165.

Joukowsky, M. 1981. *Complete Manual of Field Archaeology.* Englewood Cliffs, N.J.: Prentice-Hall.

Joyce, Rosemary. 1993. "Women's Work: Images of Production and Reproduction in Pre-Hispanic Southern Central America." *Current Anthropology* 34 (3): 255–274.

Kaczor, M. J., and J. Weymouth. 1981. "Magnetic Prospecting: Results of the 1980 Field Season at the Toltec Site, 3LN42," *Proceedings of the Southeast Archaeological Conference* 24: 118–123.

Keeley, L. H. 1980. *Experimental Determination of Stone Tool Uses.* Chicago: University of Chicago Press.

Keene, D. 1985. *Survey of Medieval Winchester.* Oxford: Clarendon Press.

Kelley, J. H., and M. P. Hanan. 1988. *Archaeology and the Methodology of Science.* Albuquerque: University of New Mexico Press.

Kelso, W. M. 1984. *Kingsmill Plantation.* Orlando, Fla.: Academic Press.

———. 1986. "Mulberry Row: Slave Life at Thomas Jefferson's Monticello," *Archaeology* 39 (5): 28–35.

Kemp, B. 1989. *Ancient Egypt: Anatomy of a Civilization.* London: Routledge and Kegan Paul.

Kent, S. 1984. *Analyzing Activity Areas: An Ethnoarchaeological Study of the Use of Space.* Albuquerque: University of New Mexico Press.

Kidder, A. V. 1924. *An Introduction to the Study of Southwestern Archaeology.* New Haven, Conn.: Yale University Press.

Killingley, J. S. 1981. "Seasonality of Mollusk Collecting Determined from 0–18 Profiles of Midden Shells," *American Antiquity* 46: 152–158.

King, C., T. Blackburn, and E. Chandonet. 1968. "The Archaeological Inventory of Three Sites on the Century Ranch, Western Los Angeles County, California," *California Archaeological Survey Annual Report* 10: 12–161.

King, M. E. 1978. "Analytical Methods and Prehistoric Textiles," *American Antiquity* 43: 89–96.

King, T. F. 1971. "Resolving a Conflict of Values in American Archaeology," *American Antiquity* 36: 255–262.

———. 1983. "Professional Responsibility in Public Archaeology," *Annual Review of Anthropology* 12: 143–164.

Kirch, P. V. 1980. "The Archaeological Study of Adaptation: Theoretical and Methodological Issues," *Advances in Archaeological Method and Theory* 3: 101–155.

———. 1984. *The Evolution of Polynesian Chiefdoms.* Cambridge: Cambridge University Press.

Kirk, R. 1974. *Hunters of the Whale.* New York: Morrow.

Klein, R. G., 1969. *Man and Culture in the Late Pleistocene.* New York: Harper and Row.

———. 1977. "Environment and Subsistence of Prehistoric Man in the Southern Cape Province, South Africa," *World Archaeology* 5: 249–284.

———. 1983. "The Stone Age Prehistory of South Africa," *Annual Review of Anthropology* 12: 25–48.

Klein, R. G., and K. Cruz-Uribe. 1983. "The Computation of Ungulate Age (Mortality) Profiles from Dental Crown Heights," *Paleobiology* 9: 70–78.

———. 1984. *The Analysis of Animal Bones from Archaeological Sites.* Chicago: University of Chicago Press.

Klepinger, L. L. 1984. "Nutritional Assessment from Bone," *Annual Review of Anthropology* 13: 75–96.

Kluckhohn, C. 1940. "The Conceptual Structure in Middle American Studies," in A. M. Tozzer, ed., *The Maya and Their Neighbors. Norwalk,* Conn.: Appleton and Lang.

———. 1943. "Bronislaw Malinowski, 1884–1942," *Journal of American Folklore* 56: 208–219.

Knudson, R. 1986. "Contemporary Cultural Resource Management," in D. J. Meltzer, D. D. Fowler, and J. A. Sabloff, eds., *American Archaeology Past and Future,* pp. 395–413. Washington, D.C.: Smithsonian Institution Press.

Kooyman, B., and others. 1992. "Verifying the Reliability of Blood Residue Analysis on Archaeological Tools," *Journal of Archaeological Science* 19: 265–269.

Kosso, Peter. 1991. "Method in Archaeology: Middle-Range Theory as Hermeneutics," *American Antiquity* 56 (4): 621–627.

Kramer, C. 1985. "Ceramic Ethnoarchaeology," *Annual Review of Anthropology* 14: 77–102.

Krause, R. E. A. 1985. *The Clay Sleeps: An Ethnoarchaeological Study of Three African Potters.* Birmingham: University of Alabama Press.

Kroeber, A. L., and C. Kluckhohn. 1952. *Culture: A Critical Review of Concepts and Definitions.* Cambridge, MA: Harvard University, Peabody Museum of American Archaeology and Ethnology.

Kroeber, T. 1965. *Ishi in Two Worlds.* Berkeley: University of California Press.

Kurtén, B. 1968. *Pleistocene Mammals in Europe.* Hawthorne, N.Y.: Aldine.

Kvamme, K. L. 1989. "Geographical Information Systems in Regional Archaeological Research and Data Management," *Archaeological Method and Theory* 1: 110–131.

Lamberg-Karlovsky, C. C. 1970. *Excavations at Tepe Yahya, Iran, 1967–1969.* Cambridge, Mass.: American School of Prehistoric Research.

———. 1975. "Third Millennium Modes of Exchange and Modes of Production," in J. A. Sabloff and C. C. Lamberg-Karlovsky, eds., *Early Civilization and Trade,* pp. 341–368. Albuquerque: University of New Mexico Press.

Larsen, C. S. 1987. "Bioarchaeological Interpretations of Subsistence Economy and Behavior from Human Skeletal Remains," *Advances in Archaeological Method and Theory* 10: 27–56.

Laville, H., and others. 1980. *Rockshelters of the Perigord.* New York: Academic Press.

Layard, A. H. 1849. *Nineveh and Its Remains.* London: John Murray.

Layton, R. 1989. *Who Needs the Past?* London: Unwin-Hyman.

———, ed. 1994. *Conflict in the Archaeology of Living Traditions.* London: Unwin-Hyman.

Leach, Edmund R. 1984. *Political Systems of Highland Burma.* London: G. Bell.

Leakey, L. S. B. 1951. *Olduvai Gorge, 1931–1951.* Cambridge: Cambridge University Press.

———. 1971. *Olduvai Gorge, vol. 1.* Cambridge: Cambridge University Press.

Leakey, M. D. 1973. *Olduvai Gorge, vol. 3.* Cambridge: Cambridge University Press.

Lee, R. B. 1979. *The !Kung San.* Cambridge: Cambridge University Press.

Lee, R. F. 1970. *The Antiquities Act of 1906.* Washington, D.C.: National Park Service.

Legge, A. J., and P. A. Rowley-Conwy. 1987. "Gazelle Killing in Stone Age Syria," *Scientific American* 257: 76–83.

———. 1988. *Star Carr Revisited.* London: Birkbeck College.

Leone, M. P. 1982. "Childe's Offspring," in I. Hodder, ed., *Structural Archaeology,* pp. 179–184. Cambridge: Cambridge University Press.

———. 1984. "Interpreting Ideology in Historical Archaeology: The William Paca Garden in Annapolis, Maryland," in D. Miller and C. Tilley, eds., *Ideology, Power, and Prehistory,* pp. 25–35. Cambridge: Cambridge University Press.

———. 1986. "Symbolic, Structural, and Critical Archaeology," in D. J. Meltzer, D. D. Fowler, and J. A. Sabloff, eds., *American Archaeology Past and Future,* pp. 415–438. Washington, D.C.: Smithsonian Institution Press.

Lepper, B. T. 1983. "Fluted Point Distributional Patterns in the Eastern United States," *Midcontinental Journal of Archaeology* 8: 269–285.

Leute, J. 1987. *Archaeometry.* Weinheim, West Germany: VCH.

Lewarch, D. E., and M. J. O'Brien. 1981. "The Expanding Role of Surface Assemblages in Archaeological Research," *Advances in Archaeological Method and Theory* 4: 297–343.

Lewin, R. 1988. *Human Evolution,* 2d ed. Oxford: Blackwell.

Lewis-Williams, J. D. 1981. *Believing and Seeing: Symbolic Meanings in Southern San Rock Paintings.* Orlando, Fla.: Academic Press.

———, and J. H. N. Loubser. 1986. "Deceptive Appearances: A Critique of Southern African Rock Art Studies," *Advances in World Archaeology* 5: 203–290.

Libby, W. F. 1955. *Radiocarbon Dating.* Chicago: University of Chicago Press.

Lightfoot, K. G., and R. M. Cerrato. 1988. "Prehistoric Shellfish Exploitation in Coastal New York," *Journal of Field Archaeology* 15: 141–149.

Limbrey, S. 1972. *Soil Science in Archaeology.* New York: Seminar Press.

Limp, F. W. 1990. "Intersite Analysis: Aboriginal Use of the Rush Locality," in G. Sabo and others, *Archaeological Investigations at 3MR80-Area D in the Rush Development Area, Buffalo National River, Arkansas, vol. 1,* pp. 285–318. Santa Fe, N.M.: Southwest Cultural Resources Center, Professional Paper 38.

———, and P. Smith. 1990. "Environmental Parameters of the Rush Locality," in G. Sabo and others, *Archaeological Investigations at 3MR80-Area D in the Rush Development Area, Buffalo National River, Arkansas, vol. 1,* pp. 25–60. Santa Fe, N.M.: Southwest Cultural Resources Center, Professional Paper 38.

Linares, Olga F. 1977 *Ecology and the Arts in Ancient Panama: On the Development of Social Rank and Symbolism in the Central Provinces.* Washington, D.C.: Dumbarton Oaks.

Lipe, W. D. 1970. "A Conservation Model for American Archaeology," *Kiva* 3: 213–243.

Lloyd, S. 1963. *Mounds of the Near East.* Hawthorne, N.Y.: Aldine.

Loew, J. J., and M. J. C. Walker. 1985. *Reconstructing Quaternary Environments.* White Plains, N.Y.: Longman.

Longacre, W. 1991. *Ceramic Ethnoarchaeology.* Tucson: University of Arizona Press.

———, and M. T. Stark. 1992. "Ceramics, Kinship and Space: A Kalinga Example," *Journal of Archaeological Science* 11: 125–136.

Lyman, R. L. 1994. *Vertebrate Taphonomy.* Cambridge: Cambridge University Press.

Lynott, Mark J., and Alison Wylie. 1995. *Ethics in American Archaeology: Challenges for the 1990s.* Washington, D.C.: Society for American Archaeology.

Lyons, T. R., ed. 1981. *Remote Sensing: Multispectral Analysis of Cultural Resources in Chaco Canyon and Bandelier National Monument.* Washington, D.C.: National Park Service.

———, and T. Avery. 1977. *Remote Sensing: A Handbook for Archaeologists and Cultural Resource Managers.* Washington, D.C.: National Park Service.

MacNeish, R. S., ed. 1970. *The Prehistory of the Tehuacán Valley, vol. 3.* Austin: University of Texas Press.

———. 1978. *The Science of Archaeology?* North Scituate, Mass.: Duxbury Press.

Macquilty, W. 1965. *Abu Simbel.* London: Macmillan.

Madsen, D. P., and J. F. O'Connell, eds. 1982. *Man and Environment in the Great Basin*. Washington, D.C.: Society for American Archaeology.

Marcus, J. 1976. "The Size of the Early Mesoamerican Village," in K. V. Flannery, ed., *The Early Mesoamerican Village*, pp. 79–88. Orlando, Fla.: Academic Press.

Marcus, Michelle. 1994. "Dressed to Kill: Women and Pins in Early Iran." *Oxford Art Journal* 17 (2): 3–15.

Marean, C. W., and others. 1992. "Captive Hyena Bone Choice and Destruction, the Schlepp Effect and Olduvai Archaeofaunas," *Journal of Archaeological Science*, 19: 101–121.

Marquardt, W. H. 1978. "Advances in Archaeological Seriation," *Advances in Archaeological Method and Theory* 1: 28–64.

Martin, P. S., and R. G. Klein, eds. 1984. *A Pleistocene Revolution*. Tucson: University of Arizona Press.

Martin, P. S., and F. T. Plog. 1973. *The Archaeology of Arizona*. Garden City, N.Y.: Doubleday.

Matson, R. G. 1981. "Prehistoric Subsistence Patterns in the Fraser Delta: The Evidence from the Glenrose Cannery Site," *BC Studies* 48: 64–85.

McBryde, I., ed. 1985. *Who Owns the Past?* Melbourne, Australia: Oxford University Press.

McDonald, J. D., and others. 1991. "The Northern Cheyenne Outbreak of 1879: Using Oral History and Archaeology as Tools of Resistance," in R. McGuire and R. Paynter, eds., *The Archaeology of Inequality*, pp. 64–78. Oxford: Blackwell.

McEwen, B. G., and J. M. Mitchum. 1984. "Indian and European Acculturation in the Eastern United States as a Result of Trade," *North American Archaeologist* 5: 271–285.

McGimsey, C. 1972. *Public Archaeology*. New York: Seminar Press.

———, and H. Davis. 1977. *The Management of Archaeological Resources*. Washington, D.C.: National Park Service.

McGuire, R. H. 1992. *A Marxist Archaeology*. Orlando, Fla.: Academic Press.

———, and R. Paynter, eds. 1991. *The Archaeology of Inequality*. Oxford: Blackwell.

McHargue, G., and M. Roberts. 1977. *A Field Guide to Conservation Archaeology in North America*. Philadelphia: Lippincott.

McKern, W. C. 1939. "The Midwestern Taxonomic System as an Aid to Archaeological Culture Study," *American Antiquity* 4: 301–313.

McManamon, F. P. 1984. "Discovering Sites Unseen," *Advances in Archaeological Method and Theory* 7: 223–292.

——— 1992. "Managing America's Archaeological Resources," in LuAnn Wandsnider, ed., *Quandaries and Quests: Visions of Archaeology's Future*. Carbondale, Ill.: Center for Archaeological Investigations. pp. 25–40.

Meehan, B. 1982. *Shell Bed to Shell Midden*. Canberra: Australian Institute of Aboriginal Studies.

Meeke, N. D., and others. 1982. "Gloss and Use-Wear Traces on Flint Sickles and Similar Phenomena," *Journal of Archaeological Science* 9: 317–340.

Mellaart, J. 1975. *The Neolithic of the Near East*. London: Thames and Hudson.

Meltzer, D. J. 1983. "The Antiquity of Man and the Development of American Archaeology," *Advances in Archaeological Method and Theory* 6: 1–51.

Meltzer, D. J., D. D. Fowler, and J. A. Sabloff, eds., 1986. *American Archaeology Past and Future*. Washington, D.C.: Smithsonian Institution Press.

Meltzer, D. J., and others. 1994. "On a Pleistocene Human Occupation at Pedra Furada, Brazil," *Antiquity* 68 (261): 695–714.

Messenger, P. M., ed. 1989. *The Ethics of Collecting Cultural Property*. Albuquerque: University of New Mexico Press.

Meyer, K. 1992. *The Plundered Past*, 2d ed. Baltimore, Md.: Pelican.

Michael, H. N., and E. K. Ralph, eds. 1971. *Dating Techniques for the Archaeologist*. Cambridge, Mass.: MIT Press.

Michels, J. W. 1973. *Dating Methods in Archaeology*. Orlando, Fla.: Academic Press.

———, and R. Tsong. 1980. "Obsidian Hydration," *Advances in Archaeological Method and Theory* 3: 233–271.

Milanich, J. T., and S. Milbrath, eds. 1989. *First Encounters*. Gainesville: University of Florida Press.

Millon, R. 1973. *The Teotihuacán Map: Urbanization of Teotihuacán, Mexico*, vol. 1. Austin: University of Texas Press.

———. 1981. "Teotihuacán: City, State, and Civilization," in J. A. Sabloff, ed., *Supplement to the Handbook of Middle American Indians*, pp. 198–243. Austin: University of Texas Press.

Mithen, S. 1989. "Evolutionary Theory and Postprocessual Archaeology," *Antiquity* 63: 483–494.

———. 1990. *Thoughtful Foragers: A Study of Prehistoric Decision Making*. Cambridge: Cambridge University Press.

Molleson, Theya. 1989. "Seed Preparation in the Neolithic: The Osteological Evidence," *Antiquity* 63 (239): 356–62.

Mommsen, H., and others. 1992. "Provenance Determination of Mycenaean Sherds Found in Tell el Amarna by Neutron Activation Analysis," *Journal of Archaeological Science* 19: 295–302.

Monks, G. C. 1981. "Seasonality Studies," *Advances in Archaeological Method and Theory* 4: 177–240.

Moore, A. M. T. 1985. "Neolithic Societies in the Near East," *Advances in World Prehistory* 4: 1–69.

———. 1989. "The Transition from Foraging to Farming in Southwest Asia: Present Problems and Future Directions," in D. Harris and G. Hillman, eds., *Foraging and Farming*, pp. 620–631. London: Unwin-Hyman.

Morgan, L. 1877. *Ancient Society*. Fort Worth, Texas: Holt, Rinehart and Winston.

Morlan, R. E. 1978. "Early Man in Northern Yukon Territory: Perspectives as of 1977," in A. L. Bryan, ed., *Early Man in America*, pp. 78–95. Edmonton, Canada: Archaeological Research International.

Moseley, M. 1992. *The Inca and Their Ancestors*. New York: Thames and Hudson.

Muckelroy, K. 1978. *Maritime Archaeology*. Cambridge: Cambridge University Press.

Mueller, J. A. 1974. *The Use of Sampling in Archaeological Survey*. Washington, D.C.: U.S. Government Printing Office.

———, ed. 1975. *Sampling in Archaeology*. Tucson: University of Arizona Press.

Muensterberger, Werner. 1994. *Collecting, an unruly passion: psychological perspectives*. Princeton, N.J.: Princeton University Press.

Muhly, J. D. 1980. "The Bronze Age Setting," in J. D. Muhly and T. A. Wertime, eds., *The Coming of the Age of Iron*, pp. 25–68. New Haven, Conn.: Yale University Press.

———, and T. A. Wertime, eds. 1980. *The Coming of the Age of Iron*. New Haven, Conn.: Yale University Press.

Munson, Cheryl Ann, Marjorie M. Jones, and Robert E. Fry 1995. "The GE Mound Case: An ARPA Case Study," *American Antiquity* 60(1): 313–359.

Murdock, G. P. 1949. *Social Structure*. New York: Macmillan.

Nance, J. D. 1983. "Regional Sampling in Archaeological Survey: The Statistical Perspective," *Advances in Archaeological Method and Theory* 6: 289–356.

Nash, C. H. 1968. *Residence Mounds: An Intermediate Middle Mississippian Settlement Pattern*. Memphis, Tenn.: Memphis State University Anthropological Research Center.

Netting, R., and others, eds. 1984. *Households*. Berkeley: University of California Press.

Nilsson, T. 1983. *The Pleistocene*. Stuttgart, West Germany: Ferdinand Enke.

Noël Hume, I. 1969. *Historical Archaeology*. New York: Knopf.

———. 1982. *Martin's Hundred*. New York: Knopf.

O'Brien, M. J., and T. D. Holland. 1992. "The Role of Adaptation in Archaeological Explanation," *American Antiquity* 57 (1): 36–59.

O'Connell, J. 1975. *The Prehistory of Surprise Valley*. Ramona, Calif.: Ballena Press.

O'Connell, J. F. O., and others. 1992. "Patterns in the Distribution, Site Structure and Assemblage Composition of Hadza Kill-Butchering Sites," *Journal of Archaeological Science* 19: 319–345.

Odell, G. H., and F. Cowan. 1986. "Experiments with Spears and Arrows on Animal Targets," *Journal of Field Archaeology* 13: 195–212.

Odell, G. H., and F. Odell-Vereechea. 1980. "Verifying the Reliability of Lithic Use-Wear: The Lower Power Approach," *Journal of Field Archaeology* 7: 87–120.

Oetelaar, Gerald A. 1993. "Identifying Site Structure in the Archaeological Record: An Illinois Mississippian Example," *American Antiquity* 58 (4): 662–687.

Olin, J. S., and A. D. Franklin, eds. 1982. *Archaeological Ceramics*. Washington, D.C.: Smithsonian Institution Press.

Olsen, S. J. 1978. *Fish, Amphibian, and Reptile Remains from Archaeological Sites*. Cambridge, Mass.: Peabody Museum.

———. 1979a. "Osteologically, What Constitutes an Early Domesticated Animal?" *Advances in Archaeological Method and Theory* 2: 175–197.

———. 1979b. *Osteology for the Archaeologist*, rev. ed. Cambridge, Mass.: Peabody Museum.

Orme, B. 1979. *Thermoluminescence Techniques in Archaeology*. Oxford: Clarendon Press.

————. 1981. *Anthropology for Archaeologists*. Ithaca, N.Y.: Cornell University Press.

Orser, C.E., and Brian M. Fagan 1995. *Historical Archaeology*. New York: HarperCollins.

Orton, Clive, Paul Tyers, and Alan Vince. 1993. *Pottery in Archaeology*. Cambridge: Cambridge University Press.

Ortner, D. J., and W. G. J. Putschar. 1982. *Identification of Pathological Conditions in Human Remains*. Washington, D.C.: Smithsonian Institution Press.

O'Shea, J. M. 1984. *Mortuary Variability: An Archaeological Investigation*. Orlando, Fla.: Academic Press.

Pallottino, M. 1968. *The Meaning of Archaeology*. New York: Abrams.

Parmalee, P., and W. E. Klippel. 1974. "Freshwater Mollusca as a Prehistoric Food Resource," *American Antiquity* 39: 421–434.

Parson, J. A., and B. J. Price. 1971. *Mesoamerican Trade and Its Role in the Emergence of Civilization*. Berkeley: University of California Press.

Paul, A., and S. A. Turpin. 1986. "The Ecstatic Shaman Theme of Paracas Textiles," *Archaeology* 39 (5): 20–27.

Pearlman, M. 1980. *Digging Up the Bible*. New York: William Morrow.

Pearsall, D. 1989. *Paleoethnobotany: A Handbook of Procedures*. Orlando, Fla.: Academic Press.

————, and D. R. Piperno. 1990. "Antiquity of Maize Cultivation in Ecuador: Summary and Reevaluation of the Evidence." *American Antiquity* 55: 324–337.

Peebles, C. S. 1987. "Moundville from 1000–1500 A.D.," in R. D. Drennan and C. A. Uribe, eds., *Chiefdoms in the Americas*, pp. 21–41. Lanham, Md.: University Press of the Americas.

Petersen, J. B., and others. 1984. "Netting Technology and the Antiquity of Fish Exploitation in Eastern North America," *Midcontinental Journal of Archaeology* 9: 199–226.

Petrie, F. 1889. "Sequences in Prehistoric Remains," *Journal of the Royal Anthropological Institute* 29: 295–301.

Phillips, P. 1988. "Traceology (Microwear) Studies in the USSR," *World Archaeology* 19: 111–125.

Piggott, S. 1979. *Ruins in a Landscape*. Edinburgh: Edinburgh University Press.

————. 1985. *Ancient Europe*. Hawthorne, N.Y.: Aldine.

Piperno, D. R. 1988. *Phytolith Analysis: An Archaeological and Geological Perspective*. Orlando, Fla.: Academic Press.

Pires-Ferreira, J. 1976. "Obsidian Exchange in Formative Mesoamerica," in K. V. Flannery, ed., *The Early Mesoamerican Village,* pp. 293–305. Orlando, Fla.: Academic Press.

Plenderleith, H. J., and A. E. A. Werner. 1973. *The Conservation of Antiquities and Works of Art*, 2d ed. London: Oxford University Press.

Plog, F. 1978. "Cultural Resource Management and the 'New Archaeology,'" in C. L. Redman and others, eds., *Social Archaeology,* pp. 421–429. Orlando, Fla.: Academic Press.

Plog, F. T., and W. Wait, eds. 1982. *The San Juan Tomorrow*. Santa Fe, N.M.: National Park Service.

Plog, S. 1976a. "Measurement of Prehistoric Interaction Between Communities," in K. V. Flannery, ed., *The Early Mesoamerican Village,* pp. 255–272. Orlando, Fla.: Academic Press.

———. 1976b. "Relative Efficiencies of Sampling Techniques for Archaeological Surveys,"in K. V. Flannery, ed., *The Early Mesoamerican Village,* pp. 136–158. Orlando, Fla.: Academic Press.

———. 1980. *Stylistic Variation in Prehistoric Ceramics.* New York: Cambridge University Press.

———. 1983. "Analysis of Style in Artifacts," *Annual Review of Anthropology* 12: 125–142.

Poirier, David A., and Kenneth L. Feder. 1995. "Sharing the Past with the Present." *CRM* 18 (3): 3–4.

Polyani, K. 1975. "Traders and Trade," in J. A. Sabloff and C. C. Lamberg-Karlovsky, eds., *Early Civilization and Trade,* pp. 133–154. Albuquerque: University of New Mexico Press.

Pope, S. T. 1923. *Hunting with the Bow and Arrow.* San Francisco: James H. Barry.

Potter, Parker B., Jr. 1994. *Public Archaeology in Annapolis.* Washington, D.C.: Smithsonian Institution Press.

Powell, S., and others. 1993. "Ethics and Ownership of the Past: The Reburial and Repatriation Controversy," *Archaeological Method and Theory* 5: 14–55.

Prott, L., and P. J. O'Keefe. 1984. *Law and the Cultural Heritage.* Abingdon, England: Professional Books.

Purdy, B., ed. 1988. *Wet Site Archaeology.* Caldwell, N.J.: Telford Press.

Raab, L. M., and A. C. Goodyear. 1984. "Middle-Range Theory in Archaeology: A Critical Review of Origins and Applications," *American Antiquity* 49: 255–268.

Rahtz, P. A. 1974. *RESCUE Archaeology.* Baltimore, Md.: Pelican.

Rapoport, A. 1968. "Foreword," in W. Buckley, ed., *Modern Systems Research for the Behavioral Sciences.* Hawthorne, N.Y.: Aldine.

Rappaport, R. A. 1968. *Pigs for the Ancestors.* New Haven, Conn.: Yale University Press.

Rathje, W. H. 1970. "Socio-political Implications of Maya Lowland Burials," *World Archaeology* 1: 359–374.

———. 1971. "The Origin and Development of Lowland Classic Mayan Civilization," *American Antiquity* 36: 275–285.

———. 1979. "Modern Material Culture Studies," *Advances in Archaeological Method and Theory* 2: 1–38.

Rathje, W. H., and W. McCarthy. 1977. "Regularity and Variability in Contemporary Garbage," in S. A. South, ed., *Method and Theory in Historical Archaeology.* Orlando, Fla.: Academic Press.

———, eds. 1984. "House Refuse Analysis," *American Behavioral Scientist* 28: 47–55.

Rathje, W. H., and C. Murphy. 1992. *The Archaeology of Garbage.* New York: HarperCollins.

Rathje, W. H., and M. B. Schiffer. 1982. *Archaeology*. Orlando, Fla.: Harcourt Brace Jovanovich.

Ravensloot, John C. 1993. "The Road to Common Ground." *Federal Archaeology* 7 (3): 36–40.

Read, D. W., and S. A. Le Blanc. 1978. "Descriptive Statistics, Covering Laws, and Theories in Archaeology," *Current Anthropology* 19: 307–335.

Redman, C. L. 1974. *Archaeological Sampling Strategies*. Reading, Mass.: Addison-Wesley.

———. 1978a. "Mesopotamian Urban Ecology: The Systemic Context of the Emergence of Urbanism," in C. L. Redman and others, eds., *Social Archaeology*, pp. 329–348. Orlando, Fla.: Academic Press.

———. 1978b. "Multivariate Artifact Analysis: A Basis for Multidimensional Interpretations," in C. L. Redman and others, eds., *Social Archaeology*, pp. 159–192. Orlando, Fla.: Academic Press.

———. 1978c. *The Rise of Civilization*. New York: Freeman.

———. 1985. *Qsar es-Seghir: An Archaeological View of Medieval Life*. Orlando, Fla.: Academic Press.

———, and others, eds. 1978. *Social Archaeology*. Orlando, Fla.: Academic Press.

———, and P. J. Watson. 1970. "Systematic, Intensive Surface Collection," *American Antiquity* 35: 279–291.

Reeves, Nicholas. 1990. *The Complete Tutankhamun*. London: Thames and Hudson.

Reinhardt, Karl J., and Vaughn M. Bryant. 1992. "Coprolite Analysis: A Biological Perspective on Archaeology," *Archaeological Method and Theory* 4: 245–288.

Renfrew, A. C. 1975. *The Emergence of Civilization*. London: Methuen.

———. 1979. "Transformations," in A. C. Renfrew and K. L. Cooke, eds., *Transformations: Mathematical Applications to Cultural Change*, pp. 3–44. Orlando, Fla.: Academic Press.

———. 1987. *The Archaeology of Language*. London: Cape.

———. 1993. "Cognitive Archaeology: Some Thoughts on the Archaeology of Thought." *Cambridge Archaeological Journal* 3 (2): 248–250.

———. 1994. "Toward a cognitive archaeology," in Colin Renfrew and Ezra Zubrow, eds., *The Ancient Mind*, pp. 1–23. Cambridge: Cambridge University Press.

———, and Paul Bahn. 1991. *Archaeology: Theories, Methods, and Practice*. 2nd. ed. New York: Thames and Hudson.

———, J. E. Dixon, and J. R. Cann. 1966. "Obsidian and Early Cultural Contact in the Near East," *Proceedings of the Prehistoric Society* 32:1–29.

———, and A. Shennan, eds. 1982. *Ranking, Resources, and Exchange*. Cambridge: Cambridge University Press.

Renfrew, J. 1973. *Paleoethnobotany*. London: Methuen.

Reynolds, B. 1967. *The Material Culture of the Gwembe Tonga*. Manchester, England: Manchester University Press.

Reynolds, P. J. 1979. *Iron Age Farm*. London: British Museum.

Rice, P. M. 1984. *Pots and Potters: Current Approaches in Ceramic Archaeology*. Los Angeles: UCLA Institute of Archaeology.

———. 1987. *Pottery Analysis: A Sourcebook*. Chicago: University of Chicago Press.

Riley, C. L. 1971. *Man Across the Sea*. Austin: University of Texas Press.

Riley, D. N. 1987. *Air Photography and Archaeology*. London: Duckworth.

Roper, D. C. 1979. "The Method and Theory of Site Catchment Analysis: A Review," *Advances in Archaeological Method and Theory* 2: 120–142.

Rosen, A. M. 1986. *Cities of Clay*. Chicago: University of Chicago Press.

Rouse, I. 1972. *Introduction to Prehistory: A Systematic Approach*. New York: McGraw-Hill.

Rovner, I. 1983. "Plant Opal Phytolith Research: Major Advances in Archaeobotanical Research," *Advances in Archaeological Method and Theory* 6: 225–266.

Rye, O. S. 1981. *Pottery Technology*. Washington, D.C.: Taraxacum.

Sabloff, J. A. 1975. *Excavations at Seibal: Ceramics*. Cambridge, Mass.: Harvard University, Peabody Museum of American Archaeology and Ethnology.

———, ed. 1981. *Simulation in Archaeology*. Albuquerque: University of New Mexico Press.

———. 1989. *The Cities of Ancient Mexico*. London: Thames and Hudson.

———, and C. C. Lamberg-Karlovsky, eds. 1975. *Early Civilization and Trade*. Albuquerque: University of New Mexico Press.

———, and W. L. Rathje, eds. 1975. *A Study of Pre-Columbian Commercial Systems: The 1972–1973 Seasons at Cozumel, Mexico*. Cambridge, Mass.: Harvard University, Peabody Museum.

Sabo, G., and others. 1990. *Archaeological Investigations at 3MR80 Area D in the Rush Development Area, Buffalo National River, Arkansas, vol. 1*. Santa Fe, N.M.: Southwest Cultural Resources Center, Professional Paper 38.

Sackett, J. 1966. "Quantitative Analysis of Upper Paleolithic Stone Tools," *American Anthropologist* 68: 356–394.

———. 1977. "The Meaning of Style in Archaeology," *American Antiquity* 43: 369–382.

———. 1981. "From de Mortillet to Bordes: A Century of French Upper Palaeolithic Research," in G. Daniel, ed., *Towards a History of Archaeology*, pp. 85–99. London: Thames and Hudson.

———. 1982. "Approaches to Style in Lithic Archaeology," *Journal of Anthropological Archaeology* 1: 59–112.

Sahlins, M., and E. Service, eds. 1960. *Evolution and Culture*. Ann Arbor: University of Michigan Press.

Salmon, M. 1978. "What Can Systems Theory Do for Archaeology?" *American Antiquity* 43: 174–183.

———. 1982. *The Philosophy of Archaeology*. Orlando, Fla.: Academic Press.

Sanders, W. T., J. R. Parsons, and R. S. Santley. 1979. *The Basin of Mexico: Ecological Processes in the Evolution of a Civilization*. 2 vols. Orlando, Fla.: Academic Press.

Sanders, W. T., and B. J. Price. 1968. *Mesoamerica: Evolution of a Civilization*. New York: Random House.

Sanders, W. T., and D. Webster. 1978. "Unilinealism, Multilinealism, and the Evolution of Complex Societies," in C. L. Redman and others, eds., *Social Archaeology*, pp. 249–302. Orlando, Fla.: Academic Press.

Scarre, C., ed. 1988. *Past Worlds: The Times Atlas of Archaeology*. London: Times Books.

Schele, L., and D. Friedel. 1990. *A Forest of Kings*. New York: William Morrow.

———. 1993. *Maya Cosmos*. New York: William Morrow.

Schele, L., and M. E. Miller. 1992. *The Blood of Kings: Dynasty and Ritual in Maya Art,* 2d ed. New York: Thames and Hudson.

Schiffer, M. B. 1976. *Behavioral Archaeology*. Orlando, Fla.: Academic Press.

———. 1979. "A Preliminary Consideration of Behavioral Change," in A. C. Renfrew, ed., *Transformations: Mathematical Approaches to Culture Change,* pp. 353–368. Orlando, Fla.: Academic Press.

———. 1987. *Site Formation Processes of the Archaeological Record*. Albuquerque: University of New Mexico Press.

Schiffer, M. B., and J. H. House. 1976. *The Cache River Archaeological Project*. Fayetteville: Arkansas Archaeological Survey.

———. 1977. "Cultural Resource Management and Archaeological Research: The Cache Project," *Current Anthropology* 18: 43–68.

Schiffer, M. B., A. P. Sullivan, and T. C. Klinger. 1978. "The Design of Archaeological Surveys," *World Archaeology* 10: 1–28.

Schoeninger, M. J. 1979. "Diet and Status at Chalcatzingo: Some Empirical and Technical Aspects of Strontium Analysis," *American Journal of Physical Anthropology* 51: 295–310.

Scollar, Irwin, and others. 1990. *Archaeological Prospecting and Remote Sensing*. Cambridge: Cambridge University Press.

Scott, Elizabeth M., ed. 1994. *Those of Little Note: Gender, Race, and Class in Historical Archaeology*. Tucson, AR: University of Arizona Press.

Scudder, T. 1962. *The Ecology of the Gwembe Tonga*. Manchester, England: Manchester University Press.

Service, E. 1971. *Primitive Social Organization*. New York: Random House.

Sever, T., and J. Wiseman. 1985. *Remote Sensing and Archaeology: Potential for the Future*. Picayune, Miss.: NASA Earth Sciences Laboratory.

Shackleton, N. J., and N. D. Opdyke. 1973. "Oxygen Isotope and Paleomagnetic Stratigraphy of Equatorial Pacific Ocean Core V28–238," *Quaternary Research* 3: 38–55.

Shackley, M. L. 1975. *Archaeological Sediments*. New York: Wiley.

———. 1985. *Environmental Archaeology*. London: Batsford.

Shanks, M., and C. Tilley. 1987a. *Reconstructing Archaeology: Theory and Practice*. Cambridge: Cambridge University Press.

———. 1987b. *Social Theory and Archaeology*. Albuquerque: University of New Mexico Press.

———. 1989. "Archaeology into the 1990s," *Norwegian Archaeological Review* 22: 1–54.

Sharer, R. J., and W. Ashmore. 1988. *Discovering Our Past*. Palo Alto, Calif.: Mayfield.

———. 1995. *Archaeology: Discovering the Past,* 3d ed. Palo Alto, Calif.: Mayfield.

Shaw, T. 1960. "Early Smoking Pipes in Africa, Europe, and America," *Journal of the Royal Anthropological Institute* 90: 272–305.

Shawcross, F. C. 1967. "Prehistoric Diet and Economy on a Coastal Site at Galatea Bay, New Zealand," *Proceedings of the Prehistoric Society* 33 (7): 125–130.

Sheets, P. D. 1992. *The Cerén Site*. New York: Harcourt Brace Jovanovich.

———, and G. R. Muto. 1972. "Pressure Blades and Total Cutting Edge," *Science* 175: 632–634.

Shennan, S. 1988. *Quantifying Archaeology*. Orlando, Fla.: Academic Press.

Shepard, A. O. 1971. *Ceramics for the Archaeologist,* 2d ed. Washington, D.C.: Smithsonian Institution.

Shipman, P. 1981. *Life History of a Fossil: An Introduction to Taphonomy and Paleoecology*. Cambridge, Mass.: Harvard University Press.

Shipman, P., and J. Rose. 1983. "Early Hominid Hunting, Butchering, and Carcass Processing Behaviors: Approaches to the Fossil Record," *Journal of Anthropological Archaeology* 2: 57–98.

Shreeve, J. 1992. "The Dating Game," *Discover* 13 (6): 76–83.

Sillen, A., and others. 1989. "Chemistry and Paleodietary Research: No More Easy Answers," *American Antiquity* 54: 504–512.

Silverberg, R. 1968. *The Mound Builders of Ancient America*. New York: New York Graphic Society.

Skibo, J. M. 1992. *Pottery Function*. New York: Plenum.

———, and others, eds. 1995. *Expanding Archaeology*. Salt Lake City: University of Utah Press.

Slotkin, J. S., ed. 1965. *Readings in Early Anthropology*. New York: Viking Penguin.

Smith, B. D. 1974. "Middle Mississippian Exploitation of Animal Populations: A Predictive Model," *American Antiquity* 39: 274–291.

———. 1986. "The Archaeology of the Southeastern United States: From Dalton to de Soto, 10,500–500 B.P.," *Advances in World Archaeology* 5: 1–92.

———. 1992. *Rivers of Change: Essays on Early Agriculture in Eastern North America*. Washington, D.C.: Smithsonian Institution Press.

———. 1994. *The Emergence of Agriculture*. New York: Scientific American Library.

Smith, E. G. 1911. *The Ancient Egyptians*. London: Macmillan.

Smith, G. S., and J. E. Ehrenhard, eds. 1991. *Protecting the Past*. Boca Raton, Fla.: CRC Press.

Snodgrass, A. M. 1987. *An Archaeology of Greece: The Present State and Future Scope of a Discipline*. Berkeley: University of California Press.

Snow, D. 1976. *The North American Indians*. New York: Viking Penguin.

Soffer, O. 1985. T*he Upper Paleolithic of the Central Russian Plain*. Orlando, Fla.: Academic Press.

Soren, D., and J. James. 1988. *Kourion: The Search for a Lost Roman City*. Garden City, N.Y.: Anchor/Doubleday.

South, S., ed. 1977. *Method and Theory in Historical Archaeology*. Orlando, Fla.: Academic Press.

Spaulding, A. C. 1953. "Statistical Techniques for the Study of Artifact Types," *American Antiquity* 18: 305–313.

———. 1960. "Statistical Description and Comparison of Artifact Assemblages," in R. F. Heizer and S. F. Cook, eds., *Quantitative Methods in Archaeology,* pp. 60–92. New York: Viking Penguin.

————. 1973. "Archaeology in the Active Voice: The New Anthropology," in C. L. Redman, ed., *Research and Theory in Current Archaeology,* pp. 337–354. New York: Wiley Interscience.

Spencer, H. 1855. *Social Statistics.* London: Macmillan.

Speth, J. D. 1983. *Bison Kills and Bone Counts: Decision Making by Ancient Hunters.* Chicago: University of Chicago Press.

Spindler, Konrad. 1994. *The Man in the Ice.* London: Weidenfeld and Nicholson.

Spooner, B., ed. 1972. *Population Growth: Anthropological Implications.* Cambridge, Mass.: MIT Press.

Spriggs, M., ed. 1984. *Marxist Perspectives in Archaeology.* Cambridge: Cambridge University Press.

Stark, B. L. 1984. "An Ethnoarchaeological Study of a Mexican Pottery Industry," *Journal of Northwest Archaeology* 6 (2): 4–14.

————, and D. L. Young. 1981. "Linear Nearest Neighbor Analysis," *American Antiquity* 46: 284–300.

Starki, E. 1982. "Advances in Urban Archaeology," *Advances in Archaeological Method and Theory* 5: 97–150.

Steffy, Richard. 1994. *Wooden Shipbuilding and the Interpretation of Shipwrecks.* College Station: Texas A & M University Press.

Stein, J. K. 1987. "Deposits for Archaeologists," *Advances in Archaeological Method and Theory* 11: 337–398.

————, ed. 1992. *Deciphering a Shell Midden.* Orlando, Fla.: Academic Press.

Stephens, J. L. 1841. *Incidents of Travel in Central America, Chiapas, and Yucatán.* New York: Harper and Row.

Steward, J. 1938. *Basin-Plateau Aboriginal Sociopolitical Groups.* Washington, D.C.: Smithsonian Institution.

————. 1955. *A Theory of Culture Change.* Urbana: University of Illinois Press.

Stimmell, C., and others. 1982. "Indian Pottery from the Mississippi Valley: Coping with Bad Raw Materials," in J. S. Olin and A. D. Franklin, eds., *Archaeological Ceramics,* pp. 219–228. Washington, D.C.: Smithsonian Institution Press.

Stirland, A. 1987. *Human Bones in Archaeology.* Aylesbury, England: Shire Press.

Stoltman, J. B., and D. A. Barreis. 1983. "The Evolution of Human Ecosystems in the Eastern and Central United States," in H. E. Wright, ed., *Late Quarternary Environments of the United States,* pp. 252–268. Minneapolis: University of Minnesota Press.

Stone-Miller, Rebecca. 1995. *Art of the Andes.* London: Thames and Hudson.

Strong, W. D. 1935. *An Introduction to Nebraska Archaeology.* Washington, D.C.: Smithsonian Institution.

Struever, Stuart. 1971. "Comments on Archaeological Data Requirements and Research Strategy," *American Antiquity* 36: 10.

————, and F. A. Holton. 1979. *Koster.* Garden City, N.Y.: Anchor/Doubleday.

————, and G. L. Houart. 1972. "An Analysis of the Hopewell Interaction Sphere," *Anthropological Papers of the University of Michigan* 46: 47–79.

Stuiver, M., and G. W. Pearson 1993. "High-precision calibration of the radiocarbon time scale, A.D. 1950–500 B.C. and 2500–6000 B.C." *Radiocarbon* 35: 1–23.

Stuiver, M., and P. J. Reimer 1993. "Extended 14C data base and revised Calib 3.0 14C age calibration program." *Radiocarbon* 35: 215–230.

Suess, H. E. 1965. "Secular Variations of the Cosmic-Ray-Produced Carbon 14 in the Atmosphere and Their Interpretations," *Journal of Geophysical Research* 70: 23–31.

Sullivan, A. P., and K. C. Rozen. 1985. "Debitage Analysis and Archaeological Interpretation," *American Antiquity* 50: 755–779.

Sullivan, Lawrence. 1989. *Icanchu's Drum*. New York: Free Press.

Swanson, E., ed. 1975. *Lithic Technology: Making and Using Stone Tools*. Hawthorne, N.Y.: Aldine.

Swisher, Carl, and others. "Age of the Earliest Known Hominids in Java, Indonesia," *Science* 263 (1994): 1118–1121.

Taylor, R. E. 1987. *Radiocarbon Dating: An Archaeological Perspective*. Orlando, Fla.: Academic Press.

———, and C. W. Meighan, eds. 1978. *Chronologies in New World Archaeology*. Orlando, Fla.: Academic Press.

Taylor, W. W. 1948. *A Study of Archaeology*. Menasha, Wisc.: American Anthropological Association.

Terrell, J. 1967. "Galatea Bay: The Excavation of a Beach-Stream Midden Site on Ponju Island in the Hauraki Gulf, New Zealand," *Transactions of the Royal Society of New Zealand* 2 (3): 31–70.

Thomas, D. H. 1978. "The Awful Truth About Statistics in Archaeology," *American Antiquity* 43: 231–244.

———. 1983a. *The Archaeology of Monitor Valley, vols. 1 and 2*. New York: Anthropological Papers of the American Museum of Natural History.

———. 1983b. "On Steward's Models of Shoshonean Sociopolitical Organization: A Great Bias in the Basin," in E. Tooker, ed., *The Development of Political Organization in Native North America*, pp. 56–68. Washington, D.C.: American Ethnological Society.

———. 1986. "Contemporary Hunter-Gatherer Archaeology in America," in D. J. Meltzer, D. D. Fowler, and J. A. Sabloff, eds., *American Archaeology Past and Future*, pp. 237–276. Washington, D.C.: Smithsonian Institution Press.

———. 1988. *Archaeology, 2d ed.* Fort Worth: Holt, Rinehart and Winston.

———. 1989. *Refiguring Anthropology*. Prospect Heights, Ill.: Waveland Press.

Thomas, M. N., and M. K. Lewis. 1961. *Eva: An Archaic Site*. Knoxville: University of Tennessee Press.

Thompson, J. E. S. 1972. *Maya Hieroglyphs Without Tears*. London: British Museum.

Thompson, R. H. 1956. "The Subjective Element in Archaeological Inference," *Southwestern Journal of Anthropology* 12: 327–332.

Tite, M. S. 1972. *Methods of Physical Examination in Archaeology*. Orlando, Fla.: Academic Press.

Tobias, P. V. 1971. *Olduvai Gorge, vol. 2*. Cambridge: Cambridge University Press.

Torrence, R. 1986. *Production and Exchange of Stone Tools*. Cambridge: Cambridge University Press.

Toth, Nicholas, and K. D. Schick 1993. *Making Silent Stones Speak: Human Evolution and the Dawn of Technology*. New York: Simon and Schuster.

Townsend, R. F. 1992. *The Aztecs*. New York: Thames and Hudson.

Townsend, W. H. 1969. "Stone and Steel Tool Use in a New Guinea Society," *Ethnology* 8: 199–205.

Trigger, B. G. 1968a. *Beyond History: The Methods of Prehistory*. Fort Worth, Texas: Holt, Rinehart and Winston.

———. 1968b. "The Determination of Settlement Patterns," in K. C. Chang, ed., *Settlement Archaeology*, pp. 53–78. Palo Alto, Calif.: National Press.

———. 1980. *Gordon Childe: Revolutions in Archaeology*. London: Thames and Hudson.

———. 1984a. "Alternative Archaeologies: Nationalist, Colonialist, Imperialist," *Man* 19: 355–370.

———. 1984b. "Archaeology at the Crossroads: What's New," *Annual Review of Anthropology* 13: 275–300.

———. 1985. "The Past as Power: Anthropology and the American Indian," in I. McBryde, ed., *Who Owns the Past?* pp. 11–40. Melbourne, Australia: Oxford University Press.

———. 1986. "Prehistoric Archaeology and American Society," in D. J. Meltzer, D. D. Fowler, and J. A. Sabloff, eds., *American Archaeology Past and Future*, pp. 187–216. Washington, D.C.: Smithsonian Institution Press.

———. 1989. *A History of Archaeological Interpretation*. Cambridge: Cambridge University Press.

———. 1991. "Distinguished Lecture in Archaeology: Constraint and Freedom," *American Anthropologist* 93 (3): 551–569.

———. 1995. "Expanding middle-range theory," *Antiquity* 69 (264): 449–58.

Tringham, Ruth. 1994. "Engendered Places in Prehistory," *Gender, Place, and Culture: a Journal of Feminist Geography* 1 (2): 169–204.

Trombold, Charles D., ed. 1992. *Ancient Road Networks and Settlement Hierarchies in the New World*. Cambridge, Eng: Cambridge University Press.

Tuck, J. A., and R. Grenier. 1989. *Red Bay, Labrador: World Whaling Capital A.D. 1550–1600*. St. John's, Newfoundland: Atlantic Archaeology.

Turner, B. L., and P. D. Harrison. 1983. *Pulltrouser Swamp: Ancient Maya Habitat, Agriculture, and Settlement in Northern Belize*. Austin: University of Texas Press.

Tuross, Noreen, and others. 1994. "Subsistence in the Florida Archaic: The Stable-Isotope and Archaeobotanical Evidence form the Windover Site." *American Antiquity* 59 (2): 288–303.

Tylecote, R. F. 1992. *A History of Metallurgy*. London: The Institute of Materials.

Tylor, E. B. 1871. *Primitive Culture*. London: John Murray.

Ucko, Peter J., ed. 1995. *Theory in Archaeology: A World Perspective*. London and New York: Routledge.

Ucko, P. J., and G. W. Dimbleby, eds. 1969. *The Domestication and Exploitation of Plants and Animals*. London: Duckworth.

United States Department of the Interior. 1976. "National Register of Historic Places: Criteria for Statewide Surveys and Plans," *Code of Federal Regulations*, Title 36, Chapter 1, Part 60. Washington, D.C.: U.S. Government Printing Office.

Van Riper, A. Bowdoin. 1993. *Men among the Mammoths: Victorian Science and the Discovery of Human Prehistory*. Chicago: University of Chicago Press.

Vaughan, C. J. 1986. "Ground Penetrating Radar Surveys Used in Archaeological Investigations," *Geoscience* 51: 595–605.

Vaughan, P. 1985. *Use-Wear Analysis of Flaked Stone Tools.* Tucson: University of Arizona Press.

Villa, P. 1982. "Conjoinable Pieces and Site Formation Processes," *American Antiquity* 47: 276–290.

———. 1983. *Terra Amata and the Middle Pleistocene Archaeological Record of Southern France.* Berkeley: University of California Press.

———, and J. Courtin. 1983. "The Interpretation of Stratified Sites: A View from Underground," *Journal of Archaeological Science* 10: 267–281.

Vinnecombe, P. 1960. "A Fishing Scene from the Tsoelike River, Southwestern Basutoland," *South African Archaeological Bulletin* 15: 15–19.

Vita-Finzi, C. 1978. *Archaeological Sites in Their Setting.* London: Thames and Hudson.

Vitelli, Karen D. 1993. *Franchthi Neolithic Pottery, Vol 1: Classification and Ceramic Phases 1 and 2.* Bloomington, Indiana University Press.

Vogt, E. Z. 1967. *A Maya Community in the Highlands of Chiapas.* Cambridge, Mass.: Belknap Press.

Waselkov, G. 1987. "Shellfish Gathering and Shell Midden Archaeology," *Advances in Archaeological Method and Theory* 10: 112–167.

Waters, M. R. 1993. *The Principles of Geoarchaeology: A North American Perspective.* Tucson: University of Arizona Press.

Watson, P. J. 1974. *Archaeology of the Mammoth Cave Area.* Orlando, Fla.: Academic Press.

Watson, P. J., and M. C. Kennedy. 1991. "The Development of Horticulture in the Eastern Woodlands," in J. M. Gero and M. W. Conkey, eds., *Engendering Archaeology,* pp. 255–276. Oxford: Blackwell.

Watson, P. J., S. A. Le Blanc, and C. L. Redman. 1984. *Archaeological Explanation: The Scientific Method in Archaeology,* 2d ed. New York: Columbia University Press.

Watson, R. A. 1976. "Inference in Archaeology," *American Antiquity* 41: 58–66.

———. 1990. "Ozymandias, King of Kings: Postprocessual Radical Archaeology at Critique," *American Antiquity* 55 (4): 673–689.

Wauchope, R. 1972. *Lost Tribes and Sunken Continents.* Chicago: University of Chicago Press.

Webb, W. S. 1939. *An Archaeological Survey of Wheeler Basin on the Tennessee River in Northern Alabama.* Washington, D.C.: Smithsonian Institution, Bureau of American Ethnology.

Webster, D., and N. Gordon. 1988. "Household Remains of the Humblest Maya," *Journal of Field Archaeology* 15: 169–180.

Wells, C. 1964. *Bones, Bodies, and Disease.* London: Thames and Hudson.

Wendorf, F., and others. 1968. *The Prehistory of Nubia.* Dallas: Southern Methodist University Press.

———. 1980. *Loaves and Fishes. The Prehistory of Wadi Kubbaniya.* Dallas: Southern Methodist University Press.

Wenke, R. J. 1981. "Explaining the Evolution of Cultural Complexity: A Review," *Advances in Archaeological Method and Theory* 4: 979–1028.

Weymouth, J. W. 1986. "Geophysical Methods of Archaeological Site Survey," *Advances in Archaeological Method and Theory* 10: 311–396.

Whallon, R. A., and J. A. Brown, eds. 1982: *Essays in Archaeological Typology.* Evanston, Ill.: Center for American Archaeology.

Wheat, J. B. 1972. *The Olsen-Chubbock Site: A Paleo-Indian Bison Kill.* Washington, D.C.: Smithsonian Institution, Society for American Archaeology.

Wheatley, P. 1971. *The Pivot of the Four Quarters.* Hawthorne, N.Y.: Aldine.

———. 1975. "Satyantra in Suvarnadvipa: from reciprocity to redistribution in ancient southeast Asia." In J. A. Sabloff and C. C. Lamberg-Karlovsky, eds. *Ancient Civilization and Trade,* pp. 227–265. Albuquerque: University of New Mexico Press.

Wheeler, A., and A. K. G. Jones. 1989. *Fishes.* Cambridge: Cambridge University Press.

Wheeler, R. E. M. 1943. *Maiden Castle.* London: Society of Antiquaries.

———. 1954. *Archaeology from the Earth.* Oxford: Clarendon Press.

White, J. P., and J. O'Connell. 1982. *A Prehistory of Australia, New Guinea, and Sahul.* Orlando, Fla.: Academic Press.

White, L. 1949. *The Evolution of Culture.* New York: McGraw-Hill.

White, R. 1986. *Dark Caves, Bright Images.* New York: American Museum of Natural History.

White, T. 1953. "Observations on the Butchery Techniques of Some Aboriginal Peoples," *American Antiquity* 19: 160–164.

White, T. D., Suwa, G, and Asfaw, B. 1994. "*Australopithecus ramidus,* a new species of early hominid from Aramis, Ethiopia," *Nature* 371: 306-12.

Wildeson, L. E. 1982. "The Study of Impacts on Archaeological Sites," *Advances in Archaeological Method and Theory* 5: 51–96.

Wilk, Richard R. 1991. *Household Ecology: Economic Change and Domestic Life Among the Kekchi Maya in Belize.* Tucson: University of Arizona Press.

Willey, G. R. 1953. *Prehistoric Settlement Patterns in the Virú Valley, Peru.* Washington, D.C.: Smithsonian Institution, Bureau of American Ethnology.

———. 1962. "The Early Great Styles and the Rise of the Pre-Columbian Civilizations," *American Anthropologist* 64: 1–14.

———. 1966. *An Introduction to American Archaeology, Volume 1: North America.* Englewood Cliffs, N.J.: Prentice-Hall.

———. 1971. *An Introduction to American Archaeology, Volume 2: Middle and South America.* Englewood Cliffs, N.J.: Prentice-Hall.

———, ed. 1974. *Archaeological Researches in Retrospect.* Cambridge, Mass.: Winthrop.

Willey, G. R., and P. Phillips. 1958. *Method and Theory in American Archaeology.* Chicago: University of Chicago Press.

Willey, G. R., and J. A. Sabloff. 1993. *A History of American Archaeology,* 3d ed. New York: W. H. Freeman.

Winter, M. C. 1976. "The Archaeological Household Cluster in the Valley of Oaxaca," in K. V. Flannery, ed., *The Early Mesoamerican Village,* pp. 25–30. Orlando, Fla.: Academic Press.

Winterhalder, B., and E. A. Smith, eds. 1981. *Hunter-Gatherer Foraging Strategies.* Chicago: University of Chicago Press.

Wolf, E. 1984. *Europe and the People Without History*. Berkeley: University of California Press.

Wolfman, D. 1984. "Geomagnetic Dating Methods in Archaeology," *Advances in Archaeological Method and Theory* 7: 363–458.

Wood, J. J. 1978. "Optimal Location in Settlement Space: A Model for Describing Location Strategies," *American Antiquity* 43: 258–270.

Wood, W. R., and D. L. Johnson. 1978. "A Survey of the Disturbance Processes in Archaeological Site Formation," *Advances in Archaeological Method and Theory* 1: 112–146.

Woodbury, J. C. 1980. "The First Archaeological Appearance of Iron," in J. D. Muhly and T. A. Wertime, eds., *The Coming of the Age of Iron,* pp. 69–98. New Haven, Conn.: Yale University Press.

Woolley, C. L. 1943. *Ur Excavations. Volume 2, The Royal Cemetery*. Philadelphia: University of Pennsylvania Museum.

————. 1954. *Excavations at Ur.* New York: Barnes and Noble.

Worsaae, J. J. A. 1843. *Danmarks Oldtid*. Copenhagen.

Wright, T. 1852. "Wanderings of an Antiquary: Part VII," *Gentleman's Magazine* (October): 569.

Wylie, A. 1985. "The Reaction Against Analogy" *Advances in Archaeological Method and Theory* 8: 63–111.

————. 1988. *The New Archaeology: Tensions in Theory and Practice*. Orlando, Fla.: Academic Press.

————. 1991. "Gender Theory and the Archaeological Record: Why Is There No Archaeology of Gender?" in J. M. Gero and M. W. Conkey, eds., *Engendering Archaeology: Women and Prehistory,* pp. 31–55. Oxford: Blackwell.

Yadin, Yigal. 1966. *Masada: Herod's Fortress and the Zealots' Last Stand*. London: Weidenfeld and Nicholson.

Yellen, J. E. 1977. *Archaeological Approaches to the Present: Models for Predicting the Past.* Orlando, Fla.: Academic Press.

Yentsch, Anne. 1994. *A Chesapeake Family and Their Slaves*. Cambridge: Cambridge University Press, 1994.

Yoffee, Norman. 1993. "Too many chiefs? (or, Safe texts for the '90s)," in Norman Yoffee and Andrew Sheratt, eds. *Archaeological Theory: Who Sets the Agenda?,* pp. 60–78. Cambridge: Cambridge University Press.

Yoffee, Norman, and Sherratt, Andrew, eds. 1993. *Archaeological Theory: Who Sets the Agenda?* Cambridge: Cambridge University Press.

Zedeño, María Nieves. 1994. *Sourcing Prehistoric Ceramics at Chodistaas Pueblo, Arizona*. Tucson: University of Arizona Press.

Zubrow, E. 1976. *Demographic Anthropology: Quantitative Approaches*. Albuquerque: University of New Mexico Press.

ILLUSTRATION CREDITS

Chapter 1: *Figure 1.1A,* Courtauld Institute of Art; London; *Figure 1.1B,* Bettmann Archive; *Figure 1.2,* Photo by Susan Einstein courtesy of UCLA Fowler Museum of Cultural History; *Figure 1.3,* Photograph by Egyptian Expedition, The Metropolitan Museum of Art; *Figure 1.5,* Photo by Kenny Barkely, courtesy of David Pollack, University of Kentucky and The Kentucky Heritage Council, and Cheryl Ann Munson, Indiana University; *Figure 1.6A,* © Plenge, Robert Harding Picture Library; *Figure 1.6B,* Metropolitan Museum of Art, Bequest of Joseph H. Durkee, gift of Darius Mills, and gift of C. Ruxton Love, by Exchange, 1972 (1972.11.10); *Figure 1.7,* George Holton/Photo Researchers; *Figure 1.8,* Colonial Williamsburg Foundation; *Figure 1.9,* Nautical Institute of Archaeology.

Chapter 2: *Figure 2.1,* Werner Forman/Art Resource, NY; *Figure 2.2,* © Spencer Grant/Monkmeyer; *Figure 2.3,* Gentlemen's Magazine, 1840; *Figure 2.4,* Courtesy of the Royal Anthropological Institute of Great Britain and Ireland. Redrawn from "The Swanscombe Skull: A Survey of Research on Pleistocene Site" (Occasional Paper No. 20, fig 23.6); *Figure 2.5,* The Bettmann Archive; *Figure 2.7,* Photo by J. Oster. Courtesy of Musée de l'Homme.

Chapter 3: *Figure 3.1,* James F. O'Connell

Chapter 4: *Figure 4.1,* National Museum, Copenhagen; *Figure 4.2,* National Museum, Copenhagen; *Figure 4.3,* Ruth Kirk with Richard D. Daugherty, Hunters of the Whale, 1974. New York. William Morrow and Company; *Figure 4.4,* to come later; *Figure 4.5,* © Wieslav Smetek/Stern, Black Star; *Figure 4.6,* Owen Beattie, University of Alberta; *Figure 4.7,* Payson Sheets, The Ceren Sites, Harcourt Brace Jovanovich, 1992.

Chapter 6: *Figure 6.1,* Bibliotheque Firenze; *Figure 6.2,* Richard Lee/Anthro-Photo; *Figure 6.3,* Granger; *Figure 6.4,* none listed in 8/e; *Figure 6.5,* © The Society of Antiquaries of London; *Figure 6.6,* from Deetz, Invitation to Archaeology, 1967. Reprinted by permission of Natural History Press/Doubleday & Company, Inc., New York; *Figure 6.7,* © 1991 G. Gerster, Comstock.

Chapter 7: *Figure 7.1,* none listed in 8/e; *Figure 7.2,* none listed in 8/e; *Figure 7.3,* Bruce Smith, The Emergence of Agriculture Scientific American Library, 1994; *Figure 7.4,* from John Alexander, The Directing of Archaeologicia Excavations, Fig. 36. London: A & C Black (Publishers) Ltd., 1970; *Figure 7.5,* none listed in 8/e; *Figure 7.6,* reprinted with permission of Macmillan Publishing

Company from Foundations of Archaeology by Jason W. Smith; *Figure 7.7,* from N.J. Shackleton and N.D. Opdyke, "Oxygen Isotope and Paleomagnetic Stratigraphy of Equatorial Pacific Ocean Core V28-238" in Quaternary Research 3:38–55. Reprinted by permission; *Figure 7.8,* The China Friendship Society: from Grahame Clark, World Prehistory, third edition, p. 140, 1977, Cambridge University Press; *Figure 7.9,* after J.G.D. Clark, Star Carr, Fig 27b. New York, Cambridge University Press, 1954. Used by permission; *Figure 7.10,* adapted from Kenneth P. Oakley, Frameworks for Dating Fossil Man, Fig 7, Chicago: Aldine Publishers and London: Weidenfeld & Nicholson, 1964; *Figure 7.11,* Colin Renfrew and Paul Bahn, Archaeology, Thames & Hudson, Ltd.; *Figure 7.12,* none in 8/e; *Figure 7.13,* from James Deetz, Invitation to Archaeology, illustrated by Eric G. Engstrom. C. 1967 by James Deetz, reprinted by permission of Doubleday & Company, Inc.; *Figure 7.14,* adapted from R. S. MacNeish, the Prehistory of the Tehuacán Valley, Vol. 3, Figs 2 and 3, C. 1970 by The University of Texas Press, Austin.

Chapter 8: *Figure 8.1,* PR Source; *Figure 8.2,* none in 8/e; *Figure 8.3,* Bruce Smith, The Emergence of Agriculture Scientific American Library, 1994, p. 39; *Figure 8.4,* adapted from D.R. Brotherwell and Eric Higgs, Science in Archaeology. London: Thames & Hudson Ltd.; *Figure 8.5,* University of Pennsylvania Museum, Philadelphia (neg #56-3-112); *Figure 8.6,* redrawn from Ivor Noel Hume, The Artifacts of Colonial America, Fig 9. New York: Seminar Press, 1973;

Chapter 9: *Figure 9.1,* Lesley Newhart; *Figure 9.2,* Joe Ben Wheat, University of Colorado Museum; *Figure 9.3,* Peabody Museum of Archaeology and Ethnology, Harvard University; *Figure 9.4,* Robert Harding Picture Library; *Figure 9.5,* Cambridge University Collection of Air Photographs. Copyright reserved.; *Figure 9.6,* JPL/NASA; *Figure 9.7,* Norman Hammond/Corozal Project; *Figure 9.8,* Vincent Gaffney, Zoran Stanicic; *Figure 9.9,* Fondazione Lerici Prospezione Archeologiche, Rome; *Figure 9.10,* Payson Sheets, The Ceren Site, Harcourt Brace Jovanovich, 1992; *Figure 9.11,* Payson D. Sheets, Dept. of Anthropology, Univ. of Colorado, Boulder.

Chapter 10: *Figure 10.1,* courtesy of Anthony Pitt Rivers, from Salisbury and South Wiltshire Museum; *Figure 10.2,* Photograph by B. Cuniliffe, courtesy of Oxford University, England; *Figure 10.3,* D. Baston, photo courtesy of the Center for American Archaeology, Kampsville, IL; *Figure 10.4,* redrawn from Stuart Struever and James A. Brown, "The Organization of Archaeological Research: An Illinois Example," Fig 1, p. 278 in Charles L. Redman, Research and Theory in Current Archaeology. New York: John Wiley and Sons, 1973; *Figure 10.5,* University of Pennsylvania Museum Philadelphia (neg #Q77-1-31); *Figure 10.6,* © Sir Mortimer Wheeler and The Society of Antiquaries of London; *Figure 10.8,* Historic St. Augustine Preservation Board; *Figure 10.11,* H.J. Deacon; *Figure 10.12,* photo by A.L. Smith, Peabody Museum of Archaeology and Ethnology, Harvard University; *Figure 10.13,* The Oriental Institute of the University of Chicago; *Figure 10.15,* Mesa Verde National Park, National Park Service; *Figure 10.16,* © The Society of Antiquaries of London; *Figure 10.17,* © H.T. Bunn,

University of Wisconsin; *Figure 10.18,* Wilfred Shawcross; *Figure 10.19,* from Rosen's Cities of Clay University of Chicago Press (1986); *Figure 10.20,* © Crown Copyright, Historic Royal Palaces.

Chapter 11: *Figure 11.1,* Phoebe Hearst Museum of Anthropology, University of California, Berkeley; *Figure 11.2,* from James Deetz's Invitation to Archaeology, Illustrated by Eric Engstrom. © 1976 by James Deetz. Reproduced by permission of Doubleday Dell Publishing; *Figure 11.4,* Reproduced by Permission of the Trustees of the British Museum; *Figure 11.5,* Lesley Newhart.

Chapter 12: *Figure 12.5,* Pitt Rivers Museum; *Figure 12.9,* Marvin Kay; *Figure 12.10,* Photo by Wyatt Davis, courtesy of The Museum of New Mexico (Neg. no. 44191); *Figure 12.11,* Courtesy National Museum of the American Indian, Smithsonian Institution; *Figure 12.12,* Art Institute of Chicago; *Figure 12.13,* Courtesy National Museum of the American Indian, Smithsonian Institution; *Figure 12.14,* from G.H. Bushnell, The First Americans: The Pre-Columbain Civilization. P. 132. London: Thames and Hudson Ltd. and New York: McGraw-Hill. © 1968 by Thames and Hudson and McGraw-Hill; *Figure 12.15,* Michael S. Bisson; *Figure 12.16,* Sackler-Freer Gallery/Smithsonian Institution; *Figure 12.17,* photograph by Jean Vartut, taken at the British Museum; *Figure 12.18,* courtesy of the University of Alaska Museum. Used by permission; *Figure 12.19,* Ruth Kirk and Richard Daugherty, Hunters of the Whale. New York: William Morrow and Company, 1974. photograph by Harvey Rice; *Figure 12.20,* © Loren McIntyre.

Chapter 13: *Figure 13.9,* Cambridge University Museum of Archaeology and Ethnology; *Figure 13.11,* © Abu Hureyra Excavation; *Figure 13.15,* Photograph by Fred Stimson, Private Collection; *Figure 13.16,* Vaughn M. Bryant.

Chapter 14: *Figure 14.1,* Smithsonian Institution; *Figure 14.2,* © The Society of Antiquaries of London; *Figure 14.4,* James F. O'Connell; *Figure 14.5,* Photograph by Lewis R. Binford, from Gordon R. Willey and Jeremy A. Sabloff, A History of American Archaeology, 2/e. New York: W.H. Freeman and Company (1980). Reproduced by permission of the authors and publisher; *Figure 14.5,* Photograph by Lewis R. Binford, from Gordon R. Willey and Jeremy A. Sabloff, A History of American Archaeology, 2/e. New York: W.H. Freeman and Company (1980). Reproduced by permission of the authors and publisher; *Figure 14.6,* Colin Renfrew and Paul Bahm, Archaeology. Thames and Hudson, Ltd.

Chapter 15: *Figure 15.2,* Ancient Art & Architecture Collection; *Figure 15.6,* reproduced by permission of the Trustees of the British Museum; *Figure 15.7,* Lee Boltin; *Figure 15.8A,* Gerald A. Oetelaar/adapted from Portnoy (1981) Academic Pres (1981); *Figure 15.8B,* Gerald A. Oetelaar, additions to original plan map by Thomas Gatlin, Center for Archaeological Excavations, copyright by Board of Trustees, Southern Illinois University, 1983.

Chapter 16: *Figure 16.1,* Courtesy Department of Library Services, American Museum of Natural History (Neg #312721); *Figure 16.4,* Institute of Nautical Archaeology; *Figure 16.6,* SEF/Art Resource, NY; *Figure 16.7,* Lesley Newhart; *Figure 16.8,* © Robert Freerck, Oddyssey/Chicago; *Figure 16.9,* University of Pennsylvania Museum, Philadelphia (neg #s8–8845); *Figure 16.10,* The University of Alabama; *Figure 16.11,* courtesy of the Trustees of the British Museum; *Figure 16.12,* courtesy of the Trustees of the British Museum; *Figure*

16.14, from Robert D. Drennan "Contextual Analysis of Ritual Paraphernalia in Formative Oaxaca" in Kent V. Flannery (ed.) The Early Mesoamerican Village (Orlando, Fla: Academic Press; 1976).

Chapter 17: *Figure 17.1a,* photo by Hillel Burger. Peabody Museum of Archaeology and Ethnology, Harvard University. Copyright Presidents and Fellows of Harvard College, 1993; *Figure 171b,* photo by Hillel Burger. Peabody Museum of Archaeology and Ethnology, Harvard University. Copyright Presidents and fellows of Harvard College, 1993; *Figure 17.2,* The Bodleian Library, Oxford, Codex Mendoze, Arch Selden A.L. Folio 60. Detail; *Figure 17.4,* South Carolina Institute of Archaeology and Anthropology, University of South Carolina, Columbia.

Chapter 18: *Figure 18.2,* © 1995 Alpamayo, John Phelan/DDB Stock Photo; *Figure 18.3,* photograph by Egyptian Expedition, The Metropolitan Museum of Art; *Figure 18.5,* Ohio Historical Society.

Chapter 20: *Figure 20.1,* Rescue: The Trust for British Archaeology; *Figure 20.2,* courtesy of the National Museum of the American Indian, Smithsonian Institution (neg #21598); *Figure 20.3,* Hester A. Davis Archaeology 24:4. C. 1971, Archaeological Institute of America; *Figure 20.3,* © Tom Wagner, Oddyssey/Chicago; *Figure 20.4,* photo David Pedlar, with permission of the Society for Pennsylvania Archaeology.

INDEX

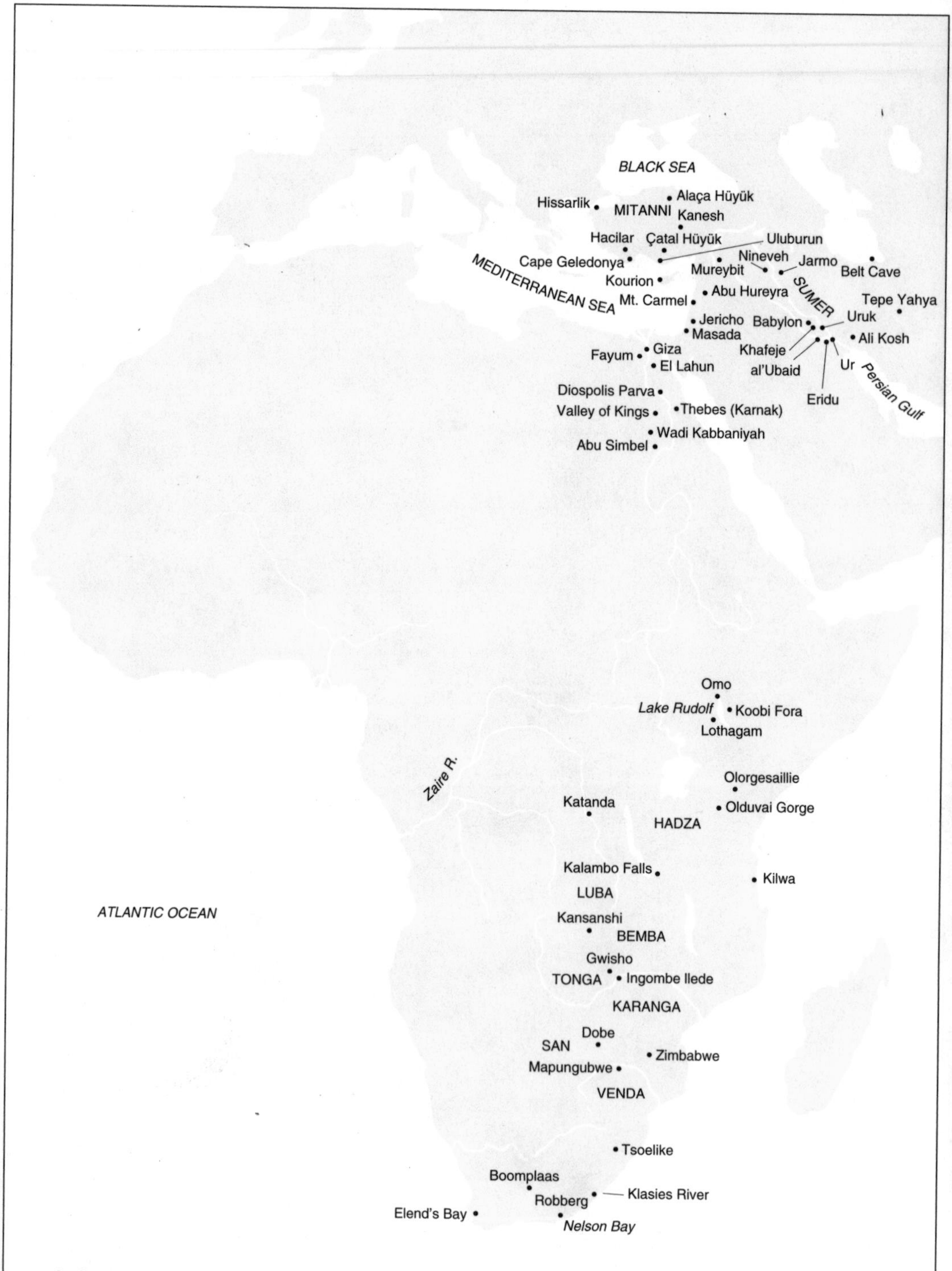

Archaeological Sites in Africa and the Near East

BLACK SEA

Hissarlik
MITANNI
Alaça Hüyük
Kanesh

Hacilar
Çatal Hüyük
Uluburun

Cape Geledonya
Nineveh
Jarmo
Belt Cave
Mureybit

Kourion
SUMER
Tepe Yahya

Mt. Carmel
Abu Hureyra

MEDITERRANEAN SEA

Jericho
Babylon
Uruk

Masada
Ali Kosh

Fayum
Giza
Khafeje

El Lahun
al'Ubaid
Ur
Persian Gulf

Diospolis Parva
Eridu

Valley of Kings
Thebes (Karnak)

Wadi Kabbaniyah

Abu Simbel

Omo

Lake Rudolf
Koobi Fora

Lothagam

Olorgesaillie

Katanda
Olduvai Gorge

HADZA

Kalambo Falls
Kilwa

LUBA

Kansanshi
BEMBA

Gwisho
TONGA
Ingombe Ilede

KARANGA

Dobe
SAN
Zimbabwe

Mapungubwe

VENDA

Tsoelike

Boomplaas
Klasies River

Robberg

Elend's Bay
Nelson Bay

Zaire R.

ATLANTIC OCEAN